Data Mining

Third Edition

The Morgan Kaufmann Series in Data Management Systems (Selected Titles)

Joe Celko's Data, Measurements, and Standards in SQL
Joe Celko

Information Modeling and Relational Databases, 2nd Edition
Terry Halpin, Tony Morgan

Joe Celko's Thinking in Sets
Joe Celko

Business Metadata
Bill Inmon, Bonnie O'Neil, Lowell Fryman

Unleashing Web 2.0
Gottfried Vossen, Stephan Hagemann

Enterprise Knowledge Management
David Loshin

The Practitioner's Guide to Data Quality Improvement
David Loshin

Business Process Change, 2nd Edition
Paul Harmon

IT Manager's Handbook, 2nd Edition
Bill Holtsnider, Brian Jaffe

Joe Celko's Puzzles and Answers, 2nd Edition
Joe Celko

Architecture and Patterns for IT Service Management, 2nd Edition, Resource Planning and Governance
Charles Betz

Joe Celko's Analytics and OLAP in SQL
Joe Celko

Data Preparation for Data Mining Using SAS
Mamdouh Refaat

Querying XML: XQuery, XPath, and SQL/ XML in Context
Jim Melton, Stephen Buxton

Data Mining: Concepts and Techniques, 3rd Edition
Jiawei Han, Micheline Kamber, Jian Pei

Database Modeling and Design: Logical Design, 5th Edition
Toby J. Teorey, Sam S. Lightstone, Thomas P. Nadeau, H. V. Jagadish

Foundations of Multidimensional and Metric Data Structures
Hanan Samet

Joe Celko's SQL for Smarties: Advanced SQL Programming, 4th Edition
Joe Celko

Moving Objects Databases
Ralf Hartmut Güting, Markus Schneider

Joe Celko's SQL Programming Style
Joe Celko

Fuzzy Modeling and Genetic Algorithms for Data Mining and Exploration
Earl Cox

Data Modeling Essentials, 3rd Edition
Graeme C. Simsion, Graham C. Witt

Developing High Quality Data Models
Matthew West

Location-Based Services
Jochen Schiller, Agnes Voisard

Managing Time in Relational Databases: How to Design, Update, and Query Temporal Data
Tom Johnston, Randall Weis

Database Modeling with Microsoft® Visio for Enterprise Architects
Terry Halpin, Ken Evans, Patrick Hallock, Bill Maclean

Designing Data-Intensive Web Applications
Stephano Ceri, Piero Fraternali, Aldo Bongio, Marco Brambilla, Sara Comai, Maristella Matera

Mining the Web: Discovering Knowledge from Hypertext Data
Soumen Chakrabarti

Advanced SQL: 1999—Understanding Object-Relational and Other Advanced Features
Jim Melton

Database Tuning: Principles, Experiments, and Troubleshooting Techniques
Dennis Shasha, Philippe Bonnet

SQL: 1999—Understanding Relational Language Components
Jim Melton, Alan R. Simon

Information Visualization in Data Mining and Knowledge Discovery
Edited by Usama Fayyad, Georges G. Grinstein, Andreas Wierse

Transactional Information Systems
Gerhard Weikum, Gottfried Vossen

Spatial Databases
Philippe Rigaux, Michel Scholl, and Agnes Voisard

Managing Reference Data in Enterprise Databases
Malcolm Chisholm

Understanding SQL and Java Together
Jim Melton, Andrew Eisenberg

Database: Principles, Programming, and Performance, 2nd Edition
Patrick and Elizabeth O'Neil

The Object Data Standard
Edited by R. G. G. Cattell, Douglas Barry

Data on the Web: From Relations to Semistructured Data and XML
Serge Abiteboul, Peter Buneman, Dan Suciu

Data Mining: Practical Machine Learning Tools and Techniques with Java Implementations, 3rd Edition
Ian Witten, Eibe Frank, Mark A. Hall

Joe Celko's Data and Databases: Concepts in Practice
Joe Celko

Developing Time-Oriented Database Applications in SQL
Richard T. Snodgrass

Web Farming for the Data Warehouse
Richard D. Hackathorn

Data Mining
Concepts and Techniques

Third Edition

Jiawei Han
University of Illinois at Urbana–Champaign

Micheline Kamber

Jian Pei
Simon Fraser University

AMSTERDAM • BOSTON • HEIDELBERG • LONDON
NEW YORK • OXFORD • PARIS • SAN DIEGO
SAN FRANCISCO • SINGAPORE • SYDNEY • TOKYO

Morgan Kaufmann is an imprint of Elsevier

Morgan Kaufmann Publishers is an imprint of Elsevier.
225 Wyman Street, Waltham, MA 02451, USA

Library of Congress Cataloging-in-Publication Data

Han, Jiawei.
  Data mining : concepts and techniques / Jiawei Han, Micheline Kamber, Jian Pei. – 3rd ed.
    p.   cm.
  ISBN 978-0-12-381479-1
  1. Data mining. I. Kamber, Micheline. II. Pei, Jian. III. Title.
  QA76.9.D343H36 2011
  006.3′12–dc22   2011010635

British Library Cataloguing-in-Publication Data
A catalogue record for this book is available from the British Library.

For information on all Morgan Kaufmann publications, visit our
Web site at *www.mkp.com* or *www.elsevierdirect.com*

Printed in the United States of America
13 14 15   10 9 8 7 6 5 4 3 2

Contents

Foreword

Analyzing large amounts of data is a necessity. Even popular science books, like "super crunchers," give compelling cases where large amounts of data yield discoveries and intuitions that surprise even experts. Every enterprise benefits from collecting and analyzing its data: Hospitals can spot trends and anomalies in their patient records, search engines can do better ranking and ad placement, and environmental and public health agencies can spot patterns and abnormalities in their data. The list continues, with cybersecurity and computer network intrusion detection; monitoring of the energy consumption of household appliances; pattern analysis in bioinformatics and pharmaceutical data; financial and business intelligence data; spotting trends in blogs, Twitter, and many more. Storage is inexpensive and getting even less so, as are data sensors. Thus, collecting and storing data is easier than ever before.

The problem then becomes *how to analyze* the data. This is exactly the focus of this Third Edition of the book. Jiawei, Micheline, and Jian give encyclopedic coverage of all the related methods, from the classic topics of clustering and classification, to database methods (e.g., association rules, data cubes) to more recent and advanced topics (e.g., SVD/PCA, wavelets, support vector machines).

The exposition is extremely accessible to beginners and advanced readers alike. The book gives the fundamental material first and the more advanced material in follow-up chapters. It also has numerous rhetorical questions, which I found extremely helpful for maintaining focus.

We have used the first two editions as textbooks in data mining courses at Carnegie Mellon and plan to continue to do so with this Third Edition. The new version has significant additions: Notably, it has more than 100 citations to works from 2006 onward, focusing on more recent material such as graphs and social networks, sensor networks, and outlier detection. This book has a new section for visualization, has expanded outlier detection into a whole chapter, and has separate chapters for advanced methods—for example, pattern mining with top-k patterns and more and clustering methods with biclustering and graph clustering.

Overall, it is an excellent book on classic and modern data mining methods, and it is ideal not only for teaching but also as a reference book.

Christos Faloutsos
Carnegie Mellon University

Foreword to Second Edition

We are deluged by data—scientific data, medical data, demographic data, financial data, and marketing data. People have no time to look at this data. Human attention has become the precious resource. So, we must find ways to automatically analyze the data, to automatically classify it, to automatically summarize it, to automatically discover and characterize trends in it, and to automatically flag anomalies. This is one of the most active and exciting areas of the database research community. Researchers in areas including statistics, visualization, artificial intelligence, and machine learning are contributing to this field. The breadth of the field makes it difficult to grasp the extraordinary progress over the last few decades.

Six years ago, Jiawei Han's and Micheline Kamber's seminal textbook organized and presented Data Mining. It heralded a golden age of innovation in the field. This revision of their book reflects that progress; more than half of the references and historical notes are to recent work. The field has matured with many new and improved algorithms, and has broadened to include many more datatypes: streams, sequences, graphs, time-series, geospatial, audio, images, and video. We are certainly not at the end of the golden age—indeed research and commercial interest in data mining continues to grow—but we are all fortunate to have this modern compendium.

The book gives quick introductions to database and data mining concepts with particular emphasis on data analysis. It then covers in a chapter-by-chapter tour the concepts and techniques that underlie classification, prediction, association, and clustering. These topics are presented with examples, a tour of the best algorithms for each problem class, and with pragmatic rules of thumb about when to apply each technique. The Socratic presentation style is both very readable and very informative. I certainly learned a lot from reading the first edition and got re-educated and updated in reading the second edition.

Jiawei Han and Micheline Kamber have been leading contributors to data mining research. This is the text they use with their students to bring them up to speed on the field. The field is evolving very rapidly, but this book is a quick way to learn the basic ideas, and to understand where the field is today. I found it very informative and stimulating, and believe you will too.

Jim Gray
In his memory

Preface

The computerization of our society has substantially enhanced our capabilities for both generating and collecting data from diverse sources. A tremendous amount of data has flooded almost every aspect of our lives. This explosive growth in stored or transient data has generated an urgent need for new techniques and automated tools that can intelligently assist us in transforming the vast amounts of data into useful information and knowledge. This has led to the generation of a promising and flourishing frontier in computer science called *data mining*, and its various applications. Data mining, also popularly referred to as *knowledge discovery from data (KDD)*, is the automated or convenient extraction of patterns representing knowledge implicitly stored or captured in large databases, data warehouses, the Web, other massive information repositories, or data streams.

This book explores the concepts and techniques of *knowledge discovery* and *data mining*. As a multidisciplinary field, data mining draws on work from areas including statistics, machine learning, pattern recognition, database technology, information retrieval, network science, knowledge-based systems, artificial intelligence, high-performance computing, and data visualization. We focus on issues relating to the feasibility, usefulness, effectiveness, and scalability of techniques for the discovery of patterns hidden in *large data sets*. As a result, this book is not intended as an introduction to statistics, machine learning, database systems, or other such areas, although we do provide some background knowledge to facilitate the reader's comprehension of their respective roles in data mining. Rather, the book is a comprehensive introduction to data mining. It is useful for computing science students, application developers, and business professionals, as well as researchers involved in any of the disciplines previously listed.

Data mining emerged during the late 1980s, made great strides during the 1990s, and continues to flourish into the new millennium. This book presents an overall picture of the field, introducing interesting data mining techniques and systems and discussing applications and research directions. An important motivation for writing this book was the need to build an organized framework for the study of data mining—a challenging task, owing to the extensive multidisciplinary nature of this fast-developing field. We hope that this book will encourage people with different backgrounds and experiences to exchange their views regarding data mining so as to contribute toward the further promotion and shaping of this exciting and dynamic field.

Organization of the Book

Since the publication of the first two editions of this book, great progress has been made in the field of data mining. Many new data mining methodologies, systems, and applications have been developed, especially for handling new kinds of data, including information networks, graphs, complex structures, and data streams, as well as text, Web, multimedia, time-series, and spatiotemporal data. Such fast development and rich, new technical contents make it difficult to cover the full spectrum of the field in a single book. Instead of continuously expanding the coverage of this book, we have decided to cover the core material in sufficient scope and depth, and leave the handling of complex data types to a separate forthcoming book.

The third edition substantially revises the first two editions of the book, with numerous enhancements and a reorganization of the technical contents. The core technical material, which handles mining on general data types, is expanded and substantially enhanced. Several individual chapters for topics from the second edition (e.g., data preprocessing, frequent pattern mining, classification, and clustering) are now augmented and each split into two chapters for this new edition. For these topics, one chapter encapsulates the basic concepts and techniques while the other presents advanced concepts and methods.

Chapters from the second edition on mining complex data types (e.g., stream data, sequence data, graph-structured data, social network data, and multirelational data, as well as text, Web, multimedia, and spatiotemporal data) are now reserved for a new book that will be dedicated to *advanced topics in data mining*. Still, to support readers in learning such advanced topics, we have placed an electronic version of the relevant chapters from the second edition onto the book's web site as companion material for the third edition.

The chapters of the third edition are described briefly as follows, with emphasis on the new material.

Chapter 1 provides an *introduction* to the multidisciplinary field of data mining. It discusses the evolutionary path of information technology, which has led to the need for data mining, and the importance of its applications. It examines the data types to be mined, including relational, transactional, and data warehouse data, as well as complex data types such as time-series, sequences, data streams, spatiotemporal data, multimedia data, text data, graphs, social networks, and Web data. The chapter presents a general classification of data mining tasks, based on the kinds of knowledge to be mined, the kinds of technologies used, and the kinds of applications that are targeted. Finally, major challenges in the field are discussed.

Chapter 2 introduces the *general data features*. It first discusses data objects and attribute types and then introduces typical measures for basic statistical data descriptions. It overviews data visualization techniques for various kinds of data. In addition to methods of numeric data visualization, methods for visualizing text, tags, graphs, and multidimensional data are introduced. Chapter 2 also introduces ways to measure similarity and dissimilarity for various kinds of data.

Chapter 3 introduces *techniques for data preprocessing*. It first introduces the concept of data quality and then discusses methods for data cleaning, data integration, data reduction, data transformation, and data discretization.

Chapters 4 and 5 provide a solid introduction to *data warehouses*, *OLAP* (online analytical processing), and *data cube technology*. **Chapter 4** introduces the basic concepts, modeling, design architectures, and general implementations of data warehouses and OLAP, as well as the relationship between data warehousing and other data generalization methods. **Chapter 5** takes an in-depth look at data cube technology, presenting a detailed study of methods of data cube computation, including Star-Cubing and high-dimensional OLAP methods. Further explorations of data cube and OLAP technologies are discussed, such as sampling cubes, ranking cubes, prediction cubes, multifeature cubes for complex analysis queries, and discovery-driven cube exploration.

Chapters 6 and 7 present methods for *mining frequent patterns, associations*, and *correlations* in large data sets. **Chapter 6** introduces fundamental concepts, such as market basket analysis, with many techniques for frequent itemset mining presented in an organized way. These range from the basic Apriori algorithm and its variations to more advanced methods that improve efficiency, including the frequent pattern growth approach, frequent pattern mining with vertical data format, and mining closed and max frequent itemsets. The chapter also discusses pattern evaluation methods and introduces measures for mining correlated patterns. **Chapter 7** is on advanced pattern mining methods. It discusses methods for pattern mining in multilevel and multidimensional space, mining rare and negative patterns, mining colossal patterns and high-dimensional data, constraint-based pattern mining, and mining compressed or approximate patterns. It also introduces methods for pattern exploration and application, including semantic annotation of frequent patterns.

Chapters 8 and 9 describe methods for *data classification*. Due to the importance and diversity of classification methods, the contents are partitioned into two chapters. **Chapter 8** introduces basic concepts and methods for classification, including decision tree induction, Bayes classification, and rule-based classification. It also discusses model evaluation and selection methods and methods for improving classification accuracy, including ensemble methods and how to handle imbalanced data. **Chapter 9** discusses advanced methods for classification, including Bayesian belief networks, the neural network technique of backpropagation, support vector machines, classification using frequent patterns, k-nearest-neighbor classifiers, case-based reasoning, genetic algorithms, rough set theory, and fuzzy set approaches. Additional topics include multiclass classification, semi-supervised classification, active learning, and transfer learning.

Cluster analysis forms the topic of Chapters 10 and 11. **Chapter 10** introduces the basic concepts and methods for data clustering, including an overview of basic cluster analysis methods, partitioning methods, hierarchical methods, density-based methods, and grid-based methods. It also introduces methods for the evaluation of clustering. **Chapter 11** discusses advanced methods for clustering, including probabilistic model-based clustering, clustering high-dimensional data, clustering graph and network data, and clustering with constraints.

Chapter 12 is dedicated to *outlier detection*. It introduces the basic concepts of outliers and outlier analysis and discusses various outlier detection methods from the view of degree of supervision (i.e., supervised, semi-supervised, and unsupervised methods), as well as from the view of approaches (i.e., statistical methods, proximity-based methods, clustering-based methods, and classification-based methods). It also discusses methods for mining contextual and collective outliers, and for outlier detection in high-dimensional data.

Finally, in **Chapter 13**, we discuss *trends, applications,* and *research frontiers* in data mining. We briefly cover mining complex data types, including mining sequence data (e.g., time series, symbolic sequences, and biological sequences), mining graphs and networks, and mining spatial, multimedia, text, and Web data. In-depth treatment of data mining methods for such data is left to a book on advanced topics in data mining, the writing of which is in progress. The chapter then moves ahead to cover other data mining methodologies, including statistical data mining, foundations of data mining, visual and audio data mining, as well as data mining applications. It discusses data mining for financial data analysis, for industries like retail and telecommunication, for use in science and engineering, and for intrusion detection and prevention. It also discusses the relationship between data mining and recommender systems. Because data mining is present in many aspects of daily life, we discuss issues regarding data mining and society, including ubiquitous and invisible data mining, as well as privacy, security, and the social impacts of data mining. We conclude our study by looking at data mining trends.

Throughout the text, *italic* font is used to emphasize terms that are defined, while **bold** font is used to highlight or summarize main ideas. Sans serif font is used for reserved words. Bold italic font is used to represent multidimensional quantities.

This book has several strong features that set it apart from other texts on data mining. It presents a very broad yet in-depth coverage of the principles of data mining. The chapters are written to be as self-contained as possible, so they may be read in order of interest by the reader. Advanced chapters offer a larger-scale view and may be considered optional for interested readers. All of the major methods of data mining are presented. The book presents important topics in data mining regarding multidimensional OLAP analysis, which is often overlooked or minimally treated in other data mining books. The book also maintains web sites with a number of online resources to aid instructors, students, and professionals in the field. These are described further in the following.

To the Instructor

This book is designed to give a broad, yet detailed overview of the data mining field. It can be used to teach an introductory course on data mining at an advanced undergraduate level or at the first-year graduate level. Sample course syllabi are provided on the book's web sites (*www.cs.uiuc.edu/~hanj/bk3* and *www.booksite.mkp.com/datamining3e*) in addition to extensive teaching resources such as lecture slides, instructors' manuals, and reading lists (see p. xxix).

Figure P.1 A suggested sequence of chapters for a short introductory course.

Depending on the length of the instruction period, the background of students, and your interests, you may select subsets of chapters to teach in various sequential orderings. For example, if you would like to give only a short introduction to students on data mining, you may follow the suggested sequence in Figure P.1. Notice that depending on the need, you can also omit some sections or subsections in a chapter if desired.

Depending on the length of the course and its technical scope, you may choose to selectively add more chapters to this preliminary sequence. For example, instructors who are more interested in advanced classification methods may first add "Chapter 9. Classification: Advanced Methods"; those more interested in pattern mining may choose to include "Chapter 7. Advanced Pattern Mining"; whereas those interested in OLAP and data cube technology may like to add "Chapter 4. Data Warehousing and Online Analytical Processing" and "Chapter 5. Data Cube Technology."

Alternatively, you may choose to teach the whole book in a two-course sequence that covers all of the chapters in the book, plus, when time permits, some advanced topics such as graph and network mining. Material for such advanced topics may be selected from the companion chapters available from the book's web site, accompanied with a set of selected research papers.

Individual chapters in this book can also be used for tutorials or for special topics in related courses, such as machine learning, pattern recognition, data warehousing, and intelligent data analysis.

Each chapter ends with a set of exercises, suitable as assigned homework. The exercises are either short questions that test basic mastery of the material covered, longer questions that require analytical thinking, or implementation projects. Some exercises can also be used as research discussion topics. The bibliographic notes at the end of each chapter can be used to find the research literature that contains the origin of the concepts and methods presented, in-depth treatment of related topics, and possible extensions.

To the Student

We hope that this textbook will spark your interest in the young yet fast-evolving field of data mining. We have attempted to present the material in a clear manner, with careful explanation of the topics covered. Each chapter ends with a summary describing the main points. We have included many figures and illustrations throughout the text to make the book more enjoyable and reader-friendly. Although this book was designed as a textbook, we have tried to organize it so that it will also be useful to you as a reference book or handbook, should you later decide to perform in-depth research in the related fields or pursue a career in data mining.

What do you need to know to read this book?

- You should have some knowledge of the concepts and terminology associated with statistics, database systems, and machine learning. However, we do try to provide enough background of the basics, so that if you are not so familiar with these fields or your memory is a bit rusty, you will not have trouble following the discussions in the book.

- You should have some programming experience. In particular, you should be able to read pseudocode and understand simple data structures such as multidimensional arrays.

To the Professional

This book was designed to cover a wide range of topics in the data mining field. As a result, it is an excellent handbook on the subject. Because each chapter is designed to be as standalone as possible, you can focus on the topics that most interest you. The book can be used by application programmers and information service managers who wish to learn about the key ideas of data mining on their own. The book would also be useful for technical data analysis staff in banking, insurance, medicine, and retailing industries who are interested in applying data mining solutions to their businesses. Moreover, the book may serve as a comprehensive survey of the data mining field, which may also benefit researchers who would like to advance the state-of-the-art in data mining and extend the scope of data mining applications.

The techniques and algorithms presented are of practical utility. Rather than selecting algorithms that perform well on small "toy" data sets, the algorithms described in the book are geared for the discovery of patterns and knowledge hidden in large, real data sets. Algorithms presented in the book are illustrated in pseudocode. The pseudocode is similar to the C programming language, yet is designed so that it should be easy to follow by programmers unfamiliar with C or C++. If you wish to implement any of the algorithms, you should find the translation of our pseudocode into the programming language of your choice to be a fairly straightforward task.

Book Web Sites with Resources

The book has a web site at *www.cs.uiuc.edu/~hanj/bk3* and another with Morgan Kaufmann Publishers at *www.booksite.mkp.com/datamining3e*. These web sites contain many supplemental materials for readers of this book or anyone else with an interest in data mining. The resources include the following:

- **Slide presentations for each chapter**. Lecture notes in Microsoft PowerPoint slides are available for each chapter.

- **Companion chapters on advanced data mining**. Chapters 8 to 10 of the second edition of the book, which cover mining complex data types, are available on the book's web sites for readers who are interested in learning more about such advanced topics, beyond the themes covered in this book.

- **Instructors' manual**. This complete set of answers to the exercises in the book is available only to instructors from the publisher's web site.

- **Course syllabi and lecture plans**. These are given for undergraduate and graduate versions of introductory and advanced courses on data mining, which use the text and slides.

- **Supplemental reading lists with hyperlinks**. Seminal papers for supplemental reading are organized per chapter.

- **Links to data mining data sets and software**. We provide a set of links to data mining data sets and sites that contain interesting data mining software packages, such as IlliMine from the University of Illinois at Urbana-Champaign (*http://illimine.cs.uiuc.edu*).

- **Sample assignments, exams, and course projects**. A set of sample assignments, exams, and course projects is available to instructors from the publisher's web site.

- **Figures from the book**. This may help you to make your own slides for your classroom teaching.

- **Contents** of the book in PDF format.

- **Errata on the different printings of the book**. We encourage you to point out any errors in this book. Once the error is confirmed, we will update the errata list and include acknowledgment of your contribution.

Comments or suggestions can be sent to *hanj@cs.uiuc.edu*. We would be happy to hear from you.

Acknowledgments

Third Edition of the Book

We would like to express our grateful thanks to all of the previous and current members of the Data Mining Group at UIUC, the faculty and students in the Data and Information Systems (DAIS) Laboratory in the Department of Computer Science at the University of Illinois at Urbana-Champaign, and many friends and colleagues, whose constant support and encouragement have made our work on this edition a rewarding experience. We would also like to thank students in CS412 and CS512 classes at UIUC of the 2010–2011 academic year, who carefully went through the early drafts of this book, identified many errors, and suggested various improvements.

We also wish to thank David Bevans and Rick Adams at Morgan Kaufmann Publishers, for their enthusiasm, patience, and support during our writing of this edition of the book. We thank Marilyn Rash, the Project Manager, and her team members, for keeping us on schedule.

We are also grateful for the invaluable feedback from all of the reviewers. Moreover, we would like to thank U.S. National Science Foundation, NASA, U.S. Air Force Office of Scientific Research, U.S. Army Research Laboratory, and Natural Science and Engineering Research Council of Canada (NSERC), as well as IBM Research, Microsoft Research, Google, Yahoo! Research, Boeing, HP Labs, and other industry research labs for their support of our research in the form of research grants, contracts, and gifts. Such research support deepens our understanding of the subjects discussed in this book. Finally, we thank our families for their wholehearted support throughout this project.

Second Edition of the Book

We would like to express our grateful thanks to all of the previous and current members of the Data Mining Group at UIUC, the faculty and students in the Data and

Information Systems (DAIS) Laboratory in the Department of Computer Science at the University of Illinois at Urbana-Champaign, and many friends and colleagues, whose constant support and encouragement have made our work on this edition a rewarding experience. These include Gul Agha, Rakesh Agrawal, Loretta Auvil, Peter Bajcsy, Geneva Belford, Deng Cai, Y. Dora Cai, Roy Cambell, Kevin C.-C. Chang, Surajit Chaudhuri, Chen Chen, Yixin Chen, Yuguo Chen, Hong Cheng, David Cheung, Shengnan Cong, Gerald DeJong, AnHai Doan, Guozhu Dong, Charios Ermopoulos, Martin Ester, Christos Faloutsos, Wei Fan, Jack C. Feng, Ada Fu, Michael Garland, Johannes Gehrke, Hector Gonzalez, Mehdi Harandi, Thomas Huang, Wen Jin, Chulyun Kim, Sangkyum Kim, Won Kim, Won-Young Kim, David Kuck, Young-Koo Lee, Harris Lewin, Xiaolei Li, Yifan Li, Chao Liu, Han Liu, Huan Liu, Hongyan Liu, Lei Liu, Ying Lu, Klara Nahrstedt, David Padua, Jian Pei, Lenny Pitt, Daniel Reed, Dan Roth, Bruce Schatz, Zheng Shao, Marc Snir, Zhaohui Tang, Bhavani M. Thuraisingham, Josep Torrellas, Peter Tzvetkov, Benjamin W. Wah, Haixun Wang, Jianyong Wang, Ke Wang, Muyuan Wang, Wei Wang, Michael Welge, Marianne Winslett, Ouri Wolfson, Andrew Wu, Tianyi Wu, Dong Xin, Xifeng Yan, Jiong Yang, Xiaoxin Yin, Hwanjo Yu, Jeffrey X. Yu, Philip S. Yu, Maria Zemankova, ChengXiang Zhai, Yuanyuan Zhou, and Wei Zou.

Deng Cai and ChengXiang Zhai have contributed to the text mining and Web mining sections, Xifeng Yan to the graph mining section, and Xiaoxin Yin to the multirelational data mining section. Hong Cheng, Charios Ermopoulos, Hector Gonzalez, David J. Hill, Chulyun Kim, Sangkyum Kim, Chao Liu, Hongyan Liu, Kasif Manzoor, Tianyi Wu, Xifeng Yan, and Xiaoxin Yin have contributed to the proofreading of the individual chapters of the manuscript.

We also wish to thank Diane Cerra, our Publisher at Morgan Kaufmann Publishers, for her constant enthusiasm, patience, and support during our writing of this book. We are indebted to Alan Rose, the book Production Project Manager, for his tireless and ever-prompt communications with us to sort out all details of the production process. We are grateful for the invaluable feedback from all of the reviewers. Finally, we thank our families for their wholehearted support throughout this project.

First Edition of the Book

We would like to express our sincere thanks to all those who have worked or are currently working with us on data mining–related research and/or the DBMiner project, or have provided us with various support in data mining. These include Rakesh Agrawal, Stella Atkins, Yvan Bedard, Binay Bhattacharya, (Yandong) Dora Cai, Nick Cercone, Surajit Chaudhuri, Sonny H. S. Chee, Jianping Chen, Ming-Syan Chen, Qing Chen, Qiming Chen, Shan Cheng, David Cheung, Shi Cong, Son Dao, Umeshwar Dayal, James Delgrande, Guozhu Dong, Carole Edwards, Max Egenhofer, Martin Ester, Usama Fayyad, Ling Feng, Ada Fu, Yongjian Fu, Daphne Gelbart, Randy Goebel, Jim Gray, Robert Grossman, Wan Gong, Yike Guo, Eli Hagen, Howard Hamilton, Jing He, Larry Henschen, Jean Hou, Mei-Chun Hsu, Kan Hu, Haiming Huang, Yue Huang, Julia Itskevitch, Wen Jin, Tiko Kameda, Hiroyuki Kawano, Rizwan Kheraj, Eddie Kim, Won Kim, Krzysztof Koperski, Hans-Peter Kriegel, Vipin Kumar, Laks V. S. Lakshmanan, Joyce

Man Lam, James Lau, Deyi Li, George (Wenmin) Li, Jin Li, Ze-Nian Li, Nancy Liao, Gang Liu, Junqiang Liu, Ling Liu, Alan (Yijun) Lu, Hongjun Lu, Tong Lu, Wei Lu, Xuebin Lu, Wo-Shun Luk, Heikki Mannila, Runying Mao, Abhay Mehta, Gabor Melli, Alberto Mendelzon, Tim Merrett, Harvey Miller, Drew Miners, Behzad Mortazavi-Asl, Richard Muntz, Raymond T. Ng, Vicent Ng, Shojiro Nishio, Beng-Chin Ooi, Tamer Ozsu, Jian Pei, Gregory Piatetsky-Shapiro, Helen Pinto, Fred Popowich, Amynmohamed Rajan, Peter Scheuermann, Shashi Shekhar, Wei-Min Shen, Avi Silberschatz, Evangelos Simoudis, Nebojsa Stefanovic, Yin Jenny Tam, Simon Tang, Zhaohui Tang, Dick Tsur, Anthony K. H. Tung, Ke Wang, Wei Wang, Zhaoxia Wang, Tony Wind, Lara Winstone, Ju Wu, Betty (Bin) Xia, Cindy M. Xin, Xiaowei Xu, Qiang Yang, Yiwen Yin, Clement Yu, Jeffrey Yu, Philip S. Yu, Osmar R. Zaiane, Carlo Zaniolo, Shuhua Zhang, Zhong Zhang, Yvonne Zheng, Xiaofang Zhou, and Hua Zhu.

We are also grateful to Jean Hou, Helen Pinto, Lara Winstone, and Hua Zhu for their help with some of the original figures in this book, and to Eugene Belchev for his careful proofreading of each chapter.

We also wish to thank Diane Cerra, our Executive Editor at Morgan Kaufmann Publishers, for her enthusiasm, patience, and support during our writing of this book, as well as Howard Severson, our Production Editor, and his staff for their conscientious efforts regarding production. We are indebted to all of the reviewers for their invaluable feedback. Finally, we thank our families for their wholehearted support throughout this project.

About the Authors

Jiawei Han is a Bliss Professor of Engineering in the Department of Computer Science at the University of Illinois at Urbana-Champaign. He has received numerous awards for his contributions on research into knowledge discovery and data mining, including ACM SIGKDD Innovation Award (2004), IEEE Computer Society Technical Achievement Award (2005), and IEEE W. Wallace McDowell Award (2009). He is a Fellow of ACM and IEEE. He served as founding Editor-in-Chief of *ACM Transactions on Knowledge Discovery from Data* (2006–2011) and as an editorial board member of several journals, including *IEEE Transactions on Knowledge and Data Engineering* and *Data Mining and Knowledge Discovery.*

Micheline Kamber has a master's degree in computer science (specializing in artificial intelligence) from Concordia University in Montreal, Quebec. She was an NSERC Scholar and has worked as a researcher at McGill University, Simon Fraser University, and in Switzerland. Her background in data mining and passion for writing in easy-to-understand terms help make this text a favorite of professionals, instructors, and students.

Jian Pei is currently an associate professor at the School of Computing Science, Simon Fraser University in British Columbia. He received a Ph.D. degree in computing science from Simon Fraser University in 2002 under Dr. Jiawei Han's supervision. He has published prolifically in the premier academic forums on data mining, databases, Web searching, and information retrieval and actively served the academic community. His publications have received thousands of citations and several prestigious awards. He is an associate editor of several data mining and data analytics journals.

Introduction

This book is an introduction to the young and fast-growing field of *data mining* (also known as *knowledge discovery from data*, or *KDD* for short). The book focuses on fundamental data mining concepts and techniques for discovering interesting patterns from data in various applications. In particular, we emphasize prominent techniques for developing effective, efficient, and scalable data mining tools.

This chapter is organized as follows. In Section 1.1, you will learn why data mining is in high demand and how it is part of the natural evolution of information technology. Section 1.2 defines data mining with respect to the knowledge discovery process. Next, you will learn about data mining from many aspects, such as the kinds of data that can be mined (Section 1.3), the kinds of knowledge to be mined (Section 1.4), the kinds of technologies to be used (Section 1.5), and targeted applications (Section 1.6). In this way, you will gain a multidimensional view of data mining. Finally, Section 1.7 outlines major data mining research and development issues.

1.1 Why Data Mining?

Necessity, who is the mother of invention. – Plato

We live in a world where vast amounts of data are collected daily. Analyzing such data is an important need. Section 1.1.1 looks at how data mining can meet this need by providing tools to discover knowledge from data. In Section 1.1.2, we observe how data mining can be viewed as a result of the natural evolution of information technology.

1.1.1 Moving toward the Information Age

"*We are living in the information age*" is a popular saying; however, *we are actually living in the data age*. Terabytes or petabytes[1] of data pour into our computer networks, the World Wide Web (WWW), and various data storage devices every day from business,

---

[1] A petabyte is a unit of information or computer storage equal to 1 quadrillion bytes, or a thousand terabytes, or 1 million gigabytes.

1

society, science and engineering, medicine, and almost every other aspect of daily life. This explosive growth of available data volume is a result of the computerization of our society and the fast development of powerful data collection and storage tools. Businesses worldwide generate gigantic data sets, including sales transactions, stock trading records, product descriptions, sales promotions, company profiles and performance, and customer feedback. For example, large stores, such as Wal-Mart, handle hundreds of millions of transactions per week at thousands of branches around the world. Scientific and engineering practices generate high orders of petabytes of data in a continuous manner, from remote sensing, process measuring, scientific experiments, system performance, engineering observations, and environment surveillance.

Global backbone telecommunication networks carry tens of petabytes of data traffic every day. The medical and health industry generates tremendous amounts of data from medical records, patient monitoring, and medical imaging. Billions of Web searches supported by search engines process tens of petabytes of data daily. Communities and social media have become increasingly important data sources, producing digital pictures and videos, blogs, Web communities, and various kinds of social networks. The list of sources that generate huge amounts of data is endless.

This explosively growing, widely available, and gigantic body of data makes our time truly the data age. Powerful and versatile tools are badly needed to automatically uncover valuable information from the tremendous amounts of data and to transform such data into organized knowledge. This necessity has led to the birth of data mining. The field is young, dynamic, and promising. Data mining has and will continue to make great strides in our journey from the data age toward the coming information age.

Example 1.1 **Data mining turns a large collection of data into knowledge.** A search engine (e.g., Google) receives hundreds of millions of queries every day. Each query can be viewed as a transaction where the user describes her or his information need. What novel and useful knowledge can a search engine learn from such a huge collection of queries collected from users over time? Interestingly, some patterns found in user search queries can disclose invaluable knowledge that cannot be obtained by reading individual data items alone. For example, Google's *Flu Trends* uses specific search terms as indicators of flu activity. It found a close relationship between the number of people who search for flu-related information and the number of people who actually have flu symptoms. A pattern emerges when all of the search queries related to flu are aggregated. Using aggregated Google search data, *Flu Trends* can estimate flu activity up to two weeks faster than traditional systems can.[2] This example shows how data mining can turn a large collection of data into knowledge that can help meet a current global challenge. ∎

1.1.2 Data Mining as the Evolution of Information Technology

Data mining can be viewed as a result of the natural evolution of information technology. The database and data management industry evolved in the development of

---

[2]This is reported in [GMP+09].

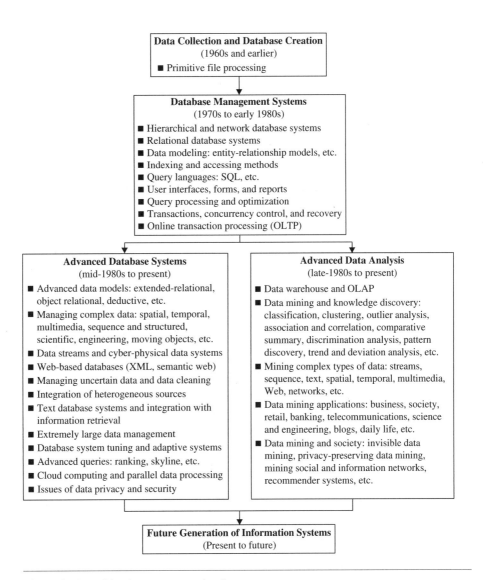

Figure 1.1 The evolution of database system technology.

several critical functionalities (Figure 1.1): *data collection and database creation, data management* (including data storage and retrieval and database transaction processing), and *advanced data analysis* (involving data warehousing and data mining). The early development of data collection and database creation mechanisms served as a prerequisite for the later development of effective mechanisms for data storage and retrieval, as well as query and transaction processing. Nowadays numerous database systems offer query and transaction processing as common practice. Advanced data analysis has naturally become the next step.

Since the 1960s, database and information technology has evolved systematically from primitive file processing systems to sophisticated and powerful database systems. The research and development in database systems since the 1970s progressed from early hierarchical and network database systems to relational database systems (where data are stored in relational table structures; see Section 1.3.1), data modeling tools, and indexing and accessing methods. In addition, users gained convenient and flexible data access through query languages, user interfaces, query optimization, and transaction management. Efficient methods for online transaction processing (OLTP), where a query is viewed as a read-only transaction, contributed substantially to the evolution and wide acceptance of relational technology as a major tool for efficient storage, retrieval, and management of large amounts of data.

After the establishment of database management systems, database technology moved toward the development of *advanced database systems*, *data warehousing*, and *data mining* for advanced data analysis and *web-based databases*. Advanced database systems, for example, resulted from an upsurge of research from the mid-1980s onward. These systems incorporate new and powerful data models such as extended-relational, object-oriented, object-relational, and deductive models. Application-oriented database systems have flourished, including spatial, temporal, multimedia, active, stream and sensor, scientific and engineering databases, knowledge bases, and office information bases. Issues related to the distribution, diversification, and sharing of data have been studied extensively.

Advanced data analysis sprang up from the late 1980s onward. The steady and dazzling progress of computer hardware technology in the past three decades led to large supplies of powerful and affordable computers, data collection equipment, and storage media. This technology provides a great boost to the database and information industry, and it enables a huge number of databases and information repositories to be available for transaction management, information retrieval, and data analysis. Data can now be stored in many different kinds of databases and information repositories.

One emerging data repository architecture is the **data warehouse** (Section 1.3.2). This is a repository of multiple heterogeneous data sources organized under a unified schema at a single site to facilitate management decision making. Data warehouse technology includes data cleaning, data integration, and online analytical processing (OLAP)—that is, analysis techniques with functionalities such as summarization, consolidation, and aggregation, as well as the ability to view information from different angles. Although OLAP tools support multidimensional analysis and decision making, additional data analysis tools are required for in-depth analysis—for example, data mining tools that provide data classification, clustering, outlier/anomaly detection, and the characterization of changes in data over time.

Huge volumes of data have been accumulated beyond databases and data warehouses. During the 1990s, the World Wide Web and web-based databases (e.g., XML databases) began to appear. Internet-based global information bases, such as the WWW and various kinds of interconnected, heterogeneous databases, have emerged and play a vital role in the information industry. The effective and efficient analysis of data from such different forms of data by integration of information retrieval, data mining, and information network analysis technologies is a challenging task.

Figure 1.2 The world is data rich but information poor.

In summary, the abundance of data, coupled with the need for powerful data analysis tools, has been described as a *data rich but information poor* situation (Figure 1.2). The fast-growing, tremendous amount of data, collected and stored in large and numerous data repositories, has far exceeded our human ability for comprehension without powerful tools. As a result, data collected in large data repositories become "data tombs"—data archives that are seldom visited. Consequently, important decisions are often made based not on the information-rich data stored in data repositories but rather on a decision maker's intuition, simply because the decision maker does not have the tools to extract the valuable knowledge embedded in the vast amounts of data. Efforts have been made to develop expert system and knowledge-based technologies, which typically rely on users or domain experts to *manually* input knowledge into knowledge bases. Unfortunately, however, the manual knowledge input procedure is prone to biases and errors and is extremely costly and time consuming. The widening gap between data and information calls for the systematic development of *data mining tools* that can turn data tombs into "golden nuggets" of knowledge.

1.2 What Is Data Mining?

It is no surprise that data mining, as a truly interdisciplinary subject, can be defined in many different ways. Even the term *data mining* does not really present all the major components in the picture. To refer to the mining of gold from rocks or sand, we say *gold mining* instead of rock or sand mining. Analogously, data mining should have been more

Figure 1.3 Data mining—searching for knowledge (interesting patterns) in data.

appropriately named "knowledge mining from data," which is unfortunately somewhat long. However, the shorter term, *knowledge mining* may not reflect the emphasis on mining from large amounts of data. Nevertheless, mining is a vivid term characterizing the process that finds a small set of precious nuggets from a great deal of raw material (Figure 1.3). Thus, such a misnomer carrying both "data" and "mining" became a popular choice. In addition, many other terms have a similar meaning to data mining—for example, *knowledge mining from data, knowledge extraction, data/pattern analysis, data archaeology,* and *data dredging.*

Many people treat data mining as a synonym for another popularly used term, **knowledge discovery from data**, or **KDD**, while others view data mining as merely an essential step in the process of knowledge discovery. The knowledge discovery process is shown in Figure 1.4 as an iterative sequence of the following steps:

1. **Data cleaning** (to remove noise and inconsistent data)

2. **Data integration** (where multiple data sources may be combined)[3]

---

[3]A popular trend in the information industry is to perform data cleaning and data integration as a preprocessing step, where the resulting data are stored in a data warehouse.

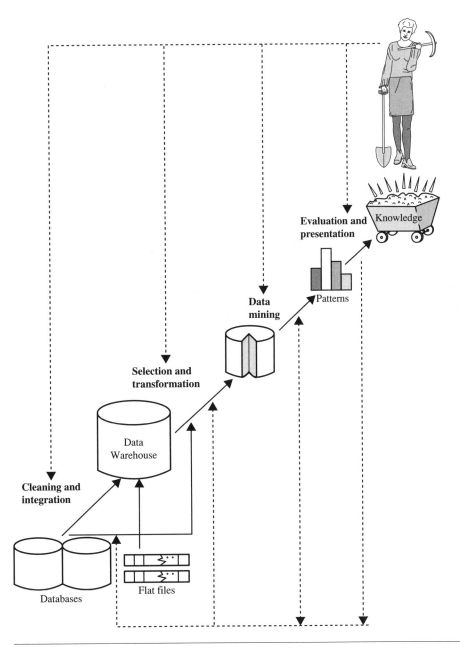

Figure 1.4 Data mining as a step in the process of knowledge discovery.

3. **Data selection** (where data relevant to the analysis task are retrieved from the database)

4. **Data transformation** (where data are transformed and consolidated into forms appropriate for mining by performing summary or aggregation operations)[4]

5. **Data mining** (an essential process where intelligent methods are applied to extract data patterns)

6. **Pattern evaluation** (to identify the truly interesting patterns representing knowledge based on *interestingness measures*—see Section 1.4.6)

7. **Knowledge presentation** (where visualization and knowledge representation techniques are used to present mined knowledge to users)

Steps 1 through 4 are different forms of data preprocessing, where data are prepared for mining. The data mining step may interact with the user or a knowledge base. The interesting patterns are presented to the user and may be stored as new knowledge in the knowledge base.

The preceding view shows data mining as one step in the knowledge discovery process, albeit an essential one because it uncovers hidden patterns for evaluation. However, in industry, in media, and in the research milieu, the term *data mining* is often used to refer to the entire knowledge discovery process (perhaps because the term is shorter than *knowledge discovery from data*). Therefore, we adopt a broad view of data mining functionality: **Data mining** is the *process* of discovering interesting patterns and knowledge from *large* amounts of data. The data sources can include databases, data warehouses, the Web, other information repositories, or data that are streamed into the system dynamically.

1.3 What Kinds of Data Can Be Mined?

As a general technology, data mining can be applied to any kind of data as long as the data are meaningful for a target application. The most basic forms of data for mining applications are database data (Section 1.3.1), data warehouse data (Section 1.3.2), and transactional data (Section 1.3.3). The concepts and techniques presented in this book focus on such data. Data mining can also be applied to other forms of data (e.g., data streams, ordered/sequence data, graph or networked data, spatial data, text data, multimedia data, and the WWW). We present an overview of such data in Section 1.3.4. Techniques for mining of these kinds of data are briefly introduced in Chapter 13. In-depth treatment is considered an advanced topic. Data mining will certainly continue to embrace new data types as they emerge.

---

[4]Sometimes data transformation and consolidation are performed before the data selection process, particularly in the case of data warehousing. *Data reduction* may also be performed to obtain a smaller representation of the original data without sacrificing its integrity.

1.3.1 Database Data

A database system, also called a **database management system** (**DBMS**), consists of a collection of interrelated data, known as a **database**, and a set of software programs to manage and access the data. The software programs provide mechanisms for defining database structures and data storage; for specifying and managing concurrent, shared, or distributed data access; and for ensuring consistency and security of the information stored despite system crashes or attempts at unauthorized access.

A **relational database** is a collection of **tables**, each of which is assigned a unique name. Each table consists of a set of **attributes** (*columns* or *fields*) and usually stores a large set of **tuples** (*records* or *rows*). Each tuple in a relational table represents an object identified by a unique *key* and described by a set of attribute values. A semantic data model, such as an **entity-relationship** (**ER**) data model, is often constructed for relational databases. An ER data model represents the database as a set of entities and their relationships.

Example 1.2 **A relational database for *AllElectronics*.** The fictitious *AllElectronics* store is used to illustrate concepts throughout this book. The company is described by the following relation tables: *customer, item, employee,* and *branch.* The headers of the tables described here are shown in Figure 1.5. (A header is also called the *schema* of a relation.)

- The relation *customer* consists of a set of attributes describing the customer information, including a unique customer identity number (*cust_ID*), customer name, address, age, occupation, annual income, credit information, and category.

- Similarly, each of the relations *item, employee,* and *branch* consists of a set of attributes describing the properties of these entities.

- Tables can also be used to represent the relationships between or among multiple entities. In our example, these include *purchases* (customer purchases items, creating a sales transaction handled by an employee), *items_sold* (lists items sold in a given transaction), and *works_at* (employee works at a branch of *AllElectronics*). ∎

customer	(*cust_ID, name, address, age, occupation, annual_income, credit_information, category,* ...)
item	(*item_ID, brand, category, type, price, place_made, supplier, cost,* ...)
employee	(*empl_ID, name, category, group, salary, commission,* ...)
branch	(*branch_ID, name, address,* ...)
purchases	(*trans_ID, cust_ID, empl_ID, date, time, method_paid, amount*)
items_sold	(*trans_ID, item_ID, qty*)
works_at	(*empl_ID, branch_ID*)

Figure 1.5 Relational schema for a relational database, *AllElectronics*.

Relational data can be accessed by **database queries** written in a relational query language (e.g., SQL) or with the assistance of graphical user interfaces. A given query is transformed into a set of relational operations, such as join, selection, and projection, and is then optimized for efficient processing. A query allows retrieval of specified subsets of the data. Suppose that your job is to analyze the *AllElectronics* data. Through the use of relational queries, you can ask things like, *"Show me a list of all items that were sold in the last quarter."* Relational languages also use aggregate functions such as sum, avg (average), count, max (maximum), and min (minimum). Using aggregates allows you to ask: *"Show me the total sales of the last month, grouped by branch,"* or *"How many sales transactions occurred in the month of December?"* or *"Which salesperson had the highest sales?"*

When **mining relational databases**, we can go further by *searching for trends* or *data patterns*. For example, data mining systems can analyze customer data to predict the credit risk of new customers based on their income, age, and previous credit information. Data mining systems may also detect deviations—that is, items with sales that are far from those expected in comparison with the previous year. Such deviations can then be further investigated. For example, data mining may discover that there has been a change in packaging of an item or a significant increase in price.

Relational databases are one of the most commonly available and richest information repositories, and thus they are a major data form in the study of data mining.

1.3.2 Data Warehouses

Suppose that *AllElectronics* is a successful international company with branches around the world. Each branch has its own set of databases. The president of *AllElectronics* has asked you to provide an analysis of the company's sales per item type per branch for the third quarter. This is a difficult task, particularly since the relevant data are spread out over several databases physically located at numerous sites.

If *AllElectronics* had a data warehouse, this task would be easy. A **data warehouse** is a repository of information collected from multiple sources, stored under a unified schema, and usually residing at a single site. Data warehouses are constructed via a process of data cleaning, data integration, data transformation, data loading, and periodic data refreshing. This process is discussed in Chapters 3 and 4. Figure 1.6 shows the typical framework for construction and use of a data warehouse for *AllElectronics*.

To facilitate decision making, the data in a data warehouse are organized around *major subjects* (e.g., customer, item, supplier, and activity). The data are stored to provide information from a *historical perspective*, such as in the past 6 to 12 months, and are typically *summarized*. For example, rather than storing the details of each sales transaction, the data warehouse may store a summary of the transactions per item type for each store or, summarized to a higher level, for each sales region.

A data warehouse is usually modeled by a multidimensional data structure, called a **data cube**, in which each **dimension** corresponds to an attribute or a set of attributes in the schema, and each **cell** stores the value of some aggregate measure such as *count*

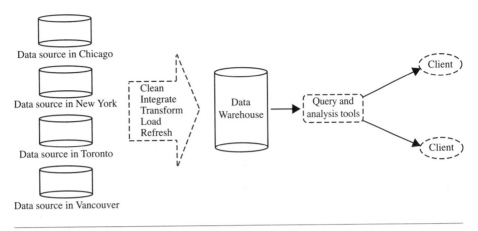

Figure 1.6 Typical framework of a data warehouse for *AllElectronics.*

or *sum(sales_amount)*. A data cube provides a multidimensional view of data and allows the precomputation and fast access of summarized data.

Example 1.3 **A data cube for *AllElectronics.*** A data cube for summarized sales data of *AllElectronics* is presented in Figure 1.7(a). The cube has three dimensions: *address* (with city values *Chicago, New York, Toronto, Vancouver*), *time* (with quarter values *Q1, Q2, Q3, Q4*), and *item* (with item type values *home entertainment, computer, phone, security*). The aggregate value stored in each cell of the cube is *sales_amount* (in thousands). For example, the total sales for the first quarter, *Q1*, for the items related to security systems in Vancouver is $400,000, as stored in cell ⟨*Vancouver, Q1, security*⟩. Additional cubes may be used to store aggregate sums over each dimension, corresponding to the aggregate values obtained using different SQL group-bys (e.g., the total sales amount per city and quarter, or per city and item, or per quarter and item, or per each individual dimension). ∎

By providing multidimensional data views and the precomputation of summarized data, data warehouse systems can provide inherent support for OLAP. Online analytical processing operations make use of background knowledge regarding the domain of the data being studied to allow the presentation of data at *different levels of abstraction*. Such operations accommodate different user viewpoints. Examples of OLAP operations include **drill-down** and **roll-up**, which allow the user to view the data at differing degrees of summarization, as illustrated in Figure 1.7(b). For instance, we can drill down on sales data summarized by *quarter* to see data summarized by *month*. Similarly, we can roll up on sales data summarized by *city* to view data summarized by *country*.

Although data warehouse tools help support data analysis, additional tools for data mining are often needed for in-depth analysis. **Multidimensional data mining** (also called **exploratory multidimensional data mining**) performs data mining in

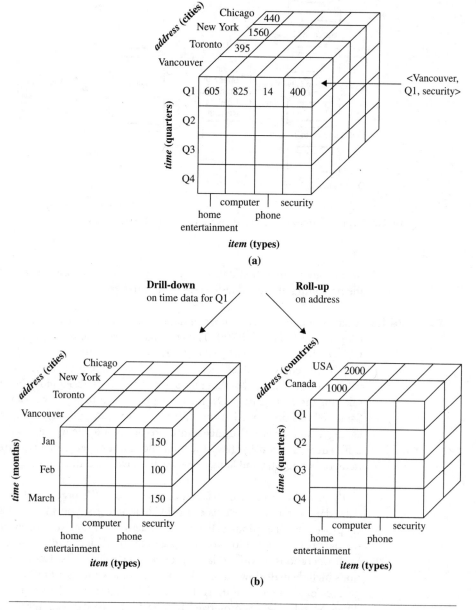

Figure 1.7 A multidimensional data cube, commonly used for data warehousing, (a) showing summarized data for *AllElectronics* and (b) showing summarized data resulting from drill-down and roll-up operations on the cube in (a). For improved readability, only some of the cube cell values are shown.

multidimensional space in an OLAP style. That is, it allows the exploration of multiple combinations of dimensions at varying levels of granularity in data mining, and thus has greater potential for discovering interesting patterns representing knowledge. An overview of data warehouse and OLAP technology is provided in Chapter 4. Advanced issues regarding data cube computation and multidimensional data mining are discussed in Chapter 5.

1.3.3 Transactional Data

In general, each record in a **transactional database** captures a transaction, such as a customer's purchase, a flight booking, or a user's clicks on a web page. A transaction typically includes a unique transaction identity number (*trans_ID*) and a list of the **items** making up the transaction, such as the items purchased in the transaction. A transactional database may have additional tables, which contain other information related to the transactions, such as item description, information about the salesperson or the branch, and so on.

Example 1.4 **A transactional database for *AllElectronics*.** Transactions can be stored in a table, with one record per transaction. A fragment of a transactional database for *AllElectronics* is shown in Figure 1.8. From the relational database point of view, the *sales* table in the figure is a nested relation because the attribute *list_of_item_IDs* contains a set of *items*. Because most relational database systems do not support nested relational structures, the transactional database is usually either stored in a flat file in a format similar to the table in Figure 1.8 or unfolded into a standard relation in a format similar to the *items_sold* table in Figure 1.5. ∎

As an analyst of *AllElectronics*, you may ask, "*Which items sold well together?*" This kind of *market basket data analysis* would enable you to bundle groups of items together as a strategy for boosting sales. For example, given the knowledge that printers are commonly purchased together with computers, you could offer certain printers at a steep discount (or even for free) to customers buying selected computers, in the hopes of selling more computers (which are often more expensive than printers). A traditional database system is not able to perform market basket data analysis. Fortunately, data mining on transactional data can do so by mining *frequent itemsets*, that is, sets

trans_ID	list_of_item_IDs
T100	I1, I3, I8, I16
T200	I2, I8
. . .	. . .

Figure 1.8 Fragment of a transactional database for sales at *AllElectronics*.

of items that are frequently sold together. The mining of such frequent patterns from transactional data is discussed in Chapters 6 and 7.

1.3.4 **Other Kinds of Data**

Besides relational database data, data warehouse data, and transaction data, there are many other kinds of data that have versatile forms and structures and rather different semantic meanings. Such kinds of data can be seen in many applications: time-related or sequence data (e.g., historical records, stock exchange data, and time-series and biological sequence data), data streams (e.g., video surveillance and sensor data, which are continuously transmitted), spatial data (e.g., maps), engineering design data (e.g., the design of buildings, system components, or integrated circuits), hypertext and multimedia data (including text, image, video, and audio data), graph and networked data (e.g., social and information networks), and the Web (a huge, widely distributed information repository made available by the Internet). These applications bring about new challenges, like how to handle data carrying special structures (e.g., sequences, trees, graphs, and networks) and specific semantics (such as ordering, image, audio and video contents, and connectivity), and how to mine patterns that carry rich structures and semantics.

Various kinds of knowledge can be mined from these kinds of data. Here, we list just a few. Regarding temporal data, for instance, we can mine banking data for changing trends, which may aid in the scheduling of bank tellers according to the volume of customer traffic. Stock exchange data can be mined to uncover trends that could help you plan investment strategies (e.g., the best time to purchase *AllElectronics* stock). We could mine computer network data streams to detect intrusions based on the anomaly of message flows, which may be discovered by clustering, dynamic construction of stream models or by comparing the current frequent patterns with those at a previous time. With spatial data, we may look for patterns that describe changes in metropolitan poverty rates based on city distances from major highways. The relationships among a set of spatial objects can be examined in order to discover which subsets of objects are spatially autocorrelated or associated. By mining text data, such as literature on data mining from the past ten years, we can identify the evolution of hot topics in the field. By mining user comments on products (which are often submitted as short text messages), we can assess customer sentiments and understand how well a product is embraced by a market. From multimedia data, we can mine images to identify objects and classify them by assigning semantic labels or tags. By mining video data of a hockey game, we can detect video sequences corresponding to goals. *Web mining* can help us learn about the distribution of information on the WWW in general, characterize and classify web pages, and uncover web dynamics and the association and other relationships among different web pages, users, communities, and web-based activities.

It is important to keep in mind that, in many applications, multiple types of data are present. For example, in web mining, there often exist text data and multimedia data (e.g., pictures and videos) on web pages, graph data like web graphs, and map data on some web sites. In bioinformatics, genomic sequences, biological networks, and

3-D spatial structures of genomes may coexist for certain biological objects. Mining multiple data sources of complex data often leads to fruitful findings due to the mutual enhancement and consolidation of such multiple sources. On the other hand, it is also challenging because of the difficulties in data cleaning and data integration, as well as the complex interactions among the multiple sources of such data.

While such data require sophisticated facilities for efficient storage, retrieval, and updating, they also provide fertile ground and raise challenging research and implementation issues for data mining. Data mining on such data is an advanced topic. The methods involved are extensions of the basic techniques presented in this book.

What Kinds of Patterns Can Be Mined?

We have observed various types of data and information repositories on which data mining can be performed. Let us now examine the kinds of patterns that can be mined.

There are a number of ***data mining functionalities***. These include characterization and discrimination (Section 1.4.1); the mining of frequent patterns, associations, and correlations (Section 1.4.2); classification and regression (Section 1.4.3); clustering analysis (Section 1.4.4); and outlier analysis (Section 1.4.5). Data mining functionalities are used to specify the kinds of patterns to be found in data mining tasks. In general, such tasks can be classified into two categories: **descriptive** and **predictive**. Descriptive mining tasks characterize properties of the data in a target data set. Predictive mining tasks perform induction on the current data in order to make predictions.

Data mining functionalities, and the kinds of patterns they can discover, are described below. In addition, Section 1.4.6 looks at what makes a pattern interesting. Interesting patterns represent *knowledge*.

1.4.1 Class/Concept Description: Characterization and Discrimination

Data entries can be associated with classes or concepts. For example, in the *AllElectronics* store, classes of items for sale include *computers* and *printers*, and concepts of customers include *bigSpenders* and *budgetSpenders*. It can be useful to describe individual classes and concepts in summarized, concise, and yet precise terms. Such descriptions of a class or a concept are called **class/concept descriptions**. These descriptions can be derived using (1) *data characterization*, by summarizing the data of the class under study (often called the **target class**) in general terms, or (2) *data discrimination*, by comparison of the target class with one or a set of comparative classes (often called the **contrasting classes**), or (3) both data characterization and discrimination.

Data characterization is a summarization of the general characteristics or features of a target class of data. The data corresponding to the user-specified class are typically collected by a query. For example, to study the characteristics of software products with sales that increased by 10% in the previous year, the data related to such products can be collected by executing an SQL query on the sales database.

There are several methods for effective data summarization and characterization. Simple data summaries based on statistical measures and plots are described in Chapter 2. The data cube-based OLAP roll-up operation (Section 1.3.2) can be used to perform user-controlled data summarization along a specified dimension. This process is further detailed in Chapters 4 and 5, which discuss data warehousing. An *attribute-oriented induction* technique can be used to perform data generalization and characterization without step-by-step user interaction. This technique is also described in Chapter 4.

The output of data characterization can be presented in various forms. Examples include **pie charts**, **bar charts**, **curves**, **multidimensional data cubes**, and **multidimensional tables**, including crosstabs. The resulting descriptions can also be presented as **generalized relations** or in rule form (called **characteristic rules**).

Example 1.5 **Data characterization.** A customer relationship manager at *AllElectronics* may order the following data mining task: *Summarize the characteristics of customers who spend more than $5000 a year at AllElectronics.* The result is a general profile of these customers, such as that they are 40 to 50 years old, employed, and have excellent credit ratings. The data mining system should allow the customer relationship manager to drill down on any dimension, such as on *occupation* to view these customers according to their type of employment. ∎

Data discrimination is a comparison of the general features of the target class data objects against the general features of objects from one or multiple contrasting classes. The target and contrasting classes can be specified by a user, and the corresponding data objects can be retrieved through database queries. For example, a user may want to compare the general features of software products with sales that increased by 10% last year against those with sales that decreased by at least 30% during the same period. The methods used for data discrimination are similar to those used for data characterization.

"*How are discrimination descriptions output?*" The forms of output presentation are similar to those for characteristic descriptions, although discrimination descriptions should include comparative measures that help to distinguish between the target and contrasting classes. Discrimination descriptions expressed in the form of rules are referred to as **discriminant rules**.

Example 1.6 **Data discrimination.** A customer relationship manager at *AllElectronics* may want to compare two groups of customers—those who shop for computer products regularly (e.g., more than twice a month) and those who rarely shop for such products (e.g., less than three times a year). The resulting description provides a general comparative profile of these customers, such as that 80% of the customers who frequently purchase computer products are between 20 and 40 years old and have a university education, whereas 60% of the customers who infrequently buy such products are either seniors or youths, and have no university degree. Drilling down on a dimension like *occupation*, or adding a new dimension like *income_level*, may help to find even more discriminative features between the two classes. ∎

Concept description, including characterization and discrimination, is described in Chapter 4.

1.4.2 Mining Frequent Patterns, Associations, and Correlations

Frequent patterns, as the name suggests, are patterns that occur frequently in data. There are many kinds of frequent patterns, including frequent itemsets, frequent subsequences (also known as sequential patterns), and frequent substructures. A *frequent itemset* typically refers to a set of items that often appear together in a transactional data set—for example, milk and bread, which are frequently bought together in grocery stores by many customers. A frequently occurring subsequence, such as the pattern that customers, tend to purchase first a laptop, followed by a digital camera, and then a memory card, is a *(frequent) sequential pattern*. A substructure can refer to different structural forms (e.g., graphs, trees, or lattices) that may be combined with itemsets or subsequences. If a substructure occurs frequently, it is called a *(frequent) structured pattern*. Mining frequent patterns leads to the discovery of interesting associations and correlations within data.

Example 1.7 **Association analysis.** Suppose that, as a marketing manager at *AllElectronics*, you want to know which items are frequently purchased together (i.e., within the same transaction). An example of such a rule, mined from the *AllElectronics* transactional database, is

$$buys(X, \text{"computer"}) \Rightarrow buys(X, \text{"software"}) \; [support = 1\%, confidence = 50\%],$$

where X is a variable representing a customer. A **confidence**, or certainty, of 50% means that if a customer buys a computer, there is a 50% chance that she will buy software as well. A 1% **support** means that 1% of all the transactions under analysis show that computer and software are purchased together. This association rule involves a single attribute or predicate (i.e., *buys*) that repeats. Association rules that contain a single predicate are referred to as **single-dimensional association rules**. Dropping the predicate notation, the rule can be written simply as "*computer* $\Rightarrow$ *software* [1%, 50%]."

Suppose, instead, that we are given the *AllElectronics* relational database related to purchases. A data mining system may find association rules like

$$age(X, \text{"20..29"}) \wedge income(X, \text{"40K..49K"}) \Rightarrow buys(X, \text{"laptop"})$$

$$[support = 2\%, confidence = 60\%].$$

The rule indicates that of the *AllElectronics* customers under study, 2% are 20 to 29 years old with an income of $40,000 to $49,000 and have purchased a laptop (computer) at *AllElectronics*. There is a 60% probability that a customer in this age and income group will purchase a laptop. Note that this is an association involving more than one attribute or predicate (i.e., *age, income,* and *buys*). Adopting the terminology used in multidimensional databases, where each attribute is referred to as a dimension, the above rule can be referred to as a **multidimensional association rule**. ∎

Typically, association rules are discarded as uninteresting if they do not satisfy both a **minimum support threshold** and a **minimum confidence threshold**. Additional analysis can be performed to uncover interesting statistical **correlations** between associated attribute–value pairs.

Frequent itemset mining is a fundamental form of frequent pattern mining. The mining of frequent patterns, associations, and correlations is discussed in Chapters 6 and 7, where particular emphasis is placed on efficient algorithms for frequent itemset mining. Sequential pattern mining and structured pattern mining are considered advanced topics.

1.4.3 Classification and Regression for Predictive Analysis

Classification is the process of finding a **model** (or function) that describes and distinguishes data classes or concepts. The model are derived based on the analysis of a set of **training data** (i.e., data objects for which the class labels are known). The model is used to predict the class label of objects for which the the class label is unknown.

"How is the derived model presented?" The derived model may be represented in various forms, such as *classification rules* (i.e., *IF-THEN rules*), *decision trees, mathematical formulae,* or *neural networks* (Figure 1.9). A **decision tree** is a flowchart-like tree structure, where each node denotes a test on an attribute value, each branch represents an outcome of the test, and tree leaves represent classes or class distributions. Decision trees can easily

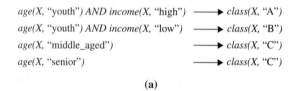

(a)

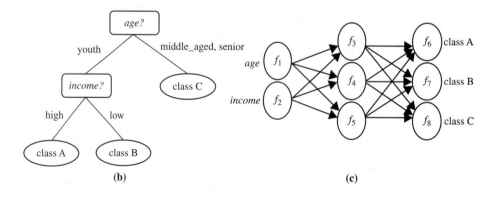

Figure 1.9 A classification model can be represented in various forms: (a) IF-THEN rules, (b) a decision tree, or (c) a neural network.

be converted to classification rules. A **neural network**, when used for classification, is typically a collection of neuron-like processing units with weighted connections between the units. There are many other methods for constructing classification models, such as naïve Bayesian classification, support vector machines, and *k*-nearest-neighbor classification.

Whereas classification predicts categorical (discrete, unordered) labels, **regression** models continuous-valued functions. That is, regression is used to predict missing or unavailable *numerical data values* rather than (discrete) class labels. The term *prediction* refers to both numeric prediction and class label prediction. **Regression analysis** is a statistical methodology that is most often used for numeric prediction, although other methods exist as well. Regression also encompasses the identification of distribution *trends* based on the available data.

Classification and regression may need to be preceded by **relevance analysis**, which attempts to identify attributes that are significantly relevant to the classification and regression process. Such attributes will be selected for the classification and regression process. Other attributes, which are irrelevant, can then be excluded from consideration.

Example 1.8 **Classification and regression.** Suppose as a sales manager of *AllElectronics* you want to classify a large set of items in the store, based on three kinds of responses to a sales campaign: *good response*, *mild response* and *no response*. You want to derive a model for each of these three classes based on the descriptive features of the items, such as *price*, *brand*, *place_made*, *type*, and *category*. The resulting classification should maximally distinguish each class from the others, presenting an organized picture of the data set.

Suppose that the resulting classification is expressed as a decision tree. The decision tree, for instance, may identify *price* as being the single factor that best distinguishes the three classes. The tree may reveal that, in addition to *price*, other features that help to further distinguish objects of each class from one another include *brand* and *place_made*. Such a decision tree may help you understand the impact of the given sales campaign and design a more effective campaign in the future.

Suppose instead, that rather than predicting categorical response labels for each store item, you would like to predict the amount of revenue that each item will generate during an upcoming sale at *AllElectronics*, based on the previous sales data. This is an example of regression analysis because the regression model constructed will predict a continuous function (or ordered value.) ■

Chapters 8 and 9 discuss classification in further detail. Regression analysis is beyond the scope of this book. Sources for further information are given in the bibliographic notes.

1.4.4 Cluster Analysis

Unlike classification and regression, which analyze class-labeled (training) data sets, **clustering** analyzes data objects without consulting class labels. In many cases, class-labeled data may simply not exist at the beginning. Clustering can be used to generate

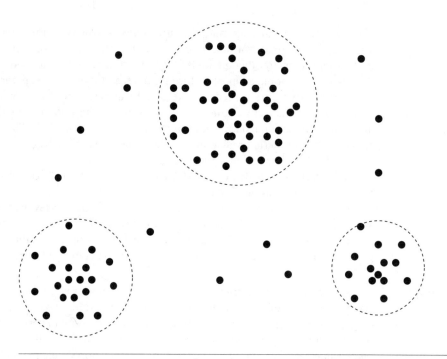

Figure 1.10 A 2-D plot of customer data with respect to customer locations in a city, showing three data clusters.

class labels for a group of data. The objects are clustered or grouped based on the principle of *maximizing the intraclass similarity and minimizing the interclass similarity*. That is, clusters of objects are formed so that objects within a cluster have high similarity in comparison to one another, but are rather dissimilar to objects in other clusters. Each cluster so formed can be viewed as a class of objects, from which rules can be derived. Clustering can also facilitate **taxonomy formation**, that is, the organization of observations into a hierarchy of classes that group similar events together.

Example 1.9 **Cluster analysis.** Cluster analysis can be performed on *AllElectronics* customer data to identify homogeneous subpopulations of customers. These clusters may represent individual target groups for marketing. Figure 1.10 shows a 2-D plot of customers with respect to customer locations in a city. Three clusters of data points are evident.   ∎

Cluster analysis forms the topic of Chapters 10 and 11.

1.4.5 Outlier Analysis

A data set may contain objects that do not comply with the general behavior or model of the data. These data objects are **outliers**. Many data mining methods discard outliers as noise or exceptions. However, in some applications (e.g., fraud detection) the rare events can be more interesting than the more regularly occurring ones. The analysis of outlier data is referred to as **outlier analysis** or **anomaly mining**.

Outliers may be detected using statistical tests that assume a distribution or probability model for the data, or using distance measures where objects that are remote from any other cluster are considered outliers. Rather than using statistical or distance measures, density-based methods may identify outliers in a local region, although they look normal from a global statistical distribution view.

Example 1.10 **Outlier analysis.** Outlier analysis may uncover fraudulent usage of credit cards by detecting purchases of unusually large amounts for a given account number in comparison to regular charges incurred by the same account. Outlier values may also be detected with respect to the locations and types of purchase, or the purchase frequency. ∎

Outlier analysis is discussed in Chapter 12.

1.4.6 Are All Patterns Interesting?

A data mining system has the potential to generate thousands or even millions of patterns, or rules.

You may ask, *"Are all of the patterns interesting?"* Typically, the answer is no—only a small fraction of the patterns potentially generated would actually be of interest to a given user.

This raises some serious questions for data mining. You may wonder, *"What makes a pattern interesting? Can a data mining system generate all of the interesting patterns? Or, Can the system generate only the interesting ones?"*

To answer the first question, a pattern is **interesting** if it is (1) *easily understood* by humans, (2) *valid* on new or test data with some degree of *certainty*, (3) potentially *useful*, and (4) *novel*. A pattern is also interesting if it validates a hypothesis that the user *sought to confirm*. An interesting pattern represents **knowledge**.

Several **objective measures of pattern interestingness** exist. These are based on the structure of discovered patterns and the statistics underlying them. An objective measure for association rules of the form $X \Rightarrow Y$ is rule **support**, representing the percentage of transactions from a transaction database that the given rule satisfies. This is taken to be the probability $P(X \cup Y)$, where $X \cup Y$ indicates that a transaction contains both X and Y, that is, the union of itemsets X and Y. Another objective measure for association rules is **confidence**, which assesses the degree of certainty of the detected association. This is taken to be the conditional probability $P(Y|X)$, that is, the probability that a transaction containing X also contains Y. More formally, support and confidence are defined as

$$support(X \Rightarrow Y) = P(X \cup Y),$$

$$confidence(X \Rightarrow Y) = P(Y|X).$$

In general, each interestingness measure is associated with a threshold, which may be controlled by the user. For example, rules that do not satisfy a confidence threshold of, say, 50% can be considered uninteresting. Rules below the threshold likely reflect noise, exceptions, or minority cases and are probably of less value.

Other objective interestingness measures include *accuracy* and *coverage* for classification (IF-THEN) rules. In general terms, accuracy tells us the percentage of data that are correctly classified by a rule. Coverage is similar to support, in that it tells us the percentage of data to which a rule applies. Regarding understandability, we may use simple objective measures that assess the complexity or length in bits of the patterns mined.

Although objective measures help identify interesting patterns, they are often insufficient unless combined with subjective measures that reflect a particular user's needs and interests. For example, patterns describing the characteristics of customers who shop frequently at *AllElectronics* should be interesting to the marketing manager, but may be of little interest to other analysts studying the same database for patterns on employee performance. Furthermore, many patterns that are interesting by objective standards may represent common sense and, therefore, are actually uninteresting.

Subjective interestingness measures are based on user beliefs in the data. These measures find patterns interesting if the patterns are **unexpected** (contradicting a user's belief) or offer strategic information on which the user can act. In the latter case, such patterns are referred to as **actionable**. For example, patterns like "a large earthquake often follows a cluster of small quakes" may be highly actionable if users can act on the information to save lives. Patterns that are **expected** can be interesting if they confirm a hypothesis that the user wishes to validate or they resemble a user's hunch.

The second question—"*Can a data mining system generate* all *of the interesting patterns?*"—refers to the **completeness** of a data mining algorithm. It is often unrealistic and inefficient for data mining systems to generate all possible patterns. Instead, user-provided constraints and interestingness measures should be used to focus the search. For some mining tasks, such as association, this is often sufficient to ensure the completeness of the algorithm. Association rule mining is an example where the use of constraints and interestingness measures can ensure the completeness of mining. The methods involved are examined in detail in Chapter 6.

Finally, the third question—"*Can a data mining system generate* only *interesting patterns?*"—is an optimization problem in data mining. It is highly desirable for data mining systems to generate only interesting patterns. This would be efficient for users and data mining systems because neither would have to search through the patterns generated to identify the truly interesting ones. Progress has been made in this direction; however, such optimization remains a challenging issue in data mining.

Measures of pattern interestingness are essential for the efficient discovery of patterns by target users. Such measures can be used after the data mining step to rank the discovered patterns according to their interestingness, filtering out the uninteresting ones. More important, such measures can be used to guide and constrain the discovery process, improving the search efficiency by pruning away subsets of the pattern space that do not satisfy prespecified interestingness constraints. Examples of such a constraint-based mining process are described in Chapter 7 (with respect to pattern discovery) and Chapter 11 (with respect to clustering).

Methods to assess pattern interestingness, and their use to improve data mining efficiency, are discussed throughout the book with respect to each kind of pattern that can be mined.

1.5 Which Technologies Are Used?

As a highly application-driven domain, data mining has incorporated many techniques from other domains such as statistics, machine learning, pattern recognition, database and data warehouse systems, information retrieval, visualization, algorithms, high-performance computing, and many application domains (Figure 1.11). The interdisciplinary nature of data mining research and development contributes significantly to the success of data mining and its extensive applications. In this section, we give examples of several disciplines that strongly influence the development of data mining methods.

1.5.1 Statistics

Statistics studies the collection, analysis, interpretation or explanation, and presentation of data. Data mining has an inherent connection with statistics.

A **statistical model** is a set of mathematical functions that describe the behavior of the objects in a target class in terms of random variables and their associated probability distributions. Statistical models are widely used to model data and data classes. For example, in data mining tasks like data characterization and classification, statistical

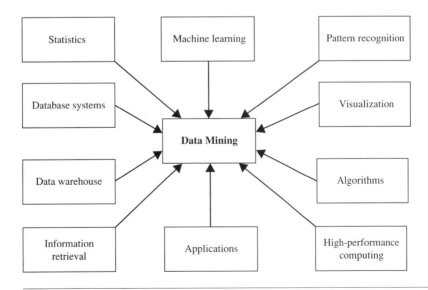

Figure 1.11 Data mining adopts techniques from many domains.

models of target classes can be built. In other words, such statistical models can be the outcome of a data mining task. Alternatively, data mining tasks can be built on top of statistical models. For example, we can use statistics to model noise and missing data values. Then, when mining patterns in a large data set, the data mining process can use the model to help identify and handle noisy or missing values in the data.

Statistics research develops tools for prediction and forecasting using data and statistical models. Statistical methods can be used to summarize or describe a collection of data. Basic **statistical descriptions** of data are introduced in Chapter 2. Statistics is useful for mining various patterns from data as well as for understanding the underlying mechanisms generating and affecting the patterns. **Inferential statistics** (or **predictive statistics**) models data in a way that accounts for randomness and uncertainty in the observations and is used to draw inferences about the process or population under investigation.

Statistical methods can also be used to verify data mining results. For example, after a classification or prediction model is mined, the model should be verified by statistical hypothesis testing. A **statistical hypothesis test** (sometimes called *confirmatory data analysis*) makes statistical decisions using experimental data. A result is called *statistically significant* if it is unlikely to have occurred by chance. If the classification or prediction model holds true, then the descriptive statistics of the model increases the soundness of the model.

Applying statistical methods in data mining is far from trivial. Often, a serious challenge is how to scale up a statistical method over a large data set. Many statistical methods have high complexity in computation. When such methods are applied on large data sets that are also distributed on multiple logical or physical sites, algorithms should be carefully designed and tuned to reduce the computational cost. This challenge becomes even tougher for online applications, such as online query suggestions in search engines, where data mining is required to continuously handle fast, real-time data streams.

1.5.2 Machine Learning

Machine learning investigates how computers can learn (or improve their performance) based on data. A main research area is for computer programs to *automatically* learn to recognize complex patterns and make intelligent decisions based on data. For example, a typical machine learning problem is to program a computer so that it can automatically recognize handwritten postal codes on mail after learning from a set of examples.

Machine learning is a fast-growing discipline. Here, we illustrate classic problems in machine learning that are highly related to data mining.

- **Supervised learning** is basically a synonym for classification. The supervision in the learning comes from the labeled examples in the training data set. For example, in the postal code recognition problem, a set of handwritten postal code images and their corresponding machine-readable translations are used as the training examples, which supervise the learning of the classification model.

- **Unsupervised learning** is essentially a synonym for clustering. The learning process is unsupervised since the input examples are not class labeled. Typically, we may use clustering to discover classes within the data. For example, an unsupervised learning method can take, as input, a set of images of handwritten digits. Suppose that it finds 10 clusters of data. These clusters may correspond to the 10 distinct digits of 0 to 9, respectively. However, since the training data are not labeled, the learned model cannot tell us the semantic meaning of the clusters found.

- **Semi-supervised learning** is a class of machine learning techniques that make use of both labeled and unlabeled examples when learning a model. In one approach, labeled examples are used to learn class models and unlabeled examples are used to refine the boundaries between classes.   For a two-class problem, we can think of the set of examples belonging to one class as the *positive examples* and those belonging to the other class as the *negative examples*. In Figure 1.12, if we do not consider the unlabeled examples, the dashed line is the decision boundary that best partitions the positive examples from the negative examples. Using the unlabeled examples, we can refine the decision boundary to the solid line. Moreover, we can detect that the two positive examples at the top right corner, though labeled, are likely noise or outliers.

- **Active learning** is a machine learning approach that lets users play an active role in the learning process. An active learning approach can ask a user (e.g., a domain expert) to label an example, which may be from a set of unlabeled examples or synthesized by the learning program. The goal is to optimize the model quality by actively acquiring knowledge from human users, given a constraint on how many examples they can be asked to label.

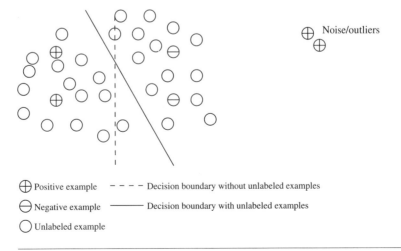

Figure 1.12 Semi-supervised learning.

You can see there are many similarities between data mining and machine learning. For classification and clustering tasks, machine learning research often focuses on the accuracy of the model. In addition to accuracy, data mining research places strong emphasis on the efficiency and scalability of mining methods on large data sets, as well as on ways to handle complex types of data and explore new, alternative methods.

1.5.3 Database Systems and Data Warehouses

Database systems research focuses on the creation, maintenance, and use of databases for organizations and end-users. Particularly, database systems researchers have established highly recognized principles in data models, query languages, query processing and optimization methods, data storage, and indexing and accessing methods. Database systems are often well known for their high scalability in processing very large, relatively structured data sets.

Many data mining tasks need to handle large data sets or even real-time, fast streaming data. Therefore, data mining can make good use of scalable database technologies to achieve high efficiency and scalability on large data sets. Moreover, data mining tasks can be used to extend the capability of existing database systems to satisfy advanced users' sophisticated data analysis requirements.

Recent database systems have built systematic data analysis capabilities on database data using data warehousing and data mining facilities. A **data warehouse** integrates data originating from multiple sources and various timeframes. It consolidates data in multidimensional space to form partially materialized data cubes. The data cube model not only facilitates OLAP in multidimensional databases but also promotes *multidimensional data mining* (see Section 1.3.2).

1.5.4 Information Retrieval

Information retrieval (**IR**) is the science of searching for documents or information in documents. Documents can be text or multimedia, and may reside on the Web. The differences between traditional information retrieval and database systems are twofold: Information retrieval assumes that (1) the data under search are unstructured; and (2) the queries are formed mainly by keywords, which do not have complex structures (unlike SQL queries in database systems).

The typical approaches in information retrieval adopt probabilistic models. For example, a text document can be regarded as a bag of words, that is, a multiset of words appearing in the document. The document's **language model** is the probability density function that generates the bag of words in the document. The similarity between two documents can be measured by the similarity between their corresponding language models.

Furthermore, a topic in a set of text documents can be modeled as a probability distribution over the vocabulary, which is called a **topic model**. A text document, which may involve one or multiple topics, can be regarded as a mixture of multiple topic models. By integrating information retrieval models and data mining techniques, we can find the major topics in a collection of documents and, for each document in the collection, the major topics involved.

Increasingly large amounts of text and multimedia data have been accumulated and made available online due to the fast growth of the Web and applications such as digital libraries, digital governments, and health care information systems. Their effective search and analysis have raised many challenging issues in data mining. Therefore, text mining and multimedia data mining, integrated with information retrieval methods, have become increasingly important.

1.6 Which Kinds of Applications Are Targeted?

Where there are data, there are data mining applications

As a highly application-driven discipline, data mining has seen great successes in many applications. It is impossible to enumerate all applications where data mining plays a critical role. Presentations of data mining in knowledge-intensive application domains, such as bioinformatics and software engineering, require more in-depth treatment and are beyond the scope of this book. To demonstrate the importance of applications as a major dimension in data mining research and development, we briefly discuss two highly successful and popular application examples of data mining: *business intelligence* and *search engines*.

1.6.1 Business Intelligence

It is critical for businesses to acquire a better understanding of the commercial context of their organization, such as their customers, the market, supply and resources, and competitors. **Business intelligence** (**BI**) technologies provide historical, current, and predictive views of business operations. Examples include reporting, online analytical processing, business performance management, competitive intelligence, benchmarking, and predictive analytics.

"How important is business intelligence?" Without data mining, many businesses may not be able to perform effective market analysis, compare customer feedback on similar products, discover the strengths and weaknesses of their competitors, retain highly valuable customers, and make smart business decisions.

Clearly, data mining is the core of business intelligence. Online analytical processing tools in business intelligence rely on data warehousing and multidimensional data mining. Classification and prediction techniques are the core of predictive analytics in business intelligence, for which there are many applications in analyzing markets, supplies, and sales. Moreover, clustering plays a central role in customer relationship management, which groups customers based on their similarities. Using characterization mining techniques, we can better understand features of each customer group and develop customized customer reward programs.

1.6.2 **Web Search Engines**

A **Web search engine** is a specialized computer server that searches for information on the Web. The search results of a user query are often returned as a list (sometimes called *hits*). The hits may consist of web pages, images, and other types of files. Some search engines also search and return data available in public databases or open directories. Search engines differ from **web directories** in that web directories are maintained by human editors whereas search engines operate algorithmically or by a mixture of algorithmic and human input.

Web search engines are essentially very large data mining applications. Various data mining techniques are used in all aspects of search engines, ranging from *crawling*[5] (e.g., deciding which pages should be crawled and the crawling frequencies), indexing (e.g., selecting pages to be indexed and deciding to which extent the index should be constructed), and searching (e.g., deciding how pages should be ranked, which advertisements should be added, and how the search results can be personalized or made "context aware").

Search engines pose grand challenges to data mining. First, they have to handle a huge and ever-growing amount of data. Typically, such data cannot be processed using one or a few machines. Instead, search engines often need to use *computer clouds*, which consist of thousands or even hundreds of thousands of computers that collaboratively mine the huge amount of data. Scaling up data mining methods over computer clouds and large distributed data sets is an area for further research.

Second, Web search engines often have to deal with online data. A search engine may be able to afford constructing a model offline on huge data sets. To do this, it may construct a query classifier that assigns a search query to predefined categories based on the query topic (i.e., whether the search query "apple" is meant to retrieve information about a fruit or a brand of computers). Whether a model is constructed offline, the application of the model online must be fast enough to answer user queries in real time.

Another challenge is maintaining and incrementally updating a model on fast-growing data streams. For example, a query classifier may need to be incrementally maintained continuously since new queries keep emerging and predefined categories and the data distribution may change. Most of the existing model training methods are offline and static and thus cannot be used in such a scenario.

Third, Web search engines often have to deal with queries that are asked only a very small number of times. Suppose a search engine wants to provide *context-aware* query recommendations. That is, when a user poses a query, the search engine tries to infer the context of the query using the user's profile and his query history in order to return more customized answers within a small fraction of a second. However, although the total number of queries asked can be huge, most of the queries may be asked only once or a few times. Such severely skewed data are challenging for many data mining and machine learning methods.

---

[5]A Web crawler is a computer program that browses the Web in a methodical, automated manner.

1.7 Major Issues in Data Mining

Life is short but art is long. – Hippocrates

Data mining is a dynamic and fast-expanding field with great strengths. In this section, we briefly outline the major issues in data mining research, partitioning them into five groups: *mining methodology, user interaction, efficiency and scalability, diversity of data types*, and *data mining and society*. Many of these issues have been addressed in recent data mining research and development *to a certain extent* and are now considered *data mining requirements*; others are still at the research stage. The issues continue to stimulate further investigation and improvement in data mining.

1.7.1 Mining Methodology

Researchers have been vigorously developing new data mining methodologies. This involves the investigation of new kinds of knowledge, mining in multidimensional space, integrating methods from other disciplines, and the consideration of semantic ties among data objects. In addition, mining methodologies should consider issues such as data uncertainty, noise, and incompleteness. Some mining methods explore how user-specified measures can be used to assess the interestingness of discovered patterns as well as guide the discovery process. Let's have a look at these various aspects of mining methodology.

- *Mining various and new kinds of knowledge:* Data mining covers a wide spectrum of data analysis and knowledge discovery tasks, from data characterization and discrimination to association and correlation analysis, classification, regression, clustering, outlier analysis, sequence analysis, and trend and evolution analysis. These tasks may use the same database in different ways and require the development of numerous data mining techniques. Due to the diversity of applications, new mining tasks continue to emerge, making data mining a dynamic and fast-growing field. For example, for effective knowledge discovery in information networks, integrated clustering and ranking may lead to the discovery of high-quality clusters and object ranks in large networks.

- *Mining knowledge in multidimensional space:* When searching for knowledge in large data sets, we can explore the data in multidimensional space. That is, we can search for interesting patterns among combinations of dimensions (attributes) at varying levels of abstraction. Such mining is known as *(exploratory) multidimensional data mining*. In many cases, data can be aggregated or viewed as a multidimensional data cube. Mining knowledge in cube space can substantially enhance the power and flexibility of data mining.

- *Data mining—an interdisciplinary effort:* The power of data mining can be substantially enhanced by integrating new methods from multiple disciplines. For example, to mine data with natural language text, it makes sense to fuse data mining methods with methods of information retrieval and natural language processing. As another example, consider the mining of software bugs in large programs. This form of mining, known as *bug mining*, benefits from the incorporation of software engineering knowledge into the data mining process.

■ *Boosting the power of discovery in a networked environment:* Most data objects reside in a linked or interconnected environment, whether it be the Web, database relations, files, or documents. Semantic links across multiple data objects can be used to advantage in data mining. Knowledge derived in one set of objects can be used to boost the discovery of knowledge in a "related" or semantically linked set of objects.

■ *Handling uncertainty, noise, or incompleteness of data:* Data often contain noise, errors, exceptions, or uncertainty, or are incomplete. Errors and noise may confuse the data mining process, leading to the derivation of erroneous patterns. Data cleaning, data preprocessing, outlier detection and removal, and uncertainty reasoning are examples of techniques that need to be integrated with the data mining process.

■ *Pattern evaluation and pattern- or constraint-guided mining:* Not all the patterns generated by data mining processes are interesting. What makes a pattern interesting may vary from user to user. Therefore, techniques are needed to assess the interestingness of discovered patterns based on subjective measures. These estimate the value of patterns with respect to a given user class, based on user beliefs or expectations. Moreover, by using interestingness measures or user-specified constraints to *guide* the discovery process, we may generate more interesting patterns and reduce the search space.

1.7.2 User Interaction

The user plays an important role in the data mining process. Interesting areas of research include *how to interact with a data mining system, how to incorporate a user's background knowledge in mining,* and *how to visualize and comprehend data mining results.* We introduce each of these here.

■ *Interactive mining:* The data mining process should be highly *interactive.* Thus, it is important to build flexible user interfaces and an exploratory mining environment, facilitating the user's interaction with the system. A user may like to first sample a set of data, explore general characteristics of the data, and estimate potential mining results. Interactive mining should allow users to dynamically change the focus of a search, to refine mining requests based on returned results, and to drill, dice, and pivot through the data and knowledge space interactively, dynamically exploring "cube space" while mining.

■ *Incorporation of background knowledge:* Background knowledge, constraints, rules, and other information regarding the domain under study should be incorporated into the knowledge discovery process. Such knowledge can be used for pattern evaluation as well as to guide the search toward interesting patterns.

■ *Ad hoc data mining and data mining query languages:* Query languages (e.g., SQL) have played an important role in flexible searching because they allow users to pose ad hoc queries. Similarly, high-level data mining query languages or other high-level flexible user interfaces will give users the freedom to define ad hoc data mining tasks. This should facilitate specification of the relevant sets of data for analysis, the domain knowledge, the kinds of knowledge to be mined, and the conditions and constraints to be enforced on the discovered patterns. Optimization of the processing of such flexible mining requests is another promising area of study.

■ *Presentation and visualization of data mining results:* How can a data mining system present data mining results, vividly and flexibly, so that the discovered knowledge can be easily understood and directly usable by humans? This is especially crucial if the data mining process is interactive. It requires the system to adopt expressive knowledge representations, user-friendly interfaces, and visualization techniques.

1.7.3 Efficiency and Scalability

Efficiency and scalability are always considered when comparing data mining algorithms. As data amounts continue to multiply, these two factors are especially critical.

■ *Efficiency and scalability of data mining algorithms:* Data mining algorithms must be efficient and scalable in order to effectively extract information from huge amounts of data in many data repositories or in dynamic data streams. In other words, the running time of a data mining algorithm must be predictable, short, and acceptable by applications. *Efficiency, scalability, performance, optimization,* and the ability to execute in *real time* are key criteria that drive the development of many new data mining algorithms.

■ *Parallel, distributed, and incremental mining algorithms:* The humongous size of many data sets, the wide distribution of data, and the computational complexity of some data mining methods are factors that motivate the development of **parallel and distributed data-intensive mining algorithms**. Such algorithms first partition the data into "pieces." Each piece is processed, in parallel, by searching for patterns. The parallel processes may interact with one another. The patterns from each partition are eventually merged.

Cloud computing and *cluster computing*, which use computers in a distributed and collaborative way to tackle very large-scale computational tasks, are also active research themes in parallel data mining. In addition, the high cost of some data mining processes and the incremental nature of input promote **incremental** data mining, which incorporates new data updates without having to mine the entire data "from scratch." Such methods perform knowledge modification incrementally to amend and strengthen what was previously discovered.

1.7.4 Diversity of Database Types

The wide diversity of database types brings about challenges to data mining. These include

- *Handling complex types of data:* Diverse applications generate a wide spectrum of new data types, from structured data such as relational and data warehouse data to semi-structured and unstructured data; from stable data repositories to dynamic data streams; from simple data objects to temporal data, biological sequences, sensor data, spatial data, hypertext data, multimedia data, software program code, Web data, and social network data. It is unrealistic to expect one data mining system to mine all kinds of data, given the diversity of data types and the different goals of data mining. Domain- or application-dedicated data mining systems are being constructed for in-depth mining of specific kinds of data. The construction of effective and efficient data mining tools for diverse applications remains a challenging and active area of research.

- *Mining dynamic, networked, and global data repositories:* Multiple sources of data are connected by the Internet and various kinds of networks, forming gigantic, distributed, and heterogeneous global information systems and networks. The discovery of knowledge from different sources of structured, semi-structured, or unstructured yet interconnected data with diverse data semantics poses great challenges to data mining. Mining such gigantic, interconnected information networks may help disclose many more patterns and knowledge in heterogeneous data sets than can be discovered from a small set of isolated data repositories. Web mining, multisource data mining, and information network mining have become challenging and fast-evolving data mining fields.

1.7.5 Data Mining and Society

How does data mining impact society? What steps can data mining take to preserve the privacy of individuals? Do we use data mining in our daily lives without even knowing that we do? These questions raise the following issues:

- *Social impacts of data mining:* With data mining penetrating our everyday lives, it is important to study the impact of data mining on society. How can we use data mining technology to benefit society? How can we guard against its misuse? The improper disclosure or use of data and the potential violation of individual privacy and data protection rights are areas of concern that need to be addressed.

- *Privacy-preserving data mining:* Data mining will help scientific discovery, business management, economy recovery, and security protection (e.g., the real-time discovery of intruders and cyberattacks). However, it poses the risk of disclosing an individual's personal information. Studies on privacy-preserving data publishing and data mining are ongoing. The philosophy is to observe data sensitivity and preserve people's privacy while performing successful data mining.

▪ *Invisible data mining:* We cannot expect everyone in society to learn and master data mining techniques. More and more systems should have data mining functions built within so that people can perform data mining or use data mining results simply by mouse clicking, without any knowledge of data mining algorithms. Intelligent search engines and Internet-based stores perform such *invisible data mining* by incorporating data mining into their components to improve their functionality and performance. This is done often unbeknownst to the user. For example, when purchasing items online, users may be unaware that the store is likely collecting data on the buying patterns of its customers, which may be used to recommend other items for purchase in the future.

These issues and many additional ones relating to the research, development, and application of data mining are discussed throughout the book.

1.8 Summary

▪ *Necessity is the mother of invention.* With the mounting growth of data in every application, data mining meets the imminent need for effective, scalable, and flexible data analysis in our society. Data mining can be considered as a natural evolution of information technology and a confluence of several related disciplines and application domains.

▪ **Data mining** is the process of discovering interesting patterns from massive amounts of data. As a *knowledge discovery process*, it typically involves data cleaning, data integration, data selection, data transformation, pattern discovery, pattern evaluation, and knowledge presentation.

▪ A pattern is *interesting* if it is valid on test data with some degree of certainty, novel, potentially useful (e.g., can be acted on or validates a hunch about which the user was curious), and easily understood by humans. Interesting patterns represent **knowledge**. Measures of **pattern interestingness**, either *objective* or *subjective*, can be used to guide the discovery process.

▪ We present a **multidimensional view** of data mining. The major dimensions are **data, knowledge, technologies**, and **applications**.

▪ Data mining can be conducted on any kind of **data** as long as the data are meaningful for a target application, such as database data, data warehouse data, transactional data, and advanced data types. Advanced data types include time-related or sequence data, data streams, spatial and spatiotemporal data, text and multimedia data, graph and networked data, and Web data.

▪ A **data warehouse** is a repository for long-term storage of data from multiple sources, organized so as to facilitate management decision making. The data are stored under a unified schema and are typically summarized. Data warehouse systems provide multidimensional data analysis capabilities, collectively referred to as **online analytical processing**.

- **Multidimensional data mining** (also called **exploratory multidimensional data mining**) integrates core data mining techniques with OLAP-based multidimensional analysis. It searches for interesting patterns among multiple combinations of dimensions (attributes) at varying levels of abstraction, thereby exploring multidimensional data space.

- **Data mining functionalities** are used to specify the kinds of patterns or **knowledge** to be found in data mining tasks. The functionalities include characterization and discrimination; the mining of frequent patterns, associations, and correlations; classification and regression; cluster analysis; and outlier detection. As new types of data, new applications, and new analysis demands continue to emerge, there is no doubt we will see more and more novel data mining tasks in the future.

- Data mining, as a highly application-driven domain, has incorporated **technologies** from many other domains. These include statistics, machine learning, database and data warehouse systems, and information retrieval. The **interdisciplinary nature of data mining research and development** contributes significantly to the success of data mining and its extensive applications.

- Data mining has many successful **applications**, such as business intelligence, Web search, bioinformatics, health informatics, finance, digital libraries, and digital governments.

- There are many challenging **issues in data mining research**. Areas include mining methodology, user interaction, efficiency and scalability, and dealing with diverse data types. Data mining research has strongly impacted society and will continue to do so in the future.

1.9 Exercises

1.1 What is *data mining*? In your answer, address the following:

(a) Is it another hype?

(b) Is it a simple transformation or application of technology developed from *databases*, *statistics*, *machine learning*, and *pattern recognition*?

(c) We have presented a view that data mining is the result of the evolution of *database technology*. Do you think that data mining is also the result of the evolution of *machine learning research*? Can you present such views based on the historical progress of this discipline? Address the same for the fields of *statistics* and *pattern recognition*.

(d) Describe the steps involved in data mining when viewed as a process of knowledge discovery.

1.2 How is a *data warehouse* different from a *database*? How are they similar?

1.3 Define each of the following *data mining functionalities*: characterization, discrimination, association and correlation analysis, classification, regression, clustering, and outlier analysis. Give examples of each data mining functionality, using a real-life database that you are familiar with.

1.4 Present an example where data mining is crucial to the success of a business. What *data mining functionalities* does this business need (e.g., think of the kinds of patterns that could be mined)? Can such patterns be generated alternatively by data query processing or simple statistical analysis?

1.5 Explain the difference and similarity between discrimination and classification, between characterization and clustering, and between classification and regression.

1.6 Based on your observations, describe another possible kind of knowledge that needs to be discovered by data mining methods but has not been listed in this chapter. Does it require a mining methodology that is quite different from those outlined in this chapter?

1.7 *Outliers* are often discarded as noise. However, one person's garbage could be another's treasure. For example, exceptions in credit card transactions can help us detect the fraudulent use of credit cards. Using fraudulence detection as an example, propose two methods that can be used to detect outliers and discuss which one is more reliable.

1.8 Describe three challenges to data mining regarding *data mining methodology* and *user interaction issues*.

1.9 What are the major challenges of mining a huge amount of data (e.g., billions of tuples) in comparison with mining a small amount of data (e.g., data set of a few hundred tuple)?

1.10 Outline the major research challenges of data mining in one specific application domain, such as stream/sensor data analysis, spatiotemporal data analysis, or bioinformatics.

1.10 Bibliographic Notes

The book *Knowledge Discovery in Databases*, edited by Piatetsky-Shapiro and Frawley [P-SF91], is an early collection of research papers on knowledge discovery from data. The book *Advances in Knowledge Discovery and Data Mining*, edited by Fayyad, Piatetsky-Shapiro, Smyth, and Uthurusamy [FPSS+96], is a collection of later research results on knowledge discovery and data mining. There have been many data mining books published in recent years, including *The Elements of Statistical Learning* by Hastie, Tibshirani, and Friedman [HTF09]; *Introduction to Data Mining* by Tan, Steinbach, and Kumar [TSK05]; *Data Mining: Practical Machine Learning Tools and Techniques with Java Implementations* by Witten, Frank, and Hall [WFH11]; *Predictive Data Mining* by Weiss and Indurkhya [WI98]; *Mastering Data Mining: The Art and Science of Customer Relationship Management* by Berry and Linoff [BL99]; *Principles of Data Mining (Adaptive Computation and Machine Learning)* by Hand, Mannila, and Smyth [HMS01]; *Mining the Web: Discovering Knowledge from Hypertext Data* by Chakrabarti [Cha03a]; *Web Data Mining: Exploring Hyperlinks, Contents, and Usage*

Data by Liu [Liu06]; *Data Mining: Introductory and Advanced Topics* by Dunham [Dun03]; and *Data Mining: Multimedia, Soft Computing, and Bioinformatics* by Mitra and Acharya [MA03].

There are also books that contain collections of papers or chapters on particular aspects of knowledge discovery—for example, *Relational Data Mining* edited by Dzeroski and Lavrac [De01]; *Mining Graph Data* edited by Cook and Holder [CH07]; *Data Streams: Models and Algorithms* edited by Aggarwal [Agg06]; *Next Generation of Data Mining* edited by Kargupta, Han, Yu, et al. [KHY+08]; *Multimedia Data Mining: A Systematic Introduction to Concepts and Theory* edited by Z. Zhang and R. Zhang [ZZ09]; *Geographic Data Mining and Knowledge Discovery* edited by Miller and Han [MH09]; and *Link Mining: Models, Algorithms and Applications* edited by Yu, Han, and Faloutsos [YHF10]. There are many tutorial notes on data mining in major databases, data mining, machine learning, statistics, and Web technology conferences.

KDNuggets is a regular electronic newsletter containing information relevant to knowledge discovery and data mining, moderated by Piatetsky-Shapiro since 1991. The Internet site *KDNuggets* (*www.kdnuggets.com*) contains a good collection of KDD-related information.

The data mining community started its first international conference on knowledge discovery and data mining in 1995. The conference evolved from the four international workshops on knowledge discovery in databases, held from 1989 to 1994. ACM-SIGKDD, a Special Interest Group on Knowledge Discovery in Databases was set up under ACM in 1998 and has been organizing the international conferences on knowledge discovery and data mining since 1999. IEEE Computer Science Society has organized its annual data mining conference, International Conference on Data Mining (ICDM), since 2001. SIAM (Society on Industrial and Applied Mathematics) has organized its annual data mining conference, SIAM Data Mining Conference (SDM), since 2002. A dedicated journal, *Data Mining and Knowledge Discovery*, published by Kluwers Publishers, has been available since 1997. An ACM journal, *ACM Transactions on Knowledge Discovery from Data*, published its first volume in 2007.

ACM-SIGKDD also publishes a bi-annual newsletter, *SIGKDD Explorations*. There are a few other international or regional conferences on data mining, such as the European Conference on Machine Learning and Principles and Practice of Knowledge Discovery in Databases (ECML PKDD), the Pacific-Asia Conference on Knowledge Discovery and Data Mining (PAKDD), and the International Conference on Data Warehousing and Knowledge Discovery (DaWaK).

Research in data mining has also been published in books, conferences, and journals on databases, statistics, machine learning, and data visualization. References to such sources are listed at the end of the book.

Popular textbooks on database systems include *Database Systems: The Complete Book* by Garcia-Molina, Ullman, and Widom [GMUW08]; *Database Management Systems* by Ramakrishnan and Gehrke [RG03]; *Database System Concepts* by Silberschatz, Korth, and Sudarshan [SKS10]; and *Fundamentals of Database Systems* by Elmasri and Navathe [EN10]. For an edited collection of seminal articles on database systems, see *Readings in Database Systems* by Hellerstein and Stonebraker [HS05].

There are also many books on data warehouse technology, systems, and applications, such as *The Data Warehouse Toolkit: The Complete Guide to Dimensional Modeling* by Kimball and Ross [KR02]; *The Data Warehouse Lifecycle Toolkit* by Kimball, Ross, Thornthwaite, and Mundy [KRTM08]; *Mastering Data Warehouse Design: Relational and Dimensional Techniques* by Imhoff, Galemmo, and Geiger [IGG03]; and *Building the Data Warehouse* by Inmon [Inm96]. A set of research papers on materialized views and data warehouse implementations were collected in *Materialized Views: Techniques, Implementations, and Applications* by Gupta and Mumick [GM99]. Chaudhuri and Dayal [CD97] present an early comprehensive overview of data warehouse technology.

Research results relating to data mining and data warehousing have been published in the proceedings of many international database conferences, including the ACM-SIGMOD International Conference on Management of Data (SIGMOD), the International Conference on Very Large Data Bases (VLDB), the ACM SIGACT-SIGMOD-SIGART Symposium on Principles of Database Systems (PODS), the International Conference on Data Engineering (ICDE), the International Conference on Extending Database Technology (EDBT), the International Conference on Database Theory (ICDT), the International Conference on Information and Knowledge Management (CIKM), the International Conference on Database and Expert Systems Applications (DEXA), and the International Symposium on Database Systems for Advanced Applications (DASFAA). Research in data mining is also published in major database journals, such as *IEEE Transactions on Knowledge and Data Engineering (TKDE), ACM Transactions on Database Systems (TODS), Information Systems, The VLDB Journal, Data and Knowledge Engineering, International Journal of Intelligent Information Systems (JIIS)*, and *Knowledge and Information Systems (KAIS)*.

Many effective data mining methods have been developed by statisticians and introduced in a rich set of textbooks. An overview of classification from a statistical pattern recognition perspective can be found in *Pattern Classification* by Duda, Hart, and Stork [DHS01]. There are also many textbooks covering regression and other topics in statistical analysis, such as *Mathematical Statistics: Basic Ideas and Selected Topics* by Bickel and Doksum [BD01]; *The Statistical Sleuth: A Course in Methods of Data Analysis* by Ramsey and Schafer [RS01]; *Applied Linear Statistical Models* by Neter, Kutner, Nachtsheim, and Wasserman [NKNW96]; *An Introduction to Generalized Linear Models* by Dobson [Dob90]; *Applied Statistical Time Series Analysis* by Shumway [Shu88]; and *Applied Multivariate Statistical Analysis* by Johnson and Wichern [JW92].

Research in statistics is published in the proceedings of several major statistical conferences, including Joint Statistical Meetings, International Conference of the Royal Statistical Society and Symposium on the Interface: Computing Science and Statistics. Other sources of publication include the *Journal of the Royal Statistical Society, The Annals of Statistics*, the *Journal of American Statistical Association, Technometrics*, and *Biometrika*.

Textbooks and reference books on machine learning and pattern recognition include *Machine Learning* by Mitchell [Mit97]; *Pattern Recognition and Machine Learning* by Bishop [Bis06]; *Pattern Recognition* by Theodoridis and Koutroumbas [TK08]; *Introduction to Machine Learning* by Alpaydin [Alp11]; *Probabilistic Graphical Models: Principles and Techniques* by Koller and Friedman [KF09]; and *Machine Learning: An Algorithmic Perspective* by Marsland [Mar09]. For an edited collection of seminal articles on machine learning, see *Machine Learning, An Artificial Intelligence Approach*, Volumes 1 through 4, edited by Michalski et al. [MCM83, MCM86, KM90, MT94], and *Readings in Machine Learning* by Shavlik and Dietterich [SD90].

Machine learning and pattern recognition research is published in the proceedings of several major machine learning, artificial intelligence, and pattern recognition conferences, including the International Conference on Machine Learning (ML), the ACM Conference on Computational Learning Theory (COLT), the IEEE Conference on Computer Vision and Pattern Recognition (CVPR), the International Conference on Pattern Recognition (ICPR), the International Joint Conference on Artificial Intelligence (IJCAI), and the American Association of Artificial Intelligence Conference (AAAI). Other sources of publication include major machine learning, artificial intelligence, pattern recognition, and knowledge system journals, some of which have been mentioned before. Others include *Machine Learning (ML), Pattern Recognition (PR), Artificial Intelligence Journal (AI), IEEE Transactions on Pattern Analysis and Machine Intelligence (PAMI)*, and *Cognitive Science*.

Textbooks and reference books on information retrieval include *Introduction to Information Retrieval* by Manning, Raghavan, and Schutz [MRS08]; *Information Retrieval: Implementing and Evaluating Search Engines* by Büttcher, Clarke, and Cormack [BCC10]; *Search Engines: Information Retrieval in Practice* by Croft, Metzler, and Strohman [CMS09]; *Modern Information Retrieval: The Concepts and Technology Behind Search* by Baeza-Yates and Ribeiro-Neto [BYRN11]; and *Information Retrieval: Algorithms and Heuristics* by Grossman and Frieder [GR04].

Information retrieval research is published in the proceedings of several information retrieval and Web search and mining conferences, including the International ACM SIGIR Conference on Research and Development in Information Retrieval (SIGIR), the International World Wide Web Conference (WWW), the ACM International Conference on Web Search and Data Mining (WSDM), the ACM Conference on Information and Knowledge Management (CIKM), the European Conference on Information Retrieval (ECIR), the Text Retrieval Conference (TREC), and the ACM/IEEE Joint Conference on Digital Libraries (JCDL). Other sources of publication include major information retrieval, information systems, and Web journals, such as *Journal of Information Retrieval, ACM Transactions on Information Systems (TOIS), Information Processing and Management, Knowledge and Information Systems (KAIS)*, and *IEEE Transactions on Knowledge and Data Engineering (TKDE)*.

Getting to Know Your Data

2

It's tempting to jump straight into mining, but first, we need to get the data ready. This involves having a closer look at attributes and data values. Real-world data are typically noisy, enormous in volume (often several gigabytes or more), and may originate from a hodge-podge of heterogenous sources. This chapter is about getting familiar with your data. Knowledge about your data is useful for data preprocessing (see Chapter 3), the first major task of the data mining process. You will want to know the following: What are the types of *attributes* or fields that make up your data? What kind of values does each attribute have? Which attributes are discrete, and which are continuous-valued? What do the data *look like*? How are the values distributed? Are there ways we can visualize the data to get a better sense of it all? Can we spot any outliers? Can we measure the similarity of some data objects with respect to others? Gaining such insight into the data will help with the subsequent analysis.

"*So what can we learn about our data that's helpful in data preprocessing?*" We begin in Section 2.1 by studying the various attribute types. These include nominal attributes, binary attributes, ordinal attributes, and numeric attributes. Basic *statistical descriptions* can be used to learn more about each attribute's values, as described in Section 2.2. Given a *temperature* attribute, for example, we can determine its **mean** (average value), **median** (middle value), and **mode** (most common value). These are **measures of central tendency**, which give us an idea of the "middle" or center of distribution.

Knowing such basic statistics regarding each attribute makes it easier to fill in missing values, smooth noisy values, and spot outliers during data preprocessing. Knowledge of the attributes and attribute values can also help in fixing inconsistencies incurred during data integration. Plotting the measures of central tendency shows us if the data are symmetric or skewed. Quantile plots, histograms, and scatter plots are other graphic displays of basic statistical descriptions. These can all be useful during data preprocessing and can provide insight into areas for mining.

The field of data visualization provides many additional techniques for viewing data through graphical means. These can help identify relations, trends, and biases "hidden" in unstructured data sets. Techniques may be as simple as scatter-plot matrices (where two attributes are mapped onto a 2-D grid) to more sophisticated methods such as tree-maps (where a hierarchical partitioning of the screen is displayed based on the attribute values). Data visualization techniques are described in Section 2.3.

Finally, we may want to examine how similar (or dissimilar) data objects are. For example, suppose we have a database where the data objects are patients, described by their symptoms. We may want to find the similarity or dissimilarity between individual patients. Such information can allow us to find clusters of like patients within the data set. The similarity/dissimilarity between objects may also be used to detect outliers in the data, or to perform nearest-neighbor classification. (Clustering is the topic of Chapters 10 and 11, while nearest-neighbor classification is discussed in Chapter 9.) There are many measures for assessing similarity and dissimilarity. In general, such measures are referred to as proximity measures. Think of the proximity of two objects as a function of the *distance* between their attribute values, although proximity can also be calculated based on probabilities rather than actual distance. Measures of data proximity are described in Section 2.4.

In summary, by the end of this chapter, you will know the different attribute types and basic statistical measures to describe the central tendency and dispersion (spread) of attribute data. You will also know techniques to visualize attribute distributions and how to compute the similarity or dissimilarity between objects.

2.1 Data Objects and Attribute Types

Data sets are made up of data objects. A **data object** represents an entity—in a sales database, the objects may be customers, store items, and sales; in a medical database, the objects may be patients; in a university database, the objects may be students, professors, and courses. Data objects are typically described by attributes. Data objects can also be referred to as *samples, examples, instances, data points,* or *objects*. If the data objects are stored in a database, they are *data tuples*. That is, the rows of a database correspond to the data objects, and the columns correspond to the attributes. In this section, we define attributes and look at the various attribute types.

2.1.1 What Is an Attribute?

An **attribute** is a data field, representing a characteristic or feature of a data object. The nouns *attribute, dimension, feature,* and *variable* are often used interchangeably in the literature. The term *dimension* is commonly used in data warehousing. Machine learning literature tends to use the term *feature*, while statisticians prefer the term *variable*. Data mining and database professionals commonly use the term *attribute*, and we do here as well. Attributes describing a customer object can include, for example, *customer_ID, name,* and *address*. Observed values for a given attribute are known as *observations*. A set of attributes used to describe a given object is called an *attribute vector* (or *feature vector*). The distribution of data involving one attribute (or variable) is called *univariate*. A *bivariate* distribution involves two attributes, and so on.

The **type** of an attribute is determined by the set of possible values—nominal, binary, ordinal, or numeric—the attribute can have. In the following subsections, we introduce each type.

2.1.2 Nominal Attributes

Nominal means "relating to names." The values of a **nominal attribute** are symbols or *names of things*. Each value represents some kind of category, code, or state, and so nominal attributes are also referred to as **categorical**. The values do not have any meaningful order. In computer science, the values are also known as *enumerations*.

Example 2.1 **Nominal attributes.** Suppose that *hair_color* and *marital_status* are two attributes describing *person* objects. In our application, possible values for *hair_color* are *black, brown, blond, red, auburn, gray,* and *white*. The attribute *marital_status* can take on the values *single, married, divorced,* and *widowed*. Both *hair_color* and *marital_status* are nominal attributes. Another example of a nominal attribute is *occupation*, with the values *teacher, dentist, programmer, farmer,* and so on. ■

Although we said that the values of a nominal attribute are symbols or "names of things," it is possible to represent such symbols or "names" with numbers. With *hair_color*, for instance, we can assign a code of 0 for *black*, 1 for *brown*, and so on. Another example is *customor_ID*, with possible values that are all numeric. However, in such cases, the numbers are not intended to be used quantitatively. That is, mathematical operations on values of nominal attributes are not meaningful. It makes no sense to subtract one customer ID number from another, unlike, say, subtracting an age value from another (where *age* is a numeric attribute). Even though a nominal attribute may have integers as values, it is not considered a numeric attribute because the integers are not meant to be used quantitatively. We will say more on numeric attributes in Section 2.1.5.

Because nominal attribute values do not have any meaningful order about them and are not quantitative, it makes no sense to find the mean (average) value or median (middle) value for such an attribute, given a set of objects. One thing that is of interest, however, is the attribute's most commonly occurring value. This value, known as the *mode*, is one of the measures of central tendency. You will learn about measures of central tendency in Section 2.2.

2.1.3 Binary Attributes

A **binary attribute** is a nominal attribute with only two categories or states: 0 or 1, where 0 typically means that the attribute is absent, and 1 means that it is present. Binary attributes are referred to as **Boolean** if the two states correspond to *true* and *false*.

Example 2.2 **Binary attributes.** Given the attribute *smoker* describing a *patient* object, 1 indicates that the patient smokes, while 0 indicates that the patient does not. Similarly, suppose the patient undergoes a medical test that has two possible outcomes. The attribute *medical_test* is binary, where a value of 1 means the result of the test for the patient is positive, while 0 means the result is negative.   ∎

A binary attribute is **symmetric** if both of its states are equally valuable and carry the same weight; that is, there is no preference on which outcome should be coded as 0 or 1. One such example could be the attribute *gender* having the states *male* and *female*.

A binary attribute is **asymmetric** if the outcomes of the states are not equally important, such as the *positive* and *negative* outcomes of a medical test for HIV. By convention, we code the most important outcome, which is usually the rarest one, by 1 (e.g., *HIV positive*) and the other by 0 (e.g., *HIV negative*).

2.1.4 Ordinal Attributes

An **ordinal attribute** is an attribute with possible values that have a meaningful order or *ranking* among them, but the magnitude between successive values is not known.

Example 2.3 **Ordinal attributes.** Suppose that *drink_size* corresponds to the size of drinks available at a fast-food restaurant. This nominal attribute has three possible values: *small*, *medium*, and *large*. The values have a meaningful sequence (which corresponds to increasing drink size); however, we cannot tell from the values *how much* bigger, say, a medium is than a large. Other examples of ordinal attributes include *grade* (e.g., A+, A, A−, B+, and so on) and *professional_rank*. Professional ranks can be enumerated in a sequential order: for example, *assistant*, *associate*, and *full* for professors, and *private, private first class, specialist, corporal*, and *sergeant* for army ranks.

Ordinal attributes are useful for registering subjective assessments of qualities that cannot be measured objectively; thus ordinal attributes are often used in surveys for ratings. In one survey, participants were asked to rate how satisfied they were as customers. Customer satisfaction had the following ordinal categories: *0: very dissatisfied, 1: somewhat dissatisfied, 2: neutral, 3: satisfied*, and *4: very satisfied*.   ∎

Ordinal attributes may also be obtained from the discretization of numeric quantities by splitting the value range into a finite number of ordered categories as described in Chapter 3 on data reduction.

The central tendency of an ordinal attribute can be represented by its mode and its median (the middle value in an ordered sequence), but the mean cannot be defined.

Note that nominal, binary, and ordinal attributes are *qualitative*. That is, they *describe* a feature of an object without giving an actual size or quantity. The values of such qualitative attributes are typically words representing categories. If integers are used, they represent computer codes for the categories, as opposed to measurable quantities (e.g., 0 for *small* drink size, 1 for *medium*, and 2 for *large*). In the following subsection we look at numeric attributes, which provide *quantitative* measurements of an object.

2.1.5 Numeric Attributes

A **numeric attribute** is *quantitative*; that is, it is a measurable quantity, represented in integer or real values. Numeric attributes can be *interval-scaled* or *ratio-scaled*.

Interval-Scaled Attributes

Interval-scaled attributes are measured on a scale of equal-size units. The values of interval-scaled attributes have order and can be positive, 0, or negative. Thus, in addition to providing a ranking of values, such attributes allow us to compare and quantify the *difference* between values.

Example 2.4 **Interval-scaled attributes.** A *temperature* attribute is interval-scaled. Suppose that we have the outdoor *temperature* value for a number of different days, where each day is an object. By ordering the values, we obtain a ranking of the objects with respect to *temperature*. In addition, we can quantify the difference between values. For example, a temperature of 20°C is five degrees higher than a temperature of 15°C. Calendar dates are another example. For instance, the years 2002 and 2010 are eight years apart. ∎

Temperatures in Celsius and Fahrenheit do not have a true zero-point, that is, neither 0°C nor 0°F indicates "no temperature." (On the Celsius scale, for example, the unit of measurement is 1/100 of the difference between the melting temperature and the boiling temperature of water in atmospheric pressure.) Although we can compute the *difference* between temperature values, we cannot talk of one temperature value as being a *multiple* of another. Without a true zero, we cannot say, for instance, that 10°C is twice as warm as 5°C. That is, we cannot speak of the values in terms of ratios. Similarly, there is no true zero-point for calendar dates. (The year 0 does not correspond to the beginning of time.) This brings us to ratio-scaled attributes, for which a true zero-point exits.

Because interval-scaled attributes are numeric, we can compute their mean value, in addition to the median and mode measures of central tendency.

Ratio-Scaled Attributes

A **ratio-scaled attribute** is a numeric attribute with an inherent zero-point. That is, if a measurement is ratio-scaled, we can speak of a value as being a multiple (or ratio) of another value. In addition, the values are ordered, and we can also compute the difference between values, as well as the mean, median, and mode.

Example 2.5 **Ratio-scaled attributes.** Unlike temperatures in Celsius and Fahrenheit, the Kelvin (K) temperature scale has what is considered a true zero-point (0°K = −273.15°C): It is the point at which the particles that comprise matter have zero kinetic energy. Other examples of ratio-scaled attributes include *count* attributes such as *years_of_experience* (e.g., the objects are employees) and *number_of_words* (e.g., the objects are documents).

Additional examples include attributes to measure weight, height, and speed, and monetary quantities (e.g., you are 100 times richer with $100 than with $1).   ■

2.1.6 Discrete versus Continuous Attributes

In our presentation, we have organized attributes into nominal, binary, ordinal, and numeric types. There are many ways to organize attribute types. The types are not mutually exclusive.

Classification algorithms developed from the field of machine learning often talk of attributes as being either *discrete* or *continuous*. Each type may be processed differently. A **discrete attribute** has a finite or countably infinite set of values, which may or may not be represented as integers. The attributes *hair_color*, *smoker*, *medical_test*, and *drink_size* each have a finite number of values, and so are discrete. Note that discrete attributes may have numeric values, such as 0 and 1 for binary attributes or, the values 0 to 110 for the attribute *age*. An attribute is *countably infinite* if the set of possible values is infinite but the values can be put in a one-to-one correspondence with natural numbers. For example, the attribute *customer_ID* is countably infinite. The number of customers can grow to infinity, but in reality, the actual set of values is countable (where the values can be put in one-to-one correspondence with the set of integers). Zip codes are another example.

If an attribute is not discrete, it is **continuous**. The terms *numeric attribute* and *continuous attribute* are often used interchangeably in the literature. (This can be confusing because, in the classic sense, continuous values are real numbers, whereas numeric values can be either integers or real numbers.) In practice, real values are represented using a finite number of digits. Continuous attributes are typically represented as floating-point variables.

2.2 Basic Statistical Descriptions of Data

For data preprocessing to be successful, it is essential to have an overall picture of your data. Basic statistical descriptions can be used to identify properties of the data and highlight which data values should be treated as noise or outliers.

This section discusses three areas of basic statistical descriptions. We start with *measures of central tendency* (Section 2.2.1), which measure the location of the middle or center of a data distribution. Intuitively speaking, given an attribute, where do most of its values fall? In particular, we discuss the mean, median, mode, and midrange.

In addition to assessing the central tendency of our data set, we also would like to have an idea of the *dispersion of the data*. That is, how are the data spread out? The most common data dispersion measures are the *range*, *quartiles*, and *interquartile range*; the *five-number summary* and *boxplots*; and the *variance* and *standard deviation* of the data. These measures are useful for identifying outliers and are described in Section 2.2.2.

Finally, we can use many graphic displays of basic statistical descriptions to visually inspect our data (Section 2.2.3). Most statistical or graphical data presentation software packages include bar charts, pie charts, and line graphs. Other popular displays of data summaries and distributions include *quantile plots, quantile–quantile plots, histograms,* and *scatter plots.*

2.2.1 Measuring the Central Tendency: Mean, Median, and Mode

In this section, we look at various ways to measure the central tendency of data. Suppose that we have some attribute X, like *salary*, which has been recorded for a set of objects. Let $x_1, x_2, \ldots, x_N$ be the set of N observed values or *observations* for X. Here, these values may also be referred to as the data set (for X). If we were to plot the observations for *salary*, where would most of the values fall? This gives us an idea of the central tendency of the data. Measures of central tendency include the mean, median, mode, and midrange.

The most common and effective numeric measure of the "center" of a set of data is the *(arithmetic) mean*. Let $x_1, x_2, \ldots, x_N$ be a set of N values or *observations*, such as for some numeric attribute X, like *salary*. The **mean** of this set of values is

$$\bar{x} = \frac{\sum_{i=1}^{N} x_i}{N} = \frac{x_1 + x_2 + \cdots + x_N}{N}. \tag{2.1}$$

This corresponds to the built-in aggregate function, *average* (avg() in SQL), provided in relational database systems.

Example 2.6 **Mean.** Suppose we have the following values for *salary* (in thousands of dollars), shown in increasing order: 30, 36, 47, 50, 52, 52, 56, 60, 63, 70, 70, 110. Using Eq. (2.1), we have

$$\bar{x} = \frac{30 + 36 + 47 + 50 + 52 + 52 + 56 + 60 + 63 + 70 + 70 + 110}{12}$$

$$= \frac{696}{12} = 58.$$

Thus, the mean salary is \$58,000.   ∎

Sometimes, each value x_i in a set may be associated with a weight w_i for $i = 1, \ldots, N$. The weights reflect the significance, importance, or occurrence frequency attached to their respective values. In this case, we can compute

$$\bar{x} = \frac{\sum_{i=1}^{N} w_i x_i}{\sum_{i=1}^{N} w_i} = \frac{w_1 x_1 + w_2 x_2 + \cdots + w_N x_N}{w_1 + w_2 + \cdots + w_N}. \tag{2.2}$$

This is called the **weighted arithmetic mean** or the **weighted average**.

Although the mean is the singlemost useful quantity for describing a data set, it is not always the best way of measuring the center of the data. A major problem with the mean is its sensitivity to extreme (e.g., outlier) values. Even a small number of extreme values can corrupt the mean. For example, the mean salary at a company may be substantially pushed up by that of a few highly paid managers. Similarly, the mean score of a class in an exam could be pulled down quite a bit by a few very low scores. To offset the effect caused by a small number of extreme values, we can instead use the **trimmed mean**, which is the mean obtained after chopping off values at the high and low extremes. For example, we can sort the values observed for *salary* and remove the top and bottom 2% before computing the mean. We should avoid trimming too large a portion (such as 20%) at both ends, as this can result in the loss of valuable information.

For skewed (asymmetric) data, a better measure of the center of data is the **median**, which is the middle value in a set of ordered data values. It is the value that separates the higher half of a data set from the lower half.

In probability and statistics, the median generally applies to numeric data; however, we may extend the concept to ordinal data. Suppose that a given data set of N values for an attribute X is sorted in increasing order. If N is odd, then the median is the *middle value* of the ordered set. If N is even, then the median is not unique; it is the two middlemost values and any value in between. If X is a numeric attribute in this case, by convention, the median is taken as the average of the two middlemost values.

Example 2.7 **Median.** Let's find the median of the data from Example 2.6. The data are already sorted in increasing order. There is an even number of observations (i.e., 12); therefore, the median is not unique. It can be any value within the two middlemost values of 52 and 56 (that is, within the sixth and seventh values in the list). By convention, we assign the average of the two middlemost values as the median; that is, $\frac{52+56}{2} = \frac{108}{2} = 54$. Thus, the median is \$54,000.

Suppose that we had only the first 11 values in the list. Given an odd number of values, the median is the middlemost value. This is the sixth value in this list, which has a value of \$52,000. ∎

The median is expensive to compute when we have a large number of observations. For numeric attributes, however, we can easily *approximate* the value. Assume that data are grouped in intervals according to their x_i data values and that the frequency (i.e., number of data values) of each interval is known. For example, employees may be grouped according to their annual salary in intervals such as \$10–20,000, \$20–30,000, and so on. Let the interval that contains the median frequency be the *median interval*. We can approximate the median of the entire data set (e.g., the median salary) by interpolation using the formula

$$median = L_1 + \left(\frac{N/2 - (\sum freq)_l}{freq_{median}} \right) width, \qquad (2.3)$$

where L_1 is the lower boundary of the median interval, N is the number of values in the entire data set, $(\sum freq)_l$ is the sum of the frequencies of all of the intervals that are lower than the median interval, $freq_{median}$ is the frequency of the median interval, and *width* is the width of the median interval.

The *mode* is another measure of central tendency. The **mode** for a set of data is the value that occurs most frequently in the set. Therefore, it can be determined for qualitative and quantitative attributes. It is possible for the greatest frequency to correspond to several different values, which results in more than one mode. Data sets with one, two, or three modes are respectively called **unimodal**, **bimodal**, and **trimodal**. In general, a data set with two or more modes is **multimodal**. At the other extreme, if each data value occurs only once, then there is no mode.

Example 2.8 **Mode.** The data from Example 2.6 are bimodal. The two modes are $52,000 and $70,000. ∎

For unimodal numeric data that are moderately skewed (asymmetrical), we have the following empirical relation:

$$mean - mode \approx 3 \times (mean - median). \tag{2.4}$$

This implies that the mode for unimodal frequency curves that are moderately skewed can easily be approximated if the mean and median values are known.

The **midrange** can also be used to assess the central tendency of a numeric data set. It is the average of the largest and smallest values in the set. This measure is easy to compute using the SQL aggregate functions, max() and min().

Example 2.9 **Midrange.** The midrange of the data of Example 2.6 is $\frac{30,000+110,000}{2} = $70,000. ∎

In a unimodal frequency curve with perfect **symmetric** data distribution, the mean, median, and mode are all at the same center value, as shown in Figure 2.1(a).

Data in most real applications are not symmetric. They may instead be either **positively skewed**, where the mode occurs at a value that is smaller than the median (Figure 2.1b), or **negatively skewed**, where the mode occurs at a value greater than the median (Figure 2.1c).

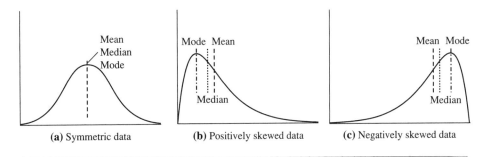

(a) Symmetric data   **(b)** Positively skewed data   **(c)** Negatively skewed data

Figure 2.1 Mean, median, and mode of symmetric versus positively and negatively skewed data.

2.2.2 Measuring the Dispersion of Data: Range, Quartiles, Variance, Standard Deviation, and Interquartile Range

We now look at measures to assess the dispersion or spread of numeric data. The measures include range, quantiles, quartiles, percentiles, and the interquartile range. The five-number summary, which can be displayed as a boxplot, is useful in identifying outliers. Variance and standard deviation also indicate the spread of a data distribution.

Range, Quartiles, and Interquartile Range

To start off, let's study the *range, quantiles, quartiles, percentiles,* and the *interquartile range* as measures of data dispersion.

Let $x_1, x_2, \ldots, x_N$ be a set of observations for some numeric attribute, X. The **range** of the set is the difference between the largest (**max()**) and smallest (**min()**) values.

Suppose that the data for attribute X are sorted in increasing numeric order. Imagine that we can pick certain data points so as to split the data distribution into equal-size consecutive sets, as in Figure 2.2. These data points are called *quantiles.* **Quantiles** are points taken at regular intervals of a data distribution, dividing it into essentially equal-size consecutive sets. (We say "essentially" because there may not be data values of X that divide the data into exactly equal-sized subsets. For readability, we will refer to them as equal.) The kth q-*quantile* for a given data distribution is the value x such that at most k/q of the data values are less than x and at most $(q - k)/q$ of the data values are more than x, where k is an integer such that $0 < k < q$. There are $q - 1$ q-quantiles.

The 2-quantile is the data point dividing the lower and upper halves of the data distribution. It corresponds to the median. The 4-quantiles are the three data points that split the data distribution into four equal parts; each part represents one-fourth of the data distribution. They are more commonly referred to as **quartiles**. The 100-quantiles are more commonly referred to as **percentiles**; they divide the data distribution into 100 equal-sized consecutive sets. The median, quartiles, and percentiles are the most widely used forms of quantiles.

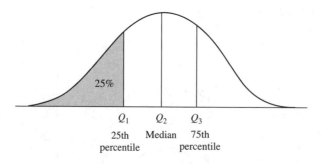

Figure 2.2 A plot of the data distribution for some attribute X. The quantiles plotted are quartiles. The three quartiles divide the distribution into four equal-size consecutive subsets. The second quartile corresponds to the median.

The quartiles give an indication of a distribution's center, spread, and shape. The **first quartile**, denoted by Q_1, is the 25th percentile. It cuts off the lowest 25% of the data. The **third quartile**, denoted by Q_3, is the 75th percentile—it cuts off the lowest 75% (or highest 25%) of the data. The second quartile is the 50th percentile. As the median, it gives the center of the data distribution.

The distance between the first and third quartiles is a simple measure of spread that gives the range covered by the middle half of the data. This distance is called the **interquartile range** (**IQR**) and is defined as

$$IQR = Q_3 - Q_1. \tag{2.5}$$

Example 2.10 Interquartile range. The quartiles are the three values that split the sorted data set into four equal parts. The data of Example 2.6 contain 12 observations, already sorted in increasing order. Thus, the quartiles for this data are the third, sixth, and ninth values, respectively, in the sorted list. Therefore, $Q_1 = \$47,000$ and Q_3 is $\$63,000$. Thus, the interquartile range is $IQR = 63 - 47 = \$16,000$. (Note that the sixth value is a median, $\$52,000$, although this data set has two medians since the number of data values is even.)   ∎

Five-Number Summary, Boxplots, and Outliers

No single numeric measure of spread (e.g., IQR) is very useful for describing skewed distributions. Have a look at the symmetric and skewed data distributions of Figure 2.1. In the symmetric distribution, the median (and other measures of central tendency) splits the data into equal-size halves. This does not occur for skewed distributions. Therefore, it is more informative to also provide the two quartiles Q_1 and Q_3, along with the median. A common rule of thumb for identifying suspected **outliers** is to single out values falling at least $1.5 \times IQR$ above the third quartile or below the first quartile.

Because Q_1, the median, and Q_3 together contain no information about the end-points (e.g., tails) of the data, a fuller summary of the shape of a distribution can be obtained by providing the lowest and highest data values as well. This is known as the *five-number summary*. The **five-number summary** of a distribution consists of the median (Q_2), the quartiles Q_1 and Q_3, and the smallest and largest individual observations, written in the order of *Minimum, Q_1, Median, Q_3, Maximum*.

Boxplots are a popular way of visualizing a distribution. A boxplot incorporates the five-number summary as follows:

- Typically, the ends of the box are at the quartiles so that the box length is the interquartile range.

- The median is marked by a line within the box.

- Two lines (called *whiskers*) outside the box extend to the smallest (*Minimum*) and largest (*Maximum*) observations.

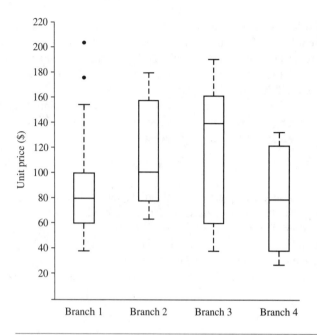

Figure 2.3 Boxplot for the unit price data for items sold at four branches of *AllElectronics* during a given time period.

When dealing with a moderate number of observations, it is worthwhile to plot potential outliers individually. To do this in a boxplot, the whiskers are extended to the extreme low and high observations *only if* these values are less than $1.5 \times IQR$ beyond the quartiles. Otherwise, the whiskers terminate at the most extreme observations occurring within $1.5 \times IQR$ of the quartiles. The remaining cases are plotted individually. Boxplots can be used in the comparisons of several sets of compatible data.

Example 2.11 Boxplot. Figure 2.3 shows boxplots for unit price data for items sold at four branches of *AllElectronics* during a given time period. For branch 1, we see that the median price of items sold is \$80, Q_1 is \$60, and Q_3 is \$100. Notice that two outlying observations for this branch were plotted individually, as their values of 175 and 202 are more than 1.5 times the IQR here of 40. ∎

Boxplots can be computed in $O(n \log n)$ time. Approximate boxplots can be computed in linear or sublinear time depending on the quality guarantee required.

Variance and Standard Deviation

Variance and standard deviation are measures of data dispersion. They indicate how spread out a data distribution is. A low standard deviation means that the data observations tend to be very close to the mean, while a high standard deviation indicates that the data are spread out over a large range of values.

The **variance** of N observations, $x_1, x_2, \ldots, x_N$, for a numeric attribute X is

$$\sigma^2 = \frac{1}{N} \sum_{i=1}^{N} (x_i - \bar{x})^2 = \left(\frac{1}{N} \sum_{i=1}^{N} x_i^2 \right) - \bar{x}^2, \tag{2.6}$$

where $\bar{x}$ is the mean value of the observations, as defined in Eq. (2.1). The **standard deviation**, σ, of the observations is the square root of the variance, σ^2.

Example 2.12 **Variance and standard deviation.** In Example 2.6, we found $\bar{x} = \$58,000$ using Eq. (2.1) for the mean. To determine the variance and standard deviation of the data from that example, we set $N = 12$ and use Eq. (2.6) to obtain

$$\sigma^2 = \frac{1}{12}(30^2 + 36^2 + 47^2 \ldots + 110^2) - 58^2$$

$$\approx 379.17$$

$$\sigma \approx \sqrt{379.17} \approx 19.47. \qquad \blacksquare$$

The basic properties of the standard deviation, σ, as a measure of spread are as follows:

- σ measures spread about the mean and should be considered only when the mean is chosen as the measure of center.

- $\sigma = 0$ only when there is no spread, that is, when all observations have the same value. Otherwise, $\sigma > 0$.

Importantly, an observation is unlikely to be more than several standard deviations away from the mean. Mathematically, using Chebyshev's inequality, it can be shown that at least $\left(1 - \frac{1}{k^2}\right) \times 100\%$ of the observations are no more than k standard deviations from the mean. Therefore, the standard deviation is a good indicator of the spread of a data set.

The computation of the variance and standard deviation is scalable in large databases.

2.2.3 Graphic Displays of Basic Statistical Descriptions of Data

In this section, we study graphic displays of basic statistical descriptions. These include *quantile plots, quantile–quantile plots, histograms,* and *scatter plots.* Such graphs are helpful for the visual inspection of data, which is useful for data preprocessing. The first three of these show univariate distributions (i.e., data for one attribute), while scatter plots show bivariate distributions (i.e., involving two attributes).

Quantile Plot

In this and the following subsections, we cover common graphic displays of data distributions. A **quantile plot** is a simple and effective way to have a first look at a univariate data distribution. First, it displays all of the data for the given attribute (allowing the user to assess both the overall behavior and unusual occurrences). Second, it plots quantile information (see Section 2.2.2). Let x_i, for $i = 1$ to N, be the data sorted in increasing order so that x_1 is the smallest observation and x_N is the largest for some ordinal or numeric attribute X. Each observation, x_i, is paired with a percentage, f_i, which indicates that approximately $f_i \times 100\%$ of the data are below the value, x_i. We say "approximately" because there may not be a value with exactly a fraction, f_i, of the data below x_i. Note that the 0.25 percentile corresponds to quartile Q_1, the 0.50 percentile is the median, and the 0.75 percentile is Q_3.

Let

$$f_i = \frac{i - 0.5}{N}. \tag{2.7}$$

These numbers increase in equal steps of $1/N$, ranging from $\frac{1}{2N}$ (which is slightly above 0) to $1 - \frac{1}{2N}$ (which is slightly below 1). On a quantile plot, x_i is graphed against f_i. This allows us to compare different distributions based on their quantiles. For example, given the quantile plots of sales data for two different time periods, we can compare their Q_1, median, Q_3, and other f_i values at a glance.

Example 2.13 Quantile plot. Figure 2.4 shows a quantile plot for the *unit price* data of Table 2.1.   ∎

Quantile–Quantile Plot

A **quantile–quantile plot**, or **q-q plot**, graphs the quantiles of one univariate distribution against the corresponding quantiles of another. It is a powerful visualization tool in that it allows the user to view whether there is a shift in going from one distribution to another.

Suppose that we have two sets of observations for the attribute or variable *unit price*, taken from two different branch locations. Let $x_1,\ldots,x_N$ be the data from the first branch, and $y_1,\ldots,y_M$ be the data from the second, where each data set is sorted in increasing order. If $M = N$ (i.e., the number of points in each set is the same), then we simply plot y_i against x_i, where y_i and x_i are both $(i - 0.5)/N$ quantiles of their respective data sets. If $M < N$ (i.e., the second branch has fewer observations than the first), there can be only M points on the q-q plot. Here, y_i is the $(i - 0.5)/M$ quantile of the y

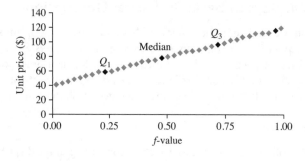

Figure 2.4 A quantile plot for the unit price data of Table 2.1.

Table 2.1 A Set of Unit Price Data for Items Sold at a Branch of *AllElectronics*

Unit price ($)	Count of items sold
40	275
43	300
47	250
—	—
74	360
75	515
78	540
—	—
115	320
117	270
120	350

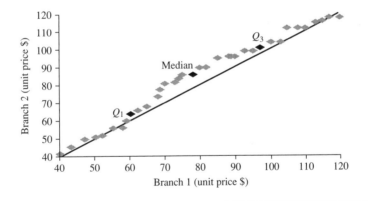

Figure 2.5 A q-q plot for unit price data from two *AllElectronics* branches.

data, which is plotted against the $(i-0.5)/M$ quantile of the x data. This computation typically involves interpolation.

Example 2.14 Quantile–quantile plot. Figure 2.5 shows a quantile–quantile plot for *unit price* data of items sold at two branches of *AllElectronics* during a given time period. Each point corresponds to the same quantile for each data set and shows the unit price of items sold at branch 1 versus branch 2 for that quantile. (To aid in comparison, the straight line represents the case where, for each given quantile, the unit price at each branch is the same. The darker points correspond to the data for Q_1, the median, and Q_3, respectively.)

We see, for example, that at Q_1, the unit price of items sold at branch 1 was slightly less than that at branch 2. In other words, 25% of items sold at branch 1 were less than or equal to $60, while 25% of items sold at branch 2 were less than or equal to $64. At the 50th percentile (marked by the median, which is also Q_2), we see that 50% of items sold at branch 1 were less than $78, while 50% of items at branch 2 were less than $85. In general, we note that there is a shift in the distribution of branch 1 with respect to branch 2 in that the unit prices of items sold at branch 1 tend to be lower than those at branch 2. ∎

Histograms

Histograms (or **frequency histograms**) are at least a century old and are widely used. "Histos" means pole or mast, and "gram" means chart, so a histogram is a chart of poles. Plotting histograms is a graphical method for summarizing the distribution of a given attribute, X. If X is nominal, such as *automobile_model* or *item_type*, then a pole or vertical bar is drawn for each known value of X. The height of the bar indicates the frequency (i.e., count) of that X value. The resulting graph is more commonly known as a **bar chart**.

If X is numeric, the term *histogram* is preferred. The range of values for X is partitioned into disjoint consecutive subranges. The subranges, referred to as *buckets* or *bins*, are disjoint subsets of the data distribution for X. The range of a bucket is known as the **width**. Typically, the buckets are of equal width. For example, a *price* attribute with a value range of $1 to $200 (rounded up to the nearest dollar) can be partitioned into subranges 1 to 20, 21 to 40, 41 to 60, and so on. For each subrange, a bar is drawn with a height that represents the total count of items observed within the subrange. Histograms and partitioning rules are further discussed in Chapter 3 on data reduction.

Example 2.15 Histogram. Figure 2.6 shows a histogram for the data set of Table 2.1, where buckets (or bins) are defined by equal-width ranges representing $20 increments and the frequency is the count of items sold. ∎

Although histograms are widely used, they may not be as effective as the quantile plot, q-q plot, and boxplot methods in comparing groups of univariate observations.

Scatter Plots and Data Correlation

A **scatter plot** is one of the most effective graphical methods for determining if there appears to be a relationship, pattern, or trend between two numeric attributes. To construct a scatter plot, each pair of values is treated as a pair of coordinates in an algebraic sense and plotted as points in the plane. Figure 2.7 shows a scatter plot for the set of data in Table 2.1.

The scatter plot is a useful method for providing a first look at bivariate data to see clusters of points and outliers, or to explore the possibility of correlation relationships. Two attributes, X, and Y, are **correlated** if one attribute implies the other. Correlations can be positive, negative, or null (uncorrelated). Figure 2.8 shows examples of positive and negative correlations between two attributes. If the plotted points pattern slopes

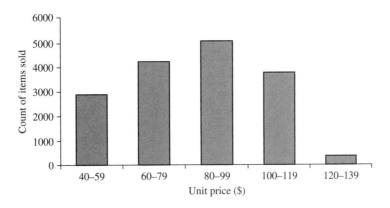

Figure 2.6 A histogram for the Table 2.1 data set.

Figure 2.7 A scatter plot for the Table 2.1 data set.

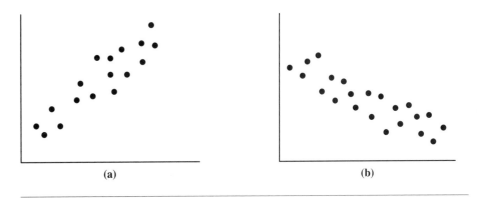

Figure 2.8 Scatter plots can be used to find (a) positive or (b) negative correlations between attributes.

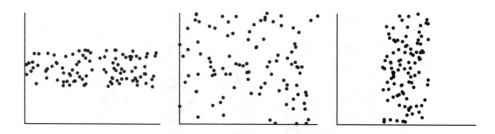

Figure 2.9 Three cases where there is no observed correlation between the two plotted attributes in each of the data sets.

from lower left to upper right, this means that the values of X increase as the values of Y increase, suggesting a *positive correlation* (Figure 2.8a). If the pattern of plotted points slopes from upper left to lower right, the values of X increase as the values of Y decrease, suggesting a *negative correlation* (Figure 2.8b). A line of best fit can be drawn to study the correlation between the variables. Statistical tests for correlation are given in Chapter 3 on data integration (Eq. (3.3)). Figure 2.9 shows three cases for which there is no correlation relationship between the two attributes in each of the given data sets. Section 2.3.2 shows how scatter plots can be extended to n attributes, resulting in a *scatter-plot matrix*.

In conclusion, basic data descriptions (e.g., measures of central tendency and measures of dispersion) and graphic statistical displays (e.g., quantile plots, histograms, and scatter plots) provide valuable insight into the overall behavior of your data. By helping to identify noise and outliers, they are especially useful for data cleaning.

2.3 Data Visualization

How can we convey data to users effectively? **Data visualization** aims to communicate data clearly and effectively through graphical representation. Data visualization has been used extensively in many applications—for example, at work for reporting, managing business operations, and tracking progress of tasks. More popularly, we can take advantage of visualization techniques to discover data relationships that are otherwise not easily observable by looking at the raw data. Nowadays, people also use data visualization to create fun and interesting graphics.

In this section, we briefly introduce the basic concepts of data visualization. We start with multidimensional data such as those stored in relational databases. We discuss several representative approaches, including pixel-oriented techniques, geometric projection techniques, icon-based techniques, and hierarchical and graph-based techniques. We then discuss the visualization of complex data and relations.

2.3.1 Pixel-Oriented Visualization Techniques

A simple way to visualize the value of a dimension is to use a pixel where the color of the pixel reflects the dimension's value. For a data set of *m* dimensions, **pixel-oriented techniques** create *m* windows on the screen, one for each dimension. The *m* dimension values of a record are mapped to *m* pixels at the corresponding positions in the windows. The colors of the pixels reflect the corresponding values.

Inside a window, the data values are arranged in some global order shared by all windows. The global order may be obtained by sorting all data records in a way that's meaningful for the task at hand.

Example 2.16 **Pixel-oriented visualization.** *AllElectronics* maintains a customer information table, which consists of four dimensions: *income*, *credit_limit*, *transaction_volume*, and *age*. Can we analyze the correlation between *income* and the other attributes by visualization?

We can sort all customers in income-ascending order, and use this order to lay out the customer data in the four visualization windows, as shown in Figure 2.10. The pixel colors are chosen so that the smaller the value, the lighter the shading. Using pixel-based visualization, we can easily observe the following: *credit_limit* increases as *income* increases; customers whose income is in the middle range are more likely to purchase more from *AllElectronics*; there is no clear correlation between *income* and *age*. ∎

In pixel-oriented techniques, data records can also be ordered in a query-dependent way. For example, given a point query, we can sort all records in descending order of similarity to the point query.

Filling a window by laying out the data records in a linear way may not work well for a wide window. The first pixel in a row is far away from the last pixel in the previous row, though they are next to each other in the global order. Moreover, a pixel is next to the one above it in the window, even though the two are not next to each other in the global order. To solve this problem, we can lay out the data records in a space-filling curve

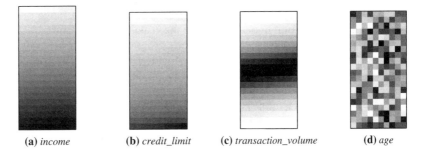

    (a) *income*   **(b)** *credit_limit*   **(c)** *transaction_volume*   **(d)** *age*

Figure 2.10 Pixel-oriented visualization of four attributes by sorting all customers in *income* ascending order.

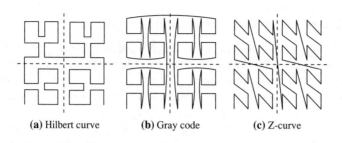

(a) Hilbert curve   (b) Gray code   (c) Z-curve

Figure 2.11 Some frequently used 2-D space-filling curves.

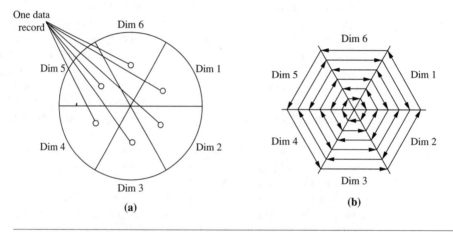

Figure 2.12 The circle segment technique. (a) Representing a data record in circle segments. (b) Laying out pixels in circle segments.

to fill the windows. A *space-filling curve* is a curve with a range that covers the entire *n*-dimensional unit hypercube. Since the visualization windows are 2-D, we can use any 2-D space-filling curve. Figure 2.11 shows some frequently used 2-D space-filling curves.

Note that the windows do not have to be rectangular. For example, the *circle segment technique* uses windows in the shape of segments of a circle, as illustrated in Figure 2.12. This technique can ease the comparison of dimensions because the dimension windows are located side by side and form a circle.

2.3.2 Geometric Projection Visualization Techniques

A drawback of pixel-oriented visualization techniques is that they cannot help us much in understanding the distribution of data in a multidimensional space. For example, they do not show whether there is a dense area in a multidimensional subspace. **Geometric**

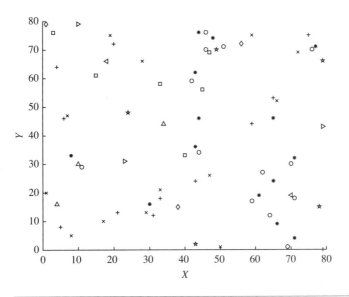

Figure 2.13 Visualization of a 2-D data set using a scatter plot. *Source: www.cs.sfu.ca/jpei/publications/ rareevent-geoinformatica06.pdf*.

projection techniques help users find interesting projections of multidimensional data sets. The central challenge the geometric projection techniques try to address is how to visualize a high-dimensional space on a 2-D display.

A **scatter plot** displays 2-D data points using Cartesian coordinates. A third dimension can be added using different colors or shapes to represent different data points. Figure 2.13 shows an example, where X and Y are two spatial attributes and the third dimension is represented by different shapes. Through this visualization, we can see that points of types "+" and "×" tend to be colocated.

A 3-D scatter plot uses three axes in a Cartesian coordinate system. If it also uses color, it can display up to 4-D data points (Figure 2.14).

For data sets with more than four dimensions, scatter plots are usually ineffective. The **scatter-plot matrix** technique is a useful extension to the scatter plot. For an n-dimensional data set, a scatter-plot matrix is an $n \times n$ grid of 2-D scatter plots that provides a visualization of each dimension with every other dimension. Figure 2.15 shows an example, which visualizes the Iris data set. The data set consists of 450 samples from each of three species of Iris flowers. There are five dimensions in the data set: length and width of sepal and petal, and species.

The scatter-plot matrix becomes less effective as the dimensionality increases. Another popular technique, called parallel coordinates, can handle higher dimensionality. To visualize n-dimensional data points, the **parallel coordinates** technique draws n equally spaced axes, one for each dimension, parallel to one of the display axes.

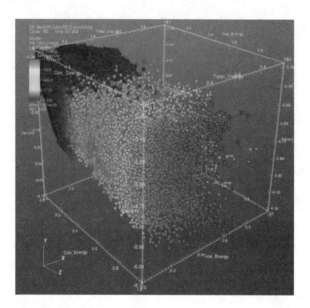

Figure 2.14 Visualization of a 3-D data set using a scatter plot. *Source: http://upload.wikimedia.org/ wikipedia/commons/c/c4/Scatter_plot.jpg.*

A data record is represented by a polygonal line that intersects each axis at the point corresponding to the associated dimension value (Figure 2.16).

A major limitation of the parallel coordinates technique is that it cannot effectively show a data set of many records. Even for a data set of several thousand records, visual clutter and overlap often reduce the readability of the visualization and make the patterns hard to find.

2.3.3 Icon-Based Visualization Techniques

Icon-based visualization techniques use small icons to represent multidimensional data values. We look at two popular icon-based techniques: *Chernoff faces* and *stick figures*.

Chernoff faces were introduced in 1973 by statistician Herman Chernoff. They display multidimensional data of up to 18 variables (or dimensions) as a cartoon human face (Figure 2.17). Chernoff faces help reveal trends in the data. Components of the face, such as the eyes, ears, mouth, and nose, represent values of the dimensions by their shape, size, placement, and orientation. For example, dimensions can be mapped to the following facial characteristics: eye size, eye spacing, nose length, nose width, mouth curvature, mouth width, mouth openness, pupil size, eyebrow slant, eye eccentricity, and head eccentricity.

Chernoff faces make use of the ability of the human mind to recognize small differences in facial characteristics and to assimilate many facial characteristics at once.

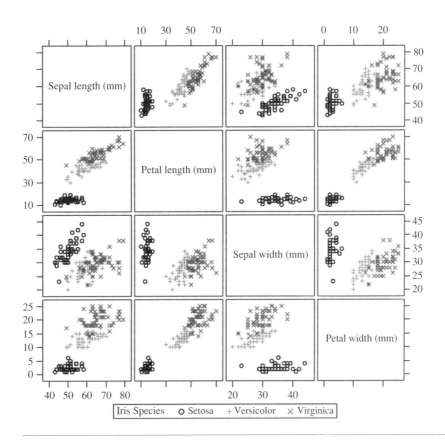

Figure 2.15 Visualization of the Iris data set using a scatter-plot matrix. *Source: http://support.sas.com/ documentation/cdl/en/grstatproc/61948/HTML/default/images/gsgscmat.gif*.

Viewing large tables of data can be tedious. By condensing the data, Chernoff faces make the data easier for users to digest. In this way, they facilitate visualization of regularities and irregularities present in the data, although their power in relating multiple relationships is limited. Another limitation is that specific data values are not shown. Furthermore, facial features vary in perceived importance. This means that the similarity of two faces (representing two multidimensional data points) can vary depending on the order in which dimensions are assigned to facial characteristics. Therefore, this mapping should be carefully chosen. Eye size and eyebrow slant have been found to be important.

Asymmetrical Chernoff faces were proposed as an extension to the original technique. Since a face has vertical symmetry (along the *y*-axis), the left and right side of a face are identical, which wastes space. Asymmetrical Chernoff faces double the number of facial characteristics, thus allowing up to 36 dimensions to be displayed.

The **stick figure** visualization technique maps multidimensional data to five-piece stick figures, where each figure has four limbs and a body. Two dimensions are mapped to the display (*x* and *y*) axes and the remaining dimensions are mapped to the angle

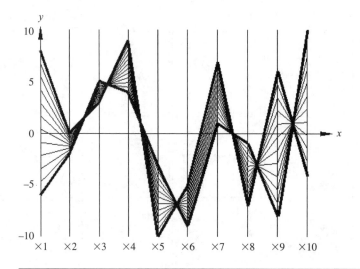

Figure 2.16 Here is a visualization that uses parallel coordinates. *Source: www.stat.columbia.edu/~cook/ movabletype/archives/2007/10/parallel_coordi.thml.*

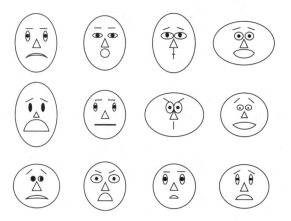

Figure 2.17 Chernoff faces. Each face represents an *n*-dimensional data point ($n \le 18$).

and/or length of the limbs. Figure 2.18 shows census data, where *age* and *income* are mapped to the display axes, and the remaining dimensions (*gender, education,* and so on) are mapped to stick figures. If the data items are relatively dense with respect to the two display dimensions, the resulting visualization shows texture patterns, reflecting data trends.

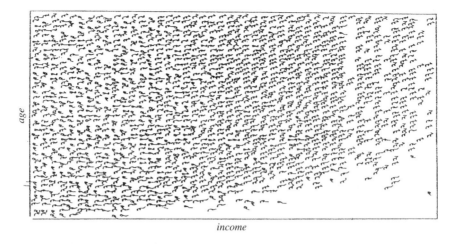

age

income

Figure 2.18 Census data represented using stick figures. *Source:* Professor G. Grinstein, Department of Computer Science, University of Massachusetts at Lowell.

2.3.4 Hierarchical Visualization Techniques

The visualization techniques discussed so far focus on visualizing multiple dimensions simultaneously. However, for a large data set of high dimensionality, it would be difficult to visualize all dimensions at the same time. **Hierarchical visualization techniques** partition all dimensions into subsets (i.e., subspaces). The subspaces are visualized in a hierarchical manner.

"**Worlds-within-Worlds,**" also known as n-Vision, is a representative hierarchical visualization method. Suppose we want to visualize a 6-D data set, where the dimensions are $F, X_1, \ldots, X_5$. We want to observe how dimension F changes with respect to the other dimensions. We can first fix the values of dimensions X_3, X_4, X_5 to some selected values, say, c_3, c_4, c_5. We can then visualize F, X_1, X_2 using a 3-D plot, called a *world*, as shown in Figure 2.19. The position of the origin of the inner world is located at the point (c_3, c_4, c_5) in the outer world, which is another 3-D plot using dimensions X_3, X_4, X_5. A user can interactively change, in the outer world, the location of the origin of the inner world. The user then views the resulting changes of the inner world. Moreover, a user can vary the dimensions used in the inner world and the outer world. Given more dimensions, more levels of worlds can be used, which is why the method is called "worlds-within-worlds."

As another example of hierarchical visualization methods, **tree-maps** display hierarchical data as a set of nested rectangles. For example, Figure 2.20 shows a tree-map visualizing Google news stories. All news stories are organized into seven categories, each shown in a large rectangle of a unique color. Within each category (i.e., each rectangle at the top level), the news stories are further partitioned into smaller subcategories.

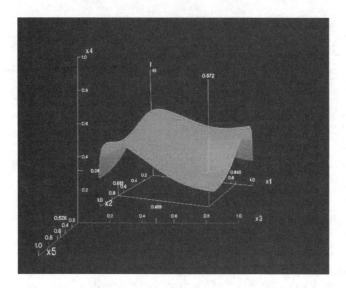

Figure 2.19 "Worlds-within-Worlds" (also known as *n*-Vision). *Source: http://graphics.cs.columbia.edu/ projects/AutoVisual/images/1.dipstick.5.gif.*

2.3.5 Visualizing Complex Data and Relations

In early days, visualization techniques were mainly for numeric data. Recently, more and more non-numeric data, such as text and social networks, have become available. Visualizing and analyzing such data attracts a lot of interest.

There are many new visualization techniques dedicated to these kinds of data. For example, many people on the Web tag various objects such as pictures, blog entries, and product reviews. A **tag cloud** is a visualization of statistics of user-generated tags. Often, in a tag cloud, tags are listed alphabetically or in a user-preferred order. The importance of a tag is indicated by font size or color. Figure 2.21 shows a tag cloud for visualizing the popular tags used in a Web site.

Tag clouds are often used in two ways. First, in a tag cloud for a single item, we can use the size of a tag to represent the number of times that the tag is applied to this item by different users. Second, when visualizing the tag statistics on multiple items, we can use the size of a tag to represent the number of items that the tag has been applied to, that is, the popularity of the tag.

In addition to complex data, complex relations among data entries also raise challenges for visualization. For example, Figure 2.22 uses a disease influence graph to visualize the correlations between diseases. The nodes in the graph are diseases, and the size of each node is proportional to the prevalence of the corresponding disease. Two nodes are linked by an edge if the corresponding diseases have a strong correlation. The width of an edge is proportional to the strength of the correlation pattern of the two corresponding diseases.

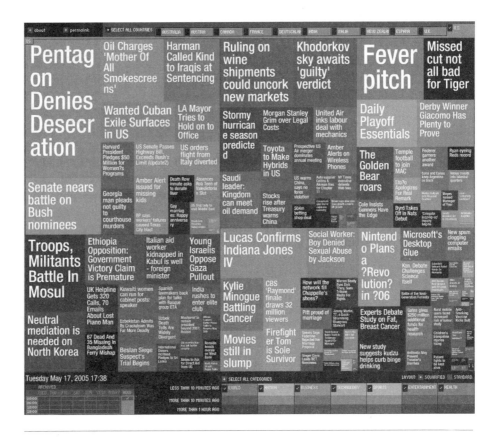

Figure 2.20 Newsmap: Use of tree-maps to visualize Google news headline stories. *Source: www.cs.umd. edu/class/spring2005/cmsc838s/viz4all/ss/newsmap.png.*

In summary, visualization provides effective tools to explore data. We have introduced several popular methods and the essential ideas behind them. There are many existing tools and methods. Moreover, visualization can be used in data mining in various aspects. In addition to visualizing data, visualization can be used to represent the data mining process, the patterns obtained from a mining method, and user interaction with the data. Visual data mining is an important research and development direction.

2.4 Measuring Data Similarity and Dissimilarity

In data mining applications, such as clustering, outlier analysis, and nearest-neighbor classification, we need ways to assess how alike or unalike objects are in comparison to one another. For example, a store may want to search for clusters of *customer* objects, resulting in groups of customers with similar characteristics (e.g., similar income, area of residence, and age). Such information can then be used for marketing. A **cluster** is animals architecture art asia australia autumn baby band barcelona beach berlin bike bird birds birthday black blackandwhite blue bw california canada canon car cat chicago china christmas church city clouds color concert cute dance day de dog england europe fall family fashion festival film florida flower flowers food football france friends fun garden geotagged germany girl girls graffiti green halloween hawaii holiday home house india iphone ireland island italia italy japan july kids la lake landscape light live london love macro me mexico model mountain mountains museum music nature new newyork newyorkcity night nikon nyc ocean old paris park party people photo photography photos portrait red river rock san sanfrancisco scotland sea seattle show sky snow spain spring street summer sun sunset taiwan texas thailand tokyo toronto tour travel tree trees trip uk urban usa vacation washington water wedding white winter yellow york zoo

Figure 2.21 Using a tag cloud to visualize popular Web site tags. *Source:* A snapshot of *www.flickr.com/photos/tags/*, January 23, 2010.

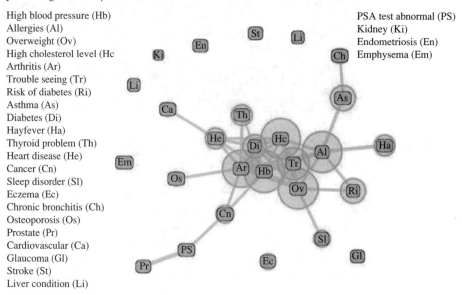

High blood pressure (Hb)
Allergies (Al)
Overweight (Ov)
High cholesterol level (Hc
Arthritis (Ar)
Trouble seeing (Tr)
Risk of diabetes (Ri)
Asthma (As)
Diabetes (Di)
Hayfever (Ha)
Thyroid problem (Th)
Heart disease (He)
Cancer (Cn)
Sleep disorder (Sl)
Eczema (Ec)
Chronic bronchitis (Ch)
Osteoporosis (Os)
Prostate (Pr)
Cardiovascular (Ca)
Glaucoma (Gl)
Stroke (St)
Liver condition (Li)

PSA test abnormal (PS)
Kidney (Ki)
Endometriosis (En)
Emphysema (Em)

Figure 2.22 Disease influence graph of people at least 20 years old in the NHANES data set.

a collection of data objects such that the objects within a cluster are *similar* to one another and *dissimilar* to the objects in other clusters. Outlier analysis also employs clustering-based techniques to identify potential outliers as objects that are highly dissimilar to others. Knowledge of object similarities can also be used in nearest-neighbor classification schemes where a given object (e.g., a *patient*) is assigned a class label (relating to, say, a *diagnosis*) based on its similarity toward other objects in the model.

This section presents similarity and dissimilarity measures, which are referred to as measures of *proximity*. Similarity and dissimilarity are related. A similarity measure for two objects, i and j, will typically return the value 0 if the objects are unalike. The higher the similarity value, the greater the similarity between objects. (Typically, a value of 1 indicates complete similarity, that is, the objects are identical.) A dissimilarity measure works the opposite way. It returns a value of 0 if the objects are the same (and therefore, far from being dissimilar). The higher the dissimilarity value, the more dissimilar the two objects are.

In Section 2.4.1 we present two data structures that are commonly used in the above types of applications: the *data matrix* (used to store the data objects) and the *dissimilarity matrix* (used to store dissimilarity values for pairs of objects). We also switch to a different notation for data objects than previously used in this chapter since now we are dealing with objects described by more than one attribute. We then discuss how object dissimilarity can be computed for objects described by *nominal* attributes (Section 2.4.2), by *binary* attributes (Section 2.4.3), by *numeric* attributes (Section 2.4.4), by *ordinal* attributes (Section 2.4.5), or by combinations of these attribute types (Section 2.4.6). Section 2.4.7 provides similarity measures for very long and sparse data vectors, such as term-frequency vectors representing documents in information retrieval. Knowing how to compute dissimilarity is useful in studying attributes and will also be referenced in later topics on clustering (Chapters 10 and 11), outlier analysis (Chapter 12), and nearest-neighbor classification (Chapter 9).

2.4.1 Data Matrix versus Dissimilarity Matrix

In Section 2.2, we looked at ways of studying the central tendency, dispersion, and spread of observed values for some attribute X. Our objects there were one-dimensional, that is, described by a single attribute. In this section, we talk about objects described by *multiple* attributes. Therefore, we need a change in notation. Suppose that we have n objects (e.g., persons, items, or courses) described by p attributes (also called *measurements* or *features*, such as age, height, weight, or gender). The objects are $x_1 = (x_{11}, x_{12}, \ldots, x_{1p})$, $x_2 = (x_{21}, x_{22}, \ldots, x_{2p})$, and so on, where x_{ij} is the value for object x_i of the jth attribute. For brevity, we hereafter refer to object x_i as object i. The objects may be tuples in a relational database, and are also referred to as *data samples* or *feature vectors*.

Main memory-based clustering and nearest-neighbor algorithms typically operate on either of the following two data structures:

■ **Data matrix** (or *object-by-attribute structure*): This structure stores the n data objects in the form of a relational table, or n-by-p matrix (n objects $\times p$ attributes):

$$\begin{bmatrix} x_{11} & \cdots & x_{1f} & \cdots & x_{1p} \\ \cdots & \cdots & \cdots & \cdots & \cdots \\ x_{i1} & \cdots & x_{if} & \cdots & x_{ip} \\ \cdots & \cdots & \cdots & \cdots & \cdots \\ x_{n1} & \cdots & x_{nf} & \cdots & x_{np} \end{bmatrix}. \tag{2.8}$$

Each row corresponds to an object. As part of our notation, we may use f to index through the p attributes.

■ **Dissimilarity matrix** (or *object-by-object structure*): This structure stores a collection of proximities that are available for all pairs of n objects. It is often represented by an n-by-n table:

$$\begin{bmatrix} 0 & & & & \\ d(2,1) & 0 & & & \\ d(3,1) & d(3,2) & 0 & & \\ \vdots & \vdots & \vdots & & \\ d(n,1) & d(n,2) & \cdots & \cdots & 0 \end{bmatrix}, \tag{2.9}$$

where $d(i,j)$ is the measured **dissimilarity** or "difference" between objects i and j. In general, $d(i,j)$ is a non-negative number that is close to 0 when objects i and j are highly similar or "near" each other, and becomes larger the more they differ. Note that $d(i,i) = 0$; that is, the difference between an object and itself is 0. Furthermore, $d(i,j) = d(j,i)$. (For readability, we do not show the $d(j,i)$ entries; the matrix is symmetric.) Measures of dissimilarity are discussed throughout the remainder of this chapter.

Measures of similarity can often be expressed as a function of measures of dissimilarity. For example, for nominal data,

$$sim(i,j) = 1 - d(i,j), \tag{2.10}$$

where $sim(i,j)$ is the similarity between objects i and j. Throughout the rest of this chapter, we will also comment on measures of similarity.

A data matrix is made up of two entities or "things," namely rows (for objects) and columns (for attributes). Therefore, the data matrix is often called a **two-mode** matrix. The dissimilarity matrix contains one kind of entity (dissimilarities) and so is called a **one-mode** matrix. Many clustering and nearest-neighbor algorithms operate on a dissimilarity matrix. Data in the form of a data matrix can be transformed into a dissimilarity matrix before applying such algorithms.

2.4.2 Proximity Measures for Nominal Attributes

A nominal attribute can take on two or more states (Section 2.1.2). For example, *map_color* is a nominal attribute that may have, say, five states: *red, yellow, green, pink,* and *blue.*

Let the number of states of a nominal attribute be M. The states can be denoted by letters, symbols, or a set of integers, such as 1, 2,..., M. Notice that such integers are used just for data handling and do not represent any specific ordering.

"*How is dissimilarity computed between objects described by nominal attributes?*" The dissimilarity between two objects i and j can be computed based on the ratio of mismatches:

$$d(i, j) = \frac{p - m}{p}, \qquad (2.11)$$

where m is the number of *matches* (i.e., the number of attributes for which i and j are in the same state), and p is the total number of attributes describing the objects. Weights can be assigned to increase the effect of m or to assign greater weight to the matches in attributes having a larger number of states.

Example 2.17 **Dissimilarity between nominal attributes.** Suppose that we have the sample data of Table 2.2, except that only the *object-identifier* and the attribute *test-1* are available, where *test-1* is nominal. (We will use *test-2* and *test-3* in later examples.) Let's compute the dissimilarity matrix (Eq. 2.9), that is,

$$\begin{bmatrix} 0 & & & \\ d(2,1) & 0 & & \\ d(3,1) & d(3,2) & 0 & \\ d(4,1) & d(4,2) & d(4,3) & 0 \end{bmatrix}.$$

Since here we have one nominal attribute, *test-1*, we set $p = 1$ in Eq. (2.11) so that $d(i, j)$ evaluates to 0 if objects i and j match, and 1 if the objects differ. Thus, we get

$$\begin{bmatrix} 0 & & & \\ 1 & 0 & & \\ 1 & 1 & 0 & \\ 0 & 1 & 1 & 0 \end{bmatrix}.$$

From this, we see that all objects are dissimilar except objects 1 and 4 (i.e., $d(4, 1) = 0$). ∎

Table 2.2 A Sample Data Table Containing Attributes of Mixed Type

Object Identifier	test-1 (nominal)	test-2 (ordinal)	test-3 (numeric)
1	code A	excellent	45
2	code B	fair	22
3	code C	good	64
4	code A	excellent	28

Alternatively, similarity can be computed as

$$sim(i, j) = 1 - d(i, j) = \frac{m}{p}.$$
(2.12)

Proximity between objects described by nominal attributes can be computed using an alternative encoding scheme. Nominal attributes can be encoded using asymmetric binary attributes by creating a new binary attribute for each of the M states. For an object with a given state value, the binary attribute representing that state is set to 1, while the remaining binary attributes are set to 0. For example, to encode the nominal attribute *map_color*, a binary attribute can be created for each of the five colors previously listed. For an object having the color *yellow*, the *yellow* attribute is set to 1, while the remaining four attributes are set to 0. Proximity measures for this form of encoding can be calculated using the methods discussed in the next subsection.

2.4.3 Proximity Measures for Binary Attributes

Let's look at dissimilarity and similarity measures for objects described by either *symmetric* or *asymmetric binary attributes*.

Recall that a binary attribute has only one of two states: 0 and 1, where 0 means that the attribute is absent, and 1 means that it is present (Section 2.1.3). Given the attribute *smoker* describing a patient, for instance, 1 indicates that the patient smokes, while 0 indicates that the patient does not. Treating binary attributes as if they are numeric can be misleading. Therefore, methods specific to binary data are necessary for computing dissimilarity.

"*So, how can we compute the dissimilarity between two binary attributes?*" One approach involves computing a dissimilarity matrix from the given binary data. If all binary attributes are thought of as having the same weight, we have the 2×2 contingency table of Table 2.3, where q is the number of attributes that equal 1 for both objects i and j, r is the number of attributes that equal 1 for object i but equal 0 for object j, s is the number of attributes that equal 0 for object i but equal 1 for object j, and t is the number of attributes that equal 0 for both objects i and j. The total number of attributes is p, where $p = q + r + s + t$.

Recall that for symmetric binary attributes, each state is equally valuable. Dissimilarity that is based on symmetric binary attributes is called **symmetric binary dissimilarity**. If objects i and j are described by symmetric binary attributes, then the

Table 2.3 Contingency Table for Binary Attributes

		Object j		
		1	0	sum
	1	q	r	$q+r$
Object i	0	s	t	$s+t$
	sum	$q+s$	$r+t$	p

dissimilarity between i and j is

$$d(i, j) = \frac{r+s}{q+r+s+t}. \tag{2.13}$$

For asymmetric binary attributes, the two states are not equally important, such as the *positive* (1) and *negative* (0) outcomes of a disease test. Given two asymmetric binary attributes, the agreement of two 1s (a positive match) is then considered more significant than that of two 0s (a negative match). Therefore, such binary attributes are often considered "monary" (having one state). The dissimilarity based on these attributes is called **asymmetric binary dissimilarity**, where the number of negative matches, t, is considered unimportant and is thus ignored in the following computation:

$$d(i, j) = \frac{r+s}{q+r+s}. \tag{2.14}$$

Complementarily, we can measure the difference between two binary attributes based on the notion of similarity instead of dissimilarity. For example, the **asymmetric binary similarity** between the objects i and j can be computed as

$$sim(i, j) = \frac{q}{q+r+s} = 1 - d(i, j). \tag{2.15}$$

The coefficient $sim(i, j)$ of Eq. (2.15) is called the **Jaccard coefficient** and is popularly referenced in the literature.

When both symmetric and asymmetric binary attributes occur in the same data set, the mixed attributes approach described in Section 2.4.6 can be applied.

Example 2.18 **Dissimilarity between binary attributes.** Suppose that a patient record table (Table 2.4) contains the attributes *name, gender, fever, cough, test-1, test-2, test-3,* and *test-4,* where *name* is an object identifier, *gender* is a symmetric attribute, and the remaining attributes are asymmetric binary.

For asymmetric attribute values, let the values Y (*yes*) and P (*positive*) be set to 1, and the value N (*no* or *negative*) be set to 0. Suppose that the distance between objects

Table 2.4 Relational Table Where Patients Are Described by Binary Attributes

name	gender	fever	cough	test-1	test-2	test-3	test-4
Jack	M	Y	N	P	N	N	N
Jim	M	Y	Y	N	N	N	N
Mary	F	Y	N	P	N	P	N
⋮	⋮	⋮	⋮	⋮	⋮	⋮	⋮

(patients) is computed based only on the asymmetric attributes. According to Eq. (2.14), the distance between each pair of the three patients—Jack, Mary, and Jim—is

$$d(Jack, Jim) = \frac{1+1}{1+1+1} = 0.67,$$

$$d(Jack, Mary) = \frac{0+1}{2+0+1} = 0.33,$$

$$d(Jim, Mary) = \frac{1+2}{1+1+2} = 0.75.$$

These measurements suggest that Jim and Mary are unlikely to have a similar disease because they have the highest dissimilarity value among the three pairs. Of the three patients, Jack and Mary are the most likely to have a similar disease. ∎

2.4.4 Dissimilarity of Numeric Data: Minkowski Distance

In this section, we describe distance measures that are commonly used for computing the dissimilarity of objects described by numeric attributes. These measures include the *Euclidean, Manhattan,* and *Minkowski distances.*

In some cases, the data are normalized before applying distance calculations. This involves transforming the data to fall within a smaller or common range, such as $[-1, 1]$ or $[0.0, 1.0]$. Consider a *height* attribute, for example, which could be measured in either meters or inches. In general, expressing an attribute in smaller units will lead to a larger range for that attribute, and thus tend to give such attributes greater effect or "weight." Normalizing the data attempts to give all attributes an equal weight. It may or may not be useful in a particular application. Methods for normalizing data are discussed in detail in Chapter 3 on data preprocessing.

The most popular distance measure is **Euclidean distance** (i.e., straight line or "as the crow flies"). Let $i = (x_{i1}, x_{i2}, \ldots, x_{ip})$ and $j = (x_{j1}, x_{j2}, \ldots, x_{jp})$ be two objects described by p numeric attributes. The Euclidean distance between objects i and j is defined as

$$d(i, j) = \sqrt{(x_{i1} - x_{j1})^2 + (x_{i2} - x_{j2})^2 + \cdots + (x_{ip} - x_{jp})^2}. \qquad (2.16)$$

Another well-known measure is the **Manhattan (or city block) distance**, named so because it is the distance in blocks between any two points in a city (such as 2 blocks down and 3 blocks over for a total of 5 blocks). It is defined as

$$d(i, j) = |x_{i1} - x_{j1}| + |x_{i2} - x_{j2}| + \cdots + |x_{ip} - x_{jp}|. \qquad (2.17)$$

Both the Euclidean and the Manhattan distance satisfy the following mathematical properties:

Non-negativity: $d(i, j) \geq 0$: Distance is a non-negative number.

Identity of indiscernibles: $d(i, i) = 0$: The distance of an object to itself is 0.

Symmetry: $d(i, j) = d(j, i)$: Distance is a symmetric function.

Triangle inequality: $d(i, j) \leq d(i, k) + d(k, j)$: Going directly from object i to object j in space is no more than making a detour over any other object k.

A measure that satisfies these conditions is known as **metric**. Please note that the non-negativity property is implied by the other three properties.

Example 2.19 **Euclidean distance and Manhattan distance.** Let $x_1 = (1, 2)$ and $x_2 = (3, 5)$ represent two objects as shown in Figure 2.23. The Euclidean distance between the two is $\sqrt{2^2 + 3^2} = 3.61$. The Manhattan distance between the two is $2 + 3 = 5$. ∎

Minkowski distance is a generalization of the Euclidean and Manhattan distances. It is defined as

$$d(i, j) = \sqrt[h]{|x_{i1} - x_{j1}|^h + |x_{i2} - x_{j2}|^h + \cdots + |x_{ip} - x_{jp}|^h}, \qquad (2.18)$$

where h is a real number such that $h \geq 1$. (Such a distance is also called L_p **norm** in some literature, where the symbol p refers to our notation of h. We have kept p as the number of attributes to be consistent with the rest of this chapter.) It represents the Manhattan distance when $h = 1$ (i.e., L_1 norm) and Euclidean distance when $h = 2$ (i.e., L_2 norm).

The **supremum distance** (also referred to as L_{max}, L_∞ **norm** and as the **Chebyshev distance**) is a generalization of the Minkowski distance for $h \to \infty$. To compute it, we find the attribute f that gives the maximum difference in values between the two objects. This difference is the supremum distance, defined more formally as:

$$d(i, j) = \lim_{h \to \infty} \left(\sum_{f=1}^{p} |x_{if} - x_{jf}|^h \right)^{\frac{1}{h}} = \max_f^p |x_{if} - x_{jf}|. \qquad (2.19)$$

The L^∞ norm is also known as the *uniform norm*.

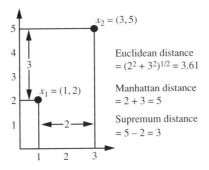

Euclidean distance
$= (2^2 + 3^2)^{1/2} = 3.61$

Manhattan distance
$= 2 + 3 = 5$

Supremum distance
$= 5 - 2 = 3$

Figure 2.23 Euclidean, Manhattan, and supremum distances between two objects.

Example 2.20   **Supremum distance.** Let's use the same two objects, $x_1 = (1, 2)$ and $x_2 = (3, 5)$, as in Figure 2.23. The second attribute gives the greatest difference between values for the objects, which is $5 - 2 = 3$. This is the supremum distance between both objects.   ∎

If each attribute is assigned a weight according to its perceived importance, the **weighted Euclidean distance** can be computed as

$$d(i, j) = \sqrt{w_1|x_{i1} - x_{j1}|^2 + w_2|x_{i2} - x_{j2}|^2 + \cdots + w_m|x_{ip} - x_{jp}|^2}. \qquad (2.20)$$

Weighting can also be applied to other distance measures as well.

2.4.5 Proximity Measures for Ordinal Attributes

The values of an ordinal attribute have a meaningful order or ranking about them, yet the magnitude between successive values is unknown (Section 2.1.4). An example includes the sequence *small, medium, large* for a *size* attribute. Ordinal attributes may also be obtained from the discretization of numeric attributes by splitting the value range into a finite number of categories. These categories are organized into ranks. That is, the range of a numeric attribute can be mapped to an ordinal attribute f having M_f states. For example, the range of the interval-scaled attribute *temperature* (in Celsius) can be organized into the following states: -30 to -10, -10 to 10, 10 to 30, representing the categories *cold temperature, moderate temperature,* and *warm temperature,* respectively. Let M represent the number of possible states that an ordinal attribute can have. These ordered states define the ranking $1, \ldots, M_f$.

"*How are ordinal attributes handled?*" The treatment of ordinal attributes is quite similar to that of numeric attributes when computing dissimilarity between objects. Suppose that f is an attribute from a set of ordinal attributes describing n objects. The dissimilarity computation with respect to f involves the following steps:

1. The value of f for the ith object is x_{if}, and f has M_f ordered states, representing the ranking $1, \ldots, M_f$. Replace each x_{if} by its corresponding rank, $r_{if} \in \{1, \ldots, M_f\}$.

2. Since each ordinal attribute can have a different number of states, it is often necessary to map the range of each attribute onto $[0.0, 1.0]$ so that each attribute has equal weight. We perform such data normalization by replacing the rank r_{if} of the ith object in the fth attribute by

$$z_{if} = \frac{r_{if} - 1}{M_f - 1}. \qquad (2.21)$$

3. Dissimilarity can then be computed using any of the distance measures described in Section 2.4.4 for numeric attributes, using z_{if} to represent the f value for the ith object.

Example 2.21 **Dissimilarity between ordinal attributes.** Suppose that we have the sample data shown earlier in Table 2.2, except that this time only the *object-identifier* and the continuous ordinal attribute, *test-2*, are available. There are three states for *test-2*: *fair, good,* and *excellent*, that is, $M_f = 3$. For step 1, if we replace each value for *test-2* by its rank, the four objects are assigned the ranks 3, 1, 2, and 3, respectively. Step 2 normalizes the ranking by mapping rank 1 to 0.0, rank 2 to 0.5, and rank 3 to 1.0. For step 3, we can use, say, the Euclidean distance (Eq. 2.16), which results in the following dissimilarity matrix:

$$
\begin{bmatrix}
0 & & & \\
1.0 & 0 & & \\
0.5 & 0.5 & 0 & \\
0 & 1.0 & 0.5 & 0
\end{bmatrix}.
$$

Therefore, objects 1 and 2 are the most dissimilar, as are objects 2 and 4 (i.e., $d(2,1) = 1.0$ and $d(4,2) = 1.0$). This makes intuitive sense since objects 1 and 4 are both *excellent*. Object 2 is *fair*, which is at the opposite end of the range of values for *test-2*. ∎

Similarity values for ordinal attributes can be interpreted from dissimilarity as $sim(i,j) = 1 - d(i,j)$.

2.4.6 Dissimilarity for Attributes of Mixed Types

Sections 2.4.2 through 2.4.5 discussed how to compute the dissimilarity between objects described by attributes of the same type, where these types may be either *nominal, symmetric binary, asymmetric binary, numeric,* or *ordinal*. However, in many real databases, objects are described by a *mixture* of attribute types. In general, a database can contain all of these attribute types.

"*So, how can we compute the dissimilarity between objects of mixed attribute types?*" One approach is to group each type of attribute together, performing separate data mining (e.g., clustering) analysis for each type. This is feasible if these analyses derive compatible results. However, in real applications, it is unlikely that a separate analysis per attribute type will generate compatible results.

A more preferable approach is to process all attribute types together, performing a single analysis. One such technique combines the different attributes into a single dissimilarity matrix, bringing all of the meaningful attributes onto a common scale of the interval [0.0, 1.0].

Suppose that the data set contains p attributes of mixed type. The dissimilarity $d(i, j)$ between objects i and j is defined as

$$
d(i, j) = \frac{\sum_{f=1}^{p} \delta_{ij}^{(f)} d_{ij}^{(f)}}{\sum_{f=1}^{p} \delta_{ij}^{(f)}}, \tag{2.22}
$$

where the indicator $\delta_{ij}^{(f)} = 0$ if either (1) x_{if} or x_{jf} is missing (i.e., there is no measurement of attribute f for object i or object j), or (2) $x_{if} = x_{jf} = 0$ and attribute f is asymmetric binary; otherwise, $\delta_{ij}^{(f)} = 1$. The contribution of attribute f to the dissimilarity between i and j (i.e., $d_{ij}^{(f)}$) is computed dependent on its type:

- If f is numeric: $d_{ij}^{(f)} = \frac{|x_{if} - x_{jf}|}{max_h x_{hf} - min_h x_{hf}}$, where h runs over all nonmissing objects for attribute f.

- If f is nominal or binary: $d_{ij}^{(f)} = 0$ if $x_{if} = x_{jf}$; otherwise, $d_{ij}^{(f)} = 1$.

- If f is ordinal: compute the ranks r_{if} and $z_{if} = \frac{r_{if} - 1}{M_f - 1}$, and treat z_{if} as numeric.

These steps are identical to what we have already seen for each of the individual attribute types. The only difference is for numeric attributes, where we normalize so that the values map to the interval [0.0, 1.0]. Thus, the dissimilarity between objects can be computed even when the attributes describing the objects are of different types.

Example 2.22 Dissimilarity between attributes of mixed type. Let's compute a dissimilarity matrix for the objects in Table 2.2. Now we will consider *all* of the attributes, which are of different types. In Examples 2.17 and 2.21, we worked out the dissimilarity matrices for each of the individual attributes. The procedures we followed for *test-1* (which is nominal) and *test-2* (which is ordinal) are the same as outlined earlier for processing attributes of mixed types. Therefore, we can use the dissimilarity matrices obtained for *test-1* and *test-2* later when we compute Eq. (2.22). First, however, we need to compute the dissimilarity matrix for the third attribute, *test-3* (which is numeric). That is, we must compute $d_{ij}^{(3)}$. Following the case for numeric attributes, we let $max_h x_h = 64$ and $min_h x_h = 22$. The difference between the two is used in Eq. (2.22) to normalize the values of the dissimilarity matrix. The resulting dissimilarity matrix for *test-3* is

$$
\begin{bmatrix}
0 & & & \\
0.55 & 0 & & \\
0.45 & 1.00 & 0 & \\
0.40 & 0.14 & 0.86 & 0
\end{bmatrix}.
$$

We can now use the dissimilarity matrices for the three attributes in our computation of Eq. (2.22). The indicator $\delta_{ij}^{(f)} = 1$ for each of the three attributes, f. We get, for example, $d(3,1) = \frac{1(1) + 1(0.50) + 1(0.45)}{3} = 0.65$. The resulting dissimilarity matrix obtained for the data described by the three attributes of mixed types is:

$$\begin{bmatrix} 0 & & & \\ 0.85 & 0 & & \\ 0.65 & 0.83 & 0 & \\ 0.13 & 0.71 & 0.79 & 0 \end{bmatrix}.$$

From Table 2.2, we can intuitively guess that objects 1 and 4 are the most similar, based on their values for *test*-1 and *test*-2. This is confirmed by the dissimilarity matrix, where $d(4, 1)$ is the lowest value for any pair of different objects. Similarly, the matrix indicates that objects 1 and 2 are the least similar.   ∎

2.4.7 Cosine Similarity

Cosine similarity measures the similarity between two vectors of an inner product space. It is measured by the cosine of the angle between two vectors and determines whether two vectors are pointing in roughly the same direction. It is often used to measure document similarity in text analysis.

A document can be represented by thousands of attributes, each recording the frequency of a particular word (such as a keyword) or phrase in the document. Thus, each document is an object represented by what is called a *term-frequency vector*. For example, in Table 2.5, we see that *Document1* contains five instances of the word *team*, while *hockey* occurs three times. The word *coach* is absent from the entire document, as indicated by a count value of 0. Such data can be highly asymmetric.

Term-frequency vectors are typically very long and **sparse** (i.e., they have many 0 values). Applications using such structures include information retrieval, text document clustering, biological taxonomy, and gene feature mapping. The traditional distance measures that we have studied in this chapter do not work well for such sparse numeric data. For example, two term-frequency vectors may have many 0 values in common, meaning that the corresponding documents do not share many words, but this does not make them similar. We need a measure that will focus on the words that the two documents *do* have in common, and the occurrence frequency of such words. In other words, we need a measure for numeric data that ignores zero-matches.

Table 2.5 Document Vector or Term-Frequency Vector

Document	team	coach	hockey	baseball	soccer	penalty	score	win	loss	season
Document1	5	0	3	0	2	0	0	2	0	0
Document2	3	0	2	0	1	1	0	1	0	1
Document3	0	7	0	2	1	0	0	3	0	0
Document4	0	1	0	0	1	2	2	0	3	0

Cosine similarity is a measure of similarity that can be used to compare documents or, say, give a ranking of documents with respect to a given vector of query words. Let x and y be two vectors for comparison. Using the cosine measure as a similarity function, we have

$$sim(x,y) = \frac{x \cdot y}{||x|| ||y||},$$
(2.23)

where $||x||$ is the Euclidean norm of vector $x = (x_1, x_2, \ldots, x_p)$, defined as $\sqrt{x_1^2 + x_2^2 + \cdots + x_p^2}$. Conceptually, it is the length of the vector. Similarly, $||y||$ is the Euclidean norm of vector y. The measure computes the cosine of the angle between vectors x and y. A cosine value of 0 means that the two vectors are at 90 degrees to each other (orthogonal) and have no match. The closer the cosine value to 1, the smaller the angle and the greater the match between vectors. Note that because the cosine similarity measure does not obey all of the properties of Section 2.4.4 defining metric measures, it is referred to as a *nonmetric measure*.

Example 2.23 **Cosine similarity between two term-frequency vectors.** Suppose that x and y are the first two term-frequency vectors in Table 2.5. That is, $x = (5,0,3,0,2,0,0,2,0,0)$ and $y = (3,0,2,0,1,1,0,1,0,1)$. How similar are x and y? Using Eq. (2.23) to compute the cosine similarity between the two vectors, we get:

$$x^t \cdot y = 5 \times 3 + 0 \times 0 + 3 \times 2 + 0 \times 0 + 2 \times 1 + 0 \times 1 + 0 \times 0 + 2 \times 1$$
$$+ 0 \times 0 + 0 \times 1 = 25$$
$$||x|| = \sqrt{5^2 + 0^2 + 3^2 + 0^2 + 2^2 + 0^2 + 0^2 + 2^2 + 0^2 + 0^2} = 6.48$$
$$||y|| = \sqrt{3^2 + 0^2 + 2^2 + 0^2 + 1^2 + 1^2 + 0^2 + 1^2 + 0^2 + 1^2} = 4.12$$
$$sim(x,y) = 0.94$$

Therefore, if we were using the cosine similarity measure to compare these documents, they would be considered quite similar. ∎

When attributes are binary-valued, the cosine similarity function can be interpreted in terms of shared features or attributes. Suppose an object x possesses the ith attribute if $x_i = 1$. Then $x^t \cdot y$ is the number of attributes possessed (i.e., shared) by both x and y, and $|x||y|$ is the *geometric mean* of the number of attributes possessed by x and the number possessed by y. Thus, $sim(x,y)$ is a measure of relative possession of common attributes.

A simple variation of cosine similarity for the preceding scenario is

$$sim(x,y) = \frac{x \cdot y}{x \cdot x + y \cdot y - x \cdot y},$$
(2.24)

which is the ratio of the number of attributes shared by x and y to the number of attributes possessed by x or y. This function, known as the **Tanimoto coefficient** or **Tanimoto distance**, is frequently used in information retrieval and biology taxonomy.

2.5 Summary

- Data sets are made up of data objects. A **data object** represents an entity. Data objects are described by attributes. Attributes can be nominal, binary, ordinal, or numeric.

- The values of a **nominal** (or **categorical**) **attribute** are symbols or names of things, where each value represents some kind of category, code, or state.

- **Binary attributes** are nominal attributes with only two possible states (such as 1 and 0 or true and false). If the two states are equally important, the attribute is *symmetric*; otherwise it is *asymmetric*.

- An **ordinal attribute** is an attribute with possible values that have a meaningful order or ranking among them, but the magnitude between successive values is not known.

- A **numeric attribute** is *quantitative* (i.e., it is a measurable quantity) represented in integer or real values. Numeric attribute types can be *interval-scaled* or *ratio-scaled*. The values of an **interval-scaled attribute** are measured in fixed and equal units. **Ratio-scaled attributes** are numeric attributes with an inherent zero-point. Measurements are ratio-scaled in that we can speak of values as being an order of magnitude larger than the unit of measurement.

- **Basic statistical descriptions** provide the analytical foundation for data preprocessing. The basic statistical measures for data summarization include *mean, weighted mean, median,* and *mode* for measuring the central tendency of data; and *range, quantiles, quartiles, interquartile range, variance,* and *standard deviation* for measuring the dispersion of data. Graphical representations (e.g., *boxplots, quantile plots, quantile–quantile plots, histograms,* and *scatter plots*) facilitate visual inspection of the data and are thus useful for data preprocessing and mining.

- **Data visualization** techniques may be *pixel-oriented, geometric-based, icon-based,* or *hierarchical*. These methods apply to multidimensional relational data. Additional techniques have been proposed for the visualization of complex data, such as text and social networks.

- Measures of object **similarity** and **dissimilarity** are used in data mining applications such as clustering, outlier analysis, and nearest-neighbor classification. Such measures of *proximity* can be computed for each attribute type studied in this chapter, or for combinations of such attributes. Examples include the *Jaccard coefficient* for asymmetric binary attributes and *Euclidean, Manhattan, Minkowski,* and *supremum* distances for numeric attributes. For applications involving sparse numeric data vectors, such as term-frequency vectors, the *cosine measure* and the *Tanimoto coefficient* are often used in the assessment of similarity.

2.6 Exercises

2.1 Give three additional commonly used statistical measures that are not already illustrated in this chapter for the characterization of *data dispersion*. Discuss how they can be computed efficiently in large databases.

2.2 Suppose that the data for analysis includes the attribute *age*. The *age* values for the data tuples are (in increasing order) 13, 15, 16, 16, 19, 20, 20, 21, 22, 22, 25, 25, 25, 25, 30, 33, 33, 35, 35, 35, 35, 36, 40, 45, 46, 52, 70.

(a) What is the *mean* of the data? What is the *median*?

(b) What is the *mode* of the data? Comment on the data's modality (i.e., bimodal, trimodal, etc.).

(c) What is the *midrange* of the data?

(d) Can you find (roughly) the first quartile (Q_1) and the third quartile (Q_3) of the data?

(e) Give the *five-number summary* of the data.

(f) Show a *boxplot* of the data.

(g) How is a *quantile–quantile plot* different from a *quantile plot*?

2.3 Suppose that the values for a given set of data are grouped into intervals. The intervals and corresponding frequencies are as follows:

age	frequency
1–5	200
6–15	450
16–20	300
21–50	1500
51–80	700
81–110	44

Compute an *approximate median* value for the data.

2.4 Suppose that a hospital tested the age and body fat data for 18 randomly selected adults with the following results:

age	23	23	27	27	39	41	47	49	50
%fat	9.5	26.5	7.8	17.8	31.4	25.9	27.4	27.2	31.2

age	52	54	54	56	57	58	58	60	61
%fat	34.6	42.5	28.8	33.4	30.2	34.1	32.9	41.2	35.7

(a) Calculate the mean, median, and standard deviation of *age* and *%fat*.

(b) Draw the boxplots for *age* and *%fat*.

(c) Draw a *scatter plot* and a *q-q plot* based on these two variables.

2.5 Briefly outline how to compute the dissimilarity between objects described by the following:

(a) Nominal attributes

(b) Asymmetric binary attributes

(c) Numeric attributes

(d) Term-frequency vectors

2.6 Given two objects represented by the tuples (22, 1, 42, 10) and (20, 0, 36, 8):

(a) Compute the *Euclidean distance* between the two objects.

(b) Compute the *Manhattan distance* between the two objects.

(c) Compute the *Minkowski distance* between the two objects, using $q = 3$.

(d) Compute the *supremum distance* between the two objects.

2.7 The *median* is one of the most important holistic measures in data analysis. Propose several methods for median approximation. Analyze their respective complexity under different parameter settings and decide to what extent the real value can be approximated. Moreover, suggest a heuristic strategy to balance between accuracy and complexity and then apply it to all methods you have given.

2.8 It is important to define or select similarity measures in data analysis. However, there is no commonly accepted subjective similarity measure. Results can vary depending on the similarity measures used. Nonetheless, seemingly different similarity measures may be equivalent after some transformation.

Suppose we have the following 2-D data set:

	A_1	A_2
x_1	1.5	1.7
x_2	2	1.9
x_3	1.6	1.8
x_4	1.2	1.5
x_5	1.5	1.0

(a) Consider the data as 2-D data points. Given a new data point, $x = (1.4, 1.6)$ as a query, rank the database points based on similarity with the query using Euclidean distance, Manhattan distance, supremum distance, and cosine similarity.

(b) Normalize the data set to make the norm of each data point equal to 1. Use Euclidean distance on the transformed data to rank the data points.

2.7 Bibliographic Notes

Methods for descriptive data summarization have been studied in the statistics literature long before the onset of computers. Good summaries of statistical descriptive data mining methods include Freedman, Pisani, and Purves [FPP07] and Devore [Dev95]. For statistics-based visualization of data using boxplots, quantile plots, quantile–quantile plots, scatter plots, and loess curves, see Cleveland [Cle93].

Pioneering work on data visualization techniques is described in *The Visual Display of Quantitative Information* [Tuf83], *Envisioning Information* [Tuf90], and *Visual Explanations: Images and Quantities, Evidence and Narrative* [Tuf97], all by Tufte, in addition to *Graphics and Graphic Information Processing* by Bertin [Ber81], *Visualizing Data* by Cleveland [Cle93], and *Information Visualization in Data Mining and Knowledge Discovery* edited by Fayyad, Grinstein, and Wierse [FGW01].

Major conferences and symposiums on visualization include *ACM Human Factors in Computing Systems (CHI)*, *Visualization*, and the *International Symposium on Information Visualization*. Research on visualization is also published in *Transactions on Visualization and Computer Graphics*, *Journal of Computational and Graphical Statistics*, and *IEEE Computer Graphics and Applications*.

Many graphical user interfaces and visualization tools have been developed and can be found in various data mining products. Several books on data mining (e.g., *Data Mining Solutions* by Westphal and Blaxton [WB98]) present many good examples and visual snapshots. For a survey of visualization techniques, see "Visual techniques for exploring databases" by Keim [Kei97].

Similarity and distance measures among various variables have been introduced in many textbooks that study cluster analysis, including Hartigan [Har75]; Jain and Dubes [JD88]; Kaufman and Rousseeuw [KR90]; and Arabie, Hubert, and de Soete [AHS96]. Methods for combining attributes of different types into a single dissimilarity matrix were introduced by Kaufman and Rousseeuw [KR90].

Data Preprocessing 3

Today's real-world databases are highly susceptible to noisy, missing, and inconsistent data due to their typically huge size (often several gigabytes or more) and their likely origin from multiple, heterogenous sources. Low-quality data will lead to low-quality mining results. *"How can the data be preprocessed in order to help improve the quality of the data and, consequently, of the mining results? How can the data be preprocessed so as to improve the efficiency and ease of the mining process?"*

There are several data preprocessing techniques. *Data cleaning* can be applied to remove noise and correct inconsistencies in data. *Data integration* merges data from multiple sources into a coherent data store such as a data warehouse. *Data reduction* can reduce data size by, for instance, aggregating, eliminating redundant features, or clustering. *Data transformations* (e.g., normalization) may be applied, where data are scaled to fall within a smaller range like 0.0 to 1.0. This can improve the accuracy and efficiency of mining algorithms involving distance measurements. These techniques are not mutually exclusive; they may work together. For example, data cleaning can involve transformations to correct wrong data, such as by transforming all entries for a *date* field to a common format.

In Chapter 2, we learned about the different attribute types and how to use basic statistical descriptions to study data characteristics. These can help identify erroneous values and outliers, which will be useful in the data cleaning and integration steps. Data processing techniques, when applied before mining, can substantially improve the overall quality of the patterns mined and/or the time required for the actual mining.

In this chapter, we introduce the basic concepts of data preprocessing in Section 3.1. The methods for data preprocessing are organized into the following categories: data cleaning (Section 3.2), data integration (Section 3.3), data reduction (Section 3.4), and data transformation (Section 3.5).

3.1 | Data Preprocessing: An Overview

This section presents an overview of data preprocessing. Section 3.1.1 illustrates the many elements defining data quality. This provides the incentive behind data preprocessing. Section 3.1.2 outlines the major tasks in data preprocessing.

3.1.1 Data Quality: Why Preprocess the Data?

Data have quality if they satisfy the requirements of the intended use. There are many factors comprising **data quality**, including *accuracy, completeness, consistency, timeliness, believability*, and *interpretability*.

Imagine that you are a manager at *AllElectronics* and have been charged with analyzing the company's data with respect to your branch's sales. You immediately set out to perform this task. You carefully inspect the company's database and data warehouse, identifying and selecting the attributes or dimensions (e.g., *item, price*, and *units_sold*) to be included in your analysis. Alas! You notice that several of the attributes for various tuples have no recorded value. For your analysis, you would like to include information as to whether each item purchased was advertised as on sale, yet you discover that this information has not been recorded. Furthermore, users of your database system have reported errors, unusual values, and inconsistencies in the data recorded for some transactions. In other words, the data you wish to analyze by data mining techniques are *incomplete* (lacking attribute values or certain attributes of interest, or containing only aggregate data); *inaccurate* or *noisy* (containing errors, or values that deviate from the expected); and *inconsistent* (e.g., containing discrepancies in the department codes used to categorize items). Welcome to the real world!

This scenario illustrates three of the elements defining data quality: **accuracy, completeness**, and **consistency**. Inaccurate, incomplete, and inconsistent data are commonplace properties of large real-world databases and data warehouses. There are many possible reasons for inaccurate data (i.e., having incorrect attribute values). The data collection instruments used may be faulty. There may have been human or computer errors occurring at data entry. Users may purposely submit incorrect data values for mandatory fields when they do not wish to submit personal information (e.g., by choosing the default value "January 1" displayed for birthday). This is known as *disguised missing data*. Errors in data transmission can also occur. There may be technology limitations such as limited buffer size for coordinating synchronized data transfer and consumption. Incorrect data may also result from inconsistencies in naming conventions or data codes, or inconsistent formats for input fields (e.g., *date*). Duplicate tuples also require data cleaning.

Incomplete data can occur for a number of reasons. Attributes of interest may not always be available, such as customer information for sales transaction data. Other data may not be included simply because they were not considered important at the time of entry. Relevant data may not be recorded due to a misunderstanding or because of equipment malfunctions. Data that were inconsistent with other recorded data may have been deleted. Furthermore, the recording of the data history or modifications may have been overlooked. Missing data, particularly for tuples with missing values for some attributes, may need to be inferred.

Recall that data quality depends on the intended use of the data. Two different users may have very different assessments of the quality of a given database. For example, a marketing analyst may need to access the database mentioned before for a list of customer addresses. Some of the addresses are outdated or incorrect, yet overall, 80% of the addresses are accurate. The marketing analyst considers this to be a large customer database for target marketing purposes and is pleased with the database's accuracy, although, as sales manager, you found the data inaccurate.

Timeliness also affects data quality. Suppose that you are overseeing the distribution of monthly sales bonuses to the top sales representatives at *AllElectronics*. Several sales representatives, however, fail to submit their sales records on time at the end of the month. There are also a number of corrections and adjustments that flow in after the month's end. For a period of time following each month, the data stored in the database are incomplete. However, once all of the data are received, it is correct. The fact that the month-end data are not updated in a timely fashion has a negative impact on the data quality.

Two other factors affecting data quality are believability and interpretability. **Believability** reflects how much the data are trusted by users, while **interpretability** reflects how easy the data are understood. Suppose that a database, at one point, had several errors, all of which have since been corrected. The past errors, however, had caused many problems for sales department users, and so they no longer trust the data. The data also use many accounting codes, which the sales department does not know how to interpret. Even though the database is now accurate, complete, consistent, and timely, sales department users may regard it as of low quality due to poor believability and interpretability.

3.1.2 Major Tasks in Data Preprocessing

In this section, we look at the major steps involved in data preprocessing, namely, data cleaning, data integration, data reduction, and data transformation.

Data cleaning routines work to "clean" the data by filling in missing values, smoothing noisy data, identifying or removing outliers, and resolving inconsistencies. If users believe the data are dirty, they are unlikely to trust the results of any data mining that has been applied. Furthermore, dirty data can cause confusion for the mining procedure, resulting in unreliable output. Although most mining routines have some procedures for dealing with incomplete or noisy data, they are not always robust. Instead, they may concentrate on avoiding overfitting the data to the function being modeled. Therefore, a useful preprocessing step is to run your data through some data cleaning routines. Section 3.2 discusses methods for data cleaning.

Getting back to your task at *AllElectronics*, suppose that you would like to include data from multiple sources in your analysis. This would involve integrating multiple databases, data cubes, or files (i.e., **data integration**). Yet some attributes representing a given concept may have different names in different databases, causing inconsistencies and redundancies. For example, the attribute for customer identification may be referred to as *customer_id* in one data store and *cust_id* in another. Naming inconsistencies may also occur for attribute values. For example, the same first name could be registered as "Bill" in one database, "William" in another, and "B." in a third. Furthermore, you suspect that some attributes may be inferred from others (e.g., annual revenue). Having a large amount of redundant data may slow down or confuse the knowledge discovery process. Clearly, in addition to data cleaning, steps must be taken to help avoid redundancies during data integration. Typically, data cleaning and data integration are performed as a preprocessing step when preparing data for a data warehouse. Additional data cleaning can be performed to detect and remove redundancies that may have resulted from data integration.

"*Hmmm,*" you wonder, as you consider your data even further. "*The data set I have selected for analysis is HUGE, which is sure to slow down the mining process. Is there a way I can reduce the size of my data set without jeopardizing the data mining results?*" **Data reduction** obtains a reduced representation of the data set that is much smaller in volume, yet produces the same (or almost the same) analytical results. Data reduction strategies include *dimensionality reduction* and *numerosity reduction.*

In **dimensionality reduction**, data encoding schemes are applied so as to obtain a reduced or "compressed" representation of the original data. Examples include data compression techniques (e.g., *wavelet transforms* and *principal components analysis*), *attribute subset selection* (e.g., removing irrelevant attributes), and *attribute construction* (e.g., where a small set of more useful attributes is derived from the original set).

In **numerosity reduction**, the data are replaced by alternative, smaller representations using parametric models (e.g., *regression* or *log-linear models*) or nonparametric models (e.g., *histograms, clusters, sampling,* or *data aggregation*). Data reduction is the topic of Section 3.4.

Getting back to your data, you have decided, say, that you would like to use a distance-based mining algorithm for your analysis, such as neural networks, nearest-neighbor classifiers, or clustering.[1] Such methods provide better results if the data to be analyzed have been *normalized*, that is, scaled to a smaller range such as [0.0, 1.0]. Your customer data, for example, contain the attributes *age* and *annual salary*. The *annual salary* attribute usually takes much larger values than *age*. Therefore, if the attributes are left unnormalized, the distance measurements taken on *annual salary* will generally outweigh distance measurements taken on *age*. *Discretization* and *concept hierarchy generation* can also be useful, where raw data values for attributes are replaced by ranges or higher conceptual levels. For example, raw values for *age* may be replaced by higher-level concepts, such as *youth, adult,* or *senior.*

Discretization and concept hierarchy generation are powerful tools for data mining in that they allow data mining at multiple abstraction levels. Normalization, data

---

[1] Neural networks and nearest-neighbor classifiers are described in Chapter 9, and clustering is discussed in Chapters 10 and 11.

discretization, and concept hierarchy generation are forms of **data transformation**. You soon realize such data transformation operations are additional data preprocessing procedures that would contribute toward the success of the mining process. Data integration and data discretization are discussed in Sections 3.5.

Figure 3.1 summarizes the data preprocessing steps described here. Note that the previous categorization is not mutually exclusive. For example, the removal of redundant data may be seen as a form of data cleaning, as well as data reduction.

In summary, real-world data tend to be dirty, incomplete, and inconsistent. Data preprocessing techniques can improve data quality, thereby helping to improve the accuracy and efficiency of the subsequent mining process. Data preprocessing is an important step in the knowledge discovery process, because quality decisions must be based on quality data. Detecting data anomalies, rectifying them early, and reducing the data to be analyzed can lead to huge payoffs for decision making.

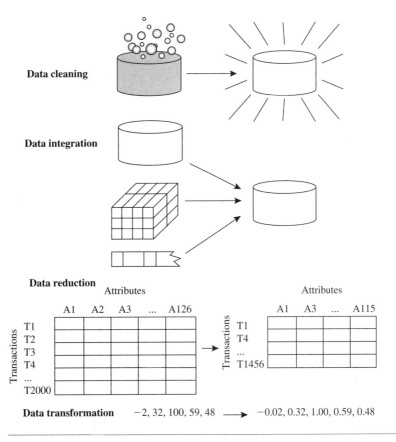

Figure 3.1 Forms of data preprocessing.

3.2 Data Cleaning

Real-world data tend to be incomplete, noisy, and inconsistent. *Data cleaning* (or *data cleansing*) routines attempt to fill in missing values, smooth out noise while identifying outliers, and correct inconsistencies in the data. In this section, you will study basic methods for data cleaning. Section 3.2.1 looks at ways of handling missing values. Section 3.2.2 explains data smoothing techniques. Section 3.2.3 discusses approaches to data cleaning as a process.

3.2.1 Missing Values

Imagine that you need to analyze *AllElectronics* sales and customer data. You note that many tuples have no recorded value for several attributes such as customer *income*. How can you go about filling in the missing values for this attribute? Let's look at the following methods.

1. **Ignore the tuple**: This is usually done when the class label is missing (assuming the mining task involves classification). This method is not very effective, unless the tuple contains several attributes with missing values. It is especially poor when the percentage of missing values per attribute varies considerably. By ignoring the tuple, we do not make use of the remaining attributes' values in the tuple. Such data could have been useful to the task at hand.

2. **Fill in the missing value manually**: In general, this approach is time consuming and may not be feasible given a large data set with many missing values.

3. **Use a global constant to fill in the missing value**: Replace all missing attribute values by the same constant such as a label like "*Unknown*" or $-\infty$. If missing values are replaced by, say, "*Unknown*," then the mining program may mistakenly think that they form an interesting concept, since they all have a value in common—that of "*Unknown*." Hence, although this method is simple, it is not foolproof.

4. **Use a measure of central tendency for the attribute (e.g., the mean or median) to fill in the missing value**: Chapter 2 discussed measures of central tendency, which indicate the "middle" value of a data distribution. For normal (symmetric) data distributions, the mean can be used, while skewed data distribution should employ the median (Section 2.2). For example, suppose that the data distribution regarding the income of *AllElectronics* customers is symmetric and that the mean income is $56,000. Use this value to replace the missing value for *income*.

5. **Use the attribute mean or median for all samples belonging to the same class as the given tuple**: For example, if classifying customers according to *credit_risk*, we may replace the missing value with the mean *income* value for customers in the same credit risk category as that of the given tuple. If the data distribution for a given class is skewed, the median value is a better choice.

6. **Use the most probable value to fill in the missing value**: This may be determined with regression, inference-based tools using a Bayesian formalism, or decision tree

induction. For example, using the other customer attributes in your data set, you may construct a decision tree to predict the missing values for *income*. Decision trees and Bayesian inference are described in detail in Chapters 8 and 9, respectively, while regression is introduced in Section 3.4.5.

Methods 3 through 6 bias the data—the filled-in value may not be correct. Method 6, however, is a popular strategy. In comparison to the other methods, it uses the most information from the present data to predict missing values. By considering the other attributes' values in its estimation of the missing value for *income*, there is a greater chance that the relationships between *income* and the other attributes are preserved.

It is important to note that, in some cases, a missing value may not imply an error in the data! For example, when applying for a credit card, candidates may be asked to supply their driver's license number. Candidates who do not have a driver's license may naturally leave this field blank. Forms should allow respondents to specify values such as "not applicable." Software routines may also be used to uncover other null values (e.g., "don't know," "?" or "none"). Ideally, each attribute should have one or more rules regarding the *null* condition. The rules may specify whether or not nulls are allowed and/or how such values should be handled or transformed. Fields may also be intentionally left blank if they are to be provided in a later step of the business process. Hence, although we can try our best to clean the data after it is seized, good database and data entry procedure design should help minimize the number of missing values or errors in the first place.

3.2.2 Noisy Data

"What is noise?" **Noise** is a random error or variance in a measured variable. In Chapter 2, we saw how some basic statistical description techniques (e.g., boxplots and scatter plots), and methods of data visualization can be used to identify outliers, which may represent noise. Given a numeric attribute such as, say, *price*, how can we "smooth" out the data to remove the noise? Let's look at the following data smoothing techniques.

Binning: Binning methods smooth a sorted data value by consulting its "neighborhood," that is, the values around it. The sorted values are distributed into a number of "buckets," or *bins*. Because binning methods consult the neighborhood of values, they perform *local* smoothing. Figure 3.2 illustrates some binning techniques. In this example, the data for *price* are first sorted and then partitioned into *equal-frequency* bins of size 3 (i.e., each bin contains three values). In **smoothing by bin means**, each value in a bin is replaced by the mean value of the bin. For example, the mean of the values 4, 8, and 15 in Bin 1 is 9. Therefore, each original value in this bin is replaced by the value 9.

Similarly, **smoothing by bin medians** can be employed, in which each bin value is replaced by the bin median. In **smoothing by bin boundaries**, the minimum and maximum values in a given bin are identified as the *bin boundaries*. Each bin value is then replaced by the closest boundary value. In general, the larger the width, the

Sorted data for *price* (in dollars): 4, 8, 15, 21, 21, 24, 25, 28, 34

Partition into (equal-frequency) bins:

Bin 1: 4, 8, 15
Bin 2: 21, 21, 24
Bin 3: 25, 28, 34

Smoothing by bin means:

Bin 1: 9, 9, 9
Bin 2: 22, 22, 22
Bin 3: 29, 29, 29

Smoothing by bin boundaries:

Bin 1: 4, 4, 15
Bin 2: 21, 21, 24
Bin 3: 25, 25, 34

Figure 3.2 Binning methods for data smoothing.

greater the effect of the smoothing. Alternatively, bins may be *equal width*, where the interval range of values in each bin is constant. Binning is also used as a discretization technique and is further discussed in Section 3.5.

Regression: Data smoothing can also be done by regression, a technique that conforms data values to a function. *Linear regression* involves finding the "best" line to fit two attributes (or variables) so that one attribute can be used to predict the other. *Multiple linear regression* is an extension of linear regression, where more than two attributes are involved and the data are fit to a multidimensional surface. Regression is further described in Section 3.4.5.

Outlier analysis: Outliers may be detected by clustering, for example, where similar values are organized into groups, or "clusters." Intuitively, values that fall outside of the set of clusters may be considered outliers (Figure 3.3). Chapter 12 is dedicated to the topic of outlier analysis.

Many data smoothing methods are also used for data discretization (a form of data transformation) and data reduction. For example, the binning techniques described before reduce the number of distinct values per attribute. This acts as a form of data reduction for logic-based data mining methods, such as decision tree induction, which repeatedly makes value comparisons on sorted data. Concept hierarchies are a form of data discretization that can also be used for data smoothing. A concept hierarchy for *price*, for example, may map real *price* values into *inexpensive, moderately_priced*, and *expensive*, thereby reducing the number of data values to be handled by the mining

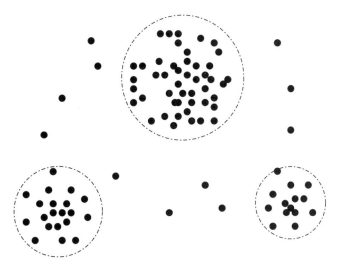

Figure 3.3 A 2-D customer data plot with respect to customer locations in a city, showing three data clusters. Outliers may be detected as values that fall outside of the cluster sets.

process. Data discretization is discussed in Section 3.5. Some methods of classification (e.g., neural networks) have built-in data smoothing mechanisms. Classification is the topic of Chapters 8 and 9.

3.2.3 Data Cleaning as a Process

Missing values, noise, and inconsistencies contribute to inaccurate data. So far, we have looked at techniques for handling missing data and for smoothing data. *"But data cleaning is a big job. What about data cleaning as a process? How exactly does one proceed in tackling this task? Are there any tools out there to help?"*

The first step in data cleaning as a process is *discrepancy detection*. Discrepancies can be caused by several factors, including poorly designed data entry forms that have many optional fields, human error in data entry, deliberate errors (e.g., respondents not wanting to divulge information about themselves), and data decay (e.g., outdated addresses). Discrepancies may also arise from inconsistent data representations and inconsistent use of codes. Other sources of discrepancies include errors in instrumentation devices that record data and system errors. Errors can also occur when the data are (inadequately) used for purposes other than originally intended. There may also be inconsistencies due to data integration (e.g., where a given attribute can have different names in different databases).[2]

---

[2]Data integration and the removal of redundant data that can result from such integration are further described in Section 3.3.

"So, how can we proceed with discrepancy detection?" As a starting point, use any knowledge you may already have regarding properties of the data. Such knowledge or "data about data" is referred to as **metadata**. This is where we can make use of the knowledge we gained about our data in Chapter 2. For example, what are the data type and domain of each attribute? What are the acceptable values for each attribute? The basic statistical data descriptions discussed in Section 2.2 are useful here to grasp data trends and identify anomalies. For example, find the mean, median, and mode values. Are the data symmetric or skewed? What is the range of values? Do all values fall within the expected range? What is the standard deviation of each attribute? Values that are more than two standard deviations away from the mean for a given attribute may be flagged as potential outliers. Are there any known dependencies between attributes? In this step, you may write your own scripts and/or use some of the tools that we discuss further later. From this, you may find noise, outliers, and unusual values that need investigation.

As a data analyst, you should be on the lookout for the inconsistent use of codes and any inconsistent data representations (e.g., "2010/12/25" and "25/12/2010" for *date*). **Field overloading** is another error source that typically results when developers squeeze new attribute definitions into unused (bit) portions of already defined attributes (e.g., an unused bit of an attribute that has a value range that uses only, say, 31 out of 32 bits).

The data should also be examined regarding unique rules, consecutive rules, and null rules. A **unique rule** says that each value of the given attribute must be different from all other values for that attribute. A **consecutive rule** says that there can be no missing values between the lowest and highest values for the attribute, and that all values must also be unique (e.g., as in check numbers). A **null rule** specifies the use of blanks, question marks, special characters, or other strings that may indicate the null condition (e.g., where a value for a given attribute is not available), and how such values should be handled. As mentioned in Section 3.2.1, reasons for missing values may include (1) the person originally asked to provide a value for the attribute refuses and/or finds that the information requested is not applicable (e.g., a *license_number* attribute left blank by nondrivers); (2) the data entry person does not know the correct value; or (3) the value is to be provided by a later step of the process. The null rule should specify how to record the null condition, for example, such as to store zero for numeric attributes, a blank for character attributes, or any other conventions that may be in use (e.g., entries like "don't know" or "?" should be transformed to blank).

There are a number of different commercial tools that can aid in the discrepancy detection step. **Data scrubbing tools** use simple domain knowledge (e.g., knowledge of postal addresses and spell-checking) to detect errors and make corrections in the data. These tools rely on parsing and fuzzy matching techniques when cleaning data from multiple sources. **Data auditing tools** find discrepancies by analyzing the data to discover rules and relationships, and detecting data that violate such conditions. They are variants of data mining tools. For example, they may employ statistical analysis to find correlations, or clustering to identify outliers. They may also use the basic statistical data descriptions presented in Section 2.2.

Some data inconsistencies may be corrected manually using external references. For example, errors made at data entry may be corrected by performing a paper trace. Most errors, however, will require *data transformations*. That is, once we find discrepancies, we typically need to define and apply (a series of) transformations to correct them.

Commercial tools can assist in the data transformation step. **Data migration tools** allow simple transformations to be specified such as to replace the string *"gender"* by *"sex."* **ETL (extraction/transformation/loading) tools** allow users to specify transforms through a graphical user interface (GUI). These tools typically support only a restricted set of transforms so that, often, we may also choose to write custom scripts for this step of the data cleaning process.

The two-step process of discrepancy detection and data transformation (to correct discrepancies) iterates. This process, however, is error-prone and time consuming. Some transformations may introduce more discrepancies. Some *nested discrepancies* may only be detected after others have been fixed. For example, a typo such as "20010" in a year field may only surface once all date values have been converted to a uniform format. Transformations are often done as a batch process while the user waits without feedback. Only after the transformation is complete can the user go back and check that no new anomalies have been mistakenly created. Typically, numerous iterations are required before the user is satisfied. Any tuples that cannot be automatically handled by a given transformation are typically written to a file without any explanation regarding the reasoning behind their failure. As a result, the entire data cleaning process also suffers from a lack of interactivity.

New approaches to data cleaning emphasize increased interactivity. Potter's Wheel, for example, is a publicly available data cleaning tool that integrates discrepancy detection and transformation. Users gradually build a series of transformations by composing and debugging individual transformations, one step at a time, on a spreadsheet-like interface. The transformations can be specified graphically or by providing examples. Results are shown immediately on the records that are visible on the screen. The user can choose to undo the transformations, so that transformations that introduced additional errors can be "erased." The tool automatically performs discrepancy checking in the background on the latest transformed view of the data. Users can gradually develop and refine transformations as discrepancies are found, leading to more effective and efficient data cleaning.

Another approach to increased interactivity in data cleaning is the development of declarative languages for the specification of data transformation operators. Such work focuses on defining powerful extensions to SQL and algorithms that enable users to express data cleaning specifications efficiently.

As we discover more about the data, it is important to keep updating the metadata to reflect this knowledge. This will help speed up data cleaning on future versions of the same data store.

3.3 Data Integration

Data mining often requires data integration—the merging of data from multiple data stores. Careful integration can help reduce and avoid redundancies and inconsistencies in the resulting data set. This can help improve the accuracy and speed of the subsequent data mining process.

The semantic heterogeneity and structure of data pose great challenges in data integration. How can we match schema and objects from different sources? This is the essence of the *entity identification problem*, described in Section 3.3.1. Are any attributes correlated? Section 3.3.2 presents correlation tests for numeric and nominal data. Tuple duplication is described in Section 3.3.3. Finally, Section 3.3.4 touches on the detection and resolution of data value conflicts.

3.3.1 Entity Identification Problem

It is likely that your data analysis task will involve *data integration*, which combines data from multiple sources into a coherent data store, as in data warehousing. These sources may include multiple databases, data cubes, or flat files.

There are a number of issues to consider during data integration. *Schema integration* and *object matching* can be tricky. How can equivalent real-world entities from multiple data sources be matched up? This is referred to as the **entity identification problem**. For example, how can the data analyst or the computer be sure that *customer_id* in one database and *cust_number* in another refer to the same attribute? Examples of metadata for each attribute include the name, meaning, data type, and range of values permitted for the attribute, and null rules for handling blank, zero, or null values (Section 3.2). Such metadata can be used to help avoid errors in schema integration. The metadata may also be used to help transform the data (e.g., where data codes for *pay_type* in one database may be "*H*" and "*S*" but *1* and *2* in another). Hence, this step also relates to data cleaning, as described earlier.

When matching attributes from one database to another during integration, special attention must be paid to the *structure* of the data. This is to ensure that any attribute functional dependencies and referential constraints in the source system match those in the target system. For example, in one system, a *discount* may be applied to the order, whereas in another system it is applied to each individual line item within the order. If this is not caught before integration, items in the target system may be improperly discounted.

3.3.2 Redundancy and Correlation Analysis

Redundancy is another important issue in data integration. An attribute (such as *annual revenue*, for instance) may be redundant if it can be "derived" from another attribute or set of attributes. Inconsistencies in attribute or dimension naming can also cause redundancies in the resulting data set.

Some redundancies can be detected by **correlation analysis**. Given two attributes, such analysis can measure how strongly one attribute implies the other, based on the available data. For nominal data, we use the χ^2 (*chi-square*) test. For numeric attributes, we can use the *correlation coefficient* and *covariance*, both of which access how one attribute's values vary from those of another.

χ^2 **Correlation Test for Nominal Data**

For nominal data, a correlation relationship between two attributes, A and B, can be discovered by a χ^2 (**chi-square**) test. Suppose A has c distinct values, namely $a_1, a_2, \ldots a_c$. B has r distinct values, namely $b_1, b_2, \ldots b_r$. The data tuples described by A and B can be shown as a **contingency table**, with the c values of A making up the columns and the r values of B making up the rows. Let (A_i, B_j) denote the joint event that attribute A takes on value a_i and attribute B takes on value b_j, that is, where $(A = a_i, B = b_j)$. Each and every possible (A_i, B_j) joint event has its own cell (or slot) in the table. The χ^2 value (also known as the *Pearson χ^2 statistic*) is computed as

$$\chi^2 = \sum_{i=1}^{c}\sum_{j=1}^{r} \frac{(o_{ij} - e_{ij})^2}{e_{ij}}, \qquad (3.1)$$

where o_{ij} is the *observed frequency* (i.e., actual count) of the joint event (A_i, B_j) and e_{ij} is the *expected frequency* of (A_i, B_j), which can be computed as

$$e_{ij} = \frac{count(A = a_i) \times count(B = b_j)}{n}, \qquad (3.2)$$

where n is the number of data tuples, $count(A = a_i)$ is the number of tuples having value a_i for A, and $count(B = b_j)$ is the number of tuples having value b_j for B. The sum in Eq. (3.1) is computed over all of the $r \times c$ cells. Note that the cells that contribute the most to the χ^2 value are those for which the actual count is very different from that expected.

The χ^2 statistic tests the hypothesis that A and B are *independent*, that is, there is no correlation between them. The test is based on a significance level, with $(r-1) \times (c-1)$ degrees of freedom. We illustrate the use of this statistic in Example 3.1. If the hypothesis can be rejected, then we say that A and B are statistically correlated.

Example 3.1 **Correlation analysis of nominal attributes using χ^2.** Suppose that a group of 1500 people was surveyed. The gender of each person was noted. Each person was polled as to whether his or her preferred type of reading material was fiction or nonfiction. Thus, we have two attributes, *gender* and *preferred_reading*. The observed frequency (or count) of each possible joint event is summarized in the contingency table shown in Table 3.1, where the numbers in parentheses are the expected frequencies. The expected frequencies are calculated based on the data distribution for both attributes using Eq. (3.2).

Using Eq. (3.2), we can verify the expected frequencies for each cell. For example, the expected frequency for the cell (*male, fiction*) is

$$e_{11} = \frac{count(male) \times count(fiction)}{n} = \frac{300 \times 450}{1500} = 90,$$

and so on. Notice that in any row, the sum of the expected frequencies must equal the total observed frequency for that row, and the sum of the expected frequencies in any column must also equal the total observed frequency for that column.

Table 3.1 Example 2.1's 2×2 Contingency Table Data

	male	female	Total
fiction	250 (90)	200 (360)	450
non_fiction	50 (210)	1000 (840)	1050
Total	300	1200	1500

Note: Are *gender* and *preferred_reading* correlated?

Using Eq. (3.1) for χ^2 computation, we get

$$\chi^2 = \frac{(250 - 90)^2}{90} + \frac{(50 - 210)^2}{210} + \frac{(200 - 360)^2}{360} + \frac{(1000 - 840)^2}{840}$$
$$= 284.44 + 121.90 + 71.11 + 30.48 = 507.93.$$

For this 2×2 table, the degrees of freedom are $(2 - 1)(2 - 1) = 1$. For 1 degree of freedom, the χ^2 value needed to reject the hypothesis at the 0.001 significance level is 10.828 (taken from the table of upper percentage points of the χ^2 distribution, typically available from any textbook on statistics). Since our computed value is above this, we can reject the hypothesis that *gender* and *preferred_reading* are independent and conclude that the two attributes are (strongly) correlated for the given group of people. ∎

Correlation Coefficient for Numeric Data

For numeric attributes, we can evaluate the correlation between two attributes, A and B, by computing the **correlation coefficient** (also known as **Pearson's product moment coefficient**, named after its inventer, Karl Pearson). This is

$$r_{A,B} = \frac{\sum_{i=1}^{n}(a_i - \bar{A})(b_i - \bar{B})}{n\sigma_A\sigma_B} = \frac{\sum_{i=1}^{n}(a_ib_i) - n\bar{A}\bar{B}}{n\sigma_A\sigma_B}, \tag{3.3}$$

where n is the number of tuples, a_i and b_i are the respective values of A and B in tuple i, $\bar{A}$ and $\bar{B}$ are the respective mean values of A and B, σ_A and σ_B are the respective standard deviations of A and B (as defined in Section 2.2.2), and $\Sigma(a_ib_i)$ is the sum of the AB cross-product (i.e., for each tuple, the value for A is multiplied by the value for B in that tuple). Note that $-1 \le r_{A,B} \le +1$. If $r_{A,B}$ is greater than 0, then A and B are *positively correlated*, meaning that the values of A increase as the values of B increase. The higher the value, the stronger the correlation (i.e., the more each attribute implies the other). Hence, a higher value may indicate that A (or B) may be removed as a redundancy.

If the resulting value is equal to 0, then A and B are *independent* and there is no correlation between them. If the resulting value is less than 0, then A and B are *negatively correlated*, where the values of one attribute increase as the values of the other attribute decrease. This means that each attribute discourages the other. Scatter plots can also be used to view correlations between attributes (Section 2.2.3). For example, Figure 2.8's scatter plots respectively show positively correlated data and negatively correlated data, while Figure 2.9 displays uncorrelated data.

Note that correlation does not imply causality. That is, if A and B are correlated, this does not necessarily imply that A causes B or that B causes A. For example, in analyzing a demographic database, we may find that attributes representing the number of hospitals and the number of car thefts in a region are correlated. This does not mean that one causes the other. Both are actually causally linked to a third attribute, namely, *population*.

Covariance of Numeric Data

In probability theory and statistics, correlation and covariance are two similar measures for assessing how much two attributes change together. Consider two numeric attributes A and B, and a set of n observations $\{(a_1, b_1), \ldots, (a_n, b_n)\}$. The mean values of A and B, respectively, are also known as the **expected values** on A and B, that is,

$$E(A) = \bar{A} = \frac{\sum_{i=1}^{n} a_i}{n}$$

and

$$E(B) = \bar{B} = \frac{\sum_{i=1}^{n} b_i}{n}.$$

The **covariance** between A and B is defined as

$$Cov(A, B) = E((A - \bar{A})(B - \bar{B})) = \frac{\sum_{i=1}^{n}(a_i - \bar{A})(b_i - \bar{B})}{n}. \tag{3.4}$$

If we compare Eq. (3.3) for $r_{A,B}$ (correlation coefficient) with Eq. (3.4) for covariance, we see that

$$r_{A,B} = \frac{Cov(A, B)}{\sigma_A \sigma_B}, \tag{3.5}$$

where σ_A and σ_B are the standard deviations of A and B, respectively. It can also be shown that

$$Cov(A, B) = E(A \cdot B) - \bar{A}\bar{B}. \tag{3.6}$$

This equation may simplify calculations.

For two attributes A and B that tend to change together, if A is larger than $\bar{A}$ (the expected value of A), then B is likely to be larger than $\bar{B}$ (the expected value of B). Therefore, the covariance between A and B is *positive*. On the other hand, if one of the attributes tends to be above its expected value when the other attribute is below its expected value, then the covariance of A and B is *negative*.

If A and B are *independent* (i.e., they do not have correlation), then $E(A \cdot B) = E(A) \cdot E(B)$. Therefore, the covariance is $Cov(A, B) = E(A \cdot B) - \bar{A}\bar{B} = E(A) \cdot E(B) - \bar{A}\bar{B} = 0$. However, the converse is not true. Some pairs of random variables (attributes) may have a covariance of 0 but are not independent. Only under some additional assumptions

Table 3.2 Stock Prices for *AllElectronics* and *HighTech*

Time point	AllElectronics	HighTech
t1	6	20
t2	5	10
t3	4	14
t4	3	5
t5	2	5

(e.g., the data follow multivariate normal distributions) does a covariance of 0 imply independence.

Example 3.2 **Covariance analysis of numeric attributes.** Consider Table 3.2, which presents a simplified example of stock prices observed at five time points for *AllElectronics* and *HighTech*, a high-tech company. If the stocks are affected by the same industry trends, will their prices rise or fall together?

$$E(AllElectronics) = \frac{6+5+4+3+2}{5} = \frac{20}{5} = \$4$$

and

$$E(HighTech) = \frac{20+10+14+5+5}{5} = \frac{54}{5} = \$10.80.$$

Thus, using Eq. (3.4), we compute

$$Cov(AllElectroncis, HighTech) = \frac{6 \times 20 + 5 \times 10 + 4 \times 14 + 3 \times 5 + 2 \times 5}{5} - 4 \times 10.80$$

$$= 50.2 - 43.2 = 7.$$

Therefore, given the positive covariance we can say that stock prices for both companies rise together. ■

Variance is a special case of covariance, where the two attributes are identical (i.e., the covariance of an attribute with itself). Variance was discussed in Chapter 2.

3.3.3 Tuple Duplication

In addition to detecting redundancies between attributes, duplication should also be detected at the tuple level (e.g., where there are two or more identical tuples for a given unique data entry case). The use of denormalized tables (often done to improve performance by avoiding joins) is another source of data redundancy. Inconsistencies often arise between various duplicates, due to inaccurate data entry or updating some but not all data occurrences. For example, if a purchase order database contains attributes for the purchaser's name and address instead of a key to this information in a purchaser database, discrepancies can occur, such as the same purchaser's name appearing with different addresses within the purchase order database.

3.3.4 Data Value Conflict Detection and Resolution

Data integration also involves the *detection and resolution of data value conflicts*. For example, for the same real-world entity, attribute values from different sources may differ. This may be due to differences in representation, scaling, or encoding. For instance, a *weight* attribute may be stored in metric units in one system and British imperial units in another. For a hotel chain, the *price* of rooms in different cities may involve not only different currencies but also different services (e.g., free breakfast) and taxes. When exchanging information between schools, for example, each school may have its own curriculum and grading scheme. One university may adopt a quarter system, offer three courses on database systems, and assign grades from A+ to F, whereas another may adopt a semester system, offer two courses on databases, and assign grades from 1 to 10. It is difficult to work out precise course-to-grade transformation rules between the two universities, making information exchange difficult.

Attributes may also differ on the abstraction level, where an attribute in one system is recorded at, say, a lower abstraction level than the "same" attribute in another. For example, the *total_sales* in one database may refer to one branch of *All_Electronics*, while an attribute of the same name in another database may refer to the total sales for *All_Electronics* stores in a given region. The topic of discrepancy detection is further described in Section 3.2.3 on data cleaning as a process.

3.4 Data Reduction

Imagine that you have selected data from the *AllElectronics* data warehouse for analysis. The data set will likely be huge! Complex data analysis and mining on huge amounts of data can take a long time, making such analysis impractical or infeasible.

Data reduction techniques can be applied to obtain a reduced representation of the data set that is much smaller in volume, yet closely maintains the integrity of the original data. That is, mining on the reduced data set should be more efficient yet produce the same (or almost the same) analytical results. In this section, we first present an overview of data reduction strategies, followed by a closer look at individual techniques.

3.4.1 Overview of Data Reduction Strategies

Data reduction strategies include *dimensionality reduction*, *numerosity reduction*, and *data compression*.

Dimensionality reduction is the process of reducing the number of random variables or attributes under consideration. Dimensionality reduction methods include *wavelet* *transforms* (Section 3.4.2) and *principal components analysis* (Section 3.4.3), which transform or project the original data onto a smaller space. *Attribute subset selection* is a method of dimensionality reduction in which irrelevant, weakly relevant, or redundant attributes or dimensions are detected and removed (Section 3.4.4).

Numerosity reduction techniques replace the original data volume by alternative, smaller forms of data representation. These techniques may be parametric or non-parametric. For *parametric methods*, a model is used to estimate the data, so that typically only the data parameters need to be stored, instead of the actual data. (Outliers may also be stored.) Regression and log-linear models (Section 3.4.5) are examples. *Nonparametric methods* for storing reduced representations of the data include *histograms* (Section 3.4.6), *clustering* (Section 3.4.7), *sampling* (Section 3.4.8), and *data cube aggregation* (Section 3.4.9).

In **data compression**, transformations are applied so as to obtain a reduced or "compressed" representation of the original data. If the original data can be *reconstructed* from the compressed data without any information loss, the data reduction is called **lossless**. If, instead, we can reconstruct only an approximation of the original data, then the data reduction is called **lossy**. There are several lossless algorithms for string compression; however, they typically allow only limited data manipulation. Dimensionality reduction and numerosity reduction techniques can also be considered forms of data compression.

There are many other ways of organizing methods of data reduction. The computational time spent on data reduction should not outweigh or "erase" the time saved by mining on a reduced data set size.

3.4.2 Wavelet Transforms

The **discrete wavelet transform (DWT)** is a linear signal processing technique that, when applied to a data vector X, transforms it to a numerically different vector, X', of **wavelet coefficients**. The two vectors are of the same length. When applying this technique to data reduction, we consider each tuple as an n-dimensional data vector, that is, $X = (x_1, x_2, \ldots, x_n)$, depicting n measurements made on the tuple from n database attributes.[3]

"How can this technique be useful for data reduction if the wavelet transformed data are of the same length as the original data?" The usefulness lies in the fact that the wavelet transformed data can be truncated. A compressed approximation of the data can be retained by storing only a small fraction of the strongest of the wavelet coefficients. For example, all wavelet coefficients larger than some user-specified threshold can be retained. All other coefficients are set to 0. The resulting data representation is therefore very sparse, so that operations that can take advantage of data sparsity are computationally very fast if performed in wavelet space. The technique also works to remove noise without smoothing out the main features of the data, making it effective for data

---

[3]In our notation, any variable representing a vector is shown in bold italic font; measurements depicting the vector are shown in italic font.

cleaning as well. Given a set of coefficients, an approximation of the original data can be constructed by applying the *inverse* of the DWT used.

The DWT is closely related to the *discrete Fourier transform (DFT)*, a signal processing technique involving sines and cosines. In general, however, the DWT achieves better lossy compression. That is, if the same number of coefficients is retained for a DWT and a DFT of a given data vector, the DWT version will provide a more accurate approximation of the original data. Hence, for an equivalent approximation, the DWT requires less space than the DFT. Unlike the DFT, wavelets are quite localized in space, contributing to the conservation of local detail.

There is only one DFT, yet there are several families of DWTs. Figure 3.4 shows some wavelet families. Popular wavelet transforms include the Haar-2, Daubechies-4, and Daubechies-6. The general procedure for applying a discrete wavelet transform uses a hierarchical *pyramid algorithm* that halves the data at each iteration, resulting in fast computational speed. The method is as follows:

1. The length, L, of the input data vector must be an integer power of 2. This condition can be met by padding the data vector with zeros as necessary ($L \geq n$).

2. Each transform involves applying two functions. The first applies some data smoothing, such as a sum or weighted average. The second performs a weighted difference, which acts to bring out the detailed features of the data.

3. The two functions are applied to pairs of data points in X, that is, to all pairs of measurements (x_{2i}, x_{2i+1}). This results in two data sets of length $L/2$. In general, these represent a smoothed or low-frequency version of the input data and the high-frequency content of it, respectively.

4. The two functions are recursively applied to the data sets obtained in the previous loop, until the resulting data sets obtained are of length 2.

5. Selected values from the data sets obtained in the previous iterations are designated the wavelet coefficients of the transformed data.

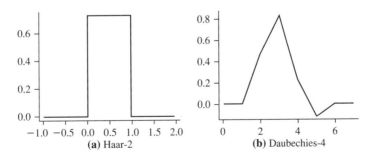

(a) Haar-2   (b) Daubechies-4

Figure 3.4 Examples of wavelet families. The number next to a wavelet name is the number of *vanishing moments* of the wavelet. This is a set of mathematical relationships that the coefficients must satisfy and is related to the number of coefficients.

Equivalently, a matrix multiplication can be applied to the input data in order to obtain the wavelet coefficients, where the matrix used depends on the given DWT. The matrix must be **orthonormal**, meaning that the columns are unit vectors and are mutually orthogonal, so that the matrix inverse is just its transpose. Although we do not have room to discuss it here, this property allows the reconstruction of the data from the smooth and smooth-difference data sets. By factoring the matrix used into a product of a few sparse matrices, the resulting "fast DWT" algorithm has a complexity of $O(n)$ for an input vector of length n.

Wavelet transforms can be applied to multidimensional data such as a data cube. This is done by first applying the transform to the first dimension, then to the second, and so on. The computational complexity involved is linear with respect to the number of cells in the cube. Wavelet transforms give good results on sparse or skewed data and on data with ordered attributes. Lossy compression by wavelets is reportedly better than JPEG compression, the current commercial standard. Wavelet transforms have many real-world applications, including the compression of fingerprint images, computer vision, analysis of time-series data, and data cleaning.

3.4.3 Principal Components Analysis

In this subsection we provide an intuitive introduction to principal components analysis as a method of dimesionality reduction. A detailed theoretical explanation is beyond the scope of this book. For additional references, please see the bibliographic notes (Section 3.8) at the end of this chapter.

Suppose that the data to be reduced consist of tuples or data vectors described by n attributes or dimensions. **Principal components analysis** (**PCA**; also called the Karhunen-Loeve, or K-L, method) searches for k n-dimensional orthogonal vectors that can best be used to represent the data, where $k \leq n$. The original data are thus projected onto a much smaller space, resulting in dimensionality reduction. Unlike attribute subset selection (Section 3.4.4), which reduces the attribute set size by retaining a subset of the initial set of attributes, PCA "combines" the essence of attributes by creating an alternative, smaller set of variables. The initial data can then be projected onto this smaller set. PCA often reveals relationships that were not previously suspected and thereby allows interpretations that would not ordinarily result.

The basic procedure is as follows:

1. The input data are normalized, so that each attribute falls within the same range. This step helps ensure that attributes with large domains will not dominate attributes with smaller domains.

2. PCA computes k orthonormal vectors that provide a basis for the normalized input data. These are unit vectors that each point in a direction perpendicular to the others. These vectors are referred to as the *principal components*. The input data are a linear combination of the principal components.

3. The principal components are sorted in order of decreasing "significance" or strength. The principal components essentially serve as a new set of axes for the data,

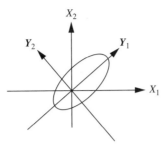

Figure 3.5 Principal components analysis. Y_1 and Y_2 are the first two principal components for the given data.

providing important information about variance. That is, the sorted axes are such that the first axis shows the most variance among the data, the second axis shows the next highest variance, and so on. For example, Figure 3.5 shows the first two principal components, Y_1 and Y_2, for the given set of data originally mapped to the axes X_1 and X_2. This information helps identify groups or patterns within the data.

4. Because the components are sorted in decreasing order of "significance," the data size can be reduced by eliminating the weaker components, that is, those with low variance. Using the strongest principal components, it should be possible to reconstruct a good approximation of the original data.

PCA can be applied to ordered and unordered attributes, and can handle sparse data and skewed data. Multidimensional data of more than two dimensions can be handled by reducing the problem to two dimensions. Principal components may be used as inputs to multiple regression and cluster analysis. In comparison with wavelet transforms, PCA tends to be better at handling sparse data, whereas wavelet transforms are more suitable for data of high dimensionality.

3.4.4 Attribute Subset Selection

Data sets for analysis may contain hundreds of attributes, many of which may be irrelevant to the mining task or redundant. For example, if the task is to classify customers based on whether or not they are likely to purchase a popular new CD at *AllElectronics* when notified of a sale, attributes such as the customer's telephone number are likely to be irrelevant, unlike attributes such as *age* or *music_taste*. Although it may be possible for a domain expert to pick out some of the useful attributes, this can be a difficult and time-consuming task, especially when the data's behavior is not well known. (Hence, a reason behind its analysis!) Leaving out relevant attributes or keeping irrelevant attributes may be detrimental, causing confusion for the mining algorithm employed. This can result in discovered patterns of poor quality. In addition, the added volume of irrelevant or redundant attributes can slow down the mining process.

Attribute subset selection[4] reduces the data set size by removing irrelevant or redundant attributes (or dimensions). The goal of attribute subset selection is to find a minimum set of attributes such that the resulting probability distribution of the data classes is as close as possible to the original distribution obtained using all attributes. Mining on a reduced set of attributes has an additional benefit: It reduces the number of attributes appearing in the discovered patterns, helping to make the patterns easier to understand.

"How can we find a 'good' subset of the original attributes?" For n attributes, there are 2^n possible subsets. An exhaustive search for the optimal subset of attributes can be prohibitively expensive, especially as n and the number of data classes increase. Therefore, heuristic methods that explore a reduced search space are commonly used for attribute subset selection. These methods are typically **greedy** in that, while searching through attribute space, they always make what looks to be the best choice at the time. Their strategy is to make a locally optimal choice in the hope that this will lead to a globally optimal solution. Such greedy methods are effective in practice and may come close to estimating an optimal solution.

The "best" (and "worst") attributes are typically determined using tests of statistical significance, which assume that the attributes are independent of one another. Many other attribute evaluation measures can be used such as the *information gain* measure used in building decision trees for classification.[5]

Basic heuristic methods of attribute subset selection include the techniques that follow, some of which are illustrated in Figure 3.6.

Forward selection	Backward elimination	Decision tree induction
Initial attribute set: $\{A_1, A_2, A_3, A_4, A_5, A_6\}$	Initial attribute set: $\{A_1, A_2, A_3, A_4, A_5, A_6\}$	Initial attribute set: $\{A_1, A_2, A_3, A_4, A_5, A_6\}$
Initial reduced set: $\{\}$ => $\{A_1\}$ => $\{A_1, A_4\}$ => Reduced attribute set: $\{A_1, A_4, A_6\}$	=> $\{A_1, A_3, A_4, A_5, A_6\}$ => $\{A_1, A_4, A_5, A_6\}$ => Reduced attribute set: $\{A_1, A_4, A_6\}$	=> Reduced attribute set: $\{A_1, A_4, A_6\}$

Figure 3.6 Greedy (heuristic) methods for attribute subset selection.

---

[4] In machine learning, attribute subset selection is known as *feature subset selection*.

[5] The information gain measure is described in detail in Chapter 8.

1. **Stepwise forward selection**: The procedure starts with an empty set of attributes as the reduced set. The best of the original attributes is determined and added to the reduced set. At each subsequent iteration or step, the best of the remaining original attributes is added to the set.

2. **Stepwise backward elimination**: The procedure starts with the full set of attributes. At each step, it removes the worst attribute remaining in the set.

3. **Combination of forward selection and backward elimination**: The stepwise forward selection and backward elimination methods can be combined so that, at each step, the procedure selects the best attribute and removes the worst from among the remaining attributes.

4. **Decision tree induction**: Decision tree algorithms (e.g., ID3, C4.5, and CART) were originally intended for classification. Decision tree induction constructs a flowchart-like structure where each internal (nonleaf) node denotes a test on an attribute, each branch corresponds to an outcome of the test, and each external (leaf) node denotes a class prediction. At each node, the algorithm chooses the "best" attribute to partition the data into individual classes.

   When decision tree induction is used for attribute subset selection, a tree is constructed from the given data. All attributes that do not appear in the tree are assumed to be irrelevant. The set of attributes appearing in the tree form the reduced subset of attributes.

The stopping criteria for the methods may vary. The procedure may employ a threshold on the measure used to determine when to stop the attribute selection process.

In some cases, we may want to create new attributes based on others. Such **attribute construction**[6] can help improve accuracy and understanding of structure in high-dimensional data. For example, we may wish to add the attribute *area* based on the attributes *height* and *width*. By combining attributes, attribute construction can discover missing information about the relationships between data attributes that can be useful for knowledge discovery.

3.4.5 Regression and Log-Linear Models: Parametric Data Reduction

Regression and log-linear models can be used to approximate the given data. In (simple) **linear regression**, the data are modeled to fit a straight line. For example, a random variable, *y* (called a *response variable*), can be modeled as a linear function of another random variable, *x* (called a *predictor variable*), with the equation

$$y = wx + b, \qquad (3.7)$$

where the variance of *y* is assumed to be constant. In the context of data mining, *x* and *y* are numeric database attributes. The coefficients, *w* and *b* (called *regression coefficients*),

---

[6]In the machine learning literature, attribute construction is known as *feature construction*.

specify the slope of the line and the *y*-intercept, respectively. These coefficients can be solved for by the *method of least squares*, which minimizes the error between the actual line separating the data and the estimate of the line. **Multiple linear regression** is an extension of (simple) linear regression, which allows a response variable, *y*, to be modeled as a linear function of two or more predictor variables.

Log-linear models approximate discrete multidimensional probability distributions. Given a set of tuples in *n* dimensions (e.g., described by *n* attributes), we can consider each tuple as a point in an *n*-dimensional space. Log-linear models can be used to estimate the probability of each point in a multidimensional space for a set of discretized attributes, based on a smaller subset of dimensional combinations. This allows a higher-dimensional data space to be constructed from lower-dimensional spaces. Log-linear models are therefore also useful for dimensionality reduction (since the lower-dimensional points together typically occupy less space than the original data points) and data smoothing (since aggregate estimates in the lower-dimensional space are less subject to sampling variations than the estimates in the higher-dimensional space).

Regression and log-linear models can both be used on sparse data, although their application may be limited. While both methods can handle skewed data, regression does exceptionally well. Regression can be computationally intensive when applied to high-dimensional data, whereas log-linear models show good scalability for up to 10 or so dimensions.

Several software packages exist to solve regression problems. Examples include SAS (*www.sas.com*), SPSS (*www.spss.com*), and S-Plus (*www.insightful.com*). Another useful resource is the book *Numerical Recipes in C*, by Press, Teukolsky, Vetterling, and Flannery [PTVF07], and its associated source code.

3.4.6 Histograms

Histograms use binning to approximate data distributions and are a popular form of data reduction. Histograms were introduced in Section 2.2.3. A **histogram** for an attribute, *A*, partitions the data distribution of *A* into disjoint subsets, referred to as *buckets* or *bins*. If each bucket represents only a single attribute–value/frequency pair, the buckets are called *singleton buckets*. Often, buckets instead represent continuous ranges for the given attribute.

Example 3.3 **Histograms.** The following data are a list of *AllElectronics* prices for commonly sold items (rounded to the nearest dollar). The numbers have been sorted: 1, 1, 5, 5, 5, 5, 5, 8, 8, 10, 10, 10, 10, 12, 14, 14, 14, 15, 15, 15, 15, 15, 15, 18, 18, 18, 18, 18, 18, 18, 18, 20, 20, 20, 20, 20, 20, 20, 21, 21, 21, 21, 25, 25, 25, 25, 25, 28, 28, 30, 30, 30.

Figure 3.7 shows a histogram for the data using singleton buckets. To further reduce the data, it is common to have each bucket denote a continuous value range for the given attribute. In Figure 3.8, each bucket represents a different $10 range for *price*. ■

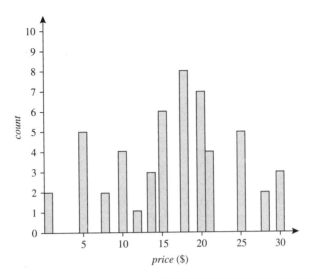

Figure 3.7 A histogram for *price* using singleton buckets—each bucket represents one price–value/frequency pair.

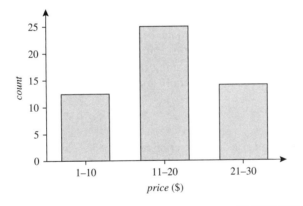

Figure 3.8 An equal-width histogram for *price*, where values are aggregated so that each bucket has a uniform width of $10.

"How are the buckets determined and the attribute values partitioned?" There are several partitioning rules, including the following:

- **Equal-width**: In an equal-width histogram, the width of each bucket range is uniform (e.g., the width of $10 for the buckets in Figure 3.8).

- **Equal-frequency** (or equal-depth): In an equal-frequency histogram, the buckets are created so that, roughly, the frequency of each bucket is constant (i.e., each bucket contains roughly the same number of contiguous data samples).

Histograms are highly effective at approximating both sparse and dense data, as well as highly skewed and uniform data. The histograms described before for single attributes can be extended for multiple attributes. *Multidimensional histograms* can capture dependencies between attributes. These histograms have been found effective in approximating data with up to five attributes. More studies are needed regarding the effectiveness of multidimensional histograms for high dimensionalities.

Singleton buckets are useful for storing high-frequency outliers.

3.4.7 Clustering

Clustering techniques consider data tuples as objects. They partition the objects into groups, or *clusters*, so that objects within a cluster are "similar" to one another and "dissimilar" to objects in other clusters. Similarity is commonly defined in terms of how "close" the objects are in space, based on a distance function. The "quality" of a cluster may be represented by its *diameter*, the maximum distance between any two objects in the cluster. **Centroid distance** is an alternative measure of cluster quality and is defined as the average distance of each cluster object from the cluster centroid (denoting the "average object," or average point in space for the cluster). Figure 3.3 showed a 2-D plot of customer data with respect to customer locations in a city. Three data clusters are visible.

In data reduction, the cluster representations of the data are used to replace the actual data. The effectiveness of this technique depends on the data's nature. It is much more effective for data that can be organized into distinct clusters than for smeared data.

There are many measures for defining clusters and cluster quality. Clustering methods are further described in Chapters 10 and 11.

3.4.8 Sampling

Sampling can be used as a data reduction technique because it allows a large data set to be represented by a much smaller random data sample (or subset). Suppose that a large data set, D, contains N tuples. Let's look at the most common ways that we could sample D for data reduction, as illustrated in Figure 3.9.

- **Simple random sample without replacement (SRSWOR) of size** s: This is created by drawing s of the N tuples from D ($s < N$), where the probability of drawing any tuple in D is $1/N$, that is, all tuples are equally likely to be sampled.

- **Simple random sample with replacement (SRSWR) of size** s: This is similar to SRSWOR, except that each time a tuple is drawn from D, it is recorded and then *replaced*. That is, after a tuple is drawn, it is placed back in D so that it may be drawn again.

- **Cluster sample:** If the tuples in D are grouped into M mutually disjoint "clusters," then an SRS of s clusters can be obtained, where $s < M$. For example, tuples in a database are usually retrieved a page at a time, so that each page can be considered

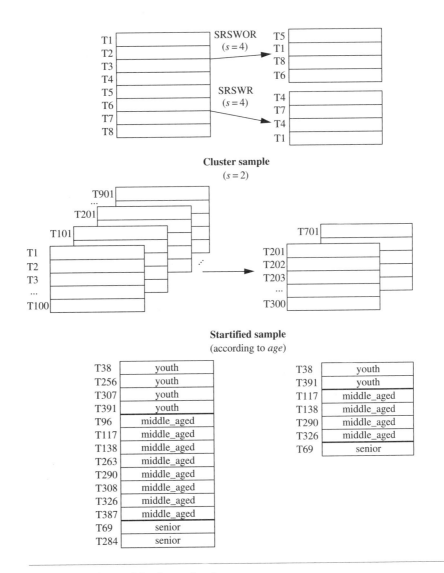

Figure 3.9 Sampling can be used for data reduction.

a cluster. A reduced data representation can be obtained by applying, say, SRSWOR to the pages, resulting in a cluster sample of the tuples. Other clustering criteria conveying rich semantics can also be explored. For example, in a spatial database, we may choose to define clusters geographically based on how closely different areas are located.

▪ **Stratified sample:** If D is divided into mutually disjoint parts called *strata*, a stratified sample of D is generated by obtaining an SRS at each stratum. This helps ensure a representative sample, especially when the data are skewed. For example, a stratified sample may be obtained from customer data, where a stratum is created for each customer age group. In this way, the age group having the smallest number of customers will be sure to be represented.

An advantage of sampling for data reduction is that the cost of obtaining a sample *is proportional to the size of the sample*, s, as opposed to N, the data set size. Hence, sampling complexity is potentially *sublinear* to the size of the data. Other data reduction techniques can require at least one complete pass through D. For a fixed sample size, sampling complexity increases only linearly as the number of data dimensions, n, increases, whereas techniques using histograms, for example, increase exponentially in n.

When applied to data reduction, sampling is most commonly used to estimate the answer to an aggregate query. It is possible (using the central limit theorem) to determine a sufficient sample size for estimating a given function within a specified degree of error. This sample size, s, may be extremely small in comparison to N. Sampling is a natural choice for the progressive refinement of a reduced data set. Such a set can be further refined by simply increasing the sample size.

3.4.9 Data Cube Aggregation

Imagine that you have collected the data for your analysis. These data consist of the *AllElectronics* sales per quarter, for the years 2008 to 2010. You are, however, interested in the annual sales (total per year), rather than the total per quarter. Thus, the data can be *aggregated* so that the resulting data summarize the total sales per year instead of per quarter. This aggregation is illustrated in Figure 3.10. The resulting data set is smaller in volume, without loss of information necessary for the analysis task.

Data cubes are discussed in detail in Chapter 4 on data warehousing and Chapter 5 on data cube technology. We briefly introduce some concepts here. Data cubes store

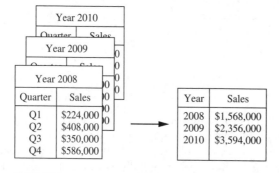

Figure 3.10 Sales data for a given branch of *AllElectronics* for the years 2008 through 2010. On the *left*, the sales are shown per quarter. On the *right*, the data are aggregated to provide the annual sales.

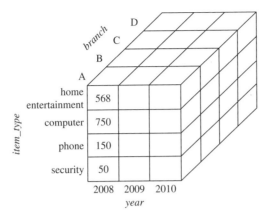

Figure 3.11 A data cube for sales at *AllElectronics*.

multidimensional aggregated information. For example, Figure 3.11 shows a data cube for multidimensional analysis of sales data with respect to annual sales per item type for each *AllElectronics* branch. Each cell holds an aggregate data value, corresponding to the data point in multidimensional space. (For readability, only some cell values are shown.) *Concept hierarchies* may exist for each attribute, allowing the analysis of data at multiple abstraction levels. For example, a hierarchy for *branch* could allow branches to be grouped into regions, based on their address. Data cubes provide fast access to precomputed, summarized data, thereby benefiting online analytical processing as well as data mining.

The cube created at the lowest abstraction level is referred to as the **base cuboid**. The base cuboid should correspond to an individual entity of interest such as *sales* or *customer*. In other words, the lowest level should be usable, or useful for the analysis. A cube at the highest level of abstraction is the **apex cuboid**. For the sales data in Figure 3.11, the apex cuboid would give one total—the total *sales* for all three years, for all item types, and for all branches. Data cubes created for varying levels of abstraction are often referred to as *cuboids*, so that a data cube may instead refer to a *lattice of cuboids*. Each higher abstraction level further reduces the resulting data size. When replying to data mining requests, the *smallest* available cuboid relevant to the given task should be used. This issue is also addressed in Chapter 4.

3.5 Data Transformation and Data Discretization

This section presents methods of data transformation. In this preprocessing step, the data are transformed or consolidated so that the resulting mining process may be more efficient, and the patterns found may be easier to understand. Data discretization, a form of data transformation, is also discussed.

3.5.1 **Data Transformation Strategies Overview**

In *data transformation*, the data are transformed or consolidated into forms appropriate for mining. Strategies for data transformation include the following:

1. **Smoothing**, which works to remove noise from the data. Techniques include binning, regression, and clustering.

2. **Attribute construction** (or *feature construction*), where new attributes are constructed and added from the given set of attributes to help the mining process.

3. **Aggregation**, where summary or aggregation operations are applied to the data. For example, the daily sales data may be aggregated so as to compute monthly and annual total amounts. This step is typically used in constructing a data cube for data analysis at multiple abstraction levels.

4. **Normalization**, where the attribute data are scaled so as to fall within a smaller range, such as -1.0 to 1.0, or 0.0 to 1.0.

5. **Discretization**, where the raw values of a numeric attribute (e.g., *age*) are replaced by interval labels (e.g., 0–10, 11–20, etc.) or conceptual labels (e.g., *youth, adult, senior*). The labels, in turn, can be recursively organized into higher-level concepts, resulting in a *concept hierarchy* for the numeric attribute. Figure 3.12 shows a concept hierarchy for the attribute *price*. More than one concept hierarchy can be defined for the same attribute to accommodate the needs of various users.

6. **Concept hierarchy generation for nominal data**, where attributes such as *street* can be generalized to higher-level concepts, like *city* or *country*. Many hierarchies for nominal attributes are implicit within the database schema and can be automatically defined at the schema definition level.

Recall that there is much overlap between the major data preprocessing tasks. The first three of these strategies were discussed earlier in this chapter. Smoothing is a form of

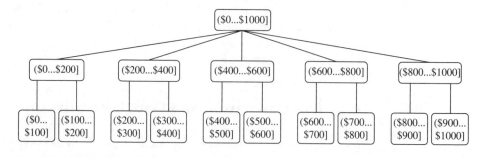

Figure 3.12 A concept hierarchy for the attribute *price*, where an interval ($X \ldots Y] denotes the range from $X (exclusive) to $Y (inclusive).

data cleaning and was addressed in Section 3.2.2. Section 3.2.3 on the data cleaning process also discussed ETL tools, where users specify transformations to correct data inconsistencies. Attribute construction and aggregation were discussed in Section 3.4 on data reduction. In this section, we therefore concentrate on the latter three strategies.

Discretization techniques can be categorized based on how the discretization is performed, such as whether it uses class information or which direction it proceeds (i.e., top-down vs. bottom-up). If the discretization process uses class information, then we say it is *supervised discretization*. Otherwise, it is *unsupervised*. If the process starts by first finding one or a few points (called *split points* or *cut points*) to split the entire attribute range, and then repeats this recursively on the resulting intervals, it is called *top-down discretization* or *splitting*. This contrasts with *bottom-up discretization* or *merging*, which starts by considering all of the continuous values as potential split-points, removes some by merging neighborhood values to form intervals, and then recursively applies this process to the resulting intervals.

Data discretization and concept hierarchy generation are also forms of data reduction. The raw data are replaced by a smaller number of interval or concept labels. This simplifies the original data and makes the mining more efficient. The resulting patterns mined are typically easier to understand. Concept hierarchies are also useful for mining at multiple abstraction levels.

The rest of this section is organized as follows. First, normalization techniques are presented in Section 3.5.2. We then describe several techniques for data discretization, each of which can be used to generate concept hierarchies for numeric attributes. The techniques include *binning* (Section 3.5.3) and *histogram analysis* (Section 3.5.4), as well as *cluster analysis*, *decision tree analysis*, and *correlation analysis* (Section 3.5.5). Finally, Section 3.5.6 describes the automatic generation of concept hierarchies for nominal data.

3.5.2 Data Transformation by Normalization

The measurement unit used can affect the data analysis. For example, changing measurement units from meters to inches for *height*, or from kilograms to pounds for *weight*, may lead to very different results. In general, expressing an attribute in smaller units will lead to a larger range for that attribute, and thus tend to give such an attribute greater effect or "weight." To help avoid dependence on the choice of measurement units, the data should be *normalized* or *standardized*. This involves transforming the data to fall within a smaller or common range such as $[-1, 1]$ or $[0.0, 1.0]$. (The terms *standardize* and *normalize* are used interchangeably in data preprocessing, although in statistics, the latter term also has other connotations.)

Normalizing the data attempts to give all attributes an equal weight. Normalization is particularly useful for classification algorithms involving neural networks or distance measurements such as nearest-neighbor classification and clustering. If using the neural network backpropagation algorithm for classification mining (Chapter 9), normalizing the input values for each attribute measured in the training tuples will help speed up the learning phase. For distance-based methods, normalization helps prevent attributes with initially large ranges (e.g., *income*) from outweighing attributes with initially smaller ranges (e.g., binary attributes). It is also useful when given no prior knowledge of the data.

There are many methods for data normalization. We study *min-max normalization, z-score normalization,* and *normalization by decimal scaling*. For our discussion, let A be a numeric attribute with n observed values, $v_1, v_2, \ldots, v_n$.

Min-max normalization performs a linear transformation on the original data. Suppose that min_A and max_A are the minimum and maximum values of an attribute, A. Min-max normalization maps a value, v_i, of A to v_i' in the range $[new\_min_A, new\_max_A]$ by computing

$$v_i' = \frac{v_i - min_A}{max_A - min_A}(new\_max_A - new\_min_A) + new\_min_A. \tag{3.8}$$

Min-max normalization preserves the relationships among the original data values. It will encounter an "out-of-bounds" error if a future input case for normalization falls outside of the original data range for A.

Example 3.4 Min-max normalization. Suppose that the minimum and maximum values for the attribute *income* are \$12,000 and \$98,000, respectively. We would like to map *income* to the range $[0.0, 1.0]$. By min-max normalization, a value of \$73,600 for *income* is transformed to $\frac{73,600 - 12,000}{98,000 - 12,000}(1.0 - 0) + 0 = 0.716$. ∎

In **z-score normalization** (or *zero-mean normalization*), the values for an attribute, A, are normalized based on the mean (i.e., average) and standard deviation of A. A value, v_i, of A is normalized to v_i' by computing

$$v_i' = \frac{v_i - \bar{A}}{\sigma_A}, \tag{3.9}$$

where $\bar{A}$ and σ_A are the mean and standard deviation, respectively, of attribute A. The mean and standard deviation were discussed in Section 2.2, where $\bar{A} = \frac{1}{n}(v_1 + v_2 + \cdots + v_n)$ and σ_A is computed as the square root of the variance of A (see Eq. (2.6)). This method of normalization is useful when the actual minimum and maximum of attribute A are unknown, or when there are outliers that dominate the min-max normalization.

Example 3.5 z-score normalization. Suppose that the mean and standard deviation of the values for the attribute *income* are \$54,000 and \$16,000, respectively. With z-score normalization, a value of \$73,600 for *income* is transformed to $\frac{73,600 - 54,000}{16,000} = 1.225$. ∎

A variation of this z-score normalization replaces the standard deviation of Eq. (3.9) by the *mean absolute deviation* of A. The *mean absolute deviation* of A, denoted s_A, is

$$s_A = \frac{1}{n}(|v_1 - \bar{A}| + |v_2 - \bar{A}| + \cdots + |v_n - \bar{A}|). \tag{3.10}$$

Thus, z-score normalization using the mean absolute deviation is

$$v'_i = \frac{v_i - \bar{A}}{s_A}.$$ (3.11)

The mean absolute deviation, s_A, is more robust to outliers than the standard deviation, σ_A. When computing the mean absolute deviation, the deviations from the mean (i.e., $|x_i - \bar{x}|$) are not squared; hence, the effect of outliers is somewhat reduced.

Normalization by decimal scaling normalizes by moving the decimal point of values of attribute A. The number of decimal points moved depends on the maximum absolute value of A. A value, v_i, of A is normalized to v'_i by computing

$$v'_i = \frac{v_i}{10^j},$$ (3.12)

where j is the smallest integer such that $max(|v'_i|) < 1$.

Example 3.6 **Decimal scaling.** Suppose that the recorded values of A range from -986 to 917. The maximum absolute value of A is 986. To normalize by decimal scaling, we therefore divide each value by 1000 (i.e., $j = 3$) so that -986 normalizes to -0.986 and 917 normalizes to 0.917. ∎

Note that normalization can change the original data quite a bit, especially when using z-score normalization or decimal scaling. It is also necessary to save the normalization parameters (e.g., the mean and standard deviation if using z-score normalization) so that future data can be normalized in a uniform manner.

3.5.3 Discretization by Binning

Binning is a top-down splitting technique based on a specified number of bins. Section 3.2.2 discussed binning methods for data smoothing. These methods are also used as discretization methods for data reduction and concept hierarchy generation. For example, attribute values can be discretized by applying equal-width or equal-frequency binning, and then replacing each bin value by the bin mean or median, as in *smoothing by bin means* or *smoothing by bin medians*, respectively. These techniques can be applied recursively to the resulting partitions to generate concept hierarchies.

Binning does not use class information and is therefore an unsupervised discretization technique. It is sensitive to the user-specified number of bins, as well as the presence of outliers.

3.5.4 Discretization by Histogram Analysis

Like binning, histogram analysis is an unsupervised discretization technique because it does not use class information. Histograms were introduced in Section 2.2.3. A histogram partitions the values of an attribute, A, into disjoint ranges called *buckets* or *bins*.

Various partitioning rules can be used to define histograms (Section 3.4.6). In an *equal-width* histogram, for example, the values are partitioned into equal-size partitions or ranges (e.g., earlier in Figure 3.8 for *price*, where each bucket has a width of $10). With an *equal-frequency* histogram, the values are partitioned so that, ideally, each partition contains the same number of data tuples. The histogram analysis algorithm can be applied recursively to each partition in order to automatically generate a multilevel concept hierarchy, with the procedure terminating once a prespecified number of concept levels has been reached. A *minimum interval size* can also be used per level to control the recursive procedure. This specifies the minimum width of a partition, or the minimum number of values for each partition at each level. Histograms can also be partitioned based on cluster analysis of the data distribution, as described next.

3.5.5 Discretization by Cluster, Decision Tree, and Correlation Analyses

Clustering, decision tree analysis, and correlation analysis can be used for data discretization. We briefly study each of these approaches.

Cluster analysis is a popular data discretization method. A clustering algorithm can be applied to discretize a numeric attribute, *A*, by partitioning the values of *A* into clusters or groups. Clustering takes the distribution of *A* into consideration, as well as the closeness of data points, and therefore is able to produce high-quality discretization results.

Clustering can be used to generate a concept hierarchy for *A* by following either a top-down splitting strategy or a bottom-up merging strategy, where each cluster forms a node of the concept hierarchy. In the former, each initial cluster or partition may be further decomposed into several subclusters, forming a lower level of the hierarchy. In the latter, clusters are formed by repeatedly grouping neighboring clusters in order to form higher-level concepts. Clustering methods for data mining are studied in Chapters 10 and 11.

Techniques to generate decision trees for classification (Chapter 8) can be applied to discretization. Such techniques employ a top-down splitting approach. Unlike the other methods mentioned so far, decision tree approaches to discretization are supervised, that is, they make use of class label information. For example, we may have a data set of patient symptoms (the attributes) where each patient has an associated *diagnosis* class label. Class distribution information is used in the calculation and determination of split-points (data values for partitioning an attribute range). Intuitively, the main idea is to select split-points so that a given resulting partition contains as many tuples of the same class as possible. *Entropy* is the most commonly used measure for this purpose. To discretize a numeric attribute, *A*, the method selects the value of *A* that has the minimum entropy as a split-point, and recursively partitions the resulting intervals to arrive at a hierarchical discretization. Such discretization forms a concept hierarchy for *A*.

Because decision tree–based discretization uses class information, it is more likely that the interval boundaries (split-points) are defined to occur in places that may help improve classification accuracy. Decision trees and the entropy measure are described in greater detail in Section 8.2.2.

Measures of correlation can be used for discretization. *ChiMerge* is a χ^2-based discretization method. The discretization methods that we have studied up to this point have all employed a top-down, splitting strategy. This contrasts with ChiMerge, which employs a bottom-up approach by finding the best neighboring intervals and then merging them to form larger intervals, recursively. As with decision tree analysis, ChiMerge is supervised in that it uses class information. The basic notion is that for accurate discretization, the relative class frequencies should be fairly consistent within an interval. Therefore, if two adjacent intervals have a very similar distribution of classes, then the intervals can be merged. Otherwise, they should remain separate.

ChiMerge proceeds as follows. Initially, each distinct value of a numeric attribute A is considered to be one interval. χ^2 tests are performed for every pair of adjacent intervals. Adjacent intervals with the least χ^2 values are merged together, because low χ^2 values for a pair indicate similar class distributions. This merging process proceeds recursively until a predefined stopping criterion is met.

3.5.6 Concept Hierarchy Generation for Nominal Data

We now look at data transformation for nominal data. In particular, we study concept hierarchy generation for nominal attributes. Nominal attributes have a finite (but possibly large) number of distinct values, with no ordering among the values. Examples include *geographic_location*, *job_category*, and *item_type*.

Manual definition of concept hierarchies can be a tedious and time-consuming task for a user or a domain expert. Fortunately, many hierarchies are implicit within the database schema and can be automatically defined at the schema definition level. The concept hierarchies can be used to transform the data into multiple levels of granularity. For example, data mining patterns regarding sales may be found relating to specific regions or countries, in addition to individual branch locations.

We study four methods for the generation of concept hierarchies for nominal data, as follows.

1. **Specification of a partial ordering of attributes explicitly at the schema level by users or experts:** Concept hierarchies for nominal attributes or dimensions typically involve a group of attributes. A user or expert can easily define a concept hierarchy by specifying a partial or total ordering of the attributes at the schema level. For example, suppose that a relational database contains the following group of attributes: *street*, *city*, *province_or_state*, and *country*. Similarly, a data warehouse *location* dimension may contain the same attributes. A hierarchy can be defined by specifying the total ordering among these attributes at the schema level such as *street* < *city* < *province_or_state* < *country*.

2. **Specification of a portion of a hierarchy by explicit data grouping:** This is essentially the manual definition of a portion of a concept hierarchy. In a large database, it is unrealistic to define an entire concept hierarchy by explicit value enumeration. On the contrary, we can easily specify explicit groupings for a small portion of intermediate-level data. For example, after specifying that *province* and *country*

form a hierarchy at the schema level, a user could define some intermediate levels manually, such as "{*Alberta, Saskatchewan, Manitoba*} ⊂ *prairies_Canada*" and "{*British Columbia, prairies_Canada*} ⊂ *Western_Canada*."

3. **Specification of a *set of attributes*, but not of their partial ordering:** A user may specify a set of attributes forming a concept hierarchy, but omit to explicitly state their partial ordering. The system can then try to automatically generate the attribute ordering so as to construct a meaningful concept hierarchy.

   "*Without knowledge of data semantics, how can a hierarchical ordering for an arbitrary set of nominal attributes be found?*" Consider the observation that since higher-level concepts generally cover several subordinate lower-level concepts, an attribute defining a high concept level (e.g., *country*) will usually contain a smaller number of distinct values than an attribute defining a lower concept level (e.g., *street*). Based on this observation, a concept hierarchy can be automatically generated based on the number of distinct values per attribute in the given attribute set. The attribute with the most distinct values is placed at the lowest hierarchy level. The lower the number of distinct values an attribute has, the higher it is in the generated concept hierarchy. This heuristic rule works well in many cases. Some local-level swapping or adjustments may be applied by users or experts, when necessary, after examination of the generated hierarchy.

   Let's examine an example of this third method.

Example 3.7 **Concept hierarchy generation based on the number of distinct values per attribute.** Suppose a user selects a set of location-oriented attributes—*street, country, province_or_state*, and *city*—from the *AllElectronics* database, but does not specify the hierarchical ordering among the attributes.

A concept hierarchy for *location* can be generated automatically, as illustrated in Figure 3.13. First, sort the attributes in ascending order based on the number of distinct values in each attribute. This results in the following (where the number of distinct values per attribute is shown in parentheses): *country* (15), *province_or_state* (365), *city* (3567), and *street* (674,339). Second, generate the hierarchy from the top down according to the sorted order, with the first attribute at the top level and the last attribute at the bottom level. Finally, the user can examine the generated hierarchy, and when necessary, modify it to reflect desired semantic relationships among the attributes. In this example, it is obvious that there is no need to modify the generated hierarchy. ∎

Note that this heuristic rule is not foolproof. For example, a time dimension in a database may contain 20 distinct years, 12 distinct months, and 7 distinct days of the week. However, this does not suggest that the time hierarchy should be "*year* < *month* < *days_of_the_week*," with *days_of_the_week* at the top of the hierarchy.

4. **Specification of only a partial set of attributes:** Sometimes a user can be careless when defining a hierarchy, or have only a vague idea about what should be included in a hierarchy. Consequently, the user may have included only a small subset of the

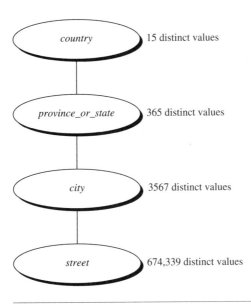

country   15 distinct values

province_or_state   365 distinct values

city   3567 distinct values

street   674,339 distinct values

Figure 3.13 Automatic generation of a schema concept hierarchy based on the number of distinct attribute values.

relevant attributes in the hierarchy specification. For example, instead of including all of the hierarchically relevant attributes for *location*, the user may have specified only *street* and *city*. To handle such partially specified hierarchies, it is important to embed data semantics in the database schema so that attributes with tight semantic connections can be pinned together. In this way, the specification of one attribute may trigger a whole group of semantically tightly linked attributes to be "dragged in" to form a complete hierarchy. Users, however, should have the option to override this feature, as necessary.

Example 3.8 **Concept hierarchy generation using prespecified semantic connections.** Suppose that a data mining expert (serving as an administrator) has pinned together the five attributes *number, street, city, province_or_state,* and *country,* because they are closely linked semantically regarding the notion of *location.* If a user were to specify only the attribute *city* for a hierarchy defining *location,* the system can automatically drag in all five semantically related attributes to form a hierarchy. The user may choose to drop any of these attributes (e.g., *number* and *street*) from the hierarchy, keeping *city* as the lowest conceptual level.   ∎

In summary, information at the schema level and on attribute–value counts can be used to generate concept hierarchies for nominal data. Transforming nominal data with the use of concept hierarchies allows higher-level knowledge patterns to be found. It allows mining at multiple levels of abstraction, which is a common requirement for data mining applications.

3.6 Summary

- **Data quality** is defined in terms of *accuracy, completeness, consistency, timeliness, believability*, and *interpretabilty*. These qualities are assessed based on the intended use of the data.

- **Data cleaning** routines attempt to fill in missing values, smooth out noise while identifying outliers, and correct inconsistencies in the data. Data cleaning is usually performed as an iterative two-step process consisting of discrepancy detection and data transformation.

- **Data integration** combines data from multiple sources to form a coherent data store. The resolution of semantic heterogeneity, metadata, correlation analysis, tuple duplication detection, and data conflict detection contribute to smooth data integration.

- **Data reduction** techniques obtain a reduced representation of the data while minimizing the loss of information content. These include methods of *dimensionality reduction, numerosity reduction*, and *data compression*. **Dimensionality reduction** reduces the number of random variables or attributes under consideration. Methods include *wavelet transforms, principal components analysis, attribute subset selection*, and *attribute creation*. **Numerosity reduction** methods use parametric or nonparatmetric models to obtain smaller representations of the original data. Parametric models store only the model parameters instead of the actual data. Examples include regression and log-linear models. Nonparamteric methods include histograms, clustering, sampling, and data cube aggregation. **Data compression** methods apply transformations to obtain a reduced or "compressed" representation of the original data. The data reduction is *lossless* if the original data can be reconstructed from the compressed data without any loss of information; otherwise, it is *lossy*.

- **Data transformation** routines convert the data into appropriate forms for mining. For example, in **normalization**, attribute data are scaled so as to fall within a small range such as 0.0 to 1.0. Other examples are **data discretization** and **concept hierarchy generation**.

- **Data discretization** transforms numeric data by mapping values to interval or concept labels. Such methods can be used to automatically generate *concept hierarchies* for the data, which allows for mining at multiple levels of granularity. Discretization techniques include binning, histogram analysis, cluster analysis, decision tree analysis, and correlation analysis. For nominal data, **concept hierarchies** may be generated based on schema definitions as well as the number of distinct values per attribute.

- Although numerous methods of data preprocessing have been developed, data preprocessing remains an active area of research, due to the huge amount of inconsistent or dirty data and the complexity of the problem.

3.7 Exercises

3.1 *Data quality* can be assessed in terms of several issues, including accuracy, completeness, and consistency. For each of the above three issues, discuss how data quality assessment can depend on the *intended use* of the data, giving examples. Propose two other dimensions of data quality.

3.2 In real-world data, tuples with *missing values* for some attributes are a common occurrence. Describe various methods for handling this problem.

3.3 Exercise 2.2 gave the following data (in increasing order) for the attribute *age*: 13, 15, 16, 16, 19, 20, 20, 21, 22, 22, 25, 25, 25, 25, 30, 33, 33, 35, 35, 35, 35, 36, 40, 45, 46, 52, 70.

   (a) Use *smoothing by bin means* to smooth these data, using a bin depth of 3. Illustrate your steps. Comment on the effect of this technique for the given data.

   (b) How might you determine *outliers* in the data?

   (c) What other methods are there for *data smoothing*?

3.4 Discuss issues to consider during *data integration*.

3.5 What are the value ranges of the following *normalization methods*?

   (a) min-max normalization

   (b) z-score normalization

   (c) z-score normalization using the mean absolute deviation instead of standard deviation

   (d) normalization by decimal scaling

3.6 Use these methods to *normalize* the following group of data:

$$200, 300, 400, 600, 1000$$

   (a) min-max normalization by setting $min = 0$ and $max = 1$

   (b) z-score normalization

   (c) z-score normalization using the mean absolute deviation instead of standard deviation

   (d) normalization by decimal scaling

3.7 Using the data for *age* given in Exercise 3.3, answer the following:

   (a) Use min-max normalization to transform the value 35 for *age* onto the range $[0.0, 1.0]$.

   (b) Use z-score normalization to transform the value 35 for *age*, where the standard deviation of *age* is 12.94 years.

   (c) Use normalization by decimal scaling to transform the value 35 for *age*.

   (d) Comment on which method you would prefer to use for the given data, giving reasons as to why.

3.8 Using the data for *age* and *body fat* given in Exercise 2.4, answer the following:

(a) Normalize the two attributes based on *z-score normalization*.

(b) Calculate the *correlation coefficient* (Pearson's product moment coefficient). Are these two attributes positively or negatively correlated? Compute their covariance.

3.9 Suppose a group of 12 *sales price* records has been sorted as follows:

$$5, 10, 11, 13, 15, 35, 50, 55, 72, 92, 204, 215.$$

Partition them into three bins by each of the following methods:

(a) equal-frequency (equal-depth) partitioning

(b) equal-width partitioning

(c) clustering

3.10 Use a flowchart to summarize the following procedures for *attribute subset selection*:

(a) stepwise forward selection

(b) stepwise backward elimination

(c) a combination of forward selection and backward elimination

3.11 Using the data for *age* given in Exercise 3.3,

(a) Plot an equal-width histogram of width 10.

(b) Sketch examples of each of the following sampling techniques: SRSWOR, SRSWR, cluster sampling, and stratified sampling. Use samples of size 5 and the strata "youth," "middle-aged," and "senior."

3.12 ChiMerge [Ker92] is a supervised, bottom-up (i.e., merge-based) *data discretization* method. It relies on χ^2 analysis: Adjacent intervals with the least χ^2 values are merged together until the chosen stopping criterion satisfies.

(a) Briefly describe how ChiMerge works.

(b) Take the IRIS data set, obtained from the University of California–Irvine Machine Learning Data Repository (*www.ics.uci.edu/~mlearn/MLRepository.html*), as a data set to be discretized. Perform data discretization for each of the four numeric attributes using the ChiMerge method. (Let the stopping criteria be: *max-interval* = 6). You need to write a small program to do this to avoid clumsy numerical computation. Submit your simple analysis and your test results: split-points, final intervals, and the documented source program.

3.13 Propose an algorithm, in pseudocode or in your favorite programming language, for the following:

(a) The automatic generation of a concept hierarchy for nominal data based on the number of distinct values of attributes in the given schema.

(b) The automatic generation of a concept hierarchy for numeric data based on the *equal-width* partitioning rule.

(c) The automatic generation of a concept hierarchy for numeric data based on the *equal-frequency* partitioning rule.

3.14 Robust data loading poses a challenge in database systems because the input data are often dirty. In many cases, an input record may miss multiple values; some records could be *contaminated*, with some data values out of range or of a different data type than expected. Work out an automated *data cleaning and loading* algorithm so that the erroneous data will be marked and contaminated data will not be mistakenly inserted into the database during data loading.

3.8 Bibliographic Notes

Data preprocessing is discussed in a number of textbooks, including English [Eng99], Pyle [Pyl99], Loshin [Los01], Redman [Red01], and Dasu and Johnson [DJ03]. More specific references to individual preprocessing techniques are given later.

For discussion regarding data quality, see Redman [Red92]; Wang, Storey, and Firth [WSF95]; Wand and Wang [WW96]; Ballou and Tayi [BT99]; and Olson [Ols03]. Potter's Wheel (*control.cx.berkely.edu/abc*), the interactive data cleaning tool described in Section 3.2.3, is presented in Raman and Hellerstein [RH01]. An example of the development of declarative languages for the specification of data transformation operators is given in Galhardas et al. [GFS$^+$01]. The handling of missing attribute values is discussed in Friedman [Fri77]; Breiman, Friedman, Olshen, and Stone [BFOS84]; and Quinlan [Qui89]. Hua and Pei [HP07] presented a heuristic approach to cleaning *disguised missing data*, where such data are captured when users falsely select default values on forms (e.g., "January 1" for *birthdate*) when they do not want to disclose personal information.

A method for the detection of outlier or "garbage" patterns in a handwritten character database is given in Guyon, Matic, and Vapnik [GMV96]. Binning and data normalization are treated in many texts, including Kennedy et al. [KLV$^+$98], Weiss and Indurkhya [WI98], and Pyle [Pyl99]. Systems that include attribute (or feature) construction include BACON by Langley, Simon, Bradshaw, and Zytkow [LSBZ87]; Stagger by Schlimmer [Sch86]; FRINGE by Pagallo [Pag89]; and AQ17-DCI by Bloedorn and Michalski [BM98]. Attribute construction is also described in Liu and Motoda [LM98a, LM98b]. Dasu et al. built a BELLMAN system and proposed a set of interesting methods for building a data quality browser by mining database structures [DJMS02].

A good survey of data reduction techniques can be found in Barbará et al. [BDF$^+$97]. For algorithms on data cubes and their precomputation, see Sarawagi and Stonebraker [SS94]; Agarwal et al. [AAD$^+$96]; Harinarayan, Rajaraman, and Ullman [HRU96]; Ross and Srivastava [RS97]; and Zhao, Deshpande, and Naughton [ZDN97]. Attribute subset selection (or *feature subset selection*) is described in many texts such as Neter, Kutner, Nachtsheim, and Wasserman [NKNW96]; Dash and Liu [DL97]; and Liu and Motoda [LM98a, LM98b]. A combination forward selection and backward elimination method was proposed in Siedlecki and Sklansky [SS88]. A wrapper approach to attribute selection is described in Kohavi and John [KJ97]. Unsupervised attribute subset selection is described in Dash, Liu, and Yao [DLY97].

For a description of wavelets for dimensionality reduction, see Press, Teukolosky, Vetterling, and Flannery [PTVF07]. A general account of wavelets can be found in Hubbard [Hub96]. For a list of wavelet software packages, see Bruce, Donoho, and Gao [BDG96]. Daubechies transforms are described in Daubechies [Dau92]. The book by Press et al. [PTVF07] includes an introduction to singular value decomposition for principal components analysis. Routines for PCA are included in most statistical software packages such as SAS (*www.sas.com/SASHome.html*).

An introduction to regression and log-linear models can be found in several textbooks such as James [Jam85]; Dobson [Dob90]; Johnson and Wichern [JW92]; Devore [Dev95]; and Neter, Kutner, Nachtsheim, and Wasserman [NKNW96]. For log-linear models (known as *multiplicative models* in the computer science literature), see Pearl [Pea88]. For a general introduction to histograms, see Barbará et al. [BDF+97] and Devore and Peck [DP97]. For extensions of single-attribute histograms to multiple attributes, see Muralikrishna and DeWitt [MD88] and Poosala and Ioannidis [PI97]. Several references to clustering algorithms are given in Chapters 10 and 11 of this book, which are devoted to the topic.

A survey of multidimensional indexing structures is given in Gaede and Günther [GG98]. The use of multidimensional index trees for data aggregation is discussed in Aoki [Aok98]. Index trees include R-trees (Guttman [Gut84]), quad-trees (Finkel and Bentley [FB74]), and their variations. For discussion on sampling and data mining, see Kivinen and Mannila [KM94] and John and Langley [JL96].

There are many methods for assessing attribute relevance. Each has its own bias. The information gain measure is biased toward attributes with many values. Many alternatives have been proposed, such as gain ratio (Quinlan [Qui93]), which considers the probability of each attribute value. Other relevance measures include the Gini index (Breiman, Friedman, Olshen, and Stone [BFOS84]), the χ^2 contingency table statistic, and the uncertainty coefficient (Johnson and Wichern [JW92]). For a comparison of attribute selection measures for decision tree induction, see Buntine and Niblett [BN92]. For additional methods, see Liu and Motoda [LM98a], Dash and Liu [DL97], and Almuallim and Dietterich [AD91].

Liu et al. [LHTD02] performed a comprehensive survey of data discretization methods. Entropy-based discretization with the C4.5 algorithm is described in Quinlan [Qui93]. In Catlett [Cat91], the D-2 system binarizes a numeric feature recursively. ChiMerge by Kerber [Ker92] and Chi2 by Liu and Setiono [LS95] are methods for the automatic discretization of numeric attributes that both employ the χ^2 statistic. Fayyad and Irani [FI93] apply the minimum description length principle to determine the number of intervals for numeric discretization. Concept hierarchies and their automatic generation from categorical data are described in Han and Fu [HF94].

Data Warehousing and Online Analytical Processing

4

Data warehouses generalize and consolidate data in multidimensional space. The construction of data warehouses involves data cleaning, data integration, and data transformation, and can be viewed as an important preprocessing step for data mining. Moreover, data warehouses provide *online analytical processing (OLAP)* tools for the interactive analysis of multidimensional data of varied granularities, which facilitates effective data generalization and data mining. Many other data mining functions, such as association, classification, prediction, and clustering, can be integrated with OLAP operations to enhance interactive mining of knowledge at multiple levels of abstraction. Hence, the data warehouse has become an increasingly important platform for data analysis and OLAP and will provide an effective platform for data mining. Therefore, data warehousing and OLAP form an essential step in the knowledge discovery process. This chapter presents an overview of data warehouse and OLAP technology. This overview is essential for understanding the overall data mining and knowledge discovery process.

In this chapter, we study a well-accepted definition of the data warehouse and see why more and more organizations are building data warehouses for the analysis of their data (Section 4.1). In particular, we study the *data cube*, a multidimensional data model for data warehouses and OLAP, as well as OLAP operations such as roll-up, drill-down, slicing, and dicing (Section 4.2). We also look at data warehouse design and usage (Section 4.3). In addition, we discuss *multidimensional data mining*, a powerful paradigm that integrates data warehouse and OLAP technology with that of data mining. An overview of data warehouse implementation examines general strategies for efficient data cube computation, OLAP data indexing, and OLAP query processing (Section 4.4). Finally, we study data generalization by attribute-oriented induction (Section 4.5). This method uses concept hierarchies to generalize data to multiple levels of abstraction.

4.1 Data Warehouse: Basic Concepts

This section gives an introduction to data warehouses. We begin with a definition of the data warehouse (Section 4.1.1). We outline the differences between operational database systems and data warehouses (Section 4.1.2), then explain the need for using data warehouses for data analysis, rather than performing the analysis directly on traditional databases (Section 4.1.3). This is followed by a presentation of data warehouse architecture (Section 4.1.4). Next, we study three data warehouse models—an enterprise model, a data mart, and a virtual warehouse (Section 4.1.5). Section 4.1.6 describes back-end utilities for data warehousing, such as extraction, transformation, and loading. Finally, Section 4.1.7 presents the metadata repository, which stores data about data.

4.1.1 What Is a Data Warehouse?

Data warehousing provides architectures and tools for business executives to systematically organize, understand, and use their data to make strategic decisions. Data warehouse systems are valuable tools in today's competitive, fast-evolving world. In the last several years, many firms have spent millions of dollars in building enterprise-wide data warehouses. Many people feel that with competition mounting in every industry, data warehousing is the latest must-have marketing weapon—a way to retain customers by learning more about their needs.

"*Then, what exactly is a data warehouse?*" Data warehouses have been defined in many ways, making it difficult to formulate a rigorous definition. Loosely speaking, a data warehouse refers to a data repository that is maintained separately from an organization's operational databases. Data warehouse systems allow for integration of a variety of application systems. They support information processing by providing a solid platform of consolidated historic data for analysis.

According to William H. Inmon, a leading architect in the construction of data warehouse systems, "A data warehouse is a subject-oriented, integrated, time-variant, and nonvolatile collection of data in support of management's decision making process" [Inm96]. This short but comprehensive definition presents the major features of a data warehouse. The four keywords—*subject-oriented, integrated, time-variant,* and *nonvolatile*—distinguish data warehouses from other data repository systems, such as relational database systems, transaction processing systems, and file systems.

Let's take a closer look at each of these key features.

■ **Subject-oriented**: A data warehouse is organized around major subjects such as customer, supplier, product, and sales. Rather than concentrating on the day-to-day operations and transaction processing of an organization, a data warehouse focuses on the modeling and analysis of data for decision makers. Hence, data warehouses typically provide a simple and concise view of particular subject issues by excluding data that are not useful in the decision support process.

■ **Integrated**: A data warehouse is usually constructed by integrating multiple heterogeneous sources, such as relational databases, flat files, and online transaction records. Data cleaning and data integration techniques are applied to ensure consistency in naming conventions, encoding structures, attribute measures, and so on.

- **Time-variant**: Data are stored to provide information from an historic perspective (e.g., the past 5–10 years). Every key structure in the data warehouse contains, either implicitly or explicitly, a time element.

- **Nonvolatile**: A data warehouse is always a physically separate store of data transformed from the application data found in the operational environment. Due to this separation, a data warehouse does not require transaction processing, recovery, and concurrency control mechanisms. It usually requires only two operations in data accessing: *initial loading of data* and *access of data*.

In sum, a data warehouse is a semantically consistent data store that serves as a physical implementation of a decision support data model. It stores the information an enterprise needs to make strategic decisions. A data warehouse is also often viewed as an architecture, constructed by integrating data from multiple heterogeneous sources to support structured and/or ad hoc queries, analytical reporting, and decision making.

Based on this information, we view **data warehousing** as the process of constructing and using data warehouses. The construction of a data warehouse requires data cleaning, data integration, and data consolidation. The utilization of a data warehouse often necessitates a collection of *decision support* technologies. This allows "knowledge workers" (e.g., managers, analysts, and executives) to use the warehouse to quickly and conveniently obtain an overview of the data, and to make sound decisions based on information in the warehouse. Some authors use the term *data warehousing* to refer only to the process of data warehouse *construction*, while the term *warehouse DBMS* is used to refer to the *management and utilization* of data warehouses. We will not make this distinction here.

"*How are organizations using the information from data warehouses?*" Many organizations use this information to support business decision-making activities, including (1) increasing customer focus, which includes the analysis of customer buying patterns (such as buying preference, buying time, budget cycles, and appetites for spending); (2) repositioning products and managing product portfolios by comparing the performance of sales by quarter, by year, and by geographic regions in order to fine-tune production strategies; (3) analyzing operations and looking for sources of profit; and (4) managing customer relationships, making environmental corrections, and managing the cost of corporate assets.

Data warehousing is also very useful from the point of view of *heterogeneous database integration*. Organizations typically collect diverse kinds of data and maintain large databases from multiple, heterogeneous, autonomous, and distributed information sources. It is highly desirable, yet challenging, to integrate such data and provide easy and efficient access to it. Much effort has been spent in the database industry and research community toward achieving this goal.

The traditional database approach to heterogeneous database integration is to build **wrappers** and **integrators** (or **mediators**) on top of multiple, heterogeneous databases. When a query is posed to a client site, a metadata dictionary is used to translate the query into queries appropriate for the individual heterogeneous sites involved. These queries are then mapped and sent to local query processors. The results returned from the different sites are integrated into a global answer set. This **query-driven approach** requires complex information filtering and integration processes, and competes with local sites for processing resources. It is inefficient and potentially expensive for frequent queries, especially queries requiring aggregations.

Data warehousing provides an interesting alternative to this traditional approach. Rather than using a query-driven approach, data warehousing employs an **update-driven** approach in which information from multiple, heterogeneous sources is integrated in advance and stored in a warehouse for direct querying and analysis. Unlike online transaction processing databases, data warehouses do not contain the most current information. However, a data warehouse brings high performance to the integrated heterogeneous database system because data are copied, preprocessed, integrated, annotated, summarized, and restructured into one semantic data store. Furthermore, query processing in data warehouses does not interfere with the processing at local sources. Moreover, data warehouses can store and integrate historic information and support complex multidimensional queries. As a result, data warehousing has become popular in industry.

4.1.2 Differences between Operational Database Systems and Data Warehouses

Because most people are familiar with commercial relational database systems, it is easy to understand what a data warehouse is by comparing these two kinds of systems.

The major task of online operational database systems is to perform online transaction and query processing. These systems are called **online transaction processing (OLTP)** systems. They cover most of the day-to-day operations of an organization such as purchasing, inventory, manufacturing, banking, payroll, registration, and accounting. Data warehouse systems, on the other hand, serve users or knowledge workers in the role of data analysis and decision making. Such systems can organize and present data in various formats in order to accommodate the diverse needs of different users. These systems are known as **online analytical processing (OLAP)** systems.

The major distinguishing features of OLTP and OLAP are summarized as follows:

- **Users and system orientation:** An OLTP system is *customer-oriented* and is used for transaction and query processing by clerks, clients, and information technology professionals. An OLAP system is *market-oriented* and is used for data analysis by knowledge workers, including managers, executives, and analysts.

- **Data contents:** An OLTP system manages current data that, typically, are too detailed to be easily used for decision making. An OLAP system manages large amounts of historic data, provides facilities for summarization and aggregation, and stores and manages information at different levels of granularity. These features make the data easier to use for informed decision making.

- **Database design**: An OLTP system usually adopts an entity-relationship (ER) data model and an application-oriented database design. An OLAP system typically adopts either a *star* or a *snowflake* model (see Section 4.2.2) and a subject-oriented database design.

- **View**: An OLTP system focuses mainly on the current data within an enterprise or department, without referring to historic data or data in different organizations. In contrast, an OLAP system often spans multiple versions of a database schema, due to the evolutionary process of an organization. OLAP systems also deal with information that originates from different organizations, integrating information from many data stores. Because of their huge volume, OLAP data are stored on multiple storage media.

- **Access patterns**: The access patterns of an OLTP system consist mainly of short, atomic transactions. Such a system requires concurrency control and recovery mechanisms. However, accesses to OLAP systems are mostly read-only operations (because most data warehouses store historic rather than up-to-date information), although many could be complex queries.

Other features that distinguish between OLTP and OLAP systems include database size, frequency of operations, and performance metrics. These are summarized in Table 4.1.

4.1.3 But, Why Have a Separate Data Warehouse?

Because operational databases store huge amounts of data, you may wonder, *"Why not perform online analytical processing directly on such databases instead of spending additional time and resources to construct a separate data warehouse?"* A major reason for such a separation is to help promote the *high performance of both systems*. An operational database is designed and tuned from known tasks and workloads like indexing and hashing using primary keys, searching for particular records, and optimizing "canned" queries. On the other hand, data warehouse queries are often complex. They involve the computation of large data groups at summarized levels, and may require the use of special data organization, access, and implementation methods based on multidimensional views. Processing OLAP queries in operational databases would substantially degrade the performance of operational tasks.

Moreover, an operational database supports the concurrent processing of multiple transactions. Concurrency control and recovery mechanisms (e.g., locking and logging) are required to ensure the consistency and robustness of transactions. An OLAP query often needs read-only access of data records for summarization and aggregation. Concurrency control and recovery mechanisms, if applied for such OLAP operations, may jeopardize the execution of concurrent transactions and thus substantially reduce the throughput of an OLTP system.

Finally, the separation of operational databases from data warehouses is based on the different structures, contents, and uses of the data in these two systems. Decision

Table 4.1 Comparison of OLTP and OLAP Systems

Feature	OLTP	OLAP
Characteristic	operational processing	informational processing
Orientation	transaction	analysis
User	clerk, DBA, database professional	knowledge worker (e.g., manager, executive, analyst)
Function	day-to-day operations	long-term informational requirements decision support
DB design	ER-based, application-oriented	star/snowflake, subject-oriented
Data	current, guaranteed up-to-date	historic, accuracy maintained over time
Summarization	primitive, highly detailed	summarized, consolidated
View	detailed, flat relational	summarized, multidimensional
Unit of work	short, simple transaction	complex query
Access	read/write	mostly read
Focus	data in	information out
Operations	index/hash on primary key	lots of scans
Number of records accessed	tens	millions
Number of users	thousands	hundreds
DB size	GB to high-order GB	$\geq$ TB
Priority	high performance, high availability	high flexibility, end-user autonomy
Metric	transaction throughput	query throughput, response time

Note: Table is partially based on Chaudhuri and Dayal [CD97].

support requires historic data, whereas operational databases do not typically maintain historic data. In this context, the data in operational databases, though abundant, are usually far from complete for decision making. Decision support requires consolidation (e.g., aggregation and summarization) of data from heterogeneous sources, resulting in high-quality, clean, integrated data. In contrast, operational databases contain only detailed raw data, such as transactions, which need to be consolidated before analysis. Because the two systems provide quite different functionalities and require different kinds of data, it is presently necessary to maintain separate databases. However, many vendors of operational relational database management systems are beginning to optimize such systems to support OLAP queries. As this trend continues, the separation between OLTP and OLAP systems is expected to decrease.

4.1.4 Data Warehousing: A Multitiered Architecture

Data warehouses often adopt a three-tier architecture, as presented in Figure 4.1.

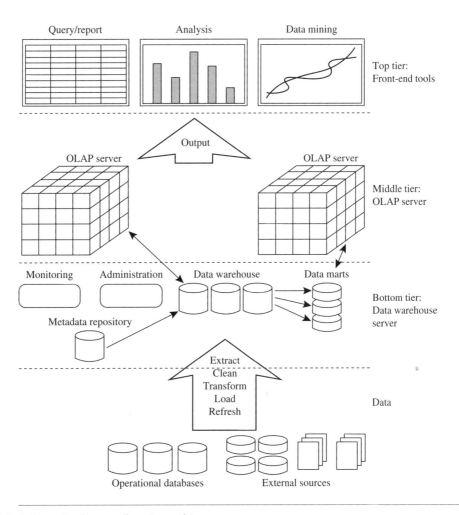

Figure 4.1 A three-tier data warehousing architecture.

1. The bottom tier is a **warehouse database server** that is almost always a relational database system. Back-end tools and utilities are used to feed data into the bottom tier from operational databases or other external sources (e.g., customer profile information provided by external consultants). These tools and utilities perform data extraction, cleaning, and transformation (e.g., to merge similar data from different sources into a unified format), as well as load and refresh functions to update the data warehouse (see Section 4.1.6). The data are extracted using application program interfaces known as **gateways**. A gateway is supported by the underlying DBMS and allows client programs to generate SQL code to be executed at a server. Examples of gateways include ODBC (Open Database Connection) and OLEDB (Object

Linking and Embedding Database) by Microsoft and JDBC (Java Database Connection). This tier also contains a metadata repository, which stores information about the data warehouse and its contents. The metadata repository is further described in Section 4.1.7.

2. The middle tier is an **OLAP server** that is typically implemented using either (1) a **relational OLAP (ROLAP)** model (i.e., an extended relational DBMS that maps operations on multidimensional data to standard relational operations); or (2) a **multidimensional OLAP (MOLAP)** model (i.e., a special-purpose server that directly implements multidimensional data and operations). OLAP servers are discussed in Section 4.4.4.

3. The top tier is a **front-end client layer**, which contains query and reporting tools, analysis tools, and/or data mining tools (e.g., trend analysis, prediction, and so on).

4.1.5 Data Warehouse Models: Enterprise Warehouse, Data Mart, and Virtual Warehouse

From the architecture point of view, there are three data warehouse models: the *enterprise warehouse*, the *data mart*, and the *virtual warehouse*.

Enterprise warehouse: An enterprise warehouse collects all of the information about subjects spanning the entire organization. It provides corporate-wide data integration, usually from one or more operational systems or external information providers, and is cross-functional in scope. It typically contains detailed data as well as summarized data, and can range in size from a few gigabytes to hundreds of gigabytes, terabytes, or beyond. An enterprise data warehouse may be implemented on traditional mainframes, computer superservers, or parallel architecture platforms. It requires extensive business modeling and may take years to design and build.

Data mart: A data mart contains a subset of corporate-wide data that is of value to a specific group of users. The scope is confined to specific selected subjects. For example, a marketing data mart may confine its subjects to customer, item, and sales. The data contained in data marts tend to be summarized.

Data marts are usually implemented on low-cost departmental servers that are Unix/Linux or Windows based. The implementation cycle of a data mart is more likely to be measured in weeks rather than months or years. However, it may involve complex integration in the long run if its design and planning were not enterprise-wide.

Depending on the source of data, data marts can be categorized as independent or dependent. *Independent* data marts are sourced from data captured from one or more operational systems or external information providers, or from data generated locally within a particular department or geographic area. *Dependent* data marts are sourced directly from enterprise data warehouses.

Virtual warehouse: A virtual warehouse is a set of views over operational databases. For efficient query processing, only some of the possible summary views may be materialized. A virtual warehouse is easy to build but requires excess capacity on operational database servers.

"What are the pros and cons of the top-down and bottom-up approaches to data warehouse development?" The top-down development of an enterprise warehouse serves as a systematic solution and minimizes integration problems. However, it is expensive, takes a long time to develop, and lacks flexibility due to the difficulty in achieving consistency and consensus for a common data model for the entire organization. The bottom-up approach to the design, development, and deployment of independent data marts provides flexibility, low cost, and rapid return of investment. It, however, can lead to problems when integrating various disparate data marts into a consistent enterprise data warehouse.

A recommended method for the development of data warehouse systems is to implement the warehouse in an incremental and evolutionary manner, as shown in Figure 4.2. First, a high-level corporate data model is defined within a reasonably short period (such as one or two months) that provides a corporate-wide, consistent, integrated view of data among different subjects and potential usages. This high-level model, although it will need to be refined in the further development of enterprise data warehouses and departmental data marts, will greatly reduce future integration problems. Second, independent data marts can be implemented in parallel with the enterprise

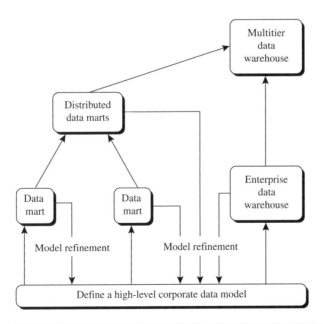

Figure 4.2 A recommended approach for data warehouse development.

warehouse based on the same corporate data model set noted before. Third, distributed data marts can be constructed to integrate different data marts via hub servers. Finally, a **multitier data warehouse** is constructed where the enterprise warehouse is the sole custodian of all warehouse data, which is then distributed to the various dependent data marts.

4.1.6 Extraction, Transformation, and Loading

Data warehouse systems use back-end tools and utilities to populate and refresh their data (Figure 4.1). These tools and utilities include the following functions:

- **Data extraction**, which typically gathers data from multiple, heterogeneous, and external sources.
- **Data cleaning**, which detects errors in the data and rectifies them when possible.
- **Data transformation**, which converts data from legacy or host format to warehouse format.
- **Load**, which sorts, summarizes, consolidates, computes views, checks integrity, and builds indices and partitions.
- **Refresh**, which propagates the updates from the data sources to the warehouse.

Besides cleaning, loading, refreshing, and metadata definition tools, data warehouse systems usually provide a good set of data warehouse management tools.

Data cleaning and data transformation are important steps in improving the data quality and, subsequently, the data mining results (see Chapter 3). Because we are mostly interested in the aspects of data warehousing technology related to data mining, we will not get into the details of the remaining tools, and recommend interested readers to consult books dedicated to data warehousing technology.

4.1.7 Metadata Repository

Metadata are data about data. When used in a data warehouse, metadata are the data that define warehouse objects. Figure 4.1 showed a metadata repository within the bottom tier of the data warehousing architecture. Metadata are created for the data names and definitions of the given warehouse. Additional metadata are created and captured for timestamping any extracted data, the source of the extracted data, and missing fields that have been added by data cleaning or integration processes.

A metadata repository should contain the following:

- A description of the *data warehouse structure*, which includes the warehouse schema, view, dimensions, hierarchies, and derived data definitions, as well as data mart locations and contents.

▣ *Operational metadata*, which include data lineage (history of migrated data and the sequence of transformations applied to it), currency of data (active, archived, or purged), and monitoring information (warehouse usage statistics, error reports, and audit trails).

▣ The *algorithms used for summarization*, which include measure and dimension definition algorithms, data on granularity, partitions, subject areas, aggregation, summarization, and predefined queries and reports.

▣ *Mapping from the operational environment to the data warehouse*, which includes source databases and their contents, gateway descriptions, data partitions, data extraction, cleaning, transformation rules and defaults, data refresh and purging rules, and security (user authorization and access control).

▣ *Data related to system performance*, which include indices and profiles that improve data access and retrieval performance, in addition to rules for the timing and scheduling of refresh, update, and replication cycles.

▣ *Business metadata*, which include business terms and definitions, data ownership information, and charging policies.

A data warehouse contains different levels of summarization, of which metadata is one. Other types include current detailed data (which are almost always on disk), older detailed data (which are usually on tertiary storage), lightly summarized data, and highly summarized data (which may or may not be physically housed).

Metadata play a very different role than other data warehouse data and are important for many reasons. For example, metadata are used as a directory to help the decision support system analyst locate the contents of the data warehouse, and as a guide to the data mapping when data are transformed from the operational environment to the data warehouse environment. Metadata also serve as a guide to the algorithms used for summarization between the current detailed data and the lightly summarized data, and between the lightly summarized data and the highly summarized data. Metadata should be stored and managed persistently (i.e., on disk).

4.2 Data Warehouse Modeling: Data Cube and OLAP

Data warehouses and OLAP tools are based on a **multidimensional data model**. This model views data in the form of a *data cube*. In this section, you will learn how data cubes model *n*-dimensional data (Section 4.2.1). In Section 4.2.2, various multidimensional models are shown: star schema, snowflake schema, and fact constellation. You will also learn about concept hierarchies (Section 4.2.3) and measures (Section 4.2.4) and how they can be used in basic OLAP operations to allow interactive mining at multiple levels of abstraction. Typical OLAP operations such as drill-down and roll-up are illustrated

(Section 4.2.5). Finally, the starnet model for querying multidimensional databases is presented (Section 4.2.6).

4.2.1 Data Cube: A Multidimensional Data Model

"What is a data cube?" A **data cube** allows data to be modeled and viewed in multiple dimensions. It is defined by dimensions and facts.

In general terms, **dimensions** are the perspectives or entities with respect to which an organization wants to keep records. For example, *AllElectronics* may create a *sales* data warehouse in order to keep records of the store's sales with respect to the dimensions *time, item, branch,* and *location*. These dimensions allow the store to keep track of things like monthly sales of items and the branches and locations at which the items were sold. Each dimension may have a table associated with it, called a **dimension table**, which further describes the dimension. For example, a dimension table for *item* may contain the attributes *item_name, brand,* and *type*. Dimension tables can be specified by users or experts, or automatically generated and adjusted based on data distributions.

A multidimensional data model is typically organized around a central theme, such as *sales*. This theme is represented by a fact table. **Facts** are numeric measures. Think of them as the quantities by which we want to analyze relationships between dimensions. Examples of facts for a sales data warehouse include *dollars_sold* (sales amount in dollars), *units_sold* (number of units sold), and *amount_budgeted*. The **fact table** contains the names of the *facts*, or measures, as well as keys to each of the related dimension tables. You will soon get a clearer picture of how this works when we look at multidimensional schemas.

Although we usually think of cubes as 3-D geometric structures, in data warehousing the data cube is *n*-dimensional. To gain a better understanding of data cubes and the multidimensional data model, let's start by looking at a simple 2-D data cube that is, in fact, a table or spreadsheet for sales data from *AllElectronics*. In particular, we will look at the *AllElectronics* sales data for items sold per quarter in the city of Vancouver. These data are shown in Table 4.2. In this 2-D representation, the sales for Vancouver are shown with respect to the *time* dimension (organized in quarters) and the *item* dimension (organized according to the types of items sold). The fact or measure displayed is *dollars_sold* (in thousands).

Now, suppose that we would like to view the sales data with a third dimension. For instance, suppose we would like to view the data according to *time* and *item*, as well as *location*, for the cities Chicago, New York, Toronto, and Vancouver. These 3-D data are shown in Table 4.3. The 3-D data in the table are represented as a series of 2-D tables. Conceptually, we may also represent the same data in the form of a 3-D data cube, as in Figure 4.3.

Suppose that we would now like to view our sales data with an additional fourth dimension such as *supplier*. Viewing things in 4-D becomes tricky. However, we can think of a 4-D cube as being a series of 3-D cubes, as shown in Figure 4.4. If we continue

Table 4.2 2-D View of Sales Data for *AllElectronics* According to *time* and *item*

	location = "Vancouver"			
	item (type)			
time (quarter)	home entertainment	computer	phone	security
Q1	605	825	14	400
Q2	680	952	31	512
Q3	812	1023	30	501
Q4	927	1038	38	580

Note: The sales are from branches located in the city of Vancouver. The measure displayed is *dollars_sold* (in thousands).

Table 4.3 3-D View of Sales Data for *AllElectronics* According to *time*, *item*, and *location*

	location = "Chicago"				location = "New York"				location = "Toronto"				location = "Vancouver"			
	item				item				item				item			
time	home ent.	comp.	phone	sec.	home ent.	comp.	phone	sec.	home ent.	comp.	phone	sec.	home ent.	comp.	phone	sec.
Q1	854	882	89	623	1087	968	38	872	818	746	43	591	605	825	14	400
Q2	943	890	64	698	1130	1024	41	925	894	769	52	682	680	952	31	512
Q3	1032	924	59	789	1034	1048	45	1002	940	795	58	728	812	1023	30	501
Q4	1129	992	63	870	1142	1091	54	984	978	864	59	784	927	1038	38	580

Note: The measure displayed is *dollars_sold* (in thousands).

in this way, we may display any n-dimensional data as a series of $(n-1)$-dimensional "cubes." The data cube is a metaphor for multidimensional data storage. The actual physical storage of such data may differ from its logical representation. The important thing to remember is that data cubes are n-dimensional and do not confine data to 3-D.

Tables 4.2 and 4.3 show the data at different degrees of summarization. In the data warehousing research literature, a data cube like those shown in Figures 4.3 and 4.4 is often referred to as a **cuboid**. Given a set of dimensions, we can generate a cuboid for each of the possible subsets of the given dimensions. The result would form a *lattice* of cuboids, each showing the data at a different level of summarization, or group-by. The lattice of cuboids is then referred to as a data cube. Figure 4.5 shows a lattice of cuboids forming a data cube for the dimensions *time*, *item*, *location*, and *supplier*.

The cuboid that holds the lowest level of summarization is called the **base cuboid**. For example, the 4-D cuboid in Figure 4.4 is the base cuboid for the given *time*, *item*, *location*, and *supplier* dimensions. Figure 4.3 is a 3-D (nonbase) cuboid for *time*, *item*,

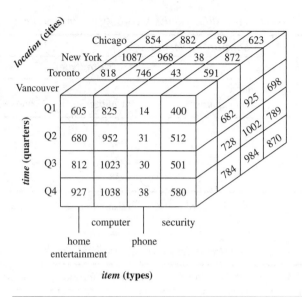

Figure 4.3 A 3-D data cube representation of the data in Table 4.3, according to *time*, *item*, and *location*. The measure displayed is *dollars_sold* (in thousands).

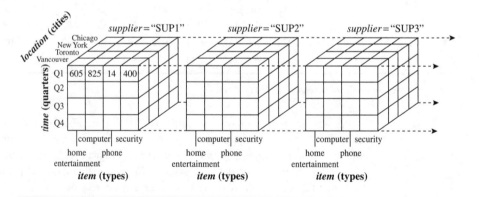

Figure 4.4 A 4-D data cube representation of sales data, according to *time*, *item*, *location*, and *supplier*. The measure displayed is *dollars_sold* (in thousands). For improved readability, only some of the cube values are shown.

and *location*, summarized for all suppliers. The 0-D cuboid, which holds the highest level of summarization, is called the **apex cuboid**. In our example, this is the total sales, or *dollars_sold*, summarized over all four dimensions. The apex cuboid is typically denoted by all.

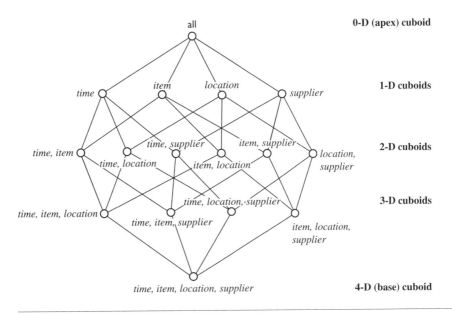

Figure 4.5 Lattice of cuboids, making up a 4-D data cube for *time*, *item*, *location*, and *supplier*. Each cuboid represents a different degree of summarization.

4.2.2 Stars, Snowflakes, and Fact Constellations: Schemas for Multidimensional Data Models

The entity-relationship data model is commonly used in the design of relational databases, where a database schema consists of a set of entities and the relationships between them. Such a data model is appropriate for online transaction processing. A data warehouse, however, requires a concise, subject-oriented schema that facilitates online data analysis.

The most popular data model for a data warehouse is a **multidimensional model**, which can exist in the form of a **star schema**, a **snowflake schema**, or a **fact constellation schema**. Let's look at each of these.

Star schema: The most common modeling paradigm is the star schema, in which the data warehouse contains (1) a large central table (**fact table**) containing the bulk of the data, with no redundancy, and (2) a set of smaller attendant tables (**dimension tables**), one for each dimension. The schema graph resembles a starburst, with the dimension tables displayed in a radial pattern around the central fact table.

Example 4.1 Star schema. A star schema for *AllElectronics* sales is shown in Figure 4.6. Sales are considered along four dimensions: *time*, *item*, *branch*, and *location*. The schema contains a central fact table for *sales* that contains keys to each of the four dimensions, along

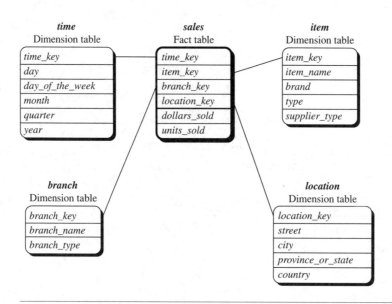

Figure 4.6 Star schema of *sales* data warehouse.

with two measures: *dollars_sold* and *units_sold*. To minimize the size of the fact table, dimension identifiers (e.g., *time_key* and *item_key*) are system-generated identifiers. ∎

Notice that in the star schema, each dimension is represented by only one table, and each table contains a set of attributes. For example, the *location* dimension table contains the attribute set {*location_key, street, city, province_or_state, country*}. This constraint may introduce some redundancy. For example, "Urbana" and "Chicago" are both cities in the state of Illinois, USA. Entries for such cities in the *location* dimension table will create redundancy among the attributes *province_or_state* and *country*; that is, (..., Urbana, IL, USA) and (..., Chicago, IL, USA). Moreover, the attributes within a dimension table may form either a hierarchy (total order) or a lattice (partial order).

Snowflake schema: The snowflake schema is a variant of the star schema model, where some dimension tables are *normalized*, thereby further splitting the data into additional tables. The resulting schema graph forms a shape similar to a snowflake.

The major difference between the snowflake and star schema models is that the dimension tables of the snowflake model may be kept in normalized form to reduce redundancies. Such a table is easy to maintain and saves storage space. However, this space savings is negligible in comparison to the typical magnitude of the fact table. Furthermore, the snowflake structure can reduce the effectiveness of browsing, since more joins will be needed to execute a query. Consequently, the system performance may be adversely impacted. Hence, although the snowflake schema reduces redundancy, it is not as popular as the star schema in data warehouse design.

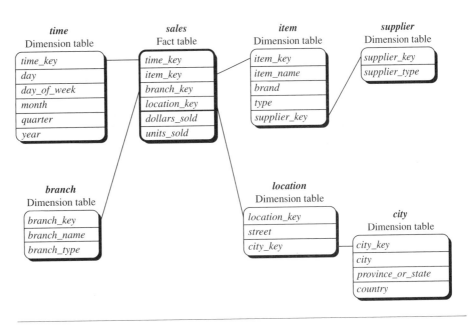

Figure 4.7 Snowflake schema of a *sales* data warehouse.

Example 4.2 Snowflake schema. A snowflake schema for *AllElectronics* sales is given in Figure 4.7. Here, the *sales* fact table is identical to that of the star schema in Figure 4.6. The main difference between the two schemas is in the definition of dimension tables. The single dimension table for *item* in the star schema is normalized in the snowflake schema, resulting in new *item* and *supplier* tables. For example, the *item* dimension table now contains the attributes *item_key, item_name, brand, type,* and *supplier_key,* where *supplier_key* is linked to the *supplier* dimension table, containing *supplier_key* and *supplier_type* information. Similarly, the single dimension table for *location* in the star schema can be normalized into two new tables: *location* and *city*. The *city_key* in the new *location* table links to the *city* dimension. Notice that, when desirable, further normalization can be performed on *province_or_state* and *country* in the snowflake schema shown in Figure 4.7. ∎

Fact constellation: Sophisticated applications may require multiple fact tables to *share* dimension tables. This kind of schema can be viewed as a collection of stars, and hence is called a **galaxy schema** or a **fact constellation**.

Example 4.3 Fact constellation. A fact constellation schema is shown in Figure 4.8. This schema specifies two fact tables, *sales* and *shipping*. The *sales* table definition is identical to that of the star schema (Figure 4.6). The *shipping* table has five dimensions, or keys—*item_key, time_key, shipper_key, from_location,* and *to_location*—and two measures—*dollars_cost*

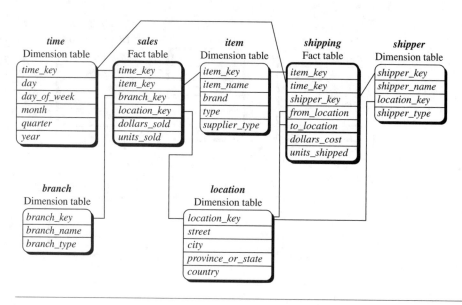

Figure 4.8 Fact constellation schema of a sales and shipping data warehouse.

and *units_shipped*. A fact constellation schema allows dimension tables to be shared between fact tables. For example, the dimensions tables for *time, item,* and *location* are shared between the *sales* and *shipping* fact tables. ∎

In data warehousing, there is a distinction between a data warehouse and a data mart. A data warehouse collects information about subjects that span the *entire organization,* such as *customers, items, sales, assets,* and *personnel,* and thus its scope is *enterprise-wide.* For data warehouses, the fact constellation schema is commonly used, since it can model multiple, interrelated subjects. A **data mart**, on the other hand, is a department subset of the data warehouse that focuses on selected subjects, and thus its scope is *department-wide.* For data marts, the *star* or *snowflake* schema is commonly used, since both are geared toward modeling single subjects, although the star schema is more popular and efficient.

4.2.3 Dimensions: The Role of Concept Hierarchies

A **concept hierarchy** defines a sequence of mappings from a set of low-level concepts to higher-level, more general concepts. Consider a concept hierarchy for the dimension *location.* City values for *location* include Vancouver, Toronto, New York, and Chicago. Each city, however, can be mapped to the province or state to which it belongs. For example, Vancouver can be mapped to British Columbia, and Chicago to Illinois. The provinces and states can in turn be mapped to the country (e.g., Canada or the United States) to which they belong. These mappings form a concept hierarchy for the dimension *location*, mapping a set of low-level concepts (i.e., cities) to higher-level, more general concepts (i.e., countries). This concept hierarchy is illustrated in Figure 4.9.

Many concept hierarchies are implicit within the database schema. For example, suppose that the dimension *location* is described by the attributes *number, street, city, province_or_state, zip_code,* and *country*. These attributes are related by a total order, forming a concept hierarchy such as "*street < city < province_or_state < country.*" This hierarchy is shown in Figure 4.10(a). Alternatively, the attributes of a dimension may

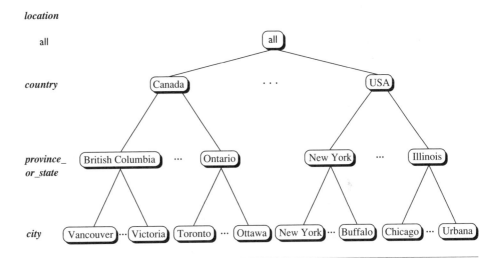

Figure 4.9 A concept hierarchy for *location*. Due to space limitations, not all of the hierarchy nodes are shown, indicated by ellipses between nodes.

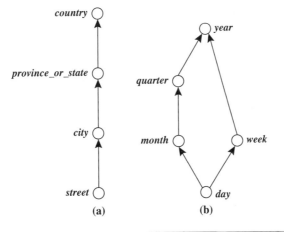

Figure 4.10 Hierarchical and lattice structures of attributes in warehouse dimensions: (a) a hierarchy for *location* and (b) a lattice for *time*.

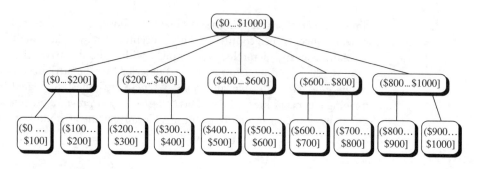

Figure 4.11 A concept hierarchy for *price*.

be organized in a partial order, forming a lattice. An example of a partial order for the *time* dimension based on the attributes *day, week, month, quarter,* and *year* is "*day* < {*month* < *quarter; week*} < *year.*"[1] This lattice structure is shown in Figure 4.10(b). A concept hierarchy that is a total or partial order among attributes in a database schema is called a **schema hierarchy**. Concept hierarchies that are common to many applications (e.g., *for time*) may be predefined in the data mining system. Data mining systems should provide users with the flexibility to tailor predefined hierarchies according to their particular needs. For example, users may want to define a fiscal year starting on April 1 or an academic year starting on September 1.

Concept hierarchies may also be defined by discretizing or grouping values for a given dimension or attribute, resulting in a **set-grouping hierarchy**. A total or partial order can be defined among groups of values. An example of a set-grouping hierarchy is shown in Figure 4.11 for the dimension *price*, where an interval ($X \ldots Y] denotes the range from $X (exclusive) to $Y (inclusive).

There may be more than one concept hierarchy for a given attribute or dimension, based on different user viewpoints. For instance, a user may prefer to organize *price* by defining ranges for *inexpensive, moderately_priced,* and *expensive.*

Concept hierarchies may be provided manually by system users, domain experts, or knowledge engineers, or may be automatically generated based on statistical analysis of the data distribution. The automatic generation of concept hierarchies is discussed in Chapter 3 as a preprocessing step in preparation for data mining.

Concept hierarchies allow data to be handled at varying levels of abstraction, as we will see in Section 4.2.4.

4.2.4 Measures: Their Categorization and Computation

"*How are measures computed?*" To answer this question, we first study how measures can be categorized. Note that a *multidimensional point* in the data cube space can be defined

---

[1]Since a *week* often crosses the boundary of two consecutive months, it is usually not treated as a lower abstraction of *month*. Instead, it is often treated as a lower abstraction of *year*, since a year contains approximately 52 weeks.

by a set of dimension–value pairs; for example, ⟨*time* = "Q1", *location* = "Vancouver", *item* = "computer"⟩. A data cube **measure** is a numeric function that can be evaluated at each point in the data cube space. A measure value is computed for a given point by aggregating the data corresponding to the respective dimension–value pairs defining the given point. We will look at concrete examples of this shortly.

Measures can be organized into three categories—distributive, algebraic, and holistic—based on the kind of aggregate functions used.

Distributive: An aggregate function is *distributive* if it can be computed in a distributed manner as follows. Suppose the data are partitioned into n sets. We apply the function to each partition, resulting in n aggregate values. If the result derived by applying the function to the n aggregate values is the same as that derived by applying the function to the entire data set (without partitioning), the function can be computed in a distributed manner. For example, sum() can be computed for a data cube by first partitioning the cube into a set of subcubes, computing sum() for each subcube, and then summing up the counts obtained for each subcube. Hence, sum() is a distributive aggregate function.

For the same reason, count(), min(), and max() are distributive aggregate functions. By treating the count value of each nonempty base cell as 1 by default, count() of any cell in a cube can be viewed as the sum of the count values of all of its corresponding child cells in its subcube. Thus, count() is distributive. A measure is *distributive* if it is obtained by applying a distributive aggregate function. Distributive measures can be computed efficiently because of the way the computation can be partitioned.

Algebraic: An aggregate function is *algebraic* if it can be computed by an algebraic function with M arguments (where M is a bounded positive integer), each of which is obtained by applying a distributive aggregate function. For example, avg() (average) can be computed by sum()/count(), where both sum() and count() are distributive aggregate functions. Similarly, it can be shown that min_N() and max_N() (which find the N minimum and N maximum values, respectively, in a given set) and standard_deviation() are algebraic aggregate functions. A measure is *algebraic* if it is obtained by applying an algebraic aggregate function.

Holistic: An aggregate function is *holistic* if there is no constant bound on the storage size needed to describe a subaggregate. That is, there does not exist an algebraic function with M arguments (where M is a constant) that characterizes the computation. Common examples of holistic functions include median(), mode(), and rank(). A measure is *holistic* if it is obtained by applying a holistic aggregate function.

Most large data cube applications require efficient computation of distributive and algebraic measures. Many efficient techniques for this exist. In contrast, it is difficult to compute holistic measures efficiently. Efficient techniques to *approximate* the computation of some holistic measures, however, do exist. For example, rather than computing the exact median(), Equation (2.3) of Chapter 2 can be used to estimate the approximate median value for a large data set. In many cases, such techniques are sufficient to overcome the difficulties of efficient computation of holistic measures.

Various methods for computing different measures in data cube construction are discussed in depth in Chapter 5. Notice that most of the current data cube technology confines the measures of multidimensional databases to *numeric data.* However, measures can also be applied to other kinds of data, such as spatial, multimedia, or text data.

4.2.5 Typical OLAP Operations

"How are concept hierarchies useful in OLAP?" In the multidimensional model, data are organized into multiple dimensions, and each dimension contains multiple levels of abstraction defined by concept hierarchies. This organization provides users with the flexibility to view data from different perspectives. A number of OLAP data cube operations exist to materialize these different views, allowing interactive querying and analysis of the data at hand. Hence, OLAP provides a user-friendly environment for interactive data analysis.

Example 4.4 **OLAP operations.** Let's look at some typical OLAP operations for multidimensional data. Each of the following operations described is illustrated in Figure 4.12. At the center of the figure is a data cube for *AllElectronics* sales. The cube contains the dimensions *location, time,* and *item,* where *location* is aggregated with respect to city values, *time* is aggregated with respect to quarters, and *item* is aggregated with respect to item types. To aid in our explanation, we refer to this cube as the central cube. The measure displayed is *dollars_sold* (in thousands). (For improved readability, only some of the cubes' cell values are shown.) The data examined are for the cities Chicago, New York, Toronto, and Vancouver.

Roll-up: The roll-up operation (also called the *drill-up* operation by some vendors) performs aggregation on a data cube, either by *climbing up a concept hierarchy* for a dimension or by *dimension reduction.* Figure 4.12 shows the result of a roll-up operation performed on the central cube by climbing up the concept hierarchy for *location* given in Figure 4.9. This hierarchy was defined as the total order "*street < city < province_or_state < country.*" The roll-up operation shown aggregates the data by ascending the *location* hierarchy from the level of *city* to the level of *country.* In other words, rather than grouping the data by city, the resulting cube groups the data by country.

When roll-up is performed by dimension reduction, one or more dimensions are removed from the given cube. For example, consider a sales data cube containing only the *location* and *time* dimensions. Roll-up may be performed by removing, say, the *time* dimension, resulting in an aggregation of the total sales by location, rather than by location and by time.

Drill-down: Drill-down is the reverse of roll-up. It navigates from less detailed data to more detailed data. Drill-down can be realized by either *stepping down a concept hierarchy* for a dimension or *introducing additional dimensions.* Figure 4.12 shows the result of a drill-down operation performed on the central cube by stepping down a

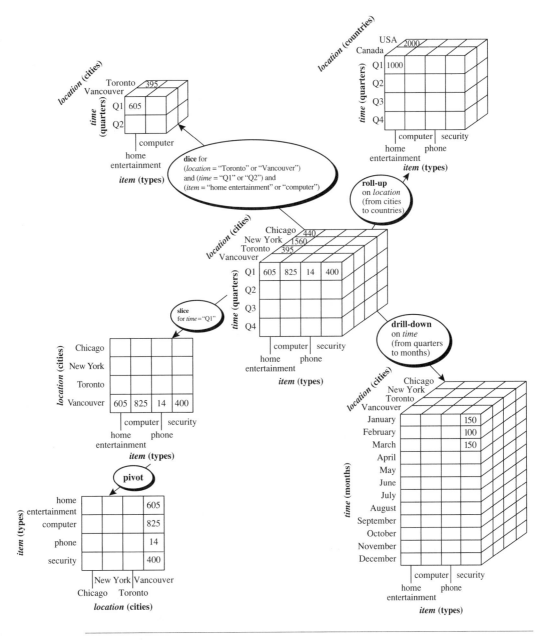

Figure 4.12 Examples of typical OLAP operations on multidimensional data.

concept hierarchy for *time* defined as "*day* < *month* < *quarter* < *year*." Drill-down occurs by descending the *time* hierarchy from the level of *quarter* to the more detailed level of *month*. The resulting data cube details the total sales per month rather than summarizing them by quarter.

Because a drill-down adds more detail to the given data, it can also be performed by adding new dimensions to a cube. For example, a drill-down on the central cube of Figure 4.12 can occur by introducing an additional dimension, such as *customer_group*.

Slice and dice: The *slice* operation performs a selection on one dimension of the given cube, resulting in a subcube. Figure 4.12 shows a slice operation where the sales data are selected from the central cube for the dimension *time* using the criterion *time* = "Q1." The *dice* operation defines a subcube by performing a selection on two or more dimensions. Figure 4.12 shows a dice operation on the central cube based on the following selection criteria that involve three dimensions: (*location* = "Toronto" or "Vancouver") and (*time* = "Q1" or "Q2") and (*item* = "home entertainment" or "computer").

Pivot (rotate): *Pivot* (also called *rotate*) is a visualization operation that rotates the data axes in view to provide an alternative data presentation. Figure 4.12 shows a pivot operation where the *item* and *location* axes in a 2-D slice are rotated. Other examples include rotating the axes in a 3-D cube, or transforming a 3-D cube into a series of 2-D planes.

Other OLAP operations: Some OLAP systems offer additional drilling operations. For example, **drill-across** executes queries involving (i.e., across) more than one fact table. The **drill-through** operation uses relational SQL facilities to drill through the bottom level of a data cube down to its back-end relational tables.

Other OLAP operations may include ranking the top N or bottom N items in lists, as well as computing moving averages, growth rates, interests, internal return rates, depreciation, currency conversions, and statistical functions. ∎

OLAP offers analytical modeling capabilities, including a calculation engine for deriving ratios, variance, and so on, and for computing measures across multiple dimensions. It can generate summarizations, aggregations, and hierarchies at each granularity level and at every dimension intersection. OLAP also supports functional models for forecasting, trend analysis, and statistical analysis. In this context, an OLAP engine is a powerful data analysis tool.

OLAP Systems versus Statistical Databases

Many OLAP systems' characteristics (e.g., the use of a multidimensional data model and concept hierarchies, the association of measures with dimensions, and the notions of roll-up and drill-down) also exist in earlier work on statistical databases (SDBs). A **statistical database** is a database system that is designed to support statistical applications. Similarities between the two types of systems are rarely discussed, mainly due to differences in terminology and application domains.

OLAP and SDB systems, however, have distinguishing differences. While SDBs tend to focus on socioeconomic applications, OLAP has been targeted for business applications. Privacy issues regarding concept hierarchies are a major concern for SDBs. For example, given summarized socioeconomic data, it is controversial to allow users to view the corresponding low-level data. Finally, unlike SDBs, OLAP systems are designed for efficiently handling huge amounts of data.

4.2.6 A Starnet Query Model for Querying Multidimensional Databases

The querying of multidimensional databases can be based on a **starnet model**, which consists of radial lines emanating from a central point, where each line represents a concept hierarchy for a dimension. Each abstraction level in the hierarchy is called a **footprint**. These represent the granularities available for use by OLAP operations such as drill-down and roll-up.

Example 4.5 Starnet. A starnet query model for the *AllElectronics* data warehouse is shown in Figure 4.13. This starnet consists of four radial lines, representing concept hierarchies for the dimensions *location, customer, item,* and *time,* respectively. Each line consists of footprints representing abstraction levels of the dimension. For example, the *time* line has four footprints: "day," "month," "quarter," and "year." A concept hierarchy may involve a single attribute (e.g., *date* for the *time* hierarchy) or several attributes (e.g., the concept hierarchy for *location* involves the attributes *street, city, province_or_state,* and *country*). In order to examine the item sales at *AllElectronics,* users can roll up along the

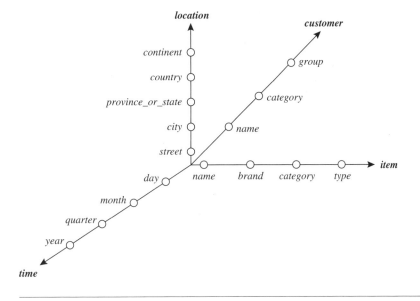

Figure 4.13 A starnet model of business queries.

time dimension from *month* to *quarter*, or, say, drill down along the *location* dimension from *country* to *city*.

Concept hierarchies can be used to **generalize** data by replacing low-level values (such as "day" for the *time* dimension) by higher-level abstractions (such as "year"), or to **specialize** data by replacing higher-level abstractions with lower-level values. ∎

4.3 Data Warehouse Design and Usage

"What goes into a data warehouse design? How are data warehouses used? How do data warehousing and OLAP relate to data mining?" This section tackles these questions. We study the design and usage of data warehousing for information processing, analytical processing, and data mining. We begin by presenting a business analysis framework for data warehouse design (Section 4.3.1). Section 4.3.2 looks at the design process, while Section 4.3.3 studies data warehouse usage. Finally, Section 4.3.4 describes *multidimensional data mining*, a powerful paradigm that integrates OLAP with data mining technology.

4.3.1 A Business Analysis Framework for Data Warehouse Design

"What can business analysts gain from having a data warehouse?" First, having a data warehouse may provide a *competitive advantage* by presenting relevant information from which to measure performance and make critical adjustments to help win over competitors. Second, a data warehouse can enhance business *productivity* because it is able to quickly and efficiently gather information that accurately describes the organization. Third, a data warehouse facilitates *customer relationship management* because it provides a consistent view of customers and items across all lines of business, all departments, and all markets. Finally, a data warehouse may bring about *cost reduction* by tracking trends, patterns, and exceptions over long periods in a consistent and reliable manner.

To design an effective data warehouse we need to understand and analyze business needs and construct a *business analysis framework*. The construction of a large and complex information system can be viewed as the construction of a large and complex building, for which the owner, architect, and builder have different views. These views are combined to form a complex framework that represents the top-down, business-driven, or owner's perspective, as well as the bottom-up, builder-driven, or implementor's view of the information system.

Four different views regarding a data warehouse design must be considered: the *top-down view*, the *data source view*, the *data warehouse view*, and the *business query view*.

- The **top-down view** allows the selection of the relevant information necessary for the data warehouse. This information matches current and future business needs.

- The **data source view** exposes the information being captured, stored, and managed by operational systems. This information may be documented at various levels of detail and accuracy, from individual data source tables to integrated data source tables. Data sources are often modeled by traditional data modeling techniques, such as the entity-relationship model or CASE (computer-aided software engineering) tools.

- The **data warehouse view** includes fact tables and dimension tables. It represents the information that is stored inside the data warehouse, including precalculated totals and counts, as well as information regarding the source, date, and time of origin, added to provide historical context.

- Finally, the **business query view** is the data perspective in the data warehouse from the end-user's viewpoint.

Building and using a data warehouse is a complex task because it requires *business skills, technology skills,* and *program management skills.* Regarding *business skills,* building a data warehouse involves understanding how systems store and manage their data, how to build **extractors** that transfer data from the operational system to the data warehouse, and how to build **warehouse refresh software** that keeps the data warehouse reasonably up-to-date with the operational system's data. Using a data warehouse involves understanding the significance of the data it contains, as well as understanding and translating the business requirements into queries that can be satisfied by the data warehouse.

Regarding *technology skills,* data analysts are required to understand how to make assessments from quantitative information and derive facts based on conclusions from historic information in the data warehouse. These skills include the ability to discover patterns and trends, to extrapolate trends based on history and look for anomalies or paradigm shifts, and to present coherent managerial recommendations based on such analysis. Finally, *program management skills* involve the need to interface with many technologies, vendors, and end-users in order to deliver results in a timely and cost-effective manner.

4.3.2 Data Warehouse Design Process

Let's look at various approaches to the data warehouse design process and the steps involved.

A data warehouse can be built using a *top-down approach,* a *bottom-up approach,* or a *combination of both.* The **top-down approach** starts with overall design and planning. It is useful in cases where the technology is mature and well known, and where the business problems that must be solved are clear and well understood. The **bottom-up approach** starts with experiments and prototypes. This is useful in the early stage of business modeling and technology development. It allows an organization to move forward at considerably less expense and to evaluate the technological benefits before making significant commitments. In the **combined approach**, an organization can exploit the planned and strategic nature of the top-down approach while retaining the rapid implementation and opportunistic application of the bottom-up approach.

From the software engineering point of view, the design and construction of a data warehouse may consist of the following steps: *planning, requirements study, problem analysis, warehouse design, data integration and testing*, and finally *deployment of the data warehouse*. Large software systems can be developed using one of two methodologies: the *waterfall method* or the *spiral method*. The **waterfall method** performs a structured and systematic analysis at each step before proceeding to the next, which is like a waterfall, falling from one step to the next. The **spiral method** involves the rapid generation of increasingly functional systems, with short intervals between successive releases. This is considered a good choice for data warehouse development, especially for data marts, because the turnaround time is short, modifications can be done quickly, and new designs and technologies can be adapted in a timely manner.

In general, the warehouse design process consists of the following steps:

1. Choose a *business process* to model (e.g., orders, invoices, shipments, inventory, account administration, sales, or the general ledger). If the business process is organizational and involves multiple complex object collections, a data warehouse model should be followed. However, if the process is departmental and focuses on the analysis of one kind of business process, a data mart model should be chosen.

2. Choose the business process *grain*, which is the fundamental, atomic level of data to be represented in the fact table for this process (e.g., individual transactions, individual daily snapshots, and so on).

3. Choose the *dimensions* that will apply to each fact table record. Typical dimensions are time, item, customer, supplier, warehouse, transaction type, and status.

4. Choose the *measures* that will populate each fact table record. Typical measures are numeric additive quantities like *dollars_sold* and *units_sold*.

Because data warehouse construction is a difficult and long-term task, its implementation scope should be clearly defined. The goals of an initial data warehouse implementation should be *specific, achievable*, and *measurable*. This involves determining the time and budget allocations, the subset of the organization that is to be modeled, the number of data sources selected, and the number and types of departments to be served.

Once a data warehouse is designed and constructed, the initial deployment of the warehouse includes initial installation, roll-out planning, training, and orientation. Platform upgrades and maintenance must also be considered. Data warehouse administration includes data refreshment, data source synchronization, planning for disaster recovery, managing access control and security, managing data growth, managing database performance, and data warehouse enhancement and extension. Scope management includes controlling the number and range of queries, dimensions, and reports; limiting the data warehouse's size; or limiting the schedule, budget, or resources.

Various kinds of data warehouse design tools are available. **Data warehouse development tools** provide functions to define and edit metadata repository contents (e.g., schemas, scripts, or rules), answer queries, output reports, and ship metadata to and from relational database system catalogs. **Planning and analysis tools** study the impact of schema changes and of refresh performance when changing refresh rates or time windows.

4.3.3 Data Warehouse Usage for Information Processing

Data warehouses and data marts are used in a wide range of applications. Business executives use the data in data warehouses and data marts to perform data analysis and make strategic decisions. In many firms, data warehouses are used as an integral part of a *plan-execute-assess* "closed-loop" feedback system for enterprise management. Data warehouses are used extensively in banking and financial services, consumer goods and retail distribution sectors, and controlled manufacturing such as demand-based production.

Typically, the longer a data warehouse has been in use, the more it will have evolved. This evolution takes place throughout a number of phases. Initially, the data warehouse is mainly used for generating reports and answering predefined queries. Progressively, it is used to analyze summarized and detailed data, where the results are presented in the form of reports and charts. Later, the data warehouse is used for strategic purposes, performing multidimensional analysis and sophisticated slice-and-dice operations. Finally, the data warehouse may be employed for knowledge discovery and strategic decision making using data mining tools. In this context, the tools for data warehousing can be categorized into *access and retrieval tools*, *database reporting tools*, *data analysis tools*, and *data mining tools*.

Business users need to have the means to know what exists in the data warehouse (through metadata), how to access the contents of the data warehouse, how to examine the contents using analysis tools, and how to present the results of such analysis.

There are three kinds of data warehouse applications: *information processing, analytical processing*, and *data mining*.

- **Information processing** supports querying, basic statistical analysis, and reporting using crosstabs, tables, charts, or graphs. A current trend in data warehouse information processing is to construct low-cost web-based accessing tools that are then integrated with web browsers.

- **Analytical processing** supports basic OLAP operations, including slice-and-dice, drill-down, roll-up, and pivoting. It generally operates on historic data in both summarized and detailed forms. The major strength of online analytical processing over information processing is the multidimensional data analysis of data warehouse data.

■ **Data mining** supports knowledge discovery by finding hidden patterns and associations, constructing analytical models, performing classification and prediction, and presenting the mining results using visualization tools.

"*How does data mining relate to information processing and online analytical processing?*" Information processing, based on queries, can find useful information. However, answers to such queries reflect the information directly stored in databases or computable by aggregate functions. They do not reflect sophisticated patterns or regularities buried in the database. Therefore, information processing is not data mining.

Online analytical processing comes a step closer to data mining because it can derive information summarized at multiple granularities from user-specified subsets of a data warehouse. Such descriptions are equivalent to the class/concept descriptions discussed in Chapter 1. Because data mining systems can also mine generalized class/concept descriptions, this raises some interesting questions: "*Do OLAP systems perform data mining? Are OLAP systems actually data mining systems?*"

The functionalities of OLAP and data mining can be viewed as disjoint: OLAP is a data summarization/aggregation *tool* that helps simplify data analysis, while data mining allows the *automated discovery* of implicit patterns and interesting knowledge hidden in large amounts of data. OLAP tools are targeted toward simplifying and supporting interactive data analysis, whereas the goal of data mining tools is to automate as much of the process as possible, while still allowing users to guide the process. In this sense, data mining goes one step beyond traditional online analytical processing.

An alternative and broader view of data mining may be adopted in which data mining covers both data description and data modeling. Because OLAP systems can present general descriptions of data from data warehouses, OLAP functions are essentially for user-directed data summarization and comparison (by drilling, pivoting, slicing, dicing, and other operations). These are, though limited, data mining functionalities. Yet according to this view, data mining covers a much broader spectrum than simple OLAP operations, because it performs not only data summarization and comparison but also association, classification, prediction, clustering, time-series analysis, and other data analysis tasks.

Data mining is not confined to the analysis of data stored in data warehouses. It may analyze data existing at more detailed granularities than the summarized data provided in a data warehouse. It may also analyze transactional, spatial, textual, and multimedia data that are difficult to model with current multidimensional database technology. In this context, data mining covers a broader spectrum than OLAP with respect to data mining functionality and the complexity of the data handled.

Because data mining involves more automated and deeper analysis than OLAP, it is expected to have broader applications. Data mining can help business managers find and reach more suitable customers, as well as gain critical business insights that may help drive market share and raise profits. In addition, data mining can help managers understand customer group characteristics and develop optimal pricing strategies accordingly. It can correct item bundling based not on intuition but on actual item groups derived from customer purchase patterns, reduce promotional spending, and at the same time increase the overall net effectiveness of promotions.

4.3.4 **From Online Analytical Processing to Multidimensional Data Mining**

The data mining field has conducted substantial research regarding mining on various data types, including relational data, data from data warehouses, transaction data, time-series data, spatial data, text data, and flat files. **Multidimensional data mining** (also known as *exploratory multidimensional data mining*, **online analytical mining**, or **OLAM**) integrates OLAP with data mining to uncover knowledge in multidimensional databases. Among the many different paradigms and architectures of data mining systems, multidimensional data mining is particularly important for the following reasons:

- **High quality of data in data warehouses:** Most data mining tools need to work on integrated, consistent, and cleaned data, which requires costly data cleaning, data integration, and data transformation as preprocessing steps. A data warehouse constructed by such preprocessing serves as a valuable source of high-quality data for OLAP as well as for data mining. Notice that data mining may serve as a valuable tool for data cleaning and data integration as well.

- **Available information processing infrastructure surrounding data warehouses:** Comprehensive information processing and data analysis infrastructures have been or will be systematically constructed surrounding data warehouses, which include accessing, integration, consolidation, and transformation of multiple heterogeneous databases, ODBC/OLEDB connections, Web accessing and service facilities, and reporting and OLAP analysis tools. It is prudent to make the best use of the available infrastructures rather than constructing everything from scratch.

- **OLAP-based exploration of multidimensional data:** Effective data mining needs exploratory data analysis. A user will often want to traverse through a database, select portions of relevant data, analyze them at different granularities, and present knowledge/results in different forms. Multidimensional data mining provides facilities for mining on different subsets of data and at varying levels of abstraction—by drilling, pivoting, filtering, dicing, and slicing on a data cube and/or intermediate data mining results. This, together with data/knowledge visualization tools, greatly enhances the power and flexibility of data mining.

- **Online selection of data mining functions:** Users may not always know the specific kinds of knowledge they want to mine. By integrating OLAP with various data mining functions, multidimensional data mining provides users with the flexibility to select desired data mining functions and swap data mining tasks dynamically.

Chapter 5 describes data warehouses on a finer level by exploring implementation issues such as data cube computation, OLAP query answering strategies, and multidimensional data mining. The chapters following it are devoted to the study of data mining techniques. As we have seen, the introduction to data warehousing and OLAP technology presented in this chapter is essential to our study of data mining. This is because data warehousing provides users with large amounts of clean, organized, and summarized data, which greatly facilitates data mining. For example, rather than storing the details of each sales transaction, a data warehouse may store a summary of the transactions per item type for each branch or, summarized to a higher level, for each country. The capability of OLAP to provide multiple and dynamic views of summarized data in a data warehouse sets a solid foundation for successful data mining.

Moreover, we also believe that data mining should be a human-centered process. Rather than asking a data mining system to generate patterns and knowledge automatically, a user will often need to interact with the system to perform exploratory data analysis. OLAP sets a good example for interactive data analysis and provides the necessary preparations for exploratory data mining. Consider the discovery of association patterns, for example. Instead of mining associations at a primitive (i.e., low) data level among transactions, users should be allowed to specify roll-up operations along any dimension.

For example, a user may want to roll up on the *item* dimension to go from viewing the data for particular TV sets that were purchased to viewing the brands of these TVs (e.g., SONY or Toshiba). Users may also navigate from the transaction level to the customer or customer-type level in the search for interesting associations. Such an OLAP data mining style is characteristic of multidimensional data mining. In our study of the principles of data mining in this book, we place particular emphasis on multidimensional data mining, that is, on the *integration of data mining and OLAP technology*.

4.4 Data Warehouse Implementation

Data warehouses contain huge volumes of data. OLAP servers demand that decision support queries be answered in the order of seconds. Therefore, it is crucial for data warehouse systems to support highly efficient cube computation techniques, access methods, and query processing techniques. In this section, we present an overview of methods for the efficient implementation of data warehouse systems. Section 4.4.1 explores how to compute data cubes efficiently. Section 4.4.2 shows how OLAP data can be indexed, using either bitmap or join indices. Next, we study how OLAP queries are processed (Section 4.4.3). Finally, Section 4.4.4 presents various types of warehouse servers for OLAP processing.

4.4.1 Efficient Data Cube Computation: An Overview

At the core of multidimensional data analysis is the efficient computation of aggregations across many sets of dimensions. In SQL terms, these aggregations are referred to as group-by's. Each group-by can be represented by a *cuboid*, where the set of group-by's forms a lattice of cuboids defining a data cube. In this subsection, we explore issues relating to the efficient computation of data cubes.

The compute cube **Operator and the Curse of Dimensionality**

One approach to cube computation extends SQL so as to include a compute cube operator. The compute cube operator computes aggregates over all subsets of the dimensions specified in the operation. This can require excessive storage space, especially for large numbers of dimensions. We start with an intuitive look at what is involved in the efficient computation of data cubes.

Example 4.6 **A data cube is a lattice of cuboids.** Suppose that you want to create a data cube for *AllElectronics* sales that contains the following: *city, item, year*, and *sales_in_dollars*. You want to be able to analyze the data, with queries such as the following:

- "*Compute the sum of sales, grouping by city and item.*"
- "*Compute the sum of sales, grouping by city.*"
- "*Compute the sum of sales, grouping by item.*"

What is the total number of cuboids, or group-by's, that can be computed for this data cube? Taking the three attributes, *city, item*, and *year*, as the dimensions for the data cube, and *sales_in_dollars* as the measure, the total number of cuboids, or group-by's, that can be computed for this data cube is $2^3 = 8$. The possible group-by's are the following: {(*city, item, year*), (*city, item*), (*city, year*), (*item, year*), (*city*), (*item*), (*year*), ()}, where () means that the group-by is empty (i.e., the dimensions are not grouped). These group-by's form a lattice of cuboids for the data cube, as shown in Figure 4.14.

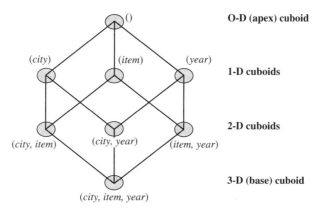

Figure 4.14 Lattice of cuboids, making up a 3-D data cube. Each cuboid represents a different group-by. The base cuboid contains *city, item*, and *year* dimensions.

The **base cuboid** contains all three dimensions, *city*, *item*, and *year*. It can return the total sales for any combination of the three dimensions. The **apex cuboid**, or 0-D cuboid, refers to the case where the group-by is empty. It contains the total sum of all sales. The base cuboid is the least generalized (most specific) of the cuboids. The apex cuboid is the most generalized (least specific) of the cuboids, and is often denoted as **all**. If we start at the apex cuboid and explore downward in the lattice, this is equivalent to drilling down within the data cube. If we start at the base cuboid and explore upward, this is akin to rolling up. ∎

An SQL query containing no group-by (e.g., "*compute the sum of total sales*") is a *zero-dimensional operation*. An SQL query containing one group-by (e.g., "*compute the sum of sales, group-by city*") is a *one-dimensional operation*. A cube operator on n dimensions is equivalent to a collection of group-by statements, one for each subset of the n dimensions. Therefore, the cube operator is the n-dimensional generalization of the group-by operator.

Similar to the SQL syntax, the data cube in Example 4.1 could be defined as

define cube sales_cube [city, item, year]: sum(sales_in_dollars)

For a cube with n dimensions, there are a total of 2^n cuboids, including the base cuboid. A statement such as

compute cube sales_cube

would explicitly instruct the system to compute the sales aggregate cuboids for all eight subsets of the set {*city, item, year*}, including the empty subset. A cube computation operator was first proposed and studied by Gray et al. [GCB+97].

Online analytical processing may need to access different cuboids for different queries. Therefore, it may seem like a good idea to compute in advance all or at least some of the cuboids in a data cube. Precomputation leads to fast response time and avoids some redundant computation. Most, if not all, OLAP products resort to some degree of precomputation of multidimensional aggregates.

A major challenge related to this precomputation, however, is that the required storage space may explode if all the cuboids in a data cube are precomputed, especially when the cube has many dimensions. The storage requirements are even more excessive when many of the dimensions have associated concept hierarchies, each with multiple levels. This problem is referred to as the **curse of dimensionality**. The extent of the curse of dimensionality is illustrated here.

"*How many cuboids are there in an* n-*dimensional data cube?*" If there were no hierarchies associated with each dimension, then the total number of cuboids for an n-dimensional data cube, as we have seen, is 2^n. However, in practice, many dimensions do have hierarchies. For example, *time* is usually explored not at only one conceptual level (e.g., *year*), but rather at multiple conceptual levels such as in the hierarchy "*day < month < quarter < year*." For an n-dimensional data cube, the total number of cuboids that can be generated (including the cuboids generated by climbing up the hierarchies along each dimension) is

$$Total\ number\ of\ cuboids = \prod_{i=1}^{n}(L_i + 1),\qquad (4.1)$$

where L_i is the number of levels associated with dimension i. One is added to L_i in Eq. (4.1) to include the *virtual* top level, all. (Note that generalizing to all is equivalent to the removal of the dimension.)

This formula is based on the fact that, at most, one abstraction level in each dimension will appear in a cuboid. For example, the time dimension as specified before has four conceptual levels, or five if we include the virtual level all. If the cube has 10 dimensions and each dimension has five levels (including all), the total number of cuboids that can be generated is $5^{10} \approx 9.8 \times 10^6$. The size of each cuboid also depends on the *cardinality* (i.e., number of distinct values) of each dimension. For example, if the *All-Electronics* branch in each city sold every item, there would be $|city| \times |item|$ tuples in the *city_item* group-by alone. As the number of dimensions, number of conceptual hierarchies, or cardinality increases, the storage space required for many of the group-by's will grossly exceed the (fixed) size of the input relation.

By now, you probably realize that it is unrealistic to precompute and materialize all of the cuboids that can possibly be generated for a data cube (i.e., from a base cuboid). If there are many cuboids, and these cuboids are large in size, a more reasonable option is *partial materialization*; that is, to materialize only *some* of the possible cuboids that can be generated.

Partial Materialization: Selected Computation of Cuboids

There are three choices for data cube materialization given a base cuboid:

1. **No materialization**: Do not precompute any of the "nonbase" cuboids. This leads to computing expensive multidimensional aggregates on-the-fly, which can be extremely slow.

2. **Full materialization**: Precompute all of the cuboids. The resulting lattice of computed cuboids is referred to as the *full cube*. This choice typically requires huge amounts of memory space in order to store all of the precomputed cuboids.

3. **Partial materialization**: Selectively compute a proper subset of the whole set of possible cuboids. Alternatively, we may compute a subset of the cube, which contains only those cells that satisfy some user-specified criterion, such as where the tuple count of each cell is above some threshold. We will use the term *subcube* to refer to the latter case, where only some of the cells may be precomputed for various cuboids. Partial materialization represents an interesting trade-off between storage space and response time.

The partial materialization of cuboids or subcubes should consider three factors: (1) identify the subset of cuboids or subcubes to materialize; (2) exploit the materialized cuboids or subcubes during query processing; and (3) efficiently update the materialized cuboids or subcubes during load and refresh.

The selection of the subset of cuboids or subcubes to materialize should take into account the queries in the workload, their frequencies, and their accessing costs. In addition, it should consider workload characteristics, the cost for incremental updates, and the total storage requirements. The selection must also consider the broad context of physical database design such as the generation and selection of indices. Several OLAP products have adopted heuristic approaches for cuboid and subcube selection. A popular approach is to materialize the cuboids set on which other frequently referenced cuboids are based. Alternatively, we can compute an **iceberg cube**, which is a data cube that stores only those cube cells with an aggregate value (e.g., count) that is above some minimum support threshold.

Another common strategy is to materialize a *shell cube*. This involves precomputing the cuboids for only a small number of dimensions (e.g., three to five) of a data cube. Queries on additional combinations of the dimensions can be computed on-the-fly. Because our aim in this chapter is to provide a solid introduction and overview of data warehousing for data mining, we defer our detailed discussion of cuboid selection and computation to Chapter 5, which studies various data cube computation methods in greater depth.

Once the selected cuboids have been materialized, it is important to take advantage of them during query processing. This involves several issues, such as how to determine the relevant cuboid(s) from among the candidate materialized cuboids, how to use available index structures on the materialized cuboids, and how to transform the OLAP operations onto the selected cuboid(s). These issues are discussed in Section 4.4.3 as well as in Chapter 5.

Finally, during load and refresh, the materialized cuboids should be updated efficiently. Parallelism and incremental update techniques for this operation should be explored.

4.4.2 Indexing OLAP Data: Bitmap Index and Join Index

To facilitate efficient data accessing, most data warehouse systems support index structures and materialized views (using cuboids). General methods to select cuboids for materialization were discussed in Section 4.4.1. In this subsection, we examine how to index OLAP data by *bitmap indexing* and *join indexing*.

The **bitmap indexing** method is popular in OLAP products because it allows quick searching in data cubes. The bitmap index is an alternative representation of the *record_ID (RID)* list. In the bitmap index for a given attribute, there is a distinct bit vector, Bv, for each value v in the attribute's domain. If a given attribute's domain consists of n values, then n bits are needed for each entry in the bitmap index (i.e., there are n bit vectors). If the attribute has the value v for a given row in the data table, then the bit representing that value is set to 1 in the corresponding row of the bitmap index. All other bits for that row are set to 0.

Example 4.7 **Bitmap indexing.** In the *AllElectronics* data warehouse, suppose the dimension *item* at the top level has four values (representing item types): *"home entertainment," "computer," "phone,"* and *"security."* Each value (e.g., *"computer"*) is represented by a bit vector in the *item* bitmap index table. Suppose that the cube is stored as a relation table with 100,000 rows. Because the domain of *item* consists of four values, the bitmap index table requires four bit vectors (or lists), each with 100,000 bits. Figure 4.15 shows a base (data) table containing the dimensions *item* and *city*, and its mapping to bitmap index tables for each of the dimensions. ∎

Base table

RID	item	city
R1	H	V
R2	C	V
R3	P	V
R4	S	V
R5	H	T
R6	C	T
R7	P	T
R8	S	T

item bitmap index table

RID	H	C	P	S
R1	1	0	0	0
R2	0	1	0	0
R3	0	0	1	0
R4	0	0	0	1
R5	1	0	0	0
R6	0	1	0	0
R7	0	0	1	0
R8	0	0	0	1

city bitmap index table

RID	V	T
R1	1	0
R2	1	0
R3	1	0
R4	1	0
R5	0	1
R6	0	1
R7	0	1
R8	0	1

Note: H for "home entertainment," C for "computer," P for "phone," S for "security,"
V for "Vancouver," T for "Toronto."

Figure 4.15 Indexing OLAP data using bitmap indices.

Bitmap indexing is advantageous compared to hash and tree indices. It is especially useful for low-cardinality domains because comparison, join, and aggregation operations are then reduced to bit arithmetic, which substantially reduces the processing time. Bitmap indexing leads to significant reductions in space and input/output (I/O) since a string of characters can be represented by a single bit. For higher-cardinality domains, the method can be adapted using compression techniques.

The **join indexing** method gained popularity from its use in relational database query processing. Traditional indexing maps the value in a given column to a list of rows having that value. In contrast, join indexing registers the joinable rows of two relations from a relational database. For example, if two relations $R(RID, A)$ and $S(B, SID)$ join on the attributes A and B, then the join index record contains the pair (RID, SID), where RID and SID are record identifiers from the R and S relations, respectively. Hence, the join index records can identify joinable tuples without performing costly join operations. Join indexing is especially useful for maintaining the relationship between a foreign key[2] and its matching primary keys, from the joinable relation.

The star schema model of data warehouses makes join indexing attractive for cross-table search, because the linkage between a fact table and its corresponding dimension tables comprises the fact table's foreign key and the dimension table's primary key. Join

---

[2]A set of attributes in a relation schema that forms a primary key for another relation schema is called a **foreign key**.

indexing maintains relationships between attribute values of a dimension (e.g., within a dimension table) and the corresponding rows in the fact table. Join indices may span multiple dimensions to form **composite join indices**. We can use join indices to identify subcubes that are of interest.

Example 4.8 **Join indexing.** In Example 3.4, we defined a star schema for *AllElectronics* of the form "*sales_star* [*time, item, branch, location*]: *dollars_sold* = sum *(sales_in_dollars)*." An example of a join index relationship between the *sales* fact table and the *location* and *item* dimension tables is shown in Figure 4.16. For example, the "Main Street" value in the *location* dimension table joins with tuples T57, T238, and T884 of the *sales* fact table. Similarly, the "Sony-TV" value in the *item* dimension table joins with tuples T57 and T459 of the *sales* fact table. The corresponding join index tables are shown in Figure 4.17.

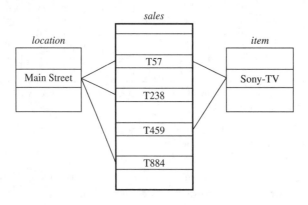

Figure 4.16 Linkages between a *sales* fact table and *location* and *item* dimension tables.

Join index table for
location/sales

location	sales_key
. . .	. . .
Main Street	T57
Main Street	T238
Main Street	T884
. . .	. . .

Join index table for
item/sales

item	sales_key
. . .	. . .
Sony-TV	T57
Sony-TV	T459
. . .	. . .

Join index table linking
location and *item* to *sales*

location	item	sales_key
. . .	. . .	. . .
Main Street	Sony-TV	T57
. . .	. . .	. . .

Figure 4.17 Join index tables based on the linkages between the *sales* fact table and the *location* and *item* dimension tables shown in Figure 4.16.

Suppose that there are 360 time values, 100 items, 50 branches, 30 locations, and 10 million sales tuples in the *sales_star* data cube. If the *sales* fact table has recorded sales for only 30 items, the remaining 70 items will obviously not participate in joins. If join indices are not used, additional I/Os have to be performed to bring the joining portions of the fact table and the dimension tables together. ∎

To further speed up query processing, the join indexing and the bitmap indexing methods can be integrated to form **bitmapped join indices**.

4.4.3 Efficient Processing of OLAP Queries

The purpose of materializing cuboids and constructing OLAP index structures is to speed up query processing in data cubes. Given materialized views, query processing should proceed as follows:

1. **Determine which operations should be performed on the available cuboids:** This involves transforming any selection, projection, roll-up (group-by), and drill-down operations specified in the query into corresponding SQL and/or OLAP operations. For example, slicing and dicing a data cube may correspond to selection and/or projection operations on a materialized cuboid.

2. **Determine to which materialized cuboid(s) the relevant operations should be applied:** This involves identifying all of the materialized cuboids that may potentially be used to answer the query, pruning the set using knowledge of "dominance" relationships among the cuboids, estimating the costs of using the remaining materialized cuboids, and selecting the cuboid with the least cost.

Example 4.9 **OLAP query processing.** Suppose that we define a data cube for *AllElectronics* of the form "*sales_cube* [*time, item, location*]: sum(*sales_in_dollars*)." The dimension hierarchies used are "*day < month < quarter < year*" for *time*; "*item_name < brand < type*" for *item*; and "*street < city < province_or_state < country*" for *location*.

Suppose that the query to be processed is on {*brand, province_or_state*}, with the selection constant "*year = 2010.*" Also, suppose that there are four materialized cuboids available, as follows:

▪ cuboid 1: {*year, item_name, city*}

▪ cuboid 2: {*year, brand, country*}

▪ cuboid 3: {*year, brand, province_or_state*}

▪ cuboid 4: {*item_name, province_or_state*}, where *year* = 2010

"*Which of these four cuboids should be selected to process the query?*" Finer-granularity data cannot be generated from coarser-granularity data. Therefore, cuboid 2 cannot be used because *country* is a more general concept than *province_or_state*. Cuboids 1, 3, and 4 can be used to process the query because (1) they have the same set or a superset of the dimensions in the query, (2) the selection clause in the query can imply the selection in the cuboid, and (3) the abstraction levels for the *item* and *location* dimensions in these cuboids are at a finer level than *brand* and *province_or_state*, respectively.

"*How would the costs of each cuboid compare if used to process the query?*" It is likely that using cuboid 1 would cost the most because both *item_name* and *city* are at a lower level than the *brand* and *province_or_state* concepts specified in the query. If there are not many *year* values associated with *items* in the cube, but there are several *item_names* for each *brand*, then cuboid 3 will be smaller than cuboid 4, and thus cuboid 3 should be chosen to process the query. However, if efficient indices are available for cuboid 4, then cuboid 4 may be a better choice. Therefore, some cost-based estimation is required to decide which set of cuboids should be selected for query processing. ∎

4.4.4 OLAP Server Architectures: ROLAP versus MOLAP versus HOLAP

Logically, OLAP servers present business users with multidimensional data from data warehouses or data marts, without concerns regarding how or where the data are stored. However, the physical architecture and implementation of OLAP servers must consider data storage issues. Implementations of a warehouse server for OLAP processing include the following:

Relational OLAP (ROLAP) servers: These are the intermediate servers that stand in between a relational back-end server and client front-end tools. They use a *relational* or *extended-relational DBMS* to store and manage warehouse data, and OLAP middleware to support missing pieces. ROLAP servers include optimization for each DBMS back end, implementation of aggregation navigation logic, and additional tools and services. ROLAP technology tends to have greater scalability than MOLAP technology. The DSS server of Microstrategy, for example, adopts the ROLAP approach.

Multidimensional OLAP (MOLAP) servers: These servers support multidimensional data views through *array-based multidimensional storage engines*. They map multidimensional views directly to data cube array structures. The advantage of using a data cube is that it allows fast indexing to precomputed summarized data. Notice that with multidimensional data stores, the storage utilization may be low if the data set is sparse. In such cases, sparse matrix compression techniques should be explored (Chapter 5).

Many MOLAP servers adopt a two-level storage representation to handle dense and sparse data sets: Denser subcubes are identified and stored as array structures, whereas sparse subcubes employ compression technology for efficient storage utilization.

Hybrid OLAP (HOLAP) servers: The hybrid OLAP approach combines ROLAP and MOLAP technology, benefiting from the greater scalability of ROLAP and the faster computation of MOLAP. For example, a HOLAP server may allow large volumes of detailed data to be stored in a relational database, while aggregations are kept in a separate MOLAP store. The Microsoft SQL Server 2000 supports a hybrid OLAP server.

Specialized SQL servers: To meet the growing demand of OLAP processing in relational databases, some database system vendors implement specialized SQL servers that provide advanced query language and query processing support for SQL queries over star and snowflake schemas in a read-only environment.

"How are data actually stored in ROLAP and MOLAP architectures?" Let's first look at ROLAP. As its name implies, ROLAP uses relational tables to store data for online analytical processing. Recall that the fact table associated with a base cuboid is referred to as a *base fact table*. The base fact table stores data at the abstraction level indicated by the join keys in the schema for the given data cube. Aggregated data can also be stored in fact tables, referred to as **summary fact tables.** Some summary fact tables store both base fact table data and aggregated data (see Example 3.10). Alternatively, separate summary fact tables can be used for each abstraction level to store only aggregated data.

Example 4.10 **A ROLAP data store.** Table 4.4 shows a summary fact table that contains both base fact data and aggregated data. The schema is "⟨*record_identifier (RID), item, ..., day, month, quarter, year, dollars_sold*⟩," where *day, month, quarter,* and *year* define the sales date, and *dollars_sold* is the sales amount. Consider the tuples with an *RID* of 1001 and 1002, respectively. The data of these tuples are at the base fact level, where the sales dates are October 15, 2010, and October 23, 2010, respectively. Consider the tuple with an *RID* of 5001. This tuple is at a more general level of abstraction than the tuples 1001 and 1002. The *day* value has been generalized to all, so that the corresponding *time* value is October 2010. That is, the *dollars_sold* amount shown is an aggregation representing the entire month of October 2010, rather than just October 15 or 23, 2010. The special value all is used to represent subtotals in summarized data. ■

MOLAP uses multidimensional array structures to store data for online analytical processing. This structure is discussed in greater detail in Chapter 5.

Most data warehouse systems adopt a client-server architecture. A relational data store always resides at the data warehouse/data mart server site. A multidimensional data store can reside at either the database server site or the client site.

Table 4.4 Single Table for Base and Summary Facts

RID	item	...	day	month	quarter	year	dollars_sold
1001	TV	...	15	10	Q4	2010	250.60
1002	TV	...	23	10	Q4	2010	175.00
...	...	...	...	...	...	...	...
5001	TV	...	all	10	Q4	2010	45,786.08
...	...	...	...	...	...	...	...

4.5 Data Generalization by Attribute-Oriented Induction

Conceptually, the data cube can be viewed as a kind of multidimensional data generalization. In general, *data generalization* summarizes data by replacing relatively low-level values (e.g., numeric values for an attribute *age*) with higher-level concepts (e.g., *young*, *middle-aged*, and *senior*), or by reducing the number of dimensions to summarize data in concept space involving fewer dimensions (e.g., removing *birth_date* and *telephone number* when summarizing the behavior of a group of students). Given the large amount of data stored in databases, it is useful to be able to describe concepts in concise and succinct terms at generalized (rather than low) levels of abstraction. Allowing data sets to be generalized at multiple levels of abstraction facilitates users in examining the general behavior of the data. Given the *AllElectronics* database, for example, instead of examining individual customer transactions, sales managers may prefer to view the data generalized to higher levels, such as summarized by customer groups according to geographic regions, frequency of purchases per group, and customer income.

This leads us to the notion of *concept description*, which is a form of data generalization. A concept typically refers to a data collection such as *frequent_buyers, graduate_students*, and so on. As a data mining task, concept description is not a simple enumeration of the data. Instead, **concept description** generates descriptions for data *characterization* and *comparison*. It is sometimes called **class description** when the concept to be described refers to a class of objects. **Characterization** provides a concise and succinct summarization of the given data collection, while concept or class **comparison** (also known as **discrimination**) provides descriptions comparing two or more data collections.

Up to this point, we have studied data cube (or OLAP) approaches to concept description using multidimensional, multilevel data generalization in data warehouses. *"Is data cube technology sufficient to accomplish all kinds of concept description tasks for large data sets?"* Consider the following cases.

- **Complex data types and aggregation**: Data warehouses and OLAP tools are based on a multidimensional data model that views data in the form of a data cube, consisting of dimensions (or attributes) and measures (aggregate functions). However, many current OLAP systems confine dimensions to non-numeric data and measures to numeric data. In reality, the database can include attributes of various data types, including numeric, non-numeric, spatial, text, or image, which ideally should be included in the concept description.

  Furthermore, the aggregation of attributes in a database may include sophisticated data types such as the collection of non-numeric data, the merging of spatial regions, the composition of images, the integration of texts, and the grouping of object pointers. Therefore, OLAP, with its restrictions on the possible dimension and measure types, represents a simplified model for data analysis. Concept description should handle complex data types of the attributes and their aggregations, as necessary.

■ **User control versus automation**: Online analytical processing in data warehouses is a user-controlled process. The selection of dimensions and the application of OLAP operations (e.g., drill-down, roll-up, slicing, and dicing) are primarily directed and controlled by users. Although the control in most OLAP systems is quite user-friendly, users do require a good understanding of the role of each dimension. Furthermore, in order to find a satisfactory description of the data, users may need to specify a long sequence of OLAP operations. It is often desirable to have a more automated process that helps users determine which dimensions (or attributes) should be included in the analysis, and the degree to which the given data set should be generalized in order to produce an interesting summarization of the data.

This section presents an alternative method for concept description, called *attribute-oriented induction*, which works for complex data types and relies on a data-driven generalization process.

4.5.1 Attribute-Oriented Induction for Data Characterization

The **attribute-oriented induction** (AOI) approach to concept description was first proposed in 1989, a few years before the introduction of the data cube approach. The data cube approach is essentially based on *materialized views* of the data, which typically have been precomputed in a data warehouse. In general, it performs offline aggregation before an OLAP or data mining query is submitted for processing. On the other hand, the attribute-oriented induction approach is basically a *query-oriented*, generalization-based, online data analysis technique. Note that there is no inherent barrier distinguishing the two approaches based on online aggregation versus offline precomputation. Some aggregations in the data cube can be computed online, while offline precomputation of multidimensional space can speed up attribute-oriented induction as well.

The general idea of attribute-oriented induction is to first collect the task-relevant data using a database query and then perform generalization based on the examination of the number of each attribute's distinct values in the relevant data set. The generalization is performed by either *attribute removal* or *attribute generalization*. Aggregation is performed by merging identical generalized tuples and accumulating their respective counts. This reduces the size of the generalized data set. The resulting generalized relation can be mapped into different forms (e.g., charts or rules) for presentation to the user.

The following illustrates the process of attribute-oriented induction. We first discuss its use for characterization. The method is extended for the mining of class comparisons in Section 4.5.3.

Example 4.11 **A data mining query for characterization.** Suppose that a user wants to describe the general characteristics of graduate students in the *Big University* database, given the attributes *name, gender, major, birth_place, birth_date, residence, phone# (telephone* *number)*, and *gpa (grade_point_average)*. A data mining query for this characterization can be expressed in the data mining query language, DMQL, as follows:

use *Big_University_DB*
mine characteristics as "Science_Students"
in relevance to *name, gender, major, birth_place, birth_date, residence,*
  phone#, gpa
from *student*
where status in "graduate"

We will see how this example of a typical data mining query can apply attribute-oriented induction to the mining of characteristic descriptions.

First, **data focusing** should be performed *before* attribute-oriented induction. This step corresponds to the specification of the task-relevant data (i.e., data for analysis). The data are collected based on the information provided in the data mining query. Because a data mining query is usually relevant to only a portion of the database, selecting the relevant data set not only makes mining more efficient, but also derives more meaningful results than mining the entire database.

Specifying the set of relevant attributes (i.e., attributes for mining, as indicated in DMQL with the in relevance to clause) may be difficult for the user. A user may select only a few attributes that he or she feels are important, while missing others that could also play a role in the description. For example, suppose that the dimension *birth_place* is defined by the attributes *city, province_or_state,* and *country*. Of these attributes, let's say that the user has only thought to specify *city*. In order to allow generalization on the *birth_place* dimension, the other attributes defining this dimension should also be included. In other words, having the system automatically include *province_or_state* and *country* as relevant attributes allows *city* to be generalized to these higher conceptual levels during the induction process.

At the other extreme, suppose that the user may have introduced too many attributes by specifying all of the possible attributes with the clause in relevance to ∗. In this case, all of the attributes in the relation specified by the from clause would be included in the analysis. Many of these attributes are unlikely to contribute to an interesting description. A correlation-based analysis method (Section 3.3.2) can be used to perform attribute *relevance analysis* and filter out statistically irrelevant or weakly relevant attributes from the descriptive mining process. Other approaches such as attribute subset selection, are also described in Chapter 3.

Table 4.5 Initial Working Relation: A Collection of Task-Relevant Data

name	gender	major	birth_place	birth_date	residence	phone#	gpa
Jim Woodman	M	CS	Vancouver, BC, Canada	12-8-76	3511 Main St., Richmond	687-4598	3.67
Scott Lachance	M	CS	Montreal, Que, Canada	7-28-75	345 1st Ave., Richmond	253-9106	3.70
Laura Lee	F	Physics	Seattle, WA, USA	8-25-70	125 Austin Ave., Burnaby	420-5232	3.83
...	...	...	...	...	...	...	...

"*What does the* 'where *status* in "graduate"' *clause mean?*" The **where** clause implies that a concept hierarchy exists for the attribute *status*. Such a concept hierarchy organizes primitive-level data values for *status* (e.g., "M.Sc.," "M.A.," "M.B.A.," "Ph.D.," "B.Sc.," and "B.A.") into higher conceptual levels (e.g., "graduate" and "undergraduate"). This use of concept hierarchies does not appear in traditional relational query languages, yet is likely to become a common feature in data mining query languages.

The data mining query presented in Example 4.11 is transformed into the following relational query for the collection of the task-relevant data set:

use *Big_University_DB*
select *name, gender, major, birth_place, birth_date, residence, phone#, gpa*
from *student*
where status in {"M.Sc.," "M.A.," "M.B.A.," "Ph.D."}

The transformed query is executed against the relational database, *Big_University_DB*, and returns the data shown earlier in Table 4.5. This table is called the (task-relevant) **initial working relation**. It is the data on which induction will be performed. Note that each tuple is, in fact, a conjunction of attribute–value pairs. Hence, we can think of a tuple within a relation as a rule of conjuncts, and of induction on the relation as the generalization of these rules. ∎

"*Now that the data are ready for attribute-oriented induction, how is attribute-oriented induction performed?*" The essential operation of attribute-oriented induction is *data generalization*, which can be performed in either of two ways on the initial working relation: *attribute removal* and *attribute generalization*.

Attribute removal is based on the following rule: *If there is a large set of distinct values for an attribute of the initial working relation, but either (case 1) there is no generalization operator on the attribute (e.g., there is no concept hierarchy defined for the attribute), or (case 2) its higher-level concepts are expressed in terms of other attributes, then the attribute should be removed from the working relation.*

Let's examine the reasoning behind this rule. An attribute–value pair represents a conjunct in a generalized tuple, or rule. The removal of a conjunct eliminates a constraint and thus generalizes the rule. If, as in case 1, there is a large set of distinct values for an attribute but there is no generalization operator for it, the attribute should be removed because it cannot be generalized. Preserving it would imply keeping a large number of disjuncts, which contradicts the goal of generating concise rules. On the other hand, consider case 2, where the attribute's higher-level concepts are expressed in terms of other attributes. For example, suppose that the attribute in question is *street*, with higher-level concepts that are represented by the attributes ⟨*city, province_or_state, country*⟩. The removal of *street* is equivalent to the application of a generalization operator. This rule corresponds to the generalization rule known as *dropping condition* in the machine learning literature on *learning from examples*.

Attribute generalization is based on the following rule: *If there is a large set of distinct values for an attribute in the initial working relation, and there exists a set of generalization operators on the attribute, then a generalization operator should be selected and applied* *to the attribute.* This rule is based on the following reasoning. Use of a generalization operator to generalize an attribute value within a tuple, or rule, in the working relation will make the rule cover more of the original data tuples, thus generalizing the concept it represents. This corresponds to the generalization rule known as *climbing generalization trees* in *learning from examples,* or *concept tree ascension.*

Both rules–*attribute removal* and *attribute generalization*–claim that if there is a *large* set of distinct values for an attribute, further generalization should be applied. This raises the question: How large is *"a large set of distinct values for an attribute"* considered to be?

Depending on the attributes or application involved, a user may prefer some attributes to remain at a rather low abstraction level while others are generalized to higher levels. The control of how high an attribute should be generalized is typically quite subjective. The control of this process is called **attribute generalization control**. If the attribute is generalized "too high," it may lead to overgeneralization, and the resulting rules may not be very informative.

On the other hand, if the attribute is not generalized to a "sufficiently high level," then undergeneralization may result, where the rules obtained may not be informative either. Thus, a balance should be attained in attribute-oriented generalization. There are many possible ways to control a generalization process. We will describe two common approaches and illustrate how they work.

The first technique, called **attribute generalization threshold control**, either sets one generalization threshold for all of the attributes, or sets one threshold for each attribute. If the number of distinct values in an attribute is greater than the attribute threshold, further attribute removal or attribute generalization should be performed. Data mining systems typically have a default attribute threshold value generally ranging from 2 to 8 and should allow experts and users to modify the threshold values as well. If a user feels that the generalization reaches too high a level for a particular attribute, the threshold can be increased. This corresponds to drilling down along the attribute. Also, to further generalize a relation, the user can reduce an attribute's threshold, which corresponds to rolling up along the attribute.

The second technique, called **generalized relation threshold control**, sets a threshold for the generalized relation. If the number of (distinct) tuples in the generalized relation is greater than the threshold, further generalization should be performed. Otherwise, no further generalization should be performed. Such a threshold may also be preset in the data mining system (usually within a range of 10 to 30), or set by an expert or user, and should be adjustable. For example, if a user feels that the generalized relation is too small, he or she can increase the threshold, which implies drilling down. Otherwise, to further generalize a relation, the threshold can be reduced, which implies rolling up.

These two techniques can be applied in sequence: First apply the attribute threshold control technique to generalize each attribute, and then apply relation threshold control to further reduce the size of the generalized relation. No matter which generalization control technique is applied, the user should be allowed to adjust the generalization thresholds in order to obtain interesting concept descriptions.

In many database-oriented induction processes, users are interested in obtaining quantitative or statistical information about the data at different abstraction levels.

Thus, it is important to accumulate count and other aggregate values in the induction process. Conceptually, this is performed as follows. The aggregate function, count(), is associated with each database tuple. Its value for each tuple in the initial working relation is initialized to 1. Through attribute removal and attribute generalization, tuples within the initial working relation may be generalized, resulting in groups of *identical tuples*. In this case, all of the identical tuples forming a group should be merged into one tuple.

The count of this new, generalized tuple is set to the total number of tuples from the initial working relation that are represented by (i.e., merged into) the new generalized tuple. For example, suppose that by attribute-oriented induction, 52 data tuples from the initial working relation are all generalized to the same tuple, T. That is, the generalization of these 52 tuples resulted in 52 identical instances of tuple T. These 52 identical tuples are merged to form one instance of T, with a count that is set to 52. Other popular aggregate functions that could also be associated with each tuple include sum() and avg(). For a given generalized tuple, sum() contains the sum of the values of a given numeric attribute for the initial working relation tuples making up the generalized tuple. Suppose that tuple T contained sum(*units_sold*) as an aggregate function. The sum value for tuple T would then be set to the total number of units sold for each of the 52 tuples. The aggregate avg() (average) is computed according to the formula avg() = sum()/count().

Example 4.12 **Attribute-oriented induction.** Here we show how attribute-oriented induction is performed on the initial working relation of Table 4.5. For each attribute of the relation, the generalization proceeds as follows:

1. *name:* Since there are a large number of distinct values for *name* and there is no generalization operation defined on it, this attribute is removed.

2. *gender:* Since there are only two distinct values for *gender*, this attribute is retained and no generalization is performed on it.

3. *major:* Suppose that a concept hierarchy has been defined that allows the attribute *major* to be generalized to the values {arts&sciences, engineering, business}. Suppose also that the attribute generalization threshold is set to 5, and that there are more than 20 distinct values for *major* in the initial working relation. By attribute generalization and attribute generalization control, *major* is therefore generalized by climbing the given concept hierarchy.

4. *birth_place:* This attribute has a large number of distinct values; therefore, we would like to generalize it. Suppose that a concept hierarchy exists for *birth_place*, defined as "*city < province_or_state < country*." If the number of distinct values for *country* in the initial working relation is greater than the attribute generalization threshold, then *birth_place* should be removed, because even though a generalization operator exists for it, the generalization threshold would not be satisfied. If, instead, the number of distinct values for *country* is less than the attribute generalization threshold, then *birth_place* should be generalized to *birth_country*.

5. *birth_date:* Suppose that a hierarchy exists that can generalize *birth_date* to *age* and *age* to *age_range*, and that the number of age ranges (or intervals) is small with

Table 4.6 Generalized Relation Obtained by Attribute-Oriented Induction on Table 4.5's Data

gender	major	birth_country	age_range	residence_city	gpa	count
M	Science	Canada	20 – 25	Richmond	very_good	16
F	Science	Foreign	25 – 30	Burnaby	excellent	22
...	...	...	...	...	...	...

respect to the attribute generalization threshold. Generalization of *birth_date* should therefore take place.

6. *residence:* Suppose that *residence* is defined by the attributes *number, street, residence_city, residence_province_or_state,* and *residence_country*. The number of distinct values for *number* and *street* will likely be very high, since these concepts are quite low level. The attributes *number* and *street* should therefore be removed so that *residence* is then generalized to *residence_city*, which contains fewer distinct values.

7. *phone#:* As with the *name* attribute, *phone#* contains too many distinct values and should therefore be removed in generalization.

8. *gpa:* Suppose that a concept hierarchy exists for *gpa* that groups values for grade point average into numeric intervals like {3.75–4.0, 3.5–3.75, ... }, which in turn are grouped into descriptive values such as {"excellent", "very_good", ... }. The attribute can therefore be generalized.

The generalization process will result in groups of identical tuples. For example, the first two tuples of Table 4.5 both generalize to the same identical tuple (namely, the first tuple shown in Table 4.6). Such identical tuples are then merged into one, with their counts accumulated. This process leads to the generalized relation shown in Table 4.6.

Based on the vocabulary used in OLAP, we may view count() as a *measure*, and the remaining attributes as *dimensions*. Note that aggregate functions, such as sum(), may be applied to numeric attributes (e.g., *salary* and *sales*). These attributes are referred to as *measure attributes*. ∎

4.5.2 Efficient Implementation of Attribute-Oriented Induction

"How is attribute-oriented induction actually implemented?" Section 4.5.1 provided an introduction to attribute-oriented induction. The general procedure is summarized in Figure 4.18. The efficiency of this algorithm is analyzed as follows:

- Step 1 of the algorithm is essentially a relational query to collect the task-relevant data into the **working relation**, *W*. Its processing efficiency depends on the query processing methods used. Given the successful implementation and commercialization of database systems, this step is expected to have good performance.

- Step 2 collects statistics on the working relation. This requires scanning the relation at most once. The cost for computing the minimum desired level and determining the mapping pairs, (v, v'), for each attribute is dependent on the number of distinct

Algorithm: Attribute-oriented induction. Mining generalized characteristics in a relational database given a user's data mining request.

Input:

- *DB*, a relational database;
- *DMQuery*, a data mining query;
- *a_list*, a list of attributes (containing attributes, a_i);
- *Gen*(a_i), a set of concept hierarchies or generalization operators on attributes, a_i;
- *a_gen_thresh*(a_i), attribute generalization thresholds for each a_i.

Output: *P*, a *Prime_generalized_relation*.

Method:

1. $W \leftarrow$ get_task_relevant_data (*DMQuery*, *DB*); // Let *W*, the working relation, hold the task-relevant data.

2. prepare_for_generalization (*W*); // This is implemented as follows.

   (a) Scan *W* and collect the distinct values for each attribute, a_i. (*Note:* If *W* is very large, this may be done by examining a sample of *W*.)

   (b) For each attribute a_i, determine whether a_i should be removed. If not, compute its minimum desired level L_i based on its given or default attribute threshold, and determine the mapping pairs (v, v'), where v is a distinct value of a_i in *W*, and v' is its corresponding generalized value at level L_i.

3. $P \leftarrow$ generalization (*W*),

   The *Prime_generalized_relation*, *P*, is derived by replacing each value v in *W* by its corresponding v' in the mapping while accumulating count and computing any other aggregate values.

   This step can be implemented efficiently using either of the two following variations:

   (a) For each generalized tuple, insert the tuple into a sorted prime relation *P* by a binary search: if the tuple is already in *P*, simply increase its count and other aggregate values accordingly; otherwise, insert it into *P*.

   (b) Since in most cases the number of distinct values at the prime relation level is small, the prime relation can be coded as an *m*-dimensional array, where *m* is the number of attributes in *P*, and each dimension contains the corresponding generalized attribute values. Each array element holds the corresponding count and other aggregation values, if any. The insertion of a generalized tuple is performed by measure aggregation in the corresponding array element.

Figure 4.18 Basic algorithm for attribute-oriented induction.

values for each attribute and is smaller than $|W|$, the number of tuples in the working relation. Notice that it may not be necessary to scan the working relation once, since if the working relation is large, a sample of such a relation will be sufficient to get statistics and determine which attributes should be generalized to a certain high level and which attributes should be removed. Moreover, such statistics may also be obtained in the process of extracting and generating a working relation in Step 1.

▪ Step 3 derives the **prime relation**, P. This is performed by scanning each tuple in the working relation and inserting generalized tuples into P. There are a total of $|W|$ tuples in W and p tuples in P. For each tuple, t, in W, we substitute its attribute values based on the derived mapping pairs. This results in a generalized tuple, t'. If variation (a) in Figure 4.18 is adopted, each t' takes $O(\log p)$ to find the location for the count increment or tuple insertion. Thus, the total time complexity is $O(|W| \times \log p)$ for all of the generalized tuples. If variation (b) is adopted, each t' takes $O(1)$ to find the tuple for the count increment. Thus, the overall time complexity is $O(N)$ for all of the generalized tuples.

Many data analysis tasks need to examine a good number of dimensions or attributes. This may involve *dynamically* introducing and testing additional attributes rather than just those specified in the mining query. Moreover, a user with little knowledge of the *truly* relevant data set may simply specify "in relevance to *" in the mining query, which includes all of the attributes in the analysis. Therefore, an advanced–concept description mining process needs to perform attribute relevance analysis on large sets of attributes to select the most relevant ones. This analysis may employ correlation measures or tests of statistical significance, as described in Chapter 3 on data preprocessing.

Example 4.13 **Presentation of generalization results.** Suppose that attribute-oriented induction was performed on a *sales* relation of the *AllElectronics* database, resulting in the generalized description of Table 4.7 for sales last year. The description is shown in the form of a generalized relation. Table 4.6 is another generalized relation example.

Such generalized relations can also be presented in the form of cross-tabulation forms, various kinds of graphic presentation (e.g., pie charts and bar charts), and quantitative characteristics rules (i.e., showing how different value combinations are distributed in the generalized relation). ▪

Table 4.7 Generalized Relation for Last Year's Sales

location	item	sales (in million dollars)	count (in thousands)
Asia	TV	15	300
Europe	TV	12	250
North America	TV	28	450
Asia	computer	120	1000
Europe	computer	150	1200
North America	computer	200	1800

4.5.3 **Attribute-Oriented Induction for Class Comparisons**

In many applications, users may not be interested in having a single class (or concept) described or characterized, but prefer to mine a description that compares or distinguishes one class (or concept) from other comparable classes (or concepts). Class discrimination or comparison (hereafter referred to as **class comparison**) mines descriptions that distinguish a target class from its contrasting classes. Notice that the target and contrasting classes must be *comparable* in the sense that they share similar dimensions and attributes. For example, the three classes *person*, *address*, and *item* are not comparable. However, sales in the last three years are comparable classes, and so are, for example, computer science students versus physics students.

Our discussions on class characterization in the previous sections handle multilevel data summarization and characterization in a single class. The techniques developed can be extended to handle class comparison across several comparable classes. For example, the attribute generalization process described for class characterization can be modified so that the generalization is performed *synchronously* among all the classes compared. This allows the attributes in all of the classes to be generalized to the *same* abstraction levels.

Suppose, for instance, that we are given the *AllElectronics* data for sales in 2009 and in 2010 and want to compare these two classes. Consider the dimension *location* with abstractions at the *city*, *province_or_state*, and *country* levels. Data in each class should be generalized to the same *location* level. That is, they are all synchronously generalized to either the *city* level, the *province_or_state* level, or the *country* level. Ideally, this is more useful than comparing, say, the sales in Vancouver in 2009 with the sales in the United States in 2010 (i.e., where each set of sales data is generalized to a different level). The users, however, should have the option to overwrite such an automated, synchronous comparison with their own choices, when preferred.

"How is class comparison performed?" In general, the procedure is as follows:

1. **Data collection**: The set of relevant data in the database is collected by query processing and is partitioned respectively into a *target class* and one or a set of *contrasting classes*.

2. **Dimension relevance analysis**: If there are many dimensions, then dimension relevance analysis should be performed on these classes to select only the highly relevant dimensions for further analysis. Correlation or entropy-based measures can be used for this step (Chapter 3).

3. **Synchronous generalization**: Generalization is performed on the target class to the level controlled by a user- or expert-specified dimension threshold, which results in a **prime target class relation**. The concepts in the contrasting class(es) are generalized to the same level as those in the prime target class relation, forming the **prime contrasting class(es) relation**.

4. **Presentation of the derived comparison**: The resulting class comparison description can be visualized in the form of tables, graphs, and rules. This presentation usually includes a "contrasting" measure such as count% (percentage count) that reflects the

comparison between the target and contrasting classes. The user can adjust the comparison description by applying drill-down, roll-up, and other OLAP operations to the target and contrasting classes, as desired.

The preceding discussion outlines a general algorithm for mining comparisons in databases. In comparison with characterization, the previous algorithm involves synchronous generalization of the target class with the contrasting classes, so that classes are simultaneously compared at the same abstraction levels.

Example 4.14 mines a class comparison describing the graduate and undergraduate students at *Big University*.

Example 4.14 Mining a class comparison. Suppose that you would like to compare the general properties of the graduate and undergraduate students at *Big_University*, given the attributes *name, gender, major, birth_place, birth_date, residence, phone#,* and *gpa*.

This data mining task can be expressed in DMQL as follows:

```
use Big_University_DB
mine comparison as "grad_vs_undergrad_students"
in relevance to name, gender, major, birth_place, birth_date, residence,
      phone#, gpa
for "graduate_students"
where status in "graduate"
versus "undergraduate_students"
where status in "undergraduate"
analyze count%
from student
```

Let's see how this typical example of a data mining query for mining comparison descriptions can be processed.

First, the query is transformed into two relational queries that collect two sets of task-relevant data: one for the *initial target-class working relation* and the other for the *initial contrasting-class working relation*, as shown in Tables 4.8 and 4.9. This can also be viewed as the construction of a data cube, where the status {graduate, undergraduate} serves as one dimension, and the other attributes form the remaining dimensions.

Second, dimension relevance analysis can be performed, when necessary, on the two classes of data. After this analysis, irrelevant or weakly relevant dimensions (e.g., *name, gender, birth_place, residence,* and *phone#*) are removed from the resulting classes. Only the highly relevant attributes are included in the subsequent analysis.

Third, synchronous generalization is performed on the target class to the levels controlled by user- or expert-specified dimension thresholds, forming the *prime target class relation*. The contrasting class is generalized to the same levels as those in the prime target class relation, forming the *prime contrasting class(es) relation*, as presented in Tables 4.10 and 4.11. In comparison with undergraduate students, graduate students tend to be older and have a higher GPA in general.

Table 4.8 Initial Working Relations: The Target Class (Graduate Students)

name	gender	major	birth_place	birth_date	residence	phone#	gpa
Jim Woodman	M	CS	Vancouver, BC, Canada	12-8-76	3511 Main St., Richmond	687-4598	3.67
Scott Lachance	M	CS	Montreal, Que, Canada	7-28-75	345 1st Ave., Vancouver	253-9106	3.70
Laura Lee	F	Physics	Seattle, WA, USA	8-25-70	125 Austin Ave., Burnaby	420-5232	3.83
…	…	…	…	…	…	…	…

Table 4.9 Initial Working Relations: The Contrasting Class (Undergraduate Students)

name	gender	major	birth_place	birth_date	residence	phone#	gpa
Bob Schumann	M	Chemistry	Calgary, Alt, Canada	1-10-78	2642 Halifax St., Burnaby	294-4291	2.96
Amy Eau	F	Biology	Golden, BC, Canada	3-30-76	463 Sunset Cres., Vancouver	681-5417	3.52
…	…	…	…	…	…	…	…

Table 4.10 Prime Generalized Relation for the Target Class (Graduate Students)

major	age_range	gpa	count%
Science	21...25	good	5.53
Science	26...30	good	5.02
Science	over_30	very good	5.86
…	…	…	…
Business	over_30	excellent	4.68

Table 4.11 Prime Generalized Relation for the Contrasting Class (Undergraduate Students)

major	age_range	gpa	count%
Science	16...20	fair	5.53
Science	16...20	good	4.53
…	…	…	…
Science	26...30	good	2.32
…	…	…	…
Business	over_30	excellent	0.68

Finally, the resulting class comparison is presented in the form of tables, graphs, and/or rules. This visualization includes a contrasting measure (e.g., count%) that compares the target class and the contrasting class. For example, 5.02% of the graduate students majoring in science are between 26 and 30 years old and have a "good" GPA, while only 2.32% of undergraduates have these same characteristics. Drilling and other

OLAP operations may be performed on the target and contrasting classes as deemed necessary by the user in order to adjust the abstraction levels of the final description. ∎

In summary, attribute-oriented induction for data characterization and generalization provides an alternative data generalization method in comparison to the data cube approach. It is not confined to relational data because such an induction can be performed on spatial, multimedia, sequence, and other kinds of data sets. In addition, there is no need to precompute a data cube because generalization can be performed online upon receiving a user's query.

Moreover, automated analysis can be added to such an induction process to automatically filter out irrelevant or unimportant attributes. However, because attribute-oriented induction automatically generalizes data to a higher level, it cannot efficiently support the process of drilling down to levels deeper than those provided in the generalized relation. The integration of data cube technology with attribute-oriented induction may provide a balance between precomputation and online computation. This would also support fast online computation when it is necessary to drill down to a level deeper than that provided in the generalized relation.

4.6 Summary

- A **data warehouse** is a *subject-oriented, integrated, time-variant,* and *nonvolatile* data collection organized in support of management decision making. Several factors distinguish data warehouses from operational databases. Because the two systems provide quite different functionalities and require different kinds of data, it is necessary to maintain data warehouses separately from operational databases.

- Data warehouses often adopt a **three-tier architecture**. The bottom tier is a *warehouse database server*, which is typically a relational database system. The middle tier is an *OLAP server*, and the top tier is a *client* that contains query and reporting tools.

- A data warehouse contains **back-end tools and utilities** for populating and refreshing the warehouse. These cover data extraction, data cleaning, data transformation, loading, refreshing, and warehouse management.

- Data warehouse **metadata** are data defining the warehouse objects. A metadata repository provides details regarding the warehouse structure, data history, the algorithms used for summarization, mappings from the source data to the warehouse form, system performance, and business terms and issues.

- A **multidimensional data model** is typically used for the design of corporate *data warehouses* and *departmental data marts*. Such a model can adopt a *star schema, snowflake schema,* or *fact constellation schema*. The core of the *multidimensional model* is the **data cube**, which consists of a large set of *facts* (or *measures*) and a number of *dimensions*. Dimensions are the entities or perspectives with respect to which an organization wants to keep records and are hierarchical in nature.

▪ A data cube consists of a **lattice of cuboids**, each corresponding to a different degree of summarization of the given multidimensional data.

▪ **Concept hierarchies** organize the values of attributes or dimensions into gradual abstraction levels. They are useful in mining at multiple abstraction levels.

▪ **Online analytical processing** can be performed in data warehouses/marts using the multidimensional data model. Typical OLAP operations include *roll-up*, and *drill-*(*down, across, through*), *slice-and-dice*, and *pivot* (*rotate*), as well as statistical operations such as ranking and computing moving averages and growth rates. OLAP operations can be implemented efficiently using the data cube structure.

▪ Data warehouses are used for *information processing* (querying and reporting), *analytical processing* (which allows users to navigate through summarized and detailed data by OLAP operations), and *data mining* (which supports knowledge discovery). OLAP-based data mining is referred to as **multidimensional data mining** (also known as exploratory multidimensional data mining, online analytical mining, or OLAM). It emphasizes the interactive and exploratory nature of data mining.

▪ OLAP servers may adopt a **relational OLAP (ROLAP)**, a **multidimensional OLAP (MOLAP)**, or a **hybrid OLAP (HOLAP)** implementation. A ROLAP server uses an extended relational DBMS that maps OLAP operations on multidimensional data to standard relational operations. A MOLAP server maps multidimensional data views directly to array structures. A HOLAP server combines ROLAP and MOLAP. For example, it may use ROLAP for historic data while maintaining frequently accessed data in a separate MOLAP store.

▪ **Full materialization** refers to the computation of all of the cuboids in the lattice defining a data cube. It typically requires an excessive amount of storage space, particularly as the number of dimensions and size of associated concept hierarchies grow. This problem is known as the **curse of dimensionality**. Alternatively, **partial materialization** is the selective computation of a subset of the cuboids or subcubes in the lattice. For example, an **iceberg cube** is a data cube that stores only those cube cells that have an aggregate value (e.g., count) above some minimum support threshold.

▪ OLAP query processing can be made more efficient with the use of indexing techniques. In **bitmap indexing**, each attribute has its own bitmap index table. Bitmap indexing reduces join, aggregation, and comparison operations to bit arithmetic. **Join indexing** registers the joinable rows of two or more relations from a relational database, reducing the overall cost of OLAP join operations. **Bitmapped join indexing**, which combines the bitmap and join index methods, can be used to further speed up OLAP query processing.

▪ **Data generalization** is a process that abstracts a large set of task-relevant data in a database from a relatively low conceptual level to higher conceptual levels. Data generalization approaches include data cube-based data aggregation and attribute-oriented induction. **Concept description** is the most basic form of descriptive data mining. It describes a given set of task-relevant data in a concise and summarative manner, presenting interesting general properties of the data. Concept (or class) description consists of **characterization** and **comparison** (or **discrimination**). The former summarizes and describes a data collection, called the **target class**, whereas the latter summarizes and distinguishes one data collection, called the **target class**, from other data collection(s), collectively called the **contrasting class(es)**.

- **Concept characterization** can be implemented using **data cube (OLAP-based) approaches** and the **attribute-oriented induction approach**. These are attribute- or dimension-based generalization approaches. The **attribute-oriented induction approach** consists of the following techniques: *data focusing, data generalization by attribute removal or attribute generalization, count and aggregate value accumulation, attribute generalization control,* and *generalization data visualization.*

- **Concept comparison** can be performed using the attribute-oriented induction or data cube approaches in a manner similar to concept characterization. Generalized tuples from the target and contrasting classes can be quantitatively compared and contrasted.

4.7 Exercises

4.1 State why, for the integration of multiple heterogeneous information sources, many companies in industry prefer the *update-driven approach* (which constructs and uses data warehouses), rather than the *query-driven approach* (which applies wrappers and integrators). Describe situations where the query-driven approach is preferable to the update-driven approach.

4.2 Briefly compare the following concepts. You may use an example to explain your point(s).

(a) Snowflake schema, fact constellation, starnet query model

(b) Data cleaning, data transformation, refresh

(c) Discovery-driven cube, multifeature cube, virtual warehouse

4.3 Suppose that a data warehouse consists of the three dimensions *time, doctor,* and *patient,* and the two measures *count* and *charge,* where *charge* is the fee that a doctor charges a patient for a visit.

(a) Enumerate three classes of schemas that are popularly used for modeling data warehouses.

(b) Draw a schema diagram for the above data warehouse using one of the schema classes listed in (a).

(c) Starting with the base cuboid [*day, doctor, patient*], what specific *OLAP operations* should be performed in order to list the total fee collected by each doctor in 2010?

(d) To obtain the same list, write an SQL query assuming the data are stored in a relational database with the schema *fee* (*day, month, year, doctor, hospital, patient, count, charge*).

4.4 Suppose that a data warehouse for *Big_University* consists of the four dimensions *student, course, semester,* and *instructor*, and two measures *count* and *avg_grade*. At the lowest conceptual level (e.g., for a given student, course, semester, and instructor combination), the *avg_grade* measure stores the actual course grade of the student. At higher conceptual levels, *avg_grade* stores the average grade for the given combination.

(a) Draw a *snowflake schema* diagram for the data warehouse.

(b) Starting with the base cuboid [*student, course, semester, instructor*], what specific *OLAP operations* (e.g., roll-up from *semester* to *year*) should you perform in order to list the average grade of *CS* courses for each *Big_University* student.

(c) If each dimension has five levels (including all), such as "*student < major < status < university < all*", how many cuboids will this cube contain (including the base and apex cuboids)?

4.5 Suppose that a data warehouse consists of the four dimensions *date, spectator, location,* and *game*, and the two measures *count* and *charge*, where *charge* is the fare that a spectator pays when watching a game on a given date. Spectators may be students, adults, or seniors, with each category having its own charge rate.

(a) Draw a *star schema* diagram for the data warehouse.

(b) Starting with the base cuboid [*date, spectator, location, game*], what specific *OLAP operations* should you perform in order to list the total charge paid by student spectators at *GM_Place* in 2010?

(c) *Bitmap indexing* is useful in data warehousing. Taking this cube as an example, briefly discuss advantages and problems of using a bitmap index structure.

4.6 A data warehouse can be modeled by either a *star schema* or a *snowflake schema*. Briefly describe the similarities and the differences of the two models, and then analyze their advantages and disadvantages with regard to one another. Give your opinion of which might be more empirically useful and state the reasons behind your answer.

4.7 Design a data warehouse for a regional weather bureau. The weather bureau has about 1000 probes, which are scattered throughout various land and ocean locations in the region to collect basic weather data, including air pressure, temperature, and precipitation at each hour. All data are sent to the central station, which has collected such data for more than 10 years. Your design should facilitate efficient querying and online analytical processing, and derive general weather patterns in multidimensional space.

4.8 A popular data warehouse implementation is to construct a multidimensional database, known as a data cube. Unfortunately, this may often generate a huge, yet very sparse, multidimensional matrix.

    (a) Present an example illustrating such a huge and sparse data cube.

    (b) Design an implementation method that can elegantly overcome this sparse matrix problem. Note that you need to explain your data structures in detail and discuss the space needed, as well as how to retrieve data from your structures.

    (c) Modify your design in (b) to handle *incremental data updates*. Give the reasoning behind your new design.

4.9 Regarding the *computation of measures* in a data cube:

    (a) Enumerate three categories of measures, based on the kind of aggregate functions used in computing a data cube.

    (b) For a data cube with the three dimensions *time, location,* and *item,* which category does the function *variance* belong to? Describe how to compute it if the cube is partitioned into many chunks.

    Hint: The formula for computing *variance* is $\frac{1}{N}\sum_{i=1}^{N}(x_i - \bar{x}_i)^2$, where $\bar{x}_i$ is the average of x_is.

    (c) Suppose the function is "*top 10 sales.*" Discuss how to efficiently compute this measure in a data cube.

4.10 Suppose a company wants to design a data warehouse to facilitate the analysis of moving vehicles in an online analytical processing manner. The company registers huge amounts of auto movement data in the format of (*Auto_ID, location, speed, time*). Each *Auto_ID* represents a vehicle associated with information (e.g., *vehicle_category, driver_category*), and each location may be associated with a street in a city. Assume that a street map is available for the city.

    (a) Design such a data warehouse to facilitate effective online analytical processing in multidimensional space.

    (b) The movement data may contain noise. Discuss how you would develop a method to automatically discover data records that were likely erroneously registered in the data repository.

    (c) The movement data may be sparse. Discuss how you would develop a method that constructs a reliable data warehouse despite the sparsity of data.

    (d) If you want to drive from A to B starting at a particular time, discuss how a system may use the data in this warehouse to work out a fast route.

4.11 Radio-frequency identification is commonly used to trace object movement and perform inventory control. An RFID reader can successfully read an RFID tag from a limited distance at any scheduled time. Suppose a company wants to design a data warehouse to facilitate the analysis of objects with RFID tags in an online analytical processing manner. The company registers huge amounts of RFID data in the format of (*RFID, at_location, time*), and also has some information about the objects carrying the RFID tag, for example, (*RFID, product_name, product_category, producer, date_produced, price*).

    (a) Design a data warehouse to facilitate effective registration and online analytical processing of such data.

(b) The RFID data may contain lots of redundant information. Discuss a method that maximally reduces redundancy during data registration in the RFID data warehouse.

(c) The RFID data may contain lots of noise such as missing registration and misread IDs. Discuss a method that effectively cleans up the noisy data in the RFID data warehouse.

(d) You may want to perform online analytical processing to determine how many TV sets were shipped from the LA seaport to BestBuy in Champaign, IL, by *month*, *brand*, and *price_range*. Outline how this could be done efficiently if you were to store such RFID data in the warehouse.

(e) If a customer returns a jug of milk and complains that is has spoiled before its expiration date, discuss how you can investigate such a case in the warehouse to find out what the problem is, either in shipping or in storage.

4.12 In many applications, new data sets are incrementally added to the existing large data sets. Thus, an important consideration is whether a measure can be computed efficiently in an incremental manner. Use *count, standard deviation*, and *median* as examples to show that a distributive or algebraic measure facilitates efficient incremental computation, whereas a holistic measure does not.

4.13 Suppose that we need to record three measures in a data cube: min(), average(), and median(). Design an efficient computation and storage method for each measure given that the cube allows data to be *deleted incrementally* (i.e., in small portions at a time) from the cube.

4.14 In data warehouse technology, a multiple dimensional view can be implemented by a relational database technique (*ROLAP*), by a multidimensional database technique (*MOLAP*), or by a hybrid database technique (*HOLAP*).

(a) Briefly describe each implementation technique.

(b) For each technique, explain how each of the following functions may be implemented:
   i. The generation of a data warehouse (including aggregation)

   ii. Roll-up

   iii. Drill-down

   iv. Incremental updating

(c) Which implementation techniques do you prefer, and why?

4.15 Suppose that a data warehouse contains 20 dimensions, each with about five levels of granularity.

(a) Users are mainly interested in four particular dimensions, each having three frequently accessed levels for rolling up and drilling down. How would you design a data cube structure to support this preference efficiently?

(b) At times, a user may want to *drill through* the cube to the raw data for one or two particular dimensions. How would you support this feature?

4.16 A data cube, *C*, has *n* dimensions, and each dimension has exactly *p* distinct values in the base cuboid. Assume that there are no concept hierarchies associated with the dimensions.

(a) What is the *maximum number of cells* possible in the base cuboid?

(b) What is the *minimum number of cells* possible in the base cuboid?

(c) What is the *maximum number of cells* possible (including both base cells and aggregate cells) in the *C* data cube?

(d) What is the *minimum number of cells* possible in *C*?

4.17 What are the differences between the three main types of data warehouse usage: *information processing, analytical processing,* and *data mining*? Discuss the motivation behind *OLAP mining (OLAM)*.

4.8 Bibliographic Notes

There are a good number of introductory-level textbooks on data warehousing and OLAP technology—for example, Kimball, Ross, Thornthwaite, et al. [KRTM08]; Imhoff, Galemmo, and Geiger [IGG03]; and Inmon [Inm96]. Chaudhuri and Dayal [CD97] provide an early overview of data warehousing and OLAP technology. A set of research papers on materialized views and data warehouse implementations were collected in *Materialized Views: Techniques, Implementations, and Applications* by Gupta and Mumick [GM99].

The history of decision support systems can be traced back to the 1960s. However, the proposal to construct large data warehouses for multidimensional data analysis is credited to Codd [CCS93] who coined the term *OLAP* for *online analytical processing*. The OLAP Council was established in 1995. Widom [Wid95] identified several research problems in data warehousing. Kimball and Ross [KR02] provide an overview of the deficiencies of SQL regarding the ability to support comparisons that are common in the business world, and present a good set of application cases that require data warehousing and OLAP technology. For an overview of OLAP systems versus statistical databases, see Shoshani [Sho97].

Gray et al. [GCB+97] proposed the data cube as a relational aggregation operator generalizing group-by, crosstabs, and subtotals. Harinarayan, Rajaraman, and Ullman [HRU96] proposed a greedy algorithm for the partial materialization of cuboids in the computation of a data cube. Data cube computation methods have been investigated by numerous studies such as Sarawagi and Stonebraker [SS94]; Agarwal et al. [AAD+96]; Zhao, Deshpande, and Naughton [ZDN97]; Ross and Srivastava [RS97]; Beyer and Ramakrishnan [BR99]; Han, Pei, Dong, and Wang [HPDW01]; and Xin, Han, Li, and Wah [XHLW03]. These methods are discussed in depth in Chapter 5.

The concept of iceberg queries was first introduced in Fang, Shivakumar, Garcia-Molina et al. [FSGM+98]. The use of join indices to speed up relational query processing was proposed by Valduriez [Val87]. O'Neil and Graefe [OG95] proposed a bitmapped join index method to speed up OLAP-based query processing. A discussion of the performance of bitmapping and other nontraditional index techniques is given in O'Neil and Quass [OQ97].

For work regarding the selection of materialized cuboids for efficient OLAP query processing, see, for example, Chaudhuri and Dayal [CD97]; Harinarayan, Rajaraman, and Ullman [HRU96]; and Sristava et al. [SDJL96]. Methods for cube size estimation can be found in Deshpande et al. [DNR$^+$97], Ross and Srivastava [RS97], and Beyer and Ramakrishnan [BR99]. Agrawal, Gupta, and Sarawagi [AGS97] proposed operations for modeling multidimensional databases. Methods for answering queries quickly by online aggregation are described in Hellerstein, Haas, and Wang [HHW97] and Hellerstein et al. [HAC$^+$99]. Techniques for estimating the top N queries are proposed in Carey and Kossman [CK98] and Donjerkovic and Ramakrishnan [DR99]. Further studies on intelligent OLAP and discovery-driven exploration of data cubes are presented in the bibliographic notes in Chapter 5.

Data Cube Technology 5

Data warehouse systems provide online analytical processing (OLAP) tools for interactive analysis of multidimensional data at varied granularity levels. OLAP tools typically use the *data cube* and a multidimensional data model to provide flexible access to summarized data. For example, a data cube can store precomputed measures (like count() and total_sales()) for multiple combinations of data dimensions (like *item*, *region*, and *customer*). Users can pose OLAP queries on the data. They can also interactively explore the data in a multidimensional way through OLAP operations like *drill-down* (to see more specialized data such as total sales per city) or *roll-up* (to see the data at a more generalized level such as total sales per country).

Although the data cube concept was originally intended for OLAP, it is also useful for data mining. **Multidimensional data mining** is an approach to data mining that integrates OLAP-based data analysis with knowledge discovery techniques. It is also known as *exploratory multidimensional data mining* and *online analytical mining* (*OLAM*). It searches for interesting patterns by exploring the data in multidimensional space. This gives users the freedom to dynamically focus on any subset of interesting dimensions. Users can interactively drill down or roll up to varying abstraction levels to find classification models, clusters, predictive rules, and outliers.

This chapter focuses on data cube technology. In particular, we study methods for data cube computation and methods for multidimensional data analysis. Precomputing a data cube (or parts of a data cube) allows for fast accessing of summarized data. Given the high dimensionality of most data, multidimensional analysis can run into performance bottlenecks. Therefore, it is important to study data cube computation techniques. Luckily, data cube technology provides many effective and scalable methods for cube computation. Studying these methods will also help in our understanding and further development of scalable methods for other data mining tasks such as the discovery of frequent patterns (Chapters 6 and 7).

We begin in Section 5.1 with preliminary concepts for cube computation. These summarize the data cube notion as a lattice of cuboids, and describe basic forms of cube materialization. General strategies for cube computation are given. Section 5.2 follows with an in-depth look at specific methods for data cube computation. We study both *full materialization* (i.e., where all the cuboids representing a data cube are precomputed and thereby ready for use) and *partial cuboid materialization* (where, say, only the more "useful" parts of the data cube are precomputed). The *multiway array aggregation* method is detailed for full cube computation. Methods for partial cube computation, including *BUC*, *Star-Cubing*, and the use of *cube shell fragments*, are discussed.

In Section 5.3, we study cube-based query processing. The techniques described build on the standard methods of cube computation presented in Section 5.2. You will learn about *sampling cubes* for OLAP query answering on sampling data (e.g., survey data, which represent a sample or subset of a target data population of interest). In addition, you will learn how to compute *ranking cubes* for efficient top-k (ranking) query processing in large relational data sets.

In Section 5.4, we describe various ways to perform multidimensional data analysis using data cubes. *Prediction cubes* are introduced, which facilitate predictive modeling in multidimensional space. We discuss *multifeature cubes*, which compute complex queries involving multiple dependent aggregates at multiple granularities. You will also learn about the *exception-based discovery-driven exploration* of cube space, where visual cues are displayed to indicate discovered data exceptions at all aggregation levels, thereby guiding the user in the data analysis process.

5.1 Data Cube Computation: Preliminary Concepts

Data cubes facilitate the online analytical processing of multidimensional data. *"But how can we compute data cubes in advance, so that they are handy and readily available for query processing?"* This section contrasts full cube materialization (i.e., precomputation) versus various strategies for partial cube materialization. For completeness, we begin with a review of the basic terminology involving data cubes. We also introduce a cube cell notation that is useful for describing data cube computation methods.

5.1.1 Cube Materialization: Full Cube, Iceberg Cube, Closed Cube, and Cube Shell

Figure 5.1 shows a 3-D data cube for the dimensions A, B, and C, and an aggregate measure, M. Commonly used measures include count(), sum(), min(), max(), and total_sales(). A data cube is a lattice of cuboids. Each cuboid represents a group-by. ABC is the base cuboid, containing all three of the dimensions. Here, the aggregate measure, M, is computed for each possible combination of the three dimensions. The base cuboid is the least generalized of all the cuboids in the data cube. The most generalized cuboid is the apex cuboid, commonly represented as all. It contains one value—it aggregates measure M for all the tuples stored in the base cuboid. To drill down in the data cube, we move from the apex cuboid downward in the lattice. To roll up, we move from the base cuboid upward. For the purposes of our discussion in this chapter, we will always use the term *data cube* to refer to a lattice of cuboids rather than an individual cuboid.

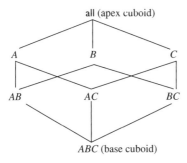

Figure 5.1 Lattice of cuboids making up a 3-D data cube with the dimensions A, B, and C for some aggregate measure, M.

A cell in the base cuboid is a **base cell**. A cell from a nonbase cuboid is an **aggregate cell**. An aggregate cell aggregates over one or more dimensions, where each aggregated dimension is indicated by a $*$ in the cell notation. Suppose we have an n-dimensional data cube. Let $a = (a_1, a_2, \ldots, a_n, measures)$ be a cell from one of the cuboids making up the data cube. We say that a is an m**-dimensional cell** (i.e., from an m-dimensional cuboid) if exactly m ($m \leq n$) values among $\{a_1, a_2, \ldots, a_n\}$ are *not* $*$. If $m = n$, then a is a base cell; otherwise, it is an aggregate cell (i.e., where $m < n$).

Example 5.1 **Base and aggregate cells.** Consider a data cube with the dimensions *month*, *city*, and *customer_group*, and the measure *sales*. (*Jan*, $*$, $*$, 2800) and ($*$, *Chicago*, $*$, 1200) are 1-D cells; (*Jan*, $*$, *Business*, 150) is a 2-D cell; and (*Jan*, *Chicago*, *Business*, 45) is a 3-D cell. Here, all base cells are 3-D, whereas 1-D and 2-D cells are aggregate cells. ∎

An ancestor–descendant relationship may exist between cells. In an n-dimensional data cube, an i-D cell $a = (a_1, a_2, \ldots, a_n, measures_a)$ is an **ancestor** of a j-D cell $b = (b_1, b_2, \ldots, b_n, measures_b)$, and b is a **descendant** of a, if and only if (1) $i < j$, and (2) for $1 \leq k \leq n$, $a_k = b_k$ whenever $a_k \neq *$. In particular, cell a is called a **parent** of cell b, and b is a **child** of a, if and only if $j = i + 1$.

Example 5.2 **Ancestor and descendant cells.** Referring to Example 5.1, 1-D cell $a = (Jan, *, *, 2800)$ and 2-D cell $b = (Jan, *, Business, 150)$ are *ancestors* of 3-D cell $c = (Jan, Chicago, Business, 45)$; c is a *descendant* of both a and b; b is a *parent* of c; and c is a *child* of b. ∎

To ensure fast OLAP, it is sometimes desirable to precompute the **full cube** (i.e., all the cells of all the cuboids for a given data cube). A method of full cube computation is given in Section 5.2.1. Full cube computation, however, is exponential to the number of dimensions. That is, a data cube of n dimensions contains 2^n cuboids. There are even more cuboids if we consider concept hierarchies for each dimension.[1] In addition, the size of each cuboid depends on the cardinality of its dimensions. Thus, precomputation of the full cube can require huge and often excessive amounts of memory.

Nonetheless, full cube computation algorithms are important. **Individual** cuboids may be stored on secondary storage and accessed when necessary. Alternatively, we can use such algorithms to compute smaller cubes, consisting of a subset of the given set of dimensions, or a smaller range of possible values for some of the dimensions. In these cases, the smaller cube is a full cube for the given subset of dimensions and/or dimension values. A thorough understanding of full cube computation methods will help us develop efficient methods for computing partial cubes. Hence, it is important to explore scalable methods for computing all the cuboids making up a data cube, that is, for full materialization. These methods must take into consideration the limited amount of main memory available for cuboid computation, the total size of the computed data cube, as well as the time required for such computation.

Partial materialization of data cubes offers an interesting trade-off between storage space and response time for OLAP. Instead of computing the full cube, we can compute only a subset of the data cube's cuboids, or subcubes consisting of subsets of cells from the various cuboids.

Many cells in a cuboid may actually be of little or no interest to the data analyst. Recall that each cell in a full cube records an aggregate value such as count or sum. For many cells in a cuboid, the measure value will be zero. When the product of the cardinalities for the dimensions in a cuboid is large relative to the number of nonzero-valued tuples that are stored in the cuboid, then we say that the cuboid is **sparse**. If a cube contains many sparse cuboids, we say that the cube is **sparse**.

In many cases, a substantial amount of the cube's space could be taken up by a large number of cells with very low measure values. This is because the cube cells are often quite sparsely distributed within a multidimensional space. For example, a customer may only buy a few items in a store at a time. Such an event will generate only a few nonempty cells, leaving most other cube cells empty. In such situations, it is useful to materialize only those cells in a cuboid (group-by) with a measure value above some minimum threshold. In a data cube for sales, say, we may wish to materialize only those cells for which *count $\geq$ 10* (i.e., where at least 10 tuples exist for the cell's given combination of dimensions), or only those cells representing *sales $\geq$ $100*. This not only saves processing time and disk space, but also leads to a more focused analysis. The cells that cannot pass the threshold are likely to be too trivial to warrant further analysis.

Such partially materialized cubes are known as **iceberg cubes**. The minimum threshold is called the **minimum support threshold**, or *minimum support (min_sup)*, for short. By materializing only a fraction of the cells in a data cube, the result is seen as the "tip of the iceberg," where the "iceberg" is the potential full cube including all cells. An iceberg cube can be specified with an SQL query, as shown in Example 5.3.

---

[1] Eq. (4.1) of Section 4.4.1 gives the total number of cuboids in a data cube where each dimension has an associated concept hierarchy.

Example 5.3 Iceberg cube.

> compute cube *sales_iceberg* as
> select *month, city, customer_group*, count(*)
> from *salesInfo*
> cube by *month, city, customer_group*
> having count(*) $>= min\_sup$

The **compute cube** statement specifies the precomputation of the iceberg cube, *sales_iceberg*, with the dimensions *month*, *city*, and *customer_group*, and the aggregate measure **count()**. The input tuples are in the *salesInfo* relation. The **cube by** clause specifies that aggregates (group-by's) are to be formed for each of the possible subsets of the given dimensions. If we were computing the full cube, each group-by would correspond to a cuboid in the data cube lattice. The constraint specified in the **having** clause is known as the **iceberg condition**. Here, the iceberg measure is **count()**. Note that the iceberg cube computed here could be used to answer group-by queries on any combination of the specified dimensions of the form **having count(*)** $>= v$, where $v \geq min\_sup$. Instead of **count()**, the iceberg condition could specify more complex measures such as **average()**.

If we were to omit the **having** clause, we would end up with the full cube. Let's call this cube *sales_cube*. The iceberg cube, *sales_iceberg*, excludes all the cells of *sales_cube* with a count that is less than *min_sup*. Obviously, if we were to set the minimum support to 1 in *sales_iceberg*, the resulting cube would be the full cube, *sales_cube*. ∎

A naïve approach to computing an iceberg cube would be to first compute the full cube and then prune the cells that do not satisfy the iceberg condition. However, this is still prohibitively expensive. An efficient approach is to compute only the iceberg cube directly without computing the full cube. Sections 5.2.2 and 5.2.3 discuss methods for efficient iceberg cube computation.

Introducing iceberg cubes will lessen the burden of computing trivial aggregate cells in a data cube. However, we could still end up with a large number of uninteresting cells to compute. For example, suppose that there are 2 base cells for a database of 100 dimensions, denoted as $\{(a_1, a_2, a_3, \ldots, a_{100}) : 10, (a_1, a_2, b_3, \ldots, b_{100}) : 10\}$, where each has a cell count of 10. If the minimum support is set to 10, there will still be an impermissible number of cells to compute and store, although most of them are not interesting. For example, there are $2^{101} - 6$ distinct aggregate cells,[2] like $\{(a_1, a_2, a_3, a_4, \ldots, a_{99}, *) : 10, \ldots, (a_1, a_2, *, a_4, \ldots, a_{99}, a_{100}) : 10, \ldots, (a_1, a_2, a_3, *, \ldots, *, *) : 10\}$, but most of them do not contain much new information. If we ignore all the aggregate cells that can be obtained by replacing some constants by *'s while keeping the same measure value, there are only three distinct cells left: $\{(a_1, a_2, a_3, \ldots, a_{100}) : 10, (a_1, a_2, b_3, \ldots, b_{100}) : 10, (a_1, a_2, *, \ldots, *) : 20\}$. That is, out of $2^{101} - 4$ distinct base and aggregate cells, only three really offer valuable information.

---

[2] The proof is left as an exercise for the reader.

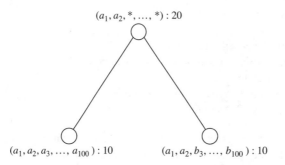

$(a_1, a_2, *, \ldots, *) : 20$

$(a_1, a_2, a_3, \ldots, a_{100}) : 10$ $(a_1, a_2, b_3, \ldots, b_{100}) : 10$

Figure 5.2 Three closed cells forming the lattice of a closed cube.

To systematically compress a data cube, we need to introduce the concept of *closed coverage*. A cell, c, is a *closed cell* if there exists no cell, d, such that d is a specialization (descendant) of cell c (i.e., where d is obtained by replacing $*$ in c with a non-$*$ value), and d has the same measure value as c. A **closed cube** is a data cube consisting of only closed cells. For example, the three cells derived in the preceding paragraph are the three closed cells of the data cube for the data set $\{(a_1, a_2, a_3, \ldots, a_{100}) : 10, (a_1, a_2, b_3, \ldots, b_{100}) : 10\}$. They form the lattice of a closed cube as shown in Figure 5.2. Other nonclosed cells can be derived from their corresponding closed cells in this lattice. For example, "$(a_1, *, *, \ldots, *) : 20$" can be derived from "$(a_1, a_2, *, \ldots, *) : 20$" because the former is a generalized nonclosed cell of the latter. Similarly, we have "$(a_1, a_2, b_3, *, \ldots, *) : 10$."

Another strategy for partial materialization is to precompute only the cuboids involving a small number of dimensions such as three to five. These cuboids form a **cube shell** for the corresponding data cube. Queries on additional combinations of the dimensions will have to be computed on-the-fly. For example, we could compute all cuboids with three dimensions or less in an n-dimensional data cube, resulting in a cube shell of size 3. This, however, can still result in a large number of cuboids to compute, particularly when n is large. Alternatively, we can choose to precompute only portions or *fragments* of the cube shell based on cuboids of interest. Section 5.2.4 discusses a method for computing **shell fragments** and explores how they can be used for efficient OLAP query processing.

5.1.2 General Strategies for Data Cube Computation

There are several methods for efficient data cube computation, based on the various kinds of cubes described in Section 5.1.1. In general, there are two basic data structures used for storing cuboids. The implementation of relational OLAP (ROLAP) uses relational tables, whereas multidimensional arrays are used in multidimensional OLAP (MOLAP). Although ROLAP and MOLAP may each explore different cube computation techniques, some optimization "tricks" can be shared among the different data representations. The following are general optimization techniques for efficient computation of data cubes.

Optimization Technique 1: Sorting, hashing, and grouping. Sorting, hashing, and grouping operations should be applied to the dimension attributes to reorder and cluster related tuples.

In cube computation, aggregation is performed on the tuples (or cells) that share the same set of dimension values. Thus, it is important to explore sorting, hashing, and grouping operations to access and group such data together to facilitate computation of such aggregates.

To compute total sales by *branch*, *day*, and *item*, for example, it can be more efficient to sort tuples or cells by *branch*, and then by *day*, and then group them according to the *item* name. Efficient implementations of such operations in large data sets have been extensively studied in the database research community. Such implementations can be extended to data cube computation.

This technique can also be further extended to perform **shared-sorts** (i.e., sharing sorting costs across multiple cuboids when sort-based methods are used), or to perform **shared-partitions** (i.e., sharing the partitioning cost across multiple cuboids when hash-based algorithms are used).

Optimization Technique 2: Simultaneous aggregation and caching of intermediate results. In cube computation, it is efficient to compute higher-level aggregates from previously computed lower-level aggregates, rather than from the base fact table. Moreover, simultaneous aggregation from cached intermediate computation results may lead to the reduction of expensive disk input/output (I/O) operations.

To compute sales by *branch*, for example, we can use the intermediate results derived from the computation of a lower-level cuboid such as sales by *branch* and *day*. This technique can be further extended to perform **amortized scans** (i.e., computing as many cuboids as possible at the same time to amortize disk reads).

Optimization Technique 3: Aggregation from the smallest child when there exist multiple child cuboids. When there exist multiple child cuboids, it is usually more efficient to compute the desired parent (i.e., more generalized) cuboid from the smallest, previously computed child cuboid.

To compute a sales cuboid, C_{branch}, when there exist two previously computed cuboids, $C_{\{branch,year\}}$ and $C_{\{branch,item\}}$, for example, it is obviously more efficient to compute C_{branch} from the former than from the latter if there are many more distinct items than distinct years.

Many other optimization techniques may further improve computational efficiency. For example, string dimension attributes can be mapped to integers with values ranging from zero to the cardinality of the attribute.

In iceberg cube computation the following optimization technique plays a particularly important role.

Optimization Technique 4: The Apriori pruning method can be explored to compute iceberg cubes efficiently. The **Apriori property**,[3] in the context of data cubes, states as follows: *If a given cell does not satisfy minimum support, then no descendant of the cell (i.e., more specialized cell) will satisfy minimum support either.* This property can be used to substantially reduce the computation of iceberg cubes.

Recall that the specification of iceberg cubes contains an iceberg condition, which is a constraint on the cells to be materialized. A common iceberg condition is that the cells must satisfy a *minimum support* threshold such as a minimum count or sum. In this situation, the Apriori property can be used to prune away the exploration of the cell's descendants. For example, if the count of a cell, c, in a cuboid is less than a minimum support threshold, v, then the count of any of c's descendant cells in the lower-level cuboids can never be greater than or equal to v, and thus can be pruned.

In other words, if a condition (e.g., the iceberg condition specified in the **having** clause) is violated for some cell c, then every descendant of c will also violate that condition. Measures that obey this property are known as **antimonotonic**.[4] This form of pruning was made popular in frequent pattern mining, yet also aids in data cube computation by cutting processing time and disk space requirements. It can lead to a more focused analysis because cells that cannot pass the threshold are unlikely to be of interest.

In the following sections, we introduce several popular methods for efficient cube computation that explore these optimization strategies.

5.2 Data Cube Computation Methods

Data cube computation is an essential task in data warehouse implementation. The precomputation of all or part of a data cube can greatly reduce the response time and enhance the performance of online analytical processing. However, such computation is challenging because it may require substantial computational time and storage space. This section explores efficient methods for data cube computation. Section 5.2.1 describes the *multiway array aggregation* (MultiWay) method for computing full cubes. Section 5.2.2 describes a method known as BUC, which computes iceberg cubes from the apex cuboid downward. Section 5.2.3 describes the Star-Cubing method, which integrates top-down and bottom-up computation.

Finally, Section 5.2.4 describes a shell-fragment cubing approach that computes shell fragments for efficient high-dimensional OLAP. To simplify our discussion, we exclude

---

[3]The Apriori property was proposed in the Apriori algorithm for association rule mining by Agrawal and Srikant [AS94b]. Many algorithms in association rule mining have adopted this property (see Chapter 6).

[4]**Antimonotone** is based on *condition violation*. This differs from **monotone**, which is based on *condition satisfaction*.

the cuboids that would be generated by climbing up any existing hierarchies for the dimensions. Those cube types can be computed by extension of the discussed methods. Methods for the efficient computation of closed cubes are left as an exercise for interested readers.

5.2.1 Multiway Array Aggregation for Full Cube Computation

The **multiway array aggregation** (or simply **MultiWay**) method computes a full data cube by using a multidimensional array as its basic data structure. It is a typical MOLAP approach that uses direct array addressing, where dimension values are accessed via the position or index of their corresponding array locations. Hence, MultiWay cannot perform any value-based reordering as an optimization technique. A different approach is developed for the array-based cube construction, as follows:

1. Partition the array into chunks. A **chunk** is a subcube that is small enough to fit into the memory available for cube computation. **Chunking** is a method for dividing an n-dimensional array into small n-dimensional chunks, where each chunk is stored as an object on disk. The chunks are compressed so as to remove wasted space resulting from *empty array cells*. A cell is *empty* if it does not contain any valid data (i.e., its cell count is 0). For instance, "*chunkID* + *offset*" can be used as a cell-addressing mechanism to **compress a sparse array structure** and when searching for cells within a chunk. Such a compression technique is powerful at handling sparse cubes, both on disk and in memory.

2. Compute aggregates by visiting (i.e., accessing the values at) cube cells. The order in which cells are visited can be optimized so as to *minimize the number of times that each cell must be revisited*, thereby reducing memory access and storage costs. The trick is to exploit this ordering so that portions of the aggregate cells in multiple cuboids can be computed simultaneously, and any unnecessary revisiting of cells is avoided.

This chunking technique involves "overlapping" some of the aggregation computations; therefore, it is referred to as multiway array aggregation. It performs **simultaneous aggregation**, that is, it computes aggregations simultaneously on multiple dimensions.

We explain this approach to array-based cube construction by looking at a concrete example.

Example 5.4 Multiway array cube computation. Consider a 3-D data array containing the three dimensions A, B, and C. The 3-D array is partitioned into small, memory-based chunks. In this example, the array is partitioned into 64 chunks as shown in Figure 5.3. Dimension A is organized into four equal-sized partitions: a_0, a_1, a_2, and a_3. Dimensions B and C are similarly organized into four partitions each. Chunks 1, 2, ..., 64 correspond to the subcubes $a_0 b_0 c_0$, $a_1 b_0 c_0$, ..., $a_3 b_3 c_3$, respectively. Suppose that the cardinality of

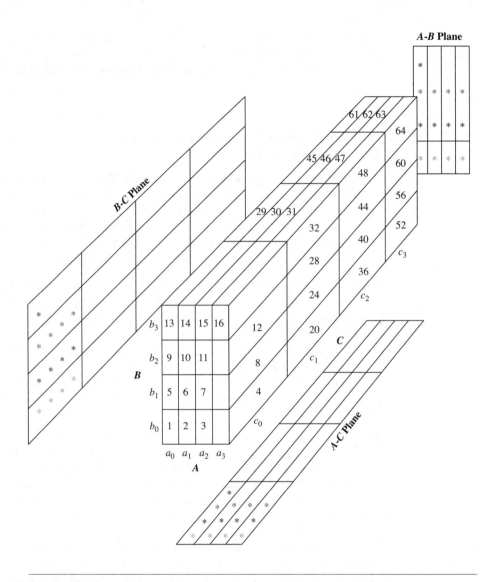

Figure 5.3 A 3-D array for the dimensions *A*, *B*, and *C*, organized into 64 *chunks*. Each chunk is small enough to fit into the memory available for cube computation. The ∗'s indicate the chunks from 1 to 13 that have been aggregated so far in the process.

the dimensions *A*, *B*, and *C* is 40, 400, and 4000, respectively. Thus, the size of the array for each dimension, *A*, *B*, and *C*, is also 40, 400, and 4000, respectively. The size of each partition in *A*, *B*, and *C* is therefore 10, 100, and 1000, respectively. Full materialization of the corresponding data cube involves the computation of all the cuboids defining this cube. The resulting full cube consists of the following cuboids:

- The base cuboid, denoted by *ABC* (from which all the other cuboids are directly or indirectly computed). This cube is already computed and corresponds to the given 3-D array.

- The 2-D cuboids, *AB*, *AC*, and *BC*, which respectively correspond to the group-by's *AB*, *AC*, and *BC*. These cuboids must be computed.

- The 1-D cuboids, *A*, *B*, and *C*, which respectively correspond to the group-by's *A*, *B*, and *C*. These cuboids must be computed.

- The 0-D (apex) cuboid, denoted by **all**, which corresponds to the group-by (); that is, there is no group-by here. This cuboid must be computed. It consists of only one value. If, say, the data cube measure is count, then the value to be computed is simply the total count of all the tuples in *ABC*.

Let's look at how the multiway array aggregation technique is used in this computation. There are many possible orderings with which chunks can be read into memory for use in cube computation. Consider the ordering labeled from 1 to 64, shown in Figure 5.3. Suppose we want to compute the $b_0 c_0$ chunk of the *BC* cuboid. We allocate space for this chunk in *chunk memory*. By scanning *ABC* chunks 1 through 4, the $b_0 c_0$ chunk is computed. That is, the cells for $b_0 c_0$ are aggregated over a_0 to a_3. The chunk memory can then be assigned to the next chunk, $b_1 c_0$, which completes its aggregation after the scanning of the next four *ABC* chunks: 5 through 8. Continuing in this way, the entire *BC* cuboid can be computed. Therefore, only *one BC* chunk needs to be in memory at a time, for the computation of all the *BC* chunks.

In computing the *BC* cuboid, we will have scanned each of the 64 chunks. *"Is there a way to avoid having to rescan all of these chunks for the computation of other cuboids such as AC and AB?"* The answer is, most definitely, *yes*. This is where the "multiway computation" or "simultaneous aggregation" idea comes in. For example, when chunk 1 (i.e., $a_0 b_0 c_0$) is being scanned (say, for the computation of the 2-D chunk $b_0 c_0$ of *BC*, as described previously), all of the other 2-D chunks relating to $a_0 b_0 c_0$ can be simultaneously computed. That is, when $a_0 b_0 c_0$ is being scanned, each of the three chunks ($b_0 c_0$, $a_0 c_0$, and $a_0 b_0$) on the three 2-D aggregation planes (*BC*, *AC*, and *AB*) should be computed then as well. In other words, multiway computation simultaneously aggregates to each of the 2-D planes while a 3-D chunk is in memory.

Now let's look at how different orderings of chunk scanning and of cuboid computation can affect the overall data cube computation efficiency. Recall that the size of the dimensions *A*, *B*, and *C* is 40, 400, and 4000, respectively. Therefore, the largest 2-D plane is *BC* (of size $400 \times 4000 = 1,600,000$). The second largest 2-D plane is *AC* (of size $40 \times 4000 = 160,000$). *AB* is the smallest 2-D plane (of size $40 \times 400 = 16,000$).

Suppose that the chunks are scanned in the order shown, from chunks 1 to 64. As previously mentioned, $b_0 c_0$ is fully aggregated after scanning the row containing chunks 1 through 4; $b_1 c_0$ is fully aggregated after scanning chunks 5 through 8, and so on. Thus, we need to scan four chunks of the 3-D array to *fully* compute one chunk of the *BC* cuboid (where *BC* is the largest of the 2-D planes). In other words, by scanning in this order, one *BC* chunk is fully computed for each row scanned. In comparison, the complete computation of one chunk of the second largest 2-D plane, *AC*, requires scanning 13 chunks, given the ordering from 1 to 64. That is, $a_0 c_0$ is fully aggregated only after the scanning of chunks 1, 5, 9, and 13.

Finally, the complete computation of one chunk of the smallest 2-D plane, *AB*, requires scanning 49 chunks. For example, $a_0 b_0$ is fully aggregated after scanning chunks 1, 17, 33, and 49. Hence, *AB* requires the longest scan of chunks to complete its computation. To avoid bringing a 3-D chunk into memory more than once, the minimum memory requirement for holding all relevant 2-D planes in chunk memory, according to the chunk ordering of 1 to 64, is as follows: 40×400 (for the whole *AB* plane) + 40×1000 (for one column of the *AC* plane) + 100×1000 (for one *BC* plane chunk) = $16,000 + 40,000 + 100,000 = 156,000$ memory units.

Suppose, instead, that the chunks are scanned in the order 1, 17, 33, 49, 5, 21, 37, 53, and so on. That is, suppose the scan is in the order of first aggregating toward the *AB* plane, and then toward the *AC* plane, and lastly toward the *BC* plane. The minimum memory requirement for holding 2-D planes in chunk memory would be as follows: 400×4000 (for the whole *BC* plane) + 10×4000 (for one *AC* plane row) + 10×100 (for one *AB* plane chunk) = $1,600,000 + 40,000 + 1000 = 1,641,000$ memory units. Notice that this is *more than 10 times* the memory requirement of the scan ordering of 1 to 64.

Similarly, we can work out the minimum memory requirements for the multiway computation of the 1-D and 0-D cuboids. Figure 5.4 shows the most efficient way to compute 1-D cuboids. Chunks for 1-D cuboids *A* and *B* are computed during the computation of the smallest 2-D cuboid, *AB*. The smallest 1-D cuboid, *A*, will have all of its chunks allocated in memory, whereas the larger 1-D cuboid, *B*, will have only one chunk allocated in memory at a time. Similarly, chunk *C* is computed during the computation of the second smallest 2-D cuboid, *AC*, requiring only one chunk in memory at a time. Based on this analysis, we see that the most efficient ordering in this array cube computation is the chunk ordering of 1 to 64, with the stated memory allocation strategy. ∎

Example 5.4 assumes that there is enough memory space for *one-pass* cube computation (i.e., to compute all of the cuboids from one scan of all the chunks). If there is insufficient memory space, the computation will require more than one pass through the 3-D array. In such cases, however, the basic principle of ordered chunk computation remains the same. MultiWay is most effective when the product of the cardinalities of dimensions is moderate and the data are not too sparse. When the dimensionality is high or the data are very sparse, the in-memory arrays become too large to fit in memory, and this method becomes infeasible.

With the use of appropriate sparse array compression techniques and careful ordering of the computation of cuboids, it has been shown by experiments that MultiWay array cube computation is significantly faster than traditional ROLAP (relational record-based) computation. Unlike ROLAP, the array structure of MultiWay does not require saving space to store search keys. Furthermore, MultiWay uses direct array addressing,

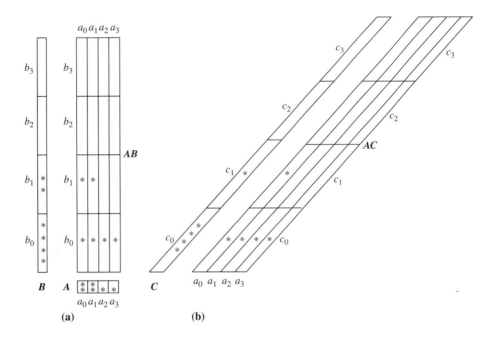

Figure 5.4 Memory allocation and computation order for computing Example 5.4's 1-D cuboids. (a) The 1-D cuboids, A and B, are aggregated during the computation of the smallest 2-D cuboid, AB. (b) The 1-D cuboid, C, is aggregated during the computation of the second smallest 2-D cuboid, AC. The $*$'s represent chunks that, so far, have been aggregated to.

which is faster than ROLAP's key-based addressing search strategy. For ROLAP cube computation, instead of cubing a table directly, it can be faster to convert the table to an array, cube the array, and then convert the result back to a table. However, this observation works only for cubes with a relatively small number of dimensions, because the number of cuboids to be computed is exponential to the number of dimensions.

"*What would happen if we tried to use MultiWay to compute iceberg cubes?*" Remember that the Apriori property states that if a given cell does not satisfy minimum support, then neither will any of its descendants. Unfortunately, MultiWay's computation starts from the base cuboid and progresses upward toward more generalized, ancestor cuboids. It cannot take advantage of Apriori pruning, which requires a parent node to be computed before its child (i.e., more specific) nodes. For example, if the count of a cell c in, say, AB, does not satisfy the minimum support specified in the iceberg condition, we cannot prune away cell c, because the count of c's ancestors in the A or B cuboids may be greater than the minimum support, and their computation will need aggregation involving the count of c.

5.2.2 **BUC: Computing Iceberg Cubes from the Apex Cuboid Downward**

BUC is an algorithm for the computation of sparse and iceberg cubes. Unlike MultiWay, BUC constructs the cube from the apex cuboid toward the base cuboid. This allows BUC to share data partitioning costs. This processing order also allows BUC to prune during construction, using the Apriori property.

Figure 5.5 shows a lattice of cuboids, making up a 3-D data cube with the dimensions *A*, *B*, and *C*. The apex (0-D) cuboid, representing the concept **all** (i.e., $(*, *, *)$), is at the top of the lattice. This is the most aggregated or generalized level. The 3-D base cuboid, *ABC*, is at the bottom of the lattice. It is the least aggregated (most detailed or specialized) level. This representation of a lattice of cuboids, with the apex at the top and the base at the bottom, is commonly accepted in data warehousing. It consolidates the notions of *drill-down* (where we can move from a highly aggregated cell to lower, more detailed cells) and *roll-up* (where we can move from detailed, low-level cells to higher-level, more aggregated cells).

BUC stands for "Bottom-Up Construction." However, according to the lattice convention described before and used throughout this book, the BUC processing order is actually top-down! The BUC authors view a lattice of cuboids in the reverse order,

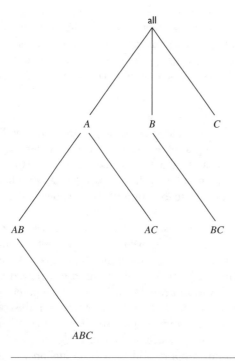

Figure 5.5 BUC's exploration for a 3-D data cube computation. Note that the computation starts from the apex cuboid.

with the apex cuboid at the bottom and the base cuboid at the top. In that view, BUC does bottom-up construction. However, because we adopt the application worldview where *drill-down* refers to drilling from the apex cuboid down toward the base cuboid, the exploration process of BUC is regarded as top-down. BUC's exploration for the computation of a 3-D data cube is shown in Figure 5.5.

The BUC algorithm is shown on the next page in Figure 5.6. We first give an explanation of the algorithm and then follow up with an example. Initially, the algorithm is called with the input relation (set of tuples). BUC aggregates the entire input (line 1) and writes the resulting total (line 3). (Line 2 is an optimization feature that is discussed later in our example.) For each dimension *d* (line 4), the input is partitioned on *d* (line 6). On return from Partition(), *dataCount* contains the total number of tuples for each distinct value of dimension *d*. Each distinct value of *d* *forms its own partition*. Line 8 iterates through each partition. Line 10 tests the partition for minimum support. That is, if the number of tuples in the partition satisfies (i.e., is $\geq$) the minimum support, then the partition becomes the input relation for a recursive call made to BUC, which computes the iceberg cube on the partitions for dimensions $d + 1$ to *numDims* (line 12).

Note that for a full cube (i.e., where minimum support in the **having** clause is 1), the minimum support condition is always satisfied. Thus, the recursive call descends one level deeper into the lattice. On return from the recursive call, we continue with the next partition for *d*. After all the partitions have been processed, the entire process is repeated for each of the remaining dimensions.

Example 5.5 **BUC construction of an iceberg cube.** Consider the iceberg cube expressed in SQL as follows:

> compute cube *iceberg_cube* as
> select *A, B, C, D*, count(*)
> from *R*
> cube by *A, B, C, D*
> having count(*) >= 3

Let's see how BUC constructs the iceberg cube for the dimensions *A, B, C,* and *D*, where 3 is the minimum support count. Suppose that dimension *A* has four distinct values, a_1, a_2, a_3, a_4; *B* has four distinct values, b_1, b_2, b_3, b_4; *C* has two distinct values, c_1, c_2; and *D* has two distinct values, d_1, d_2. If we consider each group-by to be a *partition*, then we must compute every combination of the grouping attributes that satisfy the minimum support (i.e., that have three tuples).

Figure 5.7 illustrates how the input is partitioned first according to the different attribute values of dimension *A*, and then *B, C,* and *D*. To do so, BUC scans the input, aggregating the tuples to obtain a count for **all**, corresponding to the cell $(*, *, *, *)$. Dimension *A* is used to split the input into four partitions, one for each distinct value of *A*. The number of tuples (counts) for each distinct value of *A* is recorded in *dataCount*.

BUC uses the Apriori property to save time while searching for tuples that satisfy the iceberg condition. Starting with *A* dimension value, a_1, the a_1 partition is aggregated, creating one tuple for the *A* group-by, corresponding to the cell $(a_1, *, *, *)$.

Algorithm: BUC. Algorithm for the computation of sparse and iceberg cubes.

Input:

- *input*: the relation to aggregate;
- *dim*: the starting dimension for this iteration.

Globals:

- constant *numDims*: the total number of dimensions;
- constant *cardinality[numDims]*: the cardinality of each dimension;
- constant *min_sup*: the minimum number of tuples in a partition for it to be output;
- *outputRec*: the current output record;
- *dataCount[numDims]*: stores the size of each partition. *dataCount[i]* is a list of integers of size *cardinality[i]*.

Output: Recursively output the iceberg cube cells satisfying the minimum support.

Method:

(1) Aggregate(input); // Scan *input* to compute measure, e.g., count. Place result in *outputRec*.
(2) **if** input.count() == 1 **then** // Optimization
         WriteDescendants(input[0], dim); **return**;
      endif
(3) write outputRec;
(4) **for** ($d = dim$; $d < numDims$; $d++$) **do** //Partition each dimension
(5) C = cardinality[d];
(6)   Partition(input, d, C, dataCount[d]); //create C partitions of data for dimension d
(7)   k = 0;
(8)   **for** ($i = 0$; $i < C$; $i++$) **do** // for each partition (each value of dimension d)
(9)   c = dataCount[d][i];
(10)   **if** $c >= min\_sup$ **then** // test the iceberg condition
(11)   outputRec.dim[d] = input[k].dim[d];
(12)   BUC(input[$k..k + c − 1$], $d + 1$); // aggregate on next dimension
(13)   **endif**
(14)   k +=c;
(15)   **endfor**
(16)   outputRec.dim[d] = all;
(17) **endfor**

Figure 5.6 BUC algorithm for sparse or iceberg cube computation. *Source:* Beyer and Ramakrishnan [BR99].

Suppose $(a_1, *, *, *)$ satisfies the minimum support, in which case a recursive call is made on the partition for a_1. BUC partitions a_1 on the dimension B. It checks the count of $(a_1, b_1, *, *)$ to see if it satisfies the minimum support. If it does, it outputs the aggregated tuple to the AB group-by and recurses on $(a_1, b_1, *, *)$ to partition on C, starting

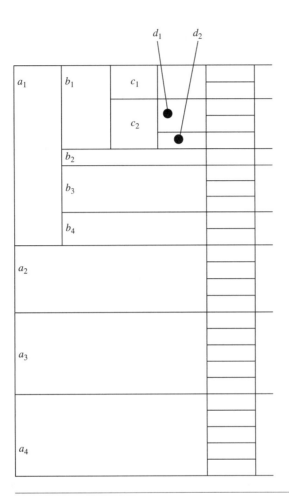

Figure 5.7 BUC partitioning snapshot given an example 4-D data set.

with c_1. Suppose the cell count for $(a_1, b_1, c_1, *)$ is 2, which does not satisfy the minimum support. According to the Apriori property, if a cell does not satisfy the minimum support, then neither can any of its descendants. Therefore, BUC prunes any further exploration of $(a_1, b_1, c_1, *)$. That is, it avoids partitioning this cell on dimension D. It backtracks to the a_1, b_1 partition and recurses on $(a_1, b_1, c_2, *)$, and so on. By checking the iceberg condition each time before performing a recursive call, BUC saves a great deal of processing time whenever a cell's count does not satisfy the minimum support.

The partition process is facilitated by a linear sorting method, CountingSort. CountingSort is fast because it does not perform any key comparisons to find partition boundaries. In addition, the counts computed during the sort can be reused to compute the group-by's in BUC. Line 2 is an optimization for partitions having a count of 1 such as $(a_1, b_2, *, *)$ in our example. To save on partitioning costs, the count is written to each of the tuple's descendant group-by's. This is particularly useful since, in practice, many partitions have a single tuple.   ∎

The BUC performance is sensitive to the order of the dimensions and to skew in the data. Ideally, the most discriminating dimensions should be processed first. Dimensions should be processed in the order of decreasing cardinality. The higher the cardinality, the smaller the partitions, and thus the more partitions there will be, thereby providing BUC with a greater opportunity for pruning. Similarly, the more uniform a dimension (i.e., having less skew), the better it is for pruning.

BUC's major contribution is the idea of sharing partitioning costs. However, unlike MultiWay, it does not share the computation of aggregates between parent and child group-by's. For example, the computation of cuboid *AB* does not help that of *ABC*. The latter needs to be computed essentially from scratch.

5.2.3 Star-Cubing: Computing Iceberg Cubes Using a Dynamic Star-Tree Structure

In this section, we describe the **Star-Cubing** algorithm for computing iceberg cubes. Star-Cubing combines the strengths of the other methods we have studied up to this point. It integrates top-down and bottom-up cube computation and explores both multidimensional aggregation (similar to MultiWay) and Apriori-like pruning (similar to BUC). It operates from a data structure called a star-tree, which performs lossless data compression, thereby reducing the computation time and memory requirements.

The Star-Cubing algorithm explores both the bottom-up and top-down computation models as follows: On the global computation order, it uses the bottom-up model. However, it has a sublayer underneath based on the top-down model, which explores the notion of *shared dimensions*, as we shall see in the following. This integration allows the algorithm to aggregate on multiple dimensions while still partitioning parent group-by's and pruning child group-by's that do not satisfy the iceberg condition.

Star-Cubing's approach is illustrated in Figure 5.8 for a 4-D data cube computation. If we were to follow only the bottom-up model (similar to MultiWay), then the cuboids marked as pruned by Star-Cubing would still be explored. Star-Cubing is able to prune the indicated cuboids because it considers shared dimensions. *ACD/A* means cuboid *ACD* has shared dimension *A*, *ABD/AB* means cuboid *ABD* has shared dimension *AB*, *ABC/ABC* means cuboid *ABC* has shared dimension *ABC*, and so on. This comes from the generalization that all the cuboids in the subtree rooted at *ACD* include dimension *A*, all those rooted at *ABD* include dimensions *AB*, and all those rooted at *ABC* include dimensions *ABC* (even though there is only one such cuboid). We call these common dimensions the **shared dimensions** of those particular subtrees.

The introduction of shared dimensions facilitates shared computation. Because the shared dimensions are identified early on in the tree expansion, we can avoid recomputing them later. For example, cuboid *AB* extending from *ABD* in Figure 5.8 would actually be pruned because *AB* was already computed in *ABD/AB*. Similarly, cuboid

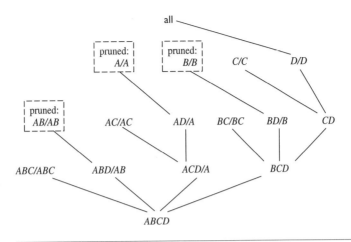

Figure 5.8 Star-Cubing: bottom-up computation with top-down expansion of shared dimensions.

A extending from AD would also be pruned because it was already computed in ACD/A.

Shared dimensions allow us to do Apriori-like pruning if the measure of an iceberg cube, such as *count*, is antimonotonic. That is, if the aggregate value on a shared dimension does not satisfy the iceberg condition, then *all the cells descending from this shared dimension cannot satisfy the iceberg condition either*. These cells and their descendants can be pruned because these descendant cells are, by definition, more specialized (i.e., contain more dimensions) than those in the shared dimension(s). The number of tuples covered by the descendant cells will be less than or equal to the number of tuples covered by the shared dimensions. Therefore, if the aggregate value on a shared dimension fails the iceberg condition, the descendant cells cannot satisfy it either.

Example 5.6 Pruning shared dimensions. If the value in the shared dimension A is a_1 and it fails to satisfy the iceberg condition, then the whole subtree rooted at a_1CD/a_1 (including a_1C/a_1C, a_1D/a_1, a_1/a_1) can be pruned because they are all more specialized versions of a_1. ∎

To explain how the Star-Cubing algorithm works, we need to explain a few more concepts, namely, *cuboid trees, star-nodes*, and *star-trees*.

We use trees to represent individual cuboids. Figure 5.9 shows a fragment of the **cuboid tree** of the base cuboid, *ABCD*. Each level in the tree represents a dimension, and each node represents an attribute value. Each node has four fields: the attribute value, aggregate value, pointer to possible first child, and pointer to possible first sibling. Tuples in the cuboid are inserted one by one into the tree. A path from the root to a leaf node represents a tuple. For example, node c_2 in the tree has an aggregate (count) value of 5,

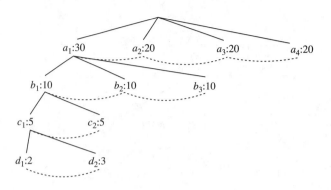

Figure 5.9 Base cuboid tree fragment.

which indicated that there are five tuples of value (a_1, b_1, c_2, *). This representation collapses the common prefixes to save memory usage and allows us to aggregate the values at internal nodes. With aggregate values at internal nodes, we can prune based on shared dimensions. For example, the *AB* cuboid tree can be used to prune possible cells in *ABD*.

If the single-dimensional aggregate on an attribute value *p* does not satisfy the iceberg condition, it is useless to distinguish such nodes in the iceberg cube computation. Thus, the node *p* can be replaced by * so that the cuboid tree can be further compressed. We say that the node *p* in an attribute *A* is a **star-node** if the single-dimensional aggregate on *p* does not satisfy the iceberg condition; otherwise, *p* is a *non-star-node*. A cuboid tree that is compressed using star-nodes is called a **star-tree**.

Example 5.7 **Star-tree construction.** A base cuboid table is shown in Table 5.1. There are five tuples and four dimensions. The cardinalities for dimensions *A*, *B*, *C*, *D* are 2, 4, 4, 4, respectively. The one-dimensional aggregates for all attributes are shown in Table 5.2. Suppose *min_sup* = 2 in the iceberg condition. Clearly, only attribute values a_1, a_2, b_1, c_3, d_4 satisfy the condition. All other values are below the threshold and thus become star-nodes. By collapsing star-nodes, the reduced base table is Table 5.3. Notice that the table contains two fewer rows and also fewer distinct values than Table 5.1.

Table 5.1 Base (Cuboid) Table: Before Star Reduction

A	B	C	D	count
a_1	b_1	c_1	d_1	1
a_1	b_1	c_4	d_3	1
a_1	b_2	c_2	d_2	1
a_2	b_3	c_3	d_4	1
a_2	b_4	c_3	d_4	1

Table 5.2 One-Dimensional Aggregates

Dimension	count $= 1$	count ≥ 2
A	—	$a_1(3), a_2(2)$
B	b_2, b_3, b_4	$b_1(2)$
C	c_1, c_2, c_4	$c_3(2)$
D	d_1, d_2, d_3	$d_4(2)$

Table 5.3 Compressed Base Table: After Star Reduction

A	B	C	D	count
a_1	b_1	$*$	$*$	2
a_1	$*$	$*$	$*$	1
a_2	$*$	c_3	d_4	2

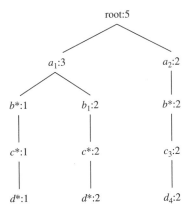

Figure 5.10 Compressed base table star-tree.

We use the reduced base table to construct the cuboid tree because it is smaller. The resultant star-tree is shown in Figure 5.10. ∎

Now, let's see how the Star-Cubing algorithm uses star-trees to compute an iceberg cube. The algorithm is given later in Figure 5.13.

Example 5.8 Star-Cubing. Using the star-tree generated in Example 5.7 (Figure 5.10), we start the aggregation process by traversing in a bottom-up fashion. Traversal is depth-first. The first stage (i.e., the processing of the first branch of the tree) is shown in Figure 5.11. The leftmost tree in the figure is the base star-tree. Each attribute value is shown with its corresponding aggregate value. In addition, subscripts by the nodes in the tree show the traversal order. The remaining four trees are *BCD*, *ACD/A*, *ABD/AB*, and *ABC/ABC*. They are the child trees of the base star-tree, and correspond to the level of 3-D cuboids above the base cuboid in Figure 5.8. The subscripts in them correspond to the same subscripts in the base tree—they denote the step or order in which they are created during the tree traversal. For example, when the algorithm is at step 1, the *BCD* child tree root is created. At step 2, the *ACD/A* child tree root is created. At step 3, the *ABD/AB* tree root and the $b*$ node in *BCD* are created.

When the algorithm has reached step 5, the trees in memory are exactly as shown in Figure 5.11. Because depth-first traversal has reached a leaf at this point, it starts backtracking. Before traversing back, the algorithm notices that all possible nodes in the base dimension (*ABC*) have been visited. This means the *ABC/ABC* tree is complete, so the count is output and the tree is destroyed. Similarly, upon moving back from $d*$ to $c*$ and seeing that $c*$ has no siblings, the count in *ABD/AB* is also output and the tree is destroyed.

When the algorithm is at $b*$ during the backtraversal, it notices that there exists a sibling in b_1. Therefore, it will keep *ACD/A* in memory and perform a depth-first search

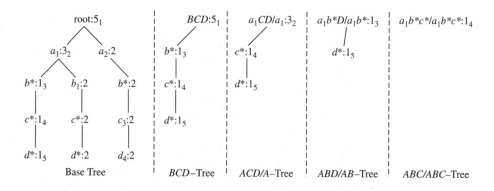

Figure 5.11 Aggregation stage one: processing the leftmost branch of the base tree.

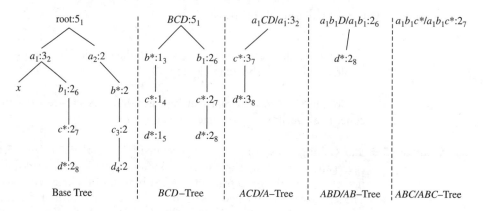

Figure 5.12 Aggregation stage two: processing the second branch of the base tree.

Algorithm: Star-Cubing. Compute iceberg cubes by Star-Cubing.

Input:

- *R*: a relational table
- *min_support*: minimum support threshold for the iceberg condition (taking **count** as the measure).

Output: The computed iceberg cube.

Method: Each star-tree corresponds to one cuboid tree node, and vice versa.

BEGIN
    scan *R* twice, **create** star-table *S* and star-tree *T*;
    output *count* of *T.root*;
  call *starcubing(T, T.root)*;
END

procedure *starcubing(T, cnode)*// cnode: current node
{
(1)   **for each** non-null *child C* of *T*'s cuboid tree
(2)   **insert or aggregate** *cnode* to the corresponding
            position or node in *C*'s star-tree;
(3)   **if** (*cnode.count* $\geq$ *min_support*) **then** {
(4)   **if** (cnode $\neq$ root) **then**
(5)   **output** cnode.count;
(6)   **if** (cnode is a leaf) **then**
(7)   **output** cnode.count;
(8)   **else** { // initiate a new cuboid tree
(9)   **create** C_C as a child of *T*'s cuboid tree;
(10)   **let** T_C be C_C's star-tree;
(11) $T_C.root's$ count $=$ cnode.count;
(12)   }
(13) }
(14) **if** (*cnode* is not a leaf) **then**
(15)   *starcubing(T, cnode.first_child)*;
(16) **if** (C_C is not null) **then** {
(17)   *starcubing(T_C, T_C.root)*;
(18)   **remove** C_C from *T*'s cuboid tree; }
(19) **if** (*cnode* has sibling) **then**
(20)   *starcubing(T, cnode.sibling)*;
(21) **remove** *T*;
}

Figure 5.13 Star-Cubing algorithm.

on b_1 just as it did on $b*$. This traversal and the resultant trees are shown in Figure 5.12. The child trees ABD/AB and ABC/ABC are created again but now with the new values from the b_1 subtree. For example, notice.that the aggregate count of $c*$ in the ACD/A tree has increased from 1 to 3. The trees that remained intact during the last traversal are reused and the new aggregate values are added on. For instance, another branch is added to the BCD tree.

Just like before, the algorithm will reach a leaf node at $d*$ and traverse back. This time, it will reach a_1 and notice that there exists a sibling in a_2. In this case, all child trees except BCD in Figure 5.12 are destroyed. Afterward, the algorithm will perform the same traversal on a_2. BCD continues to grow while the other subtrees start fresh with a_2 instead of a_1.   ∎

A node must satisfy two conditions in order to generate child trees: (1) the measure of the node must satisfy the iceberg condition; and (2) the tree to be generated must include at least one non-star-node (i.e., nontrivial). This is because if all the nodes were star-nodes, then none of them would satisfy *min_sup*. Therefore, it would be a complete waste to compute them. This pruning is observed in Figures 5.11 and 5.12. For example, the left subtree extending from node a_1 in the base tree in Figure 5.11 does not include any nonstar-nodes. Therefore, the $a_1 CD/a_1$ subtree should not have been generated. It is shown, however, for illustration of the child tree generation process.

Star-Cubing is sensitive to the ordering of dimensions, as with other iceberg cube construction algorithms. For best performance, the dimensions are processed in order of decreasing cardinality. This leads to a better chance of early pruning, because the higher the cardinality, the smaller the partitions, and therefore the higher possibility that the partition will be pruned.

Star-Cubing can also be used for full cube computation. When computing the full cube for a dense data set, Star-Cubing's performance is comparable with MultiWay and is much faster than BUC. If the data set is sparse, Star-Cubing is significantly faster than MultiWay and faster than BUC, in most cases. For iceberg cube computation, Star-Cubing is faster than BUC, where the data are skewed and the speed-up factor increases as *min_sup* decreases.

5.2.4 Precomputing Shell Fragments for Fast High-Dimensional OLAP

Recall the reason that we are interested in precomputing data cubes: Data cubes facilitate fast OLAP in a multidimensional data space. However, a full data cube of high dimensionality needs massive storage space and unrealistic computation time. Iceberg cubes provide a more feasible alternative, as we have seen, wherein the iceberg condition is used to specify the computation of only a subset of the full cube's cells. However, although an iceberg cube is smaller and requires less computation time than its corresponding full cube, it is not an ultimate solution.

For one, the computation and storage of the iceberg cube can still be costly. For example, if the base cuboid cell, $(a_1, a_2, \ldots, a_{60})$, passes minimum support (or the iceberg threshold), it will generate 2^{60} iceberg cube cells. Second, it is difficult to determine an appropriate iceberg threshold. Setting the threshold too low will result in a huge cube, whereas setting the threshold too high may invalidate many useful applications. Third, an iceberg cube cannot be incrementally updated. Once an aggregate cell falls below the iceberg threshold and is pruned, its measure value is lost. Any incremental update would require recomputing the cells from scratch. This is extremely undesirable for large real-life applications where incremental appending of new data is the norm.

One possible solution, which has been implemented in some commercial data warehouse systems, is to compute a thin **cube shell**. For example, we could compute all cuboids with three dimensions or less in a 60-dimensional data cube, resulting in a cube shell of size 3. The resulting cuboids set would require much less computation and storage than the full 60-dimensional data cube. However, there are two disadvantages to this approach. First, we would still need to compute $\binom{60}{3} + \binom{60}{2} + 60 = 36,050$ cuboids, each with many cells. Second, such a cube shell does not support high-dimensional OLAP because (1) it does not support OLAP on four or more dimensions, and (2) it cannot even support drilling along three dimensions, such as, say, (A_4, A_5, A_6), *on a subset of data* selected based on the constants provided in three *other* dimensions, such as (A_1, A_2, A_3), because this essentially requires the computation of the corresponding 6-D cuboid. (Notice that there is no cell in cuboid (A_4, A_5, A_6) computed for any particular constant set, such as (a_1, a_2, a_3), associated with dimensions (A_1, A_2, A_3).)

Instead of computing a cube shell, we can compute only portions or fragments of it. This section discusses the *shell fragment* approach for OLAP query processing. It is based on the following key observation about OLAP in high-dimensional space. Although a data cube may contain many dimensions, *most OLAP operations are performed on only a small number of dimensions at a time*. In other words, an OLAP query is likely to ignore many dimensions (i.e., treating them as irrelevant), fix some dimensions (e.g., using query constants as instantiations), and leave only a few to be manipulated (for drilling, pivoting, etc.). This is because it is neither realistic nor fruitful for anyone to comprehend the changes of thousands of cells involving tens of dimensions simultaneously in a high-dimensional space at the same time.

Instead, it is more natural to first locate some cuboids of interest and then drill along one or two dimensions to examine the changes of a few related dimensions. Most analysts will only need to examine, at any one moment, the combinations of a small number of dimensions. This implies that if multidimensional aggregates can be computed quickly on a *small number of dimensions inside a high-dimensional space*, we may still achieve fast OLAP without materializing the original high-dimensional data cube. Computing the full cube (or, often, even an iceberg cube or cube shell) can be excessive. Instead, a *semi-online computation model with certain preprocessing* may offer a more feasible solution. Given a base cuboid, some quick preparation computation can be done first (i.e., offline). After that, a query can then be computed online using the preprocessed data.

The shell fragment approach follows such a semi-online computation strategy. It involves two algorithms: one for computing cube shell fragments and the other for query processing with the cube fragments. The shell fragment approach can handle databases

Table 5.4 Original Database

TID	A	B	C	D	E
1	a_1	b_1	c_1	d_1	e_1
2	a_1	b_2	c_1	d_2	e_1
3	a_1	b_2	c_1	d_1	e_2
4	a_2	b_1	c_1	d_1	e_2
5	a_2	b_1	c_1	d_1	e_3

of high dimensionality and can quickly compute small local cubes online. It explores the *inverted index* data structure, which is popular in information retrieval and Web-based information systems.

The basic idea is as follows. Given a high-dimensional data set, we partition the dimensions into a set of disjoint dimension *fragments*, convert each fragment into its corresponding inverted index representation, and then construct *cube shell fragments* while keeping the inverted indices associated with the cube cells. Using the precomputed cubes' shell fragments, we can dynamically assemble and compute cuboid cells of the required data cube online. This is made efficient by set intersection operations on the inverted indices.

To illustrate the shell fragment approach, we use the tiny database of Table 5.4 as a running example. Let the cube measure be count(). Other measures will be discussed later. We first look at how to construct the inverted index for the given database.

Example 5.9 **Construct the inverted index.** For each attribute value in each dimension, list the tuple identifiers (*TIDs*) of all the tuples that have that value. For example, attribute value a_2 appears in tuples 4 and 5. The TID list for a_2 then contains exactly two items, namely 4 and 5. The resulting inverted index table is shown in Table 5.5. It retains all the original database's information. If each table entry takes one unit of memory, Tables 5.4 and 5.5 each takes 25 units, that is, the inverted index table uses the same amount of memory as the original database. ∎

"How do we compute shell fragments of a data cube?" The shell fragment computation algorithm, **Frag-Shells**, is summarized in Figure 5.14. We first partition all the dimensions of the given data set into independent groups of dimensions, called *fragments* (line 1). We scan the base cuboid and construct an inverted index for each attribute (lines 2 to 6). Line 3 is for when the measure is other than the tuple count(), which will be described later. For each fragment, we compute the full *local* (i.e., fragment-based) data cube while retaining the inverted indices (lines 7 to 8). Consider a database of 60 dimensions, namely, $A_1, A_2, \ldots, A_{60}$. We can first partition the 60 dimensions into 20 fragments of size 3: (A_1, A_2, A_3), (A_4, A_5, A_6), …, (A_{58}, A_{59}, A_{60}). For each fragment, we compute its full data cube while recording the inverted indices. For example, in fragment (A_1, A_2, A_3), we would compute seven cuboids: $A_1, A_2, A_3, A_1A_2, A_2A_3, A_1A_3, A_1A_2A_3$. Furthermore, an inverted index

Table 5.5 Inverted Index

Attribute Value	TID List	List Size
a_1	{1, 2, 3}	3
a_2	{4, 5}	2
b_1	{1, 4, 5}	3
b_2	{2, 3}	2
c_1	{1, 2, 3, 4, 5}	5
d_1	{1, 3, 4, 5}	4
d_2	{2}	1
e_1	{1, 2}	2
e_2	{3, 4}	2
e_3	{5}	1

Algorithm: Frag-Shells. Compute shell fragments on a given high-dimensional base table (i.e., base cuboid).

Input: A base cuboid, B, of n dimensions, namely, $(A_1, \ldots, A_n)$.

Output:

- a set of fragment partitions, $\{P_1, \ldots, P_k\}$, and their corresponding (local) fragment cubes, $\{S_1, \ldots, S_k\}$, where P_i represents some set of dimension(s) and $P_1 \cup \ldots \cup P_k$ make up all the n dimensions

- an *ID_measure* array if the measure is not the tuple count, **count()**

Method:

```
(1)    partition the set of dimensions (A₁, ..., Aₙ) into
               a set of k fragments P₁, ..., Pₖ (based on data & query distribution)
(2)    scan base cuboid, B, once and do the following {
(3)        insert each ⟨TID, measure⟩ into ID_measure array
(4)        for each attribute value aⱼ of each dimension Aᵢ
(5)            build an inverted index entry: ⟨aⱼ, TIDlist⟩
(6)    }
(7)    for each fragment partition Pᵢ
(8)        build a local fragment cube, Sᵢ, by intersecting their
               corresponding TIDlists and computing their measures
```

Figure 5.14 Shell fragment computation algorithm.

is retained for each cell in the cuboids. That is, for each cell, its associated TID list is recorded.

The benefit of computing local cubes of each shell fragment instead of computing the complete cube shell can be seen by a simple calculation. For a base cuboid of

60 dimensions, there are only $7 \times 20 = 140$ cuboids to be computed according to the preceding shell fragment partitioning. This is in contrast to the 36,050 cuboids computed for the cube shell of size 3 described earlier! Notice that the above fragment partitioning is based simply on the grouping of consecutive dimensions. A more desirable approach would be to partition based on popular dimension groupings. This information can be obtained from domain experts or the past history of OLAP queries.

Let's return to our running example to see how shell fragments are computed.

Example 5.10 **Compute shell fragments.** Suppose we are to compute the shell fragments of size 3. We first divide the five dimensions into two fragments, namely (A, B, C) and (D, E). For each fragment, we compute the full local data cube by intersecting the TID lists in Table 5.5 in a top-down depth-first order in the cuboid lattice. For example, to compute the cell $(a_1, b_2, *)$, we intersect the TID lists of a_1 and b_2 to obtain a new list of $\{2, 3\}$. Cuboid AB is shown in Table 5.6.

After computing cuboid AB, we can then compute cuboid ABC by intersecting all pairwise combinations between Table 5.6 and the row c_1 in Table 5.5. Notice that because cell (a_2, b_2) is empty, it can be effectively discarded in subsequent computations, based on the Apriori property. The same process can be applied to compute fragment (D, E), which is completely independent from computing (A, B, C). Cuboid DE is shown in Table 5.7. ∎

If the measure in the iceberg condition is **count()** (as in tuple counting), there is no need to reference the original database for this because the *length* of the TID list is equivalent to the tuple count. "*Do we need to reference the original database if computing other measures such as* **average()**?" Actually, we can build and reference an *ID_measure*

Table 5.6 Cuboid AB

Cell	Intersection	TID List	List Size
(a_1, b_1)	$\{1, 2, 3\} \cap \{1, 4, 5\}$	$\{1\}$	1
(a_1, b_2)	$\{1, 2, 3\} \cap \{2, 3\}$	$\{2, 3\}$	2
(a_2, b_1)	$\{4, 5\} \cap \{1, 4, 5\}$	$\{4, 5\}$	2
(a_2, b_2)	$\{4, 5\} \cap \{2, 3\}$	$\{\}$	0

Table 5.7 Cuboid DE

Cell	Intersection	TID List	List Size
(d_1, e_1)	$\{1, 3, 4, 5\} \cap \{1, 2\}$	$\{1\}$	1
(d_1, e_2)	$\{1, 3, 4, 5\} \cap \{3, 4\}$	$\{3, 4\}$	2
(d_1, e_3)	$\{1, 3, 4, 5\} \cap \{5\}$	$\{5\}$	1
(d_2, e_1)	$\{2\} \cap \{1, 2\}$	$\{2\}$	1

array instead, which stores what we need to compute other measures. For example, to compute **average()**, we let the *ID_measure* array hold three elements, namely, (*TID*, **item_count**, **sum**), for each cell (line 3 of the shell fragment computation algorithm in Figure 5.14). The **average()** measure for each aggregate cell can then be computed by accessing only this *ID_measure* array, using sum()/item_count(). Considering a database with 10^6 tuples, each taking 4 bytes each for *TID*, item_count, and sum, the *ID_measure* array requires 12 MB, whereas the corresponding database of 60 dimensions will require $(60 + 3) \times 4 \times 10^6 = 252$ MB (assuming each attribute value takes 4 bytes). Obviously, *ID_measure* array is a more compact data structure and is more likely to fit in memory than the corresponding high-dimensional database.

To illustrate the design of the *ID_measure* array, let's look at Example 5.11.

Example 5.11 **Computing cubes with the average() measure.** Table 5.8 shows an example sales database where each tuple has two associated values, such as **item_count** and **sum**, where **item_count** is the count of items sold.

To compute a data cube for this database with the measure **average()**, we need to have a TID list for each cell: $\{TID_1, \ldots, TID_n\}$. Because each TID is uniquely associated with a particular set of measure values, all future computation just needs to fetch the measure values associated with the tuples in the list. In other words, by keeping an *ID_measure* array in memory for online processing, we can handle complex algebraic measures, such as average, variance, and standard deviation. Table 5.9 shows what exactly should be kept for our example, which is substantially smaller than the database itself. ∎

Table 5.8 Database with Two Measure Values

TID	A	B	C	D	E	item_count	sum
1	a_1	b_1	c_1	d_1	e_1	5	70
2	a_1	b_2	c_1	d_2	e_1	3	10
3	a_1	b_2	c_1	d_1	e_2	8	20
4	a_2	b_1	c_1	d_1	e_2	5	40
5	a_2	b_1	c_1	d_1	e_3	2	30

Table 5.9 Table 5.8 *ID_measure* Array

TID	item_count	sum
1	5	70
2	3	10
3	8	20
4	5	40
5	2	30

The shell fragments are negligible in both storage space and computation time in comparison with the full data cube. Note that we can also use the Frag-Shells algorithm to compute the full data cube by including all the dimensions as a single fragment. Because the order of computation with respect to the cuboid lattice is top-down and depth-first (similar to that of BUC), the algorithm can perform Apriori pruning if applied to the construction of iceberg cubes.

"Once we have computed the shell fragments, how can they be used to answer OLAP queries?" Given the precomputed shell fragments, we can view the cube space as a virtual cube and perform OLAP queries related to the cube online. In general, two types of queries are possible: (1) *point query* and (2) *subcube query.*

In a **point query**, all of the *relevant* dimensions in the cube have been instantiated (i.e., there are no *inquired* dimensions in the relevant dimensions set). For example, in an *n*-dimensional data cube, $A_1 A_2 \ldots A_n$, a point query could be in the form of $\langle A_1, A_5, A_9 : M? \rangle$, where $A_1 = \{a_{11}, a_{18}\}$, $A_5 = \{a_{52}, a_{55}, a_{59}\}$, $A_9 = a_{94}$, and M is the inquired measure for each corresponding cube cell. For a cube with a small number of dimensions, we can use $*$ to represent a "don't care" position where the corresponding dimension is *irrelevant*, that is, neither inquired nor instantiated. For example, in the query $\langle a_2, b_1, c_1, d_1, * : \mathsf{count}()? \rangle$ for the database in Table 5.4, the first four dimension values are instantiated to a_2, b_1, c_1, and d_1, respectively, while the last dimension is irrelevant, and $\mathsf{count}()$ (which is the tuple count by context) is the inquired measure.

In a **subcube query**, at least one of the *relevant* dimensions in the cube is *inquired*. For example, in an *n*-dimensional data cube $A_1 A_2 \ldots A_n$, a subcube query could be in the form $\langle A_1, A_5?, A_9, A_{21}? : M? \rangle$, where $A_1 = \{a_{11}, a_{18}\}$ and $A_9 = a_{94}$, A_5 and A_{21} are the inquired dimensions, and M is the inquired measure. For a cube with a small number of dimensions, we can use $*$ for an irrelevant dimension and ? for an inquired one. For example, in the query $\langle a_2, ?, c_1, *, ? : \mathsf{count}() ? \rangle$ we see that the first and third dimension values are instantiated to a_2 and c_1, respectively, while the fourth is irrelevant, and the second and the fifth are inquired. *A subcube query computes all possible value combinations of the inquired dimensions.* It essentially returns a local data cube consisting of the inquired dimensions.

"How can we use shell fragments to answer a point query?" Because a point query explicitly provides the instantiated variables set on the relevant dimensions set, we can make maximal use of the precomputed shell fragments by finding the *best fitting* (i.e., *dimension-wise completely matching*) fragments to fetch and intersect the associated TID lists.

Let the point query be of the form $\langle \alpha_i, \alpha_j, \alpha_k, \alpha_p : M? \rangle$, where α_i represents a set of instantiated values of dimension A_i, and so on for $\alpha_j, \alpha_k,$ and α_p. First, we check the shell fragment schema to determine which dimensions among $A_i, A_j, A_k,$ and A_p are in the same fragment(s). Suppose A_i and A_j are in the same fragment, while A_k and A_p are in two other fragments. We fetch the corresponding TID lists on the precomputed 2-D fragment for dimensions A_i and A_j using the instantiations α_i and α_j, and fetch the TID lists on the 1-D fragments for dimensions A_k and A_p using the instantiations α_k and α_p, respectively. The obtained TID lists are intersected to derive the TID list table. This table is then used to derive the specified measure (e.g., by taking the length of the TID lists for tuple count(), or by fetching item_count() and sum() from the *ID_measure* array to compute average()) for the final set of cells.

Example 5.12 **Point query.** Suppose a user wants to compute the point query $\langle a_2, b_1, c_1, d_1, *: \mathsf{count()?}\rangle$ for our database in Table 5.4 and that the shell fragments for the partitions (A, B, C) and (D, E) are precomputed as described in Example 5.10. The query is broken down into two subqueries based on the precomputed fragments: $\langle a_2, b_1, c_1, *, *\rangle$ and $\langle *, *, *, d_1, *\rangle$. The best-fit precomputed shell fragments for the two subqueries are ABC and D. The fetch of the TID lists for the two subqueries returns two lists: $\{4, 5\}$ and $\{1, 3, 4, 5\}$. Their intersection is the list $\{4, 5\}$, which is of size 2. Thus, the final answer is count() $= 2$. ∎

"How can we use shell fragments to answer a subcube query?" A subcube query returns a local data cube based on the instantiated and inquired dimensions. Such a data cube needs to be aggregated in a multidimensional way so that online analytical processing (drilling, dicing, pivoting, etc.) can be made available to users for flexible manipulation and analysis. Because instantiated dimensions usually provide highly selective constants that dramatically reduce the size of the valid TID lists, we should make maximal use of the precomputed shell fragments by finding the fragments that best fit the set of instantiated dimensions, and fetching and intersecting the associated TID lists to derive the reduced TID list. This list can then be used to intersect the best-fitting shell fragments consisting of the inquired dimensions. This will generate the relevant and inquired base cuboid, which can then be used to compute the relevant subcube on-the-fly using an efficient online cubing algorithm.

Let the subcube query be of the form $\langle \alpha_i, \alpha_j, A_k?, \alpha_p, A_q? : M?\rangle$, where α_i, α_j, and α_p represent a set of instantiated values of dimension A_i, A_j, and A_p, respectively, and A_k and A_q represent two inquired dimensions. First, we check the shell fragment schema to determine which dimensions among (1) A_i, A_j, and A_p, and (2) A_k and A_q are in the same fragment partition. Suppose A_i and A_j belong to the same fragment, as do A_k and A_q, but that A_p is in a different fragment. We fetch the corresponding TID lists in the precomputed 2-D fragment for A_i and A_j using the instantiations α_i and α_j, then fetch the TID list on the precomputed 1-D fragment for A_p using instantiation α_p, and then fetch the TID lists on the precomputed 2-D fragments for A_k and A_q, respectively, using no instantiations (i.e., all possible values). The obtained TID lists are intersected to derive the final TID lists, which are used to fetch the corresponding measures from the *ID_measure* array to derive the "base cuboid" of a 2-D subcube for two dimensions (A_k, A_q). A fast cube computation algorithm can be applied to compute this 2-D cube based on the derived base cuboid. The computed 2-D cube is then ready for OLAP operations.

Example 5.13 **Subcube query.** Suppose that a user wants to compute the subcube query, $\langle a_2, b_1, ?, * , ? : \mathsf{count()?}\rangle$, for our database shown earlier in Table 5.4, and that the shell fragments have been precomputed as described in Example 5.10. The query can be broken into three best-fit fragments according to the instantiated and inquired dimensions: AB, C, and E, where AB has the instantiation (a_2, b_1). The fetch of the TID lists for these partitions returns (a_2, b_1): {4, 5}, (c_1): {1, 2, 3, 4, 5} and {$(e_1$: {1, 2}), $(e_2$: {3, 4}), $(e_3$: {5})}, respectively. The intersection of these corresponding TID lists contains a cuboid with two tuples: {(c_1, e_2): {4},[5] (c_1, e_3): {5}}. This base cuboid can be used to compute the 2-D data cube, which is trivial. ■

For large data sets, a fragment size of 2 or 3 typically results in reasonable storage requirements for the shell fragments and for fast query response time. Querying with shell fragments is substantially faster than answering queries using precomputed data cubes that are stored on disk. In comparison to full cube computation, Frag-Shells is recommended if there are less than four inquired dimensions. Otherwise, more efficient algorithms, such as Star-Cubing, can be used for fast online cube computation. Frag-Shells can be easily extended to allow incremental updates, the details of which are left as an exercise.

5.3 Processing Advanced Kinds of Queries by Exploring Cube Technology

Data cubes are not confined to the simple multidimensional structure illustrated in the last section for typical business data warehouse applications. The methods described in this section further develop data cube technology for effective processing of advanced kinds of queries. Section 5.3.1 explores *sampling cubes*. This extension of data cube technology can be used to answer queries on *sample data*, such as survey data, which represent a sample or subset of a target data population of interest. Section 5.3.2 explains how *ranking cubes* can be computed to answer top-k queries, such as "find the top 5 cars," according to some user-specified criteria.

The basic data cube structure has been further extended for various sophisticated data types and new applications. Here we list some examples, such as *spatial data cubes* for the design and implementation of *geospatial data warehouses*, and *multimedia data cubes* for the multidimensional analysis of *multimedia data* (those containing images and videos). *RFID data cubes* handle the compression and multidimensional analysis of *RFID* (i.e., radio-frequency identification) data. *Text cubes* and *topic cubes* were developed for the application of vector-space models and generative language models, respectively, in the analysis of *multidimensional text databases* (which contain both structure attributes and narrative text attributes).

5.3.1 Sampling Cubes: OLAP-Based Mining on Sampling Data

When collecting data, we often collect only a *subset* of the data we would ideally like to gather. In statistics, this is known as collecting a **sample** of the data population.

---

[5]That is, the intersection of the TID lists for (a_2, b_1), (c_1), and (e_2) is {4}.

The resulting data are called **sample data**. Data are often sampled to save on costs, manpower, time, and materials. In many applications, the collection of the entire data population of interest is unrealistic. In the study of TV ratings or pre-election polls, for example, it is impossible to gather the opinion of *everyone* in the population. Most published ratings or polls rely on a data sample for analysis. The results are extrapolated for the entire population, and associated with certain statistical measures such as a *confidence interval*. The confidence interval tells us how reliable a result is. Statistical surveys based on sampling are a common tool in many fields like politics, healthcare, market research, and social and natural sciences.

"*How effective is OLAP on sample data?*" OLAP traditionally has the full data population on hand, yet with sample data, we have only a small subset. If we try to apply traditional OLAP tools to sample data, we encounter three challenges. First, sample data are often sparse in the multidimensional sense. When a user drills down on the data, it is easy to reach a point with very few or no samples even when the overall sample size is large. Traditional OLAP simply uses whatever data are available to compute a query answer. To extrapolate such an answer for a population based on a small sample could be misleading: A single outlier or a slight bias in the sampling can distort the answer significantly. Second, with sample data, statistical methods are used to provide a measure of reliability (e.g., a confidence interval) to indicate the quality of the query answer as it pertains to the population. Traditional OLAP is not equipped with such tools.

A *sampling cube* framework was introduced to tackle each of the preceding challenges.

Sampling Cube Framework

The **sampling cube** is a data cube structure that stores the sample data and their multidimensional aggregates. It supports OLAP on sample data. It calculates confidence intervals as a quality measure for any multidimensional query. Given a sample data relation (i.e., base cuboid) R, the sampling cube C_R typically computes the sample mean, sample standard deviation, and other task-specific measures.

In statistics, a *confidence interval* is used to indicate the reliability of an estimate. Suppose we want to estimate the mean age of all viewers of a given TV show. We have sample data (a subset) of this data population. Let's say our sample mean is 35 years. This becomes our estimate for the entire population of viewers as well, but how confident can we be that 35 is also the mean of the true population? It is unlikely that the sample mean will be exactly equal to the true population mean because of sampling error. Therefore, we need to qualify our estimate in some way to indicate the general magnitude of this error. This is typically done by computing a **confidence interval**, which is an *estimated value range with a given high probability of covering the true population value*. A confidence interval for our example could be "*the actual mean will not vary by +/− two standard deviations 95% of the time.*" (Recall that the standard deviation is just a number, which can be computed as shown in Section 2.2.2.) A confidence interval is always qualified by a particular *confidence level*. In our example, it is 95%.

The confidence interval is calculated as follows. Let x be a set of samples. The mean of the samples is denoted by $\bar{x}$, and the number of samples in x is denoted by l. Assuming that the standard deviation of the population is unknown, the *sample* standard deviation of x is denoted by s. Given a desired confidence level, the **confidence interval** for $\bar{x}$ is

$$\bar{x} \pm t_c \hat{\sigma}_{\bar{x}}, \tag{5.1}$$

where t_c is the *critical t-value* associated with the confidence level and $\hat{\sigma}_{\bar{x}} = \frac{s}{\sqrt{l}}$ is the *estimated standard error of the mean*. To find the appropriate t_c, specify the desired confidence level (e.g., 95%) and also the *degree of freedom*, which is just $l - 1$.

The important thing to note is that the computation involved in computing a confidence interval is *algebraic*. Let's look at the three terms involved in Eq. (5.1). The first is the mean of the sample set, $\bar{x}$, which is algebraic; the second is the critical *t*-value, which is calculated by a lookup, and with respect to x, it depends on l, a distributive measure; and the third is $\hat{\sigma}_{\bar{x}} = \frac{s}{\sqrt{l}}$, which also turns out to be algebraic if one records the linear sum $(\sum_{i=1}^{l} x_i)$ and squared sum $(\sum_{i=1}^{l} x_i^2)$. Because the terms involved are either algebraic or distributive, the confidence interval computation is algebraic. Actually, since both the mean and confidence interval are algebraic, at every cell, exactly three values are sufficient to calculate them—all of which are either distributive or algebraic:

1. l
2. $sum = \sum_{i=1}^{l} x_i$
3. $squared\ sum = \sum_{i=1}^{l} x_i^2$

There are many efficient techniques for computing algebraic and distributive measures (Section 4.2.4). Therefore, any of the previously developed cubing algorithms can be used to efficiently construct a sampling cube.

Now that we have established that sampling cubes can be computed efficiently, our next step is to find a way of boosting the confidence of results obtained for queries on sample data.

Query Processing: Boosting Confidences for Small Samples

A query posed against a data cube can be either a *point query* or a *range query*. Without loss of generality, consider the case of a point query. Here, it corresponds to a cell in sampling cube C_R. The goal is to provide an accurate point estimate for the samples in that cell. Because the cube also reports the confidence interval associated with the sample mean, there is some measure of "reliability" to the returned answer. If the confidence interval is small, the reliability is deemed good; however, if the interval is large, the reliability is questionable.

"What can we do to boost the reliability of query answers?" Consider what affects the confidence interval size. There are two main factors: the variance of the sample data and the sample size. First, a rather large variance in the cell may indicate that the chosen cube

cell is poor for prediction. A better solution is probably to drill down on the query cell to a more specific one (i.e., asking more specific queries). Second, a small sample size can cause a large confidence interval. When there are very few samples, the corresponding t_c is large because of the small degree of freedom. This in turn could cause a large confidence interval. Intuitively, this makes sense. Suppose one is trying to figure out the average income of people in the United States. Just asking two or three people does not give much confidence to the returned response.

The best way to solve this small sample size problem is to get more data. Fortunately, there is usually an abundance of additional data available in the cube. The data do not match the query cell exactly; however, we can consider data from cells that are "close by." There are two ways to incorporate such data to enhance the reliability of the query answer: (1) *intracuboid query expansion*, where we consider nearby cells *within* the same cuboid, and (2) *intercuboid query expansion*, where we consider more general versions (from parent cuboids) of the query cell. Let's see how this works, starting with intracuboid query expansion.

Method 1. Intracuboid query expansion. Here, we expand the sample size by including nearby cells in the *same* cuboid as the queried cell, as shown in Figure 5.15(a). We just have to be careful that the new samples serve to increase the confidence in the answer without changing the query's semantics.

So, the first question is "*Which dimensions should be expanded?*" The best candidates should be the dimensions that are *uncorrelated* or *weakly correlated* with the measure

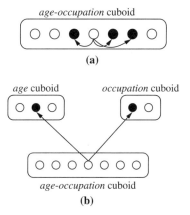

Figure 5.15 Query expansion within sampling cube: Given small data samples, both methods use strategies to boost the reliability of query answers by considering additional data cell values. (a) Intracuboid expansion considers nearby cells in the same cuboid as the queried cell. (b) Intercuboid expansion considers more general cells from parent cuboids.

value (i.e., the value to be predicted). Expanding within these dimensions will likely increase the sample size and not shift the query's answer. Consider an example of a 2-D query specifying *education* = "college" and *birth_month* = "July." Let the cube measure be *average income*. Intuitively, education has a high correlation to income while birth month does not. It would be harmful to expand the *education* dimension to include values such as "graduate" or "high school." They are likely to alter the final result. However, expansion in the *birth_month* dimension to include other month values could be helpful, because it is unlikely to change the result but will increase sampling size.

To mathematically measure the correlation of a dimension to the cube value, the correlation between the dimension's values and their aggregated cube measures is computed. *Pearson's correlation coefficient* for numeric data and the χ^2 correlation test for nominal data are popularly used correlation measures, although many other measures, such as *covariance*, can be used. (These measures were presented in Section 3.3.2.) A dimension that is strongly correlated with the value to be predicted should *not* be a candidate for expansion. Notice that since the correlation of a dimension with the cube measure is independent of a particular query, it should be precomputed and stored with the cube measure to facilitate efficient online analysis.

After selecting dimensions for expansion, the next question is "*Which values within these dimensions should the expansion use?*" This relies on the semantic knowledge of the dimensions in question. The goal should be to select semantically similar values to minimize the risk of altering the final result. Consider the *age* dimension—similarity of values in this dimension is clear. There is a definite (numeric) order to the values. Dimensions with numeric or ordinal (ranked) data (like *education*) have a definite ordering among data values. Therefore, we can select values that are close to the instantiated query value. For nominal data of a dimension that is organized in a multilevel hierarchy in a data cube (e.g., *location*), we should select those values located in the same branch of the tree (e.g., the same district or city).

By considering additional data during query expansion, we are aiming for a more accurate and reliable answer. As mentioned before, strongly correlated dimensions are precluded from expansion for this purpose. An additional strategy is to ensure that new samples share the "same" cube measure value (e.g., mean income) as the existing samples in the query cell. The two-sample *t*-test is a relatively simple statistical method that can be used to determine whether two samples have the same mean (or any other point estimate), where "same" means that they do not differ significantly. (It is described in greater detail in Section 8.5.5 on model selection using statistical tests of significance.)

The test determines whether two samples have the same mean (the null hypothesis) with the only assumption being that they are both normally distributed. The test fails if there is evidence that the two samples do not share the same mean. Furthermore, the test can be performed with a confidence level as an input. This allows the user to control how strict or loose the query expansion will be.

Example 5.14 shows how the intracuboid expansion strategies just described can be used to answer a query on sample data.

Table 5.10 Sample Customer Survey Data

gender	age	education	occupation	income
female	23	college	teacher	$85,000
female	40	college	programmer	$50,000
female	31	college	programmer	$52,000
female	50	graduate	teacher	$90,000
female	62	graduate	CEO	$500,000
male	25	high school	programmer	$50,000
male	28	high school	CEO	$250,000
male	40	college	teacher	$80,000
male	50	college	programmer	$45,000
male	57	graduate	programmer	$80,000

Example 5.14 **Intracuboid query expansion to answer a query on sample data.** Consider a book retailer trying to learn more about its customers' annual income levels. In Table 5.10, a sample of the survey data collected is shown.[6] In the survey, customers are segmented by four attributes, namely *gender, age, education,* and *occupation.*

Let a query on customer income be "*age* = 25," where the user specifies a 95% confidence level. Suppose this returns an *income* value of $50,000 with a rather large confidence interval.[7] Suppose also, that this confidence interval is larger than a preset threshold and that the *age* dimension was found to have little correlation with *income* in this data set. Therefore, intracuboid expansion starts within the *age* dimension. The nearest cell is "*age* = 23," which returns an *income* of $85,000. The two-sample t-test at the 95% confidence level passes so the query expands; it is now "*age* = {23, 25}" with a smaller confidence interval than initially. However, it is still larger than the threshold, so expansion continues to the next nearest cell: "*age* = 28," which returns an *income* of $250,000. The two sample t-test between this cell and the original query cell fails; as a result, it is ignored. Next, "*age* = 31" is checked and it passes the test.

The confidence interval of the three cells combined is now below the threshold and the expansion finishes at "*age* = {23, 25, 31}." The mean of the *income* values at these three cells is $\frac{85,000+50,000+52,000}{3}$ = $62,333, which is returned as the query answer. It has a smaller confidence interval, and thus is more reliable than the response of $50,000, which would have been returned if intracuboid expansion had not been considered. ∎

Method 2. Intercuboid query expansion. In this case, the expansion occurs by looking to a *more general cell*, as shown in Figure 5.15(b). For example, the cell in the 2-D cuboid

---

[6]For the sake of illustration, ignore the fact that the sample size is too small to be statistically significant.

[7]For the sake of the example, suppose this is true even though there is only one sample. In practice, more points are needed to calculate a legitimate value.

age-occupation can use its parent in either of the 1-D cuboids, *age* or *occupation*. Think of intercuboid expansion as just an extreme case of intracuboid expansion, where *all* the cells within a dimension are used in the expansion. This essentially sets the dimension to ∗ and thus generalizes to a higher-level cuboid.

A *k*-dimensional cell has *k* direct parents in the cuboid lattice, where each parent is $(k-1)$-dimensional. There are *many* more ancestor cells in the data cube (e.g., if multiple dimensions are rolled up simultaneously). However, we choose only one parent here to make the search space tractable and to limit the change in the query's semantics. As with intracuboid query expansion, correlated dimensions are not allowed in intercuboid expansions. Within the uncorrelated dimensions, the two-sample *t*-test can be performed to confirm that the parent and the query cell share the same sample mean. If multiple parent cells pass the test, the test's confidence level can be adjusted progressively higher until only one passes. Alternatively, multiple parent cells can be used to boost the confidence simultaneously. The choice is application dependent.

Example 5.15 **Intercuboid expansion to answer a query on sample data.** Given the input relation in Table 5.10, let the query on *income* be "*occupation* = teacher ∧ *gender* = male." There is only one sample in Table 5.10 that matches the query, and it has an *income* of $80,000. Suppose the corresponding confidence interval is larger than a preset threshold. We use intercuboid expansion to find a more reliable answer. There are two parent cells in the data cube: "*gender* = male" and "*occupation* = teacher." By moving up to "*gender* = male" (and thus setting *occupation* to ∗), the mean *income* is $101,000. A two sample *t*-test reveals that this parent's sample mean differs significantly from that of the original query cell, so it is ignored. Next, "*occupation* = teacher" is considered. It has a mean *income* of $85,000 and passes the two-sample *t*-test. As a result, the query is expanded to "*occupation* = teacher" and an *income* value of $85,000 is returned with acceptable reliability. ∎

"*How can we determine which method to choose—intracuboid expansion or intercuboid expansion?*" This is difficult to answer without knowing the data and the application. A strategy for choosing between the two is to consider what the tolerance is for change in the query's semantics. This depends on the specific dimensions chosen in the query. For instance, the user might tolerate a bigger change in semantics for the *age* dimension than *education*. The difference in tolerance could be so large that the user is willing to set *age* to ∗ (i.e., intercuboid expansion) rather than letting *education* change at all. Domain knowledge is helpful here.

So far, our discussion has only focused on full materialization of the sampling cube. In many real-world problems, this is often impossible, especially for high-dimensional cases. Real-world survey data, for example, can easily contain over 50 variables (i.e., dimensions). The sampling cube size would grow exponentially with the number of dimensions. To handle high-dimensional data, a sampling cube method called *Sampling Cube Shell* was developed. It integrates the Frag-Shell method of Section 5.2.4 with the query expansion approach. The shell computes only a subset of the full sampling cube.

The subset should consist of relatively low-dimensional cuboids (that are commonly queried) and cuboids that offer the most benefit to the user. The details are left to interested readers as an exercise. The method was tested on both real and synthetic data and found to be efficient and effective in answering queries.

5.3.2 Ranking Cubes: Efficient Computation of Top-*k* Queries

The data cube helps not only online analytical processing of multidimensional queries but also search and data mining. In this section, we introduce a new cube structure called *Ranking Cube* and examine how it contributes to the efficient processing of *top-k queries*. Instead of returning a large set of indiscriminative answers to a query, a **top-k query** (or **ranking query**) returns only the best *k* results according to a user-specified preference.

The results are returned in ranked order so that the best is at the top. The user-specified preference generally consists of two components: a *selection condition* and a *ranking function*. Top-*k* queries are common in many applications like searching web databases, *k*-nearest-neighbor searches with approximate matches, and similarity queries in multimedia databases.

Example 5.16 **A top-*k* query.** Consider an online used-car database, *R*, that maintains the following information for each car: producer (e.g., Ford, Honda), model (e.g., Taurus, Accord), type (e.g., sedan, convertible), color (e.g., red, silver), transmission (e.g., auto, manual), price, mileage, and so on. A typical top-*k* query over this database is

Q_1:   select *top* 5 * from *R*
         where *producer* = "Ford" and *type* = "sedan"
         order by $(price - 10K)^2 + (mileage - 30K)^2$ asc

Within the dimensions (or attributes) for *R*, *producer* and *type* are used here as **selection dimensions**. The **ranking function** is given in the order-by clause. It specifies the **ranking dimensions**, *price* and *mileage*. Q_1 searches for the top-5 sedans made by Ford. The entries found are ranked or sorted in ascending (asc) order, according to the ranking function. The ranking function is formulated so that entries that have price and mileage closest to the user's specified values of \$10K and 30K, respectively, appear toward the top of the list. ∎

The database may have many dimensions that could be used for selection, describing, for example, whether a car has power windows, air conditioning, or a sunroof. Users may pick any subset of dimensions and issue a top-*k* query using their preferred ranking function. There are many other similar application scenarios. For example, when searching for hotels, ranking functions are often constructed based on price and distance to an area of interest. Selection conditions can be imposed on, say, the hotel location district, the star rating, and whether the hotel offers complimentary treats or Internet access. The ranking functions may be linear, quadratic, or any other form.

As shown in the preceding examples, individual users may not only propose ad hoc ranking functions, but also have different data subsets of interest. Users often want to thoroughly study the data via *multidimensional analysis* of the top-k query results. For example, if unsatisfied by the top-5 results returned by Q_1, the user may roll up on the producer dimension to check the top-5 results on all sedans. The dynamic nature of the problem imposes a great challenge to researchers. OLAP requires offline pre-computation so that multidimensional analysis can be performed on-the-fly, yet the ad hoc ranking functions prohibit full materialization. A natural compromise is to adopt a *semi-offline materialization* and *semi-online computation* model.

Suppose a relation R has selection dimensions $(A_1, A_2, \ldots, A_S)$ and ranking dimensions $(N_1, N_2, \ldots, N_R)$. Values in each ranking dimension can be partitioned into multiple intervals according to the data and expected query distributions. Regarding the price of used cars, for example, we may have, say, these four partitions (or value ranges): $\leq 5K$, $[5 - 10K)$, $[10 - 15K)$, and $\geq 15K$. A ranking cube can be constructed by performing multidimensional aggregations on selection dimensions. We can store the count for each partition of each ranking dimension, thereby making the cube "rank-aware." The top-k queries can be answered by first accessing the cells in the more preferred value ranges before consulting the cells in the less preferred value ranges.

Example 5.17 **Using a ranking cube to answer a top-k query.** Suppose Table 5.11 shows C_{MT}, a materialized (i.e., precomputed) cuboid of a ranking cube for used-car sales. The cuboid, C_{MT}, is for the selection dimensions *producer* and *type*. It shows the count and corresponding tuple IDs (TIDs) for various partitions of the ranking dimensions, *price* and *mileage*.

Query Q_1 can be answered by using a selection condition to select the appropriate selection dimension values (i.e., *producer* = "Ford" and *type* = "sedan") in cuboid C_{MT}. In addition, the ranking function "$(price - 10K)^2 + (mileage - 30K)^2$" is used to find the tuples that most closely match the user's criteria. If there are not enough matching tuples found in the closest matching cells, the next closest matching cells will need to be accessed. We may even drill down to the corresponding lower-level cells to see the count distributions of cells that match the ranking function and additional criteria regarding, say, model, maintenance situation, or other loaded features. Only users who really want to see more detailed information, such as interior photos, will need to access the physical records stored in the database. ∎

Table 5.11 Cuboid of a Ranking Cube for Used-Car Sales

producer	type	price	mileage	count	TIDs
Ford	sedan	<5K	30–40K	7	$t_6, \ldots, t_{68}$
Ford	sedan	5–10K	30–40K	50	$t_{15}, \ldots, t_{152}$
Honda	sedan	10–15K	30–40K	20	$t_8, \ldots, t_{32}$
...	...	...	...	...	...

Most real-life top-k queries are likely to involve only a small subset of selection attributes. To support high-dimensional ranking cubes, we can carefully select the cuboids that need to be materialized. For example, we could choose to materialize only the 1-D cuboids that contain single-selection dimensions. This will achieve low space overhead and still have high performance when the number of selection dimensions is large. In some cases, there may exist many ranking dimensions to support multiple users with rather different preferences. For example, buyers may search for houses by considering various factors like price, distance to school or shopping, number of years old, floor space, and tax. In this case, a possible solution is to create multiple data partitions, each of which consists of a subset of the ranking dimensions. The query processing may need to search over a joint space involving multiple data partitions.

In summary, the general philosophy of ranking cubes is to materialize such cubes on the set of selection dimensions. Use of the interval-based partitioning in ranking dimensions makes the ranking cube efficient and flexible at supporting ad hoc user queries. Various implementation techniques and query optimization methods have been developed for efficient computation and query processing based on this framework.

5.4 Multidimensional Data Analysis in Cube Space

Data cubes create a flexible and powerful means to group and aggregate data subsets. They allow data to be explored in multiple dimensional combinations and at varying aggregate granularities. This capability greatly increases the analysis bandwidth and helps effective discovery of interesting patterns and knowledge from data. The use of cube space makes the data space both meaningful and tractable.

This section presents methods of multidimensional data analysis that make use of data cubes to organize data into intuitive regions of interest at varying granularities. Section 5.4.1 presents *prediction cubes*, a technique for multidimensional data mining that facilitates predictive modeling in multidimensional space. Section 5.4.2 describes how to construct *multifeature cubes*. These support complex analytical queries involving multiple dependent aggregates at multiple granularities. Finally, Section 5.4.3 describes an interactive method for users to systematically explore cube space. In such *exception-based, discovery-driven exploration*, interesting exceptions or anomalies in the data are automatically detected and marked for users with visual cues.

5.4.1 Prediction Cubes: Prediction Mining in Cube Space

Recently, researchers have turned their attention toward **multidimensional data mining** to uncover knowledge at varying dimensional combinations and granularities. Such mining is also known as *exploratory multidimensional data mining* and *online analytical data mining (OLAM)*. Multidimensional data space is huge. In preparing the data, how can we identify the interesting subspaces for exploration? To what granularities should we aggregate the data? Multidimensional data mining in cube space organizes data of interest into intuitive regions at various granularities. It analyzes and mines the data by applying various data mining techniques systematically over these regions.

There are at least four ways in which OLAP-style analysis can be fused with data mining techniques:

1. *Use cube space to define the data space for mining.* Each region in cube space represents a subset of data over which we wish to find interesting patterns. Cube space is defined by a set of expert-designed, informative dimension hierarchies, not just arbitrary subsets of data. Therefore, the use of cube space makes the data space both meaningful and tractable.

2. *Use OLAP queries to generate features and targets for mining.* The features and even the targets (that we wish to learn to predict) can sometimes be naturally defined as OLAP aggregate queries over regions in cube space.

3. *Use data mining models as building blocks in a multistep mining process.* Multidimensional data mining in cube space may consist of multiple steps, where data mining models can be viewed as building blocks that are used to describe the behavior of interesting data sets, rather than the end results.

4. *Use data cube computation techniques to speed up repeated model construction.* Multidimensional data mining in cube space may require building a model for each candidate data space, which is usually too expensive to be feasible. However, by carefully sharing computation across model construction for different candidates based on data cube computation techniques, efficient mining is achievable.

In this subsection we study *prediction cubes*, an example of multidimensional data mining where the cube space is explored for prediction tasks. A **prediction cube** is a cube structure that stores prediction models in multidimensional data space and supports prediction in an OLAP manner. Recall that in a data cube, each cell value is an aggregate number (e.g., count) computed over the data subset in that cell. However, each cell value in a prediction cube is computed by evaluating a predictive model built on the data subset in that cell, thereby representing that subset's predictive behavior.

Instead of seeing prediction models as the end result, prediction cubes use prediction models as building blocks to define the interestingness of data subsets, that is, they identify data subsets that indicate more accurate prediction. This is best explained with an example.

Example 5.18 Prediction cube for identification of interesting cube subspaces. Suppose a company has a customer table with the attributes *time* (with two granularity levels: *month* and *year*), *location* (with two granularity levels: *state* and *country*), *gender, salary,* and one class-label attribute: *valued_customer.* A manager wants to analyze the decision process of whether a customer is highly valued with respect to *time* and *location.* In particular, he is interested in the question "*Are there times at and locations in which the value of a* *customer depended greatly on the customer's gender?"* Notice that he believes *time* and *location* play a role in predicting valued customers, but at what granularity levels do they depend on *gender* for this task? For example, is performing analysis using {*month, country*} better than {*year, state*}?

Consider a data table **D** (e.g., the customer table). Let **X** be the attributes set for which no concept hierarchy has been defined (e.g., *gender, salary*). Let Y be the class-label attribute (e.g., *valued_customer*), and **Z** be the set of multilevel attributes, that is, attributes for which concept hierarchies have been defined (e.g., *time, location*). Let **V** be the set of attributes for which we would like to define their predictiveness. In our example, this set is {*gender*}. The predictiveness of **V** on a data subset can be quantified by the difference in accuracy between the model built on that subset using **X** to predict Y and the model built on that subset using $\mathbf{X} - \mathbf{V}$ (e.g., {*salary*}) to predict Y. The intuition is that, if the difference is large, **V** must play an important role in the prediction of class label Y.

Given a set of attributes, **V**, and a learning algorithm, the prediction cube at granularity $\langle l_1, \ldots, l_d \rangle$ (e.g., $\langle year, state \rangle$) is a d-dimensional array, in which the value in each cell (e.g., [2010, Illinois]) is the predictiveness of **V** evaluated on the subset defined by the cell (e.g., the records in the customer table with *time* in 2010 and *location* in Illinois). ∎

Supporting OLAP roll-up and drill-down operations on a prediction cube is a computational challenge requiring the materialization of cell values at many different granularities. For simplicity, we can consider only full materialization. A naïve way to fully materialize a prediction cube is to exhaustively build models and evaluate them for each cell and granularity. This method is very expensive if the base data set is large. An ensemble method called **Probability-Based Ensemble (PBE)** was developed as a more feasible alternative. It requires model construction for only the finest-grained cells. OLAP-style bottom-up aggregation is then used to generate the values of the coarser-grained cells.

The prediction of a predictive model can be seen as finding a class label that maximizes a scoring function. The PBE method was developed to approximately make the scoring function of any predictive model distributively decomposable. In our discussion of data cube measures in Section 4.2.4, we showed that distributive and algebraic measures can be computed efficiently. Therefore, if the scoring function used is distributively or algebraically decomposable, prediction cubes can also be computed with efficiency. In this way, the PBE method reduces prediction cube computation to data cube computation.

For example, previous studies have shown that the naïve Bayes classifier has an algebraically decomposable scoring function, and the kernel density–based classifier has a distributively decomposable scoring function.[8] Therefore, either of these could be used

---

[8] Naïve Bayes classifiers are detailed in Chapter 8. Kernel density–based classifiers, such as support vector machines, are described in Chapter 9.

to implement prediction cubes efficiently. The PBE method presents a novel approach to multidimensional data mining in cube space.

5.4.2 Multifeature Cubes: Complex Aggregation at Multiple Granularities

Data cubes facilitate the answering of analytical or mining-oriented queries as they allow the computation of aggregate data at multiple granularity levels. Traditional data cubes are typically constructed on commonly used dimensions (e.g., *time*, *location*, and *product*) using simple measures (e.g., count( ), average( ), and sum()). In this section, you will learn a newer way to define data cubes called **multifeature cubes**. Multifeature cubes enable more in-depth analysis. They can compute more complex queries of which the measures depend on groupings of multiple aggregates at varying granularity levels. The queries posed can be much more elaborate and task-specific than traditional queries, as we shall illustrate in the next examples. Many complex data mining queries can be answered by multifeature cubes without significant increase in computational cost, in comparison to cube computation for simple queries with traditional data cubes.

To illustrate the idea of multifeature cubes, let's first look at an example of a query on a simple data cube.

Example 5.19 **A simple data cube query.** Let the query be "*Find the total sales in 2010, broken down by item, region, and month, with subtotals for each dimension.*" To answer this query, a traditional data cube is constructed that aggregates the total sales at the following eight different granularity levels: {(*item, region, month*), (*item, region*), (*item, month*), (*month, region*), (*item*), (*month*), (*region*), ()}, where () represents **all**. This data cube is simple in that it does not involve any dependent aggregates. ∎

To illustrate what is meant by "dependent aggregates," let's examine a more complex query, which can be computed with a multifeature cube.

Example 5.20 **A complex query involving dependent aggregates.** Suppose the query is "*Grouping by all subsets of {item, region, month}, find the maximum price in 2010 for each group and the total sales among all maximum price tuples.*"

The specification of such a query using standard SQL can be long, repetitive, and difficult to optimize and maintain. Alternatively, it can be specified concisely using an extended SQL syntax as follows:

select	*item, region, month,* max(*price*), sum(*R.sales*)
from	*Purchases*
where	*year* = 2010
cube by	*item, region, month*: R
such that	*R.price* = max(*price*)

The tuples representing purchases in 2010 are first selected. The **cube by** clause computes aggregates (or group-by's) for all possible combinations of the attributes *item,* *region*, and *month*. It is an *n*-dimensional generalization of the **group-by** clause. The attributes specified in the **cube by** clause are the **grouping attributes**. Tuples with the same value on all grouping attributes form one group. Let the groups be $g_1, \ldots, g_r$. For each group of tuples g_i, the maximum price max_{g_i} among the tuples forming the group is computed. The variable R is a **grouping variable**, ranging over all tuples in group g_i that have a price equal to max_{g_i} (as specified in the **such that** clause). The sum of sales of the tuples in g_i that R ranges over is computed and returned with the values of the grouping attributes of g_i.

The resulting cube is a multifeature cube in that it supports complex data mining queries for which multiple dependent aggregates are computed at a variety of granularities. For example, the sum of sales returned in this query is dependent on the set of maximum price tuples for each group. In general, multifeature cubes give users the flexibility to define sophisticated, task-specific cubes on which multidimensional aggregation and OLAP-based mining can be performed. ∎

"How can multifeature cubes be computed efficiently?" The computation of a multifeature cube depends on the types of aggregate functions used in the cube. In Chapter 4, we saw that aggregate functions can be categorized as either distributive, algebraic, or holistic. Multifeature cubes can be organized into the same categories and computed efficiently by minor extension of the cube computation methods in Section 5.2.

5.4.3 Exception-Based, Discovery-Driven Cube Space Exploration

As studied in previous sections, a data cube may have a large number of cuboids, and each cuboid may contain a large number of (aggregate) cells. With such an overwhelmingly large space, it becomes a burden for users to even just browse a cube, let alone think of exploring it thoroughly. Tools need to be developed to assist users in intelligently exploring the huge aggregated space of a data cube.

In this section, we describe a **discovery-driven approach** to exploring cube space. Precomputed measures indicating data exceptions are used to guide the user in the data analysis process, at all aggregation levels. We hereafter refer to these measures as *exception indicators*. Intuitively, an **exception** is a data cube cell value that is significantly different from the value anticipated, based on a statistical model. The model considers variations and patterns in the measure value across *all the dimensions* to which a cell belongs. For example, if the analysis of *item-sales* data reveals an increase in sales in December in comparison to all other months, this may seem like an exception in the time dimension. However, it is not an exception if the *item* dimension is considered, since there is a similar increase in sales for other items during December.

The model considers exceptions hidden at all aggregated group-by's of a data cube. Visual cues, such as background color, are used to reflect each cell's degree of exception, based on the precomputed exception indicators. Efficient algorithms have been proposed for cube construction, as discussed in Section 5.2. The computation of exception indicators can be overlapped with cube construction, so that the overall construction of data cubes for discovery-driven exploration is efficient.

Three measures are used as exception indicators to help identify data anomalies. These measures indicate the degree of surprise that the quantity in a cell holds, with respect to its expected value. The measures are computed and associated with every cell, for all aggregation levels. They are as follows:

- **SelfExp**: This indicates the degree of surprise of the cell value, relative to other cells at the same aggregation level.

- **InExp**: This indicates the degree of surprise somewhere beneath the cell, if we were to drill down from it.

- **PathExp**: This indicates the degree of surprise for each drill-down path from the cell.

The use of these measures for discovery-driven exploration of data cubes is illustrated in Example 5.21.

Example 5.21 **Discovery-driven exploration of a data cube.** Suppose that you want to analyze the monthly sales at *AllElectronics* as a percentage difference from the previous month. The dimensions involved are *item*, *time*, and *region*. You begin by studying the data aggregated over all items and sales regions for each month, as shown in Figure 5.16.

To view the exception indicators, you click on a button marked highlight exceptions on the screen. This translates the SelfExp and InExp values into visual cues, displayed with each cell. Each cell's background color is based on its SelfExp value. In addition, a box is drawn around each cell, where the thickness and color of the box are functions of its InExp value. Thick boxes indicate high InExp values. In both cases, the darker the color, the greater the degree of exception. For example, the dark, thick boxes for sales during July, August, and September signal the user to explore the lower-level aggregations of these cells by drilling down.

Drill-downs can be executed along the aggregated *item* or *region* dimensions. *"Which path has more exceptions?"* you wonder. To find this out, you select a cell of interest and trigger a path exception module that colors each dimension based on the PathExp value of the cell. This value reflects that path's degree of surprise. Suppose that the path along *item* contains more exceptions.

A drill-down along *item* results in the cube slice of Figure 5.17, showing the sales over time for each item. At this point, you are presented with many different sales values to analyze. By clicking on the highlight exceptions button, the visual cues are displayed, bringing focus to the exceptions. Consider the sales difference of 41% for *"Sony*

Sum of sales												
							Month					
	Jan	Feb	Mar	Apr	May	Jun	Jul	Aug	Sep	Oct	Nov	Dec
Total		1%	–1%	0%	1%	3%	–1%	–9%	–1%	2%	–4%	3%

Figure 5.16 Change in sales over time.

Avg. sales	Month											
Item	Jan	Feb	Mar	Apr	May	Jun	Jul	Aug	Sep	Oct	Nov	Dec
Sony b/w printer		9%	–8%	2%	–5%	14%	–4%	0%	41%	–13%	–15%	–11%
Sony color printer		0%	0%	3%	2%	4%	–10%	–13%	0%	4%	–6%	4%
HP b/w printer		–2%	1%	2%	3%	8%	0%	–12%	–9%	3%	–3%	6%
HP color printer		0%	0%	–2%	1%	0%	–1%	–7%	–2%	1%	–4%	1%
IBM desktop computer		1%	–2%	–1%	–1%	3%	3%	–10%	4%	1%	–4%	–1%
IBM laptop computer		0%	0%	–1%	3%	4%	2%	10%	–2%	0%	–9%	3%
Toshiba desktop computer		–2%	–5%	1%	1%	–1%	1%	5%	–3%	–5%	–1%	–1%
Toshiba laptop computer		1%	0%	3%	0%	–2%	–2%	–5%	3%	2%	–1%	0%
Logitech mouse		3%	–2%	–1%	0%	4%	6%	–11%	2%	1%	–4%	0%
Ergo-way mouse		0%	0%	2%	3%	1%	–2%	–2%	–5%	0%	–5%	8%

Figure 5.17 Change in sales for each *item-time* combination.

Avg. sales	Month											
Region	Jan	Feb	Mar	Apr	May	Jun	Jul	Aug	Sep	Oct	Nov	Dec
North		–1%	–3%	–1%	0%	3%	4%	–7%	1%	0%	–3%	–3%
South		–1%	1%	–9%	6%	–1%	–39%	9%	–34%	4%	1%	7%
East		–1%	–2%	2%	–3%	1%	18%	–2%	11%	–3%	–2%	–1%
West		4%	0%	–1%	–3%	5%	1%	–18%	8%	5%	–8%	1%

Figure 5.18 Change in sales for the item *IBM desktop computer* per region.

b/w printers" in September. This cell has a dark background, indicating a high SelfExp value, meaning that the cell is an exception. Consider now the sales difference of −15% for "*Sony b/w printers*" in November and of −11% in December. The −11% value for December is marked as an exception, while the −15% value is not, even though −15% is a bigger deviation than −11%. This is because the exception indicators consider all the dimensions that a cell is in. Notice that the December sales of most of the other items have a large positive value, while the November sales do not. Therefore, by considering the cell's position in the cube, the sales difference for "*Sony b/w printers*" in December is exceptional, while the November sales difference of this item is not.

The InExp values can be used to indicate exceptions at lower levels that are not visible at the current level. Consider the cells for "*IBM desktop computers*" in July and September. These both have a dark, thick box around them, indicating high InExp values. You may decide to further explore the sales of "*IBM desktop computers*" by drilling down along *region*. The resulting sales difference by *region* is shown in Figure 5.18, where the highlight exceptions option has been invoked. The visual cues displayed make it easy to instantly notice an exception for the sales of "*IBM desktop computers*" in the southern region, where such sales have decreased by −39% and −34% in July and September, respectively. These detailed exceptions were far from obvious when we were viewing the data as an *item-time* group-by, aggregated over *region* in Figure 5.17. Thus, the InExp value is useful for searching for exceptions at lower-level cells of the cube. ∎

"*How are the exception values computed?*" The SelfExp, InExp, and PathExp measures are based on a statistical method for table analysis. They take into account all of the group-by's (aggregations) in which a given cell value participates. A cell value is considered an exception based on how much it differs from its expected value, where its expected value is determined with a statistical model. The difference between a given cell value and its expected value is called a **residual**. Intuitively, the larger the residual, the more the given cell value is an exception. The comparison of residual values requires us to scale the values based on the expected standard deviation associated with the residuals. A cell value is therefore considered an exception if its scaled residual value exceeds a prespecified threshold. The SelfExp, InExp, and PathExp measures are based on this scaled residual.

The expected value of a given cell is a function of the higher-level group-by's of the given cell. For example, given a cube with the three dimensions A, B, and C, the expected value for a cell at the ith position in A, the jth position in B, and the kth position in C is a function of γ, γ_i^A, γ_j^B, γ_k^C, γ_{ij}^{AB}, γ_{ik}^{AC}, and γ_{jk}^{BC}, which are coefficients of the statistical model used. The coefficients reflect how different the values at more detailed levels are, based on generalized impressions formed by looking at higher-level aggregations. In this way, the exception quality of a cell value is based on the exceptions of the values below it. Thus, when seeing an exception, it is natural for the user to further explore the exception by drilling down.

"*How can the data cube be efficiently constructed for discovery-driven exploration?*" This computation consists of three phases. The first step involves the computation of the aggregate values defining the cube, such as **sum** or **count**, over which exceptions will be found. The second phase consists of model fitting, in which the coefficients mentioned before are determined and used to compute the standardized residuals. This phase can be overlapped with the first phase because the computations involved are similar. The third phase computes the SelfExp, InExp, and PathExp values, based on the standardized residuals. This phase is computationally similar to phase 1. Therefore, the computation of data cubes for discovery-driven exploration can be done efficiently.

5.5 Summary

- **Data cube computation and exploration** play an essential role in data warehousing and are important for flexible data mining in multidimensional space.

- A data cube consists of a **lattice of cuboids**. Each cuboid corresponds to a different degree of summarization of the given multidimensional data. **Full materialization** refers to the computation of all the cuboids in a data cube lattice. **Partial materialization** refers to the selective computation of a subset of the cuboid cells in the lattice. Iceberg cubes and shell fragments are examples of partial materialization. An **iceberg cube** is a data cube that stores only those cube cells that have an aggregate value (e.g., count) above some minimum support threshold. For **shell fragments** of a data cube, only some cuboids involving a small number of dimensions are computed, and queries on additional combinations of the dimensions can be computed on-the-fly.

- There are several efficient **data cube computation methods**. In this chapter, we discussed four cube computation methods in detail: (1) **MultiWay** array aggregation for materializing full data cubes in sparse-array-based, bottom-up, shared computation; (2) **BUC** for computing iceberg cubes by exploring ordering and sorting for efficient top-down computation; (3) **Star-Cubing** for computing iceberg cubes by integrating top-down and bottom-up computation using a star-tree structure; and (4) **shell-fragment cubing**, which supports high-dimensional OLAP by precomputing only the partitioned cube shell fragments.

- **Multidimensional data mining in cube space** is the integration of knowledge discovery with multidimensional data cubes. It facilitates systematic and focused knowledge discovery in large structured and semi-structured data sets. It will continue to endow analysts with tremendous flexibility and power at multidimensional and multigranularity exploratory analysis. This is a vast open area for researchers to build powerful and sophisticated data mining mechanisms.

- Techniques for processing advanced queries have been proposed that take advantage of cube technology. These include **sampling cubes** for multidimensional analysis on sampling data, and **ranking cubes** for efficient top-k (ranking) query processing in large relational data sets.

- This chapter highlighted three approaches to multidimensional data analysis with data cubes. **Prediction cubes** compute prediction models in multidimensional cube space. They help users identify interesting data subsets at varying degrees of granularity for effective prediction. **Multifeature cubes** compute complex queries involving multiple dependent aggregates at multiple granularities. **Exception-based, discovery-driven exploration** of cube space displays visual cues to indicate discovered data exceptions at all aggregation levels, thereby guiding the user in the data analysis process.

5.6 Exercises

5.1 Assume that a 10-D base cuboid contains only three base cells: (1) $(a_1, d_2, d_3, d_4, \ldots, d_9, d_{10})$, (2) $(d_1, b_2, d_3, d_4, \ldots, d_9, d_{10})$, and (3) $(d_1, d_2, c_3, d_4, \ldots, d_9, d_{10})$, where $a_1 \neq d_1$, $b_2 \neq d_2$, and $c_3 \neq d_3$. The measure of the cube is count().

   (a) How many *nonempty* cuboids will a full data cube contain?

   (b) How many *nonempty* aggregate (i.e., nonbase) cells will a full cube contain?

(c) How many *nonempty* aggregate cells will an iceberg cube contain if the condition of the iceberg cube is "count $\geq$ 2"?

(d) A cell, c, is a *closed cell* if there exists no cell, d, such that d is a specialization of cell c (i.e., d is obtained by replacing a $*$ in c by a non-$*$ value) and d has the same measure value as c. A *closed cube* is a data cube consisting of only closed cells. How many closed cells are in the full cube?

5.2 There are several typical cube computation methods, such as *MultiWay* [ZDN97], *BUC* [BR99], and *Star-Cubing* [XHLW03]. Briefly describe these three methods (i.e., use one or two lines to outline the key points), and compare their feasibility and performance under the following conditions:

(a) Computing a dense full cube of low dimensionality (e.g., less than eight dimensions).

(b) Computing an iceberg cube of around 10 dimensions with a highly skewed data distribution.

(c) Computing a sparse iceberg cube of high dimensionality (e.g., over 100 dimensions).

5.3 Suppose a data cube, C, has D dimensions, and the base cuboid contains k distinct tuples.

(a) Present a formula to calculate the minimum number of cells that the cube, C, may contain.

(b) Present a formula to calculate the maximum number of cells that C may contain.

(c) Answer parts (a) and (b) as if the count in each cube cell must be no less than a threshold, v.

(d) Answer parts (a) and (b) as if only closed cells are considered (with the minimum count threshold, v).

5.4 Suppose that a base cuboid has three dimensions, A, B, C, with the following number of cells: $|A| = 1,000,000$, $|B| = 100$, and $|C| = 1000$. Suppose that each dimension is evenly partitioned into 10 portions for *chunking*.

(a) Assuming each dimension has only one level, draw the complete lattice of the cube.

(b) If each cube cell stores one measure with four bytes, what is the total size of the computed cube if the cube is *dense*?

(c) State the order for computing the chunks in the cube that requires the least amount of space, and compute the total amount of main memory space required for computing the 2-D planes.

5.5 Often, the aggregate *count* value of many cells in a large data cuboid is zero, resulting in a huge, yet sparse, multidimensional matrix.

(a) Design an implementation method that can elegantly overcome this sparse matrix problem. Note that you need to explain your data structures in detail and discuss the space needed, as well as how to retrieve data from your structures.

(b) Modify your design in (a) to handle *incremental data updates*. Give the reasoning behind your new design.

5.6 When computing a cube of high dimensionality, we encounter the inherent *curse of dimensionality* problem: There exists a huge number of subsets of combinations of dimensions.

(a) Suppose that there are only two base cells, $\{(a_1, a_2, a_3, \ldots, a_{100})$ and $(a_1, a_2, b_3, \ldots, b_{100})\}$, in a 100-D base cuboid. Compute the number of nonempty aggregate cells. Comment on the storage space and time required to compute these cells.

(b) Suppose we are to compute an iceberg cube from (a). If the minimum support count in the iceberg condition is 2, how many aggregate cells will there be in the iceberg cube? Show the cells.

(c) Introducing iceberg cubes will lessen the burden of computing trivial aggregate cells in a data cube. However, even with iceberg cubes, we could still end up having to compute a large number of trivial uninteresting cells (i.e., with small counts). Suppose that a database has 20 tuples that map to (or cover) the two following base cells in a 100-D base cuboid, each with a cell count of 10: $\{(a_1, a_2, a_3, \ldots, a_{100}) : 10,$ $(a_1, a_2, b_3, \ldots, b_{100}) : 10\}$.

    i. Let the minimum support be 10. How many distinct aggregate cells will there be like the following: $\{(a_1, a_2, a_3, a_4, \ldots, a_{99}, *) : 10, \ldots, (a_1, a_2, *, a_4, \ldots, a_{99}, a_{100}) : 10, \ldots, (a_1, a_2, a_3, *, \ldots, *, *) : 10\}$?

    ii. If we ignore all the aggregate cells that can be obtained by replacing some constants with $*$'s while keeping the same measure value, how many distinct cells remain? What are the cells?

5.7 Propose an algorithm that computes *closed iceberg cubes* efficiently.

5.8 Suppose that we want to compute an iceberg cube for the dimensions, A, B, C, D, where we wish to materialize all cells that satisfy a minimum support count of at least v, and where *cardinality(A) < cardinality(B) < cardinality(C) < cardinality(D)*. Show the *BUC* processing tree (which shows the order in which the BUC algorithm explores a data cube's lattice, starting from **all**) for the construction of this iceberg cube.

5.9 Discuss how you might extend the *Star-Cubing* algorithm to compute iceberg cubes where the iceberg condition tests for an **avg** that is no bigger than some value, v.

5.10 A flight data warehouse for a travel agent consists of six dimensions: *traveler, departure (city), departure_time, arrival, arrival_time,* and *flight*; and two measures: count() and avg_fare(), where avg_fare() stores the concrete fare at the lowest level but the average fare at other levels.

(a) Suppose the cube is fully materialized. Starting with the *base cuboid* [*traveler, departure, departure_time, arrival, arrival_time, flight*], what specific OLAP operations (e.g., roll-up *flight* to *airline*) should one perform to list the average fare per month for *each business traveler* who flies American Airlines (*AA*) from Los Angeles in 2009?

(b) Suppose we want to compute a data cube where the condition is that the minimum number of records is 10 and the average fare is over $500. Outline an efficient cube computation method (based on common sense about flight data distribution).

5.11 **(Implementation project)** There are four typical data cube computation methods: MultiWay [ZDN97], BUC [BR99], H-Cubing [HPDW01], and Star-Cubing [XHLW03].

(a) Implement any one of these cube computation algorithms and describe your implementation, experimentation, and performance. Find another student who has implemented a different algorithm on the same platform (e.g., C++ on Linux) and compare your algorithm performance with his or hers.

Input:

i.   An n-dimensional base cuboid table (for $n < 20$), which is essentially a relational table with n attributes.

ii. An iceberg condition: count $(C) \geq k$, where k is a positive integer as a parameter.

Output:

i.   The set of computed cuboids that satisfy the iceberg condition, in the order of your output generation.

ii. Summary of the set of cuboids in the form of "*cuboid ID*: the number of nonempty cells," sorted in alphabetical order of cuboids (e.g., *A*: 155, *AB*: 120, *ABC*: 22, *ABCD*: 4, *ABCE*: 6, *ABD*: 36), where the number after : represents the number of nonempty cells. (This is used to quickly check the correctness of your results.)

(b) Based on your implementation, discuss the following:

i.   What challenging computation problems are encountered as the number of dimensions grows large?

ii. How can iceberg cubing solve the problems of part (a) for some data sets (and characterize such data sets)?

iii. Give one simple example to show that sometimes iceberg cubes cannot provide a good solution.

(c) Instead of computing a high-dimensionality data cube, we may choose to materialize the cuboids that have only a small number of dimension combinations. For example, for a 30-D data cube, we may only compute the 5-D cuboids for every possible 5-D combination. The resulting cuboids form a *shell cube*. Discuss how easy or hard it is to modify your cube computation algorithm to facilitate such computation.

5.12 The *sampling cube* was proposed for multidimensional analysis of sampling data (e.g., survey data). In many real applications, sampling data can be of high dimensionality (e.g., it is not unusual to have more than 50 dimensions in a survey data set).

(a) How can we construct an efficient and scalable high-dimensional sampling cube in large sampling data sets?

(b) Design an efficient incremental update algorithm for such a high-dimensional sampling cube.

(c) Discuss how to support quality drill-down given that some low-level cells may be empty or contain too few data for reliable analysis.

5.13 The *ranking cube* was proposed for efficient computation of top-k (ranking) queries in relational databases. Recently, researchers have proposed another kind of query, called a *skyline query*. A *skyline query* returns all the objects p_i such that p_i is not dominated by any other object p_j, where dominance is defined as follows. Let the value of p_i on dimension d be $v(p_i, d)$. We say p_i is dominated by p_j if and only if for each preference dimension d, $v(p_j, d) \leq v(p_i, d)$, and there is at least one d where the equality does not hold.

(a) Design a ranking cube so that skyline queries can be processed efficiently.

(b) Skyline queries are sometimes too strict to be desirable to some users. One may generalize the concept of skyline into *generalized skyline* as follows: *Given a d-dimensional database and a query q, the **generalized skyline** is the set of the following objects: (1) the skyline objects and (2) the nonskyline objects that are ϵ-neighbors of a skyline object, where r is an ϵ-neighbor of an object p if the distance between p and r is no more than ϵ.* Design a ranking cube to process generalized skyline queries efficiently.

5.14 The ranking cube was designed to support top-k (ranking) queries in relational database systems. However, ranking queries are also posed to data warehouses, where ranking is on multidimensional aggregates instead of on measures of base facts. For example, consider a product manager who is analyzing a sales database that stores the nationwide sales history, organized by location and time. To make investment decisions, the manager may pose the following query: "*What are the top-10 (state, year) cells having the largest total product sales?*" He may further drill down and ask, "*What are the top-10 (city, month) cells?*" Suppose the system can perform such partial materialization to derive two types of materialized cuboids: a *guiding cuboid* and a *supporting cuboid*, where the former contains a number of guiding cells that provide concise, high-level data statistics to guide the ranking query processing, whereas the latter provides inverted indices for efficient online aggregation.

(a) Derive an efficient method for computing such aggregate ranking cubes.

(b) Extend your framework to handle more advanced measures. One such example could be as follows. Consider an organization donation database, where donors are grouped by "*age*," "*income*," and other attributes. Interesting questions include: "*Which age and income groups have made the top-k average amount of donation (per donor)?*" and "*Which income group of donors has the largest standard deviation in the donation amount?*"

5.15 The *prediction cube* is a good example of multidimensional data mining in cube space.

(a) Propose an efficient algorithm that computes prediction cubes in a given multidimensional database.

(b) For what kind of classification models can your algorithm be applied? Explain.

5.16 *Multifeature cubes* allow us to construct interesting data cubes based on rather sophisticated query conditions. Can you construct the following multifeature cube by translating the following user requests into queries using the form introduced in this textbook?

(a) Construct a smart shopper cube where a shopper is smart if at least 10% of the goods she buys in each shopping trip are on sale.

(b) Construct a data cube for best-deal products where best-deal products are those products for which the price is the lowest for this product in the given month.

5.17 *Discovery-driven cube exploration* is a desirable way to mark interesting points among a large number of cells in a data cube. Individual users may have different views on whether a point should be considered interesting enough to be marked. Suppose one would like to mark those objects of which the absolute value of z score is over 2 in every row and column in a d-dimensional plane.

(a) Derive an efficient computation method to identify such points during the data cube computation.

(b) Suppose a partially materialized cube has $(d-1)$-dimensional and $(d+1)$-dimensional cuboids materialized but not the d-dimensional one. Derive an efficient method to mark those $(d-1)$-dimensional cells with d-dimensional children that contain such marked points.

5.7 Bibliographic Notes

Efficient computation of multidimensional aggregates in data cubes has been studied by many researchers. Gray, Chaudhuri, Bosworth, et al. [GCB+97] proposed *cube-by* as a relational aggregation operator generalizing group-by, crosstabs, and subtotals, and categorized data cube measures into three categories: *distributive, algebraic,* and *holistic.* Harinarayan, Rajaraman, and Ullman [HRU96] proposed a greedy algorithm for the partial materialization of cuboids in the computation of a data cube. Sarawagi and Stonebraker [SS94] developed a chunk-based computation technique for the efficient organization of large multidimensional arrays. Agarwal, Agrawal, Deshpande, et al. [AAD+96] proposed several guidelines for efficient computation of multidimensional aggregates for ROLAP servers.

The chunk-based MultiWay array aggregation method for data cube computation in MOLAP was proposed in Zhao, Deshpande, and Naughton [ZDN97]. Ross and Srivastava [RS97] developed a method for computing sparse data cubes. Iceberg queries are first described in Fang, Shivakumar, Garcia-Molina, et al. [FSGM+98]. BUC, a scalable method that computes iceberg cubes from the apex cuboid downwards, was introduced by Beyer and Ramakrishnan [BR99]. Han, Pei, Dong, and Wang [HPDW01] introduced an H-Cubing method for computing iceberg cubes with complex measures using an H-tree structure.

The Star-Cubing method for computing iceberg cubes with a dynamic star-tree structure was introduced by Xin, Han, Li, and Wah [XHLW03]. MM-Cubing, an efficient iceberg cube computation method that factorizes the lattice space was developed by Shao, Han, and Xin [SHX04]. The shell-fragment-based cubing approach for efficient high-dimensional OLAP was proposed by Li, Han, and Gonzalez [LHG04].

Aside from computing iceberg cubes, another way to reduce data cube computation is to materialize condensed, dwarf, or quotient cubes, which are variants of closed cubes. Wang, Feng, Lu, and Yu proposed computing a reduced data cube, called a *condensed cube* [WLFY02]. Sismanis, Deligiannakis, Roussopoulos, and Kotids proposed computing a compressed data cube, called a *dwarf cube* [SDRK02]. Lakeshmanan, Pei, and Han proposed a *quotient cube* structure to summarize a data cube's semantics [LPH02], which has been further extended to a *qc-tree structure* by Lakshmanan, Pei, and Zhao [LPZ03]. An *aggregation-based* approach, called C-Cubing (i.e., *Closed-Cubing*), has been developed by Xin, Han, Shao, and Liu [XHSL06], which performs efficient closed-cube computation by taking advantage of a new algebraic measure *closedness*.

There are also various studies on the computation of compressed data cubes by approximation, such as *quasi-cubes* by Barbara and Sullivan [BS97]; *wavelet cubes* by Vitter, Wang, and Iyer [VWI98]; *compressed cubes* for query approximation on continuous dimensions by Shanmugasundaram, Fayyad, and Bradley [SFB99]; using log-linear models to compress data cubes by Barbara and Wu [BW00]; and OLAP over uncertain and imprecise data by Burdick, Deshpande, Jayram, et al. [BDJ$^+$05].

For works regarding the selection of materialized cuboids for efficient OLAP query processing, see Chaudhuri and Dayal [CD97]; Harinarayan, Rajaraman, and Ullman [HRU96]; Srivastava, Dar, Jagadish, and Levy [SDJL96]; Gupta [Gup97], Baralis, Paraboschi, and Teniente [BPT97]; and Shukla, Deshpande, and Naughton [SDN98]. Methods for cube size estimation can be found in Deshpande, Naughton, Ramasamy, et al. [DNR$^+$97], Ross and Srivastava [RS97], and Beyer and Ramakrishnan [BR99]. Agrawal, Gupta, and Sarawagi [AGS97] proposed operations for modeling multidimensional databases.

Data cube modeling and computation have been extended well beyond relational data. Computation of *stream cubes* for multidimensional stream data analysis has been studied by Chen, Dong, Han, et al. [CDH$^+$02]. Efficient computation of *spatial data cubes* was examined by Stefanovic, Han, and Koperski [SHK00], efficient OLAP in spatial data warehouses was studied by Papadias, Kalnis, Zhang, and Tao [PKZT01], and a map cube for visualizing spatial data warehouses was proposed by Shekhar, Lu, Tan, et al. [SLT$^+$01]. A multimedia data cube was constructed in MultiMediaMiner by Zaiane, Han, Li, et al. [ZHL$^+$98]. For analysis of multidimensional text databases, *TextCube*, based on the vector space model, was proposed by Lin, Ding, Han, et al. [LDH$^+$08], and *TopicCube*, based on a topic modeling approach, was proposed by Zhang, Zhai, and Han [ZZH09]. *RFID Cube* and *FlowCube* for analyzing RFID data were proposed by Gonzalez, Han, Li, et al. [GHLK06, GHL06].

The *sampling cube* was introduced for analyzing sampling data by Li, Han, Yin, et al. [LHY$^+$08]. The *ranking cube* was proposed by Xin, Han, Cheng, and Li [XHCL06] for efficient processing of ranking (top-k) queries in databases. This methodology has been extended by Wu, Xin, and Han [WXH08] to *ARCube*, which supports the ranking of aggregate queries in partially materialized data cubes. It has also been extended by

Wu, Xin, Mei, and Han [WXMH09] to *PromoCube*, which supports promotion query analysis in multidimensional space.

The discovery-driven exploration of OLAP data cubes was proposed by Sarawagi, Agrawal, and Megiddo [SAM98]. Further studies on integration of OLAP with data mining capabilities for intelligent exploration of multidimensional OLAP data were done by Sarawagi and Sathe [SS01]. The construction of multifeature data cubes is described by Ross, Srivastava, and Chatziantoniou [RSC98]. Methods for answering queries quickly by online aggregation are described by Hellerstein, Haas, and Wang [HHW97] and Hellerstein, Avnur, Chou, et al. [HAC$^+$99]. A cube-gradient analysis problem, called *cubegrade*, was first proposed by Imielinski, Khachiyan, and Abdulghani [IKA02]. An efficient method for multidimensional constrained gradient analysis in data cubes was studied by Dong, Han, Lam, et al. [DHL$^+$01].

Mining cube space, or integration of knowledge discovery and OLAP cubes, has been studied by many researchers. The concept of online analytical mining (OLAM), or OLAP mining, was introduced by Han [Han98]. Chen, Dong, Han, et al. developed a *regression cube* for regression-based multidimensional analysis of time-series data [CDH$^+$02, CDH$^+$06]. Fagin, Guha, Kumar, et al. [FGK$^+$05] studied data mining in *multistructured databases*. B.-C. Chen, L. Chen, Lin, and Ramakrishnan [CCLR05] proposed *prediction cubes*, which integrate prediction models with data cubes to discover interesting data subspaces for facilitated prediction. Chen, Ramakrishnan, Shavlik, and Tamma [CRST06] studied the use of data mining models as building blocks in a multistep mining process, and the use of cube space to intuitively define the space of interest for predicting global aggregates from local regions. Ramakrishnan and Chen [RC07] presented an organized picture of exploratory mining in cube space.

Mining Frequent Patterns, Associations, and Correlations: Basic Concepts and Methods

Imagine that you are a sales manager at *AllElectronics*, and you are talking to a customer who recently bought a PC and a digital camera from the store. What should you recommend to her next? Information about which products are frequently purchased by your customers following their purchases of a PC and a digital camera in sequence would be very helpful in making your recommendation. Frequent patterns and association rules are the knowledge that you want to mine in such a scenario.

Frequent patterns are patterns (e.g., itemsets, subsequences, or substructures) that appear frequently in a data set. For example, a set of items, such as milk and bread, that appear frequently together in a transaction data set is a *frequent itemset*. A subsequence, such as buying first a PC, then a digital camera, and then a memory card, if it occurs frequently in a shopping history database, is a (*frequent*) *sequential pattern*. A *substructure* can refer to different structural forms, such as subgraphs, subtrees, or sublattices, which may be combined with itemsets or subsequences. If a substructure occurs frequently, it is called a (*frequent*) *structured pattern*. Finding frequent patterns plays an essential role in mining associations, correlations, and many other interesting relationships among data. Moreover, it helps in data classification, clustering, and other data mining tasks. Thus, frequent pattern mining has become an important data mining task and a focused theme in data mining research.

In this chapter, we introduce the basic concepts of frequent patterns, associations, and correlations (Section 6.1) and study how they can be mined efficiently (Section 6.2). We also discuss how to judge whether the patterns found are interesting (Section 6.3). In Chapter 7, we extend our discussion to advanced methods of frequent pattern mining, which mine more complex forms of frequent patterns and consider user preferences or constraints to speed up the mining process.

6.1 Basic Concepts

Frequent pattern mining searches for recurring relationships in a given data set. This section introduces the basic concepts of frequent pattern mining for the discovery of interesting associations and correlations between itemsets in transactional and relational databases. We begin in Section 6.1.1 by presenting an example of market basket analysis, the earliest form of frequent pattern mining for association rules. The basic concepts of mining frequent patterns and associations are given in Section 6.1.2.

6.1.1 Market Basket Analysis: A Motivating Example

Frequent itemset mining leads to the discovery of associations and correlations among items in large transactional or relational data sets. With massive amounts of data continuously being collected and stored, many industries are becoming interested in mining such patterns from their databases. The discovery of interesting correlation relationships among huge amounts of business transaction records can help in many business decision-making processes such as catalog design, cross-marketing, and customer shopping behavior analysis.

A typical example of frequent itemset mining is **market basket analysis**. This process analyzes customer buying habits by finding associations between the different items that customers place in their "shopping baskets" (Figure 6.1). The discovery of these associations can help retailers develop marketing strategies by gaining insight into which items are frequently purchased together by customers. For instance, if customers are buying milk, how likely are they to also buy bread (and what kind of bread) on the same trip

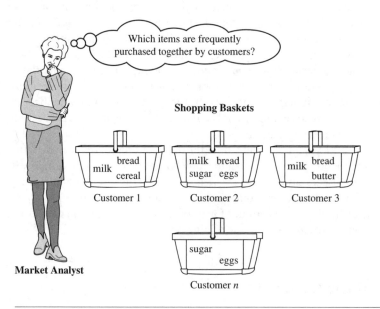

Figure 6.1 Market basket analysis.

to the supermarket? This information can lead to increased sales by helping retailers do selective marketing and plan their shelf space.

Let's look at an example of how market basket analysis can be useful.

Example 6.1 **Market basket analysis.** Suppose, as manager of an *AllElectronics* branch, you would like to learn more about the buying habits of your customers. Specifically, you wonder, *"Which groups or sets of items are customers likely to purchase on a given trip to the store?"* To answer your question, market basket analysis may be performed on the retail data of customer transactions at your store. You can then use the results to plan marketing or advertising strategies, or in the design of a new catalog. For instance, market basket analysis may help you design different store layouts. In one strategy, items that are frequently purchased together can be placed in proximity to further encourage the combined sale of such items. If customers who purchase computers also tend to buy antivirus software at the same time, then placing the hardware display close to the software display may help increase the sales of both items.

In an alternative strategy, placing hardware and software at opposite ends of the store may entice customers who purchase such items to pick up other items along the way. For instance, after deciding on an expensive computer, a customer may observe security systems for sale while heading toward the software display to purchase antivirus software, and may decide to purchase a home security system as well. Market basket analysis can also help retailers plan which items to put on sale at reduced prices. If customers tend to purchase computers and printers together, then having a sale on printers may encourage the sale of printers *as well as* computers. ∎

If we think of the universe as the set of items available at the store, then each item has a Boolean variable representing the presence or absence of that item. Each basket can then be represented by a Boolean vector of values assigned to these variables. The Boolean vectors can be analyzed for buying patterns that reflect items that are frequently *associated* or purchased together. These patterns can be represented in the form of **association rules**. For example, the information that customers who purchase computers also tend to buy antivirus software at the same time is represented in the following association rule:

$$computer \Rightarrow antivirus\_software \, [support = 2\%, confidence = 60\%]. \qquad (6.1)$$

Rule **support** and **confidence** are two measures of rule interestingness. They respectively reflect the usefulness and certainty of discovered rules. A support of 2% for Rule (6.1) means that 2% of all the transactions under analysis show that computer and antivirus software are purchased together. A confidence of 60% means that 60% of the customers who purchased a computer also bought the software. Typically, association rules are considered interesting if they satisfy both a **minimum support threshold** and a **minimum confidence threshold**. These thresholds can be a set by users or domain experts. Additional analysis can be performed to discover interesting statistical correlations between associated items.

6.1.2 Frequent Itemsets, Closed Itemsets, and Association Rules

Let $\mathcal{I} = \{I_1, I_2, \ldots, I_m\}$ be an itemset. Let D, the task-relevant data, be a set of database transactions where each transaction T is a nonempty itemset such that $T \subseteq \mathcal{I}$. Each transaction is associated with an identifier, called a *TID*. Let A be a set of items. A transaction T is said to contain A if $A \subseteq T$. An association rule is an implication of the form $A \Rightarrow B$, where $A \subset \mathcal{I}$, $B \subset \mathcal{I}$, $A \neq \emptyset$, $B \neq \emptyset$, and $A \cap B = \phi$. The rule $A \Rightarrow B$ holds in the transaction set D with **support** s, where s is the percentage of transactions in D that contain $A \cup B$ (i.e., the *union* of sets A and B say, or, both A and B). This is taken to be the probability, $P(A \cup B)$.[1] The rule $A \Rightarrow B$ has **confidence** c in the transaction set D, where c is the percentage of transactions in D containing A that also contain B. This is taken to be the conditional probability, $P(B|A)$. That is,

$$support(A \Rightarrow B) = P(A \cup B) \tag{6.2}$$

$$confidence(A \Rightarrow B) = P(B|A). \tag{6.3}$$

Rules that satisfy both a minimum support threshold (*min_sup*) and a minimum confidence threshold (*min_conf*) are called **strong**. By convention, we write support and confidence values so as to occur between 0% and 100%, rather than 0 to 1.0.

A set of items is referred to as an **itemset**.[2] An itemset that contains k items is a **k-itemset**. The set {*computer, antivirus_software*} is a 2-itemset. The **occurrence frequency of an itemset** is the number of transactions that contain the itemset. This is also known, simply, as the **frequency**, **support count**, or **count** of the itemset. Note that the itemset support defined in Eq. (6.2) is sometimes referred to as *relative support*, whereas the occurrence frequency is called the **absolute support**. If the relative support of an itemset I satisfies a prespecified **minimum support threshold** (i.e., the absolute support of I satisfies the corresponding **minimum support count threshold**), then I is a **frequent** itemset.[3] The set of frequent k-itemsets is commonly denoted by L_k.[4]

From Eq. (6.3), we have

$$confidence(A \Rightarrow B) = P(B|A) = \frac{support(A \cup B)}{support(A)} = \frac{support\_count(A \cup B)}{support\_count(A)}. \tag{6.4}$$

---

[1] Notice that the notation $P(A \cup B)$ indicates the probability that a transaction contains the *union* of sets A and B (i.e., it contains every item in A and B). This should not be confused with $P(A \text{ or } B)$, which indicates the probability that a transaction contains either A or B.

[2] In the data mining research literature, "itemset" is more commonly used than "item set."

[3] In early work, itemsets satisfying minimum support were referred to as **large**. This term, however, is somewhat confusing as it has connotations of the number of items in an itemset rather than the frequency of occurrence of the set. Hence, we use the more recent term **frequent**.

[4] Although the term **frequent** is preferred over **large**, for historic reasons frequent k-itemsets are still denoted as L_k.

Equation (6.4) shows that the confidence of rule $A \Rightarrow B$ can be easily derived from the support counts of A and $A \cup B$. That is, once the support counts of A, B, and $A \cup B$ are found, it is straightforward to derive the corresponding association rules $A \Rightarrow B$ and $B \Rightarrow A$ and check whether they are strong. Thus, the problem of mining association rules can be reduced to that of mining frequent itemsets.

In general, association rule mining can be viewed as a two-step process:

1. **Find all frequent itemsets:** By definition, each of these itemsets will occur at least as frequently as a predetermined minimum support count, *min_sup*.

2. **Generate strong association rules from the frequent itemsets:** By definition, these rules must satisfy minimum support and minimum confidence.

Additional interestingness measures can be applied for the discovery of correlation relationships between associated items, as will be discussed in Section 6.3. Because the second step is much less costly than the first, the overall performance of mining association rules is determined by the first step.

A major challenge in mining frequent itemsets from a large data set is the fact that such mining often generates a huge number of itemsets satisfying the minimum support (*min_sup*) threshold, especially when *min_sup* is set low. This is because if an itemset is frequent, each of its subsets is frequent as well. A long itemset will contain a combinatorial number of shorter, frequent sub-itemsets. For example, a frequent itemset of length 100, such as $\{a_1, a_2, \ldots, a_{100}\}$, contains $\binom{100}{1} = 100$ frequent 1-itemsets: $\{a_1\}$, $\{a_2\}$, $\ldots$, $\{a_{100}\}$; $\binom{100}{2}$ frequent 2-itemsets: $\{a_1, a_2\}$, $\{a_1, a_3\}$, $\ldots$, $\{a_{99}, a_{100}\}$; and so on. The total number of frequent itemsets that it contains is thus

$$\binom{100}{1} + \binom{100}{2} + \cdots + \binom{100}{100} = 2^{100} - 1 \approx 1.27 \times 10^{30}. \tag{6.5}$$

This is too huge a number of itemsets for any computer to compute or store. To overcome this difficulty, we introduce the concepts of *closed frequent itemset* and *maximal frequent itemset*.

An itemset X is **closed** in a data set D if there exists no proper super-itemset Y[5] such that Y has the same support count as X in D. An itemset X is a **closed frequent itemset** in set D if X is both closed and frequent in D. An itemset X is a **maximal frequent itemset** (or **max-itemset**) in a data set D if X is frequent, and there exists no super-itemset Y such that $X \subset Y$ and Y is frequent in D.

Let $\mathcal{C}$ be the set of closed frequent itemsets for a data set D satisfying a minimum support threshold, *min_sup*. Let $\mathcal{M}$ be the set of maximal frequent itemsets for D satisfying *min_sup*. Suppose that we have the support count of each itemset in $\mathcal{C}$ and $\mathcal{M}$. Notice that $\mathcal{C}$ and its count information can be used to derive the whole set of frequent itemsets.

---

[5] Y is a proper super-itemset of X if X is a proper sub-itemset of Y, that is, if $X \subset Y$. In other words, every item of X is contained in Y but there is at least one item of Y that is not in X.

Thus, we say that C contains complete information regarding its corresponding frequent itemsets. On the other hand, $\mathcal{M}$ registers only the support of the maximal itemsets. It usually does not contain the complete support information regarding its corresponding frequent itemsets. We illustrate these concepts with Example 6.2.

Example 6.2 **Closed and maximal frequent itemsets.** Suppose that a transaction database has only two transactions: $\{\langle a_1, a_2, \ldots, a_{100}\rangle; \langle a_1, a_2, \ldots, a_{50}\rangle\}$. Let the minimum support count threshold be $min\_sup = 1$. We find two closed frequent itemsets and their support counts, that is, $C = \{\{a_1, a_2, \ldots, a_{100}\} : 1; \{a_1, a_2, \ldots, a_{50}\} : 2\}$. There is only one maximal frequent itemset: $\mathcal{M} = \{\{a_1, a_2, \ldots, a_{100}\} : 1\}$. Notice that we cannot include $\{a_1, a_2, \ldots, a_{50}\}$ as a maximal frequent itemset because it has a frequent superset, $\{a_1, a_2, \ldots, a_{100}\}$. Compare this to the preceding where we determined that there are $2^{100} - 1$ frequent itemsets, which are too many to be enumerated!

The set of closed frequent itemsets contains complete information regarding the frequent itemsets. For example, from C, we can derive, say, (1) $\{a_2, a_{45} : 2\}$ since $\{a_2, a_{45}\}$ is a sub-itemset of the itemset $\{a_1, a_2, \ldots, a_{50} : 2\}$; and (2) $\{a_8, a_{55} : 1\}$ since $\{a_8, a_{55}\}$ is not a sub-itemset of the previous itemset but of the itemset $\{a_1, a_2, \ldots, a_{100} : 1\}$. However, from the maximal frequent itemset, we can only assert that both itemsets ($\{a_2, a_{45}\}$ and $\{a_8, a_{55}\}$) are frequent, but we cannot assert their actual support counts. ∎

6.2 Frequent Itemset Mining Methods

In this section, you will learn methods for mining the simplest form of frequent patterns such as those discussed for market basket analysis in Section 6.1.1. We begin by presenting **Apriori**, the basic algorithm for finding frequent itemsets (Section 6.2.1). In Section 6.2.2, we look at how to generate strong association rules from frequent itemsets. Section 6.2.3 describes several variations to the Apriori algorithm for improved efficiency and scalability. Section 6.2.4 presents pattern-growth methods for mining frequent itemsets that confine the subsequent search space to only the data sets containing the current frequent itemsets. Section 6.2.5 presents methods for mining frequent itemsets that take advantage of the vertical data format.

6.2.1 Apriori Algorithm: Finding Frequent Itemsets by Confined Candidate Generation

Apriori is a seminal algorithm proposed by R. Agrawal and R. Srikant in 1994 for mining frequent itemsets for Boolean association rules [AS94b]. The name of the algorithm is based on the fact that the algorithm uses *prior knowledge* of frequent itemset properties, as we shall see later. Apriori employs an iterative approach known as a *level-wise* search, where k-itemsets are used to explore $(k + 1)$-itemsets. First, the set of frequent 1-itemsets is found by scanning the database to accumulate the count for each item, and collecting those items that satisfy minimum support. The resulting set is denoted by L_1. Next, L_1 is used to find L_2, the set of frequent 2-itemsets, which is used to find L_3, and so on, until no more frequent k-itemsets can be found. The finding of each L_k requires one full scan of the database.

To improve the efficiency of the level-wise generation of frequent itemsets, an important property called the **Apriori property** is used to reduce the search space.

Apriori property: *All nonempty subsets of a frequent itemset must also be frequent.*

The Apriori property is based on the following observation. By definition, if an itemset I does not satisfy the minimum support threshold, *min_sup*, then I is not frequent, that is, $P(I) < min\_sup$. If an item A is added to the itemset I, then the resulting itemset (i.e., $I \cup A$) cannot occur more frequently than I. Therefore, $I \cup A$ is not frequent either, that is, $P(I \cup A) < min\_sup$.

This property belongs to a special category of properties called **antimonotonicity** in the sense that *if a set cannot pass a test, all of its supersets will fail the same test as well*. It is called *antimonotonicity* because the property is monotonic in the context of failing a test.[6]

"How is the Apriori property used in the algorithm?" To understand this, let us look at how L_{k-1} is used to find L_k for $k \geq 2$. A two-step process is followed, consisting of **join** and **prune** actions.

1. **The join step**: To find L_k, a set of **candidate** k-itemsets is generated by joining L_{k-1} with itself. This set of candidates is denoted C_k. Let l_1 and l_2 be itemsets in L_{k-1}. The notation $l_i[j]$ refers to the jth item in l_i (e.g., $l_1[k-2]$ refers to the second to the last item in l_1). For efficient implementation, Apriori assumes that items within a transaction or itemset are sorted in lexicographic order. For the $(k-1)$-itemset, l_i, this means that the items are sorted such that $l_i[1] < l_i[2] < \cdots < l_i[k-1]$. The join, $L_{k-1} \bowtie L_{k-1}$, is performed, where members of L_{k-1} are joinable if their first $(k-2)$ items are in common. That is, members l_1 and l_2 of L_{k-1} are joined if $(l_1[1] = l_2[1]) \wedge (l_1[2] = l_2[2]) \wedge \cdots \wedge (l_1[k-2] = l_2[k-2]) \wedge (l_1[k-1] < l_2[k-1])$. The condition $l_1[k-1] < l_2[k-1]$ simply ensures that no duplicates are generated. The resulting itemset formed by joining l_1 and l_2 is $\{l_1[1], l_1[2], \ldots, l_1[k-2], l_1[k-1], l_2[k-1]\}$.

2. **The prune step**: C_k is a superset of L_k, that is, its members may or may not be frequent, but all of the frequent k-itemsets are included in C_k. A database scan to determine the count of each candidate in C_k would result in the determination of L_k (i.e., all candidates having a count no less than the minimum support count are frequent by definition, and therefore belong to L_k). C_k, however, can be huge, and so this could involve heavy computation. To reduce the size of C_k, the Apriori property

---

[6]The Apriori property has many applications. For example, it can also be used to prune search during data cube computation (Chapter 5).

is used as follows. Any $(k-1)$-itemset that is not frequent cannot be a subset of a frequent k-itemset. Hence, if any $(k-1)$-subset of a candidate k-itemset is not in L_{k-1}, then the candidate cannot be frequent either and so can be removed from C_k. This **subset testing** can be done quickly by maintaining a hash tree of all frequent itemsets.

Example 6.3 **Apriori.** Let's look at a concrete example, based on the *AllElectronics* transaction database, D, of Table 6.1. There are nine transactions in this database, that is, $|D| = 9$. We use Figure 6.2 to illustrate the Apriori algorithm for finding frequent itemsets in D.

1. In the first iteration of the algorithm, each item is a member of the set of candidate 1-itemsets, C_1. The algorithm simply scans all of the transactions to count the number of occurrences of each item.

2. Suppose that the minimum support count required is 2, that is, $min\_sup = 2$. (Here, we are referring to *absolute* support because we are using a support count. The corresponding relative support is $2/9 = 22\%$.) The set of frequent 1-itemsets, L_1, can then be determined. It consists of the candidate 1-itemsets satisfying minimum support. In our example, all of the candidates in C_1 satisfy minimum support.

3. To discover the set of frequent 2-itemsets, L_2, the algorithm uses the join $L_1 \bowtie L_1$ to generate a candidate set of 2-itemsets, C_2.[7] C_2 consists of $\binom{|L_1|}{2}$ 2-itemsets. Note that no candidates are removed from C_2 during the prune step because each subset of the candidates is also frequent.

Table 6.1 Transactional Data for an *AllElectronics* Branch

TID	List of item_IDs
T100	I1, I2, I5
T200	I2, I4
T300	I2, I3
T400	I1, I2, I4
T500	I1, I3
T600	I2, I3
T700	I1, I3
T800	I1, I2, I3, I5
T900	I1, I2, I3

---

[7] $L_1 \bowtie L_1$ is equivalent to $L_1 \times L_1$, since the definition of $L_k \bowtie L_k$ requires the two joining itemsets to share $k - 1 = 0$ items.

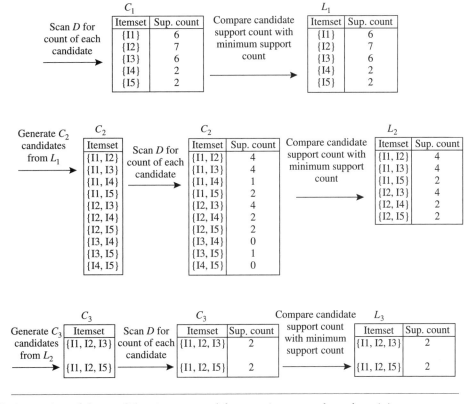

Figure 6.2 Generation of the candidate itemsets and frequent itemsets, where the minimum support count is 2.

4. Next, the transactions in D are scanned and the support count of each candidate itemset in C_2 is accumulated, as shown in the middle table of the second row in Figure 6.2.

5. The set of frequent 2-itemsets, L_2, is then determined, consisting of those candidate 2-itemsets in C_2 having minimum support.

6. The generation of the set of the candidate 3-itemsets, C_3, is detailed in Figure 6.3. From the join step, we first get $C_3 = L_2 \bowtie L_2 = \{\{I1, I2, I3\}, \{I1, I2, I5\}, \{I1, I3, I5\}, \{I2, I3, I4\}, \{I2, I3, I5\}, \{I2, I4, I5\}\}$. Based on the Apriori property that all subsets of a frequent itemset must also be frequent, we can determine that the four latter candidates cannot possibly be frequent. We therefore remove them from C_3, thereby saving the effort of unnecessarily obtaining their counts during the subsequent scan of D to determine L_3. Note that when given a candidate k-itemset, we only need to check if its $(k-1)$-subsets are frequent since the Apriori algorithm uses a level-wise

(a) Join: $C_3 = L_2 \bowtie L_2 = \{\{I1, I2\}, \{I1, I3\}, \{I1, I5\}, \{I2, I3\}, \{I2, I4\}, \{I2, I5\}\}$
$\bowtie \{\{I1, I2\}, \{I1, I3\}, \{I1, I5\}, \{I2, I3\}, \{I2, I4\}, \{I2, I5\}\}$
$= \{\{I1, I2, I3\}, \{I1, I2, I5\}, \{I1, I3, I5\}, \{I2, I3, I4\}, \{I2, I3, I5\}, \{I2, I4, I5\}\}.$

(b) Prune using the Apriori property: All nonempty subsets of a frequent itemset must also be frequent. Do any of the candidates have a subset that is not frequent?

- The 2-item subsets of $\{I1, I2, I3\}$ are $\{I1, I2\}$, $\{I1, I3\}$, and $\{I2, I3\}$. All 2-item subsets of $\{I1, I2, I3\}$ are members of L_2. Therefore, keep $\{I1, I2, I3\}$ in C_3.

- The 2-item subsets of $\{I1, I2, I5\}$ are $\{I1, I2\}$, $\{I1, I5\}$, and $\{I2, I5\}$. All 2-item subsets of $\{I1, I2, I5\}$ are members of L_2. Therefore, keep $\{I1, I2, I5\}$ in C_3.

- The 2-item subsets of $\{I1, I3, I5\}$ are $\{I1, I3\}$, $\{I1, I5\}$, and $\{I3, I5\}$. $\{I3, I5\}$ is not a member of L_2, and so it is not frequent. Therefore, remove $\{I1, I3, I5\}$ from C_3.

- The 2-item subsets of $\{I2, I3, I4\}$ are $\{I2, I3\}$, $\{I2, I4\}$, and $\{I3, I4\}$. $\{I3, I4\}$ is not a member of L_2, and so it is not frequent. Therefore, remove $\{I2, I3, I4\}$ from C_3.

- The 2-item subsets of $\{I2, I3, I5\}$ are $\{I2, I3\}$, $\{I2, I5\}$, and $\{I3, I5\}$. $\{I3, I5\}$ is not a member of L_2, and so it is not frequent. Therefore, remove $\{I2, I3, I5\}$ from C_3.

- The 2-item subsets of $\{I2, I4, I5\}$ are $\{I2, I4\}$, $\{I2, I5\}$, and $\{I4, I5\}$. $\{I4, I5\}$ is not a member of L_2, and so it is not frequent. Therefore, remove $\{I2, I4, I5\}$ from C_3.

(c) Therefore, $C_3 = \{\{I1, I2, I3\}, \{I1, I2, I5\}\}$ after pruning.

Figure 6.3 Generation and pruning of candidate 3-itemsets, C_3, from L_2 using the Apriori property.

search strategy. The resulting pruned version of C_3 is shown in the first table of the bottom row of Figure 6.2.

7. The transactions in D are scanned to determine L_3, consisting of those candidate 3-itemsets in C_3 having minimum support (Figure 6.2).

8. The algorithm uses $L_3 \bowtie L_3$ to generate a candidate set of 4-itemsets, C_4. Although the join results in $\{\{I1, I2, I3, I5\}\}$, itemset $\{I1, I2, I3, I5\}$ is pruned because its subset $\{I2, I3, I5\}$ is not frequent. Thus, $C_4 = \phi$, and the algorithm terminates, having found all of the frequent itemsets. ■

Figure 6.4 shows pseudocode for the Apriori algorithm and its related procedures. Step 1 of Apriori finds the frequent 1-itemsets, L_1. In steps 2 through 10, L_{k-1} is used to generate candidates C_k to find L_k for $k \geq 2$. The apriori_gen procedure generates the candidates and then uses the Apriori property to eliminate those having a subset that is not frequent (step 3). This procedure is described later. Once all of the candidates have been generated, the database is scanned (step 4). For each transaction, a subset function is used to find all subsets of the transaction that are candidates (step 5), and the count for each of these candidates is accumulated (steps 6 and 7). Finally, all the candidates satisfying the minimum support (step 9) form the set of frequent itemsets, L (step 11).

Algorithm: Apriori. Find frequent itemsets using an iterative level-wise approach based on candidate generation.

Input:

- D, a database of transactions;
- min_sup, the minimum support count threshold.

Output: L, frequent itemsets in D.

Method:

```
(1)    L₁ = find_frequent_1-itemsets(D);
(2)    for (k = 2; Lₖ₋₁ ≠ φ; k++) {
(3)        Cₖ = apriori_gen(Lₖ₋₁);
(4)        for each transaction t ∈ D { // scan D for counts
(5)            Cₜ = subset(Cₖ, t); // get the subsets of t that are candidates
(6)            for each candidate c ∈ Cₜ
(7)                c.count++;
(8)        }
(9)        Lₖ = {c ∈ Cₖ|c.count ≥ min_sup}
(10)   }
(11)   return L = ∪ₖLₖ;
```

procedure apriori_gen(L_{k-1}:frequent $(k-1)$-itemsets)
```
(1)    for each itemset l₁ ∈ Lₖ₋₁
(2)        for each itemset l₂ ∈ Lₖ₋₁
(3)            if (l₁[1] = l₂[1]) ∧ (l₁[2] = l₂[2])
                    ∧... ∧ (l₁[k − 2] = l₂[k − 2]) ∧ (l₁[k − 1] < l₂[k − 1]) then {
(4)                c = l₁ ⋈ l₂; // join step: generate candidates
(5)                if has_infrequent_subset(c, Lₖ₋₁) then
(6)                    delete c; // prune step: remove unfruitful candidate
(7)                else add c to Cₖ;
(8)            }
(9)    return Cₖ;
```

procedure has_infrequent_subset(c: candidate k-itemset;
            L_{k-1}: frequent $(k-1)$-itemsets); // use prior knowledge
```
(1)    for each (k − 1)-subset s of c
(2)        if s ∉ Lₖ₋₁ then
(3)            return TRUE;
(4)    return FALSE;
```

Figure 6.4 Apriori algorithm for discovering frequent itemsets for mining Boolean association rules.

A procedure can then be called to generate association rules from the frequent itemsets. Such a procedure is described in Section 6.2.2.

The apriori_gen procedure performs two kinds of actions, namely, **join** and **prune**, as described before. In the join component, L_{k-1} is joined with L_{k-1} to generate potential candidates (steps 1–4). The prune component (steps 5–7) employs the Apriori property to remove candidates that have a subset that is not frequent. The test for infrequent subsets is shown in procedure has_infrequent_subset.

6.2.2 Generating Association Rules from Frequent Itemsets

Once the frequent itemsets from transactions in a database D have been found, it is straightforward to generate strong association rules from them (where *strong* association rules satisfy both minimum support and minimum confidence). This can be done using Eq. (6.4) for confidence, which we show again here for completeness:

$$confidence(A \Rightarrow B) = P(B|A) = \frac{support\_count(A \cup B)}{support\_count(A)}.$$

The conditional probability is expressed in terms of itemset support count, where $support\_count(A \cup B)$ is the number of transactions containing the itemsets $A \cup B$, and $support\_count(A)$ is the number of transactions containing the itemset A. Based on this equation, association rules can be generated as follows:

- For each frequent itemset l, generate all nonempty subsets of l.

- For every nonempty subset s of l, output the rule "$s \Rightarrow (l - s)$" if $\frac{support\_count(l)}{support\_count(s)} \geq min\_conf$, where min_conf is the minimum confidence threshold.

Because the rules are generated from frequent itemsets, each one automatically satisfies the minimum support. Frequent itemsets can be stored ahead of time in hash tables along with their counts so that they can be accessed quickly.

Example 6.4 **Generating association rules.** Let's try an example based on the transactional data for *AllElectronics* shown before in Table 6.1. The data contain frequent itemset $X = \{I1, I2, I5\}$. What are the association rules that can be generated from X? The nonempty subsets of X are $\{I1, I2\}$, $\{I1, I5\}$, $\{I2, I5\}$, $\{I1\}$, $\{I2\}$, and $\{I5\}$. The resulting association rules are as shown below, each listed with its confidence:

$$\{I1, I2\} \Rightarrow I5, \quad confidence = 2/4 = 50\%$$
$$\{I1, I5\} \Rightarrow I2, \quad confidence = 2/2 = 100\%$$
$$\{I2, I5\} \Rightarrow I1, \quad confidence = 2/2 = 100\%$$
$$I1 \Rightarrow \{I2, I5\}, \quad confidence = 2/6 = 33\%$$
$$I2 \Rightarrow \{I1, I5\}, \quad confidence = 2/7 = 29\%$$
$$I5 \Rightarrow \{I1, I2\}, \quad confidence = 2/2 = 100\%$$

If the minimum confidence threshold is, say, 70%, then only the second, third, and last rules are output, because these are the only ones generated that are strong. Note that, unlike conventional classification rules, association rules can contain more than one conjunct in the right side of the rule. ∎

6.2.3 Improving the Efficiency of Apriori

"How can we further improve the efficiency of Apriori-based mining?" Many variations of the Apriori algorithm have been proposed that focus on improving the efficiency of the original algorithm. Several of these variations are summarized as follows:

H_2

bucket address	0	1	2	3	4	5	6
bucket count	2	2	4	2	2	4	4
bucket contents	{I1, I4}	{I1, I5}	{I2, I3}	{I2, I4}	{I2, I5}	{I1, I2}	{I1, I3}
	{I3, I5}	{I1, I5}	{I2, I3}	{I2, I4}	{I2, I5}	{I1, I2}	{I1, I3}
			{I2, I3}			{I1, I2}	{I1, I3}
			{I2, I3}			{I1, I2}	{I1, I3}

Create hash table H_2
using hash function
$h(x, y) = ((order\ of\ x) \times 10$
$+ (order\ of\ y))\ mod\ 7$

Figure 6.5 Hash table, H_2, for candidate 2-itemsets. This hash table was generated by scanning Table 6.1's transactions while determining L_1. If the minimum support count is, say, 3, then the itemsets in buckets 0, 1, 3, and 4 cannot be frequent and so they should not be included in C_2.

Hash-based technique (hashing itemsets into corresponding buckets): A hash-based technique can be used to reduce the size of the candidate k-itemsets, C_k, for $k > 1$. For example, when scanning each transaction in the database to generate the frequent 1-itemsets, L_1, we can generate all the 2-itemsets for each transaction, hash (i.e., map) them into the different *buckets* of a *hash table* structure, and increase the corresponding bucket counts (Figure 6.5). A 2-itemset with a corresponding bucket count in the hash table that is below the support threshold cannot be frequent and thus should be removed from the candidate set. Such a hash-based technique may substantially reduce the number of candidate k-itemsets examined (especially when $k = 2$).

Transaction reduction (reducing the number of transactions scanned in future iterations): A transaction that does not contain any frequent k-itemsets cannot contain any frequent $(k + 1)$-itemsets. Therefore, such a transaction can be marked or removed from further consideration because subsequent database scans for j-itemsets, where $j > k$, will not need to consider such a transaction.

Partitioning (partitioning the data to find candidate itemsets): A partitioning technique can be used that requires just two database scans to mine the frequent itemsets (Figure 6.6). It consists of two phases. In phase I, the algorithm divides the transactions of D into n nonoverlapping partitions. If the minimum relative support threshold for transactions in D is *min_sup*, then the minimum support count for a partition is *min_sup × the number of transactions in that partition*. For each partition, all the *local frequent itemsets* (i.e., the itemsets frequent within the partition) are found.

A local frequent itemset may or may not be frequent with respect to the entire database, D. However, *any itemset that is potentially frequent with respect to D must occur as a frequent itemset in at least one of the partitions.*[8] Therefore, all local frequent itemsets are candidate itemsets with respect to D. The collection of frequent itemsets from all partitions forms the *global candidate itemsets* with respect to D. In phase II,

[8]The proof of this property is left as an exercise (see Exercise 6.3d).

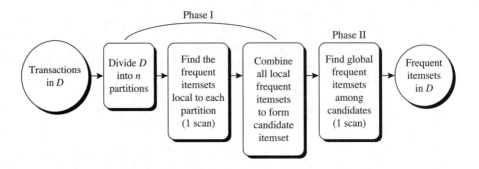

Figure 6.6 Mining by partitioning the data.

a second scan of D is conducted in which the actual support of each candidate is assessed to determine the global frequent itemsets. Partition size and the number of partitions are set so that each partition can fit into main memory and therefore be read only once in each phase.

Sampling (mining on a subset of the given data): The basic idea of the sampling approach is to pick a random sample S of the given data D, and then search for frequent itemsets in S instead of D. In this way, we trade off some degree of accuracy against efficiency. The S sample size is such that the search for frequent itemsets in S can be done in main memory, and so only one scan of the transactions in S is required overall. Because we are searching for frequent itemsets in S rather than in D, it is possible that we will miss some of the global frequent itemsets.

To reduce this possibility, we use a lower support threshold than minimum support to find the frequent itemsets local to S (denoted L^S). The rest of the database is then used to compute the actual frequencies of each itemset in L^S. A mechanism is used to determine whether all the global frequent itemsets are included in L^S. If L^S actually contains all the frequent itemsets in D, then only one scan of D is required. Otherwise, a second pass can be done to find the frequent itemsets that were missed in the first pass. The sampling approach is especially beneficial when efficiency is of utmost importance such as in computationally intensive applications that must be run frequently.

Dynamic itemset counting (adding candidate itemsets at different points during a scan): A dynamic itemset counting technique was proposed in which the database is partitioned into blocks marked by start points. In this variation, new candidate itemsets can be added at any start point, unlike in Apriori, which determines new candidate itemsets only immediately before each complete database scan. The technique uses the count-so-far as the lower bound of the actual count. If the count-so-far passes the minimum support, the itemset is added into the frequent itemset collection and can be used to generate longer candidates. This leads to fewer database scans than with Apriori for finding all the frequent itemsets.

Other variations are discussed in the next chapter.

6.2.4 A Pattern-Growth Approach for Mining Frequent Itemsets

As we have seen, in many cases the Apriori candidate generate-and-test method significantly reduces the size of candidate sets, leading to good performance gain. However, it can suffer from two nontrivial costs:

■ *It may still need to generate a huge number of candidate sets.* For example, if there are 10^4 frequent 1-itemsets, the Apriori algorithm will need to generate more than 10^7 candidate 2-itemsets.

■ *It may need to repeatedly scan the whole database and check a large set of candidates by pattern matching.* It is costly to go over each transaction in the database to determine the support of the candidate itemsets.

"Can we design a method that mines the complete set of frequent itemsets without such a costly candidate generation process?" An interesting method in this attempt is called **frequent pattern growth,** or simply **FP-growth**, which adopts a *divide-and-conquer* strategy as follows. First, it compresses the database representing frequent items into a **frequent pattern tree,** or **FP-tree**, which retains the itemset association information. It then divides the compressed database into a set of *conditional databases* (a special kind of projected database), each associated with one frequent item or "pattern fragment," and mines each database separately. For each "pattern fragment," only its associated data sets need to be examined. Therefore, this approach may substantially reduce the size of the data sets to be searched, along with the "growth" of patterns being examined. You will see how it works in Example 6.5.

Example 6.5 **FP-growth (finding frequent itemsets without candidate generation).** We reexamine the mining of transaction database, D, of Table 6.1 in Example 6.3 using the frequent pattern growth approach.

The first scan of the database is the same as Apriori, which derives the set of frequent items (1-itemsets) and their support counts (frequencies). Let the minimum support count be 2. The set of frequent items is sorted in the order of descending support count. This resulting set or *list* is denoted by L. Thus, we have $L = \{\{I2: 7\}, \{I1: 6\}, \{I3: 6\}, \{I4: 2\}, \{I5: 2\}\}$.

An FP-tree is then constructed as follows. First, create the root of the tree, labeled with "null." Scan database D a second time. The items in each transaction are processed in L order (i.e., sorted according to descending support count), and a branch is created for each transaction. For example, the scan of the first transaction, "T100: I1, I2, I5," which contains three items (I2, I1, I5 in L order), leads to the construction of the first branch of the tree with three nodes, $\langle I2: 1\rangle$, $\langle I1: 1\rangle$, and $\langle I5: 1\rangle$, where I2 is linked as a child to the root, I1 is linked to I2, and I5 is linked to I1. The second transaction, T200, contains the items I2 and I4 in L order, which would result in a branch where I2 is linked to the root and I4 is linked to I2. However, this branch would share a common **prefix**, I2, with the existing path for T100. Therefore, we instead increment the count of the I2 node by 1, and create a new node, $\langle I4: 1\rangle$, which is linked as a child to $\langle I2: 2\rangle$. In general,

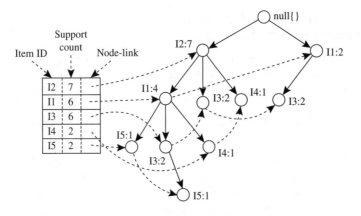

Figure 6.7 An FP-tree registers compressed, frequent pattern information.

when considering the branch to be added for a transaction, the count of each node along a common prefix is incremented by 1, and nodes for the items following the prefix are created and linked accordingly.

To facilitate tree traversal, an item header table is built so that each item points to its occurrences in the tree via a chain of **node-links**. The tree obtained after scanning all the transactions is shown in Figure 6.7 with the associated node-links. In this way, the problem of mining frequent patterns in databases is transformed into that of mining the FP-tree.

The FP-tree is mined as follows. Start from each frequent length-1 pattern (as an initial **suffix pattern**), construct its **conditional pattern base** (a "sub-database," which consists of the set of *prefix paths* in the FP-tree co-occurring with the suffix pattern), then construct its (*conditional*) FP-tree, and perform mining recursively on the tree. The pattern growth is achieved by the concatenation of the suffix pattern with the frequent patterns generated from a conditional FP-tree.

Mining of the FP-tree is summarized in Table 6.2 and detailed as follows. We first consider I5, which is the last item in *L*, rather than the first. The reason for starting at the end of the list will become apparent as we explain the FP-tree mining process. I5 occurs in two FP-tree branches of Figure 6.7. (The occurrences of I5 can easily be found by following its chain of node-links.) The paths formed by these branches are ⟨I2, I1, I5: 1⟩ and ⟨I2, I1, I3, I5: 1⟩. Therefore, considering I5 as a suffix, its corresponding two prefix paths are ⟨I2, I1: 1⟩ and ⟨I2, I1, I3: 1⟩, which form its conditional pattern base. Using this conditional pattern base as a transaction database, we build an I5-conditional FP-tree, which contains only a single path, ⟨I2: 2, I1: 2⟩; I3 is not included because its support count of 1 is less than the minimum support count. The single path generates all the combinations of frequent patterns: {I2, I5: 2}, {I1, I5: 2}, {I2, I1, I5: 2}.

For I4, its two prefix paths form the conditional pattern base, {{I2 I1: 1}, {I2: 1}}, which generates a single-node conditional FP-tree, ⟨I2: 2⟩, and derives one frequent pattern, {I2, I4: 2}.

Table 6.2 Mining the FP-Tree by Creating Conditional (Sub-)Pattern Bases

Item	Conditional Pattern Base	Conditional FP-tree	Frequent Patterns Generated
I5	{{I2, I1: 1}, {I2, I1, I3: 1}}	⟨I2: 2, I1: 2⟩	{I2, I5: 2}, {I1, I5: 2}, {I2, I1, I5: 2}
I4	{{I2, I1: 1}, {I2: 1}}	⟨I2: 2⟩	{I2, I4: 2}
I3	{{I2, I1: 2}, {I2: 2}, {I1: 2}}	⟨I2: 4, I1: 2⟩, ⟨I1: 2⟩	{I2, I3: 4}, {I1, I3: 4}, {I2, I1, I3: 2}
I1	{{I2: 4}}	⟨I2: 4⟩	{I2, I1: 4}

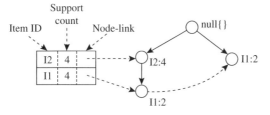

Figure 6.8 The conditional FP-tree associated with the conditional node I3.

Similar to the preceding analysis, I3's conditional pattern base is {{I2, I1: 2}, {I2: 2}, {I1: 2}}. Its conditional FP-tree has two branches, ⟨I2: 4, I1: 2⟩ and ⟨I1: 2⟩, as shown in Figure 6.8, which generates the set of patterns {{I2, I3: 4}, {I1, I3: 4}, {I2, I1, I3: 2}}. Finally, I1's conditional pattern base is {{I2: 4}}, with an FP-tree that contains only one node, ⟨I2: 4⟩, which generates one frequent pattern, {I2, I1: 4}. This mining process is summarized in Figure 6.9. ∎

The FP-growth method transforms the problem of finding long frequent patterns into searching for shorter ones in much smaller conditional databases recursively and then concatenating the suffix. It uses the least frequent items as a suffix, offering good selectivity. The method substantially reduces the search costs.

When the database is large, it is sometimes unrealistic to construct a main memory-based FP-tree. An interesting alternative is to first partition the database into a set of projected databases, and then construct an FP-tree and mine it in each projected database. This process can be recursively applied to any projected database if its FP-tree still cannot fit in main memory.

A study of the FP-growth method performance shows that it is efficient and scalable for mining both long and short frequent patterns, and is about an order of magnitude faster than the Apriori algorithm.

6.2.5 Mining Frequent Itemsets Using the Vertical Data Format

Both the Apriori and FP-growth methods mine frequent patterns from a set of trans-actions in *TID-itemset* format (i.e., {*TID* : *itemset*}), where *TID* is a transaction ID and *itemset* is the set of items bought in transaction *TID*. This is known as the **horizontal data format**. Alternatively, data can be presented in *item-TID_set* format

Algorithm: FP_growth. Mine frequent itemsets using an FP-tree by pattern fragment growth.

Input:

- *D*, a transaction database;
- *min_sup*, the minimum support count threshold.

Output: The complete set of frequent patterns.

Method:

1. The FP-tree is constructed in the following steps:

    (a) Scan the transaction database *D* once. Collect *F*, the set of frequent items, and their support counts. Sort *F* in support count descending order as *L*, the *list* of frequent items.

    (b) Create the root of an FP-tree, and label it as "null." For each transaction *Trans* in *D* do the following.
    Select and sort the frequent items in *Trans* according to the order of *L*. Let the sorted frequent item list in *Trans* be [*p*|*P*], where *p* is the first element and *P* is the remaining list. Call insert_tree([*p*|*P*], *T*), which is performed as follows. If *T* has a child *N* such that *N.item-name* = *p.item-name*, then increment *N*'s count by 1; else create a new node *N*, and let its count be 1, its parent link be linked to *T*, and its node-link to the nodes with the same *item-name* via the node-link structure. If *P* is nonempty, call insert_tree(*P*, *N*) recursively.

2. The FP-tree is mined by calling **FP_growth**(*FP_tree*, *null*), which is implemented as follows.

procedure FP_growth(*Tree*, α)

(1)   **if** *Tree* contains a single path *P* **then**
(2)   **for each** combination (denoted as β) of the nodes in the path *P*
(3)   generate pattern β ∪ α with *support_count* = *minimum support count of nodes in* β;
(4)   **else for each** a_i in the header of *Tree* {
(5)   generate pattern β = a_i ∪ α with *support_count* = a_i.*support_count*;
(6)   construct β's conditional pattern base and then β's conditional FP_tree $Tree_\beta$;
(7)   **if** $Tree_\beta$ ≠ ∅ **then**
(8)   call **FP_growth**($Tree_\beta$, β); }

Figure 6.9 FP-growth algorithm for discovering frequent itemsets without candidate generation.

(i.e., {*item* : *TID_set*}), where *item* is an item name, and *TID_set* is the set of transaction identifiers containing the item. This is known as the **vertical data format**.

In this subsection, we look at how frequent itemsets can also be mined efficiently using vertical data format, which is the essence of the **Eclat** (Equivalence Class Transformation) algorithm.

Example 6.6 **Mining frequent itemsets using the vertical data format.** Consider the horizontal data format of the transaction database, *D*, of Table 6.1 in Example 6.3. This can be transformed into the vertical data format shown in Table 6.3 by scanning the data set once.

Mining can be performed on this data set by intersecting the TID_sets of every pair of frequent single items. The minimum support count is 2. Because every single item is

Table 6.3 The Vertical Data Format of the Transaction Data Set D of Table 6.1

itemset	TID_set
I1	{T100, T400, T500, T700, T800, T900}
I2	{T100, T200, T300, T400, T600, T800, T900}
I3	{T300, T500, T600, T700, T800, T900}
I4	{T200, T400}
I5	{T100, T800}

Table 6.4 2-Itemsets in Vertical Data Format

itemset	TID_set
{I1, I2}	{T100, T400, T800, T900}
{I1, I3}	{T500, T700, T800, T900}
{I1, I4}	{T400}
{I1, I5}	{T100, T800}
{I2, I3}	{T300, T600, T800, T900}
{I2, I4}	{T200, T400}
{I2, I5}	{T100, T800}
{I3, I5}	{T800}

Table 6.5 3-Itemsets in Vertical Data Format

itemset	TID_set
{I1, I2, I3}	{T800, T900}
{I1, I2, I5}	{T100, T800}

frequent in Table 6.3, there are 10 intersections performed in total, which lead to eight nonempty 2-itemsets, as shown in Table 6.4. Notice that because the itemsets {I1, I4} and {I3, I5} each contain only one transaction, they do not belong to the set of frequent 2-itemsets.

Based on the Apriori property, a given 3-itemset is a candidate 3-itemset only if every one of its 2-itemset subsets is frequent. The candidate generation process here will generate only two 3-itemsets: {I1, I2, I3} and {I1, I2, I5}. By intersecting the TID_sets of any two corresponding 2-itemsets of these candidate 3-itemsets, it derives Table 6.5, where there are only two frequent 3-itemsets: {I1, I2, I3: 2} and {I1, I2, I5: 2}. ∎

Example 6.6 illustrates the process of mining frequent itemsets by exploring the vertical data format. First, we transform the horizontally formatted data into the vertical format by scanning the data set once. The support count of an itemset is simply the length of the TID_set of the itemset. Starting with $k = 1$, the frequent k-itemsets can be used to construct the candidate $(k + 1)$-itemsets based on the Apriori property.

The computation is done by intersection of the TID-sets of the frequent k-itemsets to compute the TID-sets of the corresponding $(k+1)$-itemsets. This process repeats, with k incremented by 1 each time, until no frequent itemsets or candidate itemsets can be found.

Besides taking advantage of the Apriori property in the generation of candidate $(k+1)$-itemset from frequent k-itemsets, another merit of this method is that there is no need to scan the database to find the support of $(k+1)$-itemsets (for $k \geq 1$). This is because the TID-set of each k-itemset carries the complete information required for counting such support. However, the TID-sets can be quite long, taking substantial memory space as well as computation time for intersecting the long sets.

To further reduce the cost of registering long TID-sets, as well as the subsequent costs of intersections, we can use a technique called *diffset*, which keeps track of only the differences of the TID-sets of a $(k+1)$-itemset and a corresponding k-itemset. For instance, in Example 6.6 we have {I1} = {T100, T400, T500, T700, T800, T900} and {I1, I2} = {T100, T400, T800, T900}. The *diffset* between the two is *diffset*({I1, I2}, {I1}) = {T500, T700}. Thus, rather than recording the four TIDs that make up the intersection of {I1} and {I2}, we can instead use *diffset* to record just two TIDs, indicating the difference between {I1} and {I1, I2}. Experiments show that in certain situations, such as when the data set contains many dense and long patterns, this technique can substantially reduce the total cost of vertical format mining of frequent itemsets.

6.2.6 Mining Closed and Max Patterns

In Section 6.1.2 we saw how frequent itemset mining may generate a huge number of frequent itemsets, especially when the *min_sup* threshold is set low or when there exist long patterns in the data set. Example 6.2 showed that closed frequent itemsets[9] can substantially reduce the number of patterns generated in frequent itemset mining while preserving the complete information regarding the set of frequent itemsets. That is, from the set of closed frequent itemsets, we can easily derive the set of frequent itemsets and their support. Thus, in practice, it is more desirable to mine the set of closed frequent itemsets rather than the set of all frequent itemsets in most cases.

"How can we mine closed frequent itemsets?" A naïve approach would be to first mine the complete set of frequent itemsets and then remove every frequent itemset that is a proper subset of, and carries the same support as, an existing frequent itemset. However, this is quite costly. As shown in Example 6.2, this method would have to first derive $2^{100} - 1$ frequent itemsets to obtain a length-100 frequent itemset, all before it could begin to eliminate redundant itemsets. This is prohibitively expensive. In fact, there exist only a very small number of closed frequent itemsets in Example 6.2's data set.

A recommended methodology is to search for closed frequent itemsets directly during the mining process. This requires us to prune the search space as soon as we

---

[9]Remember that X is a *closed frequent* itemset in a data set S if there exists no proper super-itemset Y such that Y has the same support count as X in S, and X satisfies minimum support.

can identify the case of closed itemsets during mining. Pruning strategies include the following:

Item merging: *If every transaction containing a frequent itemset X also contains an itemset Y but not any proper superset of Y, then X ∪ Y forms a frequent closed itemset and there is no need to search for any itemset containing X but no Y.*

For example, in Table 6.2 of Example 6.5, the projected conditional database for prefix itemset {I5:2} is {{I2, I1}, {I2, I1, I3}}, from which we can see that each of its transactions contains itemset {I2, I1} but no proper superset of {I2, I1}. Itemset {I2, I1} can be merged with {I5} to form the closed itemset, {I5, I2, I1: 2}, and we do not need to mine for closed itemsets that contain I5 but not {I2, I1}.

Sub-itemset pruning: *If a frequent itemset X is a proper subset of an already found frequent closed itemset Y and support_count(X)=support_count(Y), then X and all of X's descendants in the set enumeration tree cannot be frequent closed itemsets and thus can be pruned.*

Similar to Example 6.2, suppose a transaction database has only two transactions: $\{\langle a_1, a_2, \ldots, a_{100}\rangle, \langle a_1, a_2, \ldots, a_{50}\rangle\}$, and the minimum support count is $min\_sup = 2$. The projection on the first item, a_1, derives the frequent itemset, $\{a_1, a_2, \ldots, a_{50} : 2\}$, based on the *itemset merging* optimization. Because $support(\{a_2\}) = support(\{a_1, a_2, \ldots, a_{50}\}) = 2$, and $\{a_2\}$ is a proper subset of $\{a_1, a_2, \ldots, a_{50}\}$, there is no need to examine a_2 and its projected database. Similar pruning can be done for $a_3, \ldots, a_{50}$ as well. Thus, the mining of closed frequent itemsets in this data set terminates after mining a_1's projected database.

Item skipping: *In the depth-first mining of closed itemsets, at each level, there will be a prefix itemset X associated with a header table and a projected database. If a local frequent item p has the same support in several header tables at different levels, we can safely prune p from the header tables at higher levels.*

Consider, for example, the previous transaction database having only two transactions: $\{\langle a_1, a_2, \ldots, a_{100}\rangle, \langle a_1, a_2, \ldots, a_{50}\rangle\}$, where $min\_sup = 2$. Because a_2 in a_1's projected database has the same support as a_2 in the global header table, a_2 can be pruned from the global header table. Similar pruning can be done for $a_3, \ldots, a_{50}$. There is no need to mine anything more after mining a_1's projected database.

Besides pruning the search space in the closed itemset mining process, another important optimization is to perform efficient checking of each newly derived frequent itemset to see whether it is closed. This is because the mining process cannot ensure that every generated frequent itemset is closed.

When a new frequent itemset is derived, it is necessary to perform two kinds of closure checking: (1) *superset checking*, which checks if this new frequent itemset is a superset of some already found closed itemsets with the same support, and (2) *subset checking*, which checks whether the newly found itemset is a subset of an already found closed itemset with the same support.

If we adopt the *item merging* pruning method under a divide-and-conquer framework, then the superset checking is actually built-in and there is no need to explicitly perform superset checking. This is because if a frequent itemset $X \cup Y$ is found later than itemset X, and carries the same support as X, it must be in X's projected database and must have been generated during itemset merging.

To assist in subset checking, a compressed **pattern-tree** can be constructed to maintain the set of closed itemsets mined so far. The pattern-tree is similar in structure to the FP-tree except that all the closed itemsets found are stored explicitly in the corresponding tree branches. For efficient subset checking, we can use the following property: *If the current itemset* S_c *can be subsumed by another already found closed itemset* S_a, *then (1)* S_c *and* S_a *have the same support, (2) the length of* S_c *is smaller than that of* S_a, *and (3) all of the items in* S_c *are contained in* S_a.

Based on this property, a **two-level hash index structure** can be built for fast accessing of the pattern-tree: The first level uses the identifier of the last item in S_c as a hash key (since this identifier must be within the branch of S_c), and the second level uses the support of S_c as a hash key (since S_c and S_a have the same support). This will substantially speed up the subset checking process.

This discussion illustrates methods for efficient mining of closed frequent itemsets. *"Can we extend these methods for efficient mining of maximal frequent itemsets?"* Because maximal frequent itemsets share many similarities with closed frequent itemsets, many of the optimization techniques developed here can be extended to mining maximal frequent itemsets. However, we leave this method as an exercise for interested readers.

6.3 Which Patterns Are Interesting?—Pattern Evaluation Methods

Most association rule mining algorithms employ a support–confidence framework. Although minimum support and confidence thresholds *help* weed out or exclude the exploration of a good number of uninteresting rules, many of the rules generated are still not interesting to the users. Unfortunately, this is especially true *when mining at low support thresholds or mining for long patterns*. This has been a major bottleneck for successful application of association rule mining.

In this section, we first look at how even strong association rules can be uninteresting and misleading (Section 6.3.1). We then discuss how the support–confidence framework can be supplemented with additional interestingness measures based on *correlation analysis* (Section 6.3.2). Section 6.3.3 presents additional pattern evaluation measures. It then provides an overall comparison of all the measures discussed here. By the end, you will learn which pattern evaluation measures are most effective for the discovery of only interesting rules.

6.3.1 Strong Rules Are Not Necessarily Interesting

Whether or not a rule is interesting can be assessed either subjectively or objectively. Ultimately, only the user can judge if a given rule is interesting, and this judgment, being subjective, may differ from one user to another. However, objective interestingness measures, based on the statistics "behind" the data, can be used as one step toward the goal of weeding out uninteresting rules that would otherwise be presented to the user.

"*How can we tell which strong association rules are really interesting?*" Let's examine the following example.

Example 6.7 **A misleading "strong" association rule.** Suppose we are interested in analyzing transactions at *AllElectronics* with respect to the purchase of computer games and videos. Let *game* refer to the transactions containing computer games, and *video* refer to those containing videos. Of the 10,000 transactions analyzed, the data show that 6000 of the customer transactions included computer games, while 7500 included videos, and 4000 included both computer games and videos. Suppose that a data mining program for discovering association rules is run on the data, using a minimum support of, say, 30% and a minimum confidence of 60%. The following association rule is discovered:

$$buys(X, ``computer\ games") \Rightarrow buys(X, ``videos")$$

$$[support = 40\%, confidence = 66\%]. \tag{6.6}$$

Rule (6.6) is a strong association rule and would therefore be reported, since its support value of $\frac{4000}{10,000} = 40\%$ and confidence value of $\frac{4000}{6000} = 66\%$ satisfy the minimum support and minimum confidence thresholds, respectively. However, Rule (6.6) is misleading because the probability of purchasing videos is 75%, which is even larger than 66%. In fact, computer games and videos are negatively associated because the purchase of one of these items actually decreases the likelihood of purchasing the other. Without fully understanding this phenomenon, we could easily make unwise business decisions based on Rule (6.6). ∎

Example 6.7 also illustrates that the confidence of a rule $A \Rightarrow B$ can be deceiving. It does not measure the *real strength* (or lack of strength) of the *correlation* and *implication* between A and B. Hence, alternatives to the support–confidence framework can be useful in mining interesting data relationships.

6.3.2 From Association Analysis to Correlation Analysis

As we have seen so far, the support and confidence measures are insufficient at filtering out uninteresting association rules. To tackle this weakness, a correlation measure can be used to augment the support–confidence framework for association rules. This leads to *correlation rules* of the form

$$A \Rightarrow B \ [support, confidence, correlation]. \tag{6.7}$$

That is, a correlation rule is measured not only by its support and confidence but also by the correlation between itemsets A and B. There are many different correlation measures from which to choose. In this subsection, we study several correlation measures to determine which would be good for mining large data sets.

Lift is a simple correlation measure that is given as follows. The occurrence of itemset A is **independent** of the occurrence of itemset B if $P(A \cup B) = P(A)P(B)$; otherwise, itemsets A and B are **dependent** and **correlated** as events. This definition can easily be extended to more than two itemsets. The **lift** between the occurrence of A and B can be measured by computing

$$lift(A, B) = \frac{P(A \cup B)}{P(A)P(B)}. \qquad (6.8)$$

If the resulting value of Eq. (6.8) is less than 1, then the occurrence of A is *negatively correlated with* the occurrence of B, meaning that the occurrence of one likely leads to the absence of the other one. If the resulting value is greater than 1, then A and B are *positively correlated*, meaning that the occurrence of one implies the occurrence of the other. If the resulting value is equal to 1, then A and B are *independent* and there is no correlation between them.

Equation (6.8) is equivalent to $P(B|A)/P(B)$, or $conf(A \Rightarrow B)/sup(B)$, which is also referred to as the *lift* of the association (or correlation) rule $A \Rightarrow B$. In other words, it assesses the degree to which the occurrence of one "lifts" the occurrence of the other. For example, if A corresponds to the sale of computer games and B corresponds to the sale of videos, then given the current market conditions, the sale of games is said to increase or "lift" the likelihood of the sale of videos by a factor of the value returned by Eq. (6.8).

Let's go back to the computer game and video data of Example 6.7.

Example 6.8 **Correlation analysis using lift.** To help filter out misleading "strong" associations of the form $A \Rightarrow B$ from the data of Example 6.7, we need to study how the two itemsets, A and B, are correlated. Let $\overline{game}$ refer to the transactions of Example 6.7 that do not contain computer games, and $\overline{video}$ refer to those that do not contain videos. The transactions can be summarized in a *contingency table*, as shown in Table 6.6.

From the table, we can see that the probability of purchasing a computer game is $P(\{game\}) = 0.60$, the probability of purchasing a video is $P(\{video\}) = 0.75$, and the probability of purchasing both is $P(\{game, video\}) = 0.40$. By Eq. (6.8), the lift of Rule (6.6) is $P(\{game, video\})/(P(\{game\}) \times P(\{video\})) = 0.40/(0.60 \times 0.75) = 0.89$. Because this value is less than 1, there is a negative correlation between the occurrence of $\{game\}$ and $\{video\}$. The numerator is the likelihood of a customer purchasing both, while the denominator is what the likelihood would have been if the two purchases were completely independent. Such a negative correlation cannot be identified by a support–confidence framework. ∎

The second correlation measure that we study is the χ^2 measure, which was introduced in Chapter 3 (Eq. 3.1). To compute the χ^2 value, we take the squared difference between the observed and expected value for a slot (A and B pair) in the contingency table, divided by the expected value. This amount is summed for all slots of the contingency table. Let's perform a χ^2 analysis of Example 6.8.

Table 6.6 2 × 2 Contingency Table Summarizing the
Transactions with Respect to Game and
Video Purchases

	game	$\overline{game}$	Σ_{row}
video	4000	3500	7500
$\overline{video}$	2000	500	2500
Σ_{col}	6000	4000	10,000

Table 6.7 Table 6.6 Contingency Table, Now with
the Expected Values

	game	$\overline{game}$	Σ_{row}
video	4000 (4500)	3500 (3000)	7500
$\overline{video}$	2000 (1500)	500 (1000)	2500
Σ_{col}	6000	4000	10,000

Example 6.9 **Correlation analysis using χ^2.** To compute the correlation using χ^2 analysis for nominal data, we need the observed value and expected value (displayed in parenthesis) for each slot of the contingency table, as shown in Table 6.7. From the table, we can compute the χ^2 value as follows:

$$\chi^2 = \Sigma \frac{(observed - expected)^2}{expected} = \frac{(4000 - 4500)^2}{4500} + \frac{(3500 - 3000)^2}{3000}$$
$$+ \frac{(2000 - 1500)^2}{1500} + \frac{(500 - 1000)^2}{1000} = 555.6.$$

Because the χ^2 value is greater than 1, and the observed value of the slot (*game, video*) = 4000, which is less than the expected value of 4500, *buying game* and *buying video* are *negatively correlated*. This is consistent with the conclusion derived from the analysis of the *lift* measure in Example 6.8. ∎

6.3.3 A Comparison of Pattern Evaluation Measures

The above discussion shows that instead of using the simple support–confidence framework to evaluate frequent patterns, other measures, such as *lift* and χ^2, often disclose more intrinsic pattern relationships. How effective are these measures? Should we also consider other alternatives?

Researchers have studied many pattern evaluation measures even before the start of in-depth research on scalable methods for mining frequent patterns. Recently, several other pattern evaluation measures have attracted interest. In this subsection, we present four such measures: *all_confidence, max_confidence, Kulczynski*, and *cosine*. We'll then compare their effectiveness with respect to one another and with respect to the *lift* and χ^2 measures.

Given two itemsets, A and B, the **all_confidence** measure of A and B is defined as

$$all\_conf(A, B) = \frac{sup(A \cup B)}{max\{sup(A), sup(B)\}} = min\{P(A|B), P(B|A)\}, \tag{6.9}$$

where $max\{sup(A), sup(B)\}$ is the maximum support of the itemsets A and B. Thus, $all\_conf(A, B)$ is also the minimum confidence of the two association rules related to A and B, namely, "$A \Rightarrow B$" and "$B \Rightarrow A$."

Given two itemsets, A and B, the **max_confidence** measure of A and B is defined as

$$max\_conf(A, B) = max\{P(A|B), P(B|A)\}. \tag{6.10}$$

The *max_conf* measure is the maximum confidence of the two association rules, "$A \Rightarrow B$" and "$B \Rightarrow A$."

Given two itemsets, A and B, the **Kulczynski** measure of A and B (abbreviated as **Kulc**) is defined as

$$Kulc(A, B) = \frac{1}{2}(P(A|B) + P(B|A)). \tag{6.11}$$

It was proposed in 1927 by Polish mathematician S. Kulczynski. It can be viewed as an average of two confidence measures. That is, it is the average of two conditional probabilities: the probability of itemset B given itemset A, and the probability of itemset A given itemset B.

Finally, given two itemsets, A and B, the **cosine** measure of A and B is defined as

$$cosine(A, B) = \frac{P(A \cup B)}{\sqrt{P(A) \times P(B)}} = \frac{sup(A \cup B)}{\sqrt{sup(A) \times sup(B)}}$$

$$= \sqrt{P(A|B) \times P(B|A)}. \tag{6.12}$$

The *cosine* measure can be viewed as a *harmonized lift* measure: The two formulae are similar except that for cosine, the *square root* is taken on the product of the probabilities of A and B. This is an important difference, however, because by taking the square root, the cosine value is only influenced by the supports of A, B, and $A \cup B$, and not by the total number of transactions.

Each of these four measures defined has the following property: Its value is only influenced by the supports of A, B, and $A \cup B$, or more exactly, by the conditional probabilities of $P(A|B)$ and $P(B|A)$, but not by the total number of transactions. Another common property is that each measure ranges from 0 to 1, and the higher the value, the closer the relationship between A and B.

Now, together with *lift* and χ^2, we have introduced in total six pattern evaluation measures. You may wonder, "*Which is the best in assessing the discovered pattern relationships?*" To answer this question, we examine their performance on some typical data sets.

Table 6.8 2×2 Contingency Table for Two Items

	milk	$\overline{milk}$	Σ_{row}
coffee	mc	$\overline{m}c$	c
$\overline{coffee}$	$m\overline{c}$	$\overline{mc}$	$\overline{c}$
Σ_{col}	m	$\overline{m}$	Σ

Table 6.9 Comparison of Six Pattern Evaluation Measures Using Contingency Tables for a Variety of Data Sets

Data Set	mc	$\overline{m}c$	$m\overline{c}$	$\overline{mc}$	χ^2	lift	all_conf.	max_conf.	Kulc.	cosine
D_1	10,000	1000	1000	100,000	90557	9.26	0.91	0.91	0.91	0.91
D_2	10,000	1000	1000	100	0	1	0.91	0.91	0.91	0.91
D_3	100	1000	1000	100,000	670	8.44	0.09	0.09	0.09	0.09
D_4	1000	1000	1000	100,000	24740	25.75	0.5	0.5	0.5	0.5
D_5	1000	100	10,000	100,000	8173	9.18	0.09	0.91	0.5	0.29
D_6	1000	10	100,000	100,000	965	1.97	0.01	0.99	0.5	0.10

Example 6.10 **Comparison of six pattern evaluation measures on typical data sets.** The relationships between the purchases of two items, *milk* and *coffee*, can be examined by summarizing their purchase history in Table 6.8, a 2×2 contingency table, where an entry such as *mc* represents the number of transactions containing both milk and coffee.

Table 6.9 shows a set of transactional data sets with their corresponding contingency tables and the associated values for each of the six evaluation measures. Let's first examine the first four data sets, D_1 through D_4. From the table, we see that m and c are positively associated in D_1 and D_2, negatively associated in D_3, and neutral in D_4. For D_1 and D_2, m and c are positively associated because mc (10,000) is considerably greater than $\overline{m}c$ (1000) and $m\overline{c}$ (1000). Intuitively, for people who bought milk ($m = 10,000 + 1000 = 11,000$), it is very likely that they also bought coffee ($mc/m = 10/11 = 91\%$), and vice versa.

The results of the four newly introduced measures show that m and c are strongly positively associated in both data sets by producing a measure value of 0.91. However, *lift* and χ^2 generate dramatically different measure values for D_1 and D_2 due to their sensitivity to $\overline{mc}$. In fact, in many real-world scenarios, $\overline{mc}$ is usually huge and unstable. For example, in a market basket database, the total number of transactions could fluctuate on a daily basis and overwhelmingly exceed the number of transactions containing any particular itemset. Therefore, a good interestingness measure should not be affected by transactions that do not contain the itemsets of interest; otherwise, it would generate unstable results, as illustrated in D_1 and D_2.

Similarly, in D_3, the four new measures correctly show that m and c are strongly negatively associated because the m to c ratio equals the mc to m ratio, that is, $100/1100 = 9.1\%$. However, *lift* and χ^2 both contradict this in an incorrect way: Their values for D_2 are between those for D_1 and D_3.

For data set D_4, both *lift* and χ^2 indicate a highly positive association between m and c, whereas the others indicate a "neutral" association because the ratio of mc to $\overline{mc}$ equals the ratio of mc to $m\overline{c}$, which is 1. This means that if a customer buys coffee (or milk), the probability that he or she will also purchase milk (or coffee) is exactly 50%.   ∎

"*Why are* lift *and* χ^2 *so poor at distinguishing pattern association relationships in the previous transactional data sets?*" To answer this, we have to consider the *null-transactions*. A **null-transaction** is a transaction that does not contain any of the item-sets being examined. In our example, $\overline{mc}$ represents the number of null-transactions. *Lift* and χ^2 have difficulty distinguishing interesting pattern association relationships because they are both strongly influenced by $\overline{mc}$. Typically, the number of null-transactions can outweigh the number of individual purchases because, for example, many people may buy neither milk nor coffee. On the other hand, the other four measures are good indicators of interesting pattern associations because their defi-nitions remove the influence of $\overline{mc}$ (i.e., they are not influenced by the number of null-transactions).

This discussion shows that it is highly desirable to have a measure that has a value that is independent of the number of null-transactions. A measure is **null-invariant** if its value is free from the influence of null-transactions. Null-invariance is an impor-tant property for measuring association patterns in large transaction databases. Among the six discussed measures in this subsection, only *lift* and χ^2 are not null-invariant measures.

"*Among the* all_confidence, max_confidence, Kulczynski, *and* cosine *measures, which is best at indicating interesting pattern relationships?*"

To answer this question, we introduce the **imbalance ratio** (**IR**), which assesses the imbalance of two itemsets, A and B, in rule implications. It is defined as

$$IR(A, B) = \frac{|sup(A) - sup(B)|}{sup(A) + sup(B) - sup(A \cup B)}, \tag{6.13}$$

where the numerator is the absolute value of the difference between the support of the itemsets A and B, and the denominator is the number of transactions containing A or B. If the two directional implications between A and B are the same, then $IR(A, B)$ will be zero. Otherwise, the larger the difference between the two, the larger the imbalance ratio. This ratio is independent of the number of null-transactions and independent of the total number of transactions.

Let's continue examining the remaining data sets in Example 6.10.

Example 6.11 **Comparing null-invariant measures in pattern evaluation.** Although the four mea-sures introduced in this section are null-invariant, they may present dramatically different values on some subtly different data sets. Let's examine data sets D_5 and D_6, shown earlier in Table 6.9, where the two events m and c have unbalanced conditional probabilities. That is, the ratio of mc to c is greater than 0.9. This means that knowing that c occurs should strongly suggest that m occurs also. The ratio of mc to m is less than 0.1, indicating that m implies that c is quite unlikely to occur. The *all_confidence* and *cosine* measures view both cases as negatively associated and the *Kulc* measure views both as neutral. The *max_confidence* measure claims strong positive associations for these cases. The measures give very diverse results!

"*Which measure intuitively reflects the true relationship between the purchase of milk and coffee?*" Due to the "*balanced*" skewness of the data, it is difficult to argue whether the two data sets have positive or negative association. From one point of view, only $mc/(mc + m\bar{c}) = 1000/(1000 + 10,000) = 9.09\%$ of milk-related transactions contain coffee in D_5 and this percentage is $1000/(1000 + 100,000) = 0.99\%$ in D_6, both indicating a negative association. On the other hand, 90.9% of transactions in D_5 (i.e., $mc/(mc + \bar{m}c) = 1000/(1000 + 100)$) and 9% in D_6 (i.e., $1000/(1000 + 10)$) containing coffee contain milk as well, which indicates a positive association between milk and coffee. These draw very different conclusions.

For such "balanced" skewness, it could be fair to treat it as neutral, as *Kulc* does, and in the meantime indicate its skewness using the *imbalance ratio (IR)*. According to Eq. (6.13), for D_4 we have $IR(m, c) = 0$, a perfectly balanced case; for D_5, $IR(m, c) = 0.89$, a rather imbalanced case; whereas for D_6, $IR(m, c) = 0.99$, a very skewed case. Therefore, the two measures, *Kulc* and *IR*, work together, presenting a clear picture for all three data sets, D_4 through D_6. ∎

In summary, the use of only support and confidence measures to mine associations may generate a large number of rules, many of which can be uninteresting to users. Instead, we can augment the support–confidence framework with a pattern interestingness measure, which helps focus the mining toward rules with strong pattern relationships. The added measure substantially reduces the number of rules generated and leads to the discovery of more meaningful rules. Besides those introduced in this section, many other interestingness measures have been studied in the literature. Unfortunately, most of them do not have the null-invariance property. Because large data sets typically have many null-transactions, it is important to consider the null-invariance property when selecting appropriate interestingness measures for pattern evaluation. Among the four null-invariant measures studied here, namely *all_confidence*, *max_confidence*, *Kulc*, and *cosine*, we recommend using *Kulc* in conjunction with the imbalance ratio.

6.4 Summary

- The discovery of frequent patterns, associations, and correlation relationships among huge amounts of data is useful in selective marketing, decision analysis, and business management. A popular area of application is **market basket analysis**, which studies customers' buying habits by searching for itemsets that are frequently purchased together (or in sequence).

- **Association rule mining** consists of first finding **frequent itemsets** (sets of items, such as A and B, satisfying a *minimum support threshold*, or percentage of the task-relevant tuples), from which **strong** association rules in the form of $A \Rightarrow B$ are generated. These rules also satisfy a *minimum confidence threshold* (a prespecified probability of satisfying B under the condition that A is satisfied). Associations can be further analyzed to uncover **correlation rules**, which convey statistical correlations between itemsets A and B.

- Many efficient and scalable algorithms have been developed for **frequent itemset mining**, from which association and correlation rules can be derived. These algorithms can be classified into three categories: (1) *Apriori-like algorithms*, (2) *frequent pattern growth–based algorithms* such as FP-growth, and (3) *algorithms that use the vertical data format.*

- The **Apriori algorithm** is a seminal algorithm for mining frequent itemsets for Boolean association rules. It explores the level-wise mining Apriori property that *all nonempty subsets of a frequent itemset must also be frequent*. At the kth iteration (for $k \geq 2$), it forms frequent k-itemset candidates based on the frequent $(k-1)$-itemsets, and scans the database once to find the *complete* set of frequent k-itemsets, L_k.

    Variations involving hashing and transaction reduction can be used to make the procedure more efficient. Other variations include partitioning the data (mining on each partition and then combining the results) and sampling the data (mining on a data subset). These variations can reduce the number of data scans required to as little as two or even one.

- **Frequent pattern growth** is a method of mining frequent itemsets without candidate generation. It constructs a highly compact data structure (an *FP-tree*) to compress the original transaction database. Rather than employing the generate-and-test strategy of Apriori-like methods, it focuses on frequent pattern (fragment) growth, which avoids costly candidate generation, resulting in greater efficiency.

- **Mining frequent itemsets using the vertical data format (Eclat)** is a method that transforms a given data set of transactions in the horizontal data format of *TID-itemset* into the vertical data format of *item-TID_set*. It mines the transformed data set by *TID_set* intersections based on the Apriori property and additional optimization techniques such as *diffset*.

- Not all strong association rules are interesting. Therefore, the support–confidence framework should be augmented with a pattern evaluation measure, which promotes the mining of *interesting* rules. A measure is **null-invariant** if its value is free from the influence of **null-transactions** (i.e., *the transactions that do not contain any of the itemsets being examined*). Among many pattern evaluation measures, we examined *lift*, χ^2, *all_confidence, max_confidence, Kulczynski*, and *cosine*, and showed that only the latter four are null-invariant. We suggest using the Kulczynski measure, together with the imbalance ratio, to present pattern relationships among itemsets.

6.5 Exercises

6.1 Suppose you have the set C of all frequent closed itemsets on a data set D, as well as the support count for each frequent closed itemset. Describe an algorithm to determine whether a given itemset X is frequent or not, and the support of X if it is frequent.

6.2 An itemset X is called a *generator* on a data set D if there does not exist a proper sub-itemset $Y \subset X$ such that $support(X) = support(Y)$. A generator X is a *frequent generator* if $support(X)$ passes the minimum support threshold. Let G be the set of all frequent generators on a data set D.

(a) Can you determine whether an itemset A is frequent and the support of A, if it is frequent, using only G and the support counts of all frequent generators? If yes, present your algorithm. Otherwise, what other information is needed? Can you give an algorithm assuming the information needed is available?

(b) What is the relationship between closed itemsets and generators?

6.3 The Apriori algorithm makes use of *prior knowledge* of subset support properties.

(a) Prove that all nonempty subsets of a frequent itemset must also be frequent.

(b) Prove that the support of any nonempty subset s' of itemset s must be at least as great as the support of s.

(c) Given frequent itemset l and subset s of l, prove that the confidence of the rule "$s' \Rightarrow (l - s')$" cannot be more than the confidence of "$s \Rightarrow (l - s)$," where s' is a subset of s.

(d) A *partitioning* variation of Apriori subdivides the transactions of a database D into n nonoverlapping partitions. Prove that any itemset that is frequent in D must be frequent in at least one partition of D.

6.4 Let c be a candidate itemset in C_k generated by the Apriori algorithm. How many length-$(k-1)$ subsets do we need to check in the prune step? Per your previous answer, can you give an improved version of procedure has_infrequent_subset in Figure 6.4?

6.5 Section 6.2.2 describes a method for *generating association rules* from frequent itemsets. Propose a more efficient method. Explain why it is more efficient than the one proposed there. (*Hint:* Consider incorporating the properties of Exercises 6.3(b), (c) into your design.)

6.6 A database has five transactions. Let $min\_sup = 60\%$ and $min\_conf = 80\%$.

TID	items_bought
T100	{M, O, N, K, E, Y}
T200	{D, O, N, K, E, Y }
T300	{M, A, K, E}
T400	{M, U, C, K, Y}
T500	{C, O, O, K, I, E}

(a) Find all frequent itemsets using Apriori and FP-growth, respectively. Compare the efficiency of the two mining processes.

(b) List all the *strong* association rules (with support s and confidence c) matching the following metarule, where X is a variable representing customers, and *item$_i$* denotes variables representing items (e.g., "A," "B,"):

$$\forall x \in transaction, \; buys(X, item_1) \wedge buys(X, item_2) \Rightarrow buys(X, item_3) \quad [s, c]$$

6.7 (**Implementation project**) Using a programming language that you are familiar with, such as C++ or Java, implement three *frequent itemset mining* algorithms introduced in this chapter: (1) Apriori [AS94b], (2) FP-growth [HPY00], and (3) Eclat [Zak00] (mining using the vertical data format). Compare the performance of each algorithm with various kinds of large data sets. Write a report to analyze the situations (e.g., data size, data distribution, minimal support threshold setting, and pattern density) where one algorithm may perform better than the others, and state why.

6.8 A database has four transactions. Let *min_sup* = 60% and *min_conf* = 80%.

cust_ID	TID	items_bought (in the form of brand-item_category)
01	T100	{King's-Crab, Sunset-Milk, Dairyland-Cheese, Best-Bread}
02	T200	{Best-Cheese, Dairyland-Milk, Goldenfarm-Apple, Tasty-Pie, Wonder-Bread}
01	T300	{Westcoast-Apple, Dairyland-Milk, Wonder-Bread, Tasty-Pie}
03	T400	{Wonder-Bread, Sunset-Milk, Dairyland-Cheese}

(a) At the granularity of *item_category* (e.g., *item$_i$* could be "*Milk*"), for the rule template,

$$\forall X \in transaction, \; buys(X, item_1) \wedge buys(X, item_2) \Rightarrow buys(X, item_3) \quad [s, c],$$

list the frequent k-itemset for the largest k, and *all* the *strong* association rules (with their support s and confidence c) containing the frequent k-itemset for the largest k.

(b) At the granularity of *brand-item_category* (e.g., *item$_i$* could be "*Sunset-Milk*"), for the rule template,

$$\forall X \in customer, \; buys(X, item_1) \wedge buys(X, item_2) \Rightarrow buys(X, item_3),$$

list the frequent k-itemset for the largest k (but do not print any rules).

6.9 Suppose that a large store has a transactional database that is *distributed* among four locations. Transactions in each component database have the same format, namely $T_j : \{i_1, \ldots, i_m\}$, where T_j is a transaction identifier, and i_k $(1 \leq k \leq m)$ is the identifier of an item purchased in the transaction. Propose an efficient algorithm to mine global association rules. You may present your algorithm in the form of an outline. Your algorithm should not require shipping all the data to one site and should not cause excessive network communication overhead.

6.10 Suppose that frequent itemsets are saved for a large transactional database, *DB*. Discuss how to efficiently mine the (global) association rules under the same minimum support threshold, if a set of new transactions, denoted as ΔDB, is *(incrementally) added in*?

6.11 Most frequent pattern mining algorithms consider only distinct items in a transaction. However, multiple occurrences of an item in the same shopping basket, such as four cakes and three jugs of milk, can be important in transactional data analysis. How can one mine frequent itemsets efficiently considering multiple occurrences of items? Propose modifications to the well-known algorithms, such as Apriori and FP-growth, to adapt to such a situation.

6.12 (**Implementation project**) Many techniques have been proposed to further improve the performance of frequent itemset mining algorithms. Taking FP-tree–based frequent pattern growth algorithms (e.g., FP-growth) as an example, implement one of the following optimization techniques. Compare the performance of your new implementation with the unoptimized version.

(a) The frequent pattern mining method of Section 6.2.4 uses an FP-tree to generate conditional pattern bases using a bottom-up projection technique (i.e., project onto the prefix path of an item p). However, one can develop a *top-down projection* technique, that is, project onto the suffix path of an item p in the generation of a conditional pattern base. Design and implement such a top-down FP-tree mining method. Compare its performance with the bottom-up projection method.

(b) Nodes and pointers are used uniformly in an FP-tree in the FP-growth algorithm design. However, such a structure may consume a lot of space when the data are sparse. One possible alternative design is to explore *array- and pointer-based hybrid implementation*, where a node may store multiple items when it contains no splitting point to multiple sub-branches. Develop such an implementation and compare it with the original one.

(c) It is time and space consuming to generate numerous conditional pattern bases during pattern-growth mining. An interesting alternative is to *push right* the branches that have been mined for a particular item p, that is, to push them to the remaining branch(es) of the FP-tree. This is done so that fewer conditional pattern bases have to be generated and additional sharing can be explored when mining the remaining FP-tree branches. Design and implement such a method and conduct a performance study on it.

6.13 Give a short example to show that items in a strong association rule actually may be *negatively correlated.*

6.14 The following contingency table summarizes supermarket transaction data, where *hot dogs* refers to the transactions containing hot dogs, $\overline{hot\ dogs}$ refers to the transactions that do not contain hot dogs, *hamburgers* refers to the transactions containing hamburgers, and $\overline{hamburgers}$ refers to the transactions that do not contain hamburgers.

	hot dogs	$\overline{hot\ dogs}$	Σ_{row}
hamburgers	2000	500	2500
$\overline{hamburgers}$	1000	1500	2500
Σ_{col}	3000	2000	5000

(a) Suppose that the association rule "*hot dogs* $\Rightarrow$ *hamburgers*" is mined. Given a minimum support threshold of 25% and a minimum confidence threshold of 50%, is this association rule strong?

(b) Based on the given data, is the purchase of *hot dogs* independent of the purchase of *hamburgers*? If not, what kind of *correlation* relationship exists between the two?

(c) Compare the use of the *all_confidence, max_confidence, Kulczynski,* and *cosine* measures with *lift* and *correlation* on the given data.

6.15 (**Implementation project**) The DBLP data set (*www.informatik.uni-trier .de/~ley/db/*) consists of over one million entries of research papers published in computer science conferences and journals. Among these entries, there are a good number of authors that have coauthor relationships.

(a) Propose a method to efficiently mine a set of coauthor relationships that are closely correlated (e.g., often coauthoring papers together).

(b) Based on the mining results and the pattern evaluation measures discussed in this chapter, discuss which measure may convincingly uncover close collaboration patterns better than others.

(c) Based on the study in (a), develop a method that can roughly predict advisor and advisee relationships and the approximate period for such advisory supervision.

6.6 Bibliographic Notes

Association rule mining was first proposed by Agrawal, Imielinski, and Swami [AIS93]. The Apriori algorithm discussed in Section 6.2.1 for frequent itemset mining was presented in Agrawal and Srikant [AS94b]. A variation of the algorithm using a similar pruning heuristic was developed independently by Mannila, Tiovonen, and Verkamo

[MTV94]. A joint publication combining these works later appeared in Agrawal, Mannila, Srikant et al. [AMS⁺96]. A method for generating association rules from frequent itemsets is described in Agrawal and Srikant [AS94a].

References for the variations of Apriori described in Section 6.2.3 include the following. The use of hash tables to improve association mining efficiency was studied by Park, Chen, and Yu [PCY95a]. The partitioning technique was proposed by Savasere, Omiecinski, and Navathe [SON95]. The sampling approach is discussed in Toivonen [Toi96]. A dynamic itemset counting approach is given in Brin, Motwani, Ullman, and Tsur [BMUT97]. An efficient incremental updating of mined association rules was proposed by Cheung, Han, Ng, and Wong [CHNW96]. Parallel and distributed association data mining under the Apriori framework was studied by Park, Chen, and Yu [PCY95b]; Agrawal and Shafer [AS96]; and Cheung, Han, Ng, et al. [CHN⁺96]. Another parallel association mining method, which explores itemset clustering using a vertical database layout, was proposed in Zaki, Parthasarathy, Ogihara, and Li [ZPOL97].

Other scalable frequent itemset mining methods have been proposed as alternatives to the Apriori-based approach. FP-growth, a pattern-growth approach for mining frequent itemsets without candidate generation, was proposed by Han, Pei, and Yin [HPY00] (Section 6.2.4). An exploration of hyper structure mining of frequent patterns, called H-Mine, was proposed by Pei, Han, Lu, et al. [PHL⁺01]. A method that integrates top-down and bottom-up traversal of FP-trees in pattern-growth mining was proposed by Liu, Pan, Wang, and Han [LPWH02]. An array-based implementation of prefix-tree structure for efficient pattern growth mining was proposed by Grahne and Zhu [GZ03b]. Eclat, an approach for mining frequent itemsets by exploring the vertical data format, was proposed by Zaki [Zak00]. A depth-first generation of frequent itemsets by a tree projection technique was proposed by Agarwal, Aggarwal, and Prasad [AAP01]. An integration of association mining with relational database systems was studied by Sarawagi, Thomas, and Agrawal [STA98].

The mining of frequent closed itemsets was proposed in Pasquier, Bastide, Taouil, and Lakhal [PBTL99], where an Apriori-based algorithm called A-Close for such mining was presented. CLOSET, an efficient closed itemset mining algorithm based on the frequent pattern growth method, was proposed by Pei, Han, and Mao [PHM00]. CHARM by Zaki and Hsiao [ZH02] developed a compact vertical TID list structure called *diffset*, which records only the difference in the TID list of a candidate pattern from its prefix pattern. A fast hash-based approach is also used in CHARM to prune nonclosed patterns. CLOSET+ by Wang, Han, and Pei [WHP03] integrates previously proposed effective strategies as well as newly developed techniques such as hybrid tree-projection and item skipping. AFOPT, a method that explores a *right push* operation on FP-trees during the mining process, was proposed by Liu, Lu, Lou, and Yu [LLLY03]. Grahne and Zhu [GZ03b] proposed a prefix-tree–based algorithm integrated with array representation, called FPClose, for mining closed itemsets using a pattern-growth approach.

Pan, Cong, Tung, et al. [PCT⁺03] proposed CARPENTER, a method for finding closed patterns in long biological data sets, which integrates the advantages of vertical data formats and pattern growth methods. Mining max-patterns was first studied by Bayardo [Bay98], where MaxMiner, an Apriori-based, level-wise, breadth-first search method, was proposed to find *max-itemset* by performing *superset frequency pruning* and *subset infrequency pruning* for search space reduction. Another efficient method, MAFIA, developed by Burdick, Calimlim, and Gehrke [BCG01], uses vertical bitmaps to compress TID lists, thus improving the counting efficiency. A FIMI (Frequent Itemset Mining Implementation) workshop dedicated to implementation methods for frequent itemset mining was reported by Goethals and Zaki [GZ03a].

The problem of mining interesting rules has been studied by many researchers. The statistical independence of rules in data mining was studied by Piatetski-Shapiro [P-S91]. The interestingness problem of strong association rules is discussed in Chen, Han, and Yu [CHY96]; Brin, Motwani, and Silverstein [BMS97]; and Aggarwal and Yu [AY99], which cover several interestingness measures, including *lift*. An efficient method for generalizing associations to correlations is given in Brin, Motwani, and Silverstein [BMS97]. Other alternatives to the support–confidence framework for assessing the interestingness of association rules are proposed in Brin, Motwani, Ullman, and Tsur [BMUT97] and Ahmed, El-Makky, and Taha [AEMT00].

A method for mining strong gradient relationships among itemsets was proposed by Imielinski, Khachiyan, and Abdulghani [IKA02]. Silverstein, Brin, Motwani, and Ullman [SBMU98] studied the problem of mining causal structures over transaction databases. Some comparative studies of different interestingness measures were done by Hilderman and Hamilton [HH01]. The notion of null transaction invariance was introduced, together with a comparative analysis of interestingness measures, by Tan, Kumar, and Srivastava [TKS02]. The use of *all_confidence* as a correlation measure for generating interesting association rules was studied by Omiecinski [Omi03] and by Lee, Kim, Cai, and Han [LKCH03]. Wu, Chen, and Han [WCH10] introduced the Kulczynski measure for associative patterns and performed a comparative analysis of a set of measures for pattern evaluation.

Advanced Pattern Mining

Frequent pattern mining has reached far beyond the basics due to substantial research, numerous extensions of the problem scope, and broad application studies. In this chapter, you will learn methods for advanced pattern mining. We begin by laying out a general road map for pattern mining. We introduce methods for mining various kinds of patterns, and discuss extended applications of pattern mining. We include in-depth coverage of methods for mining many kinds of patterns: multilevel patterns, multidimensional patterns, patterns in continuous data, rare patterns, negative patterns, constrained frequent patterns, frequent patterns in high-dimensional data, colossal patterns, and compressed and approximate patterns. Other pattern mining themes, including mining sequential and structured patterns and mining patterns from spatiotemporal, multimedia, and stream data, are considered more advanced topics and are not covered in this book. Notice that *pattern mining* is a more general term than *frequent pattern mining* since the former covers rare and negative patterns as well. However, when there is no ambiguity, the two terms are used interchangeably.

7.1 Pattern Mining: A Road Map

Chapter 6 introduced the basic concepts, techniques, and applications of frequent pattern mining using market basket analysis as an example. Many other kinds of data, user requests, and applications have led to the development of numerous, diverse methods for mining patterns, associations, and correlation relationships. Given the rich literature in this area, it is important to lay out a clear road map to help us get an organized picture of the field and to select the best methods for pattern mining applications.

Figure 7.1 outlines a general road map on pattern mining research. Most studies mainly address three pattern mining aspects: the kinds of patterns mined, mining methodologies, and applications. Some studies, however, integrate multiple aspects; for example, different applications may need to mine different patterns, which naturally leads to the development of new mining methodologies.

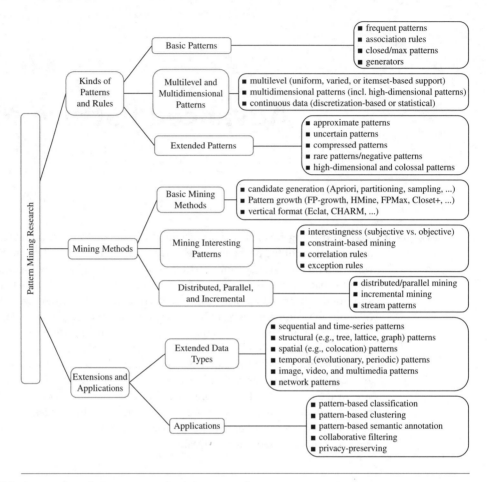

Figure 7.1 A general road map on pattern mining research.

Based on pattern diversity, pattern mining can be classified using the following criteria:

- **Basic patterns:** As discussed in Chapter 6, a frequent pattern may have several alternative forms, including a simple frequent pattern, a closed pattern, or a max-pattern. To review, a **frequent pattern** is a pattern (or itemset) that satisfies a minimum support threshold. A pattern p is a **closed pattern** if there is no superpattern p' with the same support as p. Pattern p is a **max-pattern** if there exists no frequent superpattern of p. Frequent patterns can also be mapped into **association rules**, or other kinds of rules based on interestingness measures. Sometimes we may also be interested in **infrequent** or **rare patterns** (i.e., patterns that occur rarely but are of critical importance, or **negative patterns** (i.e., patterns that reveal a negative correlation between items).

■ **Based on the *abstraction* levels involved in a pattern:** Patterns or association rules may have items or concepts residing at high, low, or multiple abstraction levels. For example, suppose that a set of association rules mined includes the following rules where X is a variable representing a customer:

$$buys(X, \text{``computer''}) \Rightarrow buys(X, \text{``printer''}) \tag{7.1}$$

$$buys(X, \text{``laptop computer''}) \Rightarrow buys(X, \text{``color laser printer''}) \tag{7.2}$$

In Rules (7.1) and (7.2), the items bought are referenced at different abstraction levels (e.g., "*computer*" is a higher-level abstraction of "*laptop computer*," and "*color laser printer*" is a lower-level abstraction of "*printer*"). We refer to the rule set mined as consisting of **multilevel association rules**. If, instead, the rules within a given set do not reference items or attributes at different abstraction levels, then the set contains **single-level association rules**.

■ **Based on the *number of dimensions* involved in the rule or pattern:** If the items or attributes in an association rule or pattern reference only one dimension, it is a **single-dimensional association rule/pattern**. For example, Rules (7.1) and (7.2) are single-dimensional association rules because they each refer to only one dimension, *buys*.[1]

If a rule/pattern references two or more dimensions, such as *age, income*, and *buys*, then it is a **multidimensional association rule/pattern**. The following is an example of a multidimensional rule:

$$age(X, \text{``20}\ldots\text{29''}) \wedge income(X, \text{``52}K\ldots\text{58}K\text{''}) \Rightarrow buys(X, \text{``iPad''}). \tag{7.3}$$

■ **Based on the *types of values* handled in the rule or pattern:** If a rule involves associations between the presence or absence of items, it is a **Boolean association rule**. For example, Rules (7.1) and (7.2) are Boolean association rules obtained from market basket analysis.

If a rule describes associations between quantitative items or attributes, then it is a **quantitative association rule**. In these rules, quantitative values for items or attributes are partitioned into intervals. Rule (7.3) can also be considered a quantitative association rule where the quantitative attributes *age* and *income* have been discretized.

■ **Based on the *constraints* or *criteria* used to mine *selective patterns*:** The patterns or rules to be discovered can be **constraint-based** (i.e., satisfying a set of user-defined constraints), **approximate**, **compressed**, **near-match** (i.e., those that tally the support count of the near or almost matching itemsets), **top-*k*** (i.e., the k most frequent itemsets for a user-specified value, k), **redundancy-aware top-*k*** (i.e., the top-k patterns with similar or redundant patterns excluded), and so on.

---

[1]Following the terminology used in multidimensional databases, we refer to each distinct predicate in a rule as a *dimension*.

Alternatively, pattern mining can be classified with respect to the kinds of data and applications involved, using the following criteria:

- **Based on *kinds of data and features* to be mined:** Given relational and data warehouse data, most people are interested in itemsets. Thus, frequent pattern mining in this context is essentially **frequent itemset mining**, that is, to mine frequent *sets of items*. However, in many other applications, patterns may involve sequences and structures. For example, by studying the order in which items are frequently purchased, we may find that customers tend to first buy a PC, followed by a digital camera, and then a memory card. This leads to **sequential patterns**, that is, frequent *subsequences* (which are often separated by some other events) in a *sequence of ordered events*.

  We may also mine **structural patterns**, that is, frequent *substructures*, in a *structured data set*. Note that *structure* is a general concept that covers many different kinds of structural forms such as directed graphs, undirected graphs, lattices, trees, sequences, sets, single items, or combinations of such structures. Single items are the simplest form of structure. Each element of a general pattern may contain a subsequence, a subtree, a subgraph, and so on, and such containment relationships can be defined recursively. Therefore, structural pattern mining can be considered as the most general form of frequent pattern mining.

- **Based on *application domain-specific semantics*:** Both data and applications can be very diverse, and therefore the patterns to be mined can differ largely based on their domain-specific semantics. Various kinds of application data include spatial data, temporal data, spatiotemporal data, multimedia data (e.g., image, audio, and video data), text data, time-series data, DNA and biological sequences, software programs, chemical compound structures, web structures, sensor networks, social and information networks, biological networks, data streams, and so on. This diversity can lead to dramatically different pattern mining methodologies.

- **Based on *data analysis usages*:** Frequent pattern mining often serves as an intermediate step for improved data understanding and more powerful data analysis. For example, it can be used as a feature extraction step for classification, which is often referred to as **pattern-based classification**. Similarly, **pattern-based clustering** has shown its strength at clustering high-dimensional data. For improved data understanding, patterns can be used for semantic annotation or contextual analysis. Pattern analysis can also be used in **recommender systems**, which recommend information items (e.g., books, movies, web pages) that are likely to be of interest to the user based on similar users' patterns. Different analysis tasks may require mining rather different kinds of patterns as well.

The next several sections present advanced methods and extensions of pattern mining, as well as their application. Section 7.2 discusses methods for mining multilevel patterns, multidimensional patterns, patterns and rules with continuous attributes, rare patterns, and negative patterns. Constraint-based pattern mining is studied in

Section 7.3. Section 7.4 explains how to mine high-dimensional and colossal patterns. The mining of compressed and approximate patterns is detailed in Section 7.5. Section 7.6 discusses the exploration and applications of pattern mining. More advanced topics regarding mining sequential and structural patterns, and pattern mining in complex and diverse kinds of data are briefly introduced in Chapter 13.

7.2 Pattern Mining in Multilevel, Multidimensional Space

This section focuses on methods for mining in multilevel, multidimensional space. In particular, you will learn about mining multilevel associations (Section 7.2.1), multidimensional associations (Section 7.2.2), quantitative association rules (Section 7.2.3), and rare patterns and negative patterns (Section 7.2.4). *Multilevel associations* involve concepts at different abstraction levels. *Multidimensional associations* involve more than one dimension or predicate (e.g., rules that relate what a customer *buys* to his or her *age*). *Quantitative association rules* involve numeric attributes that have an implicit ordering among values (e.g., *age*). *Rare patterns* are patterns that suggest interesting although rare item combinations. *Negative patterns* show negative correlations between items.

7.2.1 Mining Multilevel Associations

For many applications, strong associations discovered at high abstraction levels, though with high support, could be commonsense knowledge. We may want to drill down to find novel patterns at more detailed levels. On the other hand, there could be too many scattered patterns at low or primitive abstraction levels, some of which are just trivial specializations of patterns at higher levels. Therefore, it is interesting to examine how to develop effective methods for mining patterns at multiple abstraction levels, with sufficient flexibility for easy traversal among different abstraction spaces.

Example 7.1 **Mining multilevel association rules.** Suppose we are given the task-relevant set of transactional data in Table 7.1 for sales in an *AllElectronics* store, showing the items purchased for each transaction. The concept hierarchy for the items is shown in Figure 7.2. A concept hierarchy defines a sequence of mappings from a set of low-level concepts to a higher-level, more general concept set. Data can be generalized by replacing low-level concepts within the data by their corresponding higher-level concepts, or *ancestors*, from a concept hierarchy.

Figure 7.2's concept hierarchy has five levels, respectively referred to as levels 0 through 4, starting with level 0 at the root node for all (the most general abstraction level). Here, level 1 includes *computer, software, printer and camera*, and *computer accessory*; level 2 includes *laptop computer, desktop computer, office software, antivirus software*, etc.; and level 3 includes *Dell desktop computer, . . . , Microsoft office software*, etc. Level 4 is the most specific abstraction level of this hierarchy. It consists of the raw data values.

Table 7.1 Task-Relevant Data, *D*

TID	Items Purchased
T100	Apple 17″ MacBook Pro Notebook, HP Photosmart Pro b9180
T200	Microsoft Office Professional 2010, Microsoft Wireless Optical Mouse 5000
T300	Logitech VX Nano Cordless Laser Mouse, Fellowes GEL Wrist Rest
T400	Dell Studio XPS 16 Notebook, Canon PowerShot SD1400
T500	Lenovo ThinkPad X200 Tablet PC, Symantec Norton Antivirus 2010
...	...

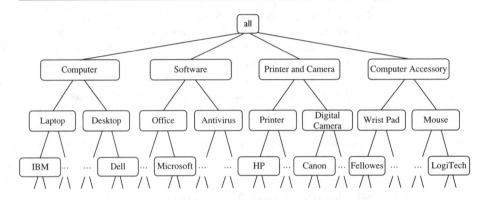

Figure 7.2 Concept hierarchy for *AllElectronics* computer items.

Concept hierarchies for nominal attributes are often implicit within the database schema, in which case they may be automatically generated using methods such as those described in Chapter 3. For our example, the concept hierarchy of Figure 7.2 was generated from data on product specifications. Concept hierarchies for numeric attributes can be generated using discretization techniques, many of which were introduced in Chapter 3. Alternatively, concept hierarchies may be specified by users familiar with the data such as store managers in the case of our example.

The items in Table 7.1 are at the lowest level of Figure 7.2's concept hierarchy. It is difficult to find interesting purchase patterns in such raw or primitive-level data. For instance, if "*Dell Studio XPS 16 Notebook*" or "*Logitech VX Nano Cordless Laser Mouse*" occurs in a very small fraction of the transactions, then it can be difficult to find strong associations involving these specific items. Few people may buy these items together, making it unlikely that the itemset will satisfy minimum support. However, we would expect that it is easier to find strong associations between generalized abstractions of these items, such as between "*Dell Notebook*" and "*Cordless Mouse.*" ∎

Association rules generated from mining data at multiple abstraction levels are called **multiple-level** or **multilevel association rules**. Multilevel association rules can be mined efficiently using concept hierarchies under a support-confidence framework. In general, a top-down strategy is employed, where counts are accumulated for the calculation of frequent itemsets at each concept level, starting at concept level 1 and working downward in the hierarchy toward the more specific concept levels, until no more frequent itemsets can be found. For each level, any algorithm for discovering frequent itemsets may be used, such as Apriori or its variations.

A number of variations to this approach are described next, where each variation involves "playing" with the support threshold in a slightly different way. The variations are illustrated in Figures 7.3 and 7.4, where nodes indicate an item or itemset that has been examined, and nodes with thick borders indicate that an examined item or itemset is frequent.

- **Using uniform minimum support for all levels** (referred to as **uniform support**): The same minimum support threshold is used when mining at each abstraction level. For example, in Figure 7.3, a minimum support threshold of 5% is used throughout (e.g., for mining from "*computer*" downward to "*laptop computer*"). Both "*computer*" and "*laptop computer*" are found to be frequent, whereas "*desktop computer*" is not.

    When a uniform minimum support threshold is used, the search procedure is simplified. The method is also simple in that users are required to specify only

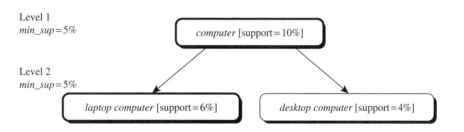

Figure 7.3 Multilevel mining with uniform support.

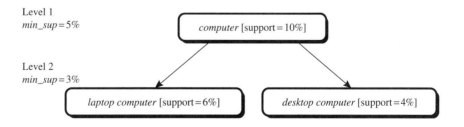

Figure 7.4 Multilevel mining with reduced support.

one minimum support threshold. An Apriori-like optimization technique can be adopted, based on the knowledge that an ancestor is a superset of its descendants: The search avoids examining itemsets containing any item of which the ancestors do not have minimum support.

The uniform support approach, however, has some drawbacks. It is unlikely that items at lower abstraction levels will occur as frequently as those at higher abstraction levels. If the minimum support threshold is set too high, it could miss some meaningful associations occurring at low abstraction levels. If the threshold is set too low, it may generate many uninteresting associations occurring at high abstraction levels. This provides the motivation for the next approach.

■ **Using reduced minimum support at lower levels** (referred to as **reduced support**): Each abstraction level has its own minimum support threshold. The deeper the abstraction level, the smaller the corresponding threshold. For example, in Figure 7.4, the minimum support thresholds for levels 1 and 2 are 5% and 3%, respectively. In this way, "*computer,*" "*laptop computer,*" and "*desktop computer*" are all considered frequent.

■ **Using item or group-based minimum support (referred to as group-based support)**: Because users or experts often have insight as to which groups are more important than others, it is sometimes more desirable to set up user-specific, item, or group-based minimal support thresholds when mining multilevel rules. For example, a user could set up the minimum support thresholds based on product price or on items of interest, such as by setting particularly low support thresholds for "*camera with price over $1000*" or "*Tablet PC,*" to pay particular attention to the association patterns containing items in these categories.

For mining patterns with mixed items from groups with different support thresholds, usually the lowest support threshold among all the participating groups is taken as the support threshold in mining. This will avoid filtering out valuable patterns containing items from the group with the lowest support threshold. In the meantime, the minimal support threshold for each individual group should be kept to avoid generating uninteresting itemsets from each group. Other interestingness measures can be used after the itemset mining to extract truly interesting rules.

Notice that the Apriori property may not always hold uniformly across all of the items when mining under reduced support and group-based support. However, efficient methods can be developed based on the extension of the property. The details are left as an exercise for interested readers.

A serious side effect of mining multilevel association rules is its generation of many redundant rules across multiple abstraction levels due to the "ancestor" relationships among items. For example, consider the following rules where "*laptop computer*" is an ancestor of "*Dell laptop computer*" based on the concept hierarchy of Figure 7.2, and where X is a variable representing customers who purchased items in *AllElectronics* transactions.

$$buys(X, \text{``laptop computer''}) \Rightarrow buys(X, \text{``HP printer''})$$
$$[support = 8\%, confidence = 70\%] \tag{7.4}$$

$$buys(X, \text{``Dell laptop computer''}) \Rightarrow buys(X, \text{``HP printer''})$$
$$[support = 2\%, confidence = 72\%] \tag{7.5}$$

"*If Rules (7.4) and (7.5) are both mined, then how useful is Rule (7.5)? Does it really provide any novel information?*" If the latter, less general rule does not provide new information, then it should be removed. Let's look at how this may be determined. A rule $R1$ is an **ancestor** of a rule $R2$, if $R1$ can be obtained by replacing the items in $R2$ by their ancestors in a concept hierarchy. For example, Rule (7.4) is an ancestor of Rule (7.5) because "*laptop computer*" is an ancestor of "*Dell laptop computer.*" Based on this definition, a rule can be considered redundant if its support and confidence are close to their "expected" values, based on an ancestor of the rule.

Example 7.2 **Checking redundancy among multilevel association rules.** Suppose that Rule (7.4) has a 70% confidence and 8% support, and that about one-quarter of all "*laptop computer*" sales are for "*Dell laptop computers.*" We may expect Rule (7.5) to have a confidence of around 70% (since all data samples of "*Dell laptop computer*" are also samples of "*laptop computer*") and a support of around 2% (i.e., $8\% \times \frac{1}{4}$). If this is indeed the case, then Rule (7.5) is not interesting because it does not offer any additional information and is less general than Rule (7.4). ∎

7.2.2 Mining Multidimensional Associations

So far, we have studied association rules that imply a single predicate, that is, the predicate *buys*. For instance, in mining our *AllElectronics* database, we may discover the Boolean association rule

$$buys(X, \text{``digital camera''}) \Rightarrow buys(X, \text{``HP printer''}). \tag{7.6}$$

Following the terminology used in multidimensional databases, we refer to each distinct predicate in a rule as a dimension. Hence, we can refer to Rule (7.6) as a **single-dimensional** or **intradimensional association rule** because it contains a single distinct predicate (e.g., *buys*) with multiple occurrences (i.e., the predicate occurs more than once within the rule). Such rules are commonly mined from transactional data.

Instead of considering transactional data only, sales and related information are often linked with relational data or integrated into a data warehouse. Such data stores are multidimensional in nature. For instance, in addition to keeping track of the items purchased in sales transactions, a relational database may record other attributes associated with the items and/or transactions such as the item description or the branch location of the sale. Additional relational information regarding the customers who purchased the items (e.g., customer age, occupation, credit rating, income, and address) may also be stored. Considering each database attribute or warehouse dimension as a predicate, we can therefore mine association rules containing *multiple* predicates such as

$$age(X, ``20\ldots29") \wedge occupation(X, ``student") \Rightarrow buys(X, ``laptop"). \quad (7.7)$$

Association rules that involve two or more dimensions or predicates can be referred to as **multidimensional association rules**. Rule (7.7) contains three predicates (*age*, *occupation*, and *buys*), each of which occurs *only once* in the rule. Hence, we say that it has **no repeated predicates**. Multidimensional association rules with no repeated predicates are called **interdimensional association rules**. We can also mine multidimensional association rules with repeated predicates, which contain multiple occurrences of some predicates. These rules are called **hybrid-dimensional association rules**. An example of such a rule is the following, where the predicate *buys* is repeated:

$$age(X, ``20\ldots29") \wedge buys(X, ``laptop") \Rightarrow buys(X, ``HP\ printer"). \quad (7.8)$$

Database attributes can be nominal or quantitative. The values of **nominal** (or categorical) attributes are "names of things." Nominal attributes have a finite number of possible values, with no ordering among the values (e.g., *occupation, brand, color*). **Quantitative** attributes are numeric and have an implicit ordering among values (e.g., *age, income, price*). Techniques for mining multidimensional association rules can be categorized into two basic approaches regarding the treatment of quantitative attributes.

In the first approach, *quantitative attributes are discretized using predefined concept hierarchies*. This discretization occurs before mining. For instance, a concept hierarchy for *income* may be used to replace the original numeric values of this attribute by interval labels such as "0..20K," "21K..30K," "31K..40K," and so on. Here, discretization is *static* and predetermined. Chapter 3 on data preprocessing gave several techniques for discretizing numeric attributes. The discretized numeric attributes, with their interval labels, can then be treated as nominal attributes (where each interval is considered a category). We refer to this as **mining multidimensional association rules using static discretization of quantitative attributes**.

In the second approach, *quantitative attributes are discretized or clustered into "bins" based on the data distribution*. These bins may be further combined during the mining process. The discretization process is *dynamic* and established so as to satisfy some mining criteria such as maximizing the confidence of the rules mined. Because this strategy treats the numeric attribute values as quantities rather than as predefined ranges or categories, association rules mined from this approach are also referred to as **(dynamic) quantitative association rules**.

Let's study each of these approaches for mining multidimensional association rules. For simplicity, we confine our discussion to interdimensional association rules. Note that rather than searching for frequent itemsets (as is done for single-dimensional association rule mining), in multidimensional association rule mining we search for frequent *predicate sets*. A **k-predicate set** is a set containing k conjunctive predicates. For instance, the set of predicates {*age, occupation, buys*} from Rule (7.7) is a 3-predicate set. Similar to the notation used for itemsets in Chapter 6, we use the notation L_k to refer to the set of frequent k-predicate sets.

7.2.3 Mining Quantitative Association Rules

As discussed earlier, relational and data warehouse data often involve quantitative attributes or measures. We can discretize quantitative attributes into multiple intervals and then treat them as nominal data in association mining. However, such simple discretization may lead to the generation of an enormous number of rules, many of which may not be useful. Here we introduce three methods that can help overcome this difficulty to discover novel association relationships: (1) a data cube method, (2) a clustering-based method, and (3) a statistical analysis method to uncover exceptional behaviors.

Data Cube–Based Mining of Quantitative Associations

In many cases quantitative attributes can be discretized before mining using predefined concept hierarchies or data discretization techniques, where numeric values are replaced by interval labels. Nominal attributes may also be generalized to higher conceptual levels if desired. If the resulting task-relevant data are stored in a relational table, then any of the frequent itemset mining algorithms we have discussed can easily be modified so as to find all frequent predicate sets. In particular, instead of searching on only one attribute like *buys*, we need to search through all of the relevant attributes, treating each attribute–value pair as an itemset.

Alternatively, the transformed multidimensional data may be used to construct a *data cube*. Data cubes are well suited for the mining of multidimensional association rules: They store aggregates (e.g., counts) in multidimensional space, which is essential for computing the support and confidence of multidimensional association rules. An overview of data cube technology was presented in Chapter 4. Detailed algorithms for data cube computation were given in Chapter 5. Figure 7.5 shows the lattice of cuboids defining a data cube for the dimensions *age, income*, and *buys*. The cells of an n-dimensional cuboid can be used to store the support counts of the corresponding n-predicate sets. The base cuboid aggregates the task-relevant data by *age, income*, and *buys*; the 2-D cuboid, (*age, income*), aggregates by *age* and *income*, and so on; the 0-D (apex) cuboid contains the total number of transactions in the task-relevant data.

Due to the ever-increasing use of data warehouse and OLAP technology, it is possible that a data cube containing the dimensions that are of interest to the user may already exist, fully or partially materialized. If this is the case, we can simply fetch the corresponding aggregate values or compute them using lower-level materialized aggregates, and return the rules needed using a rule generation algorithm. Notice that even in this case, the Apriori property can still be used to prune the search space. If a given k-predicate set has support *sup*, which does not satisfy minimum support, then further

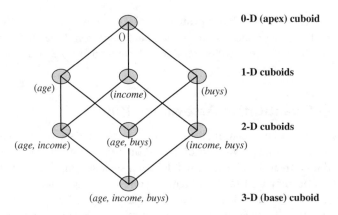

Figure 7.5 Lattice of cuboids, making up a 3-D data cube. Each cuboid represents a different group-by. The base cuboid contains the three predicates *age, income,* and *buys.*

exploration of this set should be terminated. This is because any more-specialized version of the *k*-itemset will have support no greater than *sup* and, therefore, will not satisfy minimum support either. In cases where no relevant data cube exists for the mining task, we must create one on-the-fly. This becomes an iceberg cube computation problem, where the minimum support threshold is taken as the iceberg condition (Chapter 5).

Mining Clustering-Based Quantitative Associations

Besides using discretization-based or data cube–based data sets to generate quantitative association rules, we can also generate *quantitative association rules* by clustering data in the quantitative dimensions. (Recall that objects within a cluster are similar to one another and dissimilar to those in other clusters.) The general assumption is that interesting frequent patterns or association rules are in general found at relatively dense clusters of quantitative attributes. Here, we describe a top-down approach and a bottom-up approach to clustering that finds quantitative associations.

A typical top-down approach for finding clustering-based quantitative frequent patterns is as follows. For each quantitative dimension, a standard clustering algorithm (e.g., *k*-means or a density-based clustering algorithm, as described in Chapter 10) can be applied to find clusters in this dimension that satisfy the minimum support threshold. For each cluster, we then examine the 2-D spaces generated by combining the cluster with a cluster or nominal value of another dimension to see if such a combination passes the minimum support threshold. If it does, we continue to search for clusters in this 2-D region and progress to even higher-dimensional combinations. The Apriori pruning still applies in this process: If, at any point, the support of a combination does not have minimum support, its further partitioning or combination with other dimensions cannot have minimum support either.

A bottom-up approach for finding clustering-based frequent patterns works by first clustering in high-dimensional space to form clusters with support that satisfies the minimum support threshold, and then projecting and merging those clusters in the space containing fewer dimensional combinations. However, for high-dimensional data sets, finding high-dimensional clustering itself is a tough problem. Thus, this approach is less realistic.

Using Statistical Theory to Disclose Exceptional Behavior

It is possible to discover quantitative association rules that disclose exceptional behavior, where "exceptional" is defined based on a statistical theory. For example, the following association rule may indicate exceptional behavior:

$$sex = female \Rightarrow meanwage = \$7.90/hr \ (overall\_mean\_wage = \$9.02/hr). \qquad (7.9)$$

This rule states that the average wage for females is only \$7.90/hr. This rule is (subjectively) interesting because it reveals a group of people earning a significantly lower wage than the average wage of \$9.02/hr. (If the average wage was close to \$7.90/hr, then the fact that females also earn \$7.90/hr would be "uninteresting.")

An integral aspect of our definition involves applying statistical tests to confirm the validity of our rules. That is, Rule (7.9) is only accepted if a statistical test (in this case, a Z-test) confirms that with high confidence it can be inferred that the mean wage of the female population is indeed lower than the mean wage of the rest of the population. (The above rule was mined from a real database based on a 1985 U.S. census.)

An association rule under the new definition is a rule of the form:

$$population\_subset \Rightarrow \mathbf{mean}\_of\_values\_for\_the\_subset, \qquad (7.10)$$

where the mean of the subset is significantly different from the mean of its complement in the database (and this is validated by an appropriate statistical test).

7.2.4 Mining Rare Patterns and Negative Patterns

All the methods presented so far in this chapter have been for mining frequent patterns. Sometimes, however, it is interesting to find patterns that are rare instead of frequent, or patterns that reflect a negative correlation between items. These patterns are respectively referred to as rare patterns and negative patterns. In this subsection, we consider various ways of defining rare patterns and negative patterns, which are also useful to mine.

Example 7.3 **Rare patterns and negative patterns.** In jewelry sales data, sales of diamond watches are rare; however, patterns involving the selling of diamond watches could be interesting. In supermarket data, if we find that customers frequently buy Coca-Cola Classic or Diet Coke but not both, then buying Coca-Cola Classic and buying Diet Coke together is considered a negative (correlated) pattern. In car sales data, a dealer sells a few fuel-thirsty vehicles (e.g., SUVs) to a given customer, and then later sells hybrid mini-cars to the same customer. Even though buying SUVs and buying hybrid mini-cars may be negatively correlated events, it can be interesting to discover and examine such exceptional cases. ∎

An **infrequent** (or **rare**) **pattern** is a pattern with a frequency support that is *below* (or *far below*) a user-specified minimum support threshold. However, since the occurrence frequencies of the majority of itemsets are usually below or even far below the minimum support threshold, it is desirable in practice for users to specify other conditions for rare patterns. For example, if we want to find patterns containing at least one item with a value that is over $500, we should specify such a constraint explicitly. Efficient mining of such itemsets is discussed under mining multidimensional associations (Section 7.2.1), where the strategy is to adopt multiple (e.g., item- or group-based) minimum support thresholds. Other applicable methods are discussed under constraint-based pattern mining (Section 7.3), where user-specified constraints are pushed deep into the iterative mining process.

There are various ways we could define a negative pattern. We will consider three such definitions.

Definition 7.1: If itemsets X and Y are both frequent but rarely occur together (i.e., $sup(X \cup Y) < sup(X) \times sup(Y)$), then itemsets X and Y are **negatively correlated**, and the pattern $X \cup Y$ is a **negatively correlated pattern**. If $sup(X \cup Y) \ll sup(X) \times sup(Y)$, then X and Y are **strongly negatively correlated**, and the pattern $X \cup Y$ is a **strongly negatively correlated pattern**. □

This definition can easily be extended for patterns containing k-itemsets for $k > 2$.

A problem with the definition, however, is that it is not *null-invariant*. That is, its value can be misleadingly influenced by null transactions, where a *null-transaction* is a transaction that does not contain any of the itemsets being examined (Section 6.3.3). This is illustrated in Example 7.4.

Example 7.4 **Null-transaction problem with Definition 7.1.** If there are a lot of null-transactions in the data set, then the number of null-transactions rather than the patterns observed may strongly influence a measure's assessment as to whether a pattern is negatively correlated. For example, suppose a sewing store sells needle packages A and B. The store sold 100 packages each of A and B, but only one transaction contains both A and B. Intuitively, A is negatively correlated with B since the purchase of one does not seem to encourage the purchase of the other.

Let's see how the above Definition 7.1 handles this scenario. If there are 200 transactions, we have $sup(A \cup B) = 1/200 = 0.005$ and $sup(A) \times sup(B) = 100/200 \times 100/200 = 0.25$. Thus, $sup(A \cup B) \ll sup(A) \times sup(B)$, and so Definition 7.1 indicates that A and B are strongly negatively correlated. What if, instead of only 200 transactions in the database, there are 10^6? In this case, there are many null-transactions, that is, many contain neither A nor B. How does the definition hold up? It computes $sup(A \cup B) = 1/10^6$ and $sup(X) \times sup(Y) = 100/10^6 \times 100/10^6 = 1/10^8$.

Thus, $sup(A \cup B) \gg sup(X) \times sup(Y)$, which contradicts the earlier finding even though the number of occurrences of A and B has not changed. The measure in Definition 7.1 is not null-invariant, where *null-invariance* is essential for quality interestingness measures as discussed in Section 6.3.3. ∎

Definition 7.2: If X and Y are strongly negatively correlated, then

$$sup(X \cup \overline{Y}) \times sup(\overline{X} \cup Y) \gg sup(X \cup Y) \times sup(\overline{X} \cup \overline{Y}).$$

Is this measure null-invariant? □

Example 7.5 Null-transaction problem with Definition 7.2. Given our needle package example, when there are in total 200 transactions in the database, we have

$$sup(A \cup \overline{B}) \times sup(\overline{A} \cup B) = 99/200 \times 99/200 = 0.245$$
$$\gg sup(A \cup B) \times sup(\overline{A} \cup \overline{B}) = 199/200 \times 1/200 \approx 0.005,$$

which, according to Definition 7.2, indicates that A and B are strongly negatively correlated. What if there are 10^6 transactions in the database? The measure would compute

$$sup(A \cup \overline{B}) \times sup(\overline{A} \cup B) = 99/10^6 \times 99/10^6 = 9.8 \times 10^{-9}$$
$$\ll sup(A \cup B) \times sup(\overline{A} \cup \overline{B}) = 199/10^6 \times (10^6 - 199)/10^6 \approx 1.99 \times 10^{-4}.$$

This time, the measure indicates that A and B are positively correlated, hence, a contradiction. The measure is not null-invariant. ∎

As a third alternative, consider Definition 7.3, which is based on the Kulczynski measure (i.e., the average of conditional probabilities). It follows the spirit of interestingness measures introduced in Section 6.3.3.

Definition 7.3: Suppose that itemsets X and Y are both frequent, that is, $sup(X) \geq min\_sup$ and $sup(Y) \geq min\_sup$, where min_sup is the minimum support threshold. If $(P(X|Y) + P(Y|X))/2 < \epsilon$, where ϵ is a negative pattern threshold, then pattern $X \cup Y$ is a **negatively correlated pattern**. □

Example 7.6 Negatively correlated patterns using Definition 7.3, based on the Kulczynski measure. Let's reexamine our needle package example. Let min_sup be 0.01% and $\epsilon = 0.02$. When there are 200 transactions in the database, we have $sup(A) = sup(B) = 100/200 = 0.5 > 0.01\%$ and $(P(B|A) + P(A|B))/2 = (0.01 + 0.01)/2 < 0.02$; thus A and B are negatively correlated. Does this still hold true if we have many more transactions? When there are 10^6 transactions in the database, the measure computes $sup(A) = sup(B) = 100/10^6 = 0.01\% \geq 0.01\%$ and $(P(B|A) + P(A|B))/2 = (0.01 + 0.01)/2 < 0.02$, again indicating that A and B are negatively correlated. This matches our intuition. The measure does not have the null-invariance problem of the first two definitions considered.

Let's examine another case: Suppose that among 100,000 transactions, the store sold 1000 needle packages of A but only 10 packages of B; however, every time package B is sold, package A is also sold (i.e., they appear in the same transaction). In this case, the measure computes $(P(B|A) + P(A|B))/2 = (0.01 + 1)/2 = 0.505 \gg 0.02$, which indicates that A and B are positively correlated instead of negatively correlated. This also matches our intuition. ∎

With this new definition of negative correlation, efficient methods can easily be derived for mining negative patterns in large databases. This is left as an exercise for interested readers.

7.3 Constraint-Based Frequent Pattern Mining

A data mining process may uncover thousands of rules from a given data set, most of which end up being unrelated or uninteresting to users. Often, users have a good sense of which "direction" of mining may lead to interesting patterns and the "form" of the patterns or rules they want to find. They may also have a sense of "conditions" for the rules, which would eliminate the discovery of certain rules that they know would not be of interest. Thus, a good heuristic is to have the users specify such intuition or expectations as *constraints* to confine the search space. This strategy is known as **constraint-based mining**. The constraints can include the following:

- **Knowledge type constraints:** These specify the type of knowledge to be mined, such as association, correlation, classification, or clustering.

- **Data constraints:** These specify the set of task-relevant data.

- **Dimension/level constraints:** These specify the desired dimensions (or attributes) of the data, the abstraction levels, or the level of the concept hierarchies to be used in mining.

- **Interestingness constraints:** These specify thresholds on statistical measures of rule interestingness such as support, confidence, and correlation.

- **Rule constraints:** These specify the form of, or conditions on, the rules to be mined. Such constraints may be expressed as metarules (rule templates), as the maximum or minimum number of predicates that can occur in the rule antecedent or consequent, or as relationships among attributes, attribute values, and/or aggregates.

These constraints can be specified using a high-level declarative data mining query language and user interface.

The first four constraint types have already been addressed in earlier sections of this book and this chapter. In this section, we discuss the use of *rule constraints* to focus the mining task. This form of constraint-based mining allows users to describe the rules that they would like to uncover, thereby making the data mining process more *effective*. In addition, a sophisticated mining query optimizer can be used to exploit the constraints specified by the user, thereby making the mining process more *efficient*.

Constraint-based mining encourages interactive exploratory mining and analysis. In Section 7.3.1, you will study metarule-guided mining, where syntactic rule constraints are specified in the form of rule templates. Section 7.3.2 discusses the use of *pattern space pruning* (which prunes patterns being mined) and *data space pruning* (which prunes pieces of the data space for which further exploration cannot contribute to the discovery of patterns satisfying the constraints).

For pattern space pruning, we introduce three classes of properties that facilitate constraint-based search space pruning: *antimonotonicity, monotonicity,* and *succinctness*. We also discuss a special class of constraints, called *convertible constraints*, where by proper data ordering, the constraints can be pushed deep into the iterative mining process and have the same pruning power as monotonic or antimonotonic constraints. For data space pruning, we introduce two classes of properties—*data succinctness* and *data antimonotonicty*—and study how they can be integrated within a data mining process.

For ease of discussion, we assume that the user is searching for association rules. The procedures presented can be easily extended to the mining of correlation rules by adding a correlation measure of interestingness to the support-confidence framework.

7.3.1 Metarule-Guided Mining of Association Rules

"*How are metarules useful?*" Metarules allow users to specify the syntactic form of rules that they are interested in mining. The rule forms can be used as constraints to help improve the efficiency of the mining process. Metarules may be based on the analyst's experience, expectations, or intuition regarding the data or may be automatically generated based on the database schema.

Example 7.7 **Metarule-guided mining.** Suppose that as a market analyst for *AllElectronics* you have access to the data describing customers (e.g., customer age, address, and credit rating) as well as the list of customer transactions. You are interested in finding associations between customer traits and the items that customers buy. However, rather than finding *all* of the association rules reflecting these relationships, you are interested only in determining which pairs of customer traits promote the sale of office software. A metarule can be used to specify this information describing the form of rules you are interested in finding. An example of such a metarule is

$$P_1(X, Y) \land P_2(X, W) \Rightarrow buys(X, \text{``office software''}), \tag{7.11}$$

where P_1 and P_2 are **predicate variables** that are instantiated to attributes from the given database during the mining process, X is a variable representing a customer, and Y and W take on values of the attributes assigned to P_1 and P_2, respectively. Typically, a user will specify a list of attributes to be considered for instantiation with P_1 and P_2. Otherwise, a default set may be used.

In general, a metarule forms a hypothesis regarding the relationships that the user is interested in probing or confirming. The data mining system can then search for rules that match the given metarule. For instance, Rule (7.12) matches or **complies with** Metarule (7.11):

$$age(X, \text{``}30..39\text{''}) \wedge income(X, \text{``}41K..60K\text{''}) \Rightarrow buys(X, \text{``}office\ software\text{''}). \quad (7.12)$$

∎

"*How can metarules be used to guide the mining process?*" Let's examine this problem closely. Suppose that we wish to mine interdimensional association rules such as in Example 7.7. A metarule is a rule template of the form

$$P_1 \wedge P_2 \wedge \cdots \wedge P_l \Rightarrow Q_1 \wedge Q_2 \wedge \cdots \wedge Q_r, \quad (7.13)$$

where P_i ($i = 1, \ldots, l$) and Q_j ($j = 1, \ldots, r$) are either instantiated predicates or predicate variables. Let the number of predicates in the metarule be $p = l + r$. To find interdimensional association rules satisfying the template,

- We need to find all frequent p-predicate sets, L_p.

- We must also have the support or count of the l-predicate subsets of L_p to compute the confidence of rules derived from L_p.

This is a typical case of mining multidimensional association rules. By extending such methods using the constraint-pushing techniques described in the following section, we can derive efficient methods for metarule-guided mining.

7.3.2 Constraint-Based Pattern Generation: Pruning Pattern Space and Pruning Data Space

Rule constraints specify expected set/subset relationships of the variables in the mined rules, constant initiation of variables, and constraints on aggregate functions and other forms of constraints. Users typically employ their knowledge of the application or data to specify rule constraints for the mining task. These rule constraints may be used together with, or as an alternative to, metarule-guided mining. In this section, we examine rule constraints as to how they can be used to make the mining process more efficient. Let's study an example where rule constraints are used to mine hybrid-dimensional association rules.

Example 7.8 **Constraints for mining association rules.** Suppose that *AllElectronics* has a sales multidimensional database with the following interrelated relations:

- *item(item_ID, item_name, description, category, price)*

- *sales(transaction_ID, day, month, year, store_ID, city)*

- *trans_item(item_ID, transaction_ID)*

Here, the *item* table contains attributes *item_ID, item_name, description, category*, and *price*; the *sales* table contains attributes *transaction_ID day, month, year, store_ID*, and *city*; and the two tables are linked via the foreign key attributes, *item_ID* and *transaction_ID*, in the table *trans_item*.

Suppose our association mining query is "*Find the patterns or rules about the sales of which cheap items (where the sum of the prices is less than \$10) may promote (i.e., appear in the same transaction) the sales of which expensive items (where the minimum price is \$50), shown in the sales in Chicago in 2010.*"

This query contains the following four constraints: (1) $sum(I.price) < \$10$, where I represents the *item_ID* of a cheap item; (2) $min(J.price) \geq \$50)$, where J represents the *item_ID* of an expensive item; (3) $T.city = Chicago$; and (4) $T.year = 2010$, where T represents a *transaction_ID*. For conciseness, we do not show the mining query explicitly here; however, the constraints' context is clear from the mining query semantics. ∎

Dimension/level constraints and interestingness constraints can be applied after mining to filter out discovered rules, although it is generally more efficient and less expensive to use them *during* mining to help prune the search space. Dimension/level constraints were discussed in Section 7.2, and interestingness constraints, such as support, confidence, and correlation measures, were discussed in Chapter 6. Let's focus now on rule constraints.

"*How can we use rule constraints to prune the search space? More specifically, what kind of rule constraints can be 'pushed' deep into the mining process and still ensure the completeness of the answer returned for a mining query?*"

In general, an efficient frequent pattern mining processor can prune its search space during mining in two major ways: *pruning pattern search space* and *pruning data search space*. The former checks candidate patterns and decides whether a pattern can be pruned. Applying the Apriori property, it prunes a pattern if no superpattern of it can be generated in the remaining mining process. The latter checks the data set to determine whether the particular data piece will be able to contribute to the subsequent generation of satisfiable patterns (for a particular pattern) in the remaining mining process. If not, the data piece is pruned from further exploration. A constraint that may facilitate pattern space pruning is called a *pattern pruning constraint*, whereas one that can be used for data space pruning is called a *data pruning constraint*.

Pruning Pattern Space with Pattern Pruning Constraints

Based on how a constraint may interact with the pattern mining process, there are five categories of pattern mining constraints: (1) *antimonotonic*, (2) *monotonic*, (3) *succinct*, (4) *convertible*, and (5) *inconvertible*. For each category, we use an example to show its characteristics and explain how such kinds of constraints can be used in the mining process.

The first category of constraints is **antimonotonic**. Consider the rule constraint "*sum(I.price)* ≤ $100" of Example 7.8. Suppose we are using the Apriori framework, which explores itemsets of size k at the kth iteration. If the price summation of the items in a candidate itemset is no less than $100, this itemset can be pruned from the search space, since adding more items into the set (assuming price is no less than zero) will only make it more expensive and thus will never satisfy the constraint. In other words, if an itemset does not satisfy this rule constraint, none of its supersets can satisfy the constraint. If a rule constraint obeys this property, it is **antimonotonic**. Pruning by antimonotonic constraints can be applied at each iteration of Apriori-style algorithms to help improve the efficiency of the overall mining process while guaranteeing completeness of the data mining task.

The Apriori property, which states that all nonempty subsets of a frequent itemset must also be frequent, is antimonotonic. If a given itemset does not satisfy minimum support, none of its supersets can. This property is used at each iteration of the Apriori algorithm to reduce the number of candidate itemsets examined, thereby reducing the search space for association rules.

Other examples of antimonotonic constraints include "*min(J.price)* ≥ $50," "*count(I)* ≤ 10," and so on. Any itemset that violates either of these constraints can be discarded since adding more items to such itemsets can never satisfy the constraints. Note that a constraint such as "*avg(I.price)* ≤ $10" is not antimonotonic. For a given itemset that does not satisfy this constraint, a superset created by adding some (cheap) items may result in satisfying the constraint. Hence, pushing this constraint inside the mining process will not guarantee completeness of the data mining task. A list of SQL primitives–based constraints is given in the first column of Table 7.2. The antimonotonicity of the constraints is indicated in the second column. To simplify our discussion, only existence operators (e.g., =, ∈, but not ≠, ∉) and comparison (or containment) operators with equality (e.g., ≤, ⊆) are given.

The second category of constraints is **monotonic**. If the rule constraint in Example 7.8 were "*sum(I.price)* ≥ $100," the constraint-based processing method would be quite different. If an itemset I satisfies the constraint, that is, the sum of the prices in the set is no less than $100, further addition of more items to I will increase cost and will always satisfy the constraint. Therefore, further testing of this constraint on itemset I becomes redundant. In other words, if an itemset satisfies this rule constraint, so do all of its supersets. If a rule constraint obeys this property, it is **monotonic**. Similar rule monotonic constraints include "*min(I.price)* ≤ $10," "*count(I)* ≥ 10," and so on. The monotonicity of the list of SQL primitives–based constraints is indicated in the third column of Table 7.2.

The third category is **succinct constraints**. For this constraints category, we can *enumerate all and only those sets that are guaranteed to satisfy the constraint*. That is, if a rule constraint is **succinct**, we can directly generate precisely the sets that satisfy it, even before support counting begins. This avoids the substantial overhead of the generate-and-test paradigm. In other words, such constraints are *precounting prunable*. For example, the constraint "*min(J.price)* ≥ $50" in Example 7.8 is succinct because we can explicitly and precisely generate all the itemsets that satisfy the constraint.

Table 7.2 Characterization of Commonly Used SQL-Based
Pattern Pruning Constraints

Constraint	Antimonotonic	Monotonic	Succinct
$v \in S$	no	yes	yes
$S \supseteq V$	no	yes	yes
$S \subseteq V$	yes	no	yes
$min(S) \leq v$	no	yes	yes
$min(S) \geq v$	yes	no	yes
$max(S) \leq v$	yes	no	yes
$max(S) \geq v$	no	yes	yes
$count(S) \leq v$	yes	no	weakly
$count(S) \geq v$	no	yes	weakly
$sum(S) \leq v \ (\forall a \in S, a \geq 0)$	yes	no	no
$sum(S) \geq v \ (\forall a \in S, a \geq 0)$	no	yes	no
$range(S) \leq v$	yes	no	no
$range(S) \geq v$	no	yes	no
$avg(S) \ \theta \ v, \theta \in \{\leq, \geq\}$	convertible	convertible	no
$support(S) \geq \xi$	yes	no	no
$support(S) \leq \xi$	no	yes	no
$all\_confidence(S) \geq \xi$	yes	no	no
$all\_confidence(S) \leq \xi$	no	yes	no

Specifically, such a set must consist of a nonempty set of items that have a price no less than \$50. It is of the form S, where $S \neq \emptyset$ is a subset of the set of all items with prices no less than \$50. Because there is a precise "formula" for generating all the sets satisfying a succinct constraint, there is no need to iteratively check the rule constraint during the mining process. The succinctness of the list of SQL primitives–based constraints is indicated in the fourth column of Table 7.2.[2]

The fourth category is **convertible constraints**. Some constraints belong to none of the previous three categories. However, if the items in the itemset are arranged in a particular order, the constraint may become monotonic or antimonotonic with regard to the frequent itemset mining process. For example, the constraint "$avg(I.price) \leq \$10$" is neither antimonotonic nor monotonic. However, if items in a transaction are added to an itemset in price-ascending order, the constraint becomes *antimonotonic*, because if an itemset I violates the constraint (i.e., with an average price greater than \$10), then further addition of more expensive items into the itemset will never make it

---

[2]For constraint $count(S) \leq v$ (and similarly for $count(S) \geq v$), we can have a member generation function based on a cardinality constraint (i.e., $\{X \mid X \subseteq Itemset \ \wedge \ |X| \leq v\}$). Member generation in this manner is of a different flavor and thus is called *weakly succinct*.

satisfy the constraint. Similarly, if items in a transaction are added to an itemset in price-descending order, it becomes *monotonic,* because if the itemset satisfies the constraint (i.e., with an average price no greater than \$10), then adding cheaper items into the current itemset will still make the average price no greater than \$10. Aside from "$avg(S) \leq v$" and "$avg(S) \geq v$," given in Table 7.2, there are many other convertible constraints such as "$variance(S) \geq v$" "$standard\_deviation(S) \geq v$," and so on.

Note that the previous discussion does not imply that every constraint is convertible. For example, "$sum(S)\,\theta\,v$," where $\theta \in \{\leq,\ \geq\}$ and each element in S could be of any real value, is not convertible. Therefore, there is yet a fifth category of constraints, called **inconvertible constraints**. The good news is that although there still exist some tough constraints that are not convertible, most simple SQL expressions with built-in SQL aggregates belong to one of the first four categories to which efficient constraint mining methods can be applied.

Pruning Data Space with Data Pruning Constraints

The second way of search space pruning in constraint-based frequent pattern mining is *pruning data space.* This strategy prunes pieces of data if they will not contribute to the subsequent generation of satisfiable patterns in the mining process. We consider two properties: *data succinctness* and *data antimonotonicity.*

Constraints are **data-succinct** if they can be used *at the beginning of a pattern mining process* to prune the data subsets that cannot satisfy the constraints. For example, if a mining query requires that the mined pattern must contain *digital camera*, then any transaction that does not contain *digital camera* can be pruned at the beginning of the mining process, which effectively reduces the data set to be examined.

Interestingly, many constraints are **data-antimonotonic** in the sense that *during the mining process,* if a data entry cannot satisfy a data-antimonotonic constraint based on the current pattern, then it can be pruned. We prune it because it will not be able to contribute to the generation of any superpattern of the current pattern in the remaining mining process.

Example 7.9 **Data antimonotonicity.** A mining query requires that $C_1 : sum(I.price) \geq \$100$, that is, the sum of the prices of the items in the mined pattern must be no less than \$100. Suppose that the current frequent itemset, S, does not satisfy constraint C_1 (say, because the sum of the prices of the items in S is \$50). If the remaining frequent items in a transaction T_i are such that, say, $\{i_2.price = \$5, i_5.price = \$10, i_8.price = \$20\}$, then T_i will not be able to make S satisfy the constraint. Thus, T_i cannot contribute to the patterns to be mined from S, and thus can be pruned.

Note that such pruning cannot be done at the beginning of the mining because at that time, we do not know yet if the total sum of the prices of all the items in T_i will be over \$100 (e.g., we may have $i_3.price = \$80$). However, during the iterative mining process, we may find some items (e.g., i_3) that are not frequent with S in the transaction data set, and thus they would be pruned. Therefore, such checking and pruning should be enforced at each iteration to reduce the data search space. ∎

Notice that constraint C_1 is a monotonic constraint with respect to pattern space pruning. As we have seen, this constraint has very limited power for reducing the search space in pattern pruning. However, the same constraint can be used for effective reduction of the data search space.

For an antimonotonic constraint, such as $C_2 : sum(I.price) \leq \$100$, we can prune both pattern and data search spaces at the same time. Based on our study of pattern pruning, we already know that the current itemset can be pruned if the sum of the prices in it is over \$100 (since its further expansion can never satisfy C_2). At the same time, we can also prune any remaining items in a transaction T_i that cannot make the constraint C_2 valid. For example, if the sum of the prices of items in the current itemset S is \$90, any patterns over \$10 in the remaining frequent items in T_i can be pruned. If none of the remaining items in T_i can make the constraint valid, the entire transaction T_i should be pruned.

Consider pattern constraints that are neither antimonotonic nor monotonic such as "$C_3 : avg(I.price) \leq 10$." These can be data-antimonotonic because if the remaining items in a transaction T_i cannot make the constraint valid, then T_i can be pruned as well. Therefore, data-antimonotonic constraints can be quite useful for constraint-based data space pruning.

Notice that search space pruning by data antimonotonicity is confined only to a pattern growth–based mining algorithm because the pruning of a data entry is determined based on whether it can contribute to a specific pattern. Data antimonotonicity cannot be used for pruning the data space if the Apriori algorithm is used because the data are associated with all of the currently active patterns. At any iteration, there are usually many active patterns. A data entry that cannot contribute to the formation of the superpatterns of a given pattern may still be able to contribute to the superpattern of other active patterns. Thus, the power of data space pruning can be very limited for nonpattern growth–based algorithms.

7.4 Mining High-Dimensional Data and Colossal Patterns

The frequent pattern mining methods presented so far handle large data sets having a small number of dimensions. However, some applications may need to mine *high-dimensional data* (i.e., data with hundreds or thousands of dimensions). Can we use the methods studied so far to mine high-dimensional data? The answer is unfortunately negative because the search spaces of such typical methods grow exponentially with the number of dimensions.

Researchers have overcome this difficulty in two directions. One direction extends a pattern growth approach by further exploring the vertical data format to handle data sets with a large number of *dimensions* (also called *features* or *items*, e.g., genes) but a *small* number of *rows* (also called *transactions* or *tuples*, e.g., samples). This is useful in applications like the analysis of gene expressions in bioinformatics, for example, where we often need to analyze microarray data that contain a *large* number of genes (e.g., 10,000 to 100,000) but only a *small* number of samples (e.g., 100 to 1000). The other direction develops a new mining methodology, called *Pattern-Fusion*, which mines *colossal patterns*, that is, patterns of very long length.

Let's first briefly examine the first direction, in particular, a pattern growth–based row enumeration approach. Its general philosophy is to explore the *vertical data format*, as described in Section 6.2.5, which is also known as **row enumeration**. Row enumeration differs from traditional column (i.e., item) enumeration (also known as the *horizontal data format*). In traditional column enumeration, the data set, D, is viewed as a set of rows, where each row consists of an itemset. In row enumeration, the data set is instead viewed as an itemset, each consisting of a set of *row_IDs* indicating where the item appears in the traditional view of D. The original data set, D, can easily be transformed into a transposed data set, T. A data set with a small number of rows but a large number of dimensions is then transformed into a transposed data set with a large number of rows but a small number of dimensions. Efficient pattern growth methods can then be developed on such relatively low-dimensional data sets. The details of such an approach are left as an exercise for interested readers.

The remainder of this section focuses on the second direction. We introduce Pattern-Fusion, a new mining methodology that mines *colossal patterns* (i.e., patterns of very long length). This method takes leaps in the pattern search space, leading to a good approximation of the complete set of colossal frequent patterns.

7.4.1 Mining Colossal Patterns by Pattern-Fusion

Although we have studied methods for mining frequent patterns in various situations, many applications have hidden patterns that are tough to mine, due mainly to their immense length or size. Consider bioinformatics, for example, where a common activity is DNA or microarray data analysis. This involves mapping and analyzing very long DNA and protein sequences. Researchers are more interested in finding large patterns (e.g., long sequences) than finding small ones since larger patterns usually carry more significant meaning. We call these large patterns *colossal* patterns, as distinguished from patterns with large support sets. Finding colossal patterns is challenging because incremental mining tends to get "trapped" by an explosive number of midsize patterns before it can even reach candidate patterns of large size. This is illustrated in Example 7.10.

Example 7.10 **The challenge of mining colossal patterns.** Consider a 40×40 square table where each row contains the integers 1 through 40 in increasing order. Remove the integers on the diagonal, and this gives a 40×39 table. Add 20 identical rows to the bottom of the table, where each row contains the integers 41 through 79 in increasing order, resulting in a 60×39 table (Figure 7.6). We consider each row as a transaction and set the minimum support threshold at 20. The table has an exponential number (i.e., $\binom{40}{20}$) of midsize closed/maximal frequent patterns of size 20, but only one that is colossal: $\alpha = (41, 42, \ldots, 79)$ of size 39. None of the frequent pattern mining algorithms that we have introduced so far can complete execution in a reasonable amount of time.

row/col	1	2	3	4	...	38	39
1	2	3	4	5	...	39	40
2	1	3	4	5	...	39	40
3	1	2	4	5	...	39	40
4	1	2	3	5	...	39	40
5	1	2	3	4	...	39	40
...	...	...	...	...	...	...	...
39	1	2	3	4	...	38	40
40	1	2	3	4	...	38	39
41	41	42	43	44	...	78	79
42	41	42	43	44	...	78	79
...	...	...	...	...	...	...	...
60	41	42	43	44	...	78	79

Figure 7.6 A simple colossal patterns example: The data set contains an exponential number of midsize patterns of size 20 but only one that is colossal, namely $(41, 42, \ldots, 79)$.

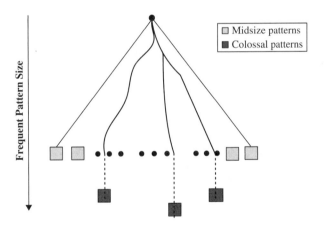

Figure 7.7 Synthetic data that contain some colossal patterns but exponentially many midsize patterns.

The pattern search space is similar to that in Figure 7.7, where midsize patterns largely outnumber colossal patterns. ∎

All of the pattern mining strategies we have studied so far, such as Apriori and FP-growth, use an incremental growth strategy by nature, that is, they increase the length of candidate patterns by one at a time. Breadth-first search methods like Apriori cannot bypass the generation of an explosive number of midsize patterns generated, making it impossible to reach colossal patterns. Even depth-first search methods like FP-growth can be easily trapped in a huge amount of subtrees before reaching colossal patterns. Clearly, a completely new mining methodology is needed to overcome such a hurdle.

A new mining strategy called *Pattern-Fusion* was developed, which fuses a small number of shorter frequent patterns into colossal pattern candidates. It thereby takes leaps in the pattern search space and avoids the pitfalls of both breadth-first and depth-first searches. This method finds a good approximation to the complete set of *colossal* frequent patterns.

The Pattern-Fusion method has the following major characteristics. First, it traverses the tree in a bounded-breadth way. Only a fixed number of patterns in a bounded-size candidate pool are used as starting nodes to search downward in the pattern tree. As such, it avoids the problem of exponential search space.

Second, Pattern-Fusion has the capability to identify "shortcuts" whenever possible. Each pattern's growth is not performed with one-item addition, but with an agglomeration of multiple patterns in the pool. These shortcuts direct Pattern-Fusion much more rapidly down the search tree toward the colossal patterns. Figure 7.8 conceptualizes this mining model.

As Pattern-Fusion is designed to give an approximation to the colossal patterns, a quality evaluation model is introduced to assess the patterns returned by the algorithm. An empirical study verifies that Pattern-Fusion is able to efficiently return high-quality results.

Let's examine the Pattern-Fusion method in more detail. First, we introduce the concept of **core pattern**. For a pattern α, an itemset $\beta \subseteq \alpha$ is said to be a τ-*core pattern* of α if $\frac{|D_\alpha|}{|D_\beta|} \geq \tau$, $0 < \tau \leq 1$, where $|D_\alpha|$ is the number of patterns containing α in database

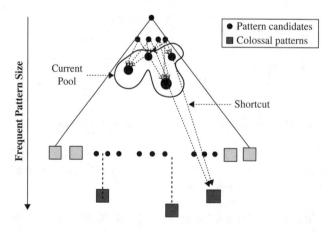

Figure 7.8 Pattern tree traversal: Candidates are taken from a pool of patterns, which results in shortcuts through pattern space to the colossal patterns.

D. τ is called the *core ratio*. A pattern α is (d, τ)-*robust* if d is the maximum number of items that can be removed from α for the resulting pattern to remain a τ-core pattern of α, that is,

$$d = \max_{\beta}\{|\alpha| - |\beta| \,\|\, \beta \subseteq \alpha, \text{ and } \beta \text{ is a } \tau\text{-core pattern of } \alpha\}.$$

Example 7.11 **Core patterns.** Figure 7.9 shows a simple transaction database of four distinct transactions, each with 100 duplicates: $\{\alpha_1 = (abe), \alpha_2 = (bcf), \alpha_3 = (acf), \alpha_4 = (abcfe)\}$. If we set $\tau = 0.5$, then (ab) is a core pattern of α_1 because (ab) is contained only by α_1 and α_4. Therefore, $\frac{|D_{\alpha_1}|}{|D_{(ab)}|} = \frac{100}{200} \geq \tau$. α_1 is $(2, 0.5)$-robust while α_4 is $(4, 0.5)$-robust. The table also shows that larger patterns (e.g., $(abcfe)$) have far more core patterns than smaller ones (e.g., (bcf)). ∎

From Example 7.11, we can deduce that large or colossal patterns have far more core patterns than smaller patterns do. Thus, a colossal pattern is more robust in the sense that *if a small number of items are removed from the pattern, the resulting pattern would have a similar support set*. The larger the pattern size, the more prominent this robustness. Such a robustness relationship between a colossal pattern and its corresponding core patterns can be extended to multiple levels. The lower-level core patterns of a colossal pattern are called **core descendants**.

Given a small c, a colossal pattern usually has far more core descendants of size c than a smaller pattern. This means that if we were to draw randomly from the complete set of patterns of size c, we would be more likely to pick a core descendant of a colossal pattern than that of a smaller pattern. In Figure 7.9, consider the complete set of patterns of size $c = 2$, which contains $\binom{5}{2} = 10$ patterns in total. For illustrative purposes, let's assume that the larger pattern, *abcef*, is colossal. The probability of being able to randomly draw a core descendant of *abcef* is 0.9. Contrast this to the probability of randomly drawing a core descendent of smaller (noncolossal) patterns, which is at most 0.3. Therefore, a colossal pattern can be generated by merging a proper set of

Transactions (# of Transactions)	Core Patterns ($\tau = 0.5$)
(abe) (100)	$(abe), (ab), (be), (ae), (e)$
(bcf) (100)	$(bcf), (bc), (bf)$
(acf) (100)	$(acf), (ac), (af)$
$(abcef)$ (100)	$(ab), (ac), (af), (ae), (bc), (bf), (be), (ce), (fe), (e), (abc),$ $(abf), (abe), (ace), (acf), (afe), (bcf), (bce), (bfe), (cfe),$ $(abcf), (abce), (bcfe), (acfe), (abfe), (abcef)$

Figure 7.9 A transaction database, which contains duplicates, and core patterns for each distinct transaction.

its core patterns. For instance, *abcef* can be generated by merging just two of its core patterns, *ab* and *cef*, instead of having to merge all of its 26 core patterns.

Now, let's see how these observations can help us leap through pattern space more directly toward colossal patterns. Consider the following scheme. First, generate a complete set of frequent patterns up to a user-specified small size, and then randomly pick a pattern, β. β will have a high probability of being a core-descendant of some colossal pattern, α. Identify all of α's core-descendants in this complete set, and merge them. This generates a much larger core-descendant of α, giving us the ability to leap along a path toward α in the core-pattern tree, T_α. In the same fashion we select K patterns. The set of larger core-descendants generated is the candidate pool for the next iteration.

A question arises: Given β, a core-descendant of a colossal pattern α, how can we find the other core-descendants of α? Given two patterns, α and β, the pattern distance between them is defined as $Dist(\alpha, \beta) = 1 - \frac{|D_\alpha \cap D_\beta|}{|D_\alpha \cup D_\beta|}$. Pattern distance satisfies the triangle inequality.

For a pattern, α, let C_α be the set of all its core patterns. It can be shown that C_α is bounded in metric space by a "ball" of diameter $r(\tau)$, where $r(\tau) = 1 - \frac{1}{2/\tau - 1}$. This means that given a core pattern $\beta \in C_\alpha$, we can identify all of α's core patterns in the current pool by posing a range query. Note that in the mining algorithm, each randomly drawn pattern could be a core-descendant of more than one colossal pattern, and as such, when merging the patterns found by the "ball," more than one larger core-descendant could be generated.

From this discussion, the Pattern-Fusion method is outlined in the following two phases:

1. **Initial Pool:** Pattern-Fusion assumes an initial pool of small frequent patterns is available. This is the complete set of frequent patterns up to a small size (e.g., 3). This initial pool can be mined with any existing efficient mining algorithm.

2. **Iterative Pattern-Fusion:** Pattern-Fusion takes as input a user-specified parameter, K, which is the maximum number of patterns to be mined. The mining process is iterative. At each iteration, K seed patterns are randomly picked from the current pool. For each of these K seeds, we find all the patterns within a ball of a size specified by τ. All the patterns in each "ball" are then fused together to generate a set of superpatterns. These superpatterns form a new pool. If the pool contains more than K patterns, the next iteration begins with this pool for the new round of random drawing. As the support set of every superpattern shrinks with each new iteration, the iteration process terminates.

Note that *Pattern-Fusion merges small subpatterns of a large pattern instead of incrementally-expanding patterns with single items*. This gives the method an advantage to circumvent midsize patterns and progress on a path leading to a potential colossal pattern. The idea is illustrated in Figure 7.10. Each point shown in the metric space

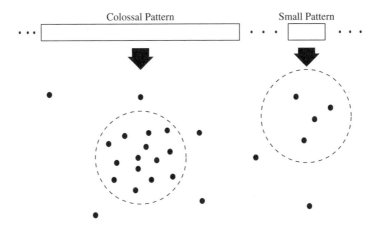

Figure 7.10 Pattern metric space: Each point represents a core pattern. The core patterns of a colossal pattern are denser than those of a small pattern, as shown within the dotted lines.

represents a core pattern. In comparison to a smaller pattern, a larger pattern has far more core patterns that are close to one another, all of which are bounded by a ball, as shown by the dotted lines. When drawing randomly from the initial pattern pool, we have a much higher probability of getting a core pattern of a large pattern, because the ball of a larger pattern is much denser.

It has been theoretically shown that Pattern-Fusion leads to a good approximation of colossal patterns. The method was tested on synthetic and real data sets constructed from program tracing data and microarray data. Experiments show that the method can find most of the colossal patterns with high efficiency.

7.5 Mining Compressed or Approximate Patterns

A major challenge in frequent pattern mining is the huge number of discovered patterns. Using a minimum support threshold to control the number of patterns found has limited effect. Too low a value can lead to the generation of an explosive number of output patterns, while too high a value can lead to the discovery of only commonsense patterns.

To reduce the huge set of frequent patterns generated in mining while maintaining high-quality patterns, we can instead mine a compressed or approximate set of frequent patterns. *Top-k most frequent closed patterns* were proposed to make the mining process concentrate on only the set of k most frequent patterns. Although interesting, they usually do not epitomize the k most representative patterns because of the uneven frequency distribution among itemsets. *Constraint-based mining* of frequent patterns (Section 7.3) incorporates user-specified constraints to filter out uninteresting patterns. Measures of pattern/rule *interestingness* and *correlation* (Section 6.3) can also be used to help confine the search to patterns/rules of interest.

In this section, we look at two forms of "compression" of frequent patterns that build on the concepts of closed patterns and max-patterns. Recall from Section 6.2.6 that a *closed pattern* is a lossless compression of the set of frequent patterns, whereas a *max-pattern* is a lossy compression. In particular, Section 7.5.1 explores *clustering-based compression of frequent patterns*, which groups patterns together based on their similarity and frequency support. Section 7.5.2 takes a "*summarization*" *approach*, where the aim is to derive redundancy-aware top-k representative patterns that cover the whole set of (closed) frequent itemsets. The approach considers not only the representativeness of patterns but also their mutual independence to avoid redundancy in the set of generated patterns. The k representatives provide compact compression over the collection of frequent patterns, making them easier to interpret and use.

7.5.1 Mining Compressed Patterns by Pattern Clustering

Pattern compression can be achieved by pattern clustering. Clustering techniques are described in detail in Chapters 10 and 11. In this section, it is not necessary to know the fine details of clustering. Rather, you will learn how the concept of clustering can be applied to compress frequent patterns. Clustering is the automatic process of grouping like objects together, so that objects within a cluster are similar to one another and dissimilar to objects in other clusters. In this case, the objects are frequent patterns. The frequent patterns are clustered using a tightness measure called δ-cluster. A representative pattern is selected for each cluster, thereby offering a compressed version of the set of frequent patterns.

Before we begin, let's review some definitions. An itemset X is a **closed frequent itemset** in a data set D if X is frequent and there exists no proper super-itemset Y of X such that Y has the same support count as X in D. An itemset X is a **maximal frequent itemset** in data set D if X is frequent and there exists no super-itemset Y such that $X \subset Y$ and Y is frequent in D. Using these concepts alone is not enough to obtain a good representative compression of a data set, as we see in Example 7.12.

Example 7.12 **Shortcomings of closed itemsets and maximal itemsets for compression.** Table 7.3 shows a subset of frequent itemsets on a large data set, where a, b, c, d, e, f represent individual items. There are no closed itemsets here; therefore, we cannot use closed frequent itemsets to compress the data. The only maximal frequent itemset is P_3. However, we observe that itemsets P_2, P_3, and P_4 are significantly different with respect to their support counts. If we were to use P_3 to represent a compressed version of the data, we would lose this support count information entirely. From visual inspection, consider the two pairs (P_1, P_2) and (P_4, P_5). The patterns within each pair are very similar with respect to their support and expression. Therefore, intuitively, P_2, P_3, and P_4, collectively, should serve as a better compressed version of the data.   ■

Table 7.3 Subset of Frequent Itemsets

ID	Itemsets	Support
P_1	$\{b,c,d,e\}$	205,227
P_2	$\{b,c,d,e,f\}$	205,211
P_3	$\{a,b,c,d,e,f\}$	101,758
P_4	$\{a,c,d,e,f\}$	161,563
P_5	$\{a,c,d,e\}$	161,576

So, let's see if we can find a way of clustering frequent patterns as a means of obtaining a compressed representation of them. We will need to define a good similarity measure, cluster patterns according to this measure, and then select and output only a *representative pattern* for each cluster. Since the set of closed frequent patterns is a lossless compression over the original frequent patterns set, it is a good idea to discover representative patterns over the collection of *closed* patterns.

We can use the following distance measure between closed patterns. Let P_1 and P_2 be two closed patterns. Their supporting transaction sets are $T(P_1)$ and $T(P_2)$, respectively. The **pattern distance** of P_1 and P_2, $Pat\_Dist(P_1, P_2)$, is defined as

$$Pat\_Dist(P_1, P_2) = 1 - \frac{|T(P_1) \cap T(P_2)|}{|T(P_1) \cup T(P_2)|}. \tag{7.14}$$

Pattern distance is a valid distance metric defined on the set of transactions. Note that it incorporates the *support* information of patterns, as desired previously.

Example 7.13 **Pattern distance.** Suppose P_1 and P_2 are two patterns such that $T(P_1) = \{t_1, t_2, t_3, t_4, t_5\}$ and $T(P_2) = \{t_1, t_2, t_3, t_4, t_6\}$, where t_i is a transaction in the database. The distance between P_1 and P_2 is $Pat\_Dist(P_1, P_2) = 1 - \frac{4}{6} = \frac{1}{3}$. ∎

Now, let's consider the *expression* of patterns. Given two patterns A and B, we say B can be **expressed** by A if $O(B) \subset O(A)$, where $O(A)$ is the corresponding itemset of pattern A. Following this definition, assume patterns $P_1, P_2, \ldots, P_k$ are in the same cluster. The representative pattern P_r of the cluster should be able to *express* all the other patterns in the cluster. Clearly, we have $\cup_{i=1}^{k} O(P_i) \subseteq O(P_r)$.

Using the distance measure, we can simply apply a clustering method, such as k-means (Section 10.2), on the collection of frequent patterns. However, this introduces two problems. First, the quality of the clusters cannot be guaranteed; second, it may not be able to find a representative pattern for each cluster (i.e., the pattern P_r may not belong to the same cluster). To overcome these problems, this is where the concept of δ-cluster comes in, where δ ($0 \leq \delta \leq 1$) measures the tightness of a cluster.

A pattern P is **δ-covered** by another pattern P' if $O(P) \subseteq O(P')$ and $Pat\_Dist(P, P') \leq \delta$. A set of patterns form a **δ-cluster** if there exists a representative pattern P_r such that for each pattern P in the set, P is δ-covered by P_r.

Note that according to the concept of δ-cluster, a pattern can belong to multiple clusters. Also, using δ-cluster, we only need to compute the distance between each pattern and the representative pattern of the cluster. Because a pattern P is δ-covered by a representative pattern P_r only if $O(P) \subseteq O(P_r)$, we can simplify the distance calculation by considering only the supports of the patterns:

$$Pat\_Dist(P, P_r) = 1 - \frac{|T(P) \cap T(P_r)|}{|T(P) \cup T(P_r)|} = 1 - \frac{|T(P_r)|}{|T(P)|}. \tag{7.15}$$

If we restrict the representative pattern to be frequent, then the number of representative patterns (i.e., clusters) is no less than the number of maximal frequent patterns. This is because a maximal frequent pattern can only be covered by itself. To achieve more succinct compression, we relax the constraints on representative patterns, that is, we allow the support of representative patterns to be *somewhat* less than *min_sup*.

For any representative pattern P_r, assume its support is k. Since it has to *cover* at least one frequent pattern (i.e., P) with support that is at least *min_sup*, we have

$$\delta \geq Pat\_Dist(P, P_r) = 1 - \frac{|T(P_r)|}{|T(P)|} \geq 1 - \frac{k}{min\_sup}. \tag{7.16}$$

That is, $k \geq (1 - \delta) \times min\_sup$. This is the minimum support for a representative pattern, denoted as min_sup_r.

Based on the preceding discussion, the pattern compression problem can be defined as follows: *Given a transaction database, a minimum support* min_sup, *and the cluster quality measure* δ, *the pattern compression problem is to find a set of representative patterns R such that for each frequent pattern P (with respect to* min_sup*), there is a representative pattern* $P_r \in R$ *(with respect to* min_sup$_r$*), which covers P, and the value of $|R|$ is minimized.*

Finding a minimum set of representative patterns is an NP-Hard problem. However, efficient methods have been developed that reduce the number of closed frequent patterns generated by orders of magnitude with respect to the original collection of closed patterns. The methods succeed in finding a high-quality compression of the pattern set.

7.5.2 Extracting Redundancy-Aware Top-*k* Patterns

Mining the top-*k* most frequent patterns is a strategy for reducing the number of patterns returned during mining. However, in many cases, frequent patterns are not mutually independent but often clustered in small regions. This is somewhat like finding 20 population centers in the world, which may result in cities clustered in a small number of countries rather than evenly distributed across the globe. Instead, most users would prefer to derive the *k* most interesting patterns, which are not only significant, but also mutually independent and containing little redundancy. A small set of *k* representative patterns that have not only high significance but also low redundancy are called **redundancy-aware top-*k* patterns**.

Example 7.14 **Redundancy-aware top-*k* strategy versus other top-*k* strategies.** Figure 7.11 illustrates the intuition behind *redundancy-aware top-k patterns* versus *traditional top-k patterns* and *k-summarized patterns*. Suppose we have the frequent patterns set shown in Figure 7.11(a), where each circle represents a pattern of which the significance is colored in grayscale. The distance between two circles reflects the redundancy of the two corresponding patterns: The closer the circles are, the more redundant the respective patterns are to one another. Let's say we want to find three patterns that will best represent the given set, that is, *k* = 3. Which three should we choose?

Arrows are used to show the patterns chosen if using redundancy-aware top-*k* patterns (Figure 7.11b), traditional top-*k* patterns (Figure 7.11c), or *k*-summarized patterns (Figure 7.11d). In Figure 7.11(c), the **traditional top-*k* strategy** relies solely on significance: It selects the three most significant patterns to represent the set.

In Figure 7.11(d), the ***k*-summarized pattern strategy** selects patterns based solely on nonredundancy. It detects three clusters, and finds the most representative patterns to

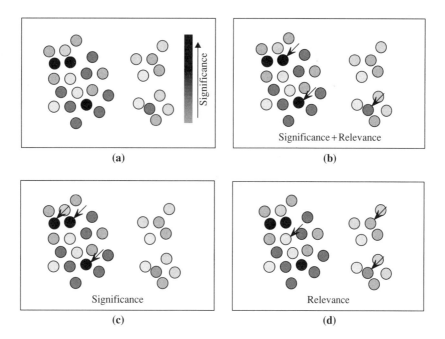

Figure 7.11 Conceptual view comparing top-*k* methodologies (where gray levels represent pattern significance, and the closer that two patterns are displayed, the more redundant they are to one another): (a) original patterns, (b) redundancy-aware top-*k* patterns, (c) traditional top-*k* patterns, and (d) *k*-summarized patterns.

be the "centermost'" pattern from each cluster. These patterns are chosen to represent the data. The selected patterns are considered "summarized patterns" in the sense that they represent or "provide a summary" of the clusters they stand for.

By contrast, in Figure 7.11(b) the **redundancy-aware top-k patterns** make a trade-off between significance and redundancy. The three patterns chosen here have high significance and low redundancy. Observe, for example, the two highly significant patterns that, based on their redundancy, are displayed next to each other. The redundancy-aware top-k strategy selects only one of them, taking into consideration that two would be redundant. To formalize the definition of redundancy-aware top-k patterns, we'll need to define the concepts of significance and redundancy. ∎

A **significance measure** S is a function mapping a pattern $p \in \mathcal{P}$ to a real value such that $S(p)$ is the degree of interestingness (or usefulness) of the pattern p. In general, significance measures can be either objective or subjective. *Objective measures* depend only on the structure of the given pattern and the underlying data used in the discovery process. Commonly used objective measures include support, confidence, correlation, and *tf-idf* (or *term frequency* versus *inverse document frequency*), where the latter is often used in information retrieval. *Subjective* measures are based on user beliefs in the data. They therefore depend on the users who examine the patterns. A subjective measure is usually a relative score based on user prior knowledge or a background model. It often measures the unexpectedness of a pattern by computing its divergence from the background model. Let $S(p, q)$ be the **combined significance** of patterns p and q, and $S(p|q) = S(p, q) - S(q)$ be the **relative significance** of p given q. Note that the combined significance, $S(p, q)$, means the collective significance of two individual patterns p and q, not the significance of a single super pattern $p \cup q$.

Given the significance measure S, the **redundancy** R **between two patterns** p and q is defined as $R(p, q) = S(p) + S(q) - S(p, q)$. Subsequently, we have $S(p|q) = S(p) - R(p, q)$.

We assume that the combined significance of two patterns is no less than the significance of any individual pattern (since it is a collective significance of two patterns) and does not exceed the sum of two individual significance patterns (since there exists redundancy). That is, the redundancy between two patterns should satisfy

$$0 \le R(p, q) \le \min(S(p), S(q)). \tag{7.17}$$

The ideal redundancy measure $R(p, q)$ is usually hard to obtain. However, we can approximate redundancy using distance between patterns such as with the distance measure defined in Section 7.5.1.

The problem of finding redundancy-aware top-k patterns can thus be transformed into finding a k-pattern set that maximizes the marginal significance, which is a well-studied problem in information retrieval. In this field, a document has high marginal relevance if it is both relevant to the query and contains minimal marginal similarity to previously selected documents, where the marginal similarity is computed by choosing the most relevant selected document. Experimental studies have shown this method to be efficient and able to find high-significance and low-redundancy top-k patterns.

7.6 Pattern Exploration and Application

For discovered frequent patterns, is there any way the mining process can return additional information that will help us to better understand the patterns? What kinds of applications exist for frequent pattern mining? These topics are discussed in this section. Section 7.6.1 looks at the automated generation of **semantic annotations** for frequent patterns. These are dictionary-like annotations. They provide semantic information relating to patterns, based on the context and usage of the patterns, which aids in their understanding. Semantically similar patterns also form part of the annotation, providing a more direct connection between discovered patterns and any other patterns already known to the users.

Section 7.6.2 presents an overview of applications of frequent pattern mining. While the applications discussed in Chapter 6 and this chapter mainly involve market basket analysis and correlation analysis, there are many other areas in which frequent pattern mining is useful. These range from data preprocessing and classification to clustering and the analysis of complex data.

7.6.1 Semantic Annotation of Frequent Patterns

Pattern mining typically generates a huge set of frequent patterns without providing enough information to interpret the meaning of the patterns. In the previous section, we introduced pattern processing techniques to shrink the size of the output set of frequent patterns such as by extracting redundancy-aware top-k patterns or compressing the pattern set. These, however, do not provide any semantic interpretation of the patterns. It would be helpful if we could also generate semantic annotations for the frequent patterns found, which would help us to better understand the patterns.

"*What is an appropriate semantic annotation for a frequent pattern?*" Think about what we find when we look up the meaning of terms in a dictionary. Suppose we are looking up the term *pattern*. A dictionary typically contains the following components to explain the term:

1. *A set of definitions*, such as "a decorative design, as for wallpaper, china, or textile fabrics, etc.; a natural or chance configuration"

2. *Example sentences*, such as "*patterns* of frost on the window; the behavior *patterns* of teenagers, ..."

3. *Synonyms from a thesaurus*, such as "model, archetype, design, exemplar, motif, ..."

Analogically, what if we could extract similar types of semantic information and provide such structured annotations for frequent patterns? This would greatly help users in interpreting the meaning of patterns and in deciding on how or whether to further explore them. Unfortunately, it is infeasible to provide such precise semantic definitions for patterns without expertise in the domain. Nevertheless, we can explore how to *approximate* such a process for frequent pattern mining.

> **Pattern: "*{frequent, pattern}*"**
>   **context indicators:**
>   "mining," "constraint," "Apriori," "FP-growth,"
>   "rakesh agrawal," "jiawei han," ...
>   **representative transactions:**
>   1) mining *frequent patterns* without candidate ...
>   2) ... mining closed *frequent* graph *patterns*
>   **semantically similar patterns:**
>   "*{frequent, sequential, pattern}*," "*{graph, pattern}*"
>   "*{maximal, pattern}*," "*{frequent, closed, pattern}*," ...

Figure 7.12 Semantic annotation of the pattern "*{frequent, pattern}*."

In general, the hidden meaning of a pattern can be inferred from patterns with similar meanings, data objects co-occurring with it, and transactions in which the pattern appears. Annotations with such information are analogous to dictionary entries, which can be regarded as annotating each term with structured semantic information. Let's examine an example.

Example 7.15 **Semantic annotation of a frequent pattern.** Figure 7.12 shows an example of a semantic annotation for the pattern "*{frequent, pattern}*." This dictionary-like annotation provides semantic information related to "*{frequent, pattern}*," consisting of its strongest *context indicators*, the most *representative data transactions*, and the most *semantically similar patterns*. This kind of semantic annotation is similar to natural language processing. The semantics of a word can be inferred from its context, and words sharing similar contexts tend to be semantically similar. The context indicators and the representative transactions provide a view of the context of the pattern from different angles to help users understand the pattern. The semantically similar patterns provide a more direct connection between the pattern and any other patterns already known to the users. ∎

"*How can we perform automated semantic annotation for a frequent pattern?*" The key to high-quality semantic annotation of a frequent pattern is the successful context modeling of the pattern. For context modeling of a pattern, p, consider the following.

- A **context unit** is a basic object in a database, D, that carries semantic information and co-occurs with at least one frequent pattern, p, in at least one transaction in D. A context unit can be an item, a pattern, or even a transaction, depending on the specific task and data.

- The **context of a pattern**, p, is a selected set of weighted context units (referred to as **context indicators**) in the database. It carries semantic information, and co-occurs with a frequent pattern, p. The context of p can be modeled using a vector space model, that is, the context of p can be represented as $C(p) = \langle w(u_1),$

$w(u_2), \ldots, w(u_n)\rangle$, where $w(u_i)$ is a weight function of term u_i. A transaction t is represented as a vector $\langle v_1, v_2, \ldots, v_m \rangle$, where $v_i = 1$ if and only if $v_i \in t$, otherwise $v_i = 0$.

Based on these concepts, we can define the basic task of **semantic pattern annotation** as follows:

1. Select context units and design a strength weight for each unit to model the contexts of frequent patterns.

2. Design similarity measures for the contexts of two patterns, and for a transaction and a pattern context.

3. For a given frequent pattern, extract the most significant context indicators, representative transactions, and semantically similar patterns to construct a structured annotation.

"*Which context units should we select as context indicators?*" Although a context unit can be an item, a transaction, or a pattern, typically, frequent patterns provide the most semantic information of the three. There are usually a large number of frequent patterns associated with a pattern, p. Therefore, we need a systematic way to select only the important and nonredundant frequent patterns from a large pattern set.

Considering that the closed patterns set is a lossless compression of frequent pattern sets, we can first derive the closed patterns set by applying efficient closed pattern mining methods. However, as discussed in Section 7.5, a closed pattern set is not compact enough, and pattern compression needs to be performed. We could use the pattern compression methods introduced in Section 7.5.1 or explore alternative compression methods such as microclustering using the Jaccard coefficient (Chapter 2) and then selecting the most representative patterns from each cluster.

"*How, then, can we assign weights for each context indicator?*" A good weighting function should obey the following properties: (1) the best semantic indicator of a pattern, p, is itself, (2) assign the same score to two patterns if they are equally strong, and (3) if two patterns are independent, neither can indicate the meaning of the other. The meaning of a pattern, p, can be inferred from either the appearance or absence of indicators.

Mutual information is one of several possible weighting functions. It is widely used in information theory to measure the mutual independency of two random variables. Intuitively, it measures how much information a random variable tells about the other. Given two frequent patterns, p_α and p_β, let $X = \{0, 1\}$ and $Y = \{0, 1\}$ be two random variables representing the appearance of p_α and p_β, respectively. **Mutual information** $I(X; Y)$ is computed as

$$I(X; Y) = \sum_{x \in X} \sum_{y \in Y} P(x, y) \log \frac{P(x, y)}{P(x)P(y)}, \tag{7.18}$$

where $P(x=1, y=1) = \frac{|D_\alpha \cap D_\beta|}{|D|}$, $P(x=0, y=1) = \frac{|D_\beta| - |D_\alpha \cap D_\beta|}{|D|}$, $P(x=1, y=0) = \frac{|D_\alpha| - |D_\alpha \cap D_\beta|}{|D|}$, and $P(x=0, y=0) = \frac{|D| - |D_\alpha \cup D_\beta|}{|D|}$. Standard Laplace smoothing can be used to avoid zero probability.

Mutual information favors strongly correlated units and thus can be used to model the indicative strength of the context units selected. With context modeling, pattern annotation can be accomplished as follows:

1. To extract the most significant context indicators, we can use cosine similarity (Chapter 2) to measure the semantic similarity between pairs of context vectors, rank the context indicators by the weight strength, and extract the strongest ones.

2. To extract representative transactions, represent each transaction as a context vector. Rank the transactions with semantic similarity to the pattern p.

3. To extract semantically similar patterns, rank each frequent pattern, p, by the semantic similarity between their context models and the context of p.

Based on these principles, experiments have been conducted on large data sets to generate semantic annotations. Example 7.16 illustrates one such experiment.

Example 7.16 **Semantic annotations generated for frequent patterns from the DBLP Computer Science Bibliography.** Table 7.4 shows annotations generated for frequent patterns from a portion of the DBLP data set.[3] The DBLP data set contains papers from the proceedings of 12 major conferences in the fields of database systems, information retrieval, and data mining. Each transaction consists of two parts: the authors and the title of the corresponding paper.

Consider two types of patterns: (1) *frequent author* or *coauthorship*, each of which is a frequent itemset of authors, and (2) *frequent title terms*, each of which is a frequent sequential pattern of the title words. The method can automatically generate dictionary-like annotations for different kinds of frequent patterns. For frequent itemsets like coauthorship or single authors, the strongest context indicators are usually the other coauthors and discriminative title terms that appear in their work. The semantically similar patterns extracted also reflect the authors and terms related to their work. However, these similar patterns may not even co-occur with the given pattern in a paper. For example, the patterns "*timos_k_selli,*" "*ramakrishnan_srikant,*" and so on, do not co-occur with the pattern "*christos_faloutsos,*" but are extracted because their contexts are similar since they all are database and/or data mining researchers; thus the annotation is meaningful.

For the title term "*information retrieval,*" which is a sequential pattern, its strongest context indicators are usually the authors who tend to use the term in the titles of their papers, or the terms that tend to coappear with it. Its semantically similar patterns usually provide interesting concepts or descriptive terms, which are close in meaning (e.g., "*information retrieval* → *information filter*)."

---

[3] *www.informatik.uni-trier.de/~ley/db/.*

Table 7.4 Annotations Generated for Frequent Patterns in the DBLP Data Set

Pattern	Type	Annotations
christos_faloutsos	Context indicator	spiros_papadimitriou; fast; use fractal; graph; use correlate
	Representative transactions	multi-attribute hash use gray code
	Representative transactions	recovery latent time-series observe sum network tomography particle filter
	Representative transactions	index multimedia database tutorial
	Semantic similar patterns	spiros_papadimitriou&christos_faloutsos; spiros_papadimitriou; flip_korn; timos_k_selli; ramakrishnan_srikant; ramakrishnan_srikant&rakesh_agrawal
information retrieval	Context indicator	w_bruce_croft; web information; monika_ rauch_henzinger; james_p_callan; full-text
	Representative transactions	web information retrieval
	Representative transactions	language model information retrieval
	Semantic similar patterns	information use; web information; probabilistic information; information filter; text information

In both scenarios, the representative transactions extracted give us the titles of papers that effectively capture the meaning of the given patterns. The experiment demonstrates the effectiveness of semantic pattern annotation to generate a dictionary-like annotation for frequent patterns, which can help a user understand the meaning of annotated patterns. ∎

The context modeling and semantic analysis method presented here is general and can deal with any type of frequent patterns with context information. Such semantic annotations can have many other applications such as ranking patterns, categorizing and clustering patterns with semantics, and summarizing databases. Applications of the pattern context model and semantical analysis method are also not limited to pattern annotation; other example applications include pattern compression, transaction clustering, pattern relations discovery, and pattern synonym discovery.

7.6.2 Applications of Pattern Mining

We have studied many aspects of frequent pattern mining, with topics ranging from efficient mining algorithms and the diversity of patterns to pattern interestingness, pattern compression/approximation, and semantic pattern annotation. Let's take a moment to consider why this field has generated so much attention. What are some of the application areas in which frequent pattern mining is useful? This section presents an overview of applications for frequent pattern mining. We have touched on several application areas already, such as market basket analysis and correlation analysis, yet frequent pattern mining can be applied to many other areas as well. These range from data preprocessing and classification to clustering and the analysis of complex data.

To summarize, frequent pattern mining is a data mining task that discovers patterns that occur frequently together and/or have some distinctive properties that distinguish them from others, often disclosing something inherent and valuable. The patterns may be itemsets, subsequences, substructures, or values. The task also includes the discovery of rare patterns, revealing items that occur very rarely together yet are of interest. Uncovering frequent patterns and rare patterns leads to many broad and interesting applications, described as follows.

Pattern mining is widely used for **noise filtering and data cleaning** as **preprocessing** in many data-intensive applications. We can use it to analyze microarray data, for instance, which typically consists of tens of thousands of dimensions (e.g., representing genes). Such data can be rather noisy. Frequent pattern data mining can help us distinguish between what is noise and what isn't. We may assume that items that occur frequently together are less likely to be random noise and should not be filtered out. On the other hand, those that occur very frequently (similar to stopwords in text documents) are likely indistinctive and may be filtered out. Frequent pattern mining can help in background information identification and noise reduction.

Pattern mining often helps in the **discovery of inherent structures and clusters hidden in the data**. Given the DBLP data set, for instance, frequent pattern mining can easily find interesting clusters like coauthor clusters (by examining authors who frequently collaborate) and conference clusters (by examining the sharing of many common authors and terms). Such structure or cluster discovery can be used as preprocessing for more sophisticated data mining.

Although there are numerous classification methods (Chapters 8 and 9), research has found that frequent patterns can be used as building blocks in the construction of high-quality classification models, hence called **pattern-based classification**. The approach is successful because (1) the appearance of very infrequent item(s) or itemset(s) can be caused by random noise and may not be reliable for model construction, yet a relatively frequent pattern often carries more information gain for constructing more reliable models; (2) patterns in general (i.e., itemsets consisting of multiple attributes) usually carry more information gain than a single attribute (feature); and (3) the patterns so generated are often intuitively understandable and easy to explain. Recent research has reported several methods that mine interesting, frequent, and discriminative patterns and use them for effective classification. Pattern-based classification methods are introduced in Chapter 9.

Frequent patterns can also be used effectively for **subspace clustering in high-dimensional space**. Clustering is challenging in high-dimensional space, where the distance between two objects is often difficult to measure. This is because such a distance is dominated by the different sets of dimensions in which the objects are residing.

Thus, instead of clustering objects in their full high-dimensional spaces, it can be more meaningful to find clusters in certain subspaces. Recently, researchers have developed subspace-based pattern growth methods that cluster objects based on their common frequent patterns. They have shown that such methods are effective for clustering microarray-based gene expression data. Subspace clustering methods are discussed in Chapter 11.

Pattern analysis is useful in the **analysis of spatiotemporal data, time-series data, image data, video data, and multimedia data**. An area of *spatiotemporal data analysis* is the discovery of **colocation patterns**. These, for example, can help determine if a certain disease is geographically colocated with certain objects like a well, a hospital, or a river. In *time-series data analysis*, researchers have discretized time-series values into multiple intervals (or levels) so that tiny fluctuations and value differences can be ignored. The data can then be summarized into sequential patterns, which can be indexed to facilitate similarity search or comparative analysis. In *image analysis and pattern recognition*, researchers have also identified frequently occurring visual fragments as "visual words," which can be used for effective clustering, classification, and comparative analysis.

Pattern mining has also been used for the **analysis of sequence or structural data** such as trees, graphs, subsequences, and networks. In software engineering, researchers have identified consecutive or gapped subsequences in program execution as sequential patterns that help identify software bugs. Copy-and-paste bugs in large software programs can be identified by extended sequential pattern analysis of source programs. Plagiarized software programs can be identified based on their essentially identical program flow/loop structures. Authors' commonly used sentence substructures can be identified and used to distinguish articles written by different authors.

Frequent and discriminative patterns can be used as primitive **indexing structures** (known as graph indices) to help search large, complex, structured data sets and networks. These support a similarity search in graph-structured data such as chemical compound databases or XML-structured databases. Such patterns can also be used for data compression and summarization.

Furthermore, frequent patterns have been used in **recommender systems**, where people can find correlations, clusters of customer behaviors, and classification models based on commonly occurring or discriminative patterns (Chapter 13).

Finally, studies on efficient computation methods in pattern mining mutually enhance many other studies on **scalable computation**. For example, the computation and materialization of **iceberg cubes** using the BUC and Star-Cubing algorithms (Chapter 5) respectively share many similarities to computing frequent patterns by the Apriori and FP-growth algorithms (Chapter 6).

7.7 Summary

- The **scope** of frequent pattern mining research reaches far beyond the basic concepts and methods introduced in Chapter 6 for mining frequent itemsets and associations. This chapter presented a road map of the field, where topics are organized with respect to the kinds of patterns and rules that can be mined, mining methods, and applications.

■ In addition to mining for basic frequent itemsets and associations, **advanced forms of patterns** can be mined such as multilevel associations and multidimensional associations, quantitative association rules, rare patterns, and negative patterns. We can also mine high-dimensional patterns and compressed or approximate patterns.

■ **Multilevel associations** involve data at more than one abstraction level (e.g., "*buys computer*" and "*buys laptop*"). These may be mined using multiple minimum support thresholds. **Multidimensional associations** contain more than one dimension. Techniques for mining such associations differ in how they handle repetitive predicates. **Quantitative association rules** involve quantitative attributes. Discretization, clustering, and statistical analysis that discloses exceptional behavior can be integrated with the pattern mining process.

■ **Rare patterns** occur rarely but are of special interest. **Negative patterns** are patterns with components that exhibit negatively correlated behavior. Care should be taken in the definition of negative patterns, with consideration of the null-invariance property. Rare and negative patterns may highlight exceptional behavior in the data, which is likely of interest.

■ **Constraint-based mining** strategies can be used to help direct the mining process toward patterns that match users' intuition or satisfy certain constraints. Many user-specified constraints can be pushed deep into the mining process. Constraints can be categorized into **pattern-pruning** and **data-pruning** constraints. Properties of such constraints include *monotonicity, antimonotonicity, data-antimonotonicity,* and *succinctness.* Constraints with such properties can be properly incorporated into efficient pattern mining processes.

■ Methods have been developed for mining patterns in **high-dimensional space**. This includes a pattern growth approach based on *row enumeration* for mining data sets where the number of dimensions is large and the number of data tuples is small (e.g., for microarray data), as well as mining **colossal patterns** (i.e., patterns of very long length) by a *Pattern-Fusion* method.

■ To reduce the number of patterns returned in mining, we can instead mine compressed patterns or approximate patterns. *Compressed patterns* can be mined with representative patterns defined based on the concept of clustering, and *approximate patterns* can be mined by extracting **redundancy-aware top-k patterns** (i.e., a small set of k-representative patterns that have not only high significance but also low redundancy with respect to one another).

■ **Semantic annotations** can be generated to help users understand the meaning of the frequent patterns found, such as for textual terms like "{*frequent, pattern*}." These are dictionary-like annotations, providing semantic information relating to the term. This information consists of *context indicators* (e.g., terms indicating the context of that pattern), the most *representative data transactions* (e.g., fragments or sentences containing the term), and the most *semantically similar patterns* (e.g., "{*maximal, pattern*}" is semantically similar to "{*frequent, pattern*}"). The annotations provide a view of the pattern's context from different angles, which aids in their understanding.

▪ Frequent pattern mining has many diverse applications, ranging from pattern-based data cleaning to pattern-based classification, clustering, and outlier or exception analysis. These methods are discussed in the subsequent chapters in this book.

7.8 Exercises

7.1 Propose and outline a **level-shared mining** approach to mining multilevel association rules in which each item is encoded by its level position. Design it so that an initial scan of the database collects the count for each item *at each concept level*, identifying frequent and subfrequent items. Comment on the processing cost of mining multilevel associations with this method in comparison to mining single-level associations.

7.2 Suppose, as manager of a chain of stores, you would like to use sales transactional data to analyze the effectiveness of your store's advertisements. In particular, you would like to study how specific factors influence the effectiveness of advertisements that announce a particular category of items on sale. The factors to study are the *region* in which customers live and the *day-of-the-week* and *time-of-the-day* of the ads. Discuss how to design an efficient method to mine the transaction data sets and explain how **multidimensional** and **multilevel mining** methods can help you derive a good solution.

7.3 **Quantitative association rules** may disclose exceptional behaviors within a data set, where "exceptional" can be defined based on statistical theory. For example, Section 7.2.3 shows the association rule

$$sex = female \Rightarrow mean\_wage = \$7.90/hr \ (overall\_mean\_wage = \$9.02/hr),$$

which suggests an exceptional pattern. The rule states that the average wage for females is only $7.90 per hour, which is a significantly lower wage than the overall average of $9.02 per hour. Discuss how such quantitative rules can be discovered systematically and efficiently in large data sets with quantitative attributes.

7.4 In multidimensional data analysis, it is interesting to extract pairs of *similar* cell characteristics associated with substantial changes in measure in a data cube, where cells are considered *similar* if they are related by roll-up (i.e, *ancestors*), drill-down (i.e, *descendants*), or 1-D mutation (i.e, *siblings*) operations. Such an analysis is called **cube gradient analysis**.

Suppose the measure of the cube is *average*. A user poses a set of *probe cells* and would like to find their corresponding sets of *gradient cells*, each of which satisfies a certain gradient threshold. For example, find the set of corresponding gradient cells that have an average sale price greater than 20% of that of the given probe cells. Develop an algorithm than mines the set of constrained gradient cells efficiently in a large data cube.

7.5 Section 7.2.4 presented various ways of defining negatively correlated patterns. Consider Definition 7.3: "Suppose that itemsets X and Y are both frequent, that is, $sup(X) \geq min\_sup$ and $sup(Y) \geq min\_sup$, where min_sup is the minimum support threshold. If $(P(X|Y) + P(Y|X))/2 < \epsilon$, where ϵ is a negative pattern threshold, then pattern $X \cup Y$ is a **negatively correlated pattern**." Design an efficient pattern growth algorithm for mining the set of negatively correlated patterns.

7.6 Prove that each entry in the following table correctly characterizes its corresponding **rule constraint** for frequent itemset mining.

	Rule Constraint	Antimonotonic	Monotonic	Succinct
(a)	$v \in S$	no	yes	yes
(b)	$S \subseteq V$	yes	no	yes
(c)	$min(S) \leq v$	no	yes	yes
(d)	$range(S) \leq v$	yes	no	no
(e)	$variance(S) \leq v$	convertible	convertible	no

7.7 The price of each item in a store is non-negative. The store manager is only interested in rules of certain forms, using the constraints given in (a)–(b). For each of the following cases, identify the kinds of **constraints** they represent and briefly discuss how to mine such association rules using **constraint-based pattern mining**.

(a) Containing at least one Blu-ray DVD movie.

(b) Containing items with a sum of the prices that is less than $150.

(c) Containing one free item and other items with a sum of the prices that is at least $200.

(d) Where the average price of all the items is between $100 and $500.

7.8 Section 7.4.1 introduced a core Pattern-Fusion method for **mining high-dimensional data**. Explain why a long pattern, if one exists in the data set, is likely to be discovered by this method.

7.9 Section 7.5.1 defined a **pattern distance measure** between closed patterns P_1 and P_2 as

$$Pat\_Dist(P_1, P_2) = 1 - \frac{|T(P_1) \cap T(P_2)|}{|T(P_1) \cup T(P_2)|},$$

where $T(P_1)$ and $T(P_2)$ are the supporting transaction sets of P_1 and P_2, respectively. Is this a valid distance metric? Show the derivation to support your answer.

7.10 Association rule mining often generates a large number of rules, many of which may be similar, thus not containing much novel information. Design an efficient algorithm that **compresses** a large set of patterns into a small compact set. Discuss whether your mining method is robust under different pattern similarity definitions.

7.11 Frequent pattern mining may generate many superfluous patterns. Therefore, it is important to develop methods that mine compressed patterns. Suppose a user would like to obtain only k patterns (where k is a small integer). Outline an efficient method that generates the **k most representative patterns**, where more distinct patterns are preferred over very similar patterns. Illustrate the effectiveness of your method using a small data set.

7.12 It is interesting to generate **semantic annotations** for mined patterns. Section 7.6.1 presented a pattern annotation method. Alternative methods are possible, such as by utilizing type information. In the DBLP data set, for example, authors, conferences, terms, and papers form multi-typed data. Develop a method for automated semantic pattern annotation that makes good use of typed information.

7.9 Bibliographic Notes

This chapter described various ways in which the basic techniques of frequent itemset mining (presented in Chapter 6) have been extended. One line of extension is mining multilevel and multidimensional association rules. Multilevel association mining was studied in Srikant and Agrawal [SA95] and Han and Fu [HF95]. In Srikant and Agrawal [SA95], such mining was studied in the context of *generalized association rules*, and an R-interest measure was proposed for removing redundant rules. Mining multidimensional association rules using static discretization of quantitative attributes and data cubes was studied by Kamber, Han, and Chiang [KHC97].

Another line of extension is to mine patterns on numeric attributes. Srikant and Agrawal [SA96] proposed a nongrid-based technique for mining quantitative association rules, which uses a measure of partial completeness. Mining quantitative association rules based on rule clustering was proposed by Lent, Swami, and Widom [LSW97]. Techniques for mining quantitative rules based on x-monotone and rectilinear regions were presented by Fukuda, Morimoto, Morishita, and Tokuyama [FMMT96] and Yoda, Fukuda, Morimoto, et al. [YFM+97]. Mining (distance-based) association rules over interval data was proposed by Miller and Yang [MY97]. Aumann and Lindell [AL99] studied the mining of quantitative association rules based on a statistical theory to present only those rules that deviate substantially from normal data.

Mining rare patterns by pushing group-based constraints was proposed by Wang, He, and Han [WHH00]. Mining negative association rules was discussed by Savasere, Omiecinski, and Navathe [SON98] and by Tan, Steinbach, and Kumar [TSK05].

Constraint-based mining directs the mining process toward patterns that are likely of interest to the user. The use of metarules as syntactic or semantic filters defining the form of interesting single-dimensional association rules was proposed in Klemettinen, Mannila, Ronkainen, et al. [KMR+94]. Metarule-guided mining, where the metarule consequent specifies an action (e.g., Bayesian clustering or plotting) to be applied to the data satisfying the metarule antecedent, was proposed in Shen, Ong, Mitbander, and Zaniolo [SOMZ96]. A relation-based approach to metarule-guided mining of association rules was studied in Fu and Han [FH95].

Methods for constraint-based mining using pattern pruning constraints were studied by Ng, Lakshmanan, Han, and Pang [NLHP98]; Lakshmanan, Ng, Han, and Pang [LNHP99]; and Pei, Han, and Lakshmanan [PHL01]. Constraint-based pattern mining by data reduction using data pruning constraints was studied by Bonchi, Giannotti, Mazzanti, and Pedreschi [BGMP03] and Zhu, Yan, Han, and Yu [ZYHY07]. An efficient method for mining constrained correlated sets was given in Grahne, Lakshmanan, and Wang [GLW00]. A dual mining approach was proposed by Bucila, Gehrke, Kifer, and White [BGKW03]. Other ideas involving the use of templates or predicate constraints in mining have been discussed in Anand and Kahn [AK93]; Dhar and Tuzhilin [DT93]; Hoschka and Klösgen [HK91]; Liu, Hsu, and Chen [LHC97]; Silberschatz and Tuzhilin [ST96]; and Srikant, Vu, and Agrawal [SVA97].

Traditional pattern mining methods encounter challenges when mining high-dimensional patterns, with applications like bioinformatics. Pan, Cong, Tung, et al. [PCT$^+$03] proposed CARPENTER, a method for finding closed patterns in high-dimensional biological data sets, which integrates the advantages of vertical data formats and pattern growth methods. Pan, Tung, Cong, and Xu [PTCX04] proposed COBBLER, which finds frequent closed itemsets by integrating row enumeration with column enumeration. Liu, Han, Xin, and Shao [LHXS06] proposed TDClose to mine frequent closed patterns in high-dimensional data by starting from the maximal rowset, integrated with a row-enumeration tree. It uses the pruning power of the minimum support threshold to reduce the search space. For mining rather long patterns, called *colossal patterns*, Zhu, Yan, Han, et al. [ZYH$^+$07] developed a core Pattern-Fusion method that leaps over an exponential number of intermediate patterns to reach colossal patterns.

To generate a reduced set of patterns, recent studies have focused on mining compressed sets of frequent patterns. Closed patterns can be viewed as a lossless compression of frequent patterns, whereas maximal patterns can be viewed as a simple lossy compression of frequent patterns. Top-k patterns, such as by Wang, Han, Lu, and Tsvetkov [WHLT05], and error-tolerant patterns, such as by Yang, Fayyad, and Bradley [YFB01], are alternative forms of interesting patterns. Afrati, Gionis, and Mannila [AGM04] proposed to use k-itemsets to cover a collection of frequent itemsets. For frequent itemset compression, Yan, Cheng, Han, and Xin [YCHX05] proposed a profile-based approach, and Xin, Han, Yan, and Cheng [XHYC05] proposed a clustering-based approach. By taking into consideration both pattern significance and pattern redundancy, Xin, Cheng, Yan, and Han [XCYH06] proposed a method for extracting redundancy-aware top-k patterns.

Automated semantic annotation of frequent patterns is useful for explaining the meaning of patterns. Mei, Xin, Cheng, et al. [MXC$^+$07] studied methods for semantic annotation of frequent patterns.

An important extension to frequent itemset mining is mining sequence and structural data. This includes mining sequential patterns (Agrawal and Srikant [AS95]; Pei, Han, Mortazavi-Asl, et al. [PHM-A$^+$01, PHM-A$^+$04]; and Zaki [Zak01]); mining frequent espisodes (Mannila, Toivonen, and Verkamo [MTV97]); mining structural patterns (Inokuchi, Washio, and Motoda [IWM98]; Kuramochi and Karypis [KK01]; and Yan and Han [YH02]); mining cyclic association rules (Özden, Ramaswamy, and Silberschatz [ORS98]); intertransaction association rule mining (Lu, Han, and Feng [LHF98]); and calendric market basket analysis (Ramaswamy, Mahajan, and Silberschatz [RMS98]). Mining such patterns is considered an advanced topic and readers are referred to these sources.

Pattern mining has been extended to help effective data classification and clustering. Pattern-based classification (Liu, Hsu, and Ma [LHM98] and Cheng, Yan, Han, and Hsu [CYHH07]) is discussed in Chapter 9. Pattern-based cluster analysis (Agrawal, Gehrke, Gunopulos, and Raghavan [AGGR98] and H. Wang, W. Wang, Yang, and Yu [WWYY02]) is discussed in Chapter 11.

Pattern mining also helps many other data analysis and processing tasks such as cube gradient mining and discriminative analysis (Imielinski, Khachiyan, and Abdulghani [IKA02]; Dong, Han, Lam, et al. [DHL$^+$04]; Ji, Bailey, and Dong [JBD05]), discriminative pattern-based indexing (Yan, Yu, and Han [YYH05]), and discriminative pattern-based similarity search (Yan, Zhu, Yu, and Han [YZYH06]).

Pattern mining has been extended to mining spatial, temporal, time-series, and multimedia data, and data streams. Mining spatial association rules or spatial collocation rules was studied by Koperski and Han [KH95]; Xiong, Shekhar, Huang, et al. [XSH$^+$04]; and Cao, Mamoulis, and Cheung [CMC05]. Pattern-based mining of time-series data is discussed in Shieh and Keogh [SK08] and Ye and Keogh [YK09]. There are many studies on pattern-based mining of multimedia data such as Zaïane, Han, and Zhu [ZHZ00] and Yuan, Wu, and Yang [YWY07]. Methods for mining frequent patterns on stream data have been proposed by many researchers, including Manku and Motwani [MM02]; Karp, Papadimitriou, and Shenker [KPS03]; and Metwally, Agrawal, and El Abbadi [MAE05]. These pattern mining methods are considered advanced topics.

Pattern mining has broad applications. Application areas include computer science such as software bug analysis, sensor network mining, and performance improvement of operating systems. For example, CP-Miner by Li, Lu, Myagmar, and Zhou [LLMZ04] uses pattern mining to identify copy-pasted code for bug isolation. PR-Miner by Li and Zhou [LZ05] uses pattern mining to extract application-specific programming rules from source code. Discriminative pattern mining is used for program failure detection to classify software behaviors (Lo, Cheng, Han, et al. [LCH$^+$09]) and for troubleshooting in sensor networks (Khan, Le, Ahmadi, et al. [KLA$^+$08]).

Classification: Basic Concepts

Classification is a form of data analysis that extracts models describing important data classes. Such models, called classifiers, predict categorical (discrete, unordered) class labels. For example, we can build a classification model to categorize bank loan applications as either safe or risky. Such analysis can help provide us with a better understanding of the data at large. Many classification methods have been proposed by researchers in machine learning, pattern recognition, and statistics. Most algorithms are memory resident, typically assuming a small data size. Recent data mining research has built on such work, developing scalable classification and prediction techniques capable of handling large amounts of disk-resident data. Classification has numerous applications, including fraud detection, target marketing, performance prediction, manufacturing, and medical diagnosis.

We start off by introducing the main ideas of classification in Section 8.1. In the rest of this chapter, you will learn the basic techniques for data classification such as how to build decision tree classifiers (Section 8.2), Bayesian classifiers (Section 8.3), and rule-based classifiers (Section 8.4). Section 8.5 discusses how to evaluate and compare different classifiers. Various measures of accuracy are given as well as techniques for obtaining reliable accuracy estimates. Methods for increasing classifier accuracy are presented in Section 8.6, including cases for when the data set is class imbalanced (i.e., where the main class of interest is rare).

8.1 Basic Concepts

We introduce the concept of classification in Section 8.1.1. Section 8.1.2 describes the general approach to classification as a two-step process. In the first step, we build a classification model based on previous data. In the second step, we determine if the model's accuracy is acceptable, and if so, we use the model to classify new data.

8.1.1 What Is Classification?

A bank loans officer needs analysis of her data to learn which loan applicants are "safe" and which are "risky" for the bank. A marketing manager at *AllElectronics* needs data analysis to help guess whether a customer with a given profile will buy a new computer. A medical researcher wants to analyze breast cancer data to predict which one of three specific treatments a patient should receive. In each of these examples, the data analysis task is **classification**, where a model or **classifier** is constructed to predict *class (categorical) labels*, such as "safe" or "risky" for the loan application data; "yes" or "no" for the marketing data; or "treatment A," "treatment B," or "treatment C" for the medical data. These categories can be represented by discrete values, where the ordering among values has no meaning. For example, the values 1, 2, and 3 may be used to represent treatments A, B, and C, where there is no ordering implied among this group of treatment regimes.

Suppose that the marketing manager wants to predict how much a given customer will spend during a sale at *AllElectronics*. This data analysis task is an example of **numeric prediction**, where the model constructed predicts a *continuous-valued function*, or *ordered value*, as opposed to a class label. This model is a **predictor**. **Regression analysis** is a statistical methodology that is most often used for numeric prediction; hence the two terms tend to be used synonymously, although other methods for numeric prediction exist. Classification and numeric prediction are the two major types of **prediction problems**. This chapter focuses on classification.

8.1.2 General Approach to Classification

"How does classification work?" **Data classification** is a two-step process, consisting of a *learning step* (where a classification model is constructed) and a *classification step* (where the model is used to predict class labels for given data). The process is shown for the loan application data of Figure 8.1. (The data are simplified for illustrative purposes. In reality, we may expect many more attributes to be considered.

In the first step, a classifier is built describing a predetermined set of data classes or concepts. This is the **learning step** (or training phase), where a classification algorithm builds the classifier by analyzing or "learning from" a **training set** made up of database tuples and their associated class labels. A tuple, X, is represented by an n-dimensional **attribute vector**, $X = (x_1, x_2, \ldots, x_n)$, depicting n measurements made on the tuple from n database attributes, respectively, $A_1, A_2, \ldots, A_n$.[1] Each tuple, X, is assumed to belong to a predefined class as determined by another database attribute called the **class label attribute**. The class label attribute is discrete-valued and unordered. It is *categorical* (or nominal) in that each value serves as a category or class. The individual tuples making up the training set are referred to as **training tuples** and are randomly sampled from the database under analysis. In the context of classification, data tuples can be referred to as *samples, examples, instances, data points*, or *objects*.[2]

---

[1] Each attribute represents a "feature" of X. Hence, the pattern recognition literature uses the term *feature vector* rather than *attribute vector*. In our discussion, we use the term attribute vector, and in our notation, any variable representing a vector is shown in bold italic font; measurements depicting the vector are shown in italic font (e.g., $X = (x_1, x_2, x_3)$).

[2] In the machine learning literature, training tuples are commonly referred to as *training samples*. Throughout this text, we prefer to use the term *tuples* instead of *samples*.

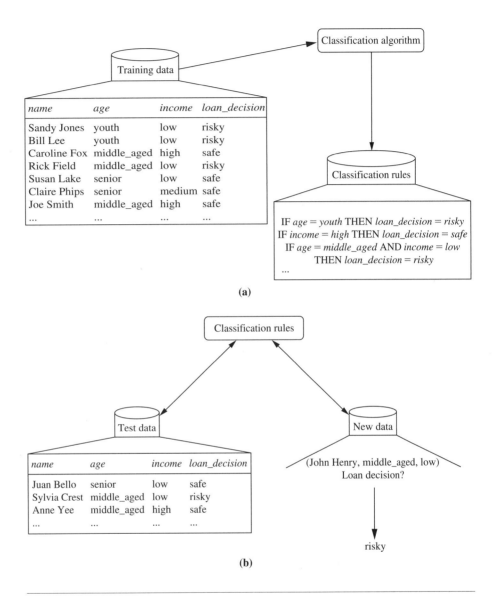

Figure 8.1 The data classification process: (a) *Learning*: Training data are analyzed by a classification algorithm. Here, the class label attribute is *loan_decision*, and the learned model or classifier is represented in the form of classification rules. (b) *Classification*: Test data are used to estimate the accuracy of the classification rules. If the accuracy is considered acceptable, the rules can be applied to the classification of new data tuples.

Because the class label of each training tuple *is provided*, this step is also known as **supervised learning** (i.e., the learning of the classifier is "supervised" in that it is told to which class each training tuple belongs). It contrasts with **unsupervised learning** (or **clustering**), in which the class label of each training tuple is not known, and the number or set of classes to be learned may not be known in advance. For example, if we did not have the *loan_decision* data available for the training set, we could use clustering to try to determine "groups of like tuples," which may correspond to risk groups within the loan application data. Clustering is the topic of Chapters 10 and 11.

This first step of the classification process can also be viewed as the learning of a mapping or function, $y = f(X)$, that can predict the associated class label y of a given tuple X. In this view, we wish to learn a mapping or function that separates the data classes. Typically, this mapping is represented in the form of classification rules, decision trees, or mathematical formulae. In our example, the mapping is represented as classification rules that identify loan applications as being either safe or risky (Figure 8.1a). The rules can be used to categorize future data tuples, as well as provide deeper insight into the data contents. They also provide a compressed data representation.

"*What about classification accuracy?*" In the second step (Figure 8.1b), the model is used for classification. First, the predictive accuracy of the classifier is estimated. If we were to use the training set to measure the classifier's accuracy, this estimate would likely be optimistic, because the classifier tends to **overfit** the data (i.e., during learning it may incorporate some particular anomalies of the training data that are not present in the general data set overall). Therefore, a **test set** is used, made up of **test tuples** and their associated class labels. They are independent of the training tuples, meaning that they were not used to construct the classifier.

The **accuracy** of a classifier on a given test set is the percentage of test set tuples that are correctly classified by the classifier. The associated class label of each test tuple is compared with the learned classifier's class prediction for that tuple. Section 8.5 describes several methods for estimating classifier accuracy. If the accuracy of the classifier is considered acceptable, the classifier can be used to classify future data tuples for which the class label is not known. (Such data are also referred to in the machine learning literature as "unknown" or "previously unseen" data.) For example, the classification rules learned in Figure 8.1(a) from the analysis of data from previous loan applications can be used to approve or reject new or future loan applicants.

8.2 Decision Tree Induction

Decision tree induction is the learning of decision trees from class-labeled training tuples. A **decision tree** is a flowchart-like tree structure, where each **internal node** (non-leaf node) denotes a test on an attribute, each **branch** represents an outcome of the test, and each **leaf node** (or *terminal node*) holds a class label. The topmost node in a tree is the **root** node. A typical decision tree is shown in Figure 8.2. It represents the concept *buys_computer*, that is, it predicts whether a customer at *AllElectronics* is

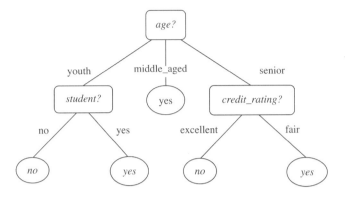

Figure 8.2 A decision tree for the concept *buys_computer*, indicating whether an *AllElectronics* customer is likely to purchase a computer. Each internal (nonleaf) node represents a test on an attribute. Each leaf node represents a class (either *buys_computer = yes* or *buys_computer = no*).

likely to purchase a computer. Internal nodes are denoted by rectangles, and leaf nodes are denoted by ovals. Some decision tree algorithms produce only *binary* trees (where each internal node branches to exactly two other nodes), whereas others can produce nonbinary trees.

"*How are decision trees used for classification?*" Given a tuple, *X*, for which the associated class label is unknown, the attribute values of the tuple are tested against the decision tree. A path is traced from the root to a leaf node, which holds the class prediction for that tuple. Decision trees can easily be converted to classification rules.

"*Why are decision tree classifiers so popular?*" The construction of decision tree classifiers does not require any domain knowledge or parameter setting, and therefore is appropriate for exploratory knowledge discovery. Decision trees can handle multidimensional data. Their representation of acquired knowledge in tree form is intuitive and generally easy to assimilate by humans. The learning and classification steps of decision tree induction are simple and fast. In general, decision tree classifiers have good accuracy. However, successful use may depend on the data at hand. Decision tree induction algorithms have been used for classification in many application areas such as medicine, manufacturing and production, financial analysis, astronomy, and molecular biology. Decision trees are the basis of several commercial rule induction systems.

In Section 8.2.1, we describe a basic algorithm for learning decision trees. During tree construction, *attribute selection measures* are used to select the attribute that best partitions the tuples into distinct classes. Popular measures of attribute selection are given in Section 8.2.2. When decision trees are built, many of the branches may reflect noise or outliers in the training data. *Tree pruning* attempts to identify and remove such branches, with the goal of improving classification accuracy on unseen data. Tree pruning is described in Section 8.2.3. Scalability issues for the induction of decision trees from large databases are discussed in Section 8.2.4. Section 8.2.5 presents a visual mining approach to decision tree induction.

8.2.1 Decision Tree Induction

During the late 1970s and early 1980s, J. Ross Quinlan, a researcher in machine learning, developed a decision tree algorithm known as **ID3** (Iterative Dichotomiser). This work expanded on earlier work on *concept learning systems*, described by E. B. Hunt, J. Marin, and P. T. Stone. Quinlan later presented **C4.5** (a successor of ID3), which became a benchmark to which newer supervised learning algorithms are often compared. In 1984, a group of statisticians (L. Breiman, J. Friedman, R. Olshen, and C. Stone) published the book *Classification and Regression Trees* (**CART**), which described the generation of binary decision trees. ID3 and CART were invented independently of one another at around the same time, yet follow a similar approach for learning decision trees from training tuples. These two cornerstone algorithms spawned a flurry of work on decision tree induction.

ID3, C4.5, and CART adopt a greedy (i.e., nonbacktracking) approach in which decision trees are constructed in a top-down recursive divide-and-conquer manner. Most algorithms for decision tree induction also follow a top-down approach, which starts with a training set of tuples and their associated class labels. The training set is recursively partitioned into smaller subsets as the tree is being built. A basic decision tree algorithm is summarized in Figure 8.3. At first glance, the algorithm may appear long, but fear not! It is quite straightforward. The strategy is as follows.

- The algorithm is called with three parameters: D, *attribute_list*, and *Attribute_selection_method*. We refer to D as a data partition. Initially, it is the complete set of training tuples and their associated class labels. The parameter *attribute_list* is a list of attributes describing the tuples. *Attribute_selection_method* specifies a heuristic procedure for selecting the attribute that "best" discriminates the given tuples according to class. This procedure employs an attribute selection measure such as information gain or the Gini index. Whether the tree is strictly binary is generally driven by the attribute selection measure. Some attribute selection measures, such as the Gini index, enforce the resulting tree to be binary. Others, like information gain, do not, therein allowing multiway splits (i.e., two or more branches to be grown from a node).

- The tree starts as a single node, N, representing the training tuples in D (step 1).[3]

---

[3]The partition of class-labeled training tuples at node N is the set of tuples that follow a path from the root of the tree to node N when being processed by the tree. This set is sometimes referred to in the literature as the *family* of tuples at node N. We have referred to this set as the "tuples represented at node N," "the tuples that reach node N," or simply "the tuples at node N." Rather than storing the actual tuples at a node, most implementations store pointers to these tuples.

Algorithm: Generate_decision_tree. Generate a decision tree from the training tuples of data partition, D.

Input:

- Data partition, D, which is a set of training tuples and their associated class labels;
- *attribute_list*, the set of candidate attributes;
- *Attribute_selection_method*, a procedure to determine the splitting criterion that "best" partitions the data tuples into individual classes. This criterion consists of a *splitting_attribute* and, possibly, either a *split-point* or *splitting subset*.

Output: A decision tree.

Method:

(1) create a node N;
(2) **if** tuples in D are all of the same class, C, **then**
(3)   return N as a leaf node labeled with the class C;
(4) **if** *attribute_list* is empty **then**
(5)   return N as a leaf node labeled with the majority class in D; // majority voting
(6) apply **Attribute_selection_method**(D, *attribute_list*) to **find** the "best" *splitting_criterion*;
(7) label node N with *splitting_criterion*;
(8) **if** *splitting_attribute* is discrete-valued **and**
       multiway splits allowed **then** // not restricted to binary trees
(9)   *attribute_list* ← *attribute_list* − *splitting_attribute*; // remove *splitting_attribute*
(10) **for each** outcome j of *splitting_criterion*
     // partition the tuples and grow subtrees for each partition
(11)   let D_j be the set of data tuples in D satisfying outcome j; // a partition
(12)   **if** D_j is empty **then**
(13)   attach a leaf labeled with the majority class in D to node N;
(14)   **else** attach the node returned by **Generate_decision_tree**(D_j, *attribute_list*) to node N;
     endfor
(15) return N;

Figure 8.3 Basic algorithm for inducing a decision tree from training tuples.

- If the tuples in D are all of the same class, then node N becomes a leaf and is labeled with that class (steps 2 and 3). Note that steps 4 and 5 are terminating conditions. All terminating conditions are explained at the end of the algorithm.

- Otherwise, the algorithm calls *Attribute_selection_method* to determine the **splitting criterion**. The splitting criterion tells us which attribute to test at node N by determining the "best" way to separate or partition the tuples in D into individual classes (step 6). The splitting criterion also tells us which branches to grow from node N with respect to the outcomes of the chosen test. More specifically, the splitting criterion indicates the **splitting attribute** and may also indicate either a **split-point** or a **splitting subset**. The splitting criterion is determined so that, ideally, the resulting partitions at each branch are as "pure" as possible. A partition is **pure** if all the tuples in it belong to the same class. In other words, if we split up the tuples in D according to the mutually exclusive outcomes of the splitting criterion, we hope for the resulting partitions to be as pure as possible.

▫ The node N is labeled with the splitting criterion, which serves as a test at the node (step 7). A branch is grown from node N for each of the outcomes of the splitting criterion. The tuples in D are partitioned accordingly (steps 10 to 11). There are three possible scenarios, as illustrated in Figure 8.4. Let A be the splitting attribute. A has v distinct values, $\{a_1, a_2, \ldots, a_v\}$, based on the training data.

1. *A is discrete-valued:* In this case, the outcomes of the test at node N correspond directly to the known values of A. A branch is created for each known value, a_j, of A and labeled with that value (Figure 8.4a). Partition D_j is the subset of class-labeled tuples in D having value a_j of A. Because all the tuples in a

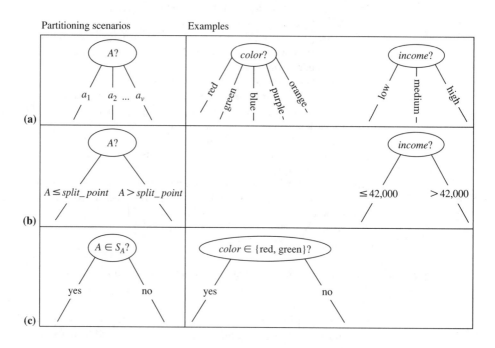

Figure 8.4 This figure shows three possibilities for partitioning tuples based on the splitting criterion, each with examples. Let A be the splitting attribute. (a) If A is discrete-valued, then one branch is grown for each known value of A. (b) If A is continuous-valued, then two branches are grown, corresponding to A ≤ *split_point* and A > *split_point*. (c) If A is discrete-valued and a binary tree must be produced, then the test is of the form $A \in S_A$, where S_A is the splitting subset for A.

given partition have the same value for A, A need not be considered in any future partitioning of the tuples. Therefore, it is removed from *attribute_list* (steps 8 and 9).

2. *A is continuous-valued:* In this case, the test at node N has two possible outcomes, corresponding to the conditions $A \leq split\_point$ and $A > split\_point$, respectively, where *split_point* is the split-point returned by *Attribute_selection_method* as part of the splitting criterion. (In practice, the split-point, a, is often taken as the midpoint of two known adjacent values of A and therefore may not actually be a preexisting value of A from the training data.) Two branches are grown from N and labeled according to the previous outcomes (Figure 8.4b). The tuples are partitioned such that D_1 holds the subset of class-labeled tuples in D for which $A \leq split\_point$, while D_2 holds the rest.

3. *A is discrete-valued* and a *binary tree* must be produced (as dictated by the attribute selection measure or algorithm being used): The test at node N is of the form "$A \in S_A$?," where S_A is the splitting subset for A, returned by *Attribute_selection_method* as part of the splitting criterion. It is a subset of the known values of A. If a given tuple has value a_j of A and if $a_j \in S_A$, then the test at node N is satisfied. Two branches are grown from N (Figure 8.4c). By convention, the left branch out of N is labeled *yes* so that D_1 corresponds to the subset of class-labeled tuples in D that satisfy the test. The right branch out of N is labeled *no* so that D_2 corresponds to the subset of class-labeled tuples from D that do not satisfy the test.

▪ The algorithm uses the same process recursively to form a decision tree for the tuples at each resulting partition, D_j, of D (step 14).

▪ The recursive partitioning stops only when any one of the following terminating conditions is true:

  1. All the tuples in partition D (represented at node N) belong to the same class (steps 2 and 3).

  2. There are no remaining attributes on which the tuples may be further partitioned (step 4). In this case, **majority voting** is employed (step 5). This involves converting node N into a leaf and labeling it with the most common class in D. Alternatively, the class distribution of the node tuples may be stored.

  3. There are no tuples for a given branch, that is, a partition D_j is empty (step 12). In this case, a leaf is created with the majority class in D (step 13).

▪ The resulting decision tree is returned (step 15).

The computational complexity of the algorithm given training set D is $O(n \times |D| \times log(|D|))$, where n is the number of attributes describing the tuples in D and $|D|$ is the number of training tuples in D. This means that the computational cost of growing a tree grows at most $n \times |D| \times log(|D|)$ with $|D|$ tuples. The proof is left as an exercise for the reader.

Incremental versions of decision tree induction have also been proposed. When given new training data, these restructure the decision tree acquired from learning on previous training data, rather than relearning a new tree from scratch.

Differences in decision tree algorithms include how the attributes are selected in creating the tree (Section 8.2.2) and the mechanisms used for pruning (Section 8.2.3). The basic algorithm described earlier requires one pass over the training tuples in D for each level of the tree. This can lead to long training times and lack of available memory when dealing with large databases. Improvements regarding the scalability of decision tree induction are discussed in Section 8.2.4. Section 8.2.5 presents a visual interactive approach to decision tree construction. A discussion of strategies for extracting rules from decision trees is given in Section 8.4.2 regarding rule-based classification.

8.2.2 Attribute Selection Measures

An **attribute selection measure** is a heuristic for selecting the splitting criterion that "best" separates a given data partition, D, of class-labeled training tuples into individual classes. If we were to split D into smaller partitions according to the outcomes of the splitting criterion, ideally each partition would be pure (i.e., all the tuples that fall into a given partition would belong to the same class). Conceptually, the "best" splitting criterion is the one that most closely results in such a scenario. Attribute selection measures are also known as **splitting rules** because they determine how the tuples at a given node are to be split.

The attribute selection measure provides a ranking for each attribute describing the given training tuples. The attribute having the best score for the measure[4] is chosen as the *splitting attribute* for the given tuples. If the splitting attribute is continuous-valued or if we are restricted to binary trees, then, respectively, either a *split point* or a *splitting subset* must also be determined as part of the splitting criterion. The tree node created for partition D is labeled with the splitting criterion, branches are grown for each outcome of the criterion, and the tuples are partitioned accordingly. This section describes three popular attribute selection measures—*information gain, gain ratio*, and *Gini index*.

The notation used herein is as follows. Let D, the data partition, be a training set of class-labeled tuples. Suppose the class label attribute has m distinct values defining m distinct classes, C_i (for $i = 1, \ldots, m$). Let $C_{i,D}$ be the set of tuples of class C_i in D. Let $|D|$ and $|C_{i,D}|$ denote the number of tuples in D and $C_{i,D}$, respectively.

Information Gain

ID3 uses **information gain** as its attribute selection measure. This measure is based on pioneering work by Claude Shannon on information theory, which studied the value or "information content" of messages. Let node N represent or hold the tuples of partition D. The attribute with the highest information gain is chosen as the splitting attribute for node N. This attribute minimizes the information needed to classify the tuples in the

---

[4]Depending on the measure, either the highest or lowest score is chosen as the best (i.e., some measures strive to maximize while others strive to minimize).

resulting partitions and reflects the least randomness or "impurity" in these partitions. Such an approach minimizes the expected number of tests needed to classify a given tuple and guarantees that a simple (but not necessarily the simplest) tree is found.

The expected information needed to classify a tuple in D is given by

$$Info(D) = -\sum_{i=1}^{m} p_i \log_2(p_i), \qquad (8.1)$$

where p_i is the nonzero probability that an arbitrary tuple in D belongs to class C_i and is estimated by $|C_{i,D}|/|D|$. A log function to the base 2 is used, because the information is encoded in bits. $Info(D)$ is just the average amount of information needed to identify the class label of a tuple in D. Note that, at this point, the information we have is based solely on the proportions of tuples of each class. $Info(D)$ is also known as the **entropy** of D.

Now, suppose we were to partition the tuples in D on some attribute A having v distinct values, $\{a_1, a_2, \ldots, a_v\}$, as observed from the training data. If A is discrete-valued, these values correspond directly to the v outcomes of a test on A. Attribute A can be used to split D into v partitions or subsets, $\{D_1, D_2, \ldots, D_v\}$, where D_j contains those tuples in D that have outcome a_j of A. These partitions would correspond to the branches grown from node N. Ideally, we would like this partitioning to produce an exact classification of the tuples. That is, we would like for each partition to be pure. However, it is quite likely that the partitions will be impure (e.g., where a partition may contain a collection of tuples from different classes rather than from a single class).

How much more information would we still need (after the partitioning) to arrive at an exact classification? This amount is measured by

$$Info_A(D) = \sum_{j=1}^{v} \frac{|D_j|}{|D|} \times Info(D_j). \qquad (8.2)$$

The term $\frac{|D_j|}{|D|}$ acts as the weight of the jth partition. $Info_A(D)$ is the expected information required to classify a tuple from D based on the partitioning by A. The smaller the expected information (still) required, the greater the purity of the partitions.

Information gain is defined as the difference between the original information requirement (i.e., based on just the proportion of classes) and the new requirement (i.e., obtained after partitioning on A). That is,

$$Gain(A) = Info(D) - Info_A(D). \qquad (8.3)$$

In other words, $Gain(A)$ tells us how much would be gained by branching on A. It is the expected reduction in the information requirement caused by knowing the value of A. The attribute A with the highest information gain, $Gain(A)$, is chosen as the splitting attribute at node N. This is equivalent to saying that we want to partition on the attribute A that would do the "best classification," so that the amount of information still required to finish classifying the tuples is minimal (i.e., minimum $Info_A(D)$).

Table 8.1 Class-Labeled Training Tuples from the *AllElectronics* Customer Database

RID	age	income	student	credit_rating	Class: buys_computer
1	youth	high	no	fair	no
2	youth	high	no	excellent	no
3	middle_aged	high	no	fair	yes
4	senior	medium	no	fair	yes
5	senior	low	yes	fair	yes
6	senior	low	yes	excellent	no
7	middle_aged	low	yes	excellent	yes
8	youth	medium	no	fair	no
9	youth	low	yes	fair	yes
10	senior	medium	yes	fair	yes
11	youth	medium	yes	excellent	yes
12	middle_aged	medium	no	excellent	yes
13	middle_aged	high	yes	fair	yes
14	senior	medium	no	excellent	no

Example 8.1 **Induction of a decision tree using information gain.** Table 8.1 presents a training set, D, of class-labeled tuples randomly selected from the *AllElectronics* customer database. (The data are adapted from Quinlan [Qui86]. In this example, each attribute is discrete-valued. Continuous-valued attributes have been generalized.) The class label attribute, *buys_computer*, has two distinct values (namely, {*yes, no*}); therefore, there are two distinct classes (i.e., $m = 2$). Let class C_1 correspond to *yes* and class C_2 correspond to *no*. There are nine tuples of class *yes* and five tuples of class *no*. A (root) node N is created for the tuples in D. To find the splitting criterion for these tuples, we must compute the information gain of each attribute. We first use Eq. (8.1) to compute the expected information needed to classify a tuple in D:

$$Info(D) = -\frac{9}{14} \log_2 \left(\frac{9}{14}\right) - \frac{5}{14} \log_2 \left(\frac{5}{14}\right) = 0.940 \text{ bits.}$$

Next, we need to compute the expected information requirement for each attribute. Let's start with the attribute *age*. We need to look at the distribution of *yes* and *no* tuples for each category of *age*. For the *age* category "youth," there are two *yes* tuples and three *no* tuples. For the category "middle_aged," there are four *yes* tuples and zero *no* tuples. For the category "senior," there are three *yes* tuples and two *no* tuples. Using Eq. (8.2), the expected information needed to classify a tuple in D if the tuples are partitioned according to *age* is

$$Info_{age}(D) = \frac{5}{14} \times \left(-\frac{2}{5} \log_2 \frac{2}{5} - \frac{3}{5} \log_2 \frac{3}{5}\right)$$

$$+ \frac{4}{14} \times \left(-\frac{4}{4} \log_2 \frac{4}{4} \right)$$

$$+ \frac{5}{14} \times \left(-\frac{3}{5} \log_2 \frac{3}{5} - \frac{2}{5} \log_2 \frac{2}{5} \right)$$

$$= 0.694 \text{ bits.}$$

Hence, the gain in information from such a partitioning would be

$$Gain(age) = Info(D) - Info_{age}(D) = 0.940 - 0.694 = 0.246 \text{ bits.}$$

Similarly, we can compute $Gain(income) = 0.029$ bits, $Gain(student) = 0.151$ bits, and $Gain(credit\_rating) = 0.048$ bits. Because *age* has the highest information gain among the attributes, it is selected as the splitting attribute. Node N is labeled with *age*, and branches are grown for each of the attribute's values. The tuples are then partitioned accordingly, as shown in Figure 8.5. Notice that the tuples falling into the partition for *age* = *middle_aged* all belong to the same class. Because they all belong to class *"yes,"* a leaf should therefore be created at the end of this branch and labeled *"yes."* The final decision tree returned by the algorithm was shown earlier in Figure 8.2.   ∎

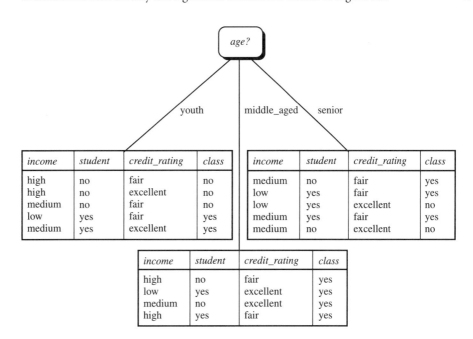

Figure 8.5 The attribute *age* has the highest information gain and therefore becomes the splitting attribute at the root node of the decision tree. Branches are grown for each outcome of *age*. The tuples are shown partitioned accordingly.

"But how can we compute the information gain of an attribute that is continuous-valued, unlike in the example?" Suppose, instead, that we have an attribute A that is continuous-valued, rather than discrete-valued. (For example, suppose that instead of the discretized version of *age* from the example, we have the raw values for this attribute.) For such a scenario, we must determine the "best" **split-point** for A, where the split-point is a threshold on A.

We first sort the values of A in increasing order. Typically, the midpoint between each pair of adjacent values is considered as a possible split-point. Therefore, given v values of A, then $v - 1$ possible splits are evaluated. For example, the midpoint between the values a_i and a_{i+1} of A is

$$\frac{a_i + a_{i+1}}{2}. \tag{8.4}$$

If the values of A are sorted in advance, then determining the best split for A requires only one pass through the values. For each possible split-point for A, we evaluate $Info_A(D)$, where the number of partitions is two, that is, $v = 2$ (or $j = 1, 2$) in Eq. (8.2). The point with the minimum expected information requirement for A is selected as the *split_point* for A. D_1 is the set of tuples in D satisfying $A \leq split\_point$, and D_2 is the set of tuples in D satisfying $A > split\_point$.

Gain Ratio

The information gain measure is biased toward tests with many outcomes. That is, it prefers to select attributes having a large number of values. For example, consider an attribute that acts as a unique identifier such as *product_ID*. A split on *product_ID* would result in a large number of partitions (as many as there are values), each one containing just one tuple. Because each partition is pure, the information required to classify data set D based on this partitioning would be $Info_{product\_ID}(D) = 0$. Therefore, the information gained by partitioning on this attribute is maximal. Clearly, such a partitioning is useless for classification.

C4.5, a successor of ID3, uses an extension to information gain known as *gain ratio*, which attempts to overcome this bias. It applies a kind of normalization to information gain using a "split information" value defined analogously with $Info(D)$ as

$$SplitInfo_A(D) = -\sum_{j=1}^{v} \frac{|D_j|}{|D|} \times \log_2 \left(\frac{|D_j|}{|D|} \right). \tag{8.5}$$

This value represents the potential information generated by splitting the training data set, D, into v partitions, corresponding to the v outcomes of a test on attribute A. Note that, for each outcome, it considers the number of tuples having that outcome with respect to the total number of tuples in D. It differs from information gain, which measures the information with respect to classification that is acquired based on the same partitioning. The gain ratio is defined as

$$GainRatio(A) = \frac{Gain(A)}{SplitInfo_A(D)}. \quad (8.6)$$

The attribute with the maximum gain ratio is selected as the splitting attribute. Note, however, that as the split information approaches 0, the ratio becomes unstable. A constraint is added to avoid this, whereby the information gain of the test selected must be large—at least as great as the average gain over all tests examined.

Example 8.2 **Computation of gain ratio for the attribute *income*.** A test on *income* splits the data of Table 8.1 into three partitions, namely *low*, *medium*, and *high*, containing four, six, and four tuples, respectively. To compute the gain ratio of *income*, we first use Eq. (8.5) to obtain

$$SplitInfo_{income}(D) = -\frac{4}{14} \times \log_2\left(\frac{4}{14}\right) - \frac{6}{14} \times \log_2\left(\frac{6}{14}\right) - \frac{4}{14} \times \log_2\left(\frac{4}{14}\right)$$

$$= 1.557.$$

From Example 8.1, we have $Gain(income) = 0.029$. Therefore, $GainRatio(income) = 0.029/1.557 = 0.019$. ∎

Gini Index

The Gini index is used in CART. Using the notation previously described, the Gini index measures the impurity of D, a data partition or set of training tuples, as

$$Gini(D) = 1 - \sum_{i=1}^{m} p_i^2, \quad (8.7)$$

where p_i is the probability that a tuple in D belongs to class C_i and is estimated by $|C_{i,D}|/|D|$. The sum is computed over m classes.

The Gini index considers a binary split for each attribute. Let's first consider the case where A is a discrete-valued attribute having v distinct values, $\{a_1, a_2, \ldots, a_v\}$, occurring in D. To determine the best binary split on A, we examine all the possible subsets that can be formed using known values of A. Each subset, S_A, can be considered as a binary test for attribute A of the form "$A \in S_A$?" Given a tuple, this test is satisfied if the value of A for the tuple is among the values listed in S_A. If A has v possible values, then there are 2^v possible subsets. For example, if *income* has three possible values, namely {*low, medium, high*}, then the possible subsets are {*low, medium, high*}, {*low, medium*}, {*low, high*}, {*medium, high*}, {*low*}, {*medium*}, {*high*}, and {}. We exclude the power set, {*low, medium, high*}, and the empty set from consideration since, conceptually, they do not represent a split. Therefore, there are $(2^v - 2)/2$ possible ways to form two partitions of the data, D, based on a binary split on A.

When considering a binary split, we compute a weighted sum of the impurity of each resulting partition. For example, if a binary split on A partitions D into D_1 and D_2, the Gini index of D given that partitioning is

$$Gini_A(D) = \frac{|D_1|}{|D|} Gini(D_1) + \frac{|D_2|}{|D|} Gini(D_2). \qquad (8.8)$$

For each attribute, each of the possible binary splits is considered. For a discrete-valued attribute, the subset that gives the minimum Gini index for that attribute is selected as its splitting subset.

For continuous-valued attributes, each possible split-point must be considered. The strategy is similar to that described earlier for information gain, where the midpoint between each pair of (sorted) adjacent values is taken as a possible split-point. The point giving the minimum Gini index for a given (continuous-valued) attribute is taken as the split-point of that attribute. Recall that for a possible split-point of A, D_1 is the set of tuples in D satisfying $A \leq split\_point$, and D_2 is the set of tuples in D satisfying $A > split\_point$.

The reduction in impurity that would be incurred by a binary split on a discrete- or continuous-valued attribute A is

$$\Delta Gini(A) = Gini(D) - Gini_A(D). \qquad (8.9)$$

The attribute that maximizes the reduction in impurity (or, equivalently, has the minimum Gini index) is selected as the splitting attribute. This attribute and either its splitting subset (for a discrete-valued splitting attribute) or split-point (for a continuous-valued splitting attribute) together form the splitting criterion.

Example 8.3 **Induction of a decision tree using the Gini index.** Let D be the training data shown earlier in Table 8.1, where there are nine tuples belonging to the class *buys_computer* = *yes* and the remaining five tuples belong to the class *buys_computer* = *no*. A (root) node N is created for the tuples in D. We first use Eq. (8.7) for the Gini index to compute the impurity of D:

$$Gini(D) = 1 - \left(\frac{9}{14}\right)^2 - \left(\frac{5}{14}\right)^2 = 0.459.$$

To find the splitting criterion for the tuples in D, we need to compute the Gini index for each attribute. Let's start with the attribute *income* and consider each of the possible splitting subsets. Consider the subset {*low, medium*}. This would result in 10 tuples in partition D_1 satisfying the condition "*income* ∈ {*low, medium*}." The remaining four tuples of D would be assigned to partition D_2. The Gini index value computed based on this partitioning is

$$Gini_{income \in \{low, medium\}}(D)$$

$$= \frac{10}{14}Gini(D_1) + \frac{4}{14}Gini(D_2)$$

$$= \frac{10}{14}\left(1 - \left(\frac{7}{10}\right)^2 - \left(\frac{3}{10}\right)^2\right) + \frac{4}{14}\left(1 - \left(\frac{2}{4}\right)^2 - \left(\frac{2}{4}\right)^2\right)$$

$$= 0.443$$

$$= Gini_{income \in \{high\}}(D).$$

Similarly, the Gini index values for splits on the remaining subsets are 0.458 (for the subsets {*low, high*} and {*medium*}) and 0.450 (for the subsets {*medium, high*} and {*low*}). Therefore, the best binary split for attribute *income* is on {*low, medium*} (or {*high*}) because it minimizes the Gini index. Evaluating *age*, we obtain {*youth, senior*} (or {*middle_aged*}) as the best split for *age* with a Gini index of 0.375; the attributes *student* and *credit_rating* are both binary, with Gini index values of 0.367 and 0.429, respectively.

The attribute *age* and splitting subset {*youth, senior*} therefore give the minimum Gini index overall, with a reduction in impurity of $0.459 - 0.357 = 0.102$. The binary split "*age* $\in$ {*youth, senior*}?" results in the maximum reduction in impurity of the tuples in D and is returned as the splitting criterion. Node N is labeled with the criterion, two branches are grown from it, and the tuples are partitioned accordingly. ∎

Other Attribute Selection Measures

This section on attribute selection measures was not intended to be exhaustive. We have shown three measures that are commonly used for building decision trees. These measures are not without their biases. Information gain, as we saw, is biased toward multivalued attributes. Although the gain ratio adjusts for this bias, it tends to prefer unbalanced splits in which one partition is much smaller than the others. The Gini index is biased toward multivalued attributes and has difficulty when the number of classes is large. It also tends to favor tests that result in equal-size partitions and purity in both partitions. Although biased, these measures give reasonably good results in practice.

Many other attribute selection measures have been proposed. CHAID, a decision tree algorithm that is popular in marketing, uses an attribute selection measure that is based on the statistical χ^2 test for independence. Other measures include C-SEP (which performs better than information gain and the Gini index in certain cases) and G-statistic (an information theoretic measure that is a close approximation to χ^2 distribution).

Attribute selection measures based on the **Minimum Description Length (MDL)** principle have the least bias toward multivalued attributes. MDL-based measures use encoding techniques to define the "best" decision tree as the one that requires the fewest number of bits to both (1) encode the tree and (2) encode the exceptions to the tree (i.e., cases that are not correctly classified by the tree). Its main idea is that the simplest of solutions is preferred.

Other attribute selection measures consider **multivariate splits** (i.e., where the partitioning of tuples is based on a *combination* of attributes, rather than on a single attribute). The CART system, for example, can find multivariate splits based on a linear combination of attributes. Multivariate splits are a form of **attribute** (or feature) **construction**, where new attributes are created based on the existing ones. (Attribute construction was also discussed in Chapter 3, as a form of data transformation.) These other measures mentioned here are beyond the scope of this book. Additional references are given in the bibliographic notes at the end of this chapter (Section 8.9).

"Which attribute selection measure is the best?" All measures have some bias. It has been shown that the time complexity of decision tree induction generally increases exponentially with tree height. Hence, measures that tend to produce shallower trees (e.g., with multiway rather than binary splits, and that favor more balanced splits) may be preferred. However, some studies have found that shallow trees tend to have a large number of leaves and higher error rates. Despite several comparative studies, no one attribute selection measure has been found to be significantly superior to others. Most measures give quite good results.

8.2.3 Tree Pruning

When a decision tree is built, many of the branches will reflect anomalies in the training data due to noise or outliers. Tree pruning methods address this problem of *overfitting* the data. Such methods typically use statistical measures to remove the least-reliable branches. An unpruned tree and a pruned version of it are shown in Figure 8.6. Pruned trees tend to be smaller and less complex and, thus, easier to comprehend. They are usually faster and better at correctly classifying independent test data (i.e., of previously unseen tuples) than unpruned trees.

"How does tree pruning work?" There are two common approaches to tree pruning: *prepruning* and *postpruning*.

In the **prepruning** approach, a tree is "pruned" by halting its construction early (e.g., by deciding not to further split or partition the subset of training tuples at a given node). Upon halting, the node becomes a leaf. The leaf may hold the most frequent class among the subset tuples or the probability distribution of those tuples.

When constructing a tree, measures such as statistical significance, information gain, Gini index, and so on, can be used to assess the goodness of a split. If partitioning the tuples at a node would result in a split that falls below a prespecified threshold, then further partitioning of the given subset is halted. There are difficulties, however, in choosing an appropriate threshold. High thresholds could result in oversimplified trees, whereas low thresholds could result in very little simplification.

The second and more common approach is **postpruning**, which removes subtrees from a "fully grown" tree. A subtree at a given node is pruned by removing its branches and replacing it with a leaf. The leaf is labeled with the most frequent class among the subtree being replaced. For example, notice the subtree at node "A_3?" in the unpruned

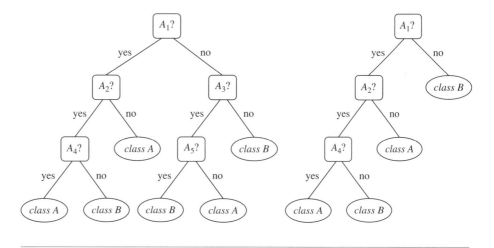

Figure 8.6 An unpruned decision tree and a pruned version of it.

tree of Figure 8.6. Suppose that the most common class within this subtree is "*class B.*" In the pruned version of the tree, the subtree in question is pruned by replacing it with the leaf "*class B.*"

The **cost complexity** pruning algorithm used in CART is an example of the postpruning approach. This approach considers the cost complexity of a tree to be a function of the number of leaves in the tree and the error rate of the tree (where the **error rate** is the percentage of tuples misclassified by the tree). It starts from the bottom of the tree. For each internal node, N, it computes the cost complexity of the subtree at N, and the cost complexity of the subtree at N if it were to be pruned (i.e., replaced by a leaf node). The two values are compared. If pruning the subtree at node N would result in a smaller cost complexity, then the subtree is pruned. Otherwise, it is kept.

A **pruning set** of class-labeled tuples is used to estimate cost complexity. This set is independent of the training set used to build the unpruned tree and of any test set used for accuracy estimation. The algorithm generates a set of progressively pruned trees. In general, the smallest decision tree that minimizes the cost complexity is preferred.

C4.5 uses a method called **pessimistic pruning**, which is similar to the cost complexity method in that it also uses error rate estimates to make decisions regarding subtree pruning. Pessimistic pruning, however, does not require the use of a prune set. Instead, it uses the training set to estimate error rates. Recall that an estimate of accuracy or error based on the training set is overly optimistic and, therefore, strongly biased. The pessimistic pruning method therefore adjusts the error rates obtained from the training set by adding a penalty, so as to counter the bias incurred.

Rather than pruning trees based on estimated error rates, we can prune trees based on the number of bits required to encode them. The "best" pruned tree is the one that minimizes the number of encoding bits. This method adopts the MDL principle, which was briefly introduced in Section 8.2.2. The basic idea is that the simplest solution is preferred. Unlike cost complexity pruning, it does not require an independent set of tuples.

Alternatively, prepruning and postpruning may be interleaved for a combined approach. Postpruning requires more computation than prepruning, yet generally leads to a more reliable tree. No single pruning method has been found to be superior over all others. Although some pruning methods do depend on the availability of additional data for pruning, this is usually not a concern when dealing with large databases.

Although pruned trees tend to be more compact than their unpruned counterparts, they may still be rather large and complex. Decision trees can suffer from *repetition* and *replication* (Figure 8.7), making them overwhelming to interpret. **Repetition** occurs when an attribute is repeatedly tested along a given branch of the tree (e.g., "*age < 60?*,"

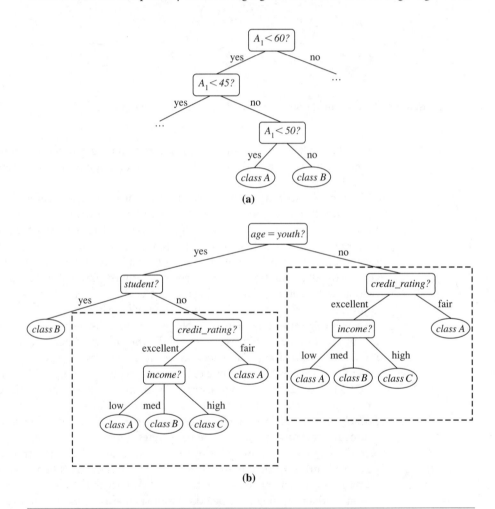

Figure 8.7 An example of: (a) subtree **repetition**, where an attribute is repeatedly tested along a given branch of the tree (e.g., *age*) and (b) subtree **replication**, where duplicate subtrees exist within a tree (e.g., the subtree headed by the node "*credit_rating?*").

followed by "*age < 45?*," and so on). In **replication**, duplicate subtrees exist within the tree. These situations can impede the accuracy and comprehensibility of a decision tree. The use of multivariate splits (splits based on a combination of attributes) can prevent these problems. Another approach is to use a different form of knowledge representation, such as rules, instead of decision trees. This is described in Section 8.4.2, which shows how a *rule-based classifier* can be constructed by extracting IF-THEN rules from a decision tree.

8.2.4 Scalability and Decision Tree Induction

"What if D, the disk-resident training set of class-labeled tuples, does not fit in memory? In other words, how scalable is decision tree induction?" The efficiency of existing decision tree algorithms, such as ID3, C4.5, and CART, has been well established for relatively small data sets. Efficiency becomes an issue of concern when these algorithms are applied to the mining of very large real-world databases. The pioneering decision tree algorithms that we have discussed so far have the restriction that the training tuples should reside *in memory*.

In data mining applications, very large training sets of millions of tuples are common. Most often, the training data will not fit in memory! Therefore, decision tree construction becomes inefficient due to swapping of the training tuples in and out of main and cache memories. More scalable approaches, capable of handling training data that are too large to fit in memory, are required. Earlier strategies to "save space" included discretizing continuous-valued attributes and sampling data at each node. These techniques, however, still assume that the training set can fit in memory.

Several scalable decision tree induction methods have been introduced in recent studies. RainForest, for example, adapts to the amount of main memory available and applies to any decision tree induction algorithm. The method maintains an **AVC-set** (where "AVC" stands for "*Attribute-Value, Classlabel*") for each attribute, at each tree node, describing the training tuples at the node. The AVC-set of an attribute A at node N gives the class label counts for each value of A for the tuples at N. Figure 8.8 shows AVC-sets for the tuple data of Table 8.1. The set of all AVC-sets at a node N is the **AVC-group** of N. The size of an AVC-set for attribute A at node N depends only on the number of distinct values of A and the number of classes in the set of tuples at N. Typically, this size should fit in memory, even for real-world data. RainForest also has techniques, however, for handling the case where the AVC-group does not fit in memory. Therefore, the method has high scalability for decision tree induction in very large data sets.

BOAT (Bootstrapped Optimistic Algorithm for Tree construction) is a decision tree algorithm that takes a completely different approach to scalability—it is not based on the use of any special data structures. Instead, it uses a statistical technique known as "bootstrapping" (Section 8.5.4) to create several smaller samples (or subsets) of the given training data, each of which fits in memory. Each subset is used to construct a tree, resulting in several trees. The trees are examined and used to construct a new tree, T', that turns out to be "very close" to the tree that would have been generated if all the original training data had fit in memory.

age	buys_computer	
	yes	no
youth	2	3
middle_aged	4	0
senior	3	2

income	buys_computer	
	yes	no
low	3	1
medium	4	2
high	2	2

student	buys_computer	
	yes	no
yes	6	1
no	3	4

credit_ratting	buys_computer	
	yes	no
fair	6	2
excellent	3	3

Figure 8.8 The use of data structures to hold aggregate information regarding the training data (e.g., these AVC-sets describing Table 8.1's data) are one approach to improving the scalability of decision tree induction.

BOAT can use any attribute selection measure that selects binary splits and that is based on the notion of purity of partitions such as the Gini index. BOAT uses a lower bound on the attribute selection measure to detect if this "very good" tree, T', is different from the "real" tree, T, that would have been generated using all of the data. It refines T' to arrive at T.

BOAT usually requires only two scans of D. This is quite an improvement, even in comparison to traditional decision tree algorithms (e.g., the basic algorithm in Figure 8.3), which require one scan per tree level! BOAT was found to be two to three times faster than RainForest, while constructing exactly the same tree. An additional advantage of BOAT is that it can be used for incremental updates. That is, BOAT can take new insertions and deletions for the training data and update the decision tree to reflect these changes, without having to reconstruct the tree from scratch.

8.2.5 Visual Mining for Decision Tree Induction

"Are there any interactive approaches to decision tree induction that allow us to visualize the data and the tree as it is being constructed? Can we use any knowledge of our data to help in building the tree?" In this section, you will learn about an approach to decision tree induction that supports these options. **Perception-based classification (PBC)** is an interactive approach based on multidimensional visualization techniques and allows the user to incorporate background knowledge about the data when building a decision tree. By visually interacting with the data, the user is also likely to develop a deeper understanding of the data. The resulting trees tend to be smaller than those built using traditional decision tree induction methods and so are easier to interpret, while achieving about the same accuracy.

"How can the data be visualized to support interactive decision tree construction?" PBC uses a pixel-oriented approach to view multidimensional data with its class label

information. The circle segments approach is adapted, which maps d-dimensional data objects to a circle that is partitioned into d segments, each representing one attribute (Section 2.3.1). Here, an attribute value of a data object is mapped to one colored pixel, reflecting the object's class label. This mapping is done for each attribute–value pair of each data object. Sorting is done for each attribute to determine the arrangement order within a segment. For example, attribute values within a given segment may be organized so as to display homogeneous (with respect to class label) regions within the same attribute value. The amount of training data that can be visualized at one time is approximately determined by the product of the number of attributes and the number of data objects.

The PBC system displays a split screen, consisting of a Data Interaction window and a Knowledge Interaction window (Figure 8.9). The Data Interaction window displays the circle segments of the data under examination, while the Knowledge Interaction window displays the decision tree constructed so far. Initially, the complete training set is visualized in the Data Interaction window, while the Knowledge Interaction window displays an empty decision tree.

Traditional decision tree algorithms allow only binary splits for numeric attributes. PBC, however, allows the user to specify multiple split-points, resulting in multiple branches to be grown from a single tree node.

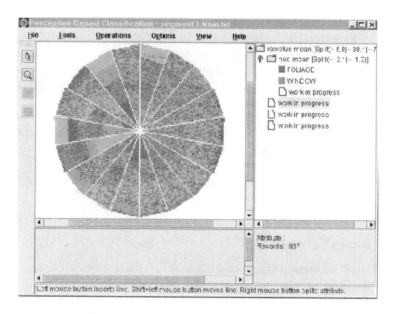

Figure 8.9 A screenshot of PBC, a system for interactive decision tree construction. Multidimensional training data are viewed as circle segments in the Data Interaction window (*left*). The Knowledge Interaction window (*right*) displays the current decision tree. *Source:* From Ankerst, Elsen, Ester, and Kriegel [AEEK99].

A tree is interactively constructed as follows. The user visualizes the multidimensional data in the Data Interaction window and selects a splitting attribute and one or more split-points. The current decision tree in the Knowledge Interaction window is expanded. The user selects a node of the decision tree. The user may either assign a class label to the node (which makes the node a leaf) or request the visualization of the training data corresponding to the node. This leads to a new visualization of every attribute except the ones used for splitting criteria on the same path from the root. The interactive process continues until a class has been assigned to each leaf of the decision tree.

The trees constructed with PBC were compared with trees generated by the CART, C4.5, and SPRINT algorithms from various data sets. The trees created with PBC were of comparable accuracy with the tree from the algorithmic approaches, yet were significantly smaller and, thus, easier to understand. Users can use their domain knowledge in building a decision tree, but also gain a deeper understanding of their data during the construction process.

8.3 Bayes Classification Methods

"What are Bayesian classifiers?" Bayesian classifiers are statistical classifiers. They can predict class membership probabilities such as the probability that a given tuple belongs to a particular class.

Bayesian classification is based on Bayes' theorem, described next. Studies comparing classification algorithms have found a simple Bayesian classifier known as the *naïve Bayesian classifier* to be comparable in performance with decision tree and selected neural network classifiers. Bayesian classifiers have also exhibited high accuracy and speed when applied to large databases.

Naïve Bayesian classifiers assume that the effect of an attribute value on a given class is independent of the values of the other attributes. This assumption is called *class-conditional independence*. It is made to simplify the computations involved and, in this sense, is considered "naïve."

Section 8.3.1 reviews basic probability notation and Bayes' theorem. In Section 8.3.2 you will learn how to do naïve Bayesian classification.

8.3.1 Bayes' Theorem

Bayes' theorem is named after Thomas Bayes, a nonconformist English clergyman who did early work in probability and decision theory during the 18th century. Let X be a data tuple. In Bayesian terms, X is considered "evidence." As usual, it is described by measurements made on a set of n attributes. Let H be some hypothesis such as that the data tuple X belongs to a specified class C. For classification problems, we want to determine $P(H|X)$, the probability that the hypothesis H holds given the "evidence" or observed data tuple X. In other words, we are looking for the probability that tuple X belongs to class C, given that we know the attribute description of X.

$P(H|X)$ is the **posterior probability**, or *a posteriori probability*, of H conditioned on X. For example, suppose our world of data tuples is confined to customers described by the attributes *age* and *income*, respectively, and that X is a 35-year-old customer with an income of \$40,000. Suppose that H is the hypothesis that our customer will buy a computer. Then $P(H|X)$ reflects the probability that customer X will buy a computer given that we know the customer's age and income.

In contrast, $P(H)$ is the **prior probability**, or *a priori probability*, of H. For our example, this is the probability that any given customer will buy a computer, regardless of age, income, or any other information, for that matter. The posterior probability, $P(H|X)$, is based on more information (e.g., customer information) than the prior probability, $P(H)$, which is independent of X.

Similarly, $P(X|H)$ is the posterior probability of X conditioned on H. That is, it is the probability that a customer, X, is 35 years old and earns \$40,000, given that we know the customer will buy a computer.

$P(X)$ is the prior probability of X. Using our example, it is the probability that a person from our set of customers is 35 years old and earns \$40,000.

"How are these probabilities estimated?" $P(H)$, $P(X|H)$, and $P(X)$ may be estimated from the given data, as we shall see next. **Bayes' theorem** is useful in that it provides a way of calculating the posterior probability, $P(H|X)$, from $P(H)$, $P(X|H)$, and $P(X)$. Bayes' theorem is

$$P(H|X) = \frac{P(X|H)P(H)}{P(X)}. \tag{8.10}$$

Now that we have that out of the way, in the next section, we will look at how Bayes' theorem is used in the naïve Bayesian classifier.

8.3.2 Naïve Bayesian Classification

The **naïve Bayesian** classifier, or **simple Bayesian** classifier, works as follows:

1. Let D be a training set of tuples and their associated class labels. As usual, each tuple is represented by an n-dimensional attribute vector, $X = (x_1, x_2, \ldots, x_n)$, depicting n measurements made on the tuple from n attributes, respectively, $A_1, A_2, \ldots, A_n$.

2. Suppose that there are m classes, $C_1, C_2, \ldots, C_m$. Given a tuple, X, the classifier will predict that X belongs to the class having the highest posterior probability, conditioned on X. That is, the naïve Bayesian classifier predicts that tuple X belongs to the class C_i if and only if

$$P(C_i|X) > P(C_j|X) \quad \text{for } 1 \leq j \leq m, j \neq i.$$

Thus, we maximize $P(C_i|X)$. The class C_i for which $P(C_i|X)$ is maximized is called the *maximum posteriori hypothesis*. By Bayes' theorem (Eq. 8.10),

$$P(C_i|X) = \frac{P(X|C_i)P(C_i)}{P(X)}. \tag{8.11}$$

3. As $P(X)$ is constant for all classes, only $P(X|C_i)P(C_i)$ needs to be maximized. If the class prior probabilities are not known, then it is commonly assumed that the classes are equally likely, that is, $P(C_1) = P(C_2) = \cdots = P(C_m)$, and we would therefore maximize $P(X|C_i)$. Otherwise, we maximize $P(X|C_i)P(C_i)$. Note that the class prior probabilities may be estimated by $P(C_i) = |C_{i,D}|/|D|$, where $|C_{i,D}|$ is the number of training tuples of class C_i in D.

4. Given data sets with many attributes, it would be extremely computationally expensive to compute $P(X|C_i)$. To reduce computation in evaluating $P(X|C_i)$, the naïve assumption of **class-conditional independence** is made. This presumes that the attributes' values are conditionally independent of one another, given the class label of the tuple (i.e., that there are no dependence relationships among the attributes). Thus,

$$P(X|C_i) = \prod_{k=1}^{n} P(x_k|C_i) \tag{8.12}$$

$$= P(x_1|C_i) \times P(x_2|C_i) \times \cdots \times P(x_n|C_i).$$

We can easily estimate the probabilities $P(x_1|C_i), P(x_2|C_i), \ldots, P(x_n|C_i)$ from the training tuples. Recall that here x_k refers to the value of attribute A_k for tuple X. For each attribute, we look at whether the attribute is categorical or continuous-valued. For instance, to compute $P(X|C_i)$, we consider the following:

(a) If A_k is categorical, then $P(x_k|C_i)$ is the number of tuples of class C_i in D having the value x_k for A_k, divided by $|C_{i,D}|$, the number of tuples of class C_i in D.

(b) If A_k is continuous-valued, then we need to do a bit more work, but the calculation is pretty straightforward. A continuous-valued attribute is typically assumed to have a Gaussian distribution with a mean μ and standard deviation σ, defined by

$$g(x, \mu, \sigma) = \frac{1}{\sqrt{2\pi}\sigma} e^{-\frac{(x-\mu)^2}{2\sigma^2}}, \tag{8.13}$$

so that

$$P(x_k|C_i) = g(x_k, \mu_{C_i}, \sigma_{C_i}). \tag{8.14}$$

These equations may appear daunting, but hold on! We need to compute μ_{C_i} and σ_{C_i}, which are the mean (i.e., average) and standard deviation, respectively, of the values of attribute A_k for training tuples of class C_i. We then plug these two quantities into Eq. (8.13), together with x_k, to estimate $P(x_k|C_i)$.

For example, let $X = (35, \$40,000)$, where A_1 and A_2 are the attributes *age* and *income*, respectively. Let the class label attribute be *buys_computer*. The associated class label for X is *yes* (i.e., *buys_computer = yes*). Let's suppose that *age* has not been discretized and therefore exists as a continuous-valued attribute. Suppose that from the training set, we find that customers in D who buy a computer are

38 ± 12 years of age. In other words, for attribute *age* and this class, we have $\mu = 38$ years and $\sigma = 12$. We can plug these quantities, along with $x_1 = 35$ for our tuple X, into Eq. (8.13) to estimate $P(age = 35|buys\_computer = yes)$. For a quick review of mean and standard deviation calculations, please see Section 2.2.

5. To predict the class label of X, $P(X|C_i)P(C_i)$ is evaluated for each class C_i. The classifier predicts that the class label of tuple X is the class C_i if and only if

$$P(X|C_i)P(C_i) > P(X|C_j)P(C_j) \quad \text{for } 1 \le j \le m, j \ne i. \tag{8.15}$$

In other words, the predicted class label is the class C_i for which $P(X|C_i)P(C_i)$ is the maximum.

"How effective are Bayesian classifiers?" Various empirical studies of this classifier in comparison to decision tree and neural network classifiers have found it to be comparable in some domains. In theory, Bayesian classifiers have the minimum error rate in comparison to all other classifiers. However, in practice this is not always the case, owing to inaccuracies in the assumptions made for its use, such as class-conditional independence, and the lack of available probability data.

Bayesian classifiers are also useful in that they provide a theoretical justification for other classifiers that do not explicitly use Bayes' theorem. For example, under certain assumptions, it can be shown that many neural network and curve-fitting algorithms output the *maximum posteriori* hypothesis, as does the naïve Bayesian classifier.

Example 8.4 **Predicting a class label using naïve Bayesian classification.** We wish to predict the class label of a tuple using naïve Bayesian classification, given the same training data as in Example 8.3 for decision tree induction. The training data were shown earlier in Table 8.1. The data tuples are described by the attributes *age, income, student,* and *credit_rating*. The class label attribute, *buys_computer*, has two distinct values (namely, {*yes, no*}). Let C_1 correspond to the class *buys_computer = yes* and C_2 correspond to *buys_computer = no*. The tuple we wish to classify is

$$X = (age = youth, income = medium, student = yes, credit\_rating = fair)$$

We need to maximize $P(X|C_i)P(C_i)$, for $i = 1, 2$. $P(C_i)$, the prior probability of each class, can be computed based on the training tuples:

$P(buys\_computer = yes) = 9/14 = 0.643$
$P(buys\_computer = no)\ = 5/14 = 0.357$

To compute $P(X|C_i)$, for $i = 1, 2$, we compute the following conditional probabilities:

$P(age = youth \mid buys\_computer = yes) \qquad = 2/9 = 0.222$
$P(age = youth \mid buys\_computer = no) \qquad = 3/5 = 0.600$
$P(income = medium \mid buys\_computer = yes) = 4/9 = 0.444$
$P(income = medium \mid buys\_computer = no) = 2/5 = 0.400$
$P(student = yes \mid buys\_computer = yes) \qquad = 6/9 = 0.667$

$$P(student = yes \mid buys\_computer = no) \qquad = 1/5 = 0.200$$
$$P(credit\_rating = fair \mid buys\_computer = yes) = 6/9 = 0.667$$
$$P(credit\_rating = fair \mid buys\_computer = no) \ = 2/5 = 0.400$$

Using these probabilities, we obtain

$$
\begin{aligned}
P(X|buys\_computer = yes) = {} & P(age = youth \mid buys\_computer = yes) \\
& \times P(income = medium \mid buys\_computer = yes) \\
& \times P(student = yes \mid buys\_computer = yes) \\
& \times P(credit\_rating = fair \mid buys\_computer = yes) \\
= {} & 0.222 \times 0.444 \times 0.667 \times 0.667 = 0.044.
\end{aligned}
$$

Similarly,

$$P(X|buys\_computer = no) = 0.600 \times 0.400 \times 0.200 \times 0.400 = 0.019.$$

To find the class, C_i, that maximizes $P(X|C_i)P(C_i)$, we compute

$$P(X|buys\_computer = yes)P(buys\_computer = yes) = 0.044 \times 0.643 = 0.028$$
$$P(X|buys\_computer = no)P(buys\_computer = no) = 0.019 \times 0.357 = 0.007$$

Therefore, the naïve Bayesian classifier predicts *buys_computer* = *yes* for tuple *X*. ∎

"*What if I encounter probability values of zero?*" Recall that in Eq. (8.12), we estimate $P(X|C_i)$ as the product of the probabilities $P(x_1|C_i)$, $P(x_2|C_i), \ldots, P(x_n|C_i)$, based on the assumption of class-conditional independence. These probabilities can be estimated from the training tuples (step 4). We need to compute $P(X|C_i)$ for *each* class ($i = 1, 2, \ldots, m$) to find the class C_i for which $P(X|C_i)P(C_i)$ is the maximum (step 5). Let's consider this calculation. For each attribute–value pair (i.e., $A_k = x_k$, for $k = 1, 2, \ldots, n$) in tuple *X*, we need to count the number of tuples having that attribute–value pair, per class (i.e., per C_i, for $i = 1, \ldots, m$). In Example 8.4, we have two classes ($m = 2$), namely *buys_computer* = *yes* and *buys_computer* = *no*. Therefore, for the attribute–value pair *student* = *yes* of *X*, say, we need two counts—the number of customers who are students and for which *buys_computer* = *yes* (which contributes to $P(X|buys\_computer = yes)$) and the number of customers who are students and for which *buys_computer* = *no* (which contributes to $P(X|buys\_computer = no)$).

But what if, say, there are no training tuples representing students for the class *buys_computer* = *no*, resulting in $P(student = yes|buys\_computer = no) = 0$? In other words, what happens if we should end up with a probability value of zero for some $P(x_k|C_i)$? Plugging this zero value into Eq. (8.12) would return a zero probability for $P(X|C_i)$, even though, without the zero probability, we may have ended up with a high probability, suggesting that *X* belonged to class C_i! A zero probability cancels the effects of all the other (posteriori) probabilities (on C_i) involved in the product.

There is a simple trick to avoid this problem. We can assume that our training database, *D*, is so large that adding one to each count that we need would only make a negligible difference in the estimated probability value, yet would conveniently avoid the case of probability values of zero. This technique for probability estimation is known as the **Laplacian correction** or **Laplace estimator**, named after Pierre Laplace, a French mathematician who lived from 1749 to 1827. If we have, say, q counts to which we each add one, then we must remember to add q to the corresponding denominator used in the probability calculation. We illustrate this technique in Example 8.5.

Example 8.5 **Using the Laplacian correction to avoid computing probability values of zero.** Suppose that for the class *buys_computer* = *yes* in some training database, D, containing 1000 tuples, we have 0 tuples with *income* = *low*, 990 tuples with *income* = *medium*, and 10 tuples with *income* = *high*. The probabilities of these events, without the Laplacian correction, are 0, 0.990 (from 990/1000), and 0.010 (from 10/1000), respectively. Using the Laplacian correction for the three quantities, we pretend that we have 1 more tuple for each income-value pair. In this way, we instead obtain the following probabilities (rounded up to three decimal places):

$$\frac{1}{1003} = 0.001, \frac{991}{1003} = 0.988, \text{ and } \frac{11}{1003} = 0.011,$$

respectively. The "corrected" probability estimates are close to their "uncorrected" counterparts, yet the zero probability value is avoided. ∎

8.4 Rule-Based Classification

In this section, we look at rule-based classifiers, where the learned model is represented as a set of IF-THEN rules. We first examine how such rules are used for classification (Section 8.4.1). We then study ways in which they can be generated, either from a decision tree (Section 8.4.2) or directly from the training data using a *sequential covering algorithm* (Section 8.4.3).

8.4.1 Using IF-THEN Rules for Classification

Rules are a good way of representing information or bits of knowledge. A **rule-based classifier** uses a set of IF-THEN rules for classification. An **IF-THEN** rule is an expression of the form

IF *condition* THEN *conclusion.*

An example is rule $R1$,

$R1$: IF *age* = *youth* AND *student* = *yes* THEN *buys_computer* = *yes*.

The "IF" part (or left side) of a rule is known as the **rule antecedent** or **precondition**. The "THEN" part (or right side) is the **rule consequent**. In the rule antecedent, the condition consists of one or more *attribute tests* (e.g., *age* = *youth* and *student* = *yes*)

that are logically ANDed. The rule's consequent contains a class prediction (in this case, we are predicting whether a customer will buy a computer). R1 can also be written as

$$R1: (age = youth) \wedge (student = yes) \Rightarrow (buys\_computer = yes).$$

If the condition (i.e., all the attribute tests) in a rule antecedent holds true for a given tuple, we say that the rule antecedent is **satisfied** (or simply, that the rule is satisfied) and that the rule **covers** the tuple.

A rule R can be assessed by its coverage and accuracy. Given a tuple, X, from a class-labeled data set, D, let n_{covers} be the number of tuples covered by R; $n_{correct}$ be the number of tuples correctly classified by R; and $|D|$ be the number of tuples in D. We can define the **coverage** and **accuracy** of R as

$$coverage(R) = \frac{n_{covers}}{|D|} \tag{8.16}$$

$$accuracy(R) = \frac{n_{correct}}{n_{covers}}. \tag{8.17}$$

That is, a rule's coverage is the percentage of tuples that are covered by the rule (i.e., their attribute values hold true for the rule's antecedent). For a rule's accuracy, we look at the tuples that it covers and see what percentage of them the rule can correctly classify.

Example 8.6 **Rule accuracy and coverage.** Let's go back to our data in Table 8.1. These are class-labeled tuples from the *AllElectronics* customer database. Our task is to predict whether a customer will buy a computer. Consider rule R1, which covers 2 of the 14 tuples. It can correctly classify both tuples. Therefore, $coverage(R1) = 2/14 = 14.28\%$ and $accuracy(R1) = 2/2 = 100\%$. ∎

Let's see how we can use rule-based classification to predict the class label of a given tuple, X. If a rule is satisfied by X, the rule is said to be **triggered**. For example, suppose we have

$$X = (age = youth, income = medium, student = yes, credit\_rating = fair).$$

We would like to classify X according to *buys_computer*. X satisfies R1, which triggers the rule.

If R1 is the only rule satisfied, then the rule **fires** by returning the class prediction for X. Note that triggering does not always mean firing because there may be more than one rule that is satisfied! If more than one rule is triggered, we have a potential problem. What if they each specify a different class? Or what if no rule is satisfied by X?

We tackle the first question. If more than one rule is triggered, we need a **conflict resolution strategy** to figure out which rule gets to fire and assign its class prediction to X. There are many possible strategies. We look at two, namely *size ordering* and *rule ordering*.

The **size ordering** scheme assigns the highest priority to the triggering rule that has the "toughest" requirements, where toughness is measured by the rule antecedent *size*. That is, the triggering rule with the most attribute tests is fired.

The **rule ordering** scheme prioritizes the rules beforehand. The ordering may be *class-based* or *rule-based*. With **class-based ordering**, the classes are sorted in order of decreasing "importance" such as by decreasing *order of prevalence*. That is, all the rules for the most prevalent (or most frequent) class come first, the rules for the next prevalent class come next, and so on. Alternatively, they may be sorted based on the misclassification cost per class. Within each class, the rules are not ordered—they don't have to be because they all predict the same class (and so there can be no class conflict!).

With **rule-based ordering**, the rules are organized into one long priority list, according to some measure of rule quality, such as accuracy, coverage, or size (number of attribute tests in the rule antecedent), or based on advice from domain experts. When rule ordering is used, the rule set is known as a **decision list**. With rule ordering, the triggering rule that appears earliest in the list has the highest priority, and so it gets to fire its class prediction. Any other rule that satisfies X is ignored. Most rule-based classification systems use a class-based rule-ordering strategy.

Note that in the first strategy, overall the rules are *unordered*. They can be applied in any order when classifying a tuple. That is, a disjunction (logical OR) is implied between each of the rules. Each rule represents a standalone nugget or piece of knowledge. This is in contrast to the rule ordering (decision list) scheme for which rules must be applied in the prescribed order so as to avoid conflicts. Each rule in a decision list implies the negation of the rules that come before it in the list. Hence, rules in a decision list are more difficult to interpret.

Now that we have seen how we can handle conflicts, let's go back to the scenario where there is no rule satisfied by X. How, then, can we determine the class label of X? In this case, a fallback or **default rule** can be set up to specify a default class, based on a training set. This may be the class in majority or the majority class of the tuples that were not covered by any rule. The default rule is evaluated at the end, if and only if no other rule covers X. The condition in the default rule is empty. In this way, the rule fires when no other rule is satisfied.

In the following sections, we examine how to build a rule-based classifier.

8.4.2 Rule Extraction from a Decision Tree

In Section 8.2, we learned how to build a decision tree classifier from a set of training data. Decision tree classifiers are a popular method of classification—it is easy to understand how decision trees work and they are known for their accuracy. Decision trees can become large and difficult to interpret. In this subsection, we look at how to build a rule-based classifier by extracting IF-THEN rules from a decision tree. In comparison with a decision tree, the IF-THEN rules may be easier for humans to understand, particularly if the decision tree is very large.

To extract rules from a decision tree, one rule is created for each path from the root to a leaf node. Each splitting criterion along a given path is logically ANDed to form the rule antecedent ("IF" part). The leaf node holds the class prediction, forming the rule consequent ("THEN" part).

Example 8.7 **Extracting classification rules from a decision tree.** The decision tree of Figure 8.2 can be converted to classification IF-THEN rules by tracing the path from the root node to each leaf node in the tree. The rules extracted from Figure 8.2 are as follows:

R1: IF *age = youth*	AND *student = no*	THEN *buys_computer = no*
R2: IF *age = youth*	AND *student = yes*	THEN *buys_computer = yes*
R3: IF *age = middle_aged*		THEN *buys_computer = yes*
R4: IF *age = senior*	AND *credit_rating = excellent*	THEN *buys_computer = yes*
R5: IF *age = senior*	AND *credit_rating = fair*	THEN *buys_computer = no*

∎

A disjunction (logical OR) is implied between each of the extracted rules. Because the rules are extracted directly from the tree, they are **mutually exclusive** and **exhaustive**. *Mutually exclusive* means that we cannot have rule conflicts here because no two rules will be triggered for the same tuple. (We have one rule per leaf, and any tuple can map to only one leaf.) *Exhaustive* means there is one rule for each possible attribute–value combination, so that this set of rules does not require a default rule. Therefore, the order of the rules does not matter—they are *unordered*.

Since we end up with one rule per leaf, the set of extracted rules is not much simpler than the corresponding decision tree! The extracted rules may be even more difficult to interpret than the original trees in some cases. As an example, Figure 8.7 showed decision trees that suffer from subtree repetition and replication. The resulting set of rules extracted can be large and difficult to follow, because some of the attribute tests may be irrelevant or redundant. So, the plot thickens. Although it is easy to extract rules from a decision tree, we may need to do some more work by pruning the resulting rule set.

"How can we prune the rule set?" For a given rule antecedent, any condition that does not improve the estimated accuracy of the rule can be pruned (i.e., removed), thereby generalizing the rule. C4.5 extracts rules from an unpruned tree, and then prunes the rules using a pessimistic approach similar to its tree pruning method. The training tuples and their associated class labels are used to estimate rule accuracy. However, because this would result in an optimistic estimate, alternatively, the estimate is adjusted to compensate for the bias, resulting in a pessimistic estimate. In addition, any rule that does not contribute to the overall accuracy of the entire rule set can also be pruned.

Other problems arise during rule pruning, however, as the rules *will no longer be* mutually exclusive and exhaustive. For conflict resolution, C4.5 adopts a **class-based ordering scheme**. It groups together all rules for a single class, and then determines a ranking of these class rule sets. Within a rule set, the rules are not ordered. C4.5 orders the class rule sets so as to minimize the number of *false-positive errors* (i.e., where a rule predicts a class, C, but the actual class is not C). The class rule set with the least number of false positives is examined first. Once pruning is complete, a final check is done to remove any duplicates. When choosing a default class, C4.5 does not choose the majority class, because this class will likely have many rules for its tuples. Instead, it selects the class that contains the most training tuples that were not covered by any rule.

8.4.3 Rule Induction Using a Sequential Covering Algorithm

IF-THEN rules can be extracted directly from the training data (i.e., without having to generate a decision tree first) using a **sequential covering algorithm**. The name comes from the notion that the rules are learned *sequentially* (one at a time), where each rule for a given class will ideally *cover* many of the class's tuples (and hopefully none of the tuples of other classes). Sequential covering algorithms are the most widely used approach to mining disjunctive sets of classification rules, and form the topic of this subsection.

There are many sequential covering algorithms. Popular variations include AQ, CN2, and the more recent RIPPER. The general strategy is as follows. Rules are learned one at a time. Each time a rule is learned, the tuples covered by the rule are removed, and the process repeats on the remaining tuples. This sequential learning of rules is in contrast to decision tree induction. Because the path to each leaf in a decision tree corresponds to a rule, we can consider decision tree induction as learning a set of rules *simultaneously*.

A basic sequential covering algorithm is shown in Figure 8.10. Here, rules are learned for one class at a time. Ideally, when learning a rule for a class, C, we would like the rule to cover all (or many) of the training tuples of class C and none (or few) of the tuples

---

Algorithm: Sequential covering. Learn a set of IF-THEN rules for classification.

Input:

    ▪ D, a data set of class-labeled tuples;

    ▪ *Att_vals*, the set of all attributes and their possible values.

Output: A set of IF-THEN rules.

Method:

(1)   *Rule_set* = {}; // initial set of rules learned is empty
(2)   **for each** class c **do**
(3)   **repeat**
(4)   Rule = **Learn_One_Rule**(D, *Att_vals*, c);
(5)   remove tuples covered by *Rule* from D;
(6)   *Rule_set* = *Rule_set* + *Rule*; // add new rule to rule set
(7)   **until** terminating condition;
(8)   **endfor**
(9)   return *Rule_Set*;

Figure 8.10 Basic sequential covering algorithm.

from other classes. In this way, the rules learned should be of high accuracy. The rules need not necessarily be of high coverage. This is because we can have more than one rule for a class, so that different rules may cover different tuples within the same class. The process continues until the terminating condition is met, such as when there are no more training tuples or the quality of a rule returned is below a user-specified threshold. The *Learn_One_Rule* procedure finds the "best" rule for the current class, given the current set of training tuples.

"How are rules learned?" Typically, rules are grown in a *general-to-specific* manner (Figure 8.11). We can think of this as a beam search, where we start off with an empty rule and then gradually keep appending attribute tests to it. We append by adding the attribute test as a logical conjunct to the existing condition of the rule antecedent. Suppose our training set, *D*, consists of loan application data. Attributes regarding each applicant include their age, income, education level, residence, credit rating, and the term of the loan. The classifying attribute is *loan_decision*, which indicates whether a loan is accepted (considered safe) or rejected (considered risky). To learn a rule for the class "accept," we start off with the most general rule possible, that is, the condition of the rule antecedent is empty. The rule is

IF THEN *loan_decision = accept.*

We then consider each possible attribute test that may be added to the rule. These can be derived from the parameter *Att_vals*, which contains a list of attributes with their associated values. For example, for an attribute–value pair (*att, val*), we can consider attribute tests such as *att = val, att ≤ val, att > val*, and so on. Typically, the training data will contain many attributes, each of which may have several possible values. Finding an optimal rule set becomes computationally explosive. Instead, *Learn_One_Rule*

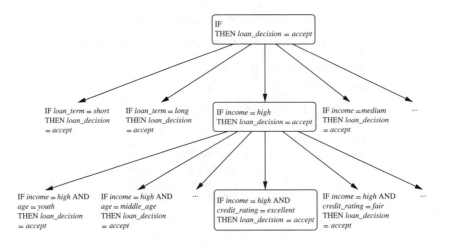

Figure 8.11 A general-to-specific search through rule space.

adopts a greedy depth-first strategy. Each time it is faced with adding a new attribute test (conjunct) to the current rule, it picks the one that most improves the rule quality, based on the training samples. We will say more about rule quality measures in a minute. For the moment, let's say we use rule accuracy as our quality measure. Getting back to our example with Figure 8.11, suppose *Learn_One_Rule* finds that the attribute test *income = high* best improves the accuracy of our current (empty) rule. We append it to the condition, so that the current rule becomes

IF *income = high* THEN *loan_decision = accept.*

Each time we add an attribute test to a rule, the resulting rule should cover relatively more of the "accept" tuples. During the next iteration, we again consider the possible attribute tests and end up selecting *credit_rating = excellent.* Our current rule grows to become

IF *income = high* AND *credit_rating = excellent* THEN *loan_decision = accept.*

The process repeats, where at each step we continue to greedily grow rules until the resulting rule meets an acceptable quality level.

Greedy search does not allow for backtracking. At each step, we *heuristically* add what appears to be the best choice at the moment. What if we unknowingly made a poor choice along the way? To lessen the chance of this happening, instead of selecting the best attribute test to append to the current rule, we can select the best k attribute tests. In this way, we perform a beam search of width k, wherein we maintain the k best candidates overall at each step, rather than a single best candidate.

Rule Quality Measures

Learn_One_Rule needs a measure of rule quality. Every time it considers an attribute test, it must check to see if appending such a test to the current rule's condition will result in an improved rule. Accuracy may seem like an obvious choice at first, but consider Example 8.8.

Example 8.8 **Choosing between two rules based on accuracy.** Consider the two rules as illustrated in Figure 8.12. Both are for the class *loan_decision = accept.* We use "*a*" to represent the tuples of class "*accept*" and "*r*" for the tuples of class "*reject.*" Rule *R1* correctly classifies 38 of the 40 tuples it covers. Rule *R2* covers only two tuples, which it correctly classifies. Their respective accuracies are 95% and 100%. Thus, *R2* has greater accuracy than *R1*, but it is not the better rule because of its small coverage. ∎

From this example, we see that accuracy on its own is not a reliable estimate of rule quality. Coverage on its own is not useful either—for a given class we could have a rule that covers many tuples, most of which belong to other classes! Thus, we seek other measures for evaluating rule quality, which may integrate aspects of accuracy and coverage. Here we will look at a few, namely *entropy*, another based on *information gain*, and a *statistical test* that considers coverage. For our discussion, suppose we are learning rules

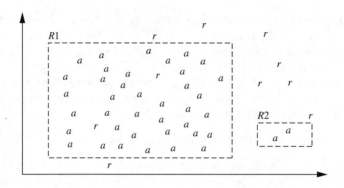

Figure 8.12 Rules for the class *loan_decision = accept*, showing *accept* (*a*) and *reject* (*r*) tuples.

for the class *c*. Our current rule is *R*: IF *condition* THEN *class = c*. We want to see if logically ANDing a given attribute test to *condition* would result in a better rule. We call the new condition, *condition'*, where *R'*: IF *condition'* THEN *class = c* is our potential new rule. In other words, we want to see if *R'* is any better than *R*.

We have already seen entropy in our discussion of the information gain measure used for attribute selection in decision tree induction (Section 8.2.2, Eq. 8.1). It is also known as the *expected information* needed to classify a tuple in data set, *D*. Here, *D* is the set of tuples covered by *condition'* and p_i is the probability of class C_i in *D*. The lower the entropy, the better *condition'* is. Entropy prefers conditions that cover a large number of tuples of a single class and few tuples of other classes.

Another measure is based on information gain and was proposed in **FOIL** (First Order Inductive Learner), a sequential covering algorithm that learns first-order logic rules. Learning first-order rules is more complex because such rules contain variables, whereas the rules we are concerned with in this section are propositional (i.e., variable-free).[5] In machine learning, the tuples of the class for which we are learning rules are called *positive* tuples, while the remaining tuples are *negative*. Let *pos* (*neg*) be the number of positive (negative) tuples covered by *R*. Let *pos'* (*neg'*) be the number of positive (negative) tuples covered by *R'*. FOIL assesses the information gained by extending *condition'* as

$$FOIL\_Gain = pos' \times \left(\log_2 \frac{pos'}{pos' + neg'} - \log_2 \frac{pos}{pos + neg} \right). \tag{8.18}$$

It favors rules that have high accuracy and cover many positive tuples.

We can also use a statistical test of significance to determine if the apparent effect of a rule is not attributed to chance but instead indicates a genuine correlation between

---

[5]Incidentally, FOIL was also proposed by Quinlan, the father of ID3.

attribute values and classes. The test compares the observed distribution among classes of tuples covered by a rule with the expected distribution that would result if the rule made predictions at random. We want to assess whether any observed differences between these two distributions may be attributed to chance. We can use the **likelihood ratio statistic**,

$$Likelihood\_Ratio = 2 \sum_{i=1}^{m} f_i \log \left(\frac{f_i}{e_i} \right), \tag{8.19}$$

where m is the number of classes.

For tuples satisfying the rule, f_i is the observed frequency of each class i among the tuples. e_i is what we would expect the frequency of each class i to be if the rule made random predictions. The statistic has a χ^2 distribution with $m-1$ degrees of freedom. The higher the likelihood ratio, the more likely that there is a *significant* difference in the number of correct predictions made by our rule in comparison with a "random guessor." That is, the performance of our rule is not due to chance. The ratio helps identify rules with insignificant coverage.

CN2 uses entropy together with the likelihood ratio test, while FOIL's information gain is used by RIPPER.

Rule Pruning

Learn_One_Rule does not employ a test set when evaluating rules. Assessments of rule quality as described previously are made with tuples from the original training data. These assessments are optimistic because the rules will likely overfit the data. That is, the rules may perform well on the training data, but less well on subsequent data. To compensate for this, we can prune the rules. A rule is pruned by removing a conjunct (attribute test). We choose to prune a rule, R, if the pruned version of R has greater quality, as assessed on an independent set of tuples. As in decision tree pruning, we refer to this set as a *pruning set*. Various pruning strategies can be used such as the pessimistic pruning approach described in the previous section.

FOIL uses a simple yet effective method. Given a rule, R,

$$FOIL\_Prune(R) = \frac{pos - neg}{pos + neg}, \tag{8.20}$$

where *pos* and *neg* are the number of positive and negative tuples covered by R, respectively. This value will increase with the accuracy of R on a pruning set. Therefore, if the *FOIL_Prune* value is higher for the pruned version of R, then we prune R.

By convention, RIPPER starts with the most recently added conjunct when considering pruning. Conjuncts are pruned one at a time as long as this results in an improvement.

8.5 Model Evaluation and Selection

Now that you may have built a classification model, there may be many questions going through your mind. For example, suppose you used data from previous sales to build a classifier to predict customer purchasing behavior. You would like an estimate of how accurately the classifier can predict the purchasing behavior of future customers, that is, future customer data on which the classifier has not been trained. You may even have tried different methods to build more than one classifier and now wish to compare their accuracy. But what is accuracy? How can we estimate it? Are some measures of a classifier's accuracy more appropriate than others? How can we obtain a *reliable* accuracy estimate? These questions are addressed in this section.

Section 8.5.1 describes various evaluation metrics for the predictive accuracy of a classifier. Holdout and random subsampling (Section 8.5.2), cross-validation (Section 8.5.3), and bootstrap methods (Section 8.5.4) are common techniques for assessing accuracy, based on randomly sampled partitions of the given data. What if we have more than one classifier and want to choose the "best" one? This is referred to as **model selection** (i.e., choosing one classifier over another). The last two sections address this issue. Section 8.5.5 discusses how to use tests of statistical significance to assess whether the difference in accuracy between two classifiers is due to chance. Section 8.5.6 presents how to compare classifiers based on cost–benefit and receiver operating characteristic (ROC) curves.

8.5.1 Metrics for Evaluating Classifier Performance

This section presents measures for assessing how good or how "accurate" your classifier is at predicting the class label of tuples. We will consider the case of where the class tuples are more or less evenly distributed, as well as the case where classes are unbalanced (e.g., where an important class of interest is rare such as in medical tests). The classifier evaluation measures presented in this section are summarized in Figure 8.13. They include accuracy (also known as recognition rate), sensitivity (or recall), specificity, precision, F_1, and F_β. Note that although accuracy is a specific measure, the word "accuracy" is also used as a general term to refer to a classifier's predictive abilities.

Using training data to derive a classifier and then estimate the accuracy of the resulting learned model can result in misleading overoptimistic estimates due to overspecialization of the learning algorithm to the data. (We will say more on this in a moment!) Instead, it is better to measure the classifier's accuracy on a *test set* consisting of class-labeled tuples that were not used to train the model.

Before we discuss the various measures, we need to become comfortable with some terminology. Recall that we can talk in terms of **positive tuples** (tuples of the main class of interest) and **negative tuples** (all other tuples).[6] Given two classes, for example, the positive tuples may be *buys_computer = yes* while the negative tuples are

---

[6]In the machine learning and pattern recognition literature, these are referred to as *positive samples* and *negative samples*, respectively.

Measure	Formula
accuracy, recognition rate	$\frac{TP+TN}{P+N}$
error rate, misclassification rate	$\frac{FP+FN}{P+N}$
sensitivity, true positive rate, recall	$\frac{TP}{P}$
specificity, true negative rate	$\frac{TN}{N}$
precision	$\frac{TP}{TP+FP}$
F, F_1, F-score, harmonic mean of precision and recall	$\frac{2 \times precision \times recall}{precision + recall}$
F_β, where β is a non-negative real number	$\frac{(1+\beta^2) \times precision \times recall}{\beta^2 \times precision + recall}$

Figure 8.13 Evaluation measures. Note that some measures are known by more than one name. TP, TN, FP, P, N refer to the number of true positive, true negative, false positive, positive, and negative samples, respectively (see text).

buys_computer = no. Suppose we use our classifier on a test set of labeled tuples. P is the number of positive tuples and N is the number of negative tuples. For each tuple, we compare the classifier's class label prediction with the tuple's known class label.

There are four additional terms we need to know that are the "building blocks" used in computing many evaluation measures. Understanding them will make it easy to grasp the meaning of the various measures.

- **True positives** (TP): These refer to the positive tuples that were correctly labeled by the classifier. Let TP be the number of true positives.

- **True negatives** (TN): These are the negative tuples that were correctly labeled by the classifier. Let TN be the number of true negatives.

- **False positives** (FP): These are the negative tuples that were incorrectly labeled as positive (e.g., tuples of class *buys_computer = no* for which the classifier predicted *buys_computer = yes*). Let FP be the number of false positives.

- **False negatives** (FN): These are the positive tuples that were mislabeled as negative (e.g., tuples of class *buys_computer = yes* for which the classifier predicted *buys_computer = no*). Let FN be the number of false negatives.

These terms are summarized in the **confusion matrix** of Figure 8.14.

The confusion matrix is a useful tool for analyzing how well your classifier can recognize tuples of different classes. TP and TN tell us when the classifier is getting things right, while FP and FN tell us when the classifier is getting things wrong (i.e.,

	Predicted class		
Actual class		yes	no	Total
	yes	TP	FN	P
	no	FP	TN	N
	Total	P'	N'	P + N

Figure 8.14 Confusion matrix, shown with totals for positive and negative tuples.

Classes	buys_computer = yes	buys_computer = no	Total	Recognition (%)
buys_computer = yes	6954	46	7000	99.34
buys_computer = no	412	2588	3000	86.27
Total	7366	2634	10,000	95.42

Figure 8.15 Confusion matrix for the classes *buys_computer = yes* and *buys_computer = no*, where an entry in row *i* and column *j* shows the number of tuples of class *i* that were labeled by the classifier as class *j*. Ideally, the nondiagonal entries should be zero or close to zero.

mislabeling). Given m classes (where $m \geq 2$), a **confusion matrix** is a table of at least size m by m. An entry, $CM_{i,j}$ in the first m rows and m columns indicates the number of tuples of class i that were labeled by the classifier as class j. For a classifier to have good accuracy, ideally most of the tuples would be represented along the diagonal of the confusion matrix, from entry $CM_{1,1}$ to entry $CM_{m,m}$, with the rest of the entries being zero or close to zero. That is, ideally, FP and FN are around zero.

The table may have additional rows or columns to provide totals. For example, in the confusion matrix of Figure 8.14, P and N are shown. In addition, P' is the number of tuples that were labeled as positive ($TP + FP$) and N' is the number of tuples that were labeled as negative ($TN + FN$). The total number of tuples is $TP + TN + FP + TN$, or $P + N$, or $P' + N'$. Note that although the confusion matrix shown is for a binary classification problem, confusion matrices can be easily drawn for multiple classes in a similar manner.

Now let's look at the evaluation measures, starting with accuracy. The **accuracy** of a classifier on a given test set is the percentage of test set tuples that are correctly classified by the classifier. That is,

$$accuracy = \frac{TP + TN}{P + N}. \tag{8.21}$$

In the pattern recognition literature, this is also referred to as the overall **recognition rate** of the classifier, that is, it reflects how well the classifier recognizes tuples of the various classes. An example of a confusion matrix for the two classes *buys_computer = yes* (positive) and *buys_computer = no* (negative) is given in Figure 8.15. Totals are shown, as well as the recognition rates per class and overall. By glancing at a confusion matrix, it is easy to see if the corresponding classifier is confusing two classes.

For example, we see that it mislabeled 412 *"no"* tuples as *"yes."* Accuracy is most effective when the class distribution is relatively balanced.

We can also speak of the **error rate** or **misclassification rate** of a classifier, M, which is simply $1 - accuracy(M)$, where $accuracy(M)$ is the accuracy of M. This also can be computed as

$$error\ rate = \frac{FP + FN}{P + N}.$$ (8.22)

If we were to use the training set (instead of a test set) to estimate the error rate of a model, this quantity is known as the **resubstitution error**. This error estimate is optimistic of the true error rate (and similarly, the corresponding accuracy estimate is optimistic) because the model is not tested on any samples that it has not already seen.

We now consider the **class imbalance problem**, where the main class of interest is rare. That is, the data set distribution reflects a significant majority of the negative class and a minority positive class. For example, in fraud detection applications, the class of interest (or positive class) is *"fraud,"* which occurs much less frequently than the negative *"nonfraudulant"* class. In medical data, there may be a rare class, such as *"cancer."* Suppose that you have trained a classifier to classify medical data tuples, where the class label attribute is *"cancer"* and the possible class values are *"yes"* and *"no."* An accuracy rate of, say, 97% may make the classifier seem quite accurate, but what if only, say, 3% of the training tuples are actually cancer? Clearly, an accuracy rate of 97% may not be acceptable—the classifier could be correctly labeling only the noncancer tuples, for instance, and misclassifying all the cancer tuples. Instead, we need other measures, which assess how well the classifier can recognize the positive tuples ($cancer = yes$) and how well it can recognize the negative tuples ($cancer = no$).

The **sensitivity** and **specificity** measures can be used, respectively, for this purpose. Sensitivity is also referred to as the *true positive (recognition) rate* (i.e., the proportion of positive tuples that are correctly identified), while specificity is the *true negative rate* (i.e., the proportion of negative tuples that are correctly identified). These measures are defined as

$$sensitivity = \frac{TP}{P}$$ (8.23)

$$specificity = \frac{TN}{N}.$$ (8.24)

It can be shown that accuracy is a function of sensitivity and specificity:

$$accuracy = sensitivity\frac{P}{(P + N)} + specificity\frac{N}{(P + N)}.$$ (8.25)

Example 8.9 Sensitivity and specificity. Figure 8.16 shows a confusion matrix for medical data where the class values are *yes* and *no* for a class label attribute, *cancer.* The sensitivity

Classes	yes	no	Total	Recognition (%)
yes	**90**	210	300	30.00
no	140	**9560**	9700	98.56
Total	230	9770	10,000	96.40

Figure 8.16 Confusion matrix for the classes *cancer* = *yes* and *cancer* = *no*.

of the classifier is $\frac{90}{300}$ = 30.00%. The specificity is $\frac{9560}{9700}$ = 98.56%. The classifier's overall accuracy is $\frac{9650}{10,000}$ = 96.50%. Thus, we note that although the classifier has a high accuracy, it's ability to correctly label the positive (rare) class is poor given its low sensitivity. It has high specificity, meaning that it can accurately recognize negative tuples. Techniques for handling class-imbalanced data are given in Section 8.6.5.   ∎

The *precision* and *recall* measures are also widely used in classification. **Precision** can be thought of as a measure of *exactness* (i.e., what percentage of tuples labeled as positive are actually such), whereas **recall** is a measure of *completeness* (what percentage of positive tuples are labeled as such). If recall seems familiar, that's because it is the same as sensitivity (or the *true positive rate*). These measures can be computed as

$$precision = \frac{TP}{TP + FP} \tag{8.26}$$

$$recall = \frac{TP}{TP + FN} = \frac{TP}{P}. \tag{8.27}$$

Example 8.10 Precision and recall. The precision of the classifier in Figure 8.16 for the *yes* class is $\frac{90}{230}$ = 39.13%. The recall is $\frac{90}{300}$ = 30.00%, which is the same calculation for sensitivity in Example 8.9.   ∎

A perfect precision score of 1.0 for a class C means that every tuple that the classifier labeled as belonging to class C does indeed belong to class C. However, it does not tell us anything about the number of class C tuples that the classifier mislabeled. A perfect recall score of 1.0 for C means that every item from class C was labeled as such, but it does not tell us how many other tuples were incorrectly labeled as belonging to class C. There tends to be an inverse relationship between precision and recall, where it is possible to increase one at the cost of reducing the other. For example, our medical classifier may achieve high precision by labeling all cancer tuples that present a certain way as *cancer*, but may have low recall if it mislabels many other instances of *cancer* tuples. Precision and recall scores are typically used together, where precision values are compared for a fixed value of recall, or vice versa. For example, we may compare precision values at a recall value of, say, 0.75.

An alternative way to use precision and recall is to combine them into a single measure. This is the approach of the *F* measure (also known as the F_1 score or *F*-score) and the F_β measure. They are defined as

$$F = \frac{2 \times precision \times recall}{precision + recall} \tag{8.28}$$

$$F_\beta = \frac{(1 + \beta^2) \times precision \times recall}{\beta^2 \times precision + recall}, \tag{8.29}$$

where β is a non-negative real number. The F measure is the *harmonic mean* of precision and recall (the proof of which is left as an exercise). It gives equal weight to precision and recall. The F_β measure is a weighted measure of precision and recall. It assigns β times as much weight to recall as to precision. Commonly used F_β measures are F_2 (which weights recall twice as much as precision) and $F_{0.5}$ (which weights precision twice as much as recall).

"Are there other cases where accuracy may not be appropriate?" In classification problems, it is commonly assumed that all tuples are uniquely classifiable, that is, that each training tuple can belong to only one class. Yet, owing to the wide diversity of data in large databases, it is not always reasonable to assume that all tuples are uniquely classifiable. Rather, it is more probable to assume that each tuple may belong to more than one class. How then can the accuracy of classifiers on large databases be measured? The accuracy measure is not appropriate, because it does not take into account the possibility of tuples belonging to more than one class.

Rather than returning a class label, it is useful to return a probability class distribution. Accuracy measures may then use a **second guess** heuristic, whereby a class prediction is judged as correct if it agrees with the first or second most probable class. Although this does take into consideration, to some degree, the nonunique classification of tuples, it is not a complete solution.

In addition to accuracy-based measures, classifiers can also be compared with respect to the following additional aspects:

- **Speed:** This refers to the computational costs involved in generating and using the given classifier.

- **Robustness:** This is the ability of the classifier to make correct predictions given noisy data or data with missing values. Robustness is typically assessed with a series of synthetic data sets representing increasing degrees of noise and missing values.

- **Scalability:** This refers to the ability to construct the classifier efficiently given large amounts of data. Scalability is typically assessed with a series of data sets of increasing size.

- **Interpretability:** This refers to the level of understanding and insight that is provided by the classifier or predictor. Interpretability is subjective and therefore more difficult to assess. Decision trees and classification rules can be easy to interpret, yet their interpretability may diminish the more they become complex. We discuss some work in this area, such as the extraction of classification rules from a "black box" neural network classifier called backpropagation, in Chapter 9.

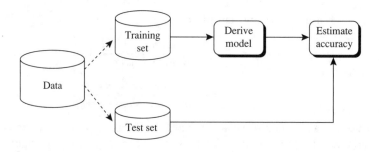

Figure 8.17 Estimating accuracy with the holdout method.

In summary, we have presented several evaluation measures. The accuracy measure works best when the data classes are fairly evenly distributed. Other measures, such as sensitivity (or recall), specificity, precision, F, and F_β, are better suited to the class imbalance problem, where the main class of interest is rare. The remaining subsections focus on obtaining reliable classifier accuracy estimates.

8.5.2 Holdout Method and Random Subsampling

The **holdout** method is what we have alluded to so far in our discussions about accuracy. In this method, the given data are randomly partitioned into two independent sets, a *training set* and a *test set*. Typically, two-thirds of the data are allocated to the training set, and the remaining one-third is allocated to the test set. The training set is used to derive the model. The model's accuracy is then estimated with the test set (Figure 8.17). The estimate is pessimistic because only a portion of the initial data is used to derive the model.

Random subsampling is a variation of the holdout method in which the holdout method is repeated k times. The overall accuracy estimate is taken as the average of the accuracies obtained from each iteration.

8.5.3 Cross-Validation

In k-**fold cross-validation**, the initial data are randomly partitioned into k mutually exclusive subsets or "folds," $D_1, D_2, \ldots, D_k$, each of approximately equal size. Training and testing is performed k times. In iteration i, partition D_i is reserved as the test set, and the remaining partitions are collectively used to train the model. That is, in the first iteration, subsets $D_2, \ldots, D_k$ collectively serve as the training set to obtain a first model, which is tested on D_1; the second iteration is trained on subsets $D_1, D_3, \ldots, D_k$ and tested on D_2; and so on. Unlike the holdout and random subsampling methods, here each sample is used the same number of times for training and once for testing. For classification, the accuracy estimate is the overall number of correct classifications from the k iterations, divided by the total number of tuples in the initial data.

Leave-one-out is a special case of k-fold cross-validation where k is set to the number of initial tuples. That is, only one sample is "left out" at a time for the test set. In **stratified cross-validation**, the folds are stratified so that the class distribution of the tuples in each fold is approximately the same as that in the initial data.

In general, stratified 10-fold cross-validation is recommended for estimating accuracy (even if computation power allows using more folds) due to its relatively low bias and variance.

8.5.4 Bootstrap

Unlike the accuracy estimation methods just mentioned, the **bootstrap method** samples the given training tuples uniformly *with replacement*. That is, each time a tuple is selected, it is equally likely to be selected again and re-added to the training set. For instance, imagine a machine that randomly selects tuples for our training set. In *sampling with replacement*, the machine is allowed to select the same tuple more than once.

There are several bootstrap methods. A commonly used one is the **.632 bootstrap**, which works as follows. Suppose we are given a data set of d tuples. The data set is sampled d times, with replacement, resulting in a *bootstrap sample* or training set of d samples. It is very likely that some of the original data tuples will occur more than once in this sample. The data tuples that did not make it into the training set end up forming the test set. Suppose we were to try this out several times. As it turns out, on average, 63.2% of the original data tuples will end up in the bootstrap sample, and the remaining 36.8% will form the test set (hence, the name, .632 bootstrap).

"*Where does the figure, 63.2%, come from?*" Each tuple has a probability of $1/d$ of being selected, so the probability of not being chosen is $(1 - 1/d)$. We have to select d times, so the probability that a tuple will not be chosen during this whole time is $(1 - 1/d)^d$. If d is large, the probability approaches $e^{-1} = 0.368$.[7] Thus, 36.8% of tuples will not be selected for training and thereby end up in the test set, and the remaining 63.2% will form the training set.

We can repeat the sampling procedure k times, where in each iteration, we use the current test set to obtain an accuracy estimate of the model obtained from the current bootstrap sample. The overall accuracy of the model, M, is then estimated as

$$Acc(M) = \frac{1}{k} \sum_{i=1}^{k} (0.632 \times Acc(M_i)_{test\_set} + 0.368 \times Acc(M_i)_{train\_set}), \qquad (8.30)$$

where $Acc(M_i)_{test\_set}$ is the accuracy of the model obtained with bootstrap sample i when it is applied to test set i. $Acc(M_i)_{train\_set}$ is the accuracy of the model obtained with bootstrap sample i when it is applied to the original set of data tuples. Bootstrapping tends to be overly optimistic. It works best with small data sets.

---

[7] e is the base of natural logarithms, that is, $e = 2.718$.

8.5.5 **Model Selection Using Statistical Tests of Significance**

Suppose that we have generated two classification models, M_1 and M_2, from our data. We have performed 10-fold cross-validation to obtain a mean error rate[8] for each. How can we determine which model is best? It may seem intuitive to select the model with the lowest error rate; however, the mean error rates are just *estimates* of error on the true population of future data cases. There can be considerable variance between error rates within any given 10-fold cross-validation experiment. Although the mean error rates obtained for M_1 and M_2 may appear different, that difference may not be statistically significant. What if any difference between the two may just be attributed to chance? This section addresses these questions.

To determine if there is any "real" difference in the mean error rates of two models, we need to employ a *test of statistical significance*. In addition, we want to obtain some confidence limits for our mean error rates so that we can make statements like, *"Any observed mean will not vary by ± two standard errors 95% of the time for future samples"* or *"One model is better than the other by a margin of error of ± 4%."*

What do we need to perform the statistical test? Suppose that for each model, we did 10-fold cross-validation, say, 10 times, each time using a different 10-fold data partitioning. Each partitioning is independently drawn. We can average the 10 error rates obtained each for M_1 and M_2, respectively, to obtain the mean error rate for each model. For a given model, the individual error rates calculated in the cross-validations may be considered as different, independent samples from a probability distribution. In general, they follow a *t-distribution with $k - 1$ degrees of freedom* where, here, $k = 10$. (This distribution looks very similar to a normal, or Gaussian, distribution even though the functions defining the two are quite different. Both are unimodal, symmetric, and bell-shaped.) This allows us to do hypothesis testing where the significance test used is the **t-test**, or **Student's t-test**. Our hypothesis is that the two models are the same, or in other words, that the difference in mean error rate between the two is zero. If we can reject this hypothesis (referred to as the *null hypothesis*), then we can conclude that the difference between the two models is statistically significant, in which case we can select the model with the lower error rate.

In data mining practice, we may often employ a single test set, that is, the same test set can be used for both M_1 and M_2. In such cases, we do a **pairwise comparison** of the two models *for each* 10-fold cross-validation round. That is, for the ith round of 10-fold cross-validation, the same cross-validation partitioning is used to obtain an error rate for M_1 and for M_2. Let $err(M_1)_i$ (or $err(M_2)_i$) be the error rate of model M_1 (or M_2) on round i. The error rates for M_1 are averaged to obtain a mean error rate for M_1, denoted $\overline{err}(M_1)$. Similarly, we can obtain $\overline{err}(M_2)$. The variance of the difference between the two models is denoted $var(M_1 - M_2)$. The t-test computes the *t-statistic with $k - 1$ degrees of freedom* for k samples. In our example we have $k = 10$ since, here, the k samples are our error rates obtained from ten 10-fold cross-validations for each

---

[8]Recall that the error rate of a model, M, is $1 - accuracy(M)$.

model. The *t*-statistic for pairwise comparison is computed as follows:

$$t = \frac{\overline{err}(M_1) - \overline{err}(M_2)}{\sqrt{var(M_1 - M_2)/k}},$$ (8.31)

where

$$var(M_1 - M_2) = \frac{1}{k} \sum_{i=1}^{k} [err(M_1)_i - err(M_2)_i - (\overline{err}(M_1) - \overline{err}(M_2))]^2.$$ (8.32)

To determine whether M_1 and M_2 are significantly different, we compute t and select a **significance level**, *sig*. In practice, a significance level of 5% or 1% is typically used. We then consult a table for the *t-distribution*, available in standard textbooks on statistics. This table is usually shown arranged by degrees of freedom as rows and significance levels as columns. Suppose we want to ascertain whether the difference between M_1 and M_2 is significantly different for 95% of the population, that is, $sig = 5\%$ or 0.05. We need to find the *t*-distribution value corresponding to $k - 1$ degrees of freedom (or 9 degrees of freedom for our example) from the table. However, because the *t*-distribution is symmetric, typically only the upper percentage points of the distribution are shown. Therefore, we look up the table value for $z = sig/2$, which in this case is 0.025, where z is also referred to as a **confidence limit**. If $t > z$ or $t < -z$, then our value of t lies in the rejection region, within the distribution's tails. This means that we can reject the null hypothesis that the means of M_1 and M_2 are the same and conclude that there is a statistically significant difference between the two models. Otherwise, if we cannot reject the null hypothesis, we conclude that any difference between M_1 and M_2 can be attributed to chance.

If two test sets are available instead of a single test set, then a nonpaired version of the *t*-test is used, where the variance between the means of the two models is estimated as

$$var(M_1 - M_2) = \sqrt{\frac{var(M_1)}{k_1} + \frac{var(M_2)}{k_2}},$$ (8.33)

and k_1 and k_2 are the number of cross-validation samples (in our case, 10-fold cross-validation rounds) used for M_1 and M_2, respectively. This is also known as the **two sample *t*-test**.[9] When consulting the table of *t*-distribution, the number of degrees of freedom used is taken as the minimum number of degrees of the two models.

8.5.6 Comparing Classifiers Based on Cost–Benefit and ROC Curves

The true positives, true negatives, false positives, and false negatives are also useful in assessing the **costs and benefits** (or risks and gains) associated with a classification

---

[9]This test was used in sampling cubes for OLAP-based mining in Chapter 5.

model. The cost associated with a false negative (such as incorrectly predicting that a cancerous patient is not cancerous) is far greater than those of a false positive (incorrectly yet conservatively labeling a noncancerous patient as cancerous). In such cases, we can outweigh one type of error over another by assigning a different cost to each. These costs may consider the danger to the patient, financial costs of resulting therapies, and other hospital costs. Similarly, the benefits associated with a true positive decision may be different than those of a true negative. Up to now, to compute classifier accuracy, we have assumed equal costs and essentially divided the sum of true positives and true negatives by the total number of test tuples.

Alternatively, we can incorporate costs and benefits by instead computing the average cost (or benefit) per decision. Other applications involving cost–benefit analysis include loan application decisions and target marketing mailouts. For example, the cost of loaning to a defaulter greatly exceeds that of the lost business incurred by denying a loan to a nondefaulter. Similarly, in an application that tries to identify households that are likely to respond to mailouts of certain promotional material, the cost of mailouts to numerous households that do not respond may outweigh the cost of lost business from not mailing to households that would have responded. Other costs to consider in the overall analysis include the costs to collect the data and to develop the classification tool.

Receiver operating characteristic curves are a useful visual tool for comparing two classification models. ROC curves come from signal detection theory that was developed during World War II for the analysis of radar images. An ROC curve for a given model shows the trade-off between the *true positive rate* (*TPR*) and the *false positive rate* (*FPR*).[10] Given a test set and a model, *TPR* is the proportion of positive (or "yes") tuples that are correctly labeled by the model; *FPR* is the proportion of negative (or "no") tuples that are mislabeled as positive. Given that *TP*, *FP*, *P*, and *N* are the number of true positive, false positive, positive, and negative tuples, respectively, from Section 8.5.1 we know that $TPR = \frac{TP}{P}$, which is sensitivity. Furthermore, $FPR = \frac{FP}{N}$, which is $1 - specificity$.

For a two-class problem, an ROC curve allows us to visualize the trade-off between the rate at which the model can accurately recognize positive cases versus the rate at which it mistakenly identifies negative cases as positive for different portions of the test set. Any increase in *TPR* occurs at the cost of an increase in *FPR*. The area under the ROC curve is a measure of the accuracy of the model.

To plot an ROC curve for a given classification model, *M*, the model must be able to return a probability of the predicted class for each test tuple. With this information, we rank and sort the tuples so that the tuple that is most likely to belong to the positive or "yes" class appears at the top of the list, and the tuple that is least likely to belong to the positive class lands at the bottom of the list. Naïve Bayesian (Section 8.3) and backpropagation (Section 9.2) classifiers return a class probability distribution for each prediction and, therefore, are appropriate, although other classifiers, such as decision tree classifiers (Section 8.2), can easily be modified to return class probability predictions. Let the value

---

[10] *TPR* and *FPR* are the two operating characteristics being compared.

that a probabilistic classifier returns for a given tuple X be $f(X) \rightarrow [0,1]$. For a binary problem, a threshold t is typically selected so that tuples where $f(X) \geq t$ are considered positive and all the other tuples are considered negative. Note that the number of true positives and the number of false positives are both functions of t, so that we could write $TP(t)$ and $FP(t)$. Both are monotonic descending functions.

We first describe the general idea behind plotting an ROC curve, and then follow up with an example. The vertical axis of an ROC curve represents TPR. The horizontal axis represents FPR. To plot an ROC curve for M, we begin as follows. Starting at the bottom left corner (where $TPR = FPR = 0$), we check the tuple's actual class label at the top of the list. If we have a true positive (i.e., a positive tuple that was correctly classified), then TP and thus TPR increase. On the graph, we move up and plot a point. If, instead, the model classifies a negative tuple as positive, we have a false positive, and so both FP and FPR increase. On the graph, we move right and plot a point. This process is repeated for each of the test tuples in ranked order, each time moving up on the graph for a true positive or toward the right for a false positive.

Example 8.11 **Plotting an ROC curve.** Figure 8.18 shows the probability value (column 3) returned by a probabilistic classifier for each of the 10 tuples in a test set, sorted by decreasing probability order. Column 1 is merely a tuple identification number, which aids in our explanation. Column 2 is the actual class label of the tuple. There are five positive tuples and five negative tuples, thus $P = 5$ and $N = 5$. As we examine the known class label of each tuple, we can determine the values of the remaining columns, TP, FP, TN, FN, TPR, and FPR. We start with tuple 1, which has the highest probability score, and take that score as our threshold, that is, $t = 0.9$. Thus, the classifier considers tuple 1 to be positive, and all the other tuples are considered negative. Since the actual class label of tuple 1 is positive, we have a true positive, hence $TP = 1$ and $FP = 0$. Among the

Tuple #	Class	Prob.	TP	FP	TN	FN	TPR	FPR
1	P	0.90	1	0	5	4	0.2	0
2	P	0.80	2	0	5	3	0.4	0
3	N	0.70	2	1	4	3	0.4	0.2
4	P	0.60	3	1	4	2	0.6	0.2
5	P	0.55	4	1	4	1	0.8	0.2
6	N	0.54	4	2	3	1	0.8	0.4
7	N	0.53	4	3	2	1	0.8	0.6
8	N	0.51	4	4	1	1	0.8	0.8
9	P	0.50	5	4	1	0	1.0	0.8
10	N	0.40	5	5	0	0	1.0	1.0

Figure 8.18 Tuples sorted by decreasing score, where the score is the value returned by a probabilistic classifier.

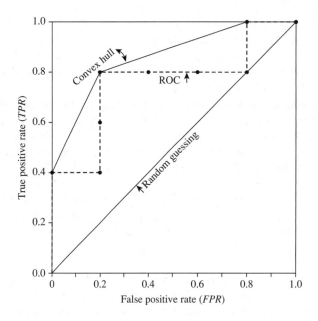

Figure 8.19 ROC curve for the data in Figure 8.18.

remaining nine tuples, which are all classified as negative, five actually are negative (thus, $TN = 5$). The remaining four are all actually positive, thus, $FN = 4$. We can therefore compute $TPR = \frac{TP}{P} = \frac{1}{5} = 0.2$, while $FPR = 0$. Thus, we have the point $(0.2, 0)$ for the ROC curve.

Next, threshold t is set to 0.8, the probability value for tuple 2, so this tuple is now also considered positive, while tuples 3 through 10 are considered negative. The actual class label of tuple 2 is positive, thus now $TP = 2$. The rest of the row can easily be computed, resulting in the point $(0.4, 0)$. Next, we examine the class label of tuple 3 and let t be 0.7, the probability value returned by the classifier for that tuple. Thus, tuple 3 is considered positive, yet its actual label is negative, and so it is a false positive. Thus, TP stays the same and FP increments so that $FP = 1$. The rest of the values in the row can also be easily computed, yielding the point $(0.4, 0.2)$. The resulting ROC graph, from examining each tuple, is the jagged line shown in Figure 8.19.

There are many methods to obtain a curve out of these points, the most common of which is to use a convex hull. The plot also shows a diagonal line where for every true positive of such a model, we are just as likely to encounter a false positive. For comparison, this line represents random guessing. ∎

Figure 8.20 shows the ROC curves of two classification models. The diagonal line representing random guessing is also shown. Thus, the closer the ROC curve of a model is to the diagonal line, the less accurate the model. If the model is really good, initially we are more likely to encounter true positives as we move down the ranked list. Thus,

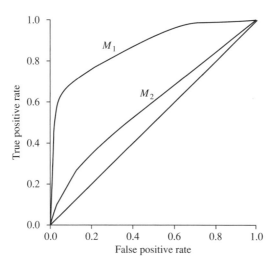

Figure 8.20 ROC curves of two classification models, M_1 and M_2. The diagonal shows where, for every true positive, we are equally likely to encounter a false positive. The closer an ROC curve is to the diagonal line, the less accurate the model is. Thus, $M1$ is more accurate here.

the curve moves steeply up from zero. Later, as we start to encounter fewer and fewer true positives, and more and more false positives, the curve eases off and becomes more horizontal.

To assess the accuracy of a model, we can measure the area under the curve. Several software packages are able to perform such calculation. The closer the area is to 0.5, the less accurate the corresponding model is. A model with perfect accuracy will have an area of 1.0.

8.6 Techniques to Improve Classification Accuracy

In this section, you will learn some tricks for increasing classification accuracy. We focus on *ensemble methods*. An ensemble for classification is a composite model, made up of a combination of classifiers. The individual classifiers vote, and a class label prediction is returned by the ensemble based on the collection of votes. Ensembles tend to be more accurate than their component classifiers. We start off in Section 8.6.1 by introducing ensemble methods in general. Bagging (Section 8.6.2), boosting (Section 8.6.3), and random forests (Section 8.6.4) are popular ensemble methods.

Traditional learning models assume that the data classes are well distributed. In many real-world data domains, however, the data are class-imbalanced, where the main class of interest is represented by only a few tuples. This is known as the *class imbalance problem.* We also study techniques for improving the classification accuracy of class-imbalanced data. These are presented in Section 8.6.5.

8.6.1 Introducing Ensemble Methods

Bagging, boosting, and *random forests* are examples of **ensemble methods** (Figure 8.21). An ensemble combines a series of k learned models (or *base classifiers*), $M_1, M_2, \ldots, M_k$, with the aim of creating an improved composite classification model, $M*$. A given data set, D, is used to create k training sets, $D_1, D_2, \ldots, D_k$, where D_i ($1 \leq i \leq k - 1$) is used to generate classifier M_i. Given a new data tuple to classify, the base classifiers each vote by returning a class prediction. The ensemble returns a class prediction based on the votes of the base classifiers.

An ensemble tends to be more accurate than its base classifiers. For example, consider an ensemble that performs majority voting. That is, given a tuple X to classify, it collects the class label predictions returned from the base classifiers and outputs the class in majority. The base classifiers may make mistakes, but the ensemble will misclassify X only if over half of the base classifiers are in error. Ensembles yield better results when there is significant diversity among the models. That is, ideally, there is little correlation among classifiers. The classifiers should also perform better than random guessing. Each base classifier can be allocated to a different CPU and so ensemble methods are parallelizable.

To help illustrate the power of an ensemble, consider a simple two-class problem described by two attributes, x_1 and x_2. The problem has a linear decision boundary. Figure 8.22(a) shows the decision boundary of a decision tree classifier on the problem. Figure 8.22(b) shows the decision boundary of an ensemble of decision tree classifiers on the same problem. Although the ensemble's decision boundary is still piecewise constant, it has a finer resolution and is better than that of a single tree.

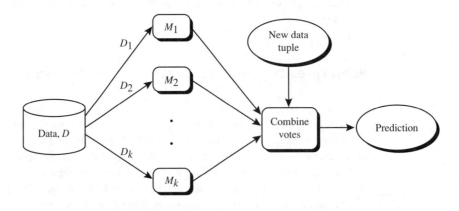

Figure 8.21 Increasing classifier accuracy: Ensemble methods generate a set of classification models, $M_1, M_2, \ldots, M_k$. Given a new data tuple to classify, each classifier "votes" for the class label of that tuple. The ensemble combines the votes to return a class prediction.

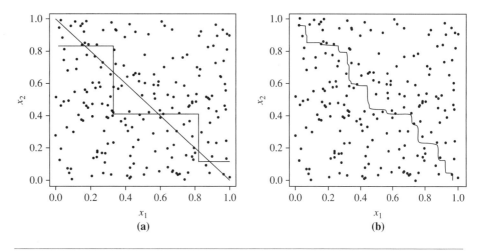

Figure 8.22 Decision boundary by (a) a single decision tree and (b) an ensemble of decision trees for a linearly separable problem (i.e., where the actual decision boundary is a straight line). The decision tree struggles with approximating a linear boundary. The decision boundary of the ensemble is closer to the true boundary. *Source:* From Seni and Elder [SE10]. © 2010 Morgan & Claypool Publishers; used with permission.

8.6.2 Bagging

We now take an intuitive look at how bagging works as a method of increasing accuracy. Suppose that you are a patient and would like to have a diagnosis made based on your symptoms. Instead of asking one doctor, you may choose to ask several. If a certain diagnosis occurs more than any other, you may choose this as the final or best diagnosis. That is, the final diagnosis is made based on a majority vote, where each doctor gets an equal vote. Now replace each doctor by a classifier, and you have the basic idea behind bagging. Intuitively, a majority vote made by a large group of doctors may be more reliable than a majority vote made by a small group.

Given a set, D, of d tuples, **bagging** works as follows. For iteration $i (i = 1, 2, \ldots, k)$, a training set, D_i, of d tuples is sampled with replacement from the original set of tuples, D. Note that the term *bagging* stands for *bootstrap aggregation*. Each training set is a bootstrap sample, as described in Section 8.5.4. Because sampling with replacement is used, some of the original tuples of D may not be included in D_i, whereas others may occur more than once. A classifier model, M_i, is learned for each training set, D_i. To classify an unknown tuple, X, each classifier, M_i, returns its class prediction, which counts as one vote. The bagged classifier, $M*$, counts the votes and assigns the class with the most votes to X. Bagging can be applied to the prediction of continuous values by taking the average value of each prediction for a given test tuple. The algorithm is summarized in Figure 8.23.

The bagged classifier often has significantly greater accuracy than a single classifier derived from D, the original training data. It will not be considerably worse and is more

Algorithm: Bagging. The bagging algorithm—create an ensemble of classification models for a learning scheme where each model gives an equally weighted prediction.

Input:

- D, a set of d training tuples;

- k, the number of models in the ensemble;

- a classification learning scheme (decision tree algorithm, naïve Bayesian, etc.).

Output: The ensemble—a composite model, $M*$.

Method:

(1) **for** $i = 1$ to k **do** // create k models:
(2)   create bootstrap sample, D_i, by sampling D with replacement;
(3)   use D_i and the learning scheme to derive a model, M_i;
(4) **endfor**

To use the ensemble to classify a tuple, X:

    let each of the k models classify X and return the majority vote;

Figure 8.23 Bagging.

robust to the effects of noisy data and overfitting. The increased accuracy occurs because the composite model reduces the variance of the individual classifiers.

8.6.3 Boosting and AdaBoost

We now look at the ensemble method of boosting. As in the previous section, suppose that as a patient, you have certain symptoms. Instead of consulting one doctor, you choose to consult several. Suppose you assign weights to the value or worth of each doctor's diagnosis, based on the accuracies of previous diagnoses they have made. The final diagnosis is then a combination of the weighted diagnoses. This is the essence behind boosting.

In **boosting**, weights are also assigned to each training tuple. A series of k classifiers is iteratively learned. After a classifier, M_i, is learned, the weights are updated to allow the subsequent classifier, M_{i+1}, to "pay more attention" to the training tuples that were misclassified by M_i. The final boosted classifier, $M*$, combines the votes of each individual classifier, where the weight of each classifier's vote is a function of its accuracy.

AdaBoost (short for Adaptive Boosting) is a popular boosting algorithm. Suppose we want to boost the accuracy of a learning method. We are given D, a data set of d class-labeled tuples, $(X_1, y_1), (X_2, y_2), \ldots, (X_d, y_d)$, where y_i is the class label of tuple X_i. Initially, AdaBoost assigns each training tuple an equal weight of $1/d$. Generating k classifiers for the ensemble requires k rounds through the rest of the algorithm. We can sample to form any sized training set, not necessarily of size d. Sampling with replacement is used—the same tuple may be selected more than once. Each tuple's chance of being selected is based on its weight. A classifier model, M_i, is derived from the training tuples of D_i. Its error is then calculated using D_i as a test set. The weights of the training tuples are then adjusted according to how they were classified.

If a tuple was incorrectly classified, its weight is increased. If a tuple was correctly classified, its weight is decreased. A tuple's weight reflects how difficult it is to classify— the higher the weight, the more often it has been misclassified. These weights will be used to generate the training samples for the classifier of the next round. The basic idea is that when we build a classifier, we want it to focus more on the misclassified tuples of the previous round. Some classifiers may be better at classifying some "difficult" tuples than others. In this way, we build a series of classifiers that complement each other. The algorithm is summarized in Figure 8.24.

Now, let's look at some of the math that's involved in the algorithm. To compute the error rate of model M_i, we sum the weights of each of the tuples in D_i that M_i misclassified. That is,

$$error(M_i) = \sum_{j=1}^{d} w_j \times err(\mathbf{X_j}), \tag{8.34}$$

where $err(\mathbf{X_j})$ is the misclassification error of tuple $\mathbf{X_j}$: If the tuple was misclassified, then $err(\mathbf{X_j})$ is 1; otherwise, it is 0. If the performance of classifier M_i is so poor that its error exceeds 0.5, then we abandon it. Instead, we try again by generating a new D_i training set, from which we derive a new M_i.

The error rate of M_i affects how the weights of the training tuples are updated. If a tuple in round i was correctly classified, its weight is multiplied by $error(M_i)/(1 - error(M_i))$. Once the weights of all the correctly classified tuples are updated, the weights for all tuples (including the misclassified ones) are normalized so that their sum remains the same as it was before. To normalize a weight, we multiply it by the sum of the old weights, divided by the sum of the new weights. As a result, the weights of mis-classified tuples are increased and the weights of correctly classified tuples are decreased, as described before.

"*Once boosting is complete, how is the ensemble of classifiers used to predict the class label of a tuple, $\mathbf{X}$?*" Unlike bagging, where each classifier was assigned an equal vote, boosting assigns a weight to each classifier's vote, based on how well the classifier performed. The lower a classifier's error rate, the more accurate it is, and therefore, the higher its weight for voting should be. The weight of classifier M_i's vote is

$$log \frac{1 - error(M_i)}{error(M_i)}. \tag{8.35}$$

For each class, c, we sum the weights of each classifier that assigned class c to $\mathbf{X}$. The class with the highest sum is the "winner" and is returned as the class prediction for tuple $\mathbf{X}$.

"*How does boosting compare with bagging?*" Because of the way boosting focuses on the misclassified tuples, it risks overfitting the resulting composite model to such data.

Algorithm: AdaBoost. A boosting algorithm—create an ensemble of classifiers. Each one gives a weighted vote.

Input:

   ▪ D, a set of d class-labeled training tuples;

   ▪ k, the number of rounds (one classifier is generated per round);

   ▪ a classification learning scheme.

Output: A composite model.

Method:

(1)   initialize the weight of each tuple in D to $1/d$;
(2)   **for** $i = 1$ to k **do** // for each round:
(3)   sample D with replacement according to the tuple weights to obtain D_i;
(4)   use training set D_i to derive a model, M_i;
(5)   compute $error(M_i)$, the error rate of M_i (Eq. 8.34)
(6)   **if** $error(M_i) > 0.5$ **then**
(7)   go back to step 3 and try again;
(8)   **endif**
(9)   **for** each tuple in D_i that was correctly classified **do**
(10)   multiply the weight of the tuple by $error(M_i)/(1 - error(M_i))$; // update weights
(11)   normalize the weight of each tuple;
(12) **endfor**

To use the ensemble to classify tuple, X:

(1)   initialize weight of each class to 0;
(2)   **for** $i = 1$ to k **do** // for each classifier:
(3) $w_i = \log \frac{1 - error(M_i)}{error(M_i)}$; // weight of the classifier's vote
(4) $c = M_i(X)$; // get class prediction for X from M_i
(5)   add w_i to weight for class c
(6)   **endfor**
(7)   return the class with the largest weight;

Figure 8.24 AdaBoost, a boosting algorithm.

Therefore, sometimes the resulting "boosted" model may be less accurate than a single model derived from the same data. Bagging is less susceptible to model overfitting. While both can significantly improve accuracy in comparison to a single model, boosting tends to achieve greater accuracy.

8.6.4 Random Forests

We now present another ensemble method called **random forests**. Imagine that each of the classifiers in the ensemble is a *decision tree* classifier so that the collection of classifiers is a "forest." The individual decision trees are generated using a random selection of attributes at each node to determine the split. More formally, each tree depends on the values of a random vector sampled independently and with the same distribution for all trees in the forest. During classification, each tree votes and the most popular class is returned.

Random forests can be built using bagging (Section 8.6.2) in tandem with random attribute selection. A training set, D, of d tuples is given. The general procedure to generate k decision trees for the ensemble is as follows. For each iteration, $i (i = 1, 2, \ldots, k)$, a training set, D_i, of d tuples is sampled with replacement from D. That is, each D_i is a bootstrap sample of D (Section 8.5.4), so that some tuples may occur more than once in D_i, while others may be excluded. Let F be the number of attributes to be used to determine the split at each node, where F is much smaller than the number of available attributes. To construct a decision tree classifier, M_i, randomly select, at each node, F attributes as candidates for the split at the node. The CART methodology is used to grow the trees. The trees are grown to maximum size and are not pruned. Random forests formed this way, with *random input selection*, are called Forest-RI.

Another form of random forest, called Forest-RC, uses *random linear combinations* of the input attributes. Instead of randomly selecting a subset of the attributes, it creates new attributes (or features) that are a linear combination of the existing attributes. That is, an attribute is generated by specifying L, the number of original attributes to be combined. At a given node, L attributes are randomly selected and added together with coefficients that are uniform random numbers on $[-1, 1]$. F linear combinations are generated, and a search is made over these for the best split. This form of random forest is useful when there are only a few attributes available, so as to reduce the correlation between individual classifiers.

Random forests are comparable in accuracy to AdaBoost, yet are more robust to errors and outliers. The generalization error for a forest converges as long as the number of trees in the forest is large. Thus, overfitting is not a problem. The accuracy of a random forest depends on the strength of the individual classifiers and a measure of the dependence between them. The ideal is to maintain the strength of individual classifiers without increasing their correlation. Random forests are insensitive to the number of attributes selected for consideration at each split. Typically, up to $log_2 d + 1$ are chosen. (An interesting empirical observation was that using a single random input attribute may result in good accuracy that is often higher than when using several attributes.) Because random forests consider many fewer attributes for each split, they are efficient on very large databases. They can be faster than either bagging or boosting. Random forests give internal estimates of variable importance.

8.6.5 Improving Classification Accuracy of Class-Imbalanced Data

In this section, we revisit the *class imbalance problem*. In particular, we study approaches to improving the classification accuracy of class-imbalanced data.

Given two-class data, the data are class-imbalanced if the main class of interest (the positive class) is represented by only a few tuples, while the majority of tuples represent the negative class. For multiclass-imbalanced data, the data distribution of each class differs substantially where, again, the main class or classes of interest are rare. The class imbalance problem is closely related to cost-sensitive learning, wherein the costs of errors, per class, are not equal. In medical diagnosis, for example, it is much more costly to falsely diagnose a cancerous patient as healthy (a false negative) than to misdiagnose a healthy patient as having cancer (a false positive). A false negative error could lead to the loss of life and therefore is much more expensive than a false positive error. Other applications involving class-imbalanced data include fraud detection, the detection of oil spills from satellite radar images, and fault monitoring.

Traditional classification algorithms aim to minimize the number of errors made during classification. They assume that the costs of false positive and false negative errors are equal. By assuming a balanced distribution of classes and equal error costs, they are therefore not suitable for class-imbalanced data. Earlier parts of this chapter presented ways of addressing the class imbalance problem. Although the accuracy measure assumes that the cost of classes are equal, alternative evaluation metrics can be used that consider the different types of classifications. Section 8.5.1, for example, presented *sensitivity* or recall (the true positive rate) and *specificity* (the true negative rate), which help to assess how well a classifier can predict the class label of imbalanced data. Additional relevant measures discussed include F_1 and F_β. Section 8.5.6 showed how ROC curves plot *sensitivity* versus $1 - specificity$ (i.e., the false positive rate). Such curves can provide insight when studying the performance of classifiers on class-imbalanced data.

In this section, we look at general approaches for *improving* the classification accuracy of class-imbalanced data. These approaches include (1) oversampling, (2) undersampling, (3) threshold moving, and (4) ensemble techniques. The first three do not involve any changes to the construction of the classification model. That is, oversampling and undersampling change the distribution of tuples in the training set; threshold moving affects how the model makes decisions when classifying new data. Ensemble methods follow the techniques described in Sections 8.6.2 through 8.6.4. For ease of explanation, we describe these general approaches with respect to the two-class imbalance data problem, where the higher-cost classes are rarer than the lower-cost classes.

Both oversampling and undersampling change the training data distribution so that the rare (positive) class is well represented. **Oversampling** works by resampling the positive tuples so that the resulting training set contains an equal number of positive and negative tuples. **Undersampling** works by decreasing the number of negative tuples. It randomly eliminates tuples from the majority (negative) class until there are an equal number of positive and negative tuples.

Example 8.12 **Oversampling and undersampling.** Suppose the original training set contains 100 positive and 1000 negative tuples. In oversampling, we replicate tuples of the rarer class to form a new training set containing 1000 positive tuples and 1000 negative tuples. In undersampling, we randomly eliminate negative tuples so that the new training set contains 100 positive tuples and 100 negative tuples. ∎

Several variations to oversampling and undersampling exist. They may vary, for instance, in how tuples are added or eliminated. For example, the SMOTE algorithm uses oversampling where synthetic tuples are added, which are "close to" the given positive tuples in tuple space.

The **threshold-moving** approach to the class imbalance problem does not involve any sampling. It applies to classifiers that, given an input tuple, return a continuous output value (just like in Section 8.5.6, where we discussed how to construct ROC curves). That is, for an input tuple, X, such a classifier returns as output a mapping, $f(X) \rightarrow [0, 1]$. Rather than manipulating the training tuples, this method returns a classification decision based on the output values. In the simplest approach, tuples for which $f(X) \geq t$, for some threshold, t, are considered positive, while all other tuples are considered negative. Other approaches may involve manipulating the outputs by weighting. In general, threshold moving moves the threshold, t, so that the rare class tuples are easier to classify (and hence, there is less chance of costly false negative errors). Examples of such classifiers include naïve Bayesian classifiers (Section 8.3) and neural network classifiers like backpropagation (Section 9.2). The threshold-moving method, although not as popular as over- and undersampling, is simple and has shown some success for the two-class-imbalanced data.

Ensemble methods (Sections 8.6.2 through 8.6.4) have also been applied to the class imbalance problem. The individual classifiers making up the ensemble may include versions of the approaches described here such as oversampling and threshold moving.

These methods work relatively well for the class imbalance problem on two-class tasks. Threshold-moving and ensemble methods were empirically observed to outperform oversampling and undersampling. Threshold moving works well even on data sets that are extremely imbalanced. The class imbalance problem on multiclass tasks is much more difficult, where oversampling and threshold moving are less effective. Although threshold-moving and ensemble methods show promise, finding a solution for the multiclass imbalance problem remains an area of future work.

8.7 Summary

- **Classification** is a form of data analysis that extracts models describing data classes. A classifier, or classification model, predicts categorical labels (classes). **Numeric prediction** models continuous-valued functions. Classification and numeric prediction are the two major types of prediction problems.

- **Decision tree induction** is a top-down recursive tree induction algorithm, which uses an attribute selection measure to select the attribute tested for each nonleaf node in the tree. **ID3**, **C4.5**, and **CART** are examples of such algorithms using different attribute selection measures. **Tree pruning** algorithms attempt to improve accuracy by removing tree branches reflecting noise in the data. Early decision tree algorithms typically assume that the data are memory resident. Several scalable algorithms, such as **RainForest**, have been proposed for scalable tree induction.

- **Naïve Bayesian classification** is based on Bayes' theorem of posterior probability. It assumes class-conditional independence—that the effect of an attribute value on a given class is independent of the values of the other attributes.

- A **rule-based classifier** uses a set of IF-THEN rules for classification. Rules can be extracted from a decision tree. Rules may also be generated directly from training data using sequential covering algorithms.

- A **confusion matrix** can be used to evaluate a classifier's quality. For a two-class problem, it shows the *true positives, true negatives, false positives*, and *false negatives*. Measures that assess a classifier's predictive ability include **accuracy, sensitivity** (also known as **recall**), **specificity, precision**, F, and F_β. Reliance on the accuracy measure can be deceiving when the main class of interest is in the minority.

- Construction and evaluation of a classifier require partitioning labeled data into a training set and a test set. **Holdout, random sampling, cross-validation**, and **bootstrapping** are typical methods used for such partitioning.

- Significance tests and ROC curves are useful tools for model selection. **Significance tests** can be used to assess whether the difference in accuracy between two classifiers is due to chance. **ROC curves** plot the true positive rate (or sensitivity) versus the false positive rate (or $1 - specificity$) of one or more classifiers.

- **Ensemble methods** can be used to increase overall accuracy by learning and combining a series of individual (base) classifier models. **Bagging, boosting**, and **random forests** are popular ensemble methods.

- The **class imbalance problem** occurs when the main class of interest is represented by only a few tuples. Strategies to address this problem include **oversampling, undersampling, threshold moving**, and **ensemble techniques**.

8.8 Exercises

8.1 Briefly outline the major steps of *decision tree classification*.

8.2 Why is *tree pruning* useful in decision tree induction? What is a drawback of using a separate set of tuples to evaluate pruning?

8.3 Given a decision tree, you have the option of (a) *converting* the decision tree to rules and then pruning the resulting rules, or (b) *pruning* the decision tree and then converting the pruned tree to rules. What advantage does (a) have over (b)?

8.4 It is important to calculate the worst-case computational complexity of the decision tree algorithm. Given data set, D, the number of attributes, n, and the number of training tuples, $|D|$, show that the computational cost of growing a tree is at most $n \times |D| \times log(|D|)$.

8.5 Given a 5-GB data set with 50 attributes (each containing 100 distinct values) and 512 MB of main memory in your laptop, outline an efficient method that constructs decision trees in such large data sets. Justify your answer by rough calculation of your main memory usage.

8.6 Why is *naïve Bayesian classification* called "naïve"? Briefly outline the major ideas of naïve Bayesian classification.

8.7 The following table consists of training data from an employee database. The data have been generalized. For example, "31 ... 35" for *age* represents the age range of 31 to 35. For a given row entry, *count* represents the number of data tuples having the values for *department, status, age*, and *salary* given in that row.

department	status	age	salary	count
sales	senior	31...35	46K...50K	30
sales	junior	26...30	26K...30K	40
sales	junior	31...35	31K...35K	40
systems	junior	21...25	46K...50K	20
systems	senior	31...35	66K...70K	5
systems	junior	26...30	46K...50K	3
systems	senior	41...45	66K...70K	3
marketing	senior	36...40	46K...50K	10
marketing	junior	31...35	41K...45K	4
secretary	senior	46...50	36K...40K	4
secretary	junior	26...30	26K...30K	6

Let *status* be the class label attribute.

(a) How would you modify the basic decision tree algorithm to take into consideration the *count* of each generalized data tuple (i.e., of each row entry)?

(b) Use your algorithm to construct a decision tree from the given data.

(c) Given a data tuple having the values "*systems*," "*26...30*," and "*46–50K*" for the attributes *department, age*, and *salary*, respectively, what would a naïve Bayesian classification of the *status* for the tuple be?

8.8 RainForest is a scalable algorithm for decision tree induction. Develop a scalable naïve Bayesian classification algorithm that requires just a single scan of the entire data set for most databases. Discuss whether such an algorithm can be refined to incorporate *boosting* to further enhance its classification accuracy.

8.9 Design an efficient method that performs effective naïve Bayesian classification over an *infinite* data stream (i.e., you can scan the data stream only once). If we wanted to discover the *evolution* of such classification schemes (e.g., comparing the classification scheme at this moment with earlier schemes such as one from a week ago), what modified design would you suggest?

8.10 Show that accuracy is a function of *sensitivity* and *specificity*, that is, prove Eq. (8.25).

8.11 The harmonic mean is one of several kinds of averages. Chapter 2 discussed how to compute the *arithmetic mean*, which is what most people typically think of when they compute an average. The **harmonic mean**, H, of the positive real numbers, $x_1, x_2, \ldots, x_n$, is defined as

$$H = \frac{n}{\frac{1}{x_1} + \frac{1}{x_2} + \cdots + \frac{1}{x_n}}$$

$$= \frac{n}{\sum_{i=1}^{n} \frac{1}{x_i}}.$$

The *F* measure is the harmonic mean of precision and recall. Use this fact to derive Eq. (8.28) for *F*. In addition, write F_β as a function of true positives, false negatives, and false positives.

8.12 The data tuples of Figure 8.25 are sorted by decreasing probability value, as returned by a classifier. For each tuple, compute the values for the number of true positives (*TP*), false positives (*FP*), true negatives (*TN*), and false negatives (*FN*). Compute the true positive rate (*TPR*) and false positive rate (*FPR*). Plot the ROC curve for the data.

8.13 It is difficult to assess classification *accuracy* when individual data objects may belong to more than one class at a time. In such cases, comment on what criteria you would use to compare different classifiers modeled after the same data.

8.14 Suppose that we want to *select between two prediction models*, M_1 and M_2. We have performed 10 rounds of 10-fold cross-validation on each model, where the same data partitioning in round *i* is used for both M_1 and M_2. The error rates obtained for M_1 are 30.5, 32.2, 20.7, 20.6, 31.0, 41.0, 27.7, 26.0, 21.5, 26.0. The error rates for M_2 are 22.4, 14.5, 22.4, 19.6, 20.7, 20.4, 22.1, 19.4, 16.2, 35.0. Comment on whether one model is significantly better than the other considering a significance level of 1%.

8.15 What is *boosting*? State why it may improve the accuracy of decision tree induction.

Tuple #	Class	Probability
1	P	0.95
2	N	0.85
3	P	0.78
4	P	0.66
5	N	0.60
6	P	0.55
7	N	0.53
8	N	0.52
9	N	0.51
10	P	0.40

Figure 8.25 Tuples sorted by decreasing score, where the score is the value returned by a probabilistic classifier.

8.16 Outline methods for addressing the *class imbalance problem*. Suppose a bank wants to develop a classifier that guards against fraudulent credit card transactions. Illustrate how you can induce a quality classifier based on a large set of nonfraudulent examples and a very small set of fraudulent cases.

8.9 Bibliographic Notes

Classification is a fundamental topic in machine learning, statistics, and pattern recognition. Many textbooks from these fields highlight classification methods such as Mitchell [Mit97]; Bishop [Bis06]; Duda, Hart, and Stork [DHS01]; Theodoridis and Koutroumbas [TK08]; Hastie, Tibshirani, and Friedman [HTF09]; Alpaydin [Alp11]; and Marsland [Mar09].

For decision tree induction, the C4.5 algorithm is described in a book by Quinlan [Qui93]. The CART system is detailed in *Classification and Regression Trees* by Breiman, Friedman, Olshen, and Stone [BFOS84]. Both books give an excellent presentation of many of the issues regarding decision tree induction. C4.5 has a commercial successor, known as C5.0, which can be found at *www.rulequest.com*. ID3, a predecessor of C4.5, is detailed in Quinlan [Qui86]. It expands on pioneering work on concept learning systems, described by Hunt, Marin, and Stone [HMS66].

Other algorithms for decision tree induction include FACT (Loh and Vanichsetakul [LV88]), QUEST (Loh and Shih [LS97]), PUBLIC (Rastogi and Shim [RS98]), and CHAID (Kass [Kas80] and Magidson [Mag94]). INFERULE (Uthurusamy, Fayyad, and Spangler [UFS91]) learns decision trees from inconclusive data, where probabilistic rather than categorical classification rules are obtained. KATE (Manago and Kodratoff [MK91]) learns decision trees from complex structured data. Incremental versions of ID3 include ID4 (Schlimmer and Fisher [SF86]) and ID5 (Utgoff [Utg88]), the latter of which is extended in Utgoff, Berkman, and Clouse [UBC97]. An incremental version of CART is described in Crawford [Cra89]. BOAT (Gehrke, Ganti, Ramakrishnan, and Loh [GGRL99]), a decision tree algorithm that addresses the scalability issue in data mining, is also incremental. Other decision tree algorithms that address scalability include SLIQ (Mehta, Agrawal, and Rissanen [MAR96]), SPRINT (Shafer, Agrawal, and Mehta [SAM96]), RainForest (Gehrke, Ramakrishnan, and Ganti [GRG98]), and earlier approaches such as Catlet [Cat91] and Chan and Stolfo [CS93a, CS93b].

For a comprehensive survey of many salient issues relating to decision tree induction, such as attribute selection and pruning, see Murthy [Mur98]. Perception-based classification (PBC), a visual and interactive approach to decision tree construction, is presented in Ankerst, Elsen, Ester, and Kriegel [AEEK99].

For a detailed discussion on attribute selection measures, see Kononenko and Hong [KH97]. Information gain was proposed by Quinlan [Qui86] and is based on pioneering work on information theory by Shannon and Weaver [SW49]. The gain ratio, proposed as an extension to information gain, is described as part of C4.5 (Quinlan [Qui93]). The Gini index was proposed for CART in Breiman, Friedman, Olshen, and

Stone [BFOS84]. The G-statistic, based on information theory, is given in Sokal and Rohlf [SR81]. Comparisons of attribute selection measures include Buntine and Niblett [BN92], Fayyad and Irani [FI92], Kononenko [Kon95], Loh and Shih [LS97], and Shih [Shi99]. Fayyad and Irani [FI92] show limitations of impurity-based measures such as information gain and the Gini index. They propose a class of attribute selection measures called C-SEP (Class SEParation), which outperform impurity-based measures in certain cases.

Kononenko [Kon95] notes that attribute selection measures based on the minimum description length principle have the least bias toward multivalued attributes. Martin and Hirschberg [MH95] proved that the time complexity of decision tree induction increases exponentially with respect to tree height in the worst case, and under fairly general conditions in the average case. Fayad and Irani [FI90] found that shallow decision trees tend to have many leaves and higher error rates for a large variety of domains. Attribute (or feature) construction is described in Liu and Motoda [LM98a, LM98b].

There are numerous algorithms for decision tree pruning, including cost complexity pruning (Breiman, Friedman, Olshen, and Stone [BFOS84]), reduced error pruning (Quinlan [Qui87]), and pessimistic pruning (Quinlan [Qui86]). PUBLIC (Rastogi and Shim [RS98]) integrates decision tree construction with tree pruning. MDL-based pruning methods can be found in Quinlan and Rivest [QR89]; Mehta, Agrawal, and Rissanen [MAR96]; and Rastogi and Shim [RS98]. Other methods include Niblett and Bratko [NB86] and Hosking, Pednault, and Sudan [HPS97]. For an empirical comparison of pruning methods, see Mingers [Min89] and Malerba, Floriana, and Semeraro [MFS95]. For a survey on simplifying decision trees, see Breslow and Aha [BA97].

Thorough presentations of Bayesian classification can be found in Duda, Hart, and Stork [DHS01], Weiss and Kulikowski [WK91], and Mitchell [Mit97]. For an analysis of the predictive power of naïve Bayesian classifiers when the class-conditional independence assumption is violated, see Domingos and Pazzani [DP96]. Experiments with kernel density estimation for continuous-valued attributes, rather than Gaussian estimation, have been reported for naïve Bayesian classifiers in John [Joh97].

There are several examples of rule-based classifiers. These include AQ15 (Hong, Mozetic, and Michalski [HMM86]), CN2 (Clark and Niblett [CN89]), ITRULE (Smyth and Goodman [SG92]), RISE (Domingos [Dom94]), IREP (Furnkranz and Widmer [FW94]), RIPPER (Cohen [Coh95]), FOIL (Quinlan and Cameron-Jones [Qui90, QC-J93]), and Swap-1 (Weiss and Indurkhya [WI98]). Rule-based classifiers that are based on frequent-pattern mining are described in Chapter 9. For the extraction of rules from decision trees, see Quinlan [Qui87, Qui93]. Rule refinement strategies that identify the most interesting rules among a given rule set can be found in Major and Mangano [MM95].

Issues involved in estimating classifier accuracy are described in Weiss and Kulikowski [WK91] and Witten and Frank [WF05]. Sensitivity, specificity, and precision are discussed in most information retrieval textbooks. For the F and F_β measures, see van Rijsbergen [vR90]. The use of stratified 10-fold cross-validation for estimating classifier accuracy is recommended over the holdout, cross-validation, leave-one-out (Stone [Sto74]), and bootstrapping (Efron and Tibshirani [ET93]) methods, based on a theoretical and empirical study by Kohavi [Koh95]. See Freedman, Pisani, and Purves [FPP07] for the confidence limits and statistical tests of significance.

For ROC analysis, see Egan [Ega75], Swets [Swe88], and Vuk and Curk [VC06]. Bagging is proposed in Breiman [Bre96]. Freund and Schapire [FS97] proposed AdaBoost. This boosting technique has been applied to several different classifiers, including decision tree induction (Quinlan [Qui96]) and naïve Bayesian classification (Elkan [Elk97]). Friedman [Fri01] proposed the gradient boosting machine for regression. The ensemble technique of random forests is described by Breiman [Bre01]. Seni and Elder [SE10] proposed the Importance Sampling Learning Ensembles (ISLE) framework, which views bagging, AdaBoost, random forests, and gradient boosting as special cases of a generic ensemble generation procedure.

Friedman and Popescu [FB08, FP05] present Rule Ensembles, an ISLE-based model where the classifiers combined are composed of simple readable rules. Such ensembles were observed to have comparable or greater accuracy and greater interpretability. There are many online software packages for ensemble routines, including bagging, AdaBoost, gradient boosting, and random forests. Studies on the class imbalance problem and/or cost-sensitive learning include Weiss [Wei04], Zhou and Liu [ZL06], Zapkowicz and Stephen [ZS02], Elkan [Elk01], and Domingos [Dom99].

The University of California at Irvine (UCI) maintains a Machine Learning Repository of data sets for the development and testing of classification algorithms. It also maintains a Knowledge Discovery in Databases (KDD) Archive, an online repository of large data sets that encompasses a wide variety of data types, analysis tasks, and application areas. For information on these two repositories, see *www.ics.uci.edu/~mlearn/ MLRepository.html* and *http://kdd.ics.uci.edu.*

No classification method is superior to all others for all data types and domains. Empirical comparisons of classification methods include Quinlan [Qui88]; Shavlik, Mooney, and Towell [SMT91]; Brown, Corruble, and Pittard [BCP93]; Curram and Mingers [CM94]; Michie, Spiegelhalter, and Taylor [MST94]; Brodley and Utgoff [BU95]; and Lim, Loh, and Shih [LLS00].

Classification: Advanced Methods

9

In this chapter, you will learn advanced techniques for data classification. We start with **Bayesian belief networks** (Section 9.1), which unlike naïve Bayesian classifiers, do not assume class conditional independence. **Backpropagation**, a neural network algorithm, is discussed in Section 9.2. In general terms, a neural network is a set of connected input/output units in which each connection has a weight associated with it. The weights are adjusted during the learning phase to help the network predict the correct class label of the input tuples. A more recent approach to classification known as support vector machines is presented in Section 9.3. A **support vector machine** transforms training data into a higher dimension, where it finds a hyperplane that separates the data by class using essential training tuples called *support vectors*. Section 9.4 describes **classification using frequent patterns**, exploring relationships between attribute–value pairs that occur frequently in data. This methodology builds on research on frequent pattern mining (Chapters 6 and 7).

Section 9.5 presents **lazy learners** or **instance-based** methods of classification, such as nearest-neighbor classifiers and case-based reasoning classifiers, which store all of the training tuples in pattern space and wait until presented with a test tuple before performing generalization. Other approaches to classification, such as genetic algorithms, rough sets, and fuzzy logic techniques, are introduced in Section 9.6. Section 9.7 introduces additional topics in classification, including multiclass classification, semi-supervised classification, active learning, and transfer learning.

9.1 Bayesian Belief Networks

Chapter 8 introduced Bayes' theorem and naïve Bayesian classification. In this chapter, we describe *Bayesian belief networks*—probabilistic graphical models, which unlike naïve Bayesian classifiers allow the representation of dependencies among subsets of attributes. Bayesian belief networks can be used for classification. Section 9.1.1 introduces the basic concepts of Bayesian belief networks. In Section 9.1.2, you will learn how to train such models.

393

9.1.1 Concepts and Mechanisms

The naïve Bayesian classifier makes the assumption of class conditional independence, that is, given the class label of a tuple, the values of the attributes are assumed to be conditionally independent of one another. This simplifies computation. When the assumption holds true, then the naïve Bayesian classifier is the most accurate in comparison with all other classifiers. In practice, however, dependencies can exist between variables. **Bayesian belief networks** specify joint conditional probability distributions. They allow class conditional independencies to be defined between subsets of variables. They provide a graphical model of causal relationships, on which learning can be performed. Trained Bayesian belief networks can be used for classification. Bayesian belief networks are also known as **belief networks**, **Bayesian networks**, and **probabilistic networks**. For brevity, we will refer to them as belief networks.

A belief network is defined by two components—a *directed acyclic graph* and a set of *conditional probability tables* (Figure 9.1). Each node in the directed acyclic graph represents a random variable. The variables may be discrete- or continuous-valued. They may correspond to actual attributes given in the data or to "hidden variables" believed to form a relationship (e.g., in the case of medical data, a hidden variable may indicate a syndrome, representing a number of symptoms that, together, characterize a specific disease). Each arc represents a probabilistic dependence. If an arc is drawn from a node Y to a node Z, then Y is a **parent** or **immediate predecessor** of Z, and Z is a **descendant**

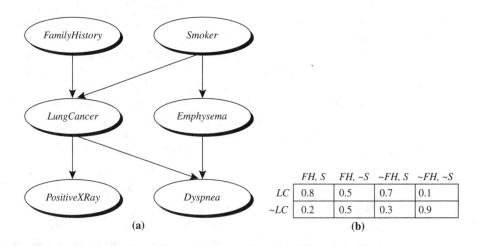

(a)

	FH, S	FH, ~S	~FH, S	~FH, ~S
LC	0.8	0.5	0.7	0.1
~LC	0.2	0.5	0.3	0.9

(b)

Figure 9.1 Simple Bayesian belief network. (a) A proposed causal model, represented by a directed acyclic graph. (b) The conditional probability table for the values of the variable *LungCancer* (*LC*) showing each possible combination of the values of its parent nodes, *FamilyHistory* (*FH*) and *Smoker* (*S*). *Source:* Adapted from Russell, Binder, Koller, and Kanazawa [RBKK95].

of Y. *Each variable is conditionally independent of its nondescendants in the graph, given its parents.*

Figure 9.1 is a simple belief network, adapted from Russell, Binder, Koller, and Kanazawa [RBKK95] for six Boolean variables. The arcs in Figure 9.1(a) allow a representation of causal knowledge. For example, having lung cancer is influenced by a person's family history of lung cancer, as well as whether or not the person is a smoker. Note that the variable *PositiveXRay* is independent of whether the patient has a family history of lung cancer or is a smoker, given that we know the patient has lung cancer. In other words, once we know the outcome of the variable *LungCancer*, then the variables *FamilyHistory* and *Smoker* do not provide any additional information regarding *PositiveXRay*. The arcs also show that the variable *LungCancer* is conditionally independent of *Emphysema*, given its parents, *FamilyHistory* and *Smoker*.

A belief network has one **conditional probability table (CPT)** for each variable. The CPT for a variable Y specifies the conditional distribution $P(Y|Parents(Y))$, where $Parents(Y)$ are the parents of Y. Figure 9.1(b) shows a CPT for the variable *LungCancer*. The conditional probability for each known value of *LungCancer* is given for each possible combination of the values of its parents. For instance, from the upper leftmost and bottom rightmost entries, respectively, we see that

$$P(LungCancer = yes \mid FamilyHistory = yes,\ Smoker = yes) = 0.8$$

$$P(LungCancer = no \mid FamilyHistory = no,\ Smoker = no) = 0.9.$$

Let $X = (x_1, \ldots, x_n)$ be a data tuple described by the variables or attributes $Y_1, \ldots, Y_n$, respectively. Recall that each variable is conditionally independent of its nondescendants in the network graph, given its parents. This allows the network to provide a complete representation of the existing joint probability distribution with the following equation:

$$P(x_1, \ldots, x_n) = \prod_{i=1}^{n} P(x_i | Parents(Y_i)), \tag{9.1}$$

where $P(x_1, \ldots, x_n)$ is the probability of a particular combination of values of X, and the values for $P(x_i | Parents(Y_i))$ correspond to the entries in the CPT for Y_i.

A node within the network can be selected as an "output" node, representing a class label attribute. There may be more than one output node. Various algorithms for inference and learning can be applied to the network. Rather than returning a single class label, the classification process can return a probability distribution that gives the probability of each class. Belief networks can be used to answer probability of evidence queries (e.g., what is the probability that an individual will have *LungCancer*, given that they have both *PositiveXRay* and *Dyspnea*) and most probable explanation queries (e.g., which group of the population is most likely to have both *PositiveXRay* and *Dyspnea*).

Belief networks have been used to model a number of well-known problems. One example is genetic linkage analysis (e.g., the mapping of genes onto a chromosome). By casting the gene linkage problem in terms of inference on Bayesian networks, and using state-of-the art algorithms, the scalability of such analysis has advanced considerably. Other applications that have benefited from the use of belief networks include computer vision (e.g., image restoration and stereo vision), document and text analysis, decision-support systems, and sensitivity analysis. The ease with which many applications can be reduced to Bayesian network inference is advantageous in that it curbs the need to invent specialized algorithms for each such application.

9.1.2 Training Bayesian Belief Networks

"*How does a Bayesian belief network learn?*" In the learning or training of a belief network, a number of scenarios are possible. The network **topology** (or "layout" of nodes and arcs) may be constructed by human experts or inferred from the data. The network variables may be *observable* or *hidden* in all or some of the training tuples. The hidden data case is also referred to as *missing values* or *incomplete data*.

Several algorithms exist for learning the network topology from the training data given observable variables. The problem is one of discrete optimization. For solutions, please see the bibliographic notes at the end of this chapter (Section 9.10). Human experts usually have a good grasp of the direct conditional dependencies that hold in the domain under analysis, which helps in network design. Experts must specify conditional probabilities for the nodes that participate in direct dependencies. These probabilities can then be used to compute the remaining probability values.

If the network topology is known and the variables are observable, then training the network is straightforward. It consists of computing the CPT entries, as is similarly done when computing the probabilities involved in naïve Bayesian classification.

When the network topology is given and some of the variables are hidden, there are various methods to choose from for training the belief network. We will describe a promising method of gradient descent. For those without an advanced math background, the description may look rather intimidating with its calculus-packed formulae. However, packaged software exists to solve these equations, and the general idea is easy to follow.

Let D be a training set of data tuples, $X_1, X_2, \ldots, X_{|D|}$. Training the belief network means that we must learn the values of the CPT entries. Let w_{ijk} be a CPT entry for the variable $Y_i = y_{ij}$ having the parents $U_i = u_{ik}$, where $w_{ijk} \equiv P(Y_i = y_{ij}|U_i = u_{ik})$. For example, if w_{ijk} is the upper leftmost CPT entry of Figure 9.1(b), then Y_i is *LungCancer*; y_{ij} is its value, "*yes*"; U_i lists the parent nodes of Y_i, namely, {*FamilyHistory, Smoker*}; and u_{ik} lists the values of the parent nodes, namely, {"*yes*", "*yes*"}. The w_{ijk} are viewed as weights, analogous to the weights in hidden units of neural networks (Section 9.2). The set of weights is collectively referred to as **W**. The weights are initialized to random probability values. A *gradient descent* strategy performs greedy hill-climbing. At each iteration, the weights are updated and will eventually converge to a local optimum solution.

A **gradient descent** strategy is used to search for the w_{ijk} values that best model the data, based on the assumption that each possible setting of w_{ijk} is equally likely. Such a strategy is iterative. It searches for a solution along the negative of the gradient (i.e., steepest descent) of a criterion function. We want to find the set of weights, W, that maximize this function. To start with, the weights are initialized to random probability values. The gradient descent method performs greedy hill-climbing in that, at each iteration or step along the way, the algorithm moves toward what appears to be the best solution at the moment, without backtracking. The weights are updated at each iteration. Eventually, they converge to a local optimum solution.

For our problem, we maximize $P_w(D) = \prod_{d=1}^{|D|} P_w(X_d)$. This can be done by following the gradient of $\ln P_w(S)$, which makes the problem simpler. Given the network topology and initialized w_{ijk}, the algorithm proceeds as follows:

1. **Compute the gradients:** For each i, j, k, compute

$$\frac{\partial \ln P_w(D)}{\partial w_{ijk}} = \sum_{d=1}^{|D|} \frac{P(Y_i = y_{ij}, U_i = u_{ik}|X_d)}{w_{ijk}}. \tag{9.2}$$

The probability on the right side of Eq. (9.2) is to be calculated for each training tuple, X_d, in D. For brevity, let's refer to this probability simply as p. When the variables represented by Y_i and U_i are hidden for some X_d, then the corresponding probability p can be computed from the observed variables of the tuple using standard algorithms for Bayesian network inference such as those available in the commercial software package HUGIN (*www.hugin.dk*).

2. **Take a small step in the direction of the gradient:** The weights are updated by

$$w_{ijk} \leftarrow w_{ijk} + (l) \frac{\partial \ln P_w(D)}{\partial w_{ijk}}, \tag{9.3}$$

where l is the **learning rate** representing the step size and $\frac{\partial \ln P_w(D)}{\partial w_{ijk}}$ is computed from Eq. (9.2). The learning rate is set to a small constant and helps with convergence.

3. **Renormalize the weights:** Because the weights w_{ijk} are probability values, they must be between 0.0 and 1.0, and $\sum_j w_{ijk}$ must equal 1 for all i, k. These criteria are achieved by renormalizing the weights after they have been updated by Eq. (9.3).

Algorithms that follow this learning form are called *adaptive probabilistic networks*. Other methods for training belief networks are referenced in the bibliographic notes at the end of this chapter (Section 9.10). Belief networks are computationally intensive. Because belief networks provide explicit representations of causal structure, a human expert can provide prior knowledge to the training process in the form of network topology and/or conditional probability values. This can significantly improve the learning rate.

9.2 Classification by Backpropagation

"*What is backpropagation?*" Backpropagation is a neural network learning algorithm. The neural networks field was originally kindled by psychologists and neurobiologists who sought to develop and test computational analogs of neurons. Roughly speaking, a **neural network** is a set of connected input/output units in which each connection has a weight associated with it. During the learning phase, the network learns by adjusting the weights so as to be able to predict the correct class label of the input tuples. Neural network learning is also referred to as **connectionist learning** due to the connections between units.

Neural networks involve long training times and are therefore more suitable for applications where this is feasible. They require a number of parameters that are typically best determined empirically such as the network topology or "structure." Neural networks have been criticized for their poor interpretability. For example, it is difficult for humans to interpret the symbolic meaning behind the learned weights and of "hidden units" in the network. These features initially made neural networks less desirable for data mining.

Advantages of neural networks, however, include their high tolerance of noisy data as well as their ability to classify patterns on which they have not been trained. They can be used when you may have little knowledge of the relationships between attributes and classes. They are well suited for continuous-valued inputs *and* outputs, unlike most decision tree algorithms. They have been successful on a wide array of real-world data, including handwritten character recognition, pathology and laboratory medicine, and training a computer to pronounce English text. Neural network algorithms are inherently parallel; parallelization techniques can be used to speed up the computation process. In addition, several techniques have been recently developed for rule extraction from trained neural networks. These factors contribute to the usefulness of neural networks for classification and numeric prediction in data mining.

There are many different kinds of neural networks and neural network algorithms. The most popular neural network algorithm is *backpropagation*, which gained repute in the 1980s. In Section 9.2.1 you will learn about multilayer feed-forward networks, the type of neural network on which the backpropagation algorithm performs. Section 9.2.2 discusses defining a network topology. The backpropagation algorithm is described in Section 9.2.3. Rule extraction from trained neural networks is discussed in Section 9.2.4.

9.2.1 A Multilayer Feed-Forward Neural Network

The backpropagation algorithm performs learning on a *multilayer feed-forward* neural network. It iteratively learns a set of weights for prediction of the class label of tuples. A **multilayer feed-forward** neural network consists of an *input layer*, one or more *hidden layers*, and an *output layer*. An example of a multilayer feed-forward network is shown in Figure 9.2.

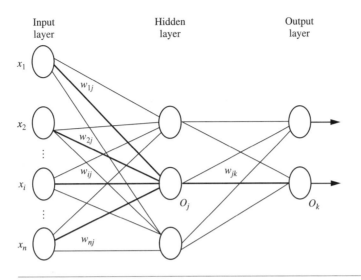

Figure 9.2 Multilayer feed-forward neural network.

Each layer is made up of units. The inputs to the network correspond to the attributes measured for each training tuple. The inputs are fed simultaneously into the units making up the **input layer**. These inputs pass through the input layer and are then weighted and fed simultaneously to a second layer of "neuronlike" units, known as a **hidden layer**. The outputs of the hidden layer units can be input to another hidden layer, and so on. The number of hidden layers is arbitrary, although in practice, usually only one is used. The weighted outputs of the last hidden layer are input to units making up the **output layer**, which emits the network's prediction for given tuples.

The units in the input layer are called **input units**. The units in the hidden layers and output layer are sometimes referred to as **neurodes**, due to their symbolic biological basis, or as **output units**. The multilayer neural network shown in Figure 9.2 has two layers of output units. Therefore, we say that it is a **two-layer** neural network. (The input layer is not counted because it serves only to pass the input values to the next layer.) Similarly, a network containing two hidden layers is called a *three-layer* neural network, and so on. It is a feed-forward network since none of the weights cycles back to an input unit or to a previous layer's output unit. It is **fully connected** in that each unit provides input to each unit in the next forward layer.

Each output unit takes, as input, a weighted sum of the outputs from units in the previous layer (see Figure 9.4 later). It applies a nonlinear (activation) function to the weighted input. Multilayer feed-forward neural networks are able to model the class prediction as a nonlinear combination of the inputs. From a statistical point of view, they perform nonlinear regression. *Multilayer feed-forward networks, given enough hidden units and enough training samples, can closely approximate any function.*

9.2.2 Defining a Network Topology

"How can I design the neural network's topology?" Before training can begin, the user must decide on the network topology by specifying the number of units in the input layer, the number of hidden layers (if more than one), the number of units in each hidden layer, and the number of units in the output layer.

Normalizing the input values for each attribute measured in the training tuples will help speed up the learning phase. Typically, input values are normalized so as to fall between 0.0 and 1.0. Discrete-valued attributes may be encoded such that there is one input unit per domain value. For example, if an attribute A has three possible or known values, namely $\{a_0, a_1, a_2\}$, then we may assign three input units to represent A. That is, we may have, say, I_0, I_1, I_2 as input units. Each unit is initialized to 0. If $A = a_0$, then I_0 is set to 1 and the rest are 0. If $A = a_1$, then I_1 is set to 1 and the rest are 0, and so on.

Neural networks can be used for both classification (to predict the class label of a given tuple) and numeric prediction (to predict a continuous-valued output). For classification, one output unit may be used to represent two classes (where the value 1 represents one class, and the value 0 represents the other). If there are more than two classes, then one output unit per class is used. (See Section 9.7.1 for more strategies on multiclass classification.)

There are no clear rules as to the "best" number of hidden layer units. Network design is a trial-and-error process and may affect the accuracy of the resulting trained network. The initial values of the weights may also affect the resulting accuracy. Once a network has been trained and its accuracy is not considered acceptable, it is common to repeat the training process with a different network topology or a different set of initial weights. Cross-validation techniques for accuracy estimation (described in Chapter 8) can be used to help decide when an acceptable network has been found. A number of automated techniques have been proposed that search for a "good" network structure. These typically use a hill-climbing approach that starts with an initial structure that is selectively modified.

9.2.3 Backpropagation

"How does backpropagation work?" Backpropagation learns by iteratively processing a data set of training tuples, comparing the network's prediction for each tuple with the actual known *target* value. The target value may be the known class label of the training tuple (for classification problems) or a continuous value (for numeric prediction). For each training tuple, the weights are modified so as to minimize the mean-squared error between the network's prediction and the actual target value. These modifications are made in the "backwards" direction (i.e., from the output layer) through each hidden layer down to the first hidden layer (hence the name *backpropagation*). Although it is not guaranteed, in general the weights will eventually converge, and the learning process stops. The algorithm is summarized in Figure 9.3. The steps involved are expressed in terms of inputs, outputs, and errors, and may seem awkward if this is your first look at

Algorithm: Backpropagation. Neural network learning for classification or numeric prediction, using the backpropagation algorithm.

Input:

- ◼ D, a data set consisting of the training tuples and their associated target values;

- ◼ l, the learning rate;

- ◼ *network*, a multilayer feed-forward network.

Output: A trained neural network.
Method:

(1)   Initialize all weights and biases in *network*;
(2)   **while** terminating condition is not satisfied {
(3)   **for** each training tuple X in D {
(4)   // Propagate the inputs forward:
(5)   **for** each input layer unit j {
(6) $O_j = I_j$; // output of an input unit is its actual input value
(7)   **for** each hidden or output layer unit j {
(8) $I_j = \sum_i w_{ij} O_i + \theta_j$; //compute the net input of unit j with respect to the previous layer, i
(9) $O_j = \frac{1}{1+e^{-I_j}}$; } // compute the output of each unit j
(10)   // Backpropagate the errors:
(11)   **for** each unit j in the output layer
(12) $Err_j = O_j(1 - O_j)(T_j - O_j)$; // compute the error
(13)   **for** each unit j in the hidden layers, from the last to the first hidden layer
(14) $Err_j = O_j(1 - O_j)\sum_k Err_k w_{jk}$; // compute the error with respect to the next higher layer, k
(15)   **for** each weight w_{ij} in *network* {
(16) $\Delta w_{ij} = (l) Err_j O_i$; // weight increment
(17) $w_{ij} = w_{ij} + \Delta w_{ij}$; } // weight update
(18)   **for** each bias θ_j in *network* {
(19) $\Delta\theta_j = (l) Err_j$; // bias increment
(20) $\theta_j = \theta_j + \Delta\theta_j$; } // bias update
(21)   } }

Figure 9.3 Backpropagation algorithm.

neural network learning. However, once you become familiar with the process, you will see that each step is inherently simple. The steps are described next.

Initialize the weights: The weights in the network are initialized to small random numbers (e.g., ranging from -1.0 to 1.0, or -0.5 to 0.5). Each unit has a *bias* associated with it, as explained later. The biases are similarly initialized to small random numbers.

Each training tuple, X, is processed by the following steps.

Propagate the inputs forward: First, the training tuple is fed to the network's input layer. The inputs pass through the input units, unchanged. That is, for an input unit, j,

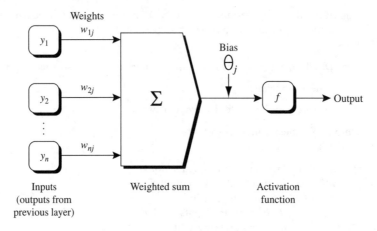

Weights

w_{1j}

y_1

Bias

θ_j

w_{2j}

y_2

Σ

f → Output

w_{nj}

y_n

Inputs
(outputs from
previous layer)

Weighted sum

Activation
function

Figure 9.4   Hidden or output layer unit *j*: The inputs to unit *j* are outputs from the previous layer. These are multiplied by their corresponding weights to form a weighted sum, which is added to the bias associated with unit *j*. A nonlinear activation function is applied to the net input. (For ease of explanation, the inputs to unit *j* are labeled $y_1, y_2, \ldots, y_n$. If unit *j* were in the first hidden layer, then these inputs would correspond to the input tuple $(x_1, x_2, \ldots, x_n)$.)

its output, O_j, is equal to its input value, I_j. Next, the net input and output of each unit in the hidden and output layers are computed. The net input to a unit in the hidden or output layers is computed as a linear combination of its inputs. To help illustrate this point, a hidden layer or output layer unit is shown in Figure 9.4. Each such unit has a number of inputs to it that are, in fact, the outputs of the units connected to it in the previous layer. Each connection has a weight. To compute the net input to the unit, each input connected to the unit is multiplied by its corresponding weight, and this is summed. Given a unit, *j* in a hidden or output layer, the net input, I_j, to unit *j* is

$$I_j = \sum_i w_{ij}O_i + \theta_j, \tag{9.4}$$

where w_{ij} is the weight of the connection from unit *i* in the previous layer to unit *j*; O_i is the output of unit *i* from the previous layer; and θ_j is the **bias** of the unit. The bias acts as a threshold in that it serves to vary the activity of the unit.

Each unit in the hidden and output layers takes its net input and then applies an **activation** function to it, as illustrated in Figure 9.4. The function symbolizes the activation of the neuron represented by the unit. The **logistic**, or **sigmoid**, function is used. Given the net input I_j to unit *j*, then O_j, the output of unit *j*, is computed as

$$O_j = \frac{1}{1 + e^{-I_j}}. \tag{9.5}$$

This function is also referred to as a *squashing function*, because it maps a large input domain onto the smaller range of 0 to 1. The logistic function is nonlinear and differentiable, allowing the backpropagation algorithm to model classification problems that are linearly inseparable.

We compute the output values, O_j, for each hidden layer, up to and including the output layer, which gives the network's prediction. In practice, it is a good idea to cache (i.e., save) the intermediate output values at each unit as they are required again later when backpropagating the error. This trick can substantially reduce the amount of computation required.

Backpropagate the error: The error is propagated backward by updating the weights and biases to reflect the error of the network's prediction. For a unit j in the output layer, the error Err_j is computed by

$$Err_j = O_j(1 - O_j)(T_j - O_j),\tag{9.6}$$

where O_j is the actual output of unit j, and T_j is the known target value of the given training tuple. Note that $O_j(1 - O_j)$ is the derivative of the logistic function.

To compute the error of a hidden layer unit j, the weighted sum of the errors of the units connected to unit j in the next layer are considered. The error of a hidden layer unit j is

$$Err_j = O_j(1 - O_j) \sum_k Err_k w_{jk},\tag{9.7}$$

where w_{jk} is the weight of the connection from unit j to a unit k in the next higher layer, and Err_k is the error of unit k.

The weights and biases are updated to reflect the propagated errors. Weights are updated by the following equations, where Δw_{ij} is the change in weight w_{ij}:

$$\Delta w_{ij} = (l) Err_j O_i.\tag{9.8}$$

$$w_{ij} = w_{ij} + \Delta w_{ij}.\tag{9.9}$$

"*What is* l *in Eq. (9.8)?*" The variable l is the **learning rate**, a constant typically having a value between 0.0 and 1.0. Backpropagation learns using a gradient descent method to search for a set of weights that fits the training data so as to minimize the mean-squared distance between the network's class prediction and the known target value of the tuples.[1] The learning rate helps avoid getting stuck at a local minimum in decision space (i.e., where the weights appear to converge, but are not the optimum solution) and encourages finding the global minimum. If the learning rate is too small, then learning will occur at a very slow pace. If the learning rate is too large, then oscillation between

---

[1] A method of gradient descent was also used for training Bayesian belief networks, as described in Section 9.1.2.

inadequate solutions may occur. A rule of thumb is to set the learning rate to $1/t$, where t is the number of iterations through the training set so far.

Biases are updated by the following equations, where $\Delta\theta_j$ is the change in bias θ_j:

$$\Delta\theta_j = (l)Err_j. \tag{9.10}$$

$$\theta_j = \theta_j + \Delta\theta_j. \tag{9.11}$$

Note that here we are updating the weights and biases after the presentation of each tuple. This is referred to as **case updating**. Alternatively, the weight and bias increments could be accumulated in variables, so that the weights and biases are updated after all the tuples in the training set have been presented. This latter strategy is called **epoch updating**, where one iteration through the training set is an **epoch**. In theory, the mathematical derivation of backpropagation employs epoch updating, yet in practice, case updating is more common because it tends to yield more accurate results.

Terminating condition: Training stops when

- All Δw_{ij} in the previous epoch are so small as to be below some specified threshold, or

- The percentage of tuples misclassified in the previous epoch is below some threshold, or

- A prespecified number of epochs has expired.

In practice, several hundreds of thousands of epochs may be required before the weights will converge.

"*How efficient is backpropagation?*" The computational efficiency depends on the time spent training the network. Given $|D|$ tuples and w weights, each epoch requires $O(|D| \times w)$ time. However, in the worst-case scenario, the number of epochs can be exponential in n, the number of inputs. In practice, the time required for the networks to converge is highly variable. A number of techniques exist that help speed up the training time. For example, a technique known as *simulated annealing* can be used, which also ensures convergence to a global optimum.

Example 9.1 **Sample calculations for learning by the backpropagation algorithm.** Figure 9.5 shows a multilayer feed-forward neural network. Let the learning rate be 0.9. The initial weight and bias values of the network are given in Table 9.1, along with the first training tuple, $X = (1, 0, 1)$, with a class label of 1.

This example shows the calculations for backpropagation, given the first training tuple, X. The tuple is fed into the network, and the net input and output of each unit are computed. These values are shown in Table 9.2. The error of each unit is computed and propagated backward. The error values are shown in Table 9.3. The weight and bias updates are shown in Table 9.4. ∎

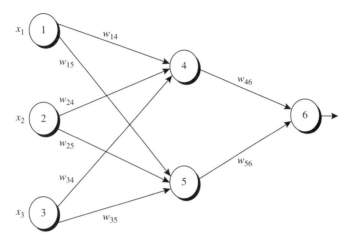

Figure 9.5 Example of a multilayer feed-forward neural network.

Table 9.1 Initial Input, Weight, and Bias Values

x_1	x_2	x_3	w_{14}	w_{15}	w_{24}	w_{25}	w_{34}	w_{35}	w_{46}	w_{56}	θ_4	θ_5	θ_6
1	0	1	0.2	−0.3	0.4	0.1	−0.5	0.2	−0.3	−0.2	−0.4	0.2	0.1

Table 9.2 Net Input and Output Calculations

Unit, j	Net Input, I_j	Output, O_j
4	$0.2 + 0 - 0.5 - 0.4 = -0.7$	$1/(1 + e^{0.7}) = 0.332$
5	$-0.3 + 0 + 0.2 + 0.2 = 0.1$	$1/(1 + e^{-0.1}) = 0.525$
6	$(-0.3)(0.332) - (0.2)(0.525) + 0.1 = -0.105$	$1/(1 + e^{0.105}) = 0.474$

Table 9.3 Calculation of the Error at Each Node

Unit, j	Err_j
6	$(0.474)(1 - 0.474)(1 - 0.474) = 0.1311$
5	$(0.525)(1 - 0.525)(0.1311)(-0.2) = -0.0065$
4	$(0.332)(1 - 0.332)(0.1311)(-0.3) = -0.0087$

Table 9.4 Calculations for Weight and Bias Updating

Weight or Bias	New Value
w_{46}	$-0.3 + (0.9)(0.1311)(0.332) = -0.261$
w_{56}	$-0.2 + (0.9)(0.1311)(0.525) = -0.138$
w_{14}	$0.2 + (0.9)(-0.0087)(1) = 0.192$
w_{15}	$-0.3 + (0.9)(-0.0065)(1) = -0.306$
w_{24}	$0.4 + (0.9)(-0.0087)(0) = 0.4$
w_{25}	$0.1 + (0.9)(-0.0065)(0) = 0.1$
w_{34}	$-0.5 + (0.9)(-0.0087)(1) = -0.508$
w_{35}	$0.2 + (0.9)(-0.0065)(1) = 0.194$
θ_6	$0.1 + (0.9)(0.1311) = 0.218$
θ_5	$0.2 + (0.9)(-0.0065) = 0.194$
θ_4	$-0.4 + (0.9)(-0.0087) = -0.408$

"*How can we classify an unknown tuple using a trained network?*" To classify an unknown tuple, X, the tuple is input to the trained network, and the net input and output of each unit are computed. (There is no need for computation and/or backpropagation of the error.) If there is one output node per class, then the output node with the highest value determines the predicted class label for X. If there is only one output node, then output values greater than or equal to 0.5 may be considered as belonging to the positive class, while values less than 0.5 may be considered negative.

Several variations and alternatives to the backpropagation algorithm have been proposed for classification in neural networks. These may involve the dynamic adjustment of the network topology and of the learning rate or other parameters, or the use of different error functions.

9.2.4 Inside the Black Box: Backpropagation and Interpretability

"*Neural networks are like a black box. How can I 'understand' what the backpropagation network has learned?*" A major disadvantage of neural networks lies in their knowledge representation. Acquired knowledge in the form of a network of units connected by weighted links is difficult for humans to interpret. This factor has motivated research in extracting the knowledge embedded in trained neural networks and in representing that knowledge symbolically. Methods include extracting rules from networks and sensitivity analysis.

Various algorithms for rule extraction have been proposed. The methods typically impose restrictions regarding procedures used in training the given neural network, the network topology, and the discretization of input values.

Fully connected networks are difficult to articulate. Hence, often the first step in extracting rules from neural networks is **network pruning**. This consists of simplifying the network structure by removing weighted links that have the least effect on the trained network. For example, a weighted link may be deleted if such removal does not result in a decrease in the classification accuracy of the network.

Once the trained network has been pruned, some approaches will then perform link, unit, or activation value clustering. In one method, for example, clustering is used to find the set of common activation values for each hidden unit in a given trained two-layer neural network (Figure 9.6). The combinations of these activation values for each hidden unit are analyzed. Rules are derived relating combinations of activation values

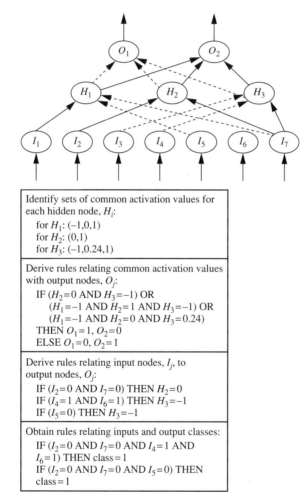

Figure 9.6 Rules can be extracted from training neural networks. *Source:* Adapted from Lu, Setiono, and Liu [LSL95].

with corresponding output unit values. Similarly, the sets of input values and activation values are studied to derive rules describing the relationship between the input layer and the hidden "layer units"? Finally, the two sets of rules may be combined to form IF-THEN rules. Other algorithms may derive rules of other forms, including M-of-N rules (where M out of a given N conditions in the rule antecedent must be true for the rule consequent to be applied), decision trees with M-of-N tests, fuzzy rules, and finite automata.

Sensitivity analysis is used to assess the impact that a given input variable has on a network output. The input to the variable is varied while the remaining input variables are fixed at some value. Meanwhile, changes in the network output are monitored. The knowledge gained from this analysis form can be represented in rules such as "*IF X decreases* 5% *THEN Y increases* 8%."

9.3 Support Vector Machines

In this section, we study **support vector machines (SVMs)**, a method for the classification of both linear and nonlinear data. In a nutshell, an **SVM** is an algorithm that works as follows. It uses a nonlinear mapping to transform the original training data into a higher dimension. Within this new dimension, it searches for the linear optimal separating hyperplane (i.e., a "decision boundary" separating the tuples of one class from another). With an appropriate nonlinear mapping to a sufficiently high dimension, data from two classes can always be separated by a hyperplane. The SVM finds this hyperplane using *support vectors* ("essential" training tuples) and *margins* (defined by the support vectors). We will delve more into these new concepts later.

"*I've heard that SVMs have attracted a great deal of attention lately. Why?*" The first paper on support vector machines was presented in 1992 by Vladimir Vapnik and colleagues Bernhard Boser and Isabelle Guyon, although the groundwork for SVMs has been around since the 1960s (including early work by Vapnik and Alexei Chervonenkis on statistical learning theory). Although the training time of even the fastest SVMs can be extremely slow, they are highly accurate, owing to their ability to model complex nonlinear decision boundaries. They are much less prone to overfitting than other methods. The support vectors found also provide a compact description of the learned model. SVMs can be used for numeric prediction as well as classification. They have been applied to a number of areas, including handwritten digit recognition, object recognition, and speaker identification, as well as benchmark time-series prediction tests.

9.3.1 The Case When the Data Are Linearly Separable

To explain the mystery of SVMs, let's first look at the simplest case—a two-class problem where the classes are linearly separable. Let the data set D be given as (X_1, y_1), $(X_2, y_2), \ldots, (X_{|D|}, y_{|D|})$, where X_i is the set of training tuples with associated class labels, y_i. Each y_i can take one of two values, either $+1$ or -1 (i.e., $y_i \in \{+1, -1\}$),

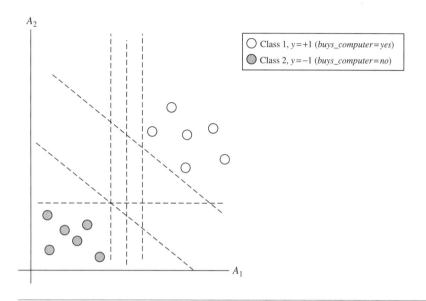

Figure 9.7 The 2-D training data are linearly separable. There are an infinite number of possible separating hyperplanes or "decision boundaries," some of which are shown here as dashed lines. Which one is best?

corresponding to the classes *buys_computer* = *yes* and *buys_computer* = *no*, respectively. To aid in visualization, let's consider an example based on two input attributes, A_1 and A_2, as shown in Figure 9.7. From the graph, we see that the 2-D data are **linearly separable** (or "linear," for short), because a straight line can be drawn to separate all the tuples of class +1 from all the tuples of class −1.

There are an infinite number of separating lines that could be drawn. We want to find the "best" one, that is, one that (we hope) will have the minimum classification error on previously unseen tuples. How can we find this best line? Note that if our data were 3-D (i.e., with three attributes), we would want to find the best separating *plane*. Generalizing to *n* dimensions, we want to find the best *hyperplane*. We will use "hyperplane" to refer to the decision boundary that we are seeking, regardless of the number of input attributes. So, in other words, how can we find the best hyperplane?

An SVM approaches this problem by searching for the **maximum marginal hyperplane**. Consider Figure 9.8, which shows two possible separating hyperplanes and their associated margins. Before we get into the definition of margins, let's take an intuitive look at this figure. Both hyperplanes can correctly classify all the given data tuples. Intuitively, however, we expect the hyperplane with the larger margin to be more accurate at classifying future data tuples than the hyperplane with the smaller margin. This is why (during the learning or training phase) the SVM searches for the hyperplane with the largest margin, that is, the *maximum marginal hyperplane* (MMH). The associated margin gives the largest separation between classes.

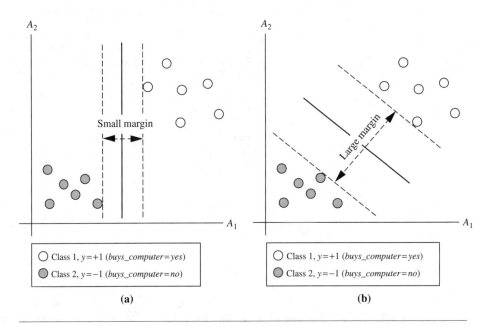

Figure 9.8 Here we see just two possible separating hyperplanes and their associated margins. Which one is better? The one with the larger margin (b) should have greater generalization accuracy.

Getting to an informal definition of **margin**, we can say that the shortest distance from a hyperplane to one side of its margin is equal to the shortest distance from the hyperplane to the other side of its margin, where the "sides" of the margin are parallel to the hyperplane. When dealing with the MMH, this distance is, in fact, the shortest distance from the MMH to the closest training tuple of either class.

A separating hyperplane can be written as

$$W \cdot X + b = 0, \tag{9.12}$$

where W is a weight vector, namely, $W = \{w_1, w_2, \ldots, w_n\}$; n is the number of attributes; and b is a scalar, often referred to as a bias. To aid in visualization, let's consider two input attributes, A_1 and A_2, as in Figure 9.8(b). Training tuples are 2-D (e.g., $X = (x_1, x_2)$), where x_1 and x_2 are the values of attributes A_1 and A_2, respectively, for X. If we think of b as an additional weight, w_0, we can rewrite Eq. (9.12) as

$$w_0 + w_1 x_1 + w_2 x_2 = 0. \tag{9.13}$$

Thus, any point that lies above the separating hyperplane satisfies

$$w_0 + w_1 x_1 + w_2 x_2 > 0. \tag{9.14}$$

Similarly, any point that lies below the separating hyperplane satisfies

$$w_0 + w_1 x_1 + w_2 x_2 < 0. \tag{9.15}$$

The weights can be adjusted so that the hyperplanes defining the "sides" of the margin can be written as

$$H_1 : w_0 + w_1 x_1 + w_2 x_2 \geq 1 \quad \text{for } y_i = +1, \tag{9.16}$$

$$H_2 : w_0 + w_1 x_1 + w_2 x_2 \leq -1 \quad \text{for } y_i = -1. \tag{9.17}$$

That is, any tuple that falls on or above H_1 belongs to class $+1$, and any tuple that falls on or below H_2 belongs to class -1. Combining the two inequalities of Eqs. (9.16) and (9.17), we get

$$y_i(w_0 + w_1 x_1 + w_2 x_2) \geq 1, \quad \forall i. \tag{9.18}$$

Any training tuples that fall on hyperplanes H_1 or H_2 (i.e., the "sides" defining the margin) satisfy Eq. (9.18) and are called **support vectors**. That is, they are equally close to the (separating) MMH. In Figure 9.9, the support vectors are shown encircled with a thicker border. Essentially, the support vectors are the most difficult tuples to classify and give the most information regarding classification.

From this, we can obtain a formula for the size of the maximal margin. The distance from the separating hyperplane to any point on H_1 is $\frac{1}{||W||}$, where $||W||$ is the Euclidean norm of W, that is, $\sqrt{W \cdot W}$.[2] By definition, this is equal to the distance from any point on H_2 to the separating hyperplane. Therefore, the maximal margin is $\frac{2}{||W||}$.

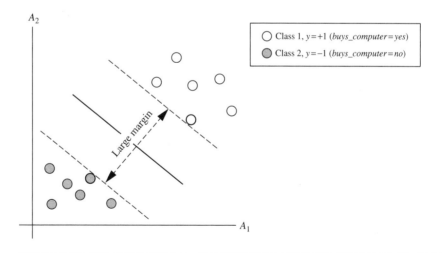

Figure 9.9 Support vectors. The SVM finds the maximum separating hyperplane, that is, the one with maximum distance between the nearest training tuples. The support vectors are shown with a thicker border.

[2]If $W = \{w_1, w_2, \ldots, w_n\}$, then $\sqrt{W \cdot W} = \sqrt{w_1^2 + w_2^2 + \cdots + w_n^2}$.

"*So, how does an SVM find the MMH and the support vectors?*" Using some "fancy math tricks," we can rewrite Eq. (9.18) so that it becomes what is known as a constrained (convex) quadratic optimization problem. Such fancy math tricks are beyond the scope of this book. Advanced readers may be interested to note that the tricks involve rewriting Eq. (9.18) using a Lagrangian formulation and then solving for the solution using Karush-Kuhn-Tucker (KKT) conditions. Details can be found in the bibliographic notes at the end of this chapter (Section 9.10).

If the data are small (say, less than 2000 training tuples), any optimization software package for solving constrained convex quadratic problems can then be used to find the support vectors and MMH. For larger data, special and more efficient algorithms for training SVMs can be used instead, the details of which exceed the scope of this book. Once we've found the support vectors and MMH (note that the support vectors define the MMH!), we have a trained support vector machine. The MMH is a linear class boundary, and so the corresponding SVM can be used to classify linearly separable data. We refer to such a trained SVM as a *linear SVM*.

"*Once I've got a trained support vector machine, how do I use it to classify test (i.e., new) tuples?*" Based on the Lagrangian formulation mentioned before, the MMH can be rewritten as the decision boundary

$$d(X^T) = \sum_{i=1}^{l} y_i \alpha_i X_i X^T + b_0,$$ \hfill (9.19)

where y_i is the class label of support vector X_i; X^T is a test tuple; α_i and b_0 are numeric parameters that were determined automatically by the optimization or SVM algorithm noted before; and l is the number of support vectors.

Interested readers may note that the α_i are Lagrangian multipliers. For linearly separable data, the support vectors are a subset of the actual training tuples (although there will be a slight twist regarding this when dealing with nonlinearly separable data, as we shall see in the following).

Given a test tuple, X^T, we plug it into Eq. (9.19), and then check to see the sign of the result. This tells us on which side of the hyperplane the test tuple falls. If the sign is positive, then X^T falls on or above the MMH, and so the SVM predicts that X^T belongs to class $+1$ (representing *buys_computer* = *yes*, in our case). If the sign is negative, then X^T falls on or below the MMH and the class prediction is -1 (representing *buys_computer* = *no*).

Notice that the Lagrangian formulation of our problem (Eq. 9.19) contains a dot product between support vector X_i and test tuple X^T. This will prove very useful for finding the MMH and support vectors for the case when the given data are nonlinearly separable, as described further in the next section.

Before we move on to the nonlinear case, there are two more important things to note. The complexity of the learned classifier is characterized by the number of support vectors rather than the dimensionality of the data. Hence, SVMs tend to be less prone to overfitting than some other methods. The support vectors are the essential or critical training tuples—they lie closest to the decision boundary (MMH). If all other training tuples were removed and training were repeated, the same separating hyperplane would be found. Furthermore, the number of support vectors found can be used to compute an (upper) bound on the expected error rate of the SVM classifier, which is independent of the data dimensionality. An SVM with a small number of support vectors can have good generalization, even when the dimensionality of the data is high.

9.3.2 The Case When the Data Are Linearly Inseparable

In Section 9.3.1 we learned about linear SVMs for classifying linearly separable data, but what if the data are not linearly separable, as in Figure 9.10? In such cases, no straight line can be found that would separate the classes. The linear SVMs we studied would not be able to find a feasible solution here. Now what?

The good news is that the approach described for linear SVMs can be extended to create *nonlinear SVMs* for the classification of *linearly inseparable data* (also called *non-linearly separable data*, or *nonlinear data* for short). Such SVMs are capable of finding nonlinear decision boundaries (i.e., nonlinear hypersurfaces) in input space.

"*So,*" you may ask, "*how can we extend the linear approach?*" We obtain a nonlinear SVM by extending the approach for linear SVMs as follows. There are two main steps. In the first step, we transform the original input data into a higher dimensional space using a nonlinear mapping. Several common nonlinear mappings can be used in this step, as we will further describe next. Once the data have been transformed into the new higher space, the second step searches for a linear separating hyperplane in the new space. We again end up with a quadratic optimization problem that can be solved using the linear SVM formulation. The maximal marginal hyperplane found in the new space corresponds to a nonlinear separating hypersurface in the original space.

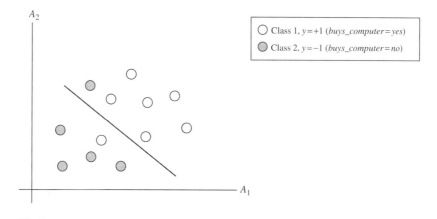

Figure 9.10 A simple 2-D case showing linearly inseparable data. Unlike the linear separable data of Figure 9.7, here it is not possible to draw a straight line to separate the classes. Instead, the decision boundary is nonlinear.

Example 9.2 **Nonlinear transformation of original input data into a higher dimensional space.**
Consider the following example. A 3-D input vector $X = (x_1, x_2, x_3)$ is mapped into
a 6-D space, Z, using the mappings $\phi_1(X) = x_1$, $\phi_2(X) = x_2$, $\phi_3(X) = x_3$, $\phi_4(X) = (x_1)^2$, $\phi_5(X) = x_1x_2$, and $\phi_6(X) = x_1x_3$. A decision hyperplane in the new space is
$d(Z) = WZ + b$, where W and Z are vectors. This is linear. We solve for W and
b and then substitute back so that the linear decision hyperplane in the new (Z)
space corresponds to a nonlinear second-order polynomial in the original 3-D input
space:

$$d(Z) = w_1x_1 + w_2x_2 + w_3x_3 + w_4(x_1)^2 + w_5x_1x_2 + w_6x_1x_3 + b$$

$$= w_1z_1 + w_2z_2 + w_3z_3 + w_4z_4 + w_5z_5 + w_6z_6 + b. \qquad ■$$

But there are some problems. First, how do we choose the nonlinear mapping to
a higher dimensional space? Second, the computation involved will be costly. Refer to
Eq. (9.19) for the classification of a test tuple, X^T. Given the test tuple, we have to compute its dot product with every one of the support vectors.[3] In training, we have to
compute a similar dot product several times in order to find the MMH. This is especially expensive. Hence, the dot product computation required is very heavy and costly.
We need another trick!

Luckily, we can use another math trick. It so happens that in solving the quadratic
optimization problem of the linear SVM (i.e., when searching for a linear SVM in the
new higher dimensional space), the training tuples appear only in the form of dot products, $\phi(X_i) \cdot \phi(X_j)$, where $\phi(X)$ is simply the nonlinear mapping function applied to
transform the training tuples. Instead of computing the dot product on the transformed
data tuples, it turns out that it is mathematically equivalent to instead apply a *kernel
function*, $K(X_i, X_j)$, to the original input data. That is,

$$K(X_i, X_j) = \phi(X_i) \cdot \phi(X_j). \qquad (9.20)$$

In other words, everywhere that $\phi(X_i) \cdot \phi(X_j)$ appears in the training algorithm, we can
replace it with $K(X_i, X_j)$. In this way, all calculations are made in the original input space,
which is of potentially much lower dimensionality! We can safely avoid the mapping—it
turns out that we don't even have to know what the mapping is! We will talk more later
about what kinds of functions can be used as kernel functions for this problem.

After applying this trick, we can then proceed to find a maximal separating hyperplane. The procedure is similar to that described in Section 9.3.1, although it involves
placing a user-specified upper bound, C, on the Lagrange multipliers, α_i. This upper
bound is best determined experimentally.

"*What are some of the kernel functions that could be used?*" Properties of the kinds of
kernel functions that could be used to replace the dot product scenario just described

---

[3]The dot product of two vectors, $X^T = (x_1^T, x_2^T, \ldots, x_n^T)$ and $X_i = (x_{i1}, x_{i2}, \ldots, x_{in})$ is $x_1^T x_{i1} + x_2^T x_{i2} + \cdots + x_n^T x_{in}$. Note that this involves one multiplication and one addition for each of the n dimensions.

have been studied. Three admissible kernel functions are

$$\text{Polynomial kernel of degree } h: \quad K(X_i, X_j) = (X_i \cdot X_j + 1)^h$$

$$\text{Gaussian radial basis function kernel:} \quad K(X_i, X_j) = e^{-\|X_i - X_j\|^2 / 2\sigma^2}$$

$$\text{Sigmoid kernel:} \quad K(X_i, X_j) = \tanh(\kappa X_i \cdot X_j - \delta)$$

Each of these results in a different nonlinear classifier in (the original) input space. Neural network aficionados will be interested to note that the resulting decision hyperplanes found for nonlinear SVMs are the same type as those found by other well-known neural network classifiers. For instance, an SVM with a Gaussian radial basis function (RBF) gives the same decision hyperplane as a type of neural network known as a radial basis function network. An SVM with a sigmoid kernel is equivalent to a simple two-layer neural network known as a multilayer perceptron (with no hidden layers).

There are no golden rules for determining which admissible kernel will result in the most accurate SVM. In practice, the kernel chosen does not generally make a large difference in resulting accuracy. SVM training always finds a global solution, unlike neural networks, such as backpropagation, where many local minima usually exist (Section 9.2.3).

So far, we have described linear and nonlinear SVMs for binary (i.e., two-class) classification. SVM classifiers can be combined for the multiclass case. See Section 9.7.1 for some strategies, such as training one classifier per class and the use of error-correcting codes.

A major research goal regarding SVMs is to improve the speed in training and testing so that SVMs may become a more feasible option for very large data sets (e.g., millions of support vectors). Other issues include determining the best kernel for a given data set and finding more efficient methods for the multiclass case.

9.4 Classification Using Frequent Patterns

Frequent patterns show interesting relationships between attribute–value pairs that occur frequently in a given data set. For example, we may find that the attribute–value pairs *age = youth* and *credit = OK* occur in 20% of data tuples describing *AllElectronics* customers who buy a computer. We can think of each attribute–value pair as an *item*, so the search for these frequent patterns is known as *frequent pattern mining* or *frequent itemset mining*. In Chapters 6 and 7, we saw how **association rules** are derived from frequent patterns, where the associations are commonly used to analyze the purchasing patterns of customers in a store. Such analysis is useful in many decision-making processes such as product placement, catalog design, and cross-marketing.

In this section, we examine how frequent patterns can be used for classification. Section 9.4.1 explores **associative classification**, where association rules are generated from frequent patterns and used for classification. The general idea is that we can search for strong associations between frequent patterns (conjunctions of attribute–value pairs) and class labels. Section 9.4.2 explores **discriminative frequent pattern–based classification**, where frequent patterns serve as combined features, which are considered in addition to single features when building a classification model. Because frequent patterns explore highly confident associations among multiple attributes, frequent pattern–based classification may overcome some constraints introduced by decision tree induction, which considers only one attribute at a time. Studies have shown many frequent pattern–based classification methods to have greater accuracy and scalability than some traditional classification methods such as C4.5.

9.4.1 Associative Classification

In this section, you will learn about associative classification. The methods discussed are CBA, CMAR, and CPAR.

Before we begin, however, let's look at association rule mining in general. Association rules are mined in a two-step process consisting of *frequent itemset mining* followed by *rule generation*. The first step searches for patterns of attribute–value pairs that occur repeatedly in a data set, where each attribute–value pair is considered an *item*. The resulting attribute–value pairs form *frequent itemsets* (also referred to as *frequent patterns*). The second step analyzes the frequent itemsets to generate association rules. All association rules must satisfy certain criteria regarding their "accuracy" (or *confidence*) and the proportion of the data set that they actually represent (referred to as *support*). For example, the following is an association rule mined from a data set, D, shown with its confidence and support:

$$age = youth \wedge credit = OK \Rightarrow buys\_computer$$
$$= yes \, [support = 20\%, confidence = 93\%], \qquad (9.21)$$

where $\wedge$ represents a logical "AND." We will say more about confidence and support later.

More formally, let D be a data set of tuples. Each tuple in D is described by n attributes, $A_1, A_2, \ldots, A_n$, and a class label attribute, A_{class}. All continuous attributes are discretized and treated as categorical (or nominal) attributes. An **item**, p, is an attribute–value pair of the form (A_i, v), where A_i is an attribute taking a value, v. A data tuple $X = (x_1, x_2, \ldots, x_n)$ satisfies an item, $p = (A_i, v)$, if and only if $x_i = v$, where x_i is the value of the ith attribute of X. Association rules can have any number of items in the rule antecedent (left side) and any number of items in the rule consequent (right side). However, when mining association rules for use in classification, we are only interested in association rules of the form $p_1 \wedge p_2 \wedge \ldots p_l \Rightarrow A_{class} = C$, where the rule antecedent is a conjunction of items, $p_1, p_2, \ldots, p_l$ $(l \leq n)$, associated with a class label, C. For a given rule, R, the percentage of tuples in D satisfying the rule antecedent that also have the class label C is called the **confidence** of R.

From a classification point of view, this is akin to rule accuracy. For example, a confidence of 93% for Rule (9.21) means that 93% of the customers in D who are young and have an OK credit rating belong to the class *buys_computer = yes*. The percentage of tuples in D satisfying the rule antecedent and having class label C is called the **support** of R. A support of 20% for Rule (9.21) means that 20% of the customers in D are young, have an OK credit rating, and belong to the class *buys_computer = yes*.

In general, associative classification consists of the following steps:

1. Mine the data for frequent itemsets, that is, find commonly occurring attribute–value pairs in the data.

2. Analyze the frequent itemsets to generate association rules per class, which satisfy confidence and support criteria.

3. Organize the rules to form a rule-based classifier.

Methods of associative classification differ primarily in the approach used for frequent itemset mining and in how the derived rules are analyzed and used for classification. We now look at some of the various methods for associative classification.

One of the earliest and simplest algorithms for associative classification is **CBA** (Classification Based on Associations). CBA uses an iterative approach to frequent itemset mining, similar to that described for Apriori in Section 6.2.1, where multiple passes are made over the data and the derived frequent itemsets are used to generate and test longer itemsets. In general, the number of passes made is equal to the length of the longest rule found. The complete set of rules satisfying minimum confidence and minimum support thresholds are found and then analyzed for inclusion in the classifier. CBA uses a heuristic method to construct the classifier, where the rules are ordered according to decreasing precedence based on their confidence and support. If a set of rules has the same antecedent, then the rule with the highest confidence is selected to represent the set. When classifying a new tuple, the first rule satisfying the tuple is used to classify it. The classifier also contains a default rule, having lowest precedence, which specifies a default class for any new tuple that is not satisfied by any other rule in the classifier. In this way, the set of rules making up the classifier form a *decision list*. In general, CBA was empirically found to be more accurate than C4.5 on a good number of data sets.

CMAR (Classification based on Multiple Association Rules) differs from CBA in its strategy for frequent itemset mining and its construction of the classifier. It also employs several rule pruning strategies with the help of a tree structure for efficient storage and retrieval of rules. CMAR adopts a variant of the *FP-growth* algorithm to find the complete set of rules satisfying the minimum confidence and minimum support thresholds. FP-growth was described in Section 6.2.4. FP-growth uses a tree structure, called an *FP-tree*, to register all the frequent itemset information contained in the given data set, D. This requires only two scans of D. The frequent itemsets are then mined from the FP-tree. CMAR uses an enhanced FP-tree that maintains the distribution of class labels among tuples satisfying each frequent itemset. In this way, it is able to combine rule generation together with frequent itemset mining in a single step.

CMAR employs another tree structure to store and retrieve rules efficiently and to prune rules based on confidence, correlation, and database coverage. Rule pruning strategies are triggered whenever a rule is inserted into the tree. For example, given two rules, $R1$ and $R2$, if the antecedent of $R1$ is more general than that of $R2$ and $conf(R1) \geq conf(R2)$, then $R2$ is pruned. The rationale is that highly specialized rules with low confidence can be pruned if a more generalized version with higher confidence exists. CMAR also prunes rules for which the rule antecedent and class are not positively correlated, based on an χ^2 test of statistical significance.

"*If more than one rule applies, which one do we use?*" As a classifier, CMAR operates differently than CBA. Suppose that we are given a tuple X to classify and that only one rule satisfies or matches X.[4] This case is trivial—we simply assign the rule's class label. Suppose, instead, that more than one rule satisfies X. These rules form a set, S. Which rule would we use to determine the class label of X? CBA would assign the class label of the most confident rule among the rule set, S. CMAR instead considers multiple rules when making its class prediction. It divides the rules into groups according to class labels. All rules within a group share the same class label and each group has a distinct class label.

CMAR uses a weighted χ^2 measure to find the "strongest" group of rules, based on the statistical correlation of rules within a group. It then assigns X the class label of the strongest group. In this way it considers multiple rules, rather than a single rule with highest confidence, when predicting the class label of a new tuple. In experiments, CMAR had slightly higher average accuracy in comparison with CBA. Its runtime, scalability, and use of memory were found to be more efficient.

"*Is there a way to cut down on the number of rules generated?*" CBA and CMAR adopt methods of frequent itemset mining to generate *candidate* association rules, which include all conjunctions of attribute–value pairs (items) satisfying minimum support. These rules are then examined, and a subset is chosen to represent the classifier. However, such methods generate quite a large number of rules. CPAR (Classification based on Predictive Association Rules) takes a different approach to rule generation, based on a rule generation algorithm for classification known as FOIL (Section 8.4.3). FOIL builds rules to distinguish positive tuples (e.g., *buys_computer* = *yes*) from negative tuples (e.g., *buys_computer* = *no*). For multiclass problems, FOIL is applied to each class. That is, for a class, C, all tuples of class C are considered positive tuples, while the rest are considered negative tuples. Rules are generated to distinguish C tuples from all others. Each time a rule is generated, the positive samples it satisfies (or *covers*) are removed until all the positive tuples in the data set are covered. In this way, fewer rules are generated. CPAR relaxes this step by allowing the covered tuples to remain under consideration, but reducing their weight. The process is repeated for each class. The resulting rules are merged to form the classifier rule set.

During classification, CPAR employs a somewhat different multiple rule strategy than CMAR. If more than one rule satisfies a new tuple, X, the rules are divided into groups according to class, similar to CMAR. However, CPAR uses the best k rules of each group to predict the class label of X, based on expected accuracy. By considering the best k rules rather than all of a group's rules, it avoids the influence of lower-ranked

---

[4]If a rule's antecedent satisfies or matches X, then we say that the rule satisfies X.

rules. CPAR's accuracy on numerous data sets was shown to be close to that of CMAR. However, since CPAR generates far fewer rules than CMAR, it shows much better efficiency with large sets of training data.

In summary, associative classification offers an alternative classification scheme by building rules based on conjunctions of attribute–value pairs that occur frequently in data.

9.4.2 Discriminative Frequent Pattern–Based Classification

From work on associative classification, we see that frequent patterns reflect strong associations between attribute–value pairs (or items) in data and are useful for classification.

"*But just how discriminative are frequent patterns for classification?*" Frequent patterns represent feature combinations. Let's compare the discriminative power of frequent patterns and single features. Figure 9.11 plots the information gain of frequent patterns and single features (i.e., of pattern length 1) for three UCI data sets.[5] The discrimination power of some frequent patterns is higher than that of single features. Frequent patterns map data to a higher dimensional space. They capture more underlying semantics of the data, and thus can hold greater expressive power than single features.

"*Why not consider frequent patterns as combined features, in addition to single features when building a classification model?*" This notion is the basis of **frequent pattern–based classification**—the learning of a classification model in the feature space of single attributes *as well as* frequent patterns. In this way, we transfer the original feature space to a larger space. This will likely increase the chance of including important features.

Let's get back to our earlier question: How discriminative are frequent patterns? Many of the frequent patterns generated in frequent itemset mining are indiscriminative because they are based solely on support, without considering predictive power. That is, by definition, a pattern must satisfy a user-specified minimum support threshold, *min_sup*, to be considered frequent. For example, if *min_sup*, is, say, 5%, a pattern is frequent if it occurs in 5% of the data tuples. Consider Figure 9.12, which plots information gain versus pattern frequency (support) for three UCI data sets. A theoretical upper bound on information gain, which was derived analytically, is also plotted. The figure shows that the discriminative power (assessed here as information gain) of low-frequency patterns is bounded by a small value. This is due to the patterns' limited coverage of the data set. Similarly, the discriminative power of very high-frequency patterns is also bounded by a small value, which is due to their commonness in the data. The upper bound of information gain is a function of pattern frequency. The information gain upper bound increases monotonically with pattern frequency. These observations can be confirmed analytically. Patterns with medium-large supports (e.g., *support* = 300 in Figure 9.12a) may be discriminative or not. Thus, not every frequent pattern is useful.

---

[5]The University of California at Irvine (UCI) archives several large data sets at *http://kdd.ics.uci.edu/*. These are commonly used by researchers for the testing and comparison of machine learning and data mining algorithms.

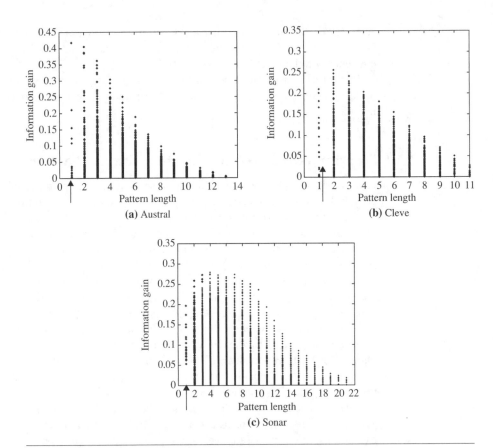

Figure 9.11 Single feature versus frequent pattern: Information gain is plotted for single features (patterns of length 1, indicated by arrows) and frequent patterns (combined features) for three UCI data sets. *Source:* Adapted from Cheng, Yan, Han, and Hsu [CYHH07].

If we were to add all the frequent patterns to the feature space, the resulting feature space would be huge. This slows down the model learning process and may also lead to decreased accuracy due to a form of overfitting in which there are too many features. Many of the patterns may be redundant. Therefore, it's a good idea to apply feature selection to eliminate the less discriminative and redundant frequent patterns as features. The *general framework for discriminative frequent pattern–based classification* is as follows.

1. **Feature generation:** The data, D, are partitioned according to class label. Use frequent itemset mining to discover frequent patterns in each partition, satisfying minimum support. The collection of frequent patterns, $\mathcal{F}$, makes up the feature candidates.

2. **Feature selection:** Apply feature selection to $\mathcal{F}$, resulting in $\mathcal{F}_S$, the set of selected (more discriminating) frequent patterns. Information gain, Fisher score, or other evaluation measures can be used for this step. Relevancy checking can also be

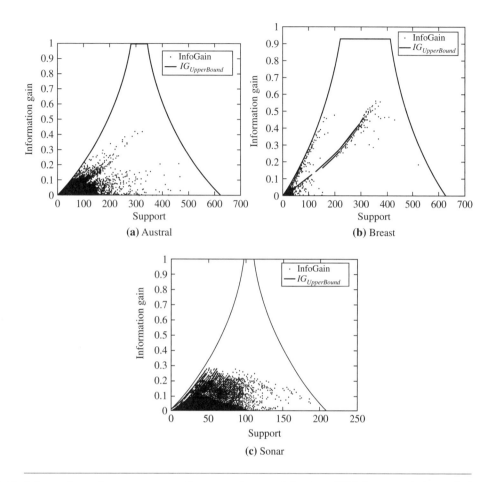

Figure 9.12 Information gain versus pattern frequency (support) for three UCI data sets. A theoretical upper bound on information gain ($IG_{UpperBound}$) is also shown. *Source:* Adapted from Cheng, Yan, Han, and Hsu [CYHH07].

incorporated into this step to weed out redundant patterns. The data set D is transformed to D', where the feature space now includes the single features as well as the selected frequent patterns, $\mathcal{F}_S$.

3. Learning of classification model: A classifier is built on the data set D'. Any learning algorithm can be used as the classification model.

The general framework is summarized in Figure 9.13(a), where the discriminative patterns are represented by dark circles. Although the approach is straightforward, we can encounter a computational bottleneck by having to first find *all* the frequent patterns, and then analyze *each one* for selection. The amount of frequent patterns found can be huge due to the explosive number of pattern combinations between items.

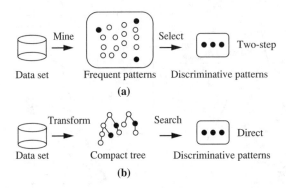

Figure 9.13 A framework for frequent pattern–based classification: (a) a two-step general approach versus (b) the direct approach of DDPMine.

To improve the efficiency of the general framework, consider condensing steps 1 and 2 into just one step. That is, rather than generating the complete set of frequent patterns, it's possible to mine only the highly discriminative ones. This more direct approach is referred to as *direct discriminative pattern mining*. The DDPMine algorithm follows this approach, as illustrated in Figure 9.13(b). It first transforms the training data into a compact tree structure known as a frequent pattern tree, or FP-tree (Section 6.2.4), which holds all of the attribute–value (itemset) association information. It then searches for discriminative patterns on the tree. The approach is direct in that it avoids generating a large number of indiscriminative patterns. It incrementally reduces the problem by eliminating training tuples, thereby progressively shrinking the FP-tree. This further speeds up the mining process.

By choosing to transform the original data to an FP-tree, DDPMine avoids generating redundant patterns because an FP-tree stores only the *closed* frequent patterns. By definition, any subpattern, β, of a closed pattern, α, is redundant with respect to α (Section 6.1.2). DDPMine directly mines the discriminative patterns and integrates feature selection into the mining framework. The theoretical upper bound on information gain is used to facilitate a branch-and-bound search, which prunes the search space significantly. Experimental results show that DDPMine achieves orders of magnitude speedup over the two-step approach without decline in classification accuracy. DDPMine also outperforms state-of-the-art associative classification methods in terms of both accuracy and efficiency.

9.5 Lazy Learners (or Learning from Your Neighbors)

The classification methods discussed so far in this book—decision tree induction, Bayesian classification, rule-based classification, classification by backpropagation, support vector machines, and classification based on association rule mining—are all examples of *eager learners*. **Eager learners**, when given a set of training tuples, will construct a generalization (i.e., classification) model before receiving new (e.g., test) tuples to classify. We can think of the learned model as being ready and eager to classify previously unseen tuples.

Imagine a contrasting lazy approach, in which the learner instead waits until the last minute before doing any model construction to classify a given test tuple. That is, when given a training tuple, a **lazy learner** simply stores it (or does only a little minor processing) and waits until it is given a test tuple. Only when it sees the test tuple does it perform generalization to classify the tuple based on its similarity to the stored training tuples. Unlike eager learning methods, lazy learners do less work when a training tuple is presented and more work when making a classification or numeric prediction. Because lazy learners store the training tuples or "instances," they are also referred to as **instance-based learners**, even though all learning is essentially based on instances.

When making a classification or numeric prediction, lazy learners can be computationally expensive. They require efficient storage techniques and are well suited to implementation on parallel hardware. They offer little explanation or insight into the data's structure. Lazy learners, however, naturally support incremental learning. They are able to model complex decision spaces having hyperpolygonal shapes that may not be as easily describable by other learning algorithms (such as hyperrectangular shapes modeled by decision trees). In this section, we look at two examples of lazy learners: *k-nearest-neighbor classifiers* (Section 9.5.1) and *case-based reasoning classifiers* (Section 9.5.2).

9.5.1 *k*-Nearest-Neighbor Classifiers

The *k*-nearest-neighbor method was first described in the early 1950s. The method is labor intensive when given large training sets, and did not gain popularity until the 1960s when increased computing power became available. It has since been widely used in the area of pattern recognition.

Nearest-neighbor classifiers are based on learning by analogy, that is, by comparing a given test tuple with training tuples that are similar to it. The training tuples are described by n attributes. Each tuple represents a point in an n-dimensional space. In this way, all the training tuples are stored in an n-dimensional pattern space. When given an unknown tuple, a **k-nearest-neighbor classifier** searches the pattern space for the k training tuples that are closest to the unknown tuple. These k training tuples are the k "nearest neighbors" of the unknown tuple.

"Closeness" is defined in terms of a distance metric, such as Euclidean distance. The Euclidean distance between two points or tuples, say, $X_1 = (x_{11}, x_{12}, \dots, x_{1n})$ and $X_2 = (x_{21}, x_{22}, \dots, x_{2n})$, is

$$dist(X_1, X_2) = \sqrt{\sum_{i=1}^{n}(x_{1i} - x_{2i})^2}. \tag{9.22}$$

In other words, for each numeric attribute, we take the difference between the corresponding values of that attribute in tuple X_1 and in tuple X_2, square this difference, and accumulate it. The square root is taken of the total accumulated distance count. Typically, we normalize the values of each attribute before using Eq. (9.22). This helps prevent attributes with initially large ranges (e.g., *income*) from outweighing attributes with initially smaller ranges (e.g., binary attributes). Min-max normalization, for example, can be used to transform a value v of a numeric attribute A to v' in the range $[0, 1]$ by computing

$$v' = \frac{v - min_A}{max_A - min_A},$$ (9.23)

where min_A and max_A are the minimum and maximum values of attribute A. Chapter 3 describes other methods for data normalization as a form of data transformation.

For k-nearest-neighbor classification, the unknown tuple is assigned the most common class among its k-nearest neighbors. When $k = 1$, the unknown tuple is assigned the class of the training tuple that is closest to it in pattern space. Nearest-neighbor classifiers can also be used for numeric prediction, that is, to return a real-valued prediction for a given unknown tuple. In this case, the classifier returns the average value of the real-valued labels associated with the k-nearest neighbors of the unknown tuple.

"*But how can distance be computed for attributes that are not numeric, but nominal (or categorical) such as color?*" The previous discussion assumes that the attributes used to describe the tuples are all numeric. For nominal attributes, a simple method is to compare the corresponding value of the attribute in tuple X_1 with that in tuple X_2. If the two are identical (e.g., tuples X_1 and X_2 both have the color blue), then the difference between the two is taken as 0. If the two are different (e.g., tuple X_1 is blue but tuple X_2 is red), then the difference is considered to be 1. Other methods may incorporate more sophisticated schemes for differential grading (e.g., where a larger difference score is assigned, say, for blue and white than for blue and black).

"*What about missing values?*" In general, if the value of a given attribute A is missing in tuple X_1 and/or in tuple X_2, we assume the maximum possible difference. Suppose that each of the attributes has been mapped to the range $[0, 1]$. For nominal attributes, we take the difference value to be 1 if either one or both of the corresponding values of A are missing. If A is numeric and missing from both tuples X_1 and X_2, then the difference is also taken to be 1. If only one value is missing and the other (which we will call v') is present and normalized, then we can take the difference to be either $|1 - v'|$ or $|0 - v'|$ (i.e., $1 - v'$ or v'), whichever is greater.

"*How can I determine a good value for k, the number of neighbors?*" This can be determined experimentally. Starting with $k = 1$, we use a test set to estimate the error rate of the classifier. This process can be repeated each time by incrementing k to allow for one more neighbor. The k value that gives the minimum error rate may be selected. In general, the larger the number of training tuples, the larger the value of k will be (so that classification and numeric prediction decisions can be based on a larger portion of the stored tuples). As the number of training tuples approaches infinity and $k = 1$, the error rate can be no worse than twice the Bayes error rate (the latter being the theoretical minimum). If k also approaches infinity, the error rate approaches the Bayes error rate.

Nearest-neighbor classifiers use distance-based comparisons that intrinsically assign equal weight to each attribute. They therefore can suffer from poor accuracy when given noisy or irrelevant attributes. The method, however, has been modified to incorporate attribute weighting and the pruning of noisy data tuples. The choice of a distance metric can be critical. The Manhattan (city block) distance (Section 2.4.4), or other distance measurements, may also be used.

Nearest-neighbor classifiers can be extremely slow when classifying test tuples. If D is a training database of $|D|$ tuples and $k = 1$, then $O(|D|)$ comparisons are required to classify a given test tuple. By presorting and arranging the stored tuples into search trees, the number of comparisons can be reduced to $O(log(|D|))$. Parallel implementation can reduce the running time to a constant, that is, $O(1)$, which is independent of $|D|$.

Other techniques to speed up classification time include the use of *partial distance* calculations and *editing* the stored tuples. In the **partial distance** method, we compute the distance based on a subset of the n attributes. If this distance exceeds a threshold, then further computation for the given stored tuple is halted, and the process moves on to the next stored tuple. The **editing** method removes training tuples that prove useless. This method is also referred to as **pruning** or **condensing** because it reduces the total number of tuples stored.

9.5.2 Case-Based Reasoning

Case-based reasoning (CBR) classifiers use a database of problem solutions to solve new problems. Unlike nearest-neighbor classifiers, which store training tuples as points in Euclidean space, CBR stores the tuples or "cases" for problem solving as complex symbolic descriptions. Business applications of CBR include problem resolution for customer service help desks, where cases describe product-related diagnostic problems. CBR has also been applied to areas such as engineering and law, where cases are either technical designs or legal rulings, respectively. Medical education is another area for CBR, where patient case histories and treatments are used to help diagnose and treat new patients.

When given a new case to classify, a case-based reasoner will first check if an identical training case exists. If one is found, then the accompanying solution to that case is returned. If no identical case is found, then the case-based reasoner will search for training cases having components that are similar to those of the new case. Conceptually, these training cases may be considered as neighbors of the new case. If cases are represented as graphs, this involves searching for subgraphs that are similar to subgraphs within the new case. The case-based reasoner tries to combine the solutions of the neighboring training cases to propose a solution for the new case. If incompatibilities arise with the individual solutions, then backtracking to search for other solutions may be necessary. The case-based reasoner may employ background knowledge and problem-solving strategies to propose a feasible combined solution.

Challenges in case-based reasoning include finding a good similarity metric (e.g., for matching subgraphs) and suitable methods for combining solutions. Other challenges include the selection of salient features for indexing training cases and the development of efficient indexing techniques. A trade-off between accuracy and efficiency evolves as the number of stored cases becomes very large. As this number increases, the case-based reasoner becomes more intelligent. After a certain point, however, the system's efficiency will suffer as the time required to search for and process relevant cases increases. As with nearest-neighbor classifiers, one solution is to edit the training database. Cases that are redundant or that have not proved useful may be discarded for the sake of improved performance. These decisions, however, are not clear-cut and their automation remains an active area of research.

9.6 Other Classification Methods

In this section, we give a brief description of several other classification methods, including genetic algorithms (Section 9.6.1), rough set approach (Section 9.6.2), and fuzzy set approaches (Section 9.6.3). In general, these methods are less commonly used for classification in commercial data mining systems than the methods described earlier in this book. However, these methods show their strength in certain applications, and hence it is worthwhile to include them here.

9.6.1 Genetic Algorithms

Genetic algorithms attempt to incorporate ideas of natural evolution. In general, genetic learning starts as follows. An initial **population** is created consisting of randomly generated rules. Each rule can be represented by a string of bits. As a simple example, suppose that samples in a given training set are described by two Boolean attributes, A_1 and A_2, and that there are two classes, C_1 and C_2. The rule "*IF A_1 AND NOT A_2 THEN C_2*" can be encoded as the bit string "100," where the two leftmost bits represent attributes A_1 and A_2, respectively, and the rightmost bit represents the class. Similarly, the rule "*IF NOT A_1 AND NOT A_2 THEN C_1*" can be encoded as "001." If an attribute has k values, where $k > 2$, then k bits may be used to encode the attribute's values. Classes can be encoded in a similar fashion.

Based on the notion of survival of the fittest, a new population is formed to consist of the *fittest* rules in the current population, as well as *offspring* of these rules. Typically, the **fitness** of a rule is assessed by its classification accuracy on a set of training samples.

Offspring are created by applying genetic operators such as crossover and mutation. In **crossover**, substrings from pairs of rules are swapped to form new pairs of rules. In **mutation**, randomly selected bits in a rule's string are inverted.

The process of generating new populations based on prior populations of rules continues until a population, P, evolves where each rule in P satisfies a prespecified fitness threshold.

Genetic algorithms are easily parallelizable and have been used for classification as well as other optimization problems. In data mining, they may be used to evaluate the fitness of other algorithms.

9.6.2 Rough Set Approach

Rough set theory can be used for classification to discover structural relationships within imprecise or noisy data. It applies to discrete-valued attributes. Continuous-valued attributes must therefore be discretized before its use.

Rough set theory is based on the establishment of **equivalence classes** within the given training data. All the data tuples forming an equivalence class are indiscernible, that is, the samples are identical with respect to the attributes describing the data. Given real-world data, it is common that some classes cannot be distinguished in terms of the available attributes. Rough sets can be used to approximately or "roughly" define such classes. A rough set definition for a given class, C, is approximated by two sets—a **lower approximation** of C and an **upper approximation** of C. The lower approximation of C consists of all the data tuples that, based on the knowledge of the attributes, are certain to belong to C without ambiguity. The upper approximation of C consists of all the tuples that, based on the knowledge of the attributes, cannot be described as not belonging to C. The lower and upper approximations for a class C are shown in Figure 9.14, where each rectangular region represents an equivalence class. Decision rules can be generated for each class. Typically, a decision table is used to represent the rules.

Rough sets can also be used for attribute subset selection (or feature reduction, where attributes that do not contribute to the classification of the given training data can be identified and removed) and relevance analysis (where the contribution or significance of each attribute is assessed with respect to the classification task). The problem of finding the minimal subsets (**reducts**) of attributes that can describe all the concepts in the given data set is NP-hard. However, algorithms to reduce the computation intensity have been proposed. In one method, for example, a **discernibility matrix** is used that stores the differences between attribute values for each pair of data tuples. Rather than

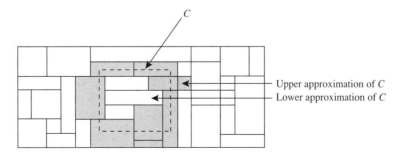

Figure 9.14 A rough set approximation of class C's set of tuples using lower and upper approximation sets of C. The rectangular regions represent equivalence classes.

searching on the entire training set, the matrix is instead searched to detect redundant attributes.

9.6.3 Fuzzy Set Approaches

Rule-based systems for classification have the disadvantage that they involve sharp cut-offs for continuous attributes. For example, consider the following rule for customer credit application approval. The rule essentially says that applications for customers who have had a job for two or more years and who have a high income (i.e., of at least $50,000) are approved:

$$IF \ (years\_employed \geq 2) \ AND \ (income \geq 50,000) \ THEN \ credit = approved. \quad (9.24)$$

By Rule (9.24), a customer who has had a job for at least two years will receive credit if her income is, say, $50,000, but not if it is $49,000. Such harsh thresholding may seem unfair.

Instead, we can discretize *income* into categories (e.g., {*low_income, medium_income, high_income*}) and then apply **fuzzy logic** to allow "fuzzy" thresholds or boundaries to be defined for each category (Figure 9.15). Rather than having a precise cutoff between categories, fuzzy logic uses truth values between 0.0 and 1.0 to represent the degree of membership that a certain value has in a given category. Each category then represents a **fuzzy set**. Hence, with fuzzy logic, we can capture the notion that an income of $49,000 is, more or less, high, although not as high as an income of $50,000. Fuzzy logic systems typically provide graphical tools to assist users in converting attribute values to fuzzy truth values.

Fuzzy set theory is also known as **possibility theory**. It was proposed by Lotfi Zadeh in 1965 as an alternative to traditional two-value logic and probability theory. It lets us work at a high abstraction level and offers a means for dealing with imprecise data

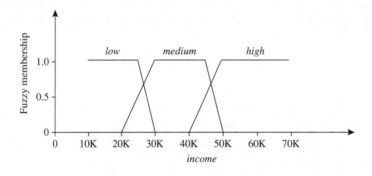

Figure 9.15 Fuzzy truth values for *income*, representing the degree of membership of *income* values with respect to the categories {*low, medium, high*}. Each category represents a fuzzy set. Note that a given income value, *x*, can have membership in more than one fuzzy set. The membership values of *x* in each fuzzy set do not have to total to 1.

measurement. Most important, fuzzy set theory allows us to deal with vague or inexact facts. For example, being a member of a set of high incomes is inexact (e.g., if $50,000 is high, then what about $49,000? or $48,000?) Unlike the notion of traditional "crisp" sets where an element belongs to either a set S or its complement, in fuzzy set theory, elements can belong to more than one fuzzy set. For example, the income value $49,000 belongs to both the *medium* and *high* fuzzy sets, but to differing degrees. Using fuzzy set notation and following Figure 9.15, this can be shown as

$$m_{medium\_income}(\$49,000) = 0.15 \ and \ m_{high\_income}(\$49,000) = 0.96,$$

where m denotes the membership function, that is operating on the fuzzy sets of *medium_income* and *high_income*, respectively. In fuzzy set theory, membership values for a given element, x (e.g., for $49,000), do not have to sum to 1. This is unlike traditional probability theory, which is constrained by a summation axiom.

Fuzzy set theory is useful for data mining systems performing rule-based classification. It provides operations for combining fuzzy measurements. Suppose that in addition to the fuzzy sets for *income*, we defined the fuzzy sets *junior_employee* and *senior_employee* for the attribute *years_employed*. Suppose also that we have a rule that, say, tests *high_income* and *senior_employee* in the rule antecedent (IF part) for a given employee, x. If these two fuzzy measures are ANDed together, the minimum of their measure is taken as the measure of the rule. In other words,

$$m_{(high\_income \ AND \ senior\_employee)}(x) = min(m_{high\_income}(x), m_{senior\_employee}(x)).$$

This is akin to saying that a chain is as strong as its weakest link. If the two measures are ORed, the maximum of their measure is taken as the measure of the rule. In other words,

$$m_{(high\_income \ OR \ senior\_employee)}(x) = max(m_{high\_income}(x), m_{senior\_employee}(x)).$$

Intuitively, this is like saying that a rope is as strong as its strongest strand.

Given a tuple to classify, more than one fuzzy rule may apply. Each applicable rule contributes a vote for membership in the categories. Typically, the truth values for each predicted category are summed, and these sums are combined. Several procedures exist for translating the resulting fuzzy output into a *defuzzified* or crisp value that is returned by the system.

Fuzzy logic systems have been used in numerous areas for classification, including market research, finance, health care, and environmental engineering.

9.7 Additional Topics Regarding Classification

Most of the classification algorithms we have studied handle multiple classes, but some, such as support vector machines, assume only two classes exist in the data. What adaptations can be made to allow for when there are more than two classes? This question is addressed in Section 9.7.1 on *multiclass classification*.

What can we do if we want to build a classifier for data where only some of the data are class-labeled, but most are not? Document classification, speech recognition, and information extraction are just a few examples of applications in which unlabeled data are abundant. Consider *document classification,* for example. Suppose we want to build a model to automatically classify text documents like articles or web pages. In particular, we want the model to distinguish between hockey and football documents. We have a vast amount of documents available, yet the documents are not class-labeled. Recall that supervised learning requires a training set, that is, a set of classlabeled data. To have a human examine and assign a class label to individual documents (to form a training set) is time consuming and expensive.

Speech recognition requires the accurate labeling of speech utterances by trained linguists. It was reported that 1 minute of speech takes 10 minutes to label, and annotating phonemes (basic units of sound) can take 400 times as long. *Information extraction systems* are trained using labeled documents with detailed annotations. These are obtained by having human experts highlight items or relations of interest in text such as the names of companies or individuals. High-level expertise may be required for certain knowledge domains such as gene and disease mentions in biomedical information extraction. Clearly, the manual assignment of class labels to prepare a training set can be extremely costly, time consuming, and tedious.

We study three approaches to classification that are suitable for situations where there is an abundance of unlabeled data. Section 9.7.2 introduces semisupervised classification, which builds a classifier using both labeled and unlabeled data. Section 9.7.3 presents *active learning,* where the learning algorithm carefully selects a few of the unlabeled data tuples and asks a human to label only those tuples. Section 9.7.4 presents *transfer learning,* which aims to extract the knowledge from one or more source tasks (e.g., classifying camera reviews) and apply the knowledge to a target task (e.g., TV reviews). Each of these strategies can reduce the need to annotate large amounts of data, resulting in cost and time savings.

9.7.1 Multiclass Classification

Some classification algorithms, such as support vector machines, are designed for binary classification. How can we extend these algorithms to allow for **multiclass classification** (i.e., classification involving more than two classes)?

A simple approach is **one-versus-all** (OVA). Given m classes, we train m binary classifiers, one for each class. Classifier j is trained using tuples of class j as the positive class, and the remaining tuples as the negative class. It learns to return a positive value for class j and a negative value for the rest. To classify an unknown tuple, X, the set of classifiers vote as an ensemble. For example, if classifier j predicts the positive class for X, then class j gets one vote. If it predicts the negative class for X, then each of the classes except j gets one vote. The class with the most votes is assigned to X.

All-versus-all (AVA) is an alternative approach that learns a classifier for each pair of classes. Given m classes, we construct $\frac{m(m-1)}{2}$ binary classifiers. A classifier is trained using tuples of the two classes it should discriminate. To classify an unknown tuple, each classifier votes. The tuple is assigned the class with the maximum number of votes. All-versus-all tends to be superior to one-versus-all.

A problem with the previous schemes is that binary classifiers are sensitive to errors. If any classifier makes an error, it can affect the vote count.

Error-correcting codes can be used to improve the accuracy of multiclass classification, not just in the previous situations, but for classification in general. Error-correcting codes were originally designed to correct errors during data transmission for communication tasks. For such tasks, the codes are used to add redundancy to the data being transmitted so that, even if some errors occur due to noise in the channel, the data can be correctly received at the other end. For multiclass classification, even if some of the individual binary classifiers make a prediction error for a given unknown tuple, we may still be able to correctly label the tuple.

An error-correcting code is assigned to each class, where each code is a bit vector. Figure 9.16 show an example of 7-bit codewords assigned to classes C_1, C_2, C_3, and C_4. We train one classifier for each bit position. Therefore, in our example we train seven classifiers. If a classifier makes an error, there is a better chance that we may still be able to predict the right class for a given unknown tuple because of the redundancy gained by having additional bits. The technique uses a distance measurement called the Hamming distance to guess the "closest" class in case of errors, and is illustrated in Example 9.3.

Example 9.3 Multiclass classification with error-correcting codes. Consider the 7-bit codewords associated with classes C_1 to C_4 in Figure 9.16. Suppose that, given an unknown tuple to label, the seven trained binary classifiers collectively output the codeword 0001010, which does not match a codeword for any of the four classes. A classification error has obviously occurred, but can we figure out what the classification most likely should be? We can try by using the **Hamming distance**, which is the number of different bits between two codewords. The Hamming distance between the output codeword and the codeword for C_1 is 5 because five bits—namely, the first, second, third, fifth, and seventh—differ. Similarly, the Hamming distance between the output code and the codewords for C_2 through C_4 are 3, 3, and 1, respectively. Note that the output codeword is closest to the codeword for C_4. That is, the smallest Hamming distance between the output and a class codeword is for class C_4. Therefore, we assign C_4 as the class label of the given tuple. ∎

Class	Error-correcting codeword
C_1	1 1 1 1 1 1 1
C_2	0 0 0 0 1 1 1
C_3	0 0 1 1 0 0 1
C_4	0 1 0 1 0 1 0

Figure 9.16 Error-correcting codes for a multiclass classification problem involving four classes.

Error-correcting codes can correct up to $\frac{h-1}{2}$ 1-bit errors, where h is the minimum Hamming distance between any two codewords. If we use one bit per class, such as for 4-bit codewords for classes C_1 through C_4, then this is equivalent to the one-versus-all approach, and the codes are not sufficient to self-correct. (Try it as an exercise.) When selecting error-correcting codes for multiclass classification, there must be good row-wise and column-wise separation between the codewords. The greater the distance, the more likely that errors will be corrected.

9.7.2 Semi-Supervised Classification

Semi-supervised classification uses labeled data and unlabeled data to build a classifier. Let $X_l = \{(x_1, y_1), \ldots, x_l, y_l)\}$ be the set of labeled data and $X_u = \{x_{l+1}, \ldots, x_n\}$ be the set of unlabeled data. Here we describe a few examples of this approach for learning.

Self-training is the simplest form of semi-supervised classification. It first builds a classifier using the labeled data. The classifier then tries to label the unlabeled data. The tuple with the most confident label prediction is added to the set of labeled data, and the process repeats (Figure 9.17). Although the method is easy to understand, a disadvantage is that it may reinforce errors.

Cotraining is another form of semi-supervised classification, where two or more classifiers teach each other. Each learner uses a different and ideally independent set of features for each tuple. Consider web page data, for example, where attributes relating to the images on the page may be used as one set of features, while attributes relating to the corresponding text constitute another set of features for the same data. Each set

Self-training

1. Select a learning method such as, say, Bayesian classification. Build the classifier using the labeled data, X_l.

2. Use the classifier to label the unlabeled data, X_u.

3. Select the tuple $x \in X_u$ having the highest confidence (most confident prediction). Add it and its predicted label to X_l.

4. Repeat (i.e., retrain the classifier using the augmented set of labeled data).

Cotraining

1. Define two separate nonoverlapping feature sets for the labeled data, X_l.

2. Train two classifiers, f_1 and f_2, on the labeled data, where f_1 is trained using one of the feature sets and f_2 is trained using the other.

3. Classify X_u with f_1 and f_2 separately.

4. Add the most confident $(x, f_1(x))$ to the set of labeled data used by f_2, where $x \in X_u$. Similarly, add the most confident $(x, f_2(x))$ to the set of labeled data used by f_1.

5. Repeat.

Figure 9.17 Self-training and cotraining methods of semi-supervised classification.

of features should be sufficient to train a good classifier. Suppose we split the feature set into two sets and train two classifiers, f_1 and f_2, where each classifier is trained on a different set. Then, f_1 and f_2 are used to predict the class labels for the unlabeled data, X_u. Each classifier then teaches the other in that the tuple having the most confident prediction from f_1 is added to the set of labeled data for f_2 (along with its label).

Similarly, the tuple having the most confident prediction from f_2 is added to the set of labeled data for f_1. The method is summarized in Figure 9.17. Cotraining is less sensitive to errors than self-training. A difficulty is that the assumptions for its usage may not hold true, that is, it may not be possible to split the features into mutually exclusive and class-conditionally independent sets.

Alternate approaches to semi-supervised learning exist. For example, we can model the joint probability distribution of the features and the labels. For the unlabeled data, the labels can then be treated as missing data. The EM algorithm (Chapter 11) can be used to maximize the likelihood of the model. Methods using support vector machines have also been proposed.

9.7.3 Active Learning

Active learning is an iterative type of supervised learning that is suitable for situations where data are abundant, yet the class labels are scarce or expensive to obtain. The learning algorithm is active in that it can purposefully query a user (e.g., a human oracle) for labels. The number of tuples used to learn a concept this way is often much smaller than the number required in typical supervised learning.

"*How does active learning work to overcome the labeling bottleneck?*" To keep costs down, the active learner aims to achieve high accuracy using as few labeled instances as possible. Let D be all of data under consideration. Various strategies exist for active learning on D. Figure 9.18 illustrates a *pool-based approach* to active learning. Suppose that a small subset of D is class-labeled. This set is denoted L. U is the set of unlabeled data in D. It is also referred to as a pool of unlabeled data. An active learner begins with L as the initial training set. It then uses a *querying function* to carefully select one or more data samples from U and requests labels for them from an oracle (e.g., a human annotator). The newly labeled samples are added to L, which the learner then uses in a standard supervised way. The process repeats. The active learning goal is to achieve high accuracy using as few labeled tuples as possible. Active learning algorithms are typically evaluated with the use of learning curves, which plot accuracy as a function of the number of instances queried.

Most of the active learning research focuses on how to *choose* the data tuples to be queried. Several frameworks have been proposed. *Uncertainty sampling* is the most common, where the active learner chooses to query the tuples which it is the least certain how to label. Other strategies work to reduce the *version space*, that is, the subset of all hypotheses that are consistent with the observed training tuples. Alternatively, we may follow a decision-theoretic approach that estimates expected error reduction. This selects tuples that would result in the greatest reduction in the total number of

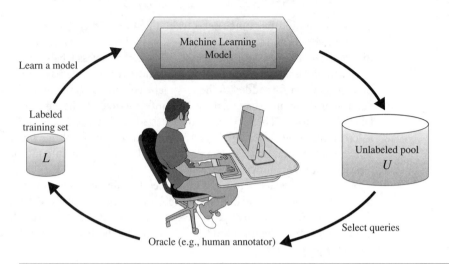

Figure 9.18 The pool-based active learning cycle. *Source:* From Settles [Set10], Burr Settles Computer Sciences Technical Report 1648, University of Wisconsin–Madison; used with permission.

incorrect predictions such as by reducing the expected entropy over U. This latter approach tends to be more computationally expensive.

9.7.4 Transfer Learning

Suppose that *AllElectronics* has collected a number of customer reviews on a product such as a brand of camera. The classification task is to automatically label the reviews as either positive or negative. This task is known as **sentiment classification**. We could examine each review and annotate it by adding a *positive* or *negative* class label. The labeled reviews can then be used to train and test a classifier to label future reviews of the product as either positive or negative. The manual effort involved in annotating the review data can be expensive and time consuming.

Suppose that *AllElectronics* has customer reviews for other products as well such as TVs. The distribution of review data for different types of products can vary greatly. We cannot assume that the TV-review data will have the same distribution as the camera-review data; thus we must build a separate classification model for the TV-review data. Examining and labeling the TV-review data to form a training set will require a lot of effort. In fact, we would need to label a large amount of the data to train the review-classification models for each product. It would be nice if we could adapt an existing classification model (e.g., the one we built for cameras) to help learn a classification model for TVs. Such *knowledge transfer* would reduce the need to annotate a large amount of data, resulting in cost and time savings. This is the essence behind *transfer learning*.

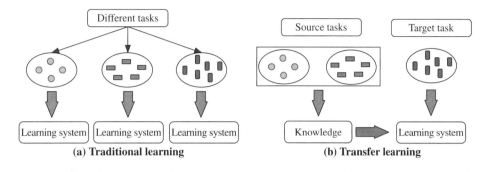

(a) Traditional learning   **(b) Transfer learning**

Figure 9.19 Transfer learning versus traditional learning. (a) Traditional learning methods build a new classifier from scratch for each classification task. (b) Transfer learning applies knowledge from a source classifier to simplify the construction of a classifier for a new, target task. *Source:* From Pan and Yang [PY10]; used with permission.

Transfer learning aims to extract the knowledge from one or more *source tasks* and apply the knowledge to a *target task*. In our example, the source task is the classification of camera reviews, and the target task is the classification of TV reviews. Figure 9.19 illustrates a comparison between traditional learning methods and transfer learning. Traditional learning methods build a new classifier for each new classification task, based on available class-labeled training and test data. Transfer learning algorithms apply knowledge about source tasks when building a classifier for a new (target) task. Construction of the resulting classifier requires fewer training data and less training time. Traditional learning algorithms assume that the training data and test data are drawn from the same distribution and the same feature space. Thus, if the distribution changes, such methods need to rebuild the models from scratch.

Transfer learning allows the distributions, tasks, and even the data domains used in training and testing to be different. Transfer learning is analogous to the way humans may apply their knowledge of a task to facilitate the learning of another task. For example, if we know how to play the recorder, we may apply our knowledge of note reading and music to simplify the task of learning to play the piano. Similarly, knowing Spanish may make it easier to learn Italian.

Transfer learning is useful for common applications where the data become outdated or the distribution changes. Here we give two more examples. Consider *web-document classification*, where we may have trained a classifier to label, say, articles from various newsgroups according to predefined categories. The web data that were used to train the classifier can easily become outdated because the topics on the Web change frequently. Another application area for transfer learning is *email spam filtering*. We could train a classifier to label email as either "*spam*" or "*not spam*," using email from a group of users. If new users come along, the distribution of their email can be different from the original group, hence the need to adapt the learned model to incorporate the new data.

There are various approaches to transfer learning, the most common of which is the *instance-based transfer learning* approach. This approach reweights some of the data from the source task and uses it to learn the target task. The **TrAdaBoost** (Transfer AdaBoost) algorithm exemplifies this approach. Consider our previous example of web-document classification, where the distribution of the old data on which the classifier was trained (the source data) is different from the newer data (the target data). TrAdaBoost assumes that the source and target domain data are each described by the same set of attributes (i.e., they have the same "feature space") and the same set of class labels, but that the distribution of the data in the two domains is very different. It extends the AdaBoost ensemble method described in Section 8.6.3. TrAdaBoost requires the labeling of only a small amount of the target data. Rather than throwing out all the old source data, TrAdaBoost assumes that a large amount of it can be useful in training the new classification model. The idea is to filter out the influence of any old data that are very different from the new data by automatically adjusting weights assigned to the training tuples.

Recall that in boosting, an ensemble is created by learning a series of classifiers. To begin, each tuple is assigned a weight. After a classifier M_i is learned, the weights are updated to allow the subsequent classifier, M_{i+1}, to "pay more attention" to the training tuples that were misclassified by M_i. TrAdaBoost follows this strategy for the target data. However, if a source data tuple is misclassified, TrAdaBoost reasons that the tuple is probably very different from the target data. It therefore *reduces* the weight of such tuples so that they will have less effect on the subsequent classifier. As a result, TrAdaBoost can learn an accurate classification model using only a small amount of new data and a large amount of old data, even when the new data alone are insufficient to train the model. Hence, in this way TrAdaBoost allows knowledge to be transferred from the old classifier to the new one.

A challenge with transfer learning is **negative transfer**, which occurs when the new classifier performs worse than if there had been no transfer at all. Work on how to avoid negative transfer is an area of future research. *Heterogeneous transfer learning*, which involves transferring knowledge from different feature spaces and multiple source domains, is another venue for further work. Much of the research on transfer learning to date has been on small-scale applications. The use of transfer learning on larger applications, such as social network analysis and video classification, is an area for further investigation.

9.8 Summary

- Unlike naïve Bayesian classification (which assumes class conditional independence), **Bayesian belief networks** allow class conditional independencies to be defined between subsets of variables. They provide a graphical model of causal relationships, on which learning can be performed. Trained Bayesian belief networks can be used for classification.

- **Backpropagation** is a neural network algorithm for classification that employs a method of gradient descent. It searches for a set of weights that can model the data so as to minimize the mean-squared distance between the network's class prediction and the actual class label of data tuples. Rules may be extracted from trained neural networks to help improve the interpretability of the learned network.

- A **support vector machine** is an algorithm for the classification of both linear and nonlinear data. It transforms the original data into a higher dimension, from where it can find a hyperplane for data separation using essential training tuples called **support vectors**.

- *Frequent patterns* reflect strong associations between attribute–value pairs (or items) in data and are used in **classification based on frequent patterns**. Approaches to this methodology include associative classification and discriminant frequent pattern–based classification. In **associative classification**, a classifier is built from association rules generated from frequent patterns. In **discriminative frequent pattern–based classification**, frequent patterns serve as combined features, which are considered in addition to single features when building a classification model.

- Decision tree classifiers, Bayesian classifiers, classification by backpropagation, support vector machines, and classification based on frequent patterns are all examples of **eager learners** in that they use training tuples to construct a generalization model and in this way are ready for classifying new tuples. This contrasts with **lazy learners** or **instance-based** methods of classification, such as nearest-neighbor classifiers and case-based reasoning classifiers, which store all of the training tuples in pattern space and wait until presented with a test tuple before performing generalization. Hence, lazy learners require efficient indexing techniques.

- In **genetic algorithms**, populations of rules "evolve" via operations of crossover and mutation until all rules within a population satisfy a specified threshold. **Rough set theory** can be used to approximately define classes that are not distinguishable based on the available attributes. **Fuzzy set** approaches replace "brittle" threshold cutoffs for continuous-valued attributes with membership degree functions.

- Binary classification schemes, such as support vector machines, can be adapted to handle **multiclass classification**. This involves constructing an ensemble of binary classifiers. Error-correcting codes can be used to increase the accuracy of the ensemble.

- **Semi-supervised classification** is useful when large amounts of unlabeled data exist. It builds a classifier using both labeled and unlabeled data. Examples of semi-supervised classification include *self-training* and *cotraining*.

- **Active learning** is a form of supervised learning that is also suitable for situations where data are abundant, yet the class labels are scarce or expensive to obtain. The learning algorithm can actively query a user (e.g., a human oracle) for labels. To keep costs down, the active learner aims to achieve high accuracy using as few labeled instances as possible.

■ **Transfer learning** aims to extract the knowledge from one or more *source tasks* and apply the knowledge to a *target task*. TrAdaBoost is an example of the *instance-based approach* to transfer learning, which reweights some of the data from the source task and uses it to learn the target task, thereby requiring fewer labeled target-task tuples.

9.9 Exercises

9.1 The following table consists of training data from an employee database. The data have been generalized. For example, "31 ... 35" for *age* represents the age range of 31 to 35. For a given row entry, *count* represents the number of data tuples having the values for *department, status, age,* and *salary* given in that row.

department	status	age	salary	count
sales	senior	31 ... 35	46K ... 50K	30
sales	junior	26 ... 30	26K ... 30K	40
sales	junior	31 ... 35	31K ... 35K	40
systems	junior	21 ... 25	46K ... 50K	20
systems	senior	31 ... 35	66K ... 70K	5
systems	junior	26 ... 30	46K ... 50K	3
systems	senior	41 ... 45	66K ... 70K	3
marketing	senior	36 ... 40	46K ... 50K	10
marketing	junior	31 ... 35	41K ... 45K	4
secretary	senior	46 ... 50	36K ... 40K	4
secretary	junior	26 ... 30	26K ... 30K	6

Let *status* be the class-label attribute.

(a) Design a multilayer feed-forward neural network for the given data. Label the nodes in the input and output layers.

(b) Using the multilayer feed-forward neural network obtained in (a), show the weight values after one iteration of the backpropagation algorithm, given the training instance "*(sales, senior, 31 ... 35, 46K ... 50K)*". Indicate your initial weight values and biases and the learning rate used.

9.2 The *support vector machine* is a highly accurate classification method. However, SVM classifiers suffer from slow processing when training with a large set of data tuples. Discuss how to overcome this difficulty and develop a scalable SVM algorithm for efficient SVM classification in large data sets.

9.3 Compare and contrast *associative classification* and *discriminative frequent pattern–based classification*. Why is classification based on frequent patterns able to achieve higher classification accuracy in many cases than a classic decision tree method?

9.4 Compare the advantages and disadvantages of *eager* classification (e.g., decision tree, Bayesian, neural network) versus *lazy* classification (e.g., *k*-nearest neighbor, case-based reasoning).

9.5 Write an algorithm for *k-nearest-neighbor classification* given *k*, the nearest number of neighbors, and *n*, the number of attributes describing each tuple.

9.6 Briefly describe the classification processes using (a) *genetic algorithms*, (b) *rough sets*, and (c) *fuzzy sets*.

9.7 Example 9.3 showed a use of error-correcting codes for a *multiclass classification* problem having four classes.

(a) Suppose that, given an unknown tuple to label, the seven trained binary classifiers collectively output the codeword 0101110, which does not match a codeword for any of the four classes. Using error correction, what class label should be assigned to the tuple?

(b) Explain why using a 4-bit vector for the codewords is insufficient for error correction.

9.8 *Semi-supervised classification*, *active learning*, and *transfer learning* are useful for situations in which unlabeled data are abundant.

(a) Describe *semi-supervised classification*, *active learning*, and *transfer learning*. Elaborate on applications for which they are useful, as well as the challenges of these approaches to classification.

(b) Research and describe an approach to semi-supervised classification other than self-training and cotraining.

(c) Research and describe an approach to active learning other than pool-based learning.

(d) Research and describe an alternative approach to instance-based transfer learning.

9.10 Bibliographic Notes

For an introduction to Bayesian belief networks, see Darwiche [Dar10] and Heckerman [Hec96]. For a thorough presentation of probabilistic networks, see Pearl [Pea88] and Koller and Friedman [KF09]. Solutions for learning the belief network structure from training data given observable variables are proposed in Cooper and Herskovits [CH92]; Buntine [Bun94]; and Heckerman, Geiger, and Chickering [HGC95]. Algorithms for inference on belief networks can be found in Russell and Norvig [RN95] and Jensen [Jen96]. The method of gradient descent, described in Section 9.1.2, for training Bayesian belief networks, is given in Russell, Binder, Koller, and Kanazawa [RBKK95]. The example given in Figure 9.1 is adapted from Russell et al. [RBKK95].

Alternative strategies for learning belief networks with hidden variables include application of Dempster, Laird, and Rubin's [DLR77] EM (Expectation Maximization) algorithm (Lauritzen [Lau95]) and methods based on the minimum description length principle (Lam [Lam98]). Cooper [Coo90] showed that the general problem of inference in unconstrained belief networks is NP-hard. Limitations of belief networks, such as their large computational complexity (Laskey and Mahoney [LM97]), have prompted the exploration of hierarchical and composable Bayesian models (Pfeffer, Koller, Milch, and Takusagawa [PKMT99] and Xiang, Olesen, and Jensen [XOJ00]). These follow an object-oriented approach to knowledge representation. Fishelson and Geiger [FG02] present a Bayesian network for genetic linkage analysis.

The perceptron is a simple neural network, proposed in 1958 by Rosenblatt [Ros58], which became a landmark in early machine learning history. Its input units are randomly connected to a single layer of output linear threshold units. In 1969, Minsky and Papert [MP69] showed that perceptrons are incapable of learning concepts that are linearly inseparable. This limitation, as well as limitations on hardware at the time, dampened enthusiasm for research in computational neuronal modeling for nearly 20 years. Renewed interest was sparked following the presentation of the backpropagation algorithm in 1986 by Rumelhart, Hinton, and Williams [RHW86], as this algorithm can learn concepts that are linearly inseparable.

Since then, many variations of backpropagation have been proposed, involving, for example, alternative error functions (Hanson and Burr [HB87]); dynamic adjustment of the network topology (Mézard and Nadal [MN89]; Fahlman and Lebiere [FL90]; Le Cun, Denker, and Solla [LDS90]; and Harp, Samad, and Guha [HSG90]); and dynamic adjustment of the learning rate and momentum parameters (Jacobs [Jac88]). Other variations are discussed in Chauvin and Rumelhart [CR95]. Books on neural networks include Rumelhart and McClelland [RM86]; Hecht-Nielsen [HN90]; Hertz, Krogh, and Palmer [HKP91]; Chauvin and Rumelhart [CR95]; Bishop [Bis95]; Ripley [Rip96]; and Haykin [Hay99]. Many books on machine learning, such as Mitchell [Mit97] and Russell and Norvig [RN95], also contain good explanations of the backpropagation algorithm.

There are several techniques for extracting rules from neural networks, such as those found in these papers: [SN88, Gal93, TS93, Avn95, LSL95, CS96, LGT97]. The method of rule extraction described in Section 9.2.4 is based on Lu, Setiono, and Liu [LSL95]. Critiques of techniques for rule extraction from neural networks can be found in Craven and Shavlik [CS97]. Roy [Roy00] proposes that the theoretical foundations of neural networks are flawed with respect to assumptions made regarding how connectionist learning models the brain. An extensive survey of applications of neural networks in industry, business, and science is provided in Widrow, Rumelhart, and Lehr [WRL94].

Support Vector Machines (SVMs) grew out of early work by Vapnik and Chervonenkis on statistical learning theory [VC71]. The first paper on SVMs was presented by Boser, Guyon, and Vapnik [BGV92]. More detailed accounts can be found in books by Vapnik [Vap95, Vap98]. Good starting points include the tutorial on SVMs by Burges [Bur98], as well as textbook coverage by Haykin [Hay08], Kecman [Kec01], and Cristianini and Shawe-Taylor [CS-T00]. For methods for solving optimization problems, see Fletcher [Fle87] and Nocedal and Wright [NW99]. These references give additional details alluded to as "fancy math tricks" in our text, such as transformation of the problem to a Lagrangian formulation and subsequent solving using Karush-Kuhn-Tucker (KKT) conditions.

For the application of SVMs to regression, see Schölkopf, Bartlett, Smola, and Williamson [SBSW99] and Drucker, Burges, Kaufman, Smola, and Vapnik [DBK+97]. Approaches to SVM for large data include the sequential minimal optimization algorithm by Platt [Pla98], decomposition approaches such as in Osuna, Freund, and Girosi [OFG97], and CB-SVM, a microclustering-based SVM algorithm for large data sets, by Yu, Yang, and Han [YYH03]. A library of software for support vector machines is provided by Chang and Lin at *www.csie.ntu.edu.tw/~cjlin/libsvm/*, which supports multiclass classification.

Many algorithms have been proposed that adapt frequent pattern mining to the task of classification. Early studies on associative classification include the CBA algorithm, proposed in Liu, Hsu, and Ma [LHM98]. A classifier that uses *emerging patterns* (itemsets with support that varies significantly from one data set to another) is proposed in Dong and Li [DL99] and Li, Dong, and Ramamohanarao [LDR00]. CMAR is presented in Li, Han, and Pei [LHP01]. CPAR is presented in Yin and Han [YH03b]. Cong, Tan, Tung, and Xu describe RCBT, a method for mining top-k covering rule groups for classifying high-dimensional gene expression data with high accuracy [CTTX05].

Wang and Karypis [WK05] present HARMONY (Highest confidence classificAtion Rule Mining fOr iNstance-centric classifYing), which directly mines the final classification rule set with the aid of pruning strategies. Lent, Swami, and Widom [LSW97] propose the ARCS system regarding mining multidimensional association rules. It combines ideas from association rule mining, clustering, and image processing, and applies them to classification. Meretakis and Wüthrich [MW99] propose constructing a naïve Bayesian classifier by mining long itemsets. Veloso, Meira, and Zaki [VMZ06] propose an association rule–based classification method based on a lazy (noneager) learning approach, in which the computation is performed on a demand-driven basis.

Studies on discriminative frequent pattern–based classification were conducted by Cheng, Yan, Han, and Hsu [CYHH07] and Cheng, Yan, Han, and Yu [CYHY08]. The former work establishes a theoretical upper bound on the discriminative power of frequent patterns (based on either information gain [Qui86] or Fisher score [DHS01]), which can be used as a strategy for setting minimum support. The latter work describes the DDPMine algorithm, which is a direct approach to mining discriminative frequent patterns for classification in that it avoids generating the complete frequent pattern set. H. Kim, S. Kim, Weninger, et al. proposed an NDPMine algorithm that performs frequent and discriminative pattern–based classification by taking *repetitive* features into consideration [KKW+10].

Nearest-neighbor classifiers were introduced in 1951 by Fix and Hodges [FH51]. A comprehensive collection of articles on nearest-neighbor classification can be found in Dasarathy [Das91]. Additional references can be found in many texts on classification, such as Duda, Hart, and Stork [DHS01] and James [Jam85], as well as articles by Cover and Hart [CH67] and Fukunaga and Hummels [FH87]. Their integration with attribute weighting and the pruning of noisy instances is described in Aha [Aha92]. The use of search trees to improve nearest-neighbor classification time is detailed in Friedman, Bentley, and Finkel [FBF77]. The partial distance method was proposed by researchers in vector quantization and compression. It is outlined in Gersho and Gray

[GG92]. The editing method for removing "useless" training tuples was first proposed by Hart [Har68].

The computational complexity of nearest-neighbor classifiers is described in Preparata and Shamos [PS85]. References on case-based reasoning include the texts by Riesbeck and Schank [RS89] and Kolodner [Kol93], as well as Leake [Lea96] and Aamodt and Plazas [AP94]. For a list of business applications, see Allen [All94]. Examples in medicine include CASEY by Koton [Kot88] and PROTOS by Bareiss, Porter, and Weir [BPW88], while Rissland and Ashley [RA87] is an example of CBR for law. CBR is available in several commercial software products. For texts on genetic algorithms, see Goldberg [Gol89], Michalewicz [Mic92], and Mitchell [Mit96].

Rough sets were introduced in Pawlak [Paw91]. Concise summaries of rough set theory in data mining include Ziarko [Zia91] and Cios, Pedrycz, and Swiniarski [CPS98]. Rough sets have been used for feature reduction and expert system design in many applications, including Ziarko [Zia91], Lenarcik and Piasta [LP97], and Swiniarski [Swi98]. Algorithms to reduce the computation intensity in finding reducts have been proposed in Skowron and Rauszer [SR92]. Fuzzy set theory was proposed by Zadeh [Zad65, Zad83]. Additional descriptions can be found in Yager and Zadeh [YZ94] and Kecman [Kec01].

Work on multiclass classification is described in Hastie and Tibshirani [HT98], Tax and Duin [TD02], and Allwein, Shapire, and Singer [ASS00]. Zhu [Zhu05] presents a comprehensive survey on semi-supervised classification. For additional references, see the book edited by Chapelle, Schölkopf, and Zien [CSZ06]. Dietterich and Bakiri [DB95] propose the use of error-correcting codes for multiclass classification. For a survey on active learning, see Settles [Set10]. Pan and Yang present a survey on transfer learning [PY10]. The TrAdaBoost boosting algorithm for transfer learning is given in Dai, Yang, Xue, and Yu [DYXY07].

Cluster Analysis: Basic Concepts and Methods

Imagine that you are the Director of Customer Relationships at *AllElectronics*, and you have five managers working for you. You would like to organize all the company's customers into five groups so that each group can be assigned to a different manager. Strategically, you would like that the customers in each group are as similar as possible. Moreover, two given customers having very different business patterns should not be placed in the same group. Your intention behind this business strategy is to develop customer relationship campaigns that specifically target each group, based on common features shared by the customers per group. What kind of data mining techniques can help you to accomplish this task?

Unlike in classification, the class label (or *group_ID*) of each customer is unknown. You need to *discover* these groupings. Given a large number of customers and many attributes describing customer profiles, it can be very costly or even infeasible to have a human study the data and manually come up with a way to partition the customers into strategic groups. You need a *clustering* tool to help.

Clustering is the process of grouping a set of data objects into multiple groups or *clusters* so that objects within a cluster have high similarity, but are very dissimilar to objects in other clusters. Dissimilarities and similarities are assessed based on the attribute values describing the objects and often involve distance measures.[1] Clustering as a data mining tool has its roots in many application areas such as biology, security, business intelligence, and Web search.

This chapter presents the basic concepts and methods of cluster analysis. In Section 10.1, we introduce the topic and study the requirements of clustering methods for massive amounts of data and various applications. You will learn several basic clustering techniques, organized into the following categories: *partitioning methods* (Section 10.2), *hierarchical methods* (Section 10.3), *density-based methods* (Section 10.4), and *grid-based methods* (Section 10.5). In Section 10.6, we briefly discuss how to evaluate

---

[1]Data similarity and dissimilarity are discussed in detail in Section 2.4. You may want to refer to that section for a quick review.

clustering methods. A discussion of advanced methods of clustering is reserved for Chapter 11.

10.1 Cluster Analysis

This section sets up the groundwork for studying cluster analysis. Section 10.1.1 defines cluster analysis and presents examples of where it is useful. In Section 10.1.2, you will learn aspects for comparing clustering methods, as well as requirements for clustering. An overview of basic clustering techniques is presented in Section 10.1.3.

10.1.1 What Is Cluster Analysis?

Cluster analysis or simply **clustering** is the process of partitioning a set of data objects (or observations) into subsets. Each subset is a **cluster**, such that objects in a cluster are similar to one another, yet dissimilar to objects in other clusters. The set of clusters resulting from a cluster analysis can be referred to as a **clustering**. In this context, different clustering methods may generate different clusterings on the same data set. The partitioning is not performed by humans, but by the clustering algorithm. Hence, clustering is useful in that it can lead to the discovery of previously unknown groups within the data.

Cluster analysis has been widely used in many applications such as business intelligence, image pattern recognition, Web search, biology, and security. In business intelligence, clustering can be used to organize a large number of customers into groups, where customers within a group share strong similar characteristics. This facilitates the development of business strategies for enhanced customer relationship management. Moreover, consider a consultant company with a large number of projects. To improve project management, clustering can be applied to partition projects into categories based on similarity so that project auditing and diagnosis (to improve project delivery and outcomes) can be conducted effectively.

In image recognition, clustering can be used to discover clusters or "subclasses" in handwritten character recognition systems. Suppose we have a data set of handwritten digits, where each digit is labeled as either 1, 2, 3, and so on. Note that there can be a large variance in the way in which people write the same digit. Take the number 2, for example. Some people may write it with a small circle at the left bottom part, while some others may not. We can use clustering to determine subclasses for "2," each of which represents a variation on the way in which 2 can be written. Using multiple models based on the subclasses can improve overall recognition accuracy.

Clustering has also found many applications in Web search. For example, a keyword search may often return a very large number of hits (i.e., pages relevant to the search) due to the extremely large number of web pages. Clustering can be used to organize the search results into groups and present the results in a concise and easily accessible way. Moreover, clustering techniques have been developed to cluster documents into topics, which are commonly used in information retrieval practice.

As a data mining function, cluster analysis can be used as a standalone tool to gain insight into the distribution of data, to observe the characteristics of each cluster, and to focus on a particular set of clusters for further analysis. Alternatively, it may serve as a preprocessing step for other algorithms, such as characterization, attribute subset selection, and classification, which would then operate on the detected clusters and the selected attributes or features.

Because a cluster is a collection of data objects that are similar to one another within the cluster and dissimilar to objects in other clusters, a cluster of data objects can be treated as an implicit class. In this sense, clustering is sometimes called **automatic classification**. Again, a critical difference here is that clustering can automatically find the groupings. This is a distinct advantage of cluster analysis.

Clustering is also called **data segmentation** in some applications because clustering partitions large data sets into groups according to their *similarity*. Clustering can also be used for **outlier detection**, where outliers (values that are "far away" from any cluster) may be more interesting than common cases. Applications of outlier detection include the detection of credit card fraud and the monitoring of criminal activities in electronic commerce. For example, exceptional cases in credit card transactions, such as very expensive and infrequent purchases, may be of interest as possible fraudulent activities. Outlier detection is the subject of Chapter 12.

Data clustering is under vigorous development. Contributing areas of research include data mining, statistics, machine learning, spatial database technology, information retrieval, Web search, biology, marketing, and many other application areas. Owing to the huge amounts of data collected in databases, cluster analysis has recently become a highly active topic in data mining research.

As a branch of statistics, cluster analysis has been extensively studied, with the main focus on *distance-based cluster analysis*. Cluster analysis tools based on k-means, k-medoids, and several other methods also have been built into many statistical analysis software packages or systems, such as S-Plus, SPSS, and SAS. In machine learning, recall that classification is known as supervised learning because the class label information is given, that is, the learning algorithm is supervised in that it is told the class membership of each training tuple. Clustering is known as **unsupervised learning** because the class label information is not present. For this reason, clustering is a form of **learning by observation**, rather than *learning by examples*. In data mining, efforts have focused on finding methods for efficient and effective cluster analysis in *large databases*. Active themes of research focus on the *scalability* of clustering methods, the effectiveness of methods for clustering *complex shapes* (e.g., nonconvex) and *types of data* (e.g., text, graphs, and images), *high-dimensional* clustering techniques (e.g., clustering objects with thousands of features), and methods for clustering *mixed numerical and nominal data* in large databases.

10.1.2 Requirements for Cluster Analysis

Clustering is a challenging research field. In this section, you will learn about the requirements for clustering as a data mining tool, as well as aspects that can be used for comparing clustering methods.

The following are typical requirements of clustering in data mining.

- **Scalability:** Many clustering algorithms work well on small data sets containing fewer than several hundred data objects; however, a large database may contain millions or even billions of objects, particularly in Web search scenarios. Clustering on only a sample of a given large data set may lead to biased results. Therefore, highly scalable clustering algorithms are needed.

- **Ability to deal with different types of attributes**: Many algorithms are designed to cluster numeric (interval-based) data. However, applications may require clustering other data types, such as binary, nominal (categorical), and ordinal data, or mixtures of these data types. Recently, more and more applications need clustering techniques for complex data types such as graphs, sequences, images, and documents.

- **Discovery of clusters with arbitrary shape**: Many clustering algorithms determine clusters based on Euclidean or Manhattan distance measures (Chapter 2). Algorithms based on such distance measures tend to find spherical clusters with similar size and density. However, a cluster could be of any shape. Consider sensors, for example, which are often deployed for environment surveillance. Cluster analysis on sensor readings can detect interesting phenomena. We may want to use clustering to find the frontier of a running forest fire, which is often not spherical. It is important to develop algorithms that can detect clusters of arbitrary shape.

- **Requirements for domain knowledge to determine input parameters**: Many clustering algorithms require users to provide domain knowledge in the form of input parameters such as the desired number of clusters. Consequently, the clustering results may be sensitive to such parameters. Parameters are often hard to determine, especially for high-dimensionality data sets and where users have yet to grasp a deep understanding of their data. Requiring the specification of domain knowledge not only burdens users, but also makes the quality of clustering difficult to control.

- **Ability to deal with noisy data**: Most real-world data sets contain outliers and/or missing, unknown, or erroneous data. Sensor readings, for example, are often noisy—some readings may be inaccurate due to the sensing mechanisms, and some readings may be erroneous due to interferences from surrounding transient objects. Clustering algorithms can be sensitive to such noise and may produce poor-quality clusters. Therefore, we need clustering methods that are robust to noise.

- **Incremental clustering and insensitivity to input order**: In many applications, incremental updates (representing newer data) may arrive at any time. Some clustering algorithms cannot incorporate incremental updates into existing clustering structures and, instead, have to recompute a new clustering from scratch. Clustering algorithms may also be sensitive to the input data order. That is, given a set of data objects, clustering algorithms may return dramatically different clusterings depending on the order in which the objects are presented. Incremental clustering algorithms and algorithms that are insensitive to the input order are needed.

- **Capability of clustering high-dimensionality data**: A data set can contain numerous dimensions or attributes. When clustering documents, for example, each keyword can be regarded as a dimension, and there are often thousands of keywords. Most clustering algorithms are good at handling low-dimensional data such as data sets involving only two or three dimensions. Finding clusters of data objects in a high-dimensional space is challenging, especially considering that such data can be very sparse and highly skewed.

- **Constraint-based clustering**: Real-world applications may need to perform clustering under various kinds of constraints. Suppose that your job is to choose the locations for a given number of new automatic teller machines (ATMs) in a city. To decide upon this, you may cluster households while considering constraints such as the city's rivers and highway networks and the types and number of customers per cluster. A challenging task is to find data groups with good clustering behavior that satisfy specified constraints.

- **Interpretability and usability**: Users want clustering results to be interpretable, comprehensible, and usable. That is, clustering may need to be tied in with specific semantic interpretations and applications. It is important to study how an application goal may influence the selection of clustering features and clustering methods.

The following are orthogonal aspects with which clustering methods can be compared:

- **The partitioning criteria**: In some methods, all the objects are partitioned so that no hierarchy exists among the clusters. That is, all the clusters are at the same level conceptually. Such a method is useful, for example, for partitioning customers into groups so that each group has its own manager. Alternatively, other methods partition data objects hierarchically, where clusters can be formed at different semantic levels. For example, in text mining, we may want to organize a corpus of documents into multiple general topics, such as "politics" and "sports," each of which may have subtopics, For instance, "football," "basketball," "baseball," and "hockey" can exist as subtopics of "sports." The latter four subtopics are at a lower level in the hierarchy than "sports."

- **Separation of clusters**: Some methods partition data objects into mutually exclusive clusters. When clustering customers into groups so that each group is taken care of by one manager, each customer may belong to only one group. In some other situations, the clusters may not be exclusive, that is, a data object may belong to more than one cluster. For example, when clustering documents into topics, a document may be related to multiple topics. Thus, the topics as clusters may not be exclusive.

- **Similarity measure**: Some methods determine the similarity between two objects by the distance between them. Such a distance can be defined on Euclidean space, a road network, a vector space, or any other space. In other methods, the similarity may be defined by connectivity based on density or contiguity, and may not rely on the absolute distance between two objects. Similarity measures play a fundamental role in the design of clustering methods. While distance-based methods can often take advantage of optimization techniques, density- and continuity-based methods can often find clusters of arbitrary shape.

- **Clustering space**: Many clustering methods search for clusters within the entire given data space. These methods are useful for low-dimensionality data sets. With high-dimensional data, however, there can be many irrelevant attributes, which can make similarity measurements unreliable. Consequently, clusters found in the full space are often meaningless. It's often better to instead search for clusters within different subspaces of the same data set. *Subspace clustering* discovers clusters and subspaces (often of low dimensionality) that manifest object similarity.

To conclude, clustering algorithms have several requirements. These factors include scalability and the ability to deal with different types of attributes, noisy data, incremental updates, clusters of arbitrary shape, and constraints. Interpretability and usability are also important. In addition, clustering methods can differ with respect to the partitioning level, whether or not clusters are mutually exclusive, the similarity measures used, and whether or not subspace clustering is performed.

10.1.3 Overview of Basic Clustering Methods

There are many clustering algorithms in the literature. It is difficult to provide a crisp categorization of clustering methods because these categories may overlap so that a method may have features from several categories. Nevertheless, it is useful to present a relatively organized picture of clustering methods. In general, the major fundamental clustering methods can be classified into the following categories, which are discussed in the rest of this chapter.

Partitioning methods: Given a set of n objects, a partitioning method constructs k partitions of the data, where each partition represents a cluster and $k \leq n$. That is, it divides the data into k groups such that each group must contain at least one object. In other words, partitioning methods conduct one-level partitioning on data sets. The basic partitioning methods typically adopt *exclusive cluster separation*. That is, each object must belong to exactly one group. This requirement may be relaxed, for example, in fuzzy partitioning techniques. References to such techniques are given in the bibliographic notes (Section 10.9).

Most partitioning methods are distance-based. Given k, the number of partitions to construct, a partitioning method creates an initial partitioning. It then uses an **iterative relocation technique** that attempts to improve the partitioning by moving objects from one group to another. The general criterion of a good partitioning is that objects in the same cluster are "close" or related to each other, whereas objects in different clusters are "far apart" or very different. There are various kinds of other criteria for judging the quality of partitions. Traditional partitioning methods can be extended for subspace clustering, rather than searching the full data space. This is useful when there are many attributes and the data are sparse.

Achieving global optimality in partitioning-based clustering is often computationally prohibitive, potentially requiring an exhaustive enumeration of all the possible partitions. Instead, most applications adopt popular heuristic methods, such as greedy approaches like the *k-means* and the *k-medoids* algorithms, which progressively improve the clustering quality and approach a local optimum. These heuristic clustering methods work well for finding spherical-shaped clusters in small- to medium-size databases. To find clusters with complex shapes and for very large data sets, partitioning-based methods need to be extended. Partitioning-based clustering methods are studied in depth in Section 10.2.

Hierarchical methods: A hierarchical method creates a hierarchical decomposition of the given set of data objects. A hierarchical method can be classified as being either *agglomerative* or *divisive*, based on how the hierarchical decomposition is formed. The *agglomerative approach*, also called the *bottom-up* approach, starts with each object forming a separate group. It successively merges the objects or groups close to one another, until all the groups are merged into one (the topmost level of the hierarchy), or a termination condition holds. The *divisive approach*, also called the *top-down* approach, starts with all the objects in the same cluster. In each successive iteration, a cluster is split into smaller clusters, until eventually each object is in one cluster, or a termination condition holds.

Hierarchical clustering methods can be distance-based or density- and continuity-based. Various extensions of hierarchical methods consider clustering in subspaces as well.

Hierarchical methods suffer from the fact that once a step (merge or split) is done, it can never be undone. This rigidity is useful in that it leads to smaller computation costs by not having to worry about a combinatorial number of different choices. Such techniques cannot correct erroneous decisions; however, methods for improving the quality of hierarchical clustering have been proposed. Hierarchical clustering methods are studied in Section 10.3.

Density-based methods: Most partitioning methods cluster objects based on the distance between objects. Such methods can find only spherical-shaped clusters and encounter difficulty in discovering clusters of arbitrary shapes. Other clustering methods have been developed based on the notion of *density*. Their general idea is to continue growing a given cluster as long as the density (number of objects or data points) in the "neighborhood" exceeds some threshold. For example, for each data point within a given cluster, the neighborhood of a given radius has to contain at least a minimum number of points. Such a method can be used to filter out noise or outliers and discover clusters of arbitrary shape.

Density-based methods can divide a set of objects into multiple exclusive clusters, or a hierarchy of clusters. Typically, density-based methods consider exclusive clusters only, and do not consider fuzzy clusters. Moreover, density-based methods can be extended from full space to subspace clustering. Density-based clustering methods are studied in Section 10.4.

Grid-based methods: Grid-based methods quantize the object space into a finite number of cells that form a grid structure. All the clustering operations are performed on the grid structure (i.e., on the quantized space). The main advantage of this approach is its fast processing time, which is typically independent of the number of data objects and dependent only on the number of cells in each dimension in the quantized space.

Using grids is often an efficient approach to many spatial data mining problems, including clustering. Therefore, grid-based methods can be integrated with other clustering methods such as density-based methods and hierarchical methods. Grid-based clustering is studied in Section 10.5.

These methods are briefly summarized in Figure 10.1. Some clustering algorithms integrate the ideas of several clustering methods, so that it is sometimes difficult to classify a given algorithm as uniquely belonging to only one clustering method category. Furthermore, some applications may have clustering criteria that require the integration of several clustering techniques.

In the following sections, we examine each clustering method in detail. Advanced clustering methods and related issues are discussed in Chapter 11. In general, the notation used is as follows. Let D be a data set of n objects to be clustered. An object is described by d variables, where each variable is also called an attribute or a dimension,

Method	General Characteristics
Partitioning methods	– Find mutually exclusive clusters of spherical shape – Distance-based – May use mean or medoid (etc.) to represent cluster center – Effective for small- to medium-size data sets
Hierarchical methods	– Clustering is a hierarchical decomposition (i.e., multiple levels) – Cannot correct erroneous merges or splits – May incorporate other techniques like microclustering or consider object "linkages"
Density-based methods	– Can find arbitrarily shaped clusters – Clusters are dense regions of objects in space that are separated by low-density regions – Cluster density: Each point must have a minimum number of points within its "neighborhood" – May filter out outliers
Grid-based methods	– Use a multiresolution grid data structure – Fast processing time (typically independent of the number of data objects, yet dependent on grid size)

Figure 10.1 Overview of clustering methods discussed in this chapter. Note that some algorithms may combine various methods.

and therefore may also be referred to as a *point* in a d-dimensional object space. Objects are represented in bold italic font (e.g., $\boldsymbol{p}$).

10.2 Partitioning Methods

The simplest and most fundamental version of cluster analysis is partitioning, which organizes the objects of a set into several exclusive groups or clusters. To keep the problem specification concise, we can assume that the number of clusters is given as background knowledge. This parameter is the starting point for partitioning methods.

Formally, given a data set, D, of n objects, and k, the number of clusters to form, a **partitioning algorithm** organizes the objects into k partitions ($k \leq n$), where each partition represents a cluster. The clusters are formed to optimize an objective partitioning criterion, such as a dissimilarity function based on distance, so that the objects within a cluster are "similar" to one another and "dissimilar" to objects in other clusters in terms of the data set attributes.

In this section you will learn the most well-known and commonly used partitioning methods—k-means (Section 10.2.1) and k-medoids (Section 10.2.2). You will also learn several variations of these classic partitioning methods and how they can be scaled up to handle large data sets.

10.2.1 *k*-Means: A Centroid-Based Technique

Suppose a data set, D, contains n objects in Euclidean space. Partitioning methods distribute the objects in D into k clusters, $C_1, \ldots, C_k$, that is, $C_i \subset D$ and $C_i \cap C_j = \emptyset$ for ($1 \leq i, j \leq k$). An objective function is used to assess the partitioning quality so that objects within a cluster are similar to one another but dissimilar to objects in other clusters. This is, the objective function aims for high intracluster similarity and low intercluster similarity.

A centroid-based partitioning technique uses the *centroid* of a cluster, C_i, to represent that cluster. Conceptually, the centroid of a cluster is its center point. The centroid can be defined in various ways such as by the mean or medoid of the objects (or points) assigned to the cluster. The difference between an object $\boldsymbol{p} \in C_i$ and $\boldsymbol{c_i}$, the representative of the cluster, is measured by $dist(\boldsymbol{p}, \boldsymbol{c_i})$, where $dist(\boldsymbol{x}, \boldsymbol{y})$ is the Euclidean distance between two points $\boldsymbol{x}$ and $\boldsymbol{y}$. The quality of cluster C_i can be measured by the **within-cluster variation**, which is the sum of *squared error* between all objects in C_i and the centroid $\boldsymbol{c_i}$, defined as

$$E = \sum_{i=1}^{k} \sum_{\boldsymbol{p} \in C_i} dist(\boldsymbol{p}, \boldsymbol{c_i})^2, \tag{10.1}$$

where E is the sum of the squared error for all objects in the data set; $\boldsymbol{p}$ is the point in space representing a given object; and $\boldsymbol{c_i}$ is the centroid of cluster C_i (both $\boldsymbol{p}$ and $\boldsymbol{c_i}$ are multidimensional). In other words, for each object in each cluster, the distance from the object to its cluster center is squared, and the distances are summed. This objective function tries to make the resulting k clusters as compact and as separate as possible.

Optimizing the within-cluster variation is computationally challenging. In the worst case, we would have to enumerate a number of possible partitionings that are exponential to the number of clusters, and check the within-cluster variation values. It has been shown that the problem is NP-hard in general Euclidean space even for two clusters (i.e., $k = 2$). Moreover, the problem is NP-hard for a general number of clusters k even in the 2-D Euclidean space. If the number of clusters k and the dimensionality of the space d are fixed, the problem can be solved in time $O(n^{dk+1} \log n)$, where n is the number of objects. To overcome the prohibitive computational cost for the exact solution, greedy approaches are often used in practice. A prime example is the k-means algorithm, which is simple and commonly used.

"How does the k-means algorithm work?" The k-means algorithm defines the centroid of a cluster as the mean value of the points within the cluster. It proceeds as follows. First, it randomly selects k of the objects in D, each of which initially represents a cluster mean or center. For each of the remaining objects, an object is assigned to the cluster to which it is the most similar, based on the Euclidean distance between the object and the cluster mean. The k-means algorithm then iteratively improves the within-cluster variation. For each cluster, it computes the new mean using the objects assigned to the cluster in the previous iteration. All the objects are then reassigned using the updated means as the new cluster centers. The iterations continue until the assignment is stable, that is, the clusters formed in the current round are the same as those formed in the previous round. The k-means procedure is summarized in Figure 10.2.

Algorithm: k-means. The k-means algorithm for partitioning, where each cluster's center is represented by the mean value of the objects in the cluster.

Input:

- k: the number of clusters,
- D: a data set containing n objects.

Output: A set of k clusters.

Method:

(1) arbitrarily choose k objects from D as the initial cluster centers;
(2) **repeat**
(3)   (re)assign each object to the cluster to which the object is the most similar,
            based on the mean value of the objects in the cluster;
(4)   update the cluster means, that is, calculate the mean value of the objects for
            each cluster;
(5) **until** no change;

Figure 10.2 The k-means partitioning algorithm.

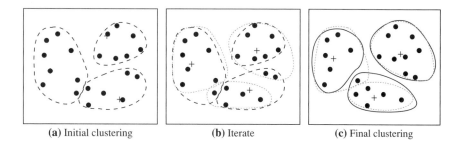

(a) Initial clustering   **(b)** Iterate   **(c)** Final clustering

Figure 10.3 Clustering of a set of objects using the k-means method; for (b) update cluster centers and reassign objects accordingly (the mean of each cluster is marked by a $+$).

Example 10.1 **Clustering by k-means partitioning.** Consider a set of objects located in 2-D space, as depicted in Figure 10.3(a). Let $k = 3$, that is, the user would like the objects to be partitioned into three clusters.

According to the algorithm in Figure 10.2, we arbitrarily choose three objects as the three initial cluster centers, where cluster centers are marked by a $+$. Each object is assigned to a cluster based on the cluster center to which it is the nearest. Such a distribution forms silhouettes encircled by dotted curves, as shown in Figure 10.3(a).

Next, the cluster centers are updated. That is, the mean value of each cluster is recalculated based on the current objects in the cluster. Using the new cluster centers, the objects are redistributed to the clusters based on which cluster center is the nearest. Such a redistribution forms new silhouettes encircled by dashed curves, as shown in Figure 10.3(b).

This process iterates, leading to Figure 10.3(c). The process of iteratively reassigning objects to clusters to improve the partitioning is referred to as *iterative relocation*. Eventually, no reassignment of the objects in any cluster occurs and so the process terminates. The resulting clusters are returned by the clustering process. ∎

The k-means method is not guaranteed to converge to the global optimum and often terminates at a local optimum. The results may depend on the initial random selection of cluster centers. (You will be asked to give an example to show this as an exercise.) To obtain good results in practice, it is common to run the k-means algorithm multiple times with different initial cluster centers.

The time complexity of the k-means algorithm is $O(nkt)$, where n is the total number of objects, k is the number of clusters, and t is the number of iterations. Normally, $k \ll n$ and $t \ll n$. Therefore, the method is relatively scalable and efficient in processing large data sets.

There are several variants of the k-means method. These can differ in the selection of the initial k-means, the calculation of dissimilarity, and the strategies for calculating cluster means.

The k-means method can be applied only when the mean of a set of objects is defined. This may not be the case in some applications such as when data with nominal attributes are involved. The **k-modes method** is a variant of k-means, which extends the k-means paradigm to cluster nominal data by replacing the means of clusters with modes. It uses new dissimilarity measures to deal with nominal objects and a frequency-based method to update modes of clusters. The k-means and the k-modes methods can be integrated to cluster data with mixed numeric and nominal values.

The necessity for users to specify k, the number of clusters, in advance can be seen as a disadvantage. There have been studies on how to overcome this difficulty, however, such as by providing an approximate range of k values, and then using an analytical technique to determine the best k by comparing the clustering results obtained for the different k values. The k-means method is not suitable for discovering clusters with nonconvex shapes or clusters of very different size. Moreover, it is sensitive to noise and outlier data points because a small number of such data can substantially influence the mean value.

"How can we make the k-means algorithm more scalable?" One approach to making the k-means method more efficient on large data sets is to use a good-sized set of samples in clustering. Another is to employ a filtering approach that uses a spatial hierarchical data index to save costs when computing means. A third approach explores the microclustering idea, which first groups nearby objects into "microclusters" and then performs k-means clustering on the microclusters. Microclustering is further discussed in Section 10.3.

10.2.2 *k*-Medoids: A Representative Object-Based Technique

The k-means algorithm is sensitive to outliers because such objects are far away from the majority of the data, and thus, when assigned to a cluster, they can dramatically distort the mean value of the cluster. This inadvertently affects the assignment of other objects to clusters. This effect is particularly exacerbated due to the use of the *squared*-error function of Eq. (10.1), as observed in Example 10.2.

Example 10.2 A drawback of *k*-means. Consider six points in 1-D space having the values $1, 2, 3, 8, 9, 10$, and 25, respectively. Intuitively, by visual inspection we may imagine the points partitioned into the clusters $\{1, 2, 3\}$ and $\{8, 9, 10\}$, where point 25 is excluded because it appears to be an outlier. How would k-means partition the values? If we apply k-means using $k = 2$ and Eq. (10.1), the partitioning $\{\{1, 2, 3\}, \{8, 9, 10, 25\}\}$ has the within-cluster variation

$$(1-2)^2 + (2-2)^2 + (3-2)^2 + (8-13)^2 + (9-13)^2 + (10-13)^2 + (25-13)^2 = 196,$$

given that the mean of cluster $\{1, 2, 3\}$ is 2 and the mean of $\{8, 9, 10, 25\}$ is 13. Compare this to the partitioning $\{\{1, 2, 3, 8\}, \{9, 10, 25\}\}$, for which k-means computes the within-cluster variation as

$$(1-3.5)^2 + (2-3.5)^2 + (3-3.5)^2 + (8-3.5)^2 + (9-14.67)^2$$
$$+ (10-14.67)^2 + (25-14.67)^2 = 189.67,$$

given that 3.5 is the mean of cluster $\{1,2,3,8\}$ and 14.67 is the mean of cluster $\{9,10,25\}$. The latter partitioning has the lowest within-cluster variation; therefore, the k-means method assigns the value 8 to a cluster different from that containing 9 and 10 due to the outlier point 25. Moreover, the center of the second cluster, 14.67, is substantially far from all the members in the cluster. ∎

"How can we modify the k-means algorithm to diminish such sensitivity to outliers?" Instead of taking the mean value of the objects in a cluster as a reference point, we can pick actual objects to represent the clusters, using one representative object per cluster. Each remaining object is assigned to the cluster of which the representative object is the most similar. The partitioning method is then performed based on the principle of minimizing the sum of the dissimilarities between each object p and its corresponding representative object. That is, an **absolute-error criterion** is used, defined as

$$E = \sum_{i=1}^{k} \sum_{p \in C_i} dist(p, o_i), \tag{10.2}$$

where E is the sum of the absolute error for all objects p in the data set, and o_i is the representative object of C_i. This is the basis for the **k-medoids method**, which groups n objects into k clusters by minimizing the absolute error (Eq. 10.2).

When $k = 1$, we can find the exact median in $O(n^2)$ time. However, when k is a general positive number, the k-medoid problem is NP-hard.

The **Partitioning Around Medoids (PAM)** algorithm (see Figure 10.5 later) is a popular realization of k-medoids clustering. It tackles the problem in an iterative, greedy way. Like the k-means algorithm, the initial representative objects (called seeds) are chosen arbitrarily. We consider whether replacing a representative object by a nonrepresentative object would improve the clustering quality. All the possible replacements are tried out. The iterative process of replacing representative objects by other objects continues until the quality of the resulting clustering cannot be improved by any replacement. This quality is measured by a cost function of the average dissimilarity between an object and the representative object of its cluster.

Specifically, let $o_1, \ldots, o_k$ be the current set of representative objects (i.e., medoids). To determine whether a nonrepresentative object, denoted by o_{random}, is a good replacement for a current medoid o_j ($1 \leq j \leq k$), we calculate the distance from every object p to the closest object in the set $\{o_1, \ldots, o_{j-1}, o_{random}, o_{j+1}, \ldots, o_k\}$, and use the distance to update the cost function. The reassignments of objects to $\{o_1, \ldots, o_{j-1}, o_{random}, o_{j+1}, \ldots, o_k\}$ are simple. Suppose object p is currently assigned to a cluster represented by medoid o_j (Figure 10.4a or b). Do we need to reassign p to a different cluster if o_j is being replaced by o_{random}? Object p needs to be reassigned to either o_{random} or some other cluster represented by o_i ($i \neq j$), whichever is the closest. For example, in Figure 10.4(a), p is closest to o_i and therefore is reassigned to o_i. In Figure 10.4(b), however, p is closest to o_{random} and so is reassigned to o_{random}. What if, instead, p is currently assigned to a cluster represented by some other object o_i, $i \neq j$?

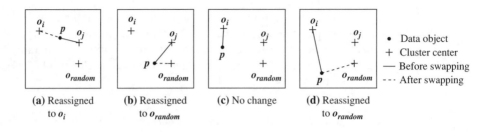

(a) Reassigned to o_i (b) Reassigned to o_{random} (c) No change   (d) Reassigned to o_{random}

Figure 10.4 Four cases of the cost function for k-medoids clustering.

Object o remains assigned to the cluster represented by o_i as long as o is still closer to o_i than to o_{random} (Figure 10.4c). Otherwise, o is reassigned to o_{random} (Figure 10.4d).

Each time a reassignment occurs, a difference in absolute error, E, is contributed to the cost function. Therefore, the cost function calculates the *difference* in absolute-error value if a current representative object is replaced by a nonrepresentative object. The total cost of swapping is the sum of costs incurred by all nonrepresentative objects. If the total cost is negative, then o_j is replaced or swapped with o_{random} because the actual absolute-error E is reduced. If the total cost is positive, the current representative object, o_j, is considered acceptable, and nothing is changed in the iteration.

"Which method is more robust—k-means or k-medoids?" The k-medoids method is more robust than k-means in the presence of noise and outliers because a medoid is less influenced by outliers or other extreme values than a mean. However, the complexity of each iteration in the k-medoids algorithm is $O(k(n-k))$. For large values of n and k, such computation becomes very costly, and much more costly than the k-means method. Both methods require the user to specify k, the number of clusters.

"How can we scale up the k-medoids method?" A typical k-medoids partitioning algorithm like PAM (Figure 10.5) works effectively for small data sets, but does not scale well for large data sets. To deal with larger data sets, a *sampling*-based method called **CLARA** (**Clustering LARge Applications**) can be used. Instead of taking the whole data set into consideration, CLARA uses a random sample of the data set. The PAM algorithm is then applied to compute the best medoids from the sample. Ideally, the sample should closely represent the original data set. In many cases, a large sample works well if it is created so that each object has equal probability of being selected into the sample. The representative objects (medoids) chosen will likely be similar to those that would have been chosen from the whole data set. CLARA builds clusterings from multiple random samples and returns the best clustering as the output. The complexity of computing the medoids on a random sample is $O(ks^2 \quad k(n-k))$, where s is the size of the sample, k is the number of clusters, and n is the total number of objects. CLARA can deal with larger data sets than PAM.

The effectiveness of CLARA depends on the sample size. Notice that PAM searches for the best k-medoids among a given data set, whereas CLARA searches for the best k-medoids among the *selected sample* of the data set. CLARA cannot find a good clustering if any of the best sampled medoids is far from the best k-medoids. If an object

Algorithm: *k*-**medoids.** PAM, a *k*-medoids algorithm for partitioning based on medoid or central objects.

Input:

- *k*: the number of clusters,

- *D*: a data set containing *n* objects.

Output: A set of *k* clusters.

Method:

(1)   arbitrarily choose *k* objects in *D* as the initial representative objects or seeds;
(2)   **repeat**
(3)   assign each remaining object to the cluster with the nearest representative object;
(4)   randomly select a nonrepresentative object, o_{random};
(5)   compute the total cost, *S*, of swapping representative object, o_j, with o_{random};
(6)   **if** $S < 0$ **then** swap o_j with o_{random} to form the new set of *k* representative objects;
(7)   **until** no change;

Figure 10.5 PAM, a *k*-medoids partitioning algorithm.

is one of the best *k*-medoids but is not selected during sampling, CLARA will never find the best clustering. (You will be asked to provide an example demonstrating this as an exercise.)

"How might we improve the quality and scalability of CLARA?" Recall that when searching for better medoids, PAM examines every object in the data set against every current medoid, whereas CLARA confines the candidate medoids to only a random sample of the data set. A randomized algorithm called **CLARANS** (Clustering Large Applications based upon RANdomized Search) presents a trade-off between the cost and the effectiveness of using samples to obtain clustering.

First, it randomly selects *k* objects in the data set as the current medoids. It then randomly selects a current medoid *x* and an object *y* that is not one of the current medoids. Can replacing *x* by *y* improve the absolute-error criterion? If yes, the replacement is made. CLARANS conducts such a randomized search *l* times. The set of the current medoids after the *l* steps is considered a local optimum. CLARANS repeats this randomized process *m* times and returns the best local optimal as the final result.

10.3 Hierarchical Methods

While partitioning methods meet the basic clustering requirement of organizing a set of objects into a number of exclusive groups, in some situations we may want to partition our data into groups at different levels such as in a hierarchy. A **hierarchical clustering method** works by grouping data objects into a hierarchy or "tree" of clusters.

Representing data objects in the form of a hierarchy is useful for data summarization and visualization. For example, as the manager of human resources at *AllElectronics*, you may organize your employees into major groups such as executives, managers, and staff. You can further partition these groups into smaller subgroups. For instance, the general group of staff can be further divided into subgroups of senior officers, officers, and trainees. All these groups form a hierarchy. We can easily summarize or characterize the data that are organized into a hierarchy, which can be used to find, say, the average salary of managers and of officers.

Consider handwritten character recognition as another example. A set of handwriting samples may be first partitioned into general groups where each group corresponds to a unique character. Some groups can be further partitioned into subgroups since a character may be written in multiple substantially different ways. If necessary, the hierarchical partitioning can be continued recursively until a desired granularity is reached.

In the previous examples, although we partitioned the data hierarchically, we did not assume that the data have a hierarchical structure (e.g., managers are at the same level in our *AllElectronics* hierarchy as staff). Our use of a hierarchy here is just to summarize and represent the underlying data in a compressed way. Such a hierarchy is particularly useful for data visualization.

Alternatively, in some applications we may believe that the data bear an underlying hierarchical structure that we want to discover. For example, hierarchical clustering may uncover a hierarchy for *AllElectronics* employees structured on, say, salary. In the study of evolution, hierarchical clustering may group animals according to their biological features to uncover evolutionary paths, which are a hierarchy of species. As another example, grouping configurations of a strategic game (e.g., chess or checkers) in a hierarchical way may help to develop game strategies that can be used to train players.

In this section, you will study hierarchical clustering methods. Section 10.3.1 begins with a discussion of agglomerative versus divisive hierarchical clustering, which organize objects into a hierarchy using a bottom-up or top-down strategy, respectively. Agglomerative methods start with individual objects as clusters, which are iteratively merged to form larger clusters. Conversely, divisive methods initially let all the given objects form one cluster, which they iteratively split into smaller clusters.

Hierarchical clustering methods can encounter difficulties regarding the selection of merge or split points. Such a decision is critical, because once a group of objects is merged or split, the process at the next step will operate on the newly generated clusters. It will neither undo what was done previously, nor perform object swapping between clusters. Thus, merge or split decisions, if not well chosen, may lead to low-quality clusters. Moreover, the methods do not scale well because each decision of merge or split needs to examine and evaluate many objects or clusters.

A promising direction for improving the clustering quality of hierarchical methods is to integrate hierarchical clustering with other clustering techniques, resulting in **multiple-phase** (or **multiphase**) **clustering**. We introduce two such methods, namely BIRCH and Chameleon. BIRCH (Section 10.3.3) begins by partitioning objects hierarchically using tree structures, where the leaf or low-level nonleaf nodes can be viewed as "microclusters" depending on the resolution scale. It then applies other clustering algorithms to perform macroclustering on the microclusters. Chameleon (Section 10.3.4) explores dynamic modeling in hierarchical clustering.

There are several orthogonal ways to categorize hierarchical clustering methods. For instance, they may be categorized into *algorithmic* methods, *probabilistic* methods, and *Bayesian* methods. Agglomerative, divisive, and multiphase methods are *algorithmic*, meaning they consider data objects as deterministic and compute clusters according to the deterministic distances between objects. Probabilistic methods use probabilistic models to capture clusters and measure the quality of clusters by the fitness of models. We discuss probabilistic hierarchical clustering in Section 10.3.5. *Bayesian methods* compute a distribution of possible clusterings. That is, instead of outputting a single deterministic clustering over a data set, they return a group of clustering structures and their probabilities, conditional on the given data. Bayesian methods are considered an advanced topic and are not discussed in this book.

10.3.1 Agglomerative versus Divisive Hierarchical Clustering

A hierarchical clustering method can be either *agglomerative* or *divisive*, depending on whether the hierarchical decomposition is formed in a bottom-up (merging) or top-down (splitting) fashion. Let's have a closer look at these strategies.

An **agglomerative hierarchical clustering method** uses a bottom-up strategy. It typically starts by letting each object form its own cluster and iteratively merges clusters into larger and larger clusters, until all the objects are in a single cluster or certain termination conditions are satisfied. The single cluster becomes the hierarchy's root. For the merging step, it finds the two clusters that are closest to each other (according to some similarity measure), and combines the two to form one cluster. Because two clusters are merged per iteration, where each cluster contains at least one object, an agglomerative method requires at most n iterations.

A **divisive hierarchical clustering method** employs a top-down strategy. It starts by placing all objects in one cluster, which is the hierarchy's root. It then divides the root cluster into several smaller subclusters, and recursively partitions those clusters into smaller ones. The partitioning process continues until each cluster at the lowest level is coherent enough—either containing only one object, or the objects within a cluster are sufficiently similar to each other.

In either agglomerative or divisive hierarchical clustering, a user can specify the desired number of clusters as a termination condition.

Example 10.3 **Agglomerative versus divisive hierarchical clustering.** Figure 10.6 shows the application of **AGNES** (AGglomerative NESting), an agglomerative hierarchical clustering method, and **DIANA** (DIvisive ANAlysis), a divisive hierarchical clustering method, on a data set of five objects, $\{a, b, c, d, e\}$. Initially, AGNES, the agglomerative method, places each object into a cluster of its own. The clusters are then merged step-by-step according to some criterion. For example, clusters C_1 and C_2 may be merged if an object in C_1 and an object in C_2 form the minimum Euclidean distance between any two objects from

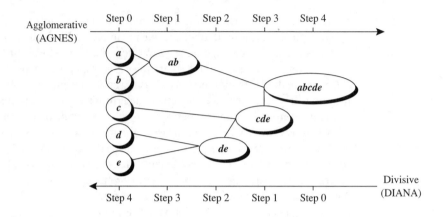

Figure 10.6 Agglomerative and divisive hierarchical clustering on data objects $\{a, b, c, d, e\}$.

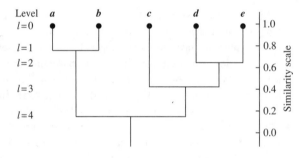

Figure 10.7 Dendrogram representation for hierarchical clustering of data objects $\{a, b, c, d, e\}$.

different clusters. This is a **single-linkage** approach in that each cluster is represented by all the objects in the cluster, and the similarity between two clusters is measured by the similarity of the *closest* pair of data points belonging to different clusters. The cluster-merging process repeats until all the objects are eventually merged to form one cluster.

DIANA, the divisive method, proceeds in the contrasting way. All the objects are used to form one initial cluster. The cluster is split according to some principle such as the maximum Euclidean distance between the closest neighboring objects in the cluster. The cluster-splitting process repeats until, eventually, each new cluster contains only a single object. ∎

A tree structure called a **dendrogram** is commonly used to represent the process of hierarchical clustering. It shows how objects are grouped together (in an agglomerative method) or partitioned (in a divisive method) step-by-step. Figure 10.7 shows a dendrogram for the five objects presented in Figure 10.6, where $l = 0$ shows the five objects as singleton clusters at level 0. At $l = 1$, objects a and b are grouped together to form the first cluster, and they stay together at all subsequent levels. We can also use a vertical axis to show the similarity scale between clusters. For example, when the similarity of two groups of objects, $\{a, b\}$ and $\{c, d, e\}$, is roughly 0.16, they are merged together to form a single cluster.

A challenge with divisive methods is how to partition a large cluster into several smaller ones. For example, there are $2^{n-1} - 1$ possible ways to partition a set of n objects into two exclusive subsets, where n is the number of objects. When n is large, it is computationally prohibitive to examine all possibilities. Consequently, a divisive method typically uses heuristics in partitioning, which can lead to inaccurate results. For the sake of efficiency, divisive methods typically do not backtrack on partitioning decisions that have been made. Once a cluster is partitioned, any alternative partitioning of this cluster will not be considered again. Due to the challenges in divisive methods, there are many more agglomerative methods than divisive methods.

10.3.2 Distance Measures in Algorithmic Methods

Whether using an agglomerative method or a divisive method, a core need is to measure the distance between two clusters, where each cluster is generally a set of objects.

Four widely used measures for distance between clusters are as follows, where $|p - p'|$ is the distance between two objects or points, p and p'; m_i is the mean for cluster, C_i; and n_i is the number of objects in C_i. They are also known as *linkage measures*.

$$\text{Minimum distance:} \quad dist_{min}(C_i, C_j) = \min_{p \in C_i, p' \in C_j} \{|p - p'|\} \tag{10.3}$$

$$\text{Maximum distance:} \quad dist_{max}(C_i, C_j) = \max_{p \in C_i, p' \in C_j} \{|p - p'|\} \tag{10.4}$$

$$\text{Mean distance:} \quad dist_{mean}(C_i, C_j) = |m_i - m_j| \tag{10.5}$$

$$\text{Average distance:} \quad dist_{avg}(C_i, C_j) = \frac{1}{n_i n_j} \sum_{p \in C_i, p' \in C_j} |p - p'| \tag{10.6}$$

When an algorithm uses the *minimum distance*, $d_{min}(C_i, C_j)$, to measure the distance between clusters, it is sometimes called a **nearest-neighbor clustering algorithm**. Moreover, if the clustering process is terminated when the distance between nearest clusters exceeds a user-defined threshold, it is called a **single-linkage algorithm**. If we view the data points as nodes of a graph, with edges forming a path between the nodes in a cluster, then the merging of two clusters, C_i and C_j, corresponds to adding an edge between the nearest pair of nodes in C_i and C_j. Because edges linking clusters always go between distinct clusters, the resulting graph will generate a tree. Thus, an agglomerative hierarchical clustering algorithm that uses the minimum distance measure is also called a

minimal spanning tree algorithm, where a spanning tree of a graph is a tree that connects all vertices, and a minimal spanning tree is the one with the least sum of edge weights.

When an algorithm uses the *maximum distance*, $d_{max}(C_i, C_j)$, to measure the distance between clusters, it is sometimes called a **farthest-neighbor clustering algorithm**. If the clustering process is terminated when the maximum distance between nearest clusters exceeds a user-defined threshold, it is called a **complete-linkage algorithm**. By viewing data points as nodes of a graph, with edges linking nodes, we can think of each cluster as a *complete* subgraph, that is, with edges connecting all the nodes in the clusters. The distance between two clusters is determined by the most distant nodes in the two clusters. Farthest-neighbor algorithms tend to minimize the increase in diameter of the clusters at each iteration. If the true clusters are rather compact and approximately equal size, the method will produce high-quality clusters. Otherwise, the clusters produced can be meaningless.

The previous minimum and maximum measures represent two extremes in measuring the distance between clusters. They tend to be overly sensitive to outliers or noisy data. The use of *mean* or *average distance* is a compromise between the minimum and maximum distances and overcomes the outlier sensitivity problem. Whereas the *mean distance* is the simplest to compute, the *average distance* is advantageous in that it can handle categoric as well as numeric data. The computation of the mean vector for categoric data can be difficult or impossible to define.

Example 10.4 **Single versus complete linkages.** Let us apply hierarchical clustering to the data set of Figure 10.8(a). Figure 10.8(b) shows the dendrogram using single linkage. Figure 10.8(c) shows the case using complete linkage, where the edges between clusters $\{A, B, J, H\}$ and $\{C, D, G, F, E\}$ are omitted for ease of presentation. This example shows that by using single linkages we can find hierarchical clusters defined by local proximity, whereas complete linkage tends to find clusters opting for global closeness. ∎

There are variations of the four essential linkage measures just discussed. For example, we can measure the distance between two clusters by the distance between the centroids (i.e., the central objects) of the clusters.

10.3.3 BIRCH: Multiphase Hierarchical Clustering Using Clustering Feature Trees

Balanced Iterative Reducing and Clustering using Hierarchies (BIRCH) is designed for clustering a large amount of numeric data by integrating hierarchical clustering (at the initial *microclustering* stage) and other clustering methods such as iterative partitioning (at the later *macroclustering* stage). It overcomes the two difficulties in agglomerative clustering methods: (1) scalability and (2) the inability to undo what was done in the previous step.

BIRCH uses the notions of *clustering feature* to summarize a cluster, and *clustering feature tree* (*CF-tree*) to represent a cluster hierarchy. These structures help

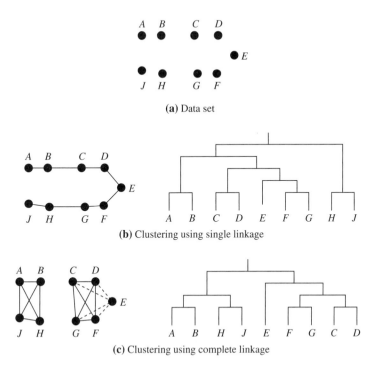

(a) Data set

(b) Clustering using single linkage

(c) Clustering using complete linkage

Figure 10.8 Hierarchical clustering using single and complete linkages.

the clustering method achieve good speed and scalability in large or even streaming databases, and also make it effective for incremental and dynamic clustering of incoming objects.

Consider a cluster of n d-dimensional data objects or points. The **clustering feature** (**CF**) of the cluster is a 3-D vector summarizing information about clusters of objects. It is defined as

$$CF = \langle n, LS, SS \rangle, \tag{10.7}$$

where LS is the linear sum of the n points (i.e., $\sum_{i=1}^{n} x_i$), and SS is the square sum of the data points (i.e., $\sum_{i=1}^{n} x_i^2$).

A clustering feature is essentially a summary of the statistics for the given cluster. Using a clustering feature, we can easily derive many useful statistics of a cluster. For example, the cluster's centroid, x_0, radius, R, and diameter, D, are

$$x_0 = \frac{\sum_{i=1}^{n} x_i}{n} = \frac{LS}{n}, \tag{10.8}$$

$$R = \sqrt{\frac{\sum_{i=1}^{n}(x_i - x_0)^2}{n}} = \sqrt{\frac{nSS - 2LS^2 + nLS}{n^2}}, \tag{10.9}$$

$$D = \sqrt{\frac{\sum_{i=1}^{n}\sum_{j=1}^{n}(x_i - x_j)^2}{n(n-1)}} = \sqrt{\frac{2nSS - 2LS^2}{n(n-1)}}. \tag{10.10}$$

Here, R is the average distance from member objects to the centroid, and D is the average pairwise distance within a cluster. Both R and D reflect the tightness of the cluster around the centroid.

Summarizing a cluster using the clustering feature can avoid storing the detailed information about individual objects or points. Instead, we only need a constant size of space to store the clustering feature. This is the key to BIRCH efficiency in space. Moreover, clustering features are *additive*. That is, for two disjoint clusters, C_1 and C_2, with the clustering features $CF_1 = \langle n_1, LS_1, SS_1 \rangle$ and $CF_2 = \langle n_2, LS_2, SS_2 \rangle$, respectively, the clustering feature for the cluster that formed by merging C_1 and C_2 is simply

$$CF_1 + CF_2 = \langle n_1 + n_2, LS_1 + LS_2, SS_1 + SS_2 \rangle. \tag{10.11}$$

Example 10.5 Clustering feature. Suppose there are three points, $(2,5),(3,2)$, and $(4,3)$, in a cluster, C_1. The clustering feature of C_1 is

$$CF_1 = \langle 3, (2+3+4, 5+2+3), (2^2 + 3^2 + 4^2, 5^2 + 2^2 + 3^2) \rangle = \langle 3, (9, 10), (29, 38) \rangle.$$

Suppose that C_1 is disjoint to a second cluster, C_2, where $CF_2 = \langle 3, (35, 36), (417, 440) \rangle$. The clustering feature of a new cluster, C_3, that is formed by merging C_1 and C_2, is derived by adding CF_1 and CF_2. That is,

$$CF_3 = \langle 3+3, (9+35, 10+36), (29+417, 38+440) \rangle = \langle 6, (44, 46), (446, 478) \rangle. \quad \blacksquare$$

A **CF-tree** is a height-balanced tree that stores the clustering features for a hierarchical clustering. An example is shown in Figure 10.9. By definition, a nonleaf node in a tree has descendants or "children." The nonleaf nodes store sums of the CFs of their children, and thus summarize clustering information about their children. A CF-tree has two parameters: *branching factor, B,* and *threshold, T*. The branching factor specifies the maximum number of children per nonleaf node. The threshold parameter specifies the maximum diameter of subclusters stored at the leaf nodes of the tree. These two parameters implicitly control the resulting tree's size.

Given a limited amount of main memory, an important consideration in BIRCH is to minimize the time required for input/output (I/O). BIRCH applies a *multiphase* clustering technique: A single scan of the data set yields a basic, good clustering, and

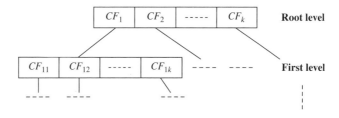

Figure 10.9 CF-tree structure.

one or more additional scans can optionally be used to further improve the quality. The primary phases are

- **Phase 1:** BIRCH scans the database to build an initial in-memory CF-tree, which can be viewed as a multilevel compression of the data that tries to preserve the data's inherent clustering structure.

- **Phase 2:** BIRCH applies a (selected) clustering algorithm to cluster the leaf nodes of the CF-tree, which removes sparse clusters as outliers and groups dense clusters into larger ones.

For Phase 1, the CF-tree is built dynamically as objects are inserted. Thus, the method is incremental. An object is inserted into the closest leaf entry (subcluster). If the diameter of the subcluster stored in the leaf node after insertion is larger than the threshold value, then the leaf node and possibly other nodes are split. After the insertion of the new object, information about the object is passed toward the root of the tree. The size of the CF-tree can be changed by modifying the threshold. If the size of the memory that is needed for storing the CF-tree is larger than the size of the main memory, then a larger threshold value can be specified and the CF-tree is rebuilt.

The rebuild process is performed by building a new tree from the leaf nodes of the old tree. Thus, the process of rebuilding the tree is done without the necessity of rereading all the objects or points. This is similar to the insertion and node split in the construction of B+-trees. Therefore, for building the tree, data has to be read just once. Some heuristics and methods have been introduced to deal with outliers and improve the quality of CF-trees by additional scans of the data. Once the CF-tree is built, any clustering algorithm, such as a typical partitioning algorithm, can be used with the CF-tree in Phase 2.

"*How effective is BIRCH?*" The time complexity of the algorithm is $O(n)$, where n is the number of objects to be clustered. Experiments have shown the linear scalability of the algorithm with respect to the number of objects, and good quality of clustering of the data. However, since each node in a CF-tree can hold only a limited number of entries due to its size, a CF-tree node does not always correspond to what a user may consider a natural cluster. Moreover, if the clusters are not spherical in shape, BIRCH does not perform well because it uses the notion of radius or diameter to control the boundary of a cluster.

The ideas of clustering features and CF-trees have been applied beyond BIRCH. The ideas have been borrowed by many others to tackle problems of clustering streaming and dynamic data.

10.3.4 Chameleon: Multiphase Hierarchical Clustering Using Dynamic Modeling

Chameleon is a hierarchical clustering algorithm that uses dynamic modeling to determine the similarity between pairs of clusters. In Chameleon, cluster similarity is assessed based on (1) how well connected objects are within a cluster and (2) the proximity of clusters. That is, two clusters are merged if their *interconnectivity* is high and they are *close together*. Thus, Chameleon does not depend on a static, user-supplied model and can automatically adapt to the internal characteristics of the clusters being merged. The merge process facilitates the discovery of natural and homogeneous clusters and applies to all data types as long as a similarity function can be specified.

Figure 10.10 illustrates how Chameleon works. Chameleon uses a k-nearest-neighbor graph approach to construct a sparse graph, where each vertex of the graph represents a data object, and there exists an edge between two vertices (objects) if one object is among the k-most similar objects to the other. The edges are weighted to reflect the similarity between objects. Chameleon uses a graph partitioning algorithm to partition the k-nearest-neighbor graph into a large number of relatively small subclusters such that it minimizes the **edge cut**. That is, a cluster C is partitioned into subclusters C_i and C_j so as to minimize the *weight of the edges* that would be cut should C be bisected into C_i and C_j. It assesses the *absolute* interconnectivity between clusters C_i and C_j.

Chameleon then uses an agglomerative hierarchical clustering algorithm that iteratively merges subclusters based on their similarity. To determine the pairs of most similar subclusters, it takes into account both the interconnectivity and the closeness of the clusters. Specifically, Chameleon determines the similarity between each pair of clusters C_i and C_j according to their *relative interconnectivity*, $RI(C_i, C_j)$, and their *relative closeness*, $RC(C_i, C_j)$.

■ The **relative interconnectivity**, $RI(C_i, C_j)$, between two clusters, C_i and C_j, is defined as the absolute interconnectivity between C_i and C_j, normalized with respect to the

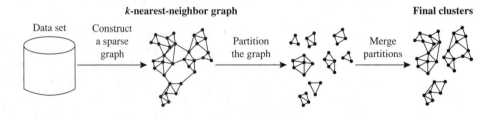

Figure 10.10 Chameleon: hierarchical clustering based on k-nearest neighbors and dynamic modeling. *Source:* Based on Karypis, Han, and Kumar [KHK99].

internal interconnectivity of the two clusters, C_i and C_j. That is,

$$RI(C_i, C_j) = \frac{|EC_{\{C_i,C_j\}}|}{\frac{1}{2}(|EC_{C_i}| + |EC_{C_j}|)}, \qquad (10.12)$$

where $EC_{\{C_i,C_j\}}$ is the edge cut as previously defined for a cluster containing both C_i and C_j. Similarly, EC_{C_i} (or EC_{C_j}) is the minimum sum of the cut edges that partition C_i (or C_j) into two roughly equal parts.

- The **relative closeness**, $RC(C_i, C_j)$, between a pair of clusters, C_i and C_j, is the absolute closeness between C_i and C_j, normalized with respect to the internal closeness of the two clusters, C_i and C_j. It is defined as

$$RC(C_i, C_j) = \frac{\overline{S}_{EC_{\{C_i,C_j\}}}}{\frac{|C_i|}{|C_i|+|C_j|}\overline{S}_{EC_{C_i}} + \frac{|C_j|}{|C_i|+|C_j|}\overline{S}_{EC_{C_j}}}, \qquad (10.13)$$

where $\overline{S}_{EC_{\{C_i,C_j\}}}$ is the average weight of the edges that connect vertices in C_i to vertices in C_j, and $\overline{S}_{EC_{C_i}}$ (or $\overline{S}_{EC_{C_j}}$) is the average weight of the edges that belong to the min-cut bisector of cluster C_i (or C_j).

Chameleon has been shown to have greater power at discovering arbitrarily shaped clusters of high quality than several well-known algorithms such as BIRCH and density-based DBSCAN (Section 10.4.1). However, the processing cost for high-dimensional data may require $O(n^2)$ time for n objects in the worst case.

10.3.5 Probabilistic Hierarchical Clustering

Algorithmic hierarchical clustering methods using linkage measures tend to be easy to understand and are often efficient in clustering. They are commonly used in many clustering analysis applications. However, algorithmic hierarchical clustering methods can suffer from several drawbacks. First, choosing a good distance measure for hierarchical clustering is often far from trivial. Second, to apply an algorithmic method, the data objects cannot have any missing attribute values. In the case of data that are partially observed (i.e., some attribute values of some objects are missing), it is not easy to apply an algorithmic hierarchical clustering method because the distance computation cannot be conducted. Third, most of the algorithmic hierarchical clustering methods are heuristic, and at each step locally search for a good merging/splitting decision. Consequently, the optimization goal of the resulting cluster hierarchy can be unclear.

Probabilistic hierarchical clustering aims to overcome some of these disadvantages by using probabilistic models to measure distances between clusters.

One way to look at the clustering problem is to regard the set of data objects to be clustered as a sample of the underlying data generation mechanism to be analyzed or, formally, the *generative model*. For example, when we conduct clustering analysis on a set of marketing surveys, we assume that the surveys collected are a sample of the opinions of all possible customers. Here, the data generation mechanism is a probability distribution of opinions with respect to different customers, which cannot be obtained directly and completely. The task of clustering is to estimate the generative model as accurately as possible using the observed data objects to be clustered.

In practice, we can assume that the data generative models adopt common distribution functions, such as Gaussian distribution or Bernoulli distribution, which are governed by parameters. The task of learning a generative model is then reduced to finding the parameter values for which the model best fits the observed data set.

Example 10.6 **Generative model.** Suppose we are given a set of 1-D points $X = \{x_1, \ldots, x_n\}$ for clustering analysis. Let us assume that the data points are generated by a Gaussian distribution,

$$\mathcal{N}(\mu, \sigma^2) = \frac{1}{\sqrt{2\pi\sigma^2}} e^{-\frac{(x-\mu)^2}{2\sigma^2}}, \tag{10.14}$$

where the parameters are μ (the mean) and σ^2 (the variance).

The probability that a point $x_i \in X$ is then generated by the model is

$$P(x_i|\mu, \sigma^2) = \frac{1}{\sqrt{2\pi\sigma^2}} e^{-\frac{(x_i-\mu)^2}{2\sigma^2}}. \tag{10.15}$$

Consequently, the likelihood that X is generated by the model is

$$L(\mathcal{N}(\mu, \sigma^2) : X) = P(X|\mu, \sigma^2) = \prod_{i=1}^{n} \frac{1}{\sqrt{2\pi\sigma^2}} e^{-\frac{(x_i-\mu)^2}{2\sigma^2}}. \tag{10.16}$$

The task of learning the generative model is to find the parameters μ and σ^2 such that the likelihood $L(\mathcal{N}(\mu, \sigma^2) : X)$ is maximized, that is, finding

$$\mathcal{N}(\mu_0, \sigma_0^2) = \arg\max\{L(\mathcal{N}(\mu, \sigma^2) : X)\}, \tag{10.17}$$

where $\max\{L(\mathcal{N}(\mu, \sigma^2) : X)\}$ is called the *maximum likelihood*. ∎

Given a set of objects, the quality of a cluster formed by all the objects can be measured by the maximum likelihood. For a set of objects partitioned into m clusters $C_1, \ldots, C_m$, the quality can be measured by

$$Q(\{C_1, \ldots, C_m\}) = \prod_{i=1}^{m} P(C_i), \tag{10.18}$$

where $P()$ is the maximum likelihood. If we merge two clusters, C_{j_1} and C_{j_2}, into a cluster, $C_{j_1} \cup C_{j_2}$, then, the change in quality of the overall clustering is

$$Q((\{C_1, \ldots, C_m\} - \{C_{j_1}, C_{j_2}\}) \cup \{C_{j_1} \cup C_{j_2}\}) - Q(\{C_1, \ldots, C_m\})$$

$$= \frac{\prod_{i=1}^{m} P(C_i) \cdot P(C_{j_1} \cup C_{j_2})}{P(C_{j_1}) P(C_{j_2})} - \prod_{i=1}^{m} P(C_i)$$

$$= \prod_{i=1}^{m} P(C_i) \left(\frac{P(C_{j_1} \cup C_{j_2})}{P(C_{j_1}) P(C_{j_2})} - 1 \right). \tag{10.19}$$

When choosing to merge two clusters in hierarchical clustering, $\prod_{i=1}^{m} P(C_i)$ is constant for any pair of clusters. Therefore, given clusters C_1 and C_2, the distance between them can be measured by

$$dist(C_i, C_j) = -\log \frac{P(C_1 \cup C_2)}{P(C_1) P(C_2)}. \tag{10.20}$$

A probabilistic hierarchical clustering method can adopt the agglomerative clustering framework, but use probabilistic models (Eq. 10.20) to measure the distance between clusters.

Upon close observation of Eq. (10.19), we see that merging two clusters may not always lead to an improvement in clustering quality, that is, $\frac{P(C_{j_1} \cup C_{j_2})}{P(C_{j_1}) P(C_{j_2})}$ may be less than 1. For example, assume that Gaussian distribution functions are used in the model of Figure 10.11. Although merging clusters C_1 and C_2 results in a cluster that better fits a Gaussian distribution, merging clusters C_3 and C_4 lowers the clustering quality because no Gaussian functions can fit the merged cluster well.

Based on this observation, a probabilistic hierarchical clustering scheme can start with one cluster per object, and merge two clusters, C_i and C_j, if the distance between them is negative. In each iteration, we try to find C_i and C_j so as to maximize $\log \frac{P(C_i \cup C_j)}{P(C_i) P(C_j)}$. The iteration continues as long as $\log \frac{P(C_i \cup C_j)}{P(C_i) P(C_j)} > 0$, that is, as long as there is an improvement in clustering quality. The pseudocode is given in Figure 10.12.

Probabilistic hierarchical clustering methods are easy to understand, and generally have the same efficiency as algorithmic agglomerative hierarchical clustering methods; in fact, they share the same framework. Probabilistic models are more interpretable, but sometimes less flexible than distance metrics. Probabilistic models can handle partially observed data. For example, given a multidimensional data set where some objects have missing values on some dimensions, we can learn a Gaussian model on each dimension independently using the observed values on the dimension. The resulting cluster hierarchy accomplishes the optimization goal of fitting data to the selected probabilistic models.

A drawback of using probabilistic hierarchical clustering is that it outputs only one hierarchy with respect to a chosen probabilistic model. It cannot handle the uncertainty of cluster hierarchies. Given a data set, there may exist multiple hierarchies that

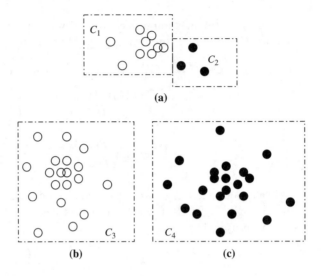

(a)

(b)   **(c)**

Figure 10.11 Merging clusters in probabilistic hierarchical clustering: (a) Merging clusters C_1 and C_2 leads to an increase in overall cluster quality, but merging clusters (b) C_3 and (c) C_4 does not.

Algorithm: A probabilistic hierarchical clustering algorithm.

Input:

- $D = \{o_1, \ldots, o_n\}$: a data set containing n objects;

Output: A hierarchy of clusters.

Method:

    (1)   **create** a cluster for each object $C_i = \{o_i\}$, $1 \leq i \leq n$;

    (2)   **for** $i = 1$ to n

    (3)   **find** pair of clusters C_i and C_j such that $C_i, C_j = \arg\max_{i \neq j} \log \frac{P(C_i \cup C_j)}{P(C_i)P(C_j)}$;

    (4)   **if** $\log \frac{P(C_i \cup C_j)}{P(C_i)P(C_j)} > 0$ then merge C_i and C_j;

    (5)   **else** stop;

Figure 10.12 A probabilistic hierarchical clustering algorithm.

fit the observed data. Neither algorithmic approaches nor probabilistic approaches can find the distribution of such hierarchies. Recently, Bayesian tree-structured models have been developed to handle such problems. Bayesian and other sophisticated probabilistic clustering methods are considered advanced topics and are not covered in this book.

10.4 Density-Based Methods

Partitioning and hierarchical methods are designed to find spherical-shaped clusters. They have difficulty finding clusters of arbitrary shape such as the "S" shape and oval clusters in Figure 10.13. Given such data, they would likely inaccurately identify convex regions, where noise or outliers are included in the clusters.

To find clusters of arbitrary shape, alternatively, we can model clusters as dense regions in the data space, separated by sparse regions. This is the main strategy behind *density-based clustering methods*, which can discover clusters of nonspherical shape. In this section, you will learn the basic techniques of density-based clustering by studying three representative methods, namely, DBSCAN (Section 10.4.1), OPTICS (Section 10.4.2), and DENCLUE (Section 10.4.3).

10.4.1 DBSCAN: Density-Based Clustering Based on Connected Regions with High Density

"How can we find dense regions in density-based clustering?" The *density* of an object o can be measured by the number of objects close to o. DBSCAN (Density-Based Spatial Clustering of Applications with Noise) finds *core objects*, that is, objects that have dense neighborhoods. It connects core objects and their neighborhoods to form dense regions as clusters.

"How does **DBSCAN** *quantify the neighborhood of an object?"* A user-specified parameter $\epsilon > 0$ is used to specify the radius of a neighborhood we consider for every object. The ϵ-**neighborhood** of an object o is the space within a radius ϵ centered at o.

Due to the fixed neighborhood size parameterized by ϵ, the **density of a neighborhood** can be measured simply by the number of objects in the neighborhood. To determine whether a neighborhood is dense or not, DBSCAN uses another user-specified

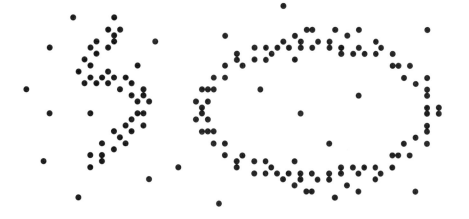

Figure 10.13 Clusters of arbitrary shape.

parameter, *MinPts*, which specifies the density threshold of dense regions. An object is a **core object** if the ϵ-neighborhood of the object contains at least *MinPts* objects. Core objects are the pillars of dense regions.

Given a set, D, of objects, we can identify all core objects with respect to the given parameters, ϵ and *MinPts*. The clustering task is therein reduced to using core objects and their neighborhoods to form dense regions, where the dense regions are clusters. For a core object q and an object p, we say that p is **directly density-reachable** from q (with respect to ϵ and *MinPts*) if p is within the ϵ-neighborhood of q. Clearly, an object p is directly density-reachable from another object q if and only if q is a core object and p is in the ϵ-neighborhood of q. Using the directly density-reachable relation, a core object can "bring" all objects from its ϵ-neighborhood into a dense region.

"How can we assemble a large dense region using small dense regions centered by core objects?" In DBSCAN, p is **density-reachable** from q (with respect to ϵ and *MinPts* in D) if there is a chain of objects $p_1, \ldots, p_n$, such that $p_1 = q$, $p_n = p$, and p_{i+1} is directly density-reachable from p_i with respect to ϵ and *MinPts*, for $1 \leq i \leq n$, $p_i \in D$. Note that density-reachability is not an equivalence relation because it is not symmetric. If both o_1 and o_2 are core objects and o_1 is density-reachable from o_2, then o_2 is density-reachable from o_1. However, if o_2 is a core object but o_1 is not, then o_1 may be density-reachable from o_2, but not vice versa.

To connect core objects as well as their neighbors in a dense region, **DBSCAN** uses the notion of density-connectedness. Two objects $p_1, p_2 \in D$ are **density-connected** with respect to ϵ and *MinPts* if there is an object $q \in D$ such that both p_1 and p_2 are density-reachable from q with respect to ϵ and *MinPts*. Unlike density-reachability, density-connectedness is an equivalence relation. It is easy to show that, for objects o_1, o_2, and o_3, if o_1 and o_2 are density-connected, and o_2 and o_3 are density-connected, then so are o_1 and o_3.

Example 10.7 Density-reachability and density-connectivity. Consider Figure 10.14 for a given ϵ represented by the radius of the circles, and, say, let *MinPts* = 3.

Of the labeled points, m, p, o, r are core objects because each is in an ϵ-neighborhood containing at least three points. Object q is directly density-reachable from m. Object m is directly density-reachable from p and vice versa.

Object q is (indirectly) density-reachable from p because q is directly density-reachable from m and m is directly density-reachable from p. However, p is not density-reachable from q because q is not a core object. Similarly, r and s are density-reachable from o and o is density-reachable from r. Thus, o, r, and s are all density-connected. ∎

We can use the closure of density-connectedness to find connected dense regions as clusters. Each closed set is a **density-based cluster**. A subset $C \subseteq D$ is a cluster if (1) for any two objects $o_1, o_2 \in C$, o_1 and o_2 are density-connected; and (2) there does not exist an object $o \in C$ and another object $o' \in (D - C)$ such that o and o' are density-connected.

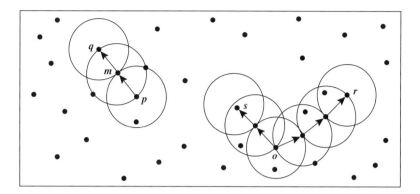

Figure 10.14 Density-reachability and density-connectivity in density-based clustering. *Source:* Based on Ester, Kriegel, Sander, and Xu [EKSX96].

"How does DBSCAN find clusters?" Initially, all objects in a given data set D are marked as "unvisited." DBSCAN randomly selects an unvisited object p, marks p as "visited," and checks whether the ϵ-neighborhood of p contains at least *MinPts* objects. If not, p is marked as a noise point. Otherwise, a new cluster C is created for p, and all the objects in the ϵ-neighborhood of p are added to a candidate set, N. DBSCAN iteratively adds to C those objects in N that do not belong to any cluster. In this process, for an object p' in N that carries the label "unvisited," DBSCAN marks it as "visited" and checks its ϵ-neighborhood. If the ϵ-neighborhood of p' has at least *MinPts* objects, those objects in the ϵ-neighborhood of p' are added to N. DBSCAN continues adding objects to C until C can no longer be expanded, that is, N is empty. At this time, cluster C is completed, and thus is output.

To find the next cluster, DBSCAN randomly selects an unvisited object from the remaining ones. The clustering process continues until all objects are visited. The pseudocode of the DBSCAN algorithm is given in Figure 10.15.

If a spatial index is used, the computational complexity of DBSCAN is $O(n\log n)$, where n is the number of database objects. Otherwise, the complexity is $O(n^2)$. With appropriate settings of the user-defined parameters, ϵ and *MinPts*, the algorithm is effective in finding arbitrary-shaped clusters.

10.4.2 OPTICS: Ordering Points to Identify the Clustering Structure

Although DBSCAN can cluster objects given input parameters such as ϵ (the maximum radius of a neighborhood) and *MinPts* (the minimum number of points required in the neighborhood of a core object), it encumbers users with the responsibility of selecting parameter values that will lead to the discovery of acceptable clusters. This is a problem associated with many other clustering algorithms. Such parameter settings

Algorithm: DBSCAN: a density-based clustering algorithm.

Input:

- D: a data set containing n objects,
- ϵ: the radius parameter, and
- *MinPts*: the neighborhood density threshold.

Output: A set of density-based clusters.

Method:

```
(1)   mark all objects as unvisited;
(2)   do
(3)       randomly select an unvisited object p;
(4)       mark p as visited;
(5)       if the ε-neighborhood of p has at least MinPts objects
(6)           create a new cluster C, and add p to C;
(7)           let N be the set of objects in the ε-neighborhood of p;
(8)           for each point p′ in N
(9)               if p′ is unvisited
(10)                  mark p′ as visited;
(11)                  if the ε-neighborhood of p′ has at least MinPts points,
                          add those points to N;
(12)              if p′ is not yet a member of any cluster, add p′ to C;
(13)          end for
(14)          output C;
(15)      else mark p as noise;
(16)  until no object is unvisited;
```

Figure 10.15 DBSCAN algorithm.

are usually empirically set and difficult to determine, especially for real-world, high-dimensional data sets. Most algorithms are sensitive to these parameter values: Slightly different settings may lead to very different clusterings of the data. Moreover, real-world, high-dimensional data sets often have very skewed distributions such that their intrinsic clustering structure may not be well characterized by a single set of *global* density parameters.

Note that density-based clusters are monotonic with respect to the neighborhood threshold. That is, in DBSCAN, for a fixed *MinPts* value and two neighborhood thresholds, $\epsilon_1 < \epsilon_2$, a cluster C with respect to ϵ_1 and *MinPts* must be a subset of a cluster C' with respect to ϵ_2 and *MinPts*. This means that if two objects are in a density-based cluster, they must also be in a cluster with a lower density requirement.

To overcome the difficulty in using one set of global parameters in clustering analysis, a cluster analysis method called **OPTICS** was proposed. OPTICS does not explicitly produce a data set clustering. Instead, it outputs a **cluster ordering**. This is a linear list of all objects under analysis and represents the *density-based clustering structure* of the data. Objects in a denser cluster are listed closer to each other in the cluster ordering. This ordering is equivalent to density-based clustering obtained from a wide range of parameter settings. Thus, OPTICS does not require the user to provide a specific density threshold. The cluster ordering can be used to extract basic clustering information (e.g., cluster centers, or arbitrary-shaped clusters), derive the intrinsic clustering structure, as well as provide a visualization of the clustering.

To construct the different clusterings simultaneously, the objects are processed in a specific order. This order selects an object that is density-reachable with respect to the lowest ϵ value so that clusters with higher density (lower ϵ) will be finished first. Based on this idea, OPTICS needs two important pieces of information per object:

- The **core-distance** of an object p is the smallest value ϵ' such that the ϵ'-neighborhood of p has at least *MinPts* objects. That is, ϵ' is the minimum distance threshold that makes p a core object. If p is not a core object with respect to ϵ and *MinPts*, the core-distance of p is undefined.

- The **reachability-distance** to object p from q is the minimum radius value that makes p density-reachable from q. According to the definition of density-reachability, q has to be a core object and p must be in the neighborhood of q. Therefore, the reachability-distance from q to p is max$\{core\text{-}distance(q), dist(p, q)\}$. If q is not a core object with respect to ϵ and *MinPts*, the reachability-distance to p from q is undefined.

  An object p may be directly reachable from multiple core objects. Therefore, p may have multiple reachability-distances with respect to different core objects. The smallest reachability-distance of p is of particular interest because it gives the shortest path for which p is connected to a dense cluster.

Example 10.8 Core-distance and reachability-distance. Figure 10.16 illustrates the concepts of core-distance and reachability-distance. Suppose that $\epsilon = 6$ mm and *MinPts* $= 5$. The core-distance of p is the distance, ϵ', between p and the fourth closest data object from p. The reachability-distance of q_1 from p is the core-distance of p (i.e., $\epsilon' = 3$ mm) because this is greater than the Euclidean distance from p to q_1. The reachability-distance of q_2 with respect to p is the Euclidean distance from p to q_2 because this is greater than the core-distance of p. ∎

OPTICS computes an ordering of all objects in a given database and, for each object in the database, stores the core-distance and a suitable reachability-distance. OPTICS maintains a list called OrderSeeds to generate the output ordering. Objects in Order-Seeds are sorted by the reachability-distance from their respective closest core objects, that is, by the smallest reachability-distance of each object.

OPTICS begins with an arbitrary object from the input database as the current object, p. It retrieves the ϵ-neighborhood of p, determines the core-distance, and sets the reachability-distance to *undefined*. The current object, p, is then written to output.

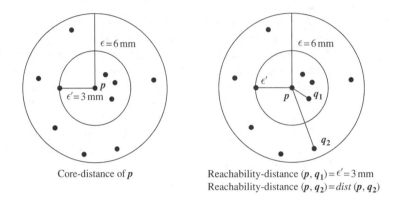

Core-distance of p

Reachability-distance $(p, q_1) = \epsilon' = 3\,\text{mm}$
Reachability-distance $(p, q_2) = dist\,(p, q_2)$

Figure 10.16 OPTICS terminology. *Source:* Based on Ankerst, Breunig, Kriegel, and Sander [ABKS99].

If p is not a core object, OPTICS simply moves on to the next object in the OrderSeeds list (or the input database if OrderSeeds is empty). If p is a core object, then for each object, q, in the ϵ-neighborhood of p, OPTICS updates its reachability-distance from p and inserts q into OrderSeeds if q has not yet been processed. The iteration continues until the input is fully consumed and OrderSeeds is empty.

A data set's cluster ordering can be represented graphically, which helps to visualize and understand the clustering structure in a data set. For example, Figure 10.17 is the reachability plot for a simple 2-D data set, which presents a general overview of how the data are structured and clustered. The data objects are plotted in the clustering order (horizontal axis) together with their respective reachability-distances (vertical axis). The three Gaussian "bumps" in the plot reflect three clusters in the data set. Methods have also been developed for viewing clustering structures of high-dimensional data at various levels of detail.

The structure of the OPTICS algorithm is very similar to that of DBSCAN. Consequently, the two algorithms have the same time complexity. The complexity is $O(n \log n)$ if a spatial index is used, and $O(n^2)$ otherwise, where n is the number of objects.

10.4.3 DENCLUE: Clustering Based on Density Distribution Functions

Density estimation is a core issue in density-based clustering methods. **DENCLUE** (DENsity-based CLUstEring) is a clustering method based on a set of density distribution functions. We first give some background on density estimation, and then describe the DENCLUE algorithm.

In probability and statistics, **density estimation** is the estimation of an unobservable underlying probability density function based on a set of observed data. In the context of density-based clustering, the unobservable underlying probability density function is the true distribution of the population of all possible objects to be analyzed. The observed data set is regarded as a random sample from that population.

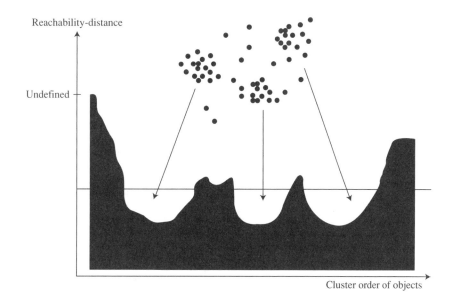

Figure 10.17 Cluster ordering in OPTICS. *Source:* Adapted from Ankerst, Breunig, Kriegel, and Sander [ABKS99].

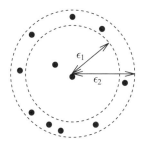

Figure 10.18 The subtlety in density estimation in DBSCAN and OPTICS: Increasing the neighborhood radius slightly from ϵ_1 to ϵ_2 results in a much higher density.

In DBSCAN and OPTICS, density is calculated by counting the number of objects in a neighborhood defined by a radius parameter, ϵ. Such density estimates can be highly sensitive to the radius value used. For example, in Figure 10.18, the density changes significantly as the radius increases by a small amount.

To overcome this problem, **kernel density estimation** can be used, which is a nonparametric density estimation approach from statistics. The general idea behind kernel density estimation is simple. We treat an observed object as an indicator of high-probability density in the surrounding region. The probability density at a point depends on the distances from this point to the observed objects.

Formally, let $x_1, \ldots, x_n$ be an independent and identically distributed sample of a random variable f. The *kernel density approximation of the probability density function* is

$$\hat{f}_h(x) = \frac{1}{nh} \sum_{i=1}^{n} K\left(\frac{x - x_i}{h}\right),$$ (10.21)

where $K()$ is a kernel and h is the bandwidth serving as a smoothing parameter. A **kernel** can be regarded as a function modeling the influence of a sample point within its neighborhood. Technically, a kernel $K()$ is a non-negative real-valued integrable function that should satisfy two requirements: $\int_{-\infty}^{+\infty} K(u)\,du = 1$ and $K(-u) = K(u)$ for all values of u. A frequently used kernel is a standard Gaussian function with a mean of 0 and a variance of 1:

$$K\left(\frac{x - x_i}{h}\right) = \frac{1}{\sqrt{2\pi}} e^{-\frac{(x - x_i)^2}{2h^2}}.$$ (10.22)

DENCLUE uses a Gaussian kernel to estimate density based on the given set of objects to be clustered. A point x^* is called a **density attractor** if it is a local maximum of the estimated density function. To avoid trivial local maximum points, DENCLUE uses a noise threshold, ξ, and only considers those density attractors x^* such that $\hat{f}(x^*) \geq \xi$. These nontrivial density attractors are the centers of clusters.

Objects under analysis are assigned to clusters through density attractors using a stepwise hill-climbing procedure. For an object, x, the hill-climbing procedure starts from x and is guided by the gradient of the estimated density function. That is, the density attractor for x is computed as

$$x^0 = x$$

$$x^{j+1} = x^j + \delta \frac{\nabla \hat{f}(x^j)}{|\nabla \hat{f}(x^j)|},$$ (10.23)

where δ is a parameter to control the speed of convergence, and

$$\nabla \hat{f}(x) = \frac{1}{h^{d+2} n \sum_{i=1}^{n} K\left(\frac{x - x_i}{h}\right) (x_i - x)}.$$ (10.24)

The hill-climbing procedure stops at step $k > 0$ if $\hat{f}(x^{k+1}) < \hat{f}(x^k)$, and assigns x to the density attractor $x^* = x^k$. An object x is an outlier or noise if it converges in the hill-climbing procedure to a local maximum x^* with $\hat{f}(x^*) < \xi$.

A cluster in DENCLUE is a set of density attractors X and a set of input objects C such that each object in C is assigned to a density attractor in X, and there exists a path between every pair of density attractors where the density is above ξ. By using multiple density attractors connected by paths, DENCLUE can find clusters of arbitrary shape.

DENCLUE has several advantages. It can be regarded as a generalization of several well-known clustering methods such as single-linkage approaches and DBSCAN. Moreover, DENCLUE is invariant against noise. The kernel density estimation can effectively reduce the influence of noise by uniformly distributing noise into the input data.

10.5 Grid-Based Methods

The clustering methods discussed so far are data-driven—they partition the set of objects and adapt to the distribution of the objects in the embedding space. Alternatively, a **grid-based clustering** method takes a space-driven approach by partitioning the embedding space into *cells* independent of the distribution of the input objects.

The *grid-based clustering* approach uses a multiresolution grid data structure. It quantizes the object space into a finite number of cells that form a grid structure on which all of the operations for clustering are performed. The main advantage of the approach is its fast processing time, which is typically independent of the number of data objects, yet dependent on only the number of cells in each dimension in the quantized space.

In this section, we illustrate grid-based clustering using two typical examples. STING (Section 10.5.1) explores statistical information stored in the grid cells. CLIQUE (Section 10.5.2) represents a grid- and density-based approach for subspace clustering in a high-dimensional data space.

10.5.1 STING: STatistical INformation Grid

STING is a grid-based multiresolution clustering technique in which the embedding spatial area of the input objects is divided into rectangular cells. The space can be divided in a hierarchical and recursive way. Several levels of such rectangular cells correspond to different levels of resolution and form a hierarchical structure: Each cell at a high level is partitioned to form a number of cells at the next lower level. Statistical information regarding the attributes in each grid cell, such as the mean, maximum, and minimum values, is precomputed and stored as *statistical parameters*. These statistical parameters are useful for query processing and for other data analysis tasks.

Figure 10.19 shows a hierarchical structure for STING clustering. The statistical parameters of higher-level cells can easily be computed from the parameters of the lower-level cells. These parameters include the following: the attribute-independent parameter, *count*; and the attribute-dependent parameters, *mean*, *stdev* (standard deviation), *min* (minimum), *max* (maximum), and the type of *distribution* that the attribute value in the cell follows such as *normal, uniform, exponential,* or *none* (if the distribution is unknown). Here, the attribute is a selected measure for analysis such as *price* for house objects. When the data are loaded into the database, the parameters *count*, *mean*, *stdev*, *min*, and *max* of the bottom-level cells are calculated directly from the data. The value of *distribution* may either be assigned by the user if the distribution type is known

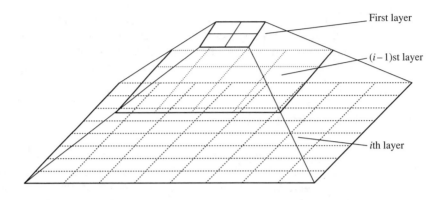

Figure 10.19 Hierarchical structure for STING clustering.

beforehand or obtained by hypothesis tests such as the χ^2 test. The type of distribution of a higher-level cell can be computed based on the majority of distribution types of its corresponding lower-level cells in conjunction with a threshold filtering process. If the distributions of the lower-level cells disagree with each other and fail the threshold test, the distribution type of the high-level cell is set to *none*.

"*How is this statistical information useful for query answering?*" The statistical parameters can be used in a top-down, grid-based manner as follows. First, a layer within the hierarchical structure is determined from which the query-answering process is to start. This layer typically contains a small number of cells. For each cell in the current layer, we compute the confidence interval (or estimated probability range) reflecting the cell's relevancy to the given query. The irrelevant cells are removed from further consideration. Processing of the next lower level examines only the remaining relevant cells. This process is repeated until the bottom layer is reached. At this time, if the query specification is met, the regions of relevant cells that satisfy the query are returned. Otherwise, the data that fall into the relevant cells are retrieved and further processed until they meet the query's requirements.

An interesting property of STING is that it approaches the clustering result of DBSCAN if the granularity approaches 0 (i.e., toward very low-level data). In other words, using the count and cell size information, dense clusters can be identified approximately using STING. Therefore, STING can also be regarded as a density-based clustering method.

"*What advantages does STING offer over other clustering methods?*" STING offers several advantages: (1) the grid-based computation is *query-independent* because the statistical information stored in each cell represents the summary information of the data in the grid cell, independent of the query; (2) the grid structure facilitates parallel processing and incremental updating; and (3) the method's efficiency is a major advantage: STING goes through the database once to compute the statistical parameters of the cells, and hence the time complexity of generating clusters is $O(n)$, where n is the total number of objects. After generating the hierarchical structure, the query processing time is $O(g)$, where g is the total number of grid cells at the lowest level, which is usually much smaller than n.

Because STING uses a multiresolution approach to cluster analysis, the quality of STING clustering depends on the granularity of the lowest level of the grid structure. If the granularity is very fine, the cost of processing will increase substantially; however, if the bottom level of the grid structure is too coarse, it may reduce the quality of cluster analysis. Moreover, STING does not consider the spatial relationship between the children and their neighboring cells for construction of a parent cell. As a result, the shapes of the resulting clusters are isothetic, that is, all the cluster boundaries are either horizontal or vertical, and no diagonal boundary is detected. This may lower the quality and accuracy of the clusters despite the fast processing time of the technique.

10.5.2 CLIQUE: An Apriori-like Subspace Clustering Method

A data object often has tens of attributes, many of which may be irrelevant. The values of attributes may vary considerably. These factors can make it difficult to locate clusters that span the entire data space. It may be more meaningful to instead search for clusters within different *subspaces* of the data. For example, consider a health-informatics application where patient records contain extensive attributes describing personal information, numerous symptoms, conditions, and family history.

Finding a nontrivial group of patients for which all or even most of the attributes strongly agree is unlikely. In bird flu patients, for instance, the *age*, *gender*, and *job* attributes may vary dramatically within a wide range of values. Thus, it can be difficult to find such a cluster within the entire data space. Instead, by searching in subspaces, we may find a cluster of similar patients in a lower-dimensional space (e.g., patients who are similar to one other with respect to symptoms like high fever, cough but no runny nose, and aged between 3 and 16).

CLIQUE (CLustering In QUEst) is a simple grid-based method for finding density-based clusters in subspaces. CLIQUE partitions each dimension into nonoverlapping intervals, thereby partitioning the entire embedding space of the data objects into cells. It uses a density threshold to identify *dense* cells and *sparse* ones. A cell is dense if the number of objects mapped to it exceeds the density threshold.

The main strategy behind CLIQUE for identifying a candidate search space uses the monotonicity of dense cells with respect to dimensionality. This is based on the *Apriori property* used in frequent pattern and association rule mining (Chapter 6). In the context of clusters in subspaces, the monotonicity says the following. A k-dimensional cell c ($k > 1$) can have at least l points only if every $(k-1)$-dimensional projection of c, which is a cell in a $(k-1)$-dimensional subspace, has at least l points. Consider Figure 10.20, where the embedding data space contains three dimensions: *age*, *salary*, and *vacation*. A 2-D cell, say in the subspace formed by *age* and *salary*, contains l points only if the projection of this cell in every dimension, that is, *age* and *salary*, respectively, contains at least l points.

CLIQUE performs clustering in two steps. In the first step, CLIQUE partitions the d-dimensional data space into nonoverlapping rectangular units, identifying the dense units among these. CLIQUE finds dense cells in all of the subspaces. To do so,

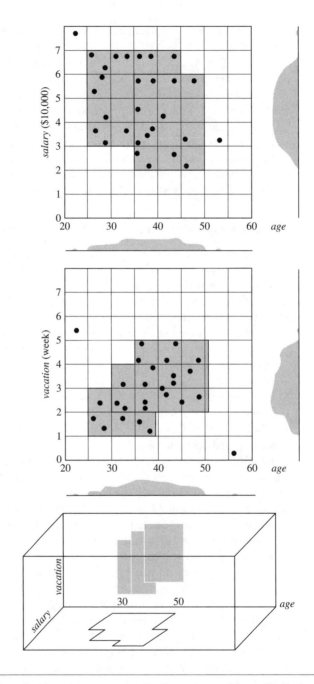

Figure 10.20 Dense units found with respect to *age* for the dimensions *salary* and *vacation* are intersected to provide a candidate search space for dense units of higher dimensionality.

CLIQUE partitions every dimension into intervals, and identifies intervals containing at least l points, where l is the density threshold. CLIQUE then iteratively joins two k-dimensional dense cells, c_1 and c_2, in subspaces $(D_{i_1}, \ldots, D_{i_k})$ and $(D_{j_1}, \ldots, D_{j_k})$, respectively, if $D_{i_1} = D_{j_1}, \ldots, D_{i_{k-1}} = D_{j_{k-1}}$, and c_1 and c_2 share the same intervals in those dimensions. The join operation generates a new $(k + 1)$-dimensional candidate cell c in space $(D_{i_1}, \ldots, D_{i_{k-1}}, D_{i_k}, D_{j_k})$. CLIQUE checks whether the number of points in c passes the density threshold. The iteration terminates when no candidates can be generated or no candidate cells are dense.

In the second step, CLIQUE uses the dense cells in each subspace to assemble clusters, which can be of arbitrary shape. The idea is to apply the Minimum Description Length (MDL) principle (Chapter 8) to use the *maximal regions* to cover connected dense cells, where a maximal region is a hyperrectangle where every cell falling into this region is dense, and the region cannot be extended further in any dimension in the subspace. Finding the best description of a cluster in general is NP-Hard. Thus, CLIQUE adopts a simple greedy approach. It starts with an arbitrary dense cell, finds a maximal region covering the cell, and then works on the remaining dense cells that have not yet been covered. The greedy method terminates when all dense cells are covered.

"How effective is CLIQUE?" CLIQUE automatically finds subspaces of the highest dimensionality such that high-density clusters exist in those subspaces. It is insensitive to the order of input objects and does not presume any canonical data distribution. It scales linearly with the size of the input and has good scalability as the number of dimensions in the data is increased. However, obtaining a meaningful clustering is dependent on proper tuning of the grid size (which is a stable structure here) and the density threshold. This can be difficult in practice because the grid size and density threshold are used across all combinations of dimensions in the data set. Thus, the accuracy of the clustering results may be degraded at the expense of the method's simplicity. Moreover, for a given dense region, all projections of the region onto lower-dimensionality subspaces will also be dense. This can result in a large overlap among the reported dense regions. Furthermore, it is difficult to find clusters of rather different densities within different dimensional subspaces.

Several extensions to this approach follow a similar philosophy. For example, we can think of a grid as a set of fixed bins. Instead of using fixed bins for each of the dimensions, we can use an adaptive, data-driven strategy to dynamically determine the bins for each dimension based on data distribution statistics. Alternatively, instead of using a density threshold, we may use entropy (Chapter 8) as a measure of the quality of subspace clusters.

10.6 Evaluation of Clustering

By now you have learned what clustering is and know several popular clustering methods. You may ask, *"When I try out a clustering method on a data set, how can I evaluate whether the clustering results are good?"* In general, *cluster evaluation* assesses the feasibility of clustering analysis on a data set and the quality of the results generated by a clustering method. The major tasks of clustering evaluation include the following:

- *Assessing clustering tendency.* In this task, for a given data set, we assess whether a nonrandom structure exists in the data. Blindly applying a clustering method on a data set will return clusters; however, the clusters mined may be misleading. Clustering analysis on a data set is meaningful only when there is a nonrandom structure in the data.

- *Determining the number of clusters in a data set.* A few algorithms, such as k-means, require the number of clusters in a data set as the parameter. Moreover, the number of clusters can be regarded as an interesting and important summary statistic of a data set. Therefore, it is desirable to estimate this number even before a clustering algorithm is used to derive detailed clusters.

- *Measuring clustering quality.* After applying a clustering method on a data set, we want to assess how good the resulting clusters are. A number of measures can be used. Some methods measure how well the clusters fit the data set, while others measure how well the clusters match the ground truth, if such truth is available. There are also measures that score clusterings and thus can compare two sets of clustering results on the same data set.

In the rest of this section, we discuss each of these three topics.

10.6.1 Assessing Clustering Tendency

Clustering tendency assessment determines whether a given data set has a non-random structure, which may lead to meaningful clusters. Consider a data set that does not have any non-random structure, such as a set of uniformly distributed points in a data space. Even though a clustering algorithm may return clusters for the data, those clusters are random and are not meaningful.

Example 10.9 Clustering requires nonuniform distribution of data. Figure 10.21 shows a data set that is uniformly distributed in 2-D data space. Although a clustering algorithm may still artificially partition the points into groups, the groups will unlikely mean anything significant to the application due to the uniform distribution of the data. ∎

"How can we assess the clustering tendency of a data set?" Intuitively, we can try to measure the probability that the data set is generated by a uniform data distribution. This can be achieved using statistical tests for spatial randomness. To illustrate this idea, let's look at a simple yet effective statistic called the Hopkins Statistic.

The **Hopkins Statistic** is a spatial statistic that tests the spatial randomness of a variable as distributed in a space. Given a data set, D, which is regarded as a sample of

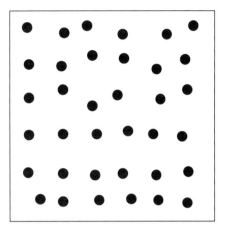

Figure 10.21 A data set that is uniformly distributed in the data space.

a random variable, o, we want to determine how far away o is from being uniformly distributed in the data space. We calculate the Hopkins Statistic as follows:

1. Sample n points, $p_1, \ldots, p_n$, uniformly from D. That is, each point in D has the same probability of being included in this sample. For each point, p_i, we find the nearest neighbor of p_i ($1 \le i \le n$) in D, and let x_i be the distance between p_i and its nearest neighbor in D. That is,

$$x_i = \min_{v \in D}\{dist(p_i, v)\}. \tag{10.25}$$

2. Sample n points, $q_1, \ldots, q_n$, uniformly from D. For each q_i ($1 \le i \le n$), we find the nearest neighbor of q_i in $D - \{q_i\}$, and let y_i be the distance between q_i and its nearest neighbor in $D - \{q_i\}$. That is,

$$y_i = \min_{v \in D, v \ne q_i}\{dist(q_i, v)\}. \tag{10.26}$$

3. Calculate the Hopkins Statistic, H, as

$$H = \frac{\sum_{i=1}^{n} y_i}{\sum_{i=1}^{n} x_i + \sum_{i=1}^{n} y_i}. \tag{10.27}$$

"*What does the Hopkins Statistic tell us about how likely data set* D *follows a uniform distribution in the data space?*" If D were uniformly distributed, then $\sum_{i=1}^{n} y_i$ and $\sum_{i=1}^{n} x_i$ would be close to each other, and thus H would be about 0.5. However, if D were highly skewed, then $\sum_{i=1}^{n} y_i$ would be substantially smaller than $\sum_{i=1}^{n} x_i$ in expectation, and thus H would be close to 0.

Our null hypothesis is the *homogeneous hypothesis*—that D is uniformly distributed and thus contains no meaningful clusters. The *nonhomogeneous hypothesis* (i.e., that D is not uniformly distributed and thus contains clusters) is the alternative hypothesis. We can conduct the Hopkins Statistic test iteratively, using 0.5 as the threshold to reject the alternative hypothesis. That is, if $H > 0.5$, then it is unlikely that D has statistically significant clusters.

10.6.2 Determining the Number of Clusters

Determining the "right" number of clusters in a data set is important, not only because some clustering algorithms like k-means require such a parameter, but also because the appropriate number of clusters controls the proper granularity of cluster analysis. It can be regarded as finding a good balance between *compressibility* and *accuracy* in cluster analysis. Consider two extreme cases. What if you were to treat the entire data set as a cluster? This would maximize the compression of the data, but such a cluster analysis has no value. On the other hand, treating each object in a data set as a cluster gives the finest clustering resolution (i.e., most accurate due to the zero distance between an object and the corresponding cluster center). In some methods like k-means, this even achieves the best cost. However, having one object per cluster does not enable any data summarization.

Determining the number of clusters is far from easy, often because the "right" number is ambiguous. Figuring out what the right number of clusters should be often depends on the distribution's shape and scale in the data set, as well as the clustering resolution required by the user. There are many possible ways to estimate the number of clusters. Here, we briefly introduce a few simple yet popular and effective methods.

A simple method is to set the number of clusters to about $\sqrt{\frac{n}{2}}$ for a data set of n points. In expectation, each cluster has $\sqrt{2n}$ points.

The **elbow method** is based on the observation that increasing the number of clusters can help to reduce the sum of within-cluster variance of each cluster. This is because having more clusters allows one to capture finer groups of data objects that are more similar to each other. However, the marginal effect of reducing the sum of within-cluster variances may drop if too many clusters are formed, because splitting a cohesive cluster into two gives only a small reduction. Consequently, a heuristic for selecting the right number of clusters is to use the turning point in the curve of the sum of within-cluster variances with respect to the number of clusters.

Technically, given a number, $k > 0$, we can form k clusters on the data set in question using a clustering algorithm like k-means, and calculate the sum of within-cluster variances, $var(k)$. We can then plot the curve of var with respect to k. The first (or most significant) turning point of the curve suggests the "right" number.

More advanced methods can determine the number of clusters using information criteria or information theoretic approaches. Please refer to the bibliographic notes for further information (Section 10.9).

The "right" number of clusters in a data set can also be determined by **cross-validation**, a technique often used in classification (Chapter 8). First, divide the given data set, D, into m parts. Next, use $m-1$ parts to build a clustering model, and use the remaining part to test the quality of the clustering. For example, for each point in the test set, we can find the closest centroid. Consequently, we can use the sum of the squared distances between all points in the test set and the closest centroids to measure how well the clustering model fits the test set. For any integer $k > 0$, we repeat this process m times to derive clusterings of k clusters by using each part in turn as the test set. The average of the quality measure is taken as the overall quality measure. We can then compare the overall quality measure with respect to different values of k, and find the number of clusters that best fits the data.

10.6.3 Measuring Clustering Quality

Suppose you have assessed the clustering tendency of a given data set. You may have also tried to predetermine the number of clusters in the set. You can now apply one or multiple clustering methods to obtain clusterings of the data set. *"How good is the clustering generated by a method, and how can we compare the clusterings generated by different methods?"*

We have a few methods to choose from for measuring the quality of a clustering. In general, these methods can be categorized into two groups according to whether ground truth is available. Here, *ground truth* is the ideal clustering that is often built using human experts.

If ground truth is available, it can be used by **extrinsic methods**, which compare the clustering against the group truth and measure. If the ground truth is unavailable, we can use **intrinsic methods**, which evaluate the goodness of a clustering by considering how well the clusters are separated. Ground truth can be considered as supervision in the form of "cluster labels." Hence, extrinsic methods are also known as *supervised methods*, while intrinsic methods are *unsupervised methods*.

Let's have a look at simple methods from each category.

Extrinsic Methods

When the ground truth is available, we can compare it with a clustering to assess the clustering. Thus, the core task in extrinsic methods is to assign a score, $Q(\mathcal{C}, \mathcal{C}_g)$, to a clustering, $\mathcal{C}$, given the ground truth, $\mathcal{C}_g$. Whether an extrinsic method is effective largely depends on the measure, Q, it uses.

In general, a measure Q on clustering quality is effective if it satisfies the following four essential criteria:

- **Cluster homogeneity.** This requires that the more pure the clusters in a clustering are, the better the clustering. Suppose that ground truth says that the objects in a data set, D, can belong to categories $L_1, \ldots, L_n$. Consider clustering, $\mathcal{C}_1$, wherein a cluster $C \in \mathcal{C}_1$ contains objects from two categories L_i, L_j ($1 \le i < j \le n$). Also consider clustering C_2, which is identical to C_1 except that C_2 is split into two clusters containing the objects in L_i and L_j, respectively. A clustering quality measure, Q, respecting cluster homogeneity should give a higher score to C_2 than C_1, that is, $Q(C_2, C_g) > Q(C_1, C_g)$.

- **Cluster completeness.** This is the counterpart of cluster homogeneity. Cluster completeness requires that for a clustering, if any two objects belong to the same category according to ground truth, then they should be assigned to the same cluster. Cluster completeness requires that a clustering should assign objects belonging to the same category (according to ground truth) to the same cluster. Consider clustering C_1, which contains clusters C_1 and C_2, of which the members belong to the same category according to ground truth. Let clustering C_2 be identical to C_1 except that C_1 and C_2 are merged into one cluster in C_2. Then, a clustering quality measure, Q, respecting cluster completeness should give a higher score to C_2, that is, $Q(C_2, C_g) > Q(C_1, C_g)$.

- **Rag bag.** In many practical scenarios, there is often a "rag bag" category containing objects that cannot be merged with other objects. Such a category is often called "miscellaneous," "other," and so on. The rag bag criterion states that putting a heterogeneous object into a pure cluster should be penalized more than putting it into a rag bag. Consider a clustering C_1 and a cluster $C \in C_1$ such that all objects in C except for one, denoted by o, belong to the same category according to ground truth. Consider a clustering C_2 identical to C_1 except that o is assigned to a cluster $C' \neq C$ in C_2 such that C' contains objects from various categories according to ground truth, and thus is noisy. In other words, C' in C_2 is a rag bag. Then, a clustering quality measure Q respecting the rag bag criterion should give a higher score to C_2, that is, $Q(C_2, C_g) > Q(C_1, C_g)$.

- **Small cluster preservation.** If a small category is split into small pieces in a clustering, those small pieces may likely become noise and thus the small category cannot be discovered from the clustering. The small cluster preservation criterion states that splitting a small category into pieces is more harmful than splitting a large category into pieces. Consider an extreme case. Let D be a data set of $n + 2$ objects such that, according to ground truth, n objects, denoted by $o_1, \ldots, o_n$, belong to one category and the other two objects, denoted by o_{n+1}, o_{n+2}, belong to another category. Suppose clustering C_1 has three clusters, $C_1 = \{o_1, \ldots, o_n\}$, $C_2 = \{o_{n+1}\}$, and $C_3 = \{o_{n+2}\}$. Let clustering C_2 have three clusters, too, namely $C_1 = \{o_1, \ldots, o_{n-1}\}$, $C_2 = \{o_n\}$, and $C_3 = \{o_{n+1}, o_{n+2}\}$. In other words, C_1 splits the small category and C_2 splits the big category. A clustering quality measure Q preserving small clusters should give a higher score to C_2, that is, $Q(C_2, C_g) > Q(C_1, C_g)$.

Many clustering quality measures satisfy some of these four criteria. Here, we introduce the *BCubed precision* and *recall* metrics, which satisfy all four criteria.

BCubed evaluates the precision and recall for every object in a clustering on a given data set according to ground truth. The precision of an object indicates how many other objects in the same cluster belong to the same category as the object. The recall of an object reflects how many objects of the same category are assigned to the same cluster.

Formally, let $D = \{o_1, \ldots, o_n\}$ be a set of objects, and C be a clustering on D. Let $L(o_i)$ $(1 \leq i \leq n)$ be the category of o_i given by ground truth, and $C(o_i)$ be the *cluster_ID* of o_i in C. Then, for two objects, o_i and o_j, $(1 \leq i, j, \leq n, i \neq j)$, the *correctness* of the relation between o_i and o_j in clustering C is given by

$$
\text{Correctness}(o_i, o_j) = \begin{cases} 1 & \text{if } L(o_i) = L(o_j) \Leftrightarrow C(o_i) = C(o_j) \\ 0 & \text{otherwise.} \end{cases} \tag{10.28}
$$

BCubed precision is defined as

$$
\text{Precision BCubed} = \frac{\sum_{i=1}^{n} \dfrac{\sum_{o_j : i \neq j, C(o_i) = C(o_j)} \text{Correctness}(o_i, o_j)}{\|\{o_j | i \neq j, C(o_i) = C(o_j)\}\|}}{n}. \tag{10.29}
$$

BCubed recall is defined as

$$
\text{Recall BCubed} = \frac{\sum_{i=1}^{n} \dfrac{\sum_{o_j : i \neq j, L(o_i) = L(o_j)} \text{Correctness}(o_i, o_j)}{\|\{o_j | i \neq j, L(o_i) = L(o_j)\}\|}}{n}. \tag{10.30}
$$

Intrinsic Methods

When the ground truth of a data set is not available, we have to use an intrinsic method to assess the clustering quality. In general, intrinsic methods evaluate a clustering by examining how well the clusters are separated and how compact the clusters are. Many intrinsic methods have the advantage of a similarity metric between objects in the data set.

The **silhouette coefficient** is such a measure. For a data set, D, of n objects, suppose D is partitioned into k clusters, $C_1, \ldots, C_k$. For each object $o \in D$, we calculate $a(o)$ as the average distance between o and all other objects in the cluster to which o belongs. Similarly, $b(o)$ is the minimum average distance from o to all clusters to which o does not belong. Formally, suppose $o \in C_i$ $(1 \leq i \leq k)$; then

$$
a(o) = \frac{\sum_{o' \in C_i, o \neq o'} dist(o, o')}{|C_i| - 1} \tag{10.31}
$$

and

$$b(o) = \min_{C_j:1\leq j\leq k, j\neq i} \left\{ \frac{\sum_{o'\in C_j} dist(o,o')}{|C_j|} \right\}. \tag{10.32}$$

The **silhouette coefficient** of o is then defined as

$$s(o) = \frac{b(o) - a(o)}{\max\{a(o), b(o)\}}. \tag{10.33}$$

The value of the silhouette coefficient is between -1 and 1. The value of $a(o)$ reflects the compactness of the cluster to which o belongs. The smaller the value, the more compact the cluster. The value of $b(o)$ captures the degree to which o is separated from other clusters. The larger $b(o)$ is, the more separated o is from other clusters. Therefore, when the silhouette coefficient value of o approaches 1, the cluster containing o is compact and o is far away from other clusters, which is the preferable case. However, when the silhouette coefficient value is negative (i.e., $b(o) < a(o)$), this means that, in expectation, o is closer to the objects in another cluster than to the objects in the same cluster as o. In many cases, this is a bad situation and should be avoided.

To measure a cluster's fitness within a clustering, we can compute the average silhouette coefficient value of all objects in the cluster. To measure the quality of a clustering, we can use the average silhouette coefficient value of all objects in the data set. The silhouette coefficient and other intrinsic measures can also be used in the elbow method to heuristically derive the number of clusters in a data set by replacing the sum of within-cluster variances.

10.7 Summary

- A **cluster** is a collection of data objects that are *similar* to one another within the same cluster and are *dissimilar* to the objects in other clusters. The process of grouping a set of physical or abstract objects into classes of *similar* objects is called **clustering**.

- Cluster analysis has extensive **applications**, including business intelligence, image pattern recognition, Web search, biology, and security. Cluster analysis can be used as a standalone data mining tool to gain insight into the data distribution, or as a preprocessing step for other data mining algorithms operating on the detected clusters.

- Clustering is a dynamic field of research in data mining. It is related to **unsupervised learning** in machine learning.

- Clustering is a challenging field. Typical **requirements** of it include scalability, the ability to deal with different types of data and attributes, the discovery of clusters in arbitrary shape, minimal requirements for domain knowledge to determine input parameters, the ability to deal with noisy data, incremental clustering and insensitivity to input order, the capability of clustering high-dimensionality data, constraint-based clustering, as well as interpretability and usability.

▪ Many clustering algorithms have been developed. These can be categorized from several **orthogonal aspects** such as those regarding partitioning criteria, separation of clusters, similarity measures used, and clustering space. This chapter discusses major fundamental clustering methods of the following categories: *partitioning methods, hierarchical methods, density-based methods*, and *grid-based methods*. Some algorithms may belong to more than one category.

▪ A **partitioning method** first creates an initial set of k partitions, where parameter k is the number of partitions to construct. It then uses an *iterative relocation technique* that attempts to improve the partitioning by moving objects from one group to another. Typical partitioning methods include k-means, k-medoids, and CLARANS.

▪ A **hierarchical method** creates a hierarchical decomposition of the given set of data objects. The method can be classified as being either *agglomerative (bottom-up)* or *divisive (top-down)*, based on how the hierarchical decomposition is formed. To compensate for the rigidity of *merge* or *split*, the quality of hierarchical agglomeration can be improved by analyzing object linkages at each hierarchical partitioning (e.g., in Chameleon), or by first performing *microclustering* (that is, grouping objects into "microclusters") and then operating on the microclusters with other clustering techniques such as iterative relocation (as in BIRCH).

▪ A **density-based method** clusters objects based on the notion of density. It grows clusters either according to the density of neighborhood objects (e.g., in DBSCAN) or according to a density function (e.g., in DENCLUE). OPTICS is a density-based method that generates an augmented ordering of the data's clustering structure.

▪ A **grid-based method** first quantizes the object space into a finite number of cells that form a grid structure, and then performs clustering on the grid structure. STING is a typical example of a grid-based method based on statistical information stored in grid cells. CLIQUE is a grid-based and subspace clustering algorithm.

▪ **Clustering evaluation** assesses the feasibility of clustering analysis on a data set and the quality of the results generated by a clustering method. The tasks include assessing clustering tendency, determining the number of clusters, and measuring clustering quality.

10.8 Exercises

10.1 Briefly describe and give examples of each of the following approaches to clustering: *partitioning* methods, *hierarchical* methods, *density-based* methods, and *grid-based* methods.

10.2 Suppose that the data mining task is to cluster points (with (x, y) representing location) into three clusters, where the points are

$$A_1(2, 10), A_2(2, 5), A_3(8, 4), B_1(5, 8), B_2(7, 5), B_3(6, 4), C_1(1, 2), C_2(4, 9).$$

The distance function is Euclidean distance. Suppose initially we assign A_1, B_1, and C_1 as the center of each cluster, respectively. Use the *k-means* algorithm to show *only*

(a) The three cluster centers after the first round of execution.

(b) The final three clusters.

10.3 Use an example to show why the *k*-means algorithm may not find the global optimum, that is, optimizing the within-cluster variation.

10.4 For the *k*-means algorithm, it is interesting to note that by choosing the initial cluster centers carefully, we may be able to not only speed up the algorithm's convergence, but also guarantee the quality of the final clustering. The **k-means++** algorithm is a variant of *k*-means, which chooses the initial centers as follows. First, it selects one center uniformly at random from the objects in the data set. Iteratively, for each object p other than the chosen center, it chooses an object as the new center. This object is chosen at random with probability proportional to $dist(p)^2$, where $dist(p)$ is the distance from p to the closest center that has already been chosen. The iteration continues until k centers are selected.

Explain why this method will not only speed up the convergence of the *k*-means algorithm, but also guarantee the quality of the final clustering results.

10.5 Provide the pseudocode of the object reassignment step of the PAM algorithm.

10.6 Both *k-means* and *k-medoids* algorithms can perform effective clustering.

(a) Illustrate the strength and weakness of *k-means* in comparison with *k-medoids*.

(b) Illustrate the strength and weakness of these schemes in comparison with a hierarchical clustering scheme (e.g., AGNES).

10.7 Prove that in DBSCAN, the density-connectedness is an equivalence relation.

10.8 Prove that in DBSCAN, for a fixed *MinPts* value and two neighborhood thresholds, $\epsilon_1 < \epsilon_2$, a cluster C with respect to ϵ_1 and *MinPts* must be a subset of a cluster C' with respect to ϵ_2 and *MinPts*.

10.9 Provide the pseudocode of the OPTICS algorithm.

10.10 Why is it that BIRCH encounters difficulties in finding clusters of arbitrary shape but OPTICS does not? Propose modifications to BIRCH to help it find clusters of arbitrary shape.

10.11 Provide the pseudocode of the step in CLIQUE that finds dense cells in all subspaces.

10.12 Present conditions under which density-based clustering is more suitable than partitioning-based clustering and hierarchical clustering. Give application examples to support your argument.

10.13 Give an example of how specific clustering methods can be *integrated*, for example, where one clustering algorithm is used as a preprocessing step for another. In addition, provide reasoning as to why the integration of two methods may sometimes lead to improved clustering quality and efficiency.

10.14 Clustering is recognized as an important data mining task with broad applications. Give one application example for each of the following cases:

(a) An application that uses clustering as a major data mining function.

(b) An application that uses clustering as a preprocessing tool for data preparation for other data mining tasks.

10.15 Data cubes and multidimensional databases contain nominal, ordinal, and numeric data in hierarchical or aggregate forms. Based on what you have learned about the clustering methods, design a clustering method that finds clusters in large data cubes effectively and efficiently.

10.16 Describe each of the following clustering algorithms in terms of the following criteria: (1) shapes of clusters that can be determined; (2) input parameters that must be specified; and (3) limitations.

(a) k-means

(b) k-medoids

(c) CLARA

(d) BIRCH

(e) CHAMELEON

(f) DBSCAN

10.17 Human eyes are fast and effective at judging the quality of clustering methods for 2-D data. Can you design a data visualization method that may help humans visualize data clusters and judge the clustering quality for 3-D data? What about for even higher-dimensional data?

10.18 Suppose that you are to allocate a number of automatic teller machines (ATMs) in a given region so as to satisfy a number of constraints. Households or workplaces may be clustered so that typically one ATM is assigned per cluster. The clustering, however, may be constrained by two factors: (1) obstacle objects (i.e., there are bridges, rivers, and highways that can affect ATM accessibility), and (2) additional user-specified constraints such as that each ATM should serve at least 10,000 households. How can a clustering algorithm such as k-means be modified for quality clustering under *both* constraints?

10.19 For *constraint-based clustering*, aside from having the minimum number of customers in each cluster (for ATM allocation) as a constraint, there can be many other kinds of constraints. For example, a constraint could be in the form of the maximum number of customers per cluster, average income of customers per cluster, maximum distance between every two clusters, and so on. Categorize the kinds of constraints that can be imposed on the clusters produced and discuss how to perform clustering efficiently under such kinds of constraints.

10.20 Design a *privacy-preserving clustering* method so that a data owner would be able to ask a third party to mine the data for quality clustering without worrying about the potential inappropriate disclosure of certain private or sensitive information stored in the data.

10.21 Show that BCubed metrics satisfy the four essential requirements for extrinsic clustering evaluation methods.

10.9 Bibliographic Notes

Clustering has been extensively studied for over 40 years and across many disciplines due to its broad applications. Most books on pattern classification and machine learning contain chapters on cluster analysis or unsupervised learning. Several textbooks are dedicated to the methods of cluster analysis, including Hartigan [Har75]; Jain and Dubes [JD88]; Kaufman and Rousseeuw [KR90]; and Arabie, Hubert, and De Sorte [AHS96]. There are also many survey articles on different aspects of clustering methods. Recent ones include Jain, Murty, and Flynn [JMF99]; Parsons, Haque, and Liu [PHL04]; and Jain [Jai10].

For partitioning methods, the k-means algorithm was first introduced by Lloyd [Llo57], and then by MacQueen [Mac67]. Arthur and Vassilvitskii [AV07] presented the k-means++ algorithm. A filtering algorithm, which uses a spatial hierarchical data index to speed up the computation of cluster means, is given in Kanungo, Mount, Netanyahu, et al. [KMN+02].

The k-medoids algorithms of PAM and CLARA were proposed by Kaufman and Rousseeuw [KR90]. The k-modes (for clustering nominal data) and k-prototypes (for clustering hybrid data) algorithms were proposed by Huang [Hua98]. The k-modes clustering algorithm was also proposed independently by Chaturvedi, Green, and Carroll [CGC94, CGC01]. The CLARANS algorithm was proposed by Ng and Han [NH94]. Ester, Kriegel, and Xu [EKX95] proposed techniques for further improvement of the performance of CLARANS using efficient spatial access methods such as R*-tree and focusing techniques. A k-means-based scalable clustering algorithm was proposed by Bradley, Fayyad, and Reina [BFR98].

An early survey of agglomerative hierarchical clustering algorithms was conducted by Day and Edelsbrunner [DE84]. Agglomerative hierarchical clustering, such as AGNES, and divisive hierarchical clustering, such as DIANA, were introduced by Kaufman and Rousseeuw [KR90]. An interesting direction for improving the clustering quality of hierarchical clustering methods is to integrate hierarchical clustering with distance-based iterative relocation or other nonhierarchical clustering methods. For example, BIRCH, by Zhang, Ramakrishnan, and Livny [ZRL96], first performs hierarchical clustering with a CF-tree before applying other techniques. Hierarchical clustering can also be performed by sophisticated linkage analysis, transformation, or nearest-neighbor analysis, such as CURE by Guha, Rastogi, and Shim [GRS98]; ROCK (for clustering nominal attributes) by Guha, Rastogi, and Shim [GRS99]; and Chameleon by Karypis, Han, and Kumar [KHK99].

A probabilistic hierarchical clustering framework following normal linkage algorithms and using probabilistic models to define cluster similarity was developed by Friedman [Fri03] and Heller and Ghahramani [HG05].

For density-based clustering methods, DBSCAN was proposed by Ester, Kriegel, Sander, and Xu [EKSX96]. Ankerst, Breunig, Kriegel, and Sander [ABKS99] developed OPTICS, a cluster-ordering method that facilitates density-based clustering without worrying about parameter specification. The DENCLUE algorithm, based on a set of density distribution functions, was proposed by Hinneburg and Keim [HK98]. Hinneburg and Gabriel [HG07] developed DENCLUE 2.0, which includes a new hill-climbing procedure for Gaussian kernels that adjusts the step size automatically.

STING, a grid-based multiresolution approach that collects statistical information in grid cells, was proposed by Wang, Yang, and Muntz [WYM97]. WaveCluster, developed by Sheikholeslami, Chatterjee, and Zhang [SCZ98], is a multiresolution clustering approach that transforms the original feature space by wavelet transform.

Scalable methods for clustering nominal data were studied by Gibson, Kleinberg, and Raghavan [GKR98]; Guha, Rastogi, and Shim [GRS99]; and Ganti, Gehrke, and Ramakrishnan [GGR99]. There are also many other clustering paradigms. For example, fuzzy clustering methods are discussed in Kaufman and Rousseeuw [KR90], Bezdek [Bez81], and Bezdek and Pal [BP92].

For high-dimensional clustering, an Apriori-based dimension-growth subspace clustering algorithm called CLIQUE was proposed by Agrawal, Gehrke, Gunopulos, and Raghavan [AGGR98]. It integrates density-based and grid-based clustering methods.

Recent studies have proceeded to clustering stream data Babcock, Badu, Datar, et al. [BBD$^+$02]. A k-median-based data stream clustering algorithm was proposed by Guha, Mishra, Motwani, and O'Callaghan [GMMO00] and by O'Callaghan et al. [OMM$^+$02]. A method for clustering evolving data streams was proposed by Aggarwal, Han, Wang, and Yu [AHWY03]. A framework for projected clustering of high-dimensional data streams was proposed by Aggarwal, Han, Wang, and Yu [AHWY04a].

Clustering evaluation is discussed in a few monographs and survey articles such as Jain and Dubes [JD88] and Halkidi, Batistakis, and Vazirgiannis [HBV01]. The extrinsic methods for clustering quality evaluation are extensively explored. Some recent studies include Meilă [Mei03, Mei05] and Amigó, Gonzalo, Artiles, and Verdejo [AGAV09]. The four essential criteria introduced in this chapter are formulated in Amigó, Gonzalo, Artiles, and Verdejo [AGAV09], while some individual criteria were also mentioned earlier, for example, in Meilă [Mei03] and Rosenberg and Hirschberg [RH07]. Bagga and Baldwin [BB98] introduced the BCubed metrics. The silhouette coefficient is described in Kaufman and Rousseeuw [KR90].

Advanced Cluster Analysis

You learned the fundamentals of cluster analysis in Chapter 10. In this chapter, we discuss advanced topics of cluster analysis. Specifically, we investigate four major perspectives:

- **Probabilistic model-based clustering**: Section 11.1 introduces a general framework and a method for deriving clusters where each object is assigned a probability of belonging to a cluster. Probabilistic model-based clustering is widely used in many data mining applications such as text mining.

- **Clustering high-dimensional data**: When the dimensionality is high, conventional distance measures can be dominated by noise. Section 11.2 introduces fundamental methods for cluster analysis on high-dimensional data.

- **Clustering graph and network data**: Graph and network data are increasingly popular in applications such as online social networks, the World Wide Web, and digital libraries. In Section 11.3, you will study the key issues in clustering graph and network data, including similarity measurement and clustering methods.

- **Clustering with constraints**: In our discussion so far, we do not assume any constraints in clustering. In some applications, however, various constraints may exist. These constraints may rise from background knowledge or spatial distribution of the objects. You will learn how to conduct cluster analysis with different kinds of constraints in Section 11.4.

By the end of this chapter, you will have a good grasp of the issues and techniques regarding advanced cluster analysis.

Probabilistic Model-Based Clustering

In all the cluster analysis methods we have discussed so far, each data object can be assigned to only one of a number of clusters. This cluster assignment rule is required in some applications such as assigning customers to marketing managers. However, in other applications, this rigid requirement may not be desirable. In this section, we demonstrate the need for fuzzy or flexible cluster assignment in some applications, and introduce a general method to compute probabilistic clusters and assignments.

"In what situations may a data object belong to more than one cluster?" Consider Example 11.1.

Example 11.1 **Clustering product reviews.** *AllElectronics* has an online store, where customers not only purchase online, but also create reviews of products. Not every product receives reviews; instead, some products may have many reviews, while many others have none or only a few. Moreover, a review may involve multiple products. Thus, as the review editor of *AllElectronics*, your task is to cluster the reviews.

Ideally, a cluster is about a *topic*, for example, a group of products, services, or issues that are highly related. Assigning a review to one cluster exclusively would not work well for your task. Suppose there is a cluster for "cameras and camcorders" and another for "computers." What if a review talks about the compatibility between a camcorder and a computer? The review relates to both clusters; however, it does not exclusively belong to either cluster.

You would like to use a clustering method that allows a review to belong to more than one cluster if the review indeed involves more than one topic. To reflect the strength that a review belongs to a cluster, you want the assignment of a review to a cluster to carry a weight representing the partial membership. ∎

The scenario where an object may belong to multiple clusters occurs often in many applications. This is illustrated in Example 11.2.

Example 11.2 **Clustering to study user search intent**. The *AllElectronics* online store records all customer browsing and purchasing behavior in a log. An important data mining task is to use the log data to categorize and understand *user search intent*. For example, consider a user *session* (a short period in which a user interacts with the online store). Is the user searching for a product, making comparisons among different products, or looking for customer support information? Clustering analysis helps here because it is difficult to predefine user behavior patterns thoroughly. A cluster that contains similar user browsing trajectories may represent similar user behavior.

However, not every session belongs to only one cluster. For example, suppose user sessions involving the purchase of digital cameras form one cluster, and user sessions that compare laptop computers form another cluster. What if a user in one session makes an order for a digital camera, and at the same time compares several laptop computers? Such a session should belong to both clusters to some extent. ∎

In this section, we systematically study the theme of clustering that allows an object to belong to more than one cluster. We start with the notion of fuzzy clusters in Section 11.1.1. We then generalize the concept to probabilistic model-based clusters in Section 11.1.2. In Section 11.1.3, we introduce the expectation-maximization algorithm, a general framework for mining such clusters.

11.1.1 Fuzzy Clusters

Given a set of objects, $X = \{x_1, \ldots, x_n\}$, a **fuzzy set** S is a subset of X that allows each object in X to have a membership degree between 0 and 1. Formally, a fuzzy set, S, can be modeled as a function, $F_S : X \rightarrow [0, 1]$.

Example 11.3 **Fuzzy set.** The more digital camera units that are sold, the more popular the camera is. In *AllElectronics*, we can use the following formula to compute the degree of popularity of a digital camera, o, given the sales of o:

$$pop(o) = \begin{cases} 1 & \text{if 1000 or more units of } o \text{ are sold} \\ \frac{i}{1000} & \text{if } i \, (i < 1000) \text{ units of } o \text{ are sold.} \end{cases} \quad (11.1)$$

Function $pop()$ defines a fuzzy set of popular digital cameras. For example, suppose the sales of digital cameras at *AllElectronics* are as shown in Table 11.1. The fuzzy set of popular digital cameras is $\{A(0.05), B(1), C(0.86), D(0.27)\}$, where the degrees of membership are written in parentheses. ∎

We can apply the fuzzy set idea on clusters. That is, given a set of objects, a cluster is a fuzzy set of objects. Such a cluster is called a fuzzy cluster. Consequently, a clustering contains multiple *fuzzy clusters.*

Formally, given a set of objects, $o_1, \ldots, o_n$, a **fuzzy clustering** of k **fuzzy clusters**, $C_1, \ldots, C_k$, can be represented using a **partition matrix**, $M = [w_{ij}]$ $(1 \le i \le n, 1 \le j \le k)$, where w_{ij} is the membership degree of o_i in fuzzy cluster C_j. The partition matrix should satisfy the following three requirements:

- For each object, o_i, and cluster, C_j, $0 \le w_{ij} \le 1$. This requirement enforces that a fuzzy cluster is a fuzzy set.

- For each object, o_i, $\sum_{j=1}^{k} w_{ij} = 1$. This requirement ensures that every object participates in the clustering equivalently.

Table 11.1 Set of Digital Cameras and Their Sales at *AllElectronics*

Camera	Sales (units)
A	50
B	1320
C	860
D	270

- For each cluster, C_j, $0 < \sum_{i=1}^{n} w_{ij} < n$. This requirement ensures that for every cluster, there is at least one object for which the membership value is nonzero.

Example 11.4 **Fuzzy clusters.** Suppose the *AllElectronics* online store has six reviews. The keywords contained in these reviews are listed in Table 11.2.

We can group the reviews into two fuzzy clusters, C_1 and C_2. C_1 is for "digital camera" and "lens," and C_2 is for "computer." The partition matrix is

$$
M = \begin{bmatrix} 1 & 0 \\ 1 & 0 \\ 1 & 0 \\ \frac{2}{3} & \frac{1}{3} \\ 0 & 1 \\ 0 & 1 \end{bmatrix}.
$$

Here, we use the keywords "digital camera" and "lens" as the features of cluster C_1, and "computer" as the feature of cluster C_2. For review, R_i, and cluster, C_j ($1 \le i \le 6, 1 \le j \le 2$), w_{ij} is defined as

$$
w_{ij} = \frac{|R_i \cap C_j|}{|R_i \cap (C_1 \cup C_2)|} = \frac{|R_i \cap C_j|}{|R_i \cap \{digital\ camera, lens, computer\}|}.
$$

In this fuzzy clustering, review R_4 belongs to clusters C_1 and C_2 with membership degrees $\frac{2}{3}$ and $\frac{1}{3}$, respectively. ∎

"How can we evaluate how well a fuzzy clustering describes a data set?" Consider a set of objects, $o_1, \ldots, o_n$, and a fuzzy clustering $\mathcal{C}$ of k clusters, $C_1, \ldots, C_k$. Let $M = [w_{ij}]$ ($1 \le i \le n, 1 \le j \le k$) be the partition matrix. Let $c_1, \ldots, c_k$ be the *centers* of clusters $C_1, \ldots, C_k$, respectively. Here, a center can be defined either as the mean or the medoid, or in other ways specific to the application.

As discussed in Chapter 10, the distance or similarity between an object and the center of the cluster to which the object is assigned can be used to measure how well the

Table 11.2 Set of Reviews and the Keywords Used

Review_ID	Keywords
R_1	digital camera, lens
R_2	digital camera
R_3	lens
R_4	digital camera, lens, computer
R_5	computer, CPU
R_6	computer, computer game

object belongs to the cluster. This idea can be extended to fuzzy clustering. For any object, o_i, and cluster, C_j, if $w_{ij} > 0$, then $dist(o_i, c_j)$ measures how well o_i is represented by c_j, and thus belongs to cluster C_j. Because an object can participate in more than one cluster, the sum of distances to the corresponding cluster centers weighted by the degrees of membership captures how well the object fits the clustering.

Formally, for an object o_i, the **sum of the squared error** (SSE) is given by

$$SSE(o_i) = \sum_{j=1}^{k} w_{ij}^p dist(o_i, c_j)^2,$$ (11.2)

where the parameter $p(p \geq 1)$ controls the influence of the degrees of membership. The larger the value of p, the larger the influence of the degrees of membership. Orthogonally, the SSE for a cluster, C_j, is

$$SSE(C_j) = \sum_{i=1}^{n} w_{ij}^p dist(o_i, c_j)^2.$$ (11.3)

Finally, the SSE of the clustering is defined as

$$SSE(\mathcal{C}) = \sum_{i=1}^{n} \sum_{j=1}^{k} w_{ij}^p dist(o_i, c_j)^2.$$ (11.4)

The SSE can be used to measure how well a fuzzy clustering fits a data set.

Fuzzy clustering is also called *soft clustering* because it allows an object to belong to more than one cluster. It is easy to see that traditional (rigid) clustering, which enforces each object to belong to only one cluster exclusively, is a special case of fuzzy clustering. We defer the discussion of how to compute fuzzy clustering to Section 11.1.3.

11.1.2 Probabilistic Model-Based Clusters

"Fuzzy clusters (Section 11.1.1) provide the flexibility of allowing an object to participate in multiple clusters. Is there a general framework to specify clusterings where objects may participate in multiple clusters in a probabilistic way?" In this section, we introduce the general notion of probabilistic model-based clusters to answer this question.

As discussed in Chapter 10, we conduct cluster analysis on a data set because we assume that the objects in the data set in fact belong to different inherent categories. Recall that clustering tendency analysis (Section 10.6.1) can be used to examine whether a data set contains objects that may lead to meaningful clusters. Here, the inherent categories hidden in the data are *latent*, which means they cannot be directly observed. Instead, we have to infer them using the data observed. For example, the topics hidden in a set of reviews in the *AllElectronics* online store are latent because one cannot read the topics directly. However, the topics can be inferred from the reviews because each review is about one or multiple topics.

Therefore, the goal of cluster analysis is to find hidden categories. A data set that is the subject of cluster analysis can be regarded as a sample of the possible instances of the hidden categories, but without any category labels. The clusters derived from cluster analysis are inferred using the data set, and are designed to approach the hidden categories.

Statistically, we can assume that a hidden category is a distribution over the data space, which can be mathematically represented using a probability density function (or distribution function). We call such a hidden category a *probabilistic cluster*. For a probabilistic cluster, C, its probability density function, f, and a point, o, in the data space, $f(o)$ is the relative likelihood that an instance of C appears at o.

Example 11.5 **Probabilistic clusters**. Suppose the digital cameras sold by *AllElectronics* can be divided into two categories: C_1, a consumer line (e.g., point-and-shoot cameras), and C_2, a professional line (e.g., single-lens reflex cameras). Their respective probability density functions, f_1 and f_2, are shown in Figure 11.1 with respect to the attribute *price*.

For a price value of, say, $1000, $f_1(1000)$ is the relative likelihood that the price of a consumer-line camera is $1000. Similarly, $f_2(1000)$ is the relative likelihood that the price of a professional-line camera is $1000.

The probability density functions, f_1 and f_2, cannot be observed directly. Instead, *AllElectronics* can only infer these distributions by analyzing the prices of the digital cameras it sells. Moreover, a camera often does not come with a well-determined category (e.g., "consumer line" or "professional line"). Instead, such categories are typically based on user background knowledge and can vary. For example, a camera in the *prosumer* segment may be regarded at the high end of the consumer line by some customers, and the low end of the professional line by others.

As an analyst at *AllElectronics*, you can consider each category as a probabilistic cluster, and conduct cluster analysis on the price of cameras to approach these categories. ■

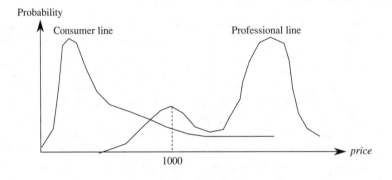

Figure 11.1 The probability density functions of two probabilistic clusters.

Suppose we want to find k probabilistic clusters, $C_1, \ldots, C_k$, through cluster analysis. For a data set, D, of n objects, we can regard D as a finite sample of the possible instances of the clusters. Conceptually, we can assume that D is formed as follows. Each cluster, C_j ($1 \leq j \leq k$), is associated with a probability, ω_j, that some instance is sampled from the cluster. It is often assumed that $\omega_1, \ldots, \omega_k$ are given as part of the problem setting, and that $\sum_{j=1}^{k} \omega_j = 1$, which ensures that all objects are generated by the k clusters. Here, parameter ω_j captures background knowledge about the relative population of cluster C_j.

We then run the following two steps to generate an object in D. The steps are executed n times in total to generate n objects, $o_1, \ldots, o_n$, in D.

1. Choose a cluster, C_j, according to probabilities $\omega_1, \ldots, \omega_k$.

2. Choose an instance of C_j according to its probability density function, f_j.

The data generation process here is the basic assumption in mixture models. Formally, a **mixture model** assumes that a set of observed objects is a mixture of instances from multiple probabilistic clusters. Conceptually, each observed object is generated independently by two steps: first choosing a probabilistic cluster according to the probabilities of the clusters, and then choosing a sample according to the probability density function of the chosen cluster.

Given data set, D, and k, the number of clusters required, the task of *probabilistic model-based cluster analysis* is to infer a set of k probabilistic clusters that is most likely to generate D using this data generation process. An important question remaining is how we can measure the likelihood that a set of k probabilistic clusters and their probabilities will generate an observed data set.

Consider a set, $\boldsymbol{C}$, of k probabilistic clusters, $C_1, \ldots, C_k$, with probability density functions $f_1, \ldots, f_k$, respectively, and their probabilities, $\omega_1, \ldots, \omega_k$. For an object, o, the probability that o is generated by cluster C_j ($1 \leq j \leq k$) is given by $P(o|C_j) = \omega_j f_j(o)$. Therefore, the probability that o is generated by the set $\boldsymbol{C}$ of clusters is

$$P(o|\boldsymbol{C}) = \sum_{j=1}^{k} \omega_j f_j(o). \tag{11.5}$$

Since the objects are assumed to have been generated independently, for a data set, $D = \{o_1, \ldots, o_n\}$, of n objects, we have

$$P(D|\boldsymbol{C}) = \prod_{i=1}^{n} P(o_i|\boldsymbol{C}) = \prod_{i=1}^{n} \sum_{j=1}^{k} \omega_j f_j(o_i). \tag{11.6}$$

Now, it is clear that the task of probabilistic model-based cluster analysis on a data set, D, is to find a set $\boldsymbol{C}$ of k probabilistic clusters such that $P(D|\boldsymbol{C})$ is maximized. Maximizing $P(D|\boldsymbol{C})$ is often intractable because, in general, the probability density function of a cluster can take an arbitrarily complicated form. To make probabilistic model-based clusters computationally feasible, we often compromise by assuming that the probability density functions are parameterized distributions.

Formally, let $o_1,\ldots,o_n$ be the n observed objects, and $\Theta_1,\ldots,\Theta_k$ be the parameters of the k distributions, denoted by $\mathbf{O} = \{o_1,\ldots,o_n\}$ and $\Theta = \{\Theta_1,\ldots,\Theta_k\}$, respectively. Then, for any object, $o_i \in \mathbf{O}$ $(1 \leq i \leq n)$, Eq. (11.5) can be rewritten as

$$P(o_i|\Theta) = \sum_{j=1}^{k} \omega_j P_j(o_i|\Theta_j), \tag{11.7}$$

where $P_j(o_i|\Theta_j)$ is the probability that o_i is generated from the jth distribution using parameter Θ_j. Consequently, Eq. (11.6) can be rewritten as

$$P(\mathbf{O}|\Theta) = \prod_{i=1}^{n}\sum_{j=1}^{k} \omega_j P_j(o_i|\Theta_j). \tag{11.8}$$

Using the parameterized probability distribution models, the task of probabilistic model-based cluster analysis is to infer a set of parameters, Θ, that maximizes Eq. (11.8).

Example 11.6 **Univariate Gaussian mixture model.** Let's use univariate Gaussian distributions as an example. That is, we assume that the probability density function of each cluster follows a 1-D Gaussian distribution. Suppose there are k clusters. The two parameters for the probability density function of each cluster are center, μ_j, and standard deviation, σ_j $(1 \leq j \leq k)$. We denote the parameters as $\Theta_j = (\mu_j, \sigma_j)$ and $\Theta = \{\Theta_1,\ldots,\Theta_k\}$. Let the data set be $\mathbf{O} = \{o_1,\ldots,o_n\}$, where o_i $(1 \leq i \leq n)$ is a real number. For any point, $o_i \in \mathbf{O}$, we have

$$P(o_i|\Theta_j) = \frac{1}{\sqrt{2\pi}\sigma_j} e^{-\frac{(o_i-\mu_j)^2}{2\sigma^2}}. \tag{11.9}$$

Assuming that each cluster has the same probability, that is $\omega_1 = \omega_2 = \cdots = \omega_k = \frac{1}{k}$, and plugging Eq. (11.9) into Eq. (11.7), we have

$$P(o_i|\Theta) = \frac{1}{k}\sum_{j=1}^{k} \frac{1}{\sqrt{2\pi}\sigma_j} e^{-\frac{(o_i-\mu_j)^2}{2\sigma^2}}. \tag{11.10}$$

Applying Eq. (11.8), we have

$$P(\mathbf{O}|\Theta) = \frac{1}{k}\prod_{i=1}^{n}\sum_{j=1}^{k} \frac{1}{\sqrt{2\pi}\sigma_j} e^{-\frac{(o_i-\mu_j)^2}{2\sigma^2}}. \tag{11.11}$$

The task of probabilistic model-based cluster analysis using a univariate Gaussian mixture model is to infer Θ such that Eq. (11.11) is maximized. ∎

11.1.3 Expectation-Maximization Algorithm

"How can we compute fuzzy clusterings and probabilistic model-based clusterings?" In this section, we introduce a principled approach. Let's start with a review of the k-means clustering problem and the k-means algorithm studied in Chapter 10.

It can easily be shown that k-means clustering is a special case of fuzzy clustering (Exercise 11.1). The k-means algorithm iterates until the clustering cannot be improved. Each iteration consists of two steps:

The expectation step (E-step): Given the current cluster centers, each object is assigned to the cluster with a center that is closest to the object. Here, an object is expected to belong to the closest cluster.

The maximization step (M-step): Given the cluster assignment, for each cluster, the algorithm adjusts the center so that the sum of the distances from the objects assigned to this cluster and the new center is minimized. That is, the similarity of objects assigned to a cluster is maximized.

We can generalize this two-step method to tackle fuzzy clustering and probabilistic model-based clustering. In general, an **expectation-maximization (EM) algorithm** is a framework that approaches maximum likelihood or maximum a posteriori estimates of parameters in statistical models. In the context of fuzzy or probabilistic model-based clustering, an EM algorithm starts with an initial set of parameters and iterates until the clustering cannot be improved, that is, until the clustering converges or the change is sufficiently small (less than a preset threshold). Each iteration also consists of two steps:

- The **expectation step** assigns objects to clusters according to the current fuzzy clustering or parameters of probabilistic clusters.

- The **maximization step** finds the new clustering or parameters than minimize the SSE in fuzzy clustering (Eq. 11.4) or the expected likelihood in probabilistic model-based clustering.

Example 11.7 **Fuzzy clustering using the EM algorithm.** Consider the six points in Figure 11.2, where the coordinates of the points are also shown. Let's compute two fuzzy clusters using the EM algorithm.

We randomly select two points, say $c_1 = a$ and $c_2 = b$, as the initial centers of the two clusters. The first iteration conducts the expectation step and the maximization step as follows.

In the **E-step**, for each point we calculate its membership degree in each cluster. For any point, o, we assign o to c_1 and c_2 with membership weights

$$\frac{\frac{1}{dist(o,c_1)^2}}{\frac{1}{dist(o,c_1)^2}+\frac{1}{dist(o,c_2)^2}} = \frac{dist(o,c_2)^2}{dist(o,c_1)^2+dist(o,c_2)^2} \text{ and } \frac{dist(o,c_1)^2}{dist(o,c_1)^2+dist(o,c_2)^2},$$

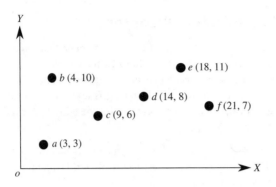

Figure 11.2 Data set for fuzzy clustering.

Table 11.3 Intermediate Results from the First Three Iterations of Example 11.7's EM Algorithm

Iteration	E-Step	M-Step
1	$M^T = \begin{bmatrix} 1 & 0 & 0.48 & 0.42 & 0.41 & 0.47 \\ 0 & 1 & 0.52 & 0.58 & 0.59 & 0.53 \end{bmatrix}$	$c_1 = (8.47, 5.12)$ $c_2 = (10.42, 8.99)$
2	$M^T = \begin{bmatrix} 0.73 & 0.49 & 0.91 & 0.26 & 0.33 & 0.42 \\ 0.27 & 0.51 & 0.09 & 0.74 & 0.67 & 0.58 \end{bmatrix}$	$c_1 = (8.51, 6.11)$ $c_2 = (14.42, 8.69)$
3.	$M^T = \begin{bmatrix} 0.80 & 0.76 & 0.99 & 0.02 & 0.14 & 0.23 \\ 0.20 & 0.24 & 0.01 & 0.98 & 0.86 & 0.77 \end{bmatrix}$	$c_1 = (6.40, 6.24)$ $c_2 = (16.55, 8.64)$

respectively, where $dist(,)$ is the Euclidean distance. The rationale is that, if o is close to c_1 and $dist(o, c_1)$ is small, the membership degree of o with respect to c_1 should be high. We also normalize the membership degrees so that the sum of degrees for an object is equal to 1.

For point a, we have $w_{a,c_1} = 1$ and $w_{a,c_2} = 0$. That is, a exclusively belongs to c_1. For point b, we have $w_{b,c_1} = 0$ and $w_{b,c_2} = 1$. For point c, we have $w_{c,c_1} = \frac{41}{45+41} = 0.48$ and $w_{c,c_2} = \frac{45}{45+41} = 0.52$. The degrees of membership of the other points are shown in the partition matrix in Table 11.3. ■

In the **M-step**, we recalculate the centroids according to the partition matrix, minimizing the SSE given in Eq. (11.4). The new centroid should be adjusted to

$$c_j = \frac{\sum_{\text{each point } o} w_{o,c_j}^2 o}{\sum_{\text{each point } o} w_{o,c_j}^2}, \tag{11.12}$$

where $j = 1, 2$.

In this example,

$$c_1 = \left(\frac{1^2 \times 3 + 0^2 \times 4 + 0.48^2 \times 9 + 0.42^2 \times 14 + 0.41^2 \times 18 + 0.47^2 \times 21}{1^2 + 0^2 + 0.48^2 + 0.42^2 + 0.41^2 + 0.47^2}, \right.$$

$$\left. \frac{1^2 \times 3 + 0^2 \times 10 + 0.48^2 \times 6 + 0.42^2 \times 8 + 0.41^2 \times 11 + 0.47^2 \times 7}{1^2 + 0^2 + 0.48^2 + 0.42^2 + 0.41^2 + 0.47^2} \right)$$

$$= (8.47, 5.12)$$

and

$$c_2 = \left(\frac{0^2 \times 3 + 1^2 \times 4 + 0.52^2 \times 9 + 0.58^2 \times 14 + 0.59^2 \times 18 + 0.53^2 \times 21}{0^2 + 1^2 + 0.52^2 + 0.58^2 + 0.59^2 + 0.53^2}, \right.$$

$$\left. \frac{0^2 \times 3 + 1^2 \times 10 + 0.52^2 \times 6 + 0.58^2 \times 8 + 0.59^2 \times 11 + 0.53^2 \times 7}{0^2 + 1^2 + 0.52^2 + 0.58^2 + 0.59^2 + 0.53^2} \right)$$

$$= (10.42, 8.99).$$

We repeat the iterations, where each iteration contains an E-step and an M-step. Table 11.3 shows the results from the first three iterations. The algorithm stops when the cluster centers converge or the change is small enough.

"How can we apply the EM algorithm to compute probabilistic model-based clustering?" Let's use a univariate Gaussian mixture model (Example 11.6) to illustrate.

Example 11.8 Using the EM algorithm for mixture models. Given a set of objects, $O = \{o_1, \ldots, o_n\}$, we want to mine a set of parameters, $\Theta = \{\Theta_1, \ldots, \Theta_k\}$, such that $P(O|\Theta)$ in Eq. (11.11) is maximized, where $\Theta_j = (\mu_j, \sigma_j)$ are the mean and standard deviation, respectively, of the jth univariate Gaussian distribution, $(1 \le j \le k)$.

We can apply the EM algorithm. We assign random values to parameters Θ as the initial values. We then iteratively conduct the E-step and the M-step as follows until the parameters converge or the change is sufficiently small.

In the **E-step**, for each object, $o_i \in O$ $(1 \le i \le n)$, we calculate the probability that o_i belongs to each distribution, that is,

$$P(\Theta_j | o_i, \Theta) = \frac{P(o_i | \Theta_j)}{\sum_{l=1}^{k} P(o_i | \Theta_l)}. \tag{11.13}$$

In the **M-step**, we adjust the parameters Θ so that the expected likelihood $P(O|\Theta)$ in Eq. (11.11) is maximized. This can be achieved by setting

$$\mu_j = \frac{1}{k} \sum_{i=1}^{n} o_i \frac{P(\Theta_j | o_i, \Theta)}{\sum_{l=1}^{n} P(\Theta_j | o_l, \Theta)} = \frac{1}{k} \frac{\sum_{i=1}^{n} o_i P(\Theta_j | o_i, \Theta)}{\sum_{i=1}^{n} P(\Theta_j | o_i, \Theta)} \tag{11.14}$$

and

$$\sigma_j = \sqrt{\frac{\sum_{i=1}^{n} P(\Theta_j | o_i, \Theta)(o_i - u_j)^2}{\sum_{i=1}^{n} P(\Theta_j | o_i, \Theta)}}.$$ (11.15)

∎

In many applications, probabilistic model-based clustering has been shown to be effective because it is more general than partitioning methods and fuzzy clustering methods. A distinct advantage is that appropriate statistical models can be used to capture latent clusters. The EM algorithm is commonly used to handle many learning problems in data mining and statistics due to its simplicity. Note that, in general, the EM algorithm may not converge to the optimal solution. It may instead converge to a local maximum. Many heuristics have been explored to avoid this. For example, we could run the EM process multiple times using different random initial values. Furthermore, the EM algorithm can be very costly if the number of distributions is large or the data set contains very few observed data points.

11.2 Clustering High-Dimensional Data

The clustering methods we have studied so far work well when the dimensionality is not high, that is, having less than 10 attributes. There are, however, important applications of high dimensionality. *"How can we conduct cluster analysis on high-dimensional data?"*

In this section, we study approaches to clustering high-dimensional data. Section 11.2.1 starts with an overview of the major challenges and the approaches used. Methods for high-dimensional data clustering can be divided into two categories: subspace clustering methods (Sections 11.2.2 and 11.2.3) and dimensionality reduction methods (Section 11.2.4).

11.2.1 Clustering High-Dimensional Data: Problems, Challenges, and Major Methodologies

Before we present any specific methods for clustering high-dimensional data, let's first demonstrate the needs of cluster analysis on high-dimensional data using examples. We examine the challenges that call for new methods. We then categorize the major methods according to whether they search for clusters in subspaces of the original space, or whether they create a new lower-dimensionality space and search for clusters there.

In some applications, a data object may be described by 10 or more attributes. Such objects are referred to as a high-dimensional data space.

Example 11.9 High-dimensional data and clustering. *AllElectronics* keeps track of the products purchased by every customer. As a customer-relationship manager, you want to cluster customers into groups according to what they purchased from *AllElectronics*.

Table 11.4 Customer Purchase Data

Customer	P_1	P_2	P_3	P_4	P_5	P_6	P_7	P_8	P_9	P_{10}
Ada	1	0	0	0	0	0	0	0	0	0
Bob	0	0	0	0	0	0	0	0	0	1
Cathy	1	0	0	0	1	0	0	0	0	1

The customer purchase data are of very high dimensionality. *AllElectronics* carries tens of thousands of products. Therefore, a customer's purchase profile, which is a vector of the products carried by the company, has tens of thousands of dimensions.

"Are the traditional distance measures, which are frequently used in low-dimensional cluster analysis, also effective on high-dimensional data?" Consider the customers in Table 11.4, where 10 products, $P_1, \ldots, P_{10}$, are used in demonstration. If a customer purchases a product, a 1 is set at the corresponding bit; otherwise, a 0 appears. Let's calculate the Euclidean distances (Eq. 2.16) among Ada, Bob, and Cathy. It is easy to see that

$$dist(\text{Ada}, \text{Bob}) = dist(\text{Bob}, \text{Cathy}) = dist(\text{Ada}, \text{Cathy}) = \sqrt{2}.$$

According to Euclidean distance, the three customers are equivalently similar (or dissimilar) to each other. However, a close look tells us that Ada should be more similar to Cathy than to Bob because Ada and Cathy share one common purchased item, P_1. ■

As shown in Example 11.9, the traditional distance measures can be ineffective on high-dimensional data. Such distance measures may be dominated by the noise in many dimensions. Therefore, clusters in the full, high-dimensional space can be unreliable, and finding such clusters may not be meaningful.

"Then what kinds of clusters are meaningful on high-dimensional data?" For cluster analysis of high-dimensional data, we still want to group similar objects together. However, the data space is often too big and too messy. An additional challenge is that we need to find not only clusters, but, for each cluster, a set of attributes that manifest the cluster. In other words, a cluster on high-dimensional data often is defined using a small set of attributes instead of the full data space. Essentially, clustering high-dimensional data should return groups of objects as clusters (as conventional cluster analysis does), *in addition to*, for each cluster, the set of attributes that characterize the cluster. For example, in Table 11.4, to characterize the similarity between Ada and Cathy, P_1 may be returned as the attribute because Ada and Cathy both purchased P_1.

Clustering high-dimensional data is the search for clusters and the space in which they exist. Thus, there are two major kinds of methods:

▪ *Subspace clustering approaches* search for clusters existing in subspaces of the given high-dimensional data space, where a subspace is defined using a subset of attributes in the full space. Subspace clustering approaches are discussed in Section 11.2.2.

▪ *Dimensionality reduction approaches* try to construct a much lower-dimensional space and search for clusters in such a space. Often, a method may construct new dimensions by combining some dimensions from the original data. Dimensionality reduction methods are the topic of Section 11.2.4.

In general, clustering high-dimensional data raises several new challenges in addition to those of conventional clustering:

▪ A major issue is how to create appropriate models for clusters in high-dimensional data. Unlike conventional clusters in low-dimensional spaces, clusters hidden in high-dimensional data are often significantly smaller. For example, when clustering customer-purchase data, we would not expect many users to have similar purchase patterns. Searching for such small but meaningful clusters is like finding needles in a haystack. As shown before, the conventional distance measures can be ineffective. Instead, we often have to consider various more sophisticated techniques that can model correlations and consistency among objects in subspaces.

▪ There are typically an exponential number of possible subspaces or dimensionality reduction options, and thus the optimal solutions are often computationally prohibitive. For example, if the original data space has 1000 dimensions, and we want to find clusters of dimensionality 10, then there are $\binom{1000}{10} = 2.63 \times 10^{23}$ possible subspaces.

11.2.2 Subspace Clustering Methods

"How can we find subspace clusters from high-dimensional data?" Many methods have been proposed. They generally can be categorized into three major groups: *subspace search methods*, *correlation-based clustering methods*, and *biclustering methods*.

Subspace Search Methods

A subspace search method searches various subspaces for clusters. Here, a cluster is a subset of objects that are similar to each other in a subspace. The similarity is often captured by conventional measures such as distance or density. For example, the CLIQUE algorithm introduced in Section 10.5.2 is a subspace clustering method. It enumerates subspaces and the clusters in those subspaces in a dimensionality-increasing order, and applies antimonotonicity to prune subspaces in which no cluster may exist.

A major challenge that subspace search methods face is how to search a series of subspaces effectively and efficiently. Generally there are two kinds of strategies:

▪ *Bottom-up approaches* start from low-dimensional subspaces and search higher-dimensional subspaces only when there may be clusters in those higher-dimensional subspaces. Various pruning techniques are explored to reduce the number of higher-dimensional subspaces that need to be searched. CLIQUE is an example of a bottom-up approach.

- *Top-down approaches* start from the full space and search smaller and smaller subspaces recursively. Top-down approaches are effective only if the *locality assumption* holds, which require that the subspace of a cluster can be determined by the local neighborhood.

Example 11.10 **PROCLUS, a top-down subspace approach.** PROCLUS is a k-medoid-like method that first generates k potential cluster centers for a high-dimensional data set using a sample of the data set. It then refines the subspace clusters iteratively. In each iteration, for each of the current k-medoids, PROCLUS considers the local neighborhood of the medoid in the whole data set, and identifies a subspace for the cluster by minimizing the standard deviation of the distances of the points in the neighborhood to the medoid on each dimension. Once all the subspaces for the medoids are determined, each point in the data set is assigned to the closest medoid according to the corresponding subspace. Clusters and possible outliers are identified. In the next iteration, new medoids replace existing ones if doing so improves the clustering quality. ∎

Correlation-Based Clustering Methods

While subspace search methods search for clusters with a similarity that is measured using conventional metrics like distance or density, *correlation-based approaches* can further discover clusters that are defined by advanced correlation models.

Example 11.11 **A correlation-based approach using PCA.** As an example, a *PCA-based approach* first applies PCA (Principal Components Analysis; see Chapter 3) to derive a set of new, uncorrelated dimensions, and then mine clusters in the new space or its subspaces. In addition to PCA, other space transformations may be used, such as the Hough transform or fractal dimensions. ∎

For additional details on subspace search methods and correlation-based clustering methods, please refer to the bibliographic notes (Section 11.7).

Biclustering Methods

In some applications, we want to cluster both objects and attributes simultaneously. The resulting clusters are known as *biclusters* and meet four requirements: (1) only a small set of objects participate in a cluster; (2) a cluster only involves a small number of attributes; (3) an object may participate in multiple clusters, or does not participate in any cluster; and (4) an attribute may be involved in multiple clusters, or is not involved in any cluster. Section 11.2.3 discusses biclustering in detail.

11.2.3 **Biclustering**

In the cluster analysis discussed so far, we cluster objects according to their attribute values. Objects and attributes are not treated in the same way. However, in some applications, objects and attributes are defined in a symmetric way, where data analysis involves searching data matrices for submatrices that show unique patterns as clusters. This kind of clustering technique belongs to the category of biclustering.

This section first introduces two motivating application examples of biclustering— gene expression and recommender systems. You will then learn about the different types of biclusters. Last, we present biclustering methods.

Application Examples

Biclustering techniques were first proposed to address the needs for analyzing gene expression data. A *gene* is a unit of the passing-on of traits from a living organism to its offspring. Typically, a gene resides on a segment of DNA. Genes are critical for all living things because they specify all proteins and functional RNA chains. They hold the information to build and maintain a living organism's cells and pass genetic traits to offspring. Synthesis of a functional gene product, either RNA or protein, relies on the process of gene expression. A *genotype* is the genetic makeup of a cell, an organism, or an individual. *Phenotypes* are observable characteristics of an organism. *Gene expression* is the most fundamental level in genetics in that genotypes cause phenotypes.

Using *DNA chips* (also known as *DNA microarrays*) and other biological engineering techniques, we can measure the expression level of a large number (possibly all) of an organism's genes, in a number of different experimental conditions. Such conditions may correspond to different time points in an experiment or samples from different organs. Roughly speaking, the *gene expression data* or *DNA microarray data* are conceptually a gene-sample/condition matrix, where each row corresponds to one gene, and each column corresponds to one sample or condition. Each element in the matrix is a real number and records the expression level of a gene under a specific condition. Figure 11.3 shows an illustration.

From the clustering viewpoint, an interesting issue is that a gene expression data matrix can be analyzed in two dimensions—the gene dimension and the sample/ condition dimension.

- When analyzing in the *gene dimension*, we treat each gene as an object and treat the samples/conditions as attributes. By mining in the gene dimension, we may find patterns shared by multiple genes, or cluster genes into groups. For example, we may find a group of genes that express themselves similarly, which is highly interesting in bioinformatics, such as in finding pathways.

- When analyzing in the *sample/condition dimension*, we treat each sample/condition as an object and treat the genes as attributes. In this way, we may find patterns of samples/conditions, or cluster samples/conditions into groups. For example, we may find the differences in gene expression by comparing a group of tumor samples and nontumor samples.

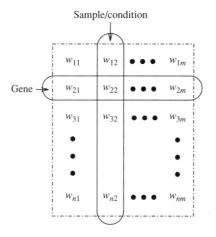

Figure 11.3 Microarrary data matrix.

Example 11.12 **Gene expression.** Gene expression matrices are popular in bioinformatics research and development. For example, an important task is to classify a new gene using the expression data of the gene and that of other genes in known classes. Symmetrically, we may classify a new sample (e.g., a new patient) using the expression data of the sample and that of samples in known classes (e.g., tumor and nontumor). Such tasks are invaluable in understanding the mechanisms of diseases and in clinical treatment. ∎

As can be seen, many gene expression data mining problems are highly related to cluster analysis. However, a challenge here is that, instead of clustering in one dimension (e.g., gene or sample/condition), in many cases we need to cluster in two dimensions simultaneously (e.g., both gene and sample/condition). Moreover, unlike the clustering models we have discussed so far, a cluster in a gene expression data matrix is a *submatrix* and usually has the following characteristics:

- Only a small set of genes participate in the cluster.
- The cluster involves only a small subset of samples/conditions.
- A gene may participate in multiple clusters, or may not participate in any cluster.
- A sample/condition may be involved in multiple clusters, or may not be involved in any cluster.

To find clusters in gene-sample/condition matrices, we need new clustering techniques that meet the following requirements for *biclustering*:

- A cluster of genes is defined using only a subset of samples/conditions.
- A cluster of samples/conditions is defined using only a subset of genes.

- The clusters are neither *exclusive* (e.g., where one gene can participate in multiple clusters) nor *exhaustive* (e.g., where a gene may not participate in any cluster).

Biclustering is useful not only in bioinformatics, but also in other applications as well. Consider recommender systems as an example.

Example 11.13 Using biclustering for a recommender system. *AllElectronics* collects data from customers' evaluations of products and uses the data to recommend products to customers. The data can be modeled as a customer-product matrix, where each row represents a customer, and each column represents a product. Each element in the matrix represents a customer's evaluation of a product, which may be a score (e.g., like, like somewhat, not like) or purchase behavior (e.g., buy or not). Figure 11.4 illustrates the structure.

The customer-product matrix can be analyzed in two dimensions: the *customer* dimension and the *product* dimension. Treating each customer as an object and products as attributes, *AllElectronics* can find customer groups that have similar preferences or purchase patterns. Using products as objects and customers as attributes, *AllElectronics* can mine product groups that are similar in customer interest.

Moreover, *AllElectronics* can mine clusters in both customers and products simultaneously. Such a cluster contains a subset of customers and involves a subset of products. For example, *AllElectronics* is highly interested in finding a group of customers who all like the same group of products. Such a cluster is a submatrix in the customer-product matrix, where all elements have a high value. Using such a cluster, *AllElectronics* can make recommendations in two directions. First, the company can recommend products to new customers who are similar to the customers in the cluster. Second, the company can recommend to customers new products that are similar to those involved in the cluster. ∎

As with biclusters in a gene expression data matrix, the biclusters in a customer-product matrix usually have the following characteristics:

- Only a small set of customers participate in a cluster.

- A cluster involves only a small subset of products.

- A customer can participate in multiple clusters, or may not participate in any cluster.

$$
\begin{array}{c}
\text{Products} \\
\begin{array}{ccccc}
w_{11} & w_{12} & \cdots & w_{1m} \\
\text{Customers} \quad w_{21} & w_{22} & \cdots & w_{2m} \\
\cdots & \cdots & \cdots & \cdots \\
w_{n1} & w_{n2} & \cdots & w_{nm}
\end{array}
\end{array}
$$

Figure 11.4 Customer–product matrix.

▪ A product may be involved in multiple clusters, or may not be involved in any cluster.

Biclustering can be applied to customer-product matrices to mine clusters satisfying these requirements.

Types of Biclusters

"How can we model biclusters and mine them?" Let's start with some basic notation. For the sake of simplicity, we will use "genes" and "conditions" to refer to the two dimensions in our discussion. Our discussion can easily be extended to other applications. For example, we can simply replace "genes" and "conditions" by "customers" and "products" to tackle the customer-product biclustering problem.

Let $A = \{a_1, \ldots, a_n\}$ be a set of genes and $B = \{b_1, \ldots, b_m\}$ be a set of conditions. Let $E = [e_{ij}]$ be a gene expression data matrix, that is, a gene-condition matrix, where $1 \leq i \leq n$ and $1 \leq j \leq m$. A submatrix $I \times J$ is defined by a subset $I \subseteq A$ of genes and a subset $J \subseteq B$ of conditions. For example, in the matrix shown in Figure 11.5, $\{a_1, a_{33}, a_{86}\} \times \{b_6, b_{12}, b_{36}, b_{99}\}$ is a submatrix.

A bicluster is a submatrix where genes and conditions follow consistent patterns. We can define different types of biclusters based on such patterns.

▪ As the simplest case, a submatrix $I \times J$ ($I \subseteq A, J \subseteq B$) is a **bicluster with constant values** if for any $i \in I$ and $j \in J$, $e_{ij} = c$, where c is a constant. For example, the submatrix $\{a_1, a_{33}, a_{86}\} \times \{b_6, b_{12}, b_{36}, b_{99}\}$ in Figure 11.5 is a bicluster with constant values.

▪ A bicluster is interesting if each row has a constant value, though different rows may have different values. A **bicluster with constant values on rows** is a submatrix $I \times J$ such that for any $i \in I$ and $j \in J$, $e_{ij} = c + \alpha_i$, where α_i is the adjustment for row i. For example, Figure 11.6 shows a bicluster with constant values on rows.

Symmetrically, a **bicluster with constant values on columns** is a submatrix $I \times J$ such that for any $i \in I$ and $j \in J$, $e_{ij} = c + \beta_j$, where β_j is the adjustment for column j.

	$\cdots$	b_6	$\cdots$	b_{12}	$\cdots$	b_{36}	$\cdots$	b_{99} $\cdots$
a_1	$\cdots$	60	$\cdots$	60	$\cdots$	60	$\cdots$	60 $\cdots$
$\cdots$	$\cdots$	$\cdots$	$\cdots$	$\cdots$	$\cdots$	$\cdots$	$\cdots$	$\cdots$ $\cdots$
a_{33}	$\cdots$	60	$\cdots$	60	$\cdots$	60	$\cdots$	60 $\cdots$
$\cdots$	$\cdots$	$\cdots$	$\cdots$	$\cdots$	$\cdots$	$\cdots$	$\cdots$	$\cdots$ $\cdots$
a_{86}	$\cdots$	60	$\cdots$	60	$\cdots$	60	$\cdots$	60 $\cdots$
$\cdots$	$\cdots$	$\cdots$	$\cdots$	$\cdots$	$\cdots$	$\cdots$	$\cdots$	$\cdots$ $\cdots$

Figure 11.5 Gene-condition matrix, a submatrix, and a bicluster.

■ More generally, a bicluster is interesting if the rows change in a synchronized way with respect to the columns and vice versa. Mathematically, a **bicluster with coherent values** (also known as **a pattern-based cluster**) is a submatrix $I \times J$ such that for any $i \in I$ and $j \in J$, $e_{ij} = c + \alpha_i + \beta_j$, where α_i and β_j are the adjustment for row i and column j, respectively. For example, Figure 11.7 shows a bicluster with coherent values.

It can be shown that $I \times J$ is a bicluster with coherent values if and only if for any $i_1, i_2 \in I$ and $j_1, j_2 \in J$, then $e_{i_1 j_1} - e_{i_2 j_1} = e_{i_1 j_2} - e_{i_2 j_2}$. Moreover, instead of using addition, we can define a bicluster with coherent values using multiplication, that is, $e_{ij} = c \cdot (\alpha_i \cdot \beta_j)$. Clearly, biclusters with constant values on rows or columns are special cases of biclusters with coherent values.

■ In some applications, we may only be interested in the up- or down-regulated changes across genes or conditions without constraining the exact values. A **bicluster with coherent evolutions on rows** is a submatrix $I \times J$ such that for any $i_1, i_2 \in I$ and $j_1, j_2 \in J$, $(e_{i_1 j_1} - e_{i_1 j_2})(e_{i_2 j_1} - e_{i_2 j_2}) \geq 0$. For example, Figure 11.8 shows a bicluster with coherent evolutions on rows. Symmetrically, we can define biclusters with coherent evolutions on columns.

Next, we study how to mine biclusters.

10	10	10	10	10
20	20	20	20	20
50	50	50	50	50
0	0	0	0	0

Figure 11.6 Bicluster with constant values on rows.

10	50	30	70	20
20	60	40	80	30
50	90	70	110	60
0	40	20	60	10

Figure 11.7 Bicluster with coherent values.

10	50	30	70	20
20	100	50	1000	30
50	100	90	120	80
0	80	20	100	10

Figure 11.8 Bicluster with coherent evolutions on rows.

Biclustering Methods

The previous specification of the types of biclusters only considers ideal cases. In real data sets, such perfect biclusters rarely exist. When they do exist, they are usually very small. Instead, random noise can affect the readings of e_{ij} and thus prevent a bicluster in nature from appearing in a perfect shape.

There are two major types of methods for discovering biclusters in data that may come with noise. **Optimization-based methods** conduct an iterative search. At each iteration, the submatrix with the highest significance score is identified as a bicluster. The process terminates when a user-specified condition is met. Due to cost concerns in computation, greedy search is often employed to find local optimal biclusters. **Enumeration methods** use a tolerance threshold to specify the degree of noise allowed in the biclusters to be mined, and then tries to enumerate all submatrices of biclusters that satisfy the requirements. We use the δ-Cluster and MaPle algorithms as examples to illustrate these ideas.

Optimization Using the δ-Cluster Algorithm

For a submatrix, $I \times J$, the mean of the ith row is

$$e_{iJ} = \frac{1}{|J|} \sum_{j \in J} e_{ij}. \tag{11.16}$$

Symmetrically, the mean of the jth column is

$$e_{Ij} = \frac{1}{|I|} \sum_{i \in I} e_{ij}. \tag{11.17}$$

The mean of all elements in the submatrix is

$$e_{IJ} = \frac{1}{|I||J|} \sum_{i \in I, j \in J} e_{ij} = \frac{1}{|I|} \sum_{i \in I} e_{iJ} = \frac{1}{|J|} \sum_{j \in J} e_{Ij}. \tag{11.18}$$

The quality of the submatrix as a bicluster can be measured by the *mean-squared residue* value as

$$H(I \times J) = \frac{1}{|I||J|} \sum_{i \in I, j \in J} (e_{ij} - e_{iJ} - e_{Ij} + e_{IJ})^2. \tag{11.19}$$

Submatrix $I \times J$ is a δ-**bicluster** if $H(I \times J) \leq \delta$, where $\delta \geq 0$ is a threshold. When $\delta = 0$, $I \times J$ is a perfect bicluster with coherent values. By setting $\delta > 0$, a user can specify the tolerance of average noise per element against a perfect bicluster, because in Eq. (11.19) the residue on each element is

$$\text{residue}(e_{ij}) = e_{ij} - e_{iJ} - e_{Ij} + e_{IJ}. \tag{11.20}$$

A *maximal δ-bicluster* is a δ-bicluster $I \times J$ such that there does not exist another δ-bicluster $I' \times J'$, and $I \subseteq I'$, $J \subseteq J'$, and at least one inequality holds. Finding the maximal δ-bicluster of the largest size is computationally costly. Therefore, we can use a heuristic greedy search method to obtain a local optimal cluster. The algorithm works in two phases.

- In the *deletion phase*, we start from the whole matrix. While the mean-squared residue of the matrix is over δ, we iteratively remove rows and columns. At each iteration, for each row i, we compute the *mean-squared residue* as

$$d(i) = \frac{1}{|J|} \sum_{j \in J} (e_{ij} - e_{iJ} - e_{Ij} + e_{IJ})^2.$$ (11.21)

Moreover, for each column j, we compute the *mean-squared residue* as

$$d(j) = \frac{1}{|I|} \sum_{i \in I} (e_{ij} - e_{iJ} - e_{Ij} + e_{IJ})^2.$$ (11.22)

We remove the row or column of the largest mean-squared residue. At the end of this phase, we obtain a submatrix $I \times J$ that is a δ-bicluster. However, the submatrix may not be maximal.

- In the *addition phase*, we iteratively expand the δ-bicluster $I \times J$ obtained in the deletion phase as long as the δ-bicluster requirement is maintained. At each iteration, we consider rows and columns that are not involved in the current bicluster $I \times J$ by calculating their mean-squared residues. A row or column of the smallest mean-squared residue is added into the current δ-bicluster.

This greedy algorithm can find one δ-bicluster only. To find multiple biclusters that do not have heavy overlaps, we can run the algorithm multiple times. After each execution where a δ-bicluster is output, we can replace the elements in the output bicluster by random numbers. Although the greedy algorithm may find neither the optimal biclusters nor all biclusters, it is very fast even on large matrices.

Enumerating All Biclusters Using MaPle

As mentioned, a submatrix $I \times J$ is a bicluster with coherent values if and only if for any $i_1, i_2 \in I$ and $j_1, j_2 \in J$, $e_{i_1 j_1} - e_{i_2 j_1} = e_{i_1 j_2} - e_{i_2 j_2}$. For any 2×2 submatrix of $I \times J$, we can define a *p-score* as

$$p\text{-score} \begin{pmatrix} e_{i_1 j_1} & e_{i_1 j_2} \\ e_{i_2 j_1} & e_{i_2 j_2} \end{pmatrix} = |(e_{i_1 j_1} - e_{i_2 j_1}) - (e_{i_1 j_2} - e_{i_2 j_2})|.$$ (11.23)

A submatrix $I \times J$ is a δ-**pCluster** (for *pattern-based cluster*) if the *p*-score of every 2×2 submatrix of $I \times J$ is at most δ, where $\delta \geq 0$ is a threshold specifying a user's tolerance of noise against a perfect bicluster. Here, the *p*-score controls the noise on every element in a bicluster, while the mean-squared residue captures the average noise.

An interesting property of δ-pCluster is that if $I \times J$ is a δ-pCluster, then every $x \times y$ $(x, y \geq 2)$ submatrix of $I \times J$ is also a δ-pCluster. This monotonicity enables us to obtain a succinct representation of nonredundant δ-pClusters. A δ-pCluster is maximal if no more rows or columns can be added into the cluster while maintaining the δ-pCluster property. To avoid redundancy, instead of finding all δ-pClusters, we only need to compute all maximal δ-pClusters.

MaPle is an algorithm that enumerates all maximal δ-pClusters. It systematically enumerates every combination of conditions using a set enumeration tree and a depth-first search. This enumeration framework is the same as the pattern-growth methods for frequent pattern mining (Chapter 6). Consider gene expression data. For each condition combination, J, MaPle finds the maximal subsets of genes, I, such that $I \times J$ is a δ-pCluster. If $I \times J$ is not a submatrix of another δ-pCluster, then $I \times J$ is a maximal δ-pCluster.

There may be a huge number of condition combinations. MaPle prunes many unfruitful combinations using the monotonicity of δ-pClusters. For a condition combination, J, if there does not exist a set of genes, I, such that $I \times J$ is a δ-pCluster, then we do not need to consider any superset of J. Moreover, we should consider $I \times J$ as a candidate of a δ-pCluster only if for every $(|J| - 1)$-subset J' of J, $I \times J'$ is a δ-pCluster. MaPle also employs several pruning techniques to speed up the search while retaining the completeness of returning all maximal δ-pClusters. For example, when examining a current δ-pCluster, $I \times J$, MaPle collects all the genes and conditions that may be added to expand the cluster. If these candidate genes and conditions together with I and J form a submatrix of a δ-pCluster that has already been found, then the search of $I \times J$ and any superset of J can be pruned. Interested readers may refer to the bibliographic notes for additional information on the MaPle algorithm (Section 11.7).

An interesting observation here is that the search for maximal δ-pClusters in MaPle is somewhat similar to mining frequent closed itemsets. Consequently, MaPle borrows the depth-first search framework and ideas from the pruning techniques of pattern-growth methods for frequent pattern mining. This is an example where frequent pattern mining and cluster analysis may share similar techniques and ideas.

An advantage of MaPle and the other algorithms that enumerate all biclusters is that they guarantee the completeness of the results and do not miss any overlapping biclusters. However, a challenge for such enumeration algorithms is that they may become very time consuming if a matrix becomes very large, such as a customer-purchase matrix of hundreds of thousands of customers and millions of products.

11.2.4 Dimensionality Reduction Methods and Spectral Clustering

Subspace clustering methods try to find clusters in subspaces of the original data space. In some situations, it is more effective to construct a new space instead of using subspaces of the original data. This is the motivation behind dimensionality reduction methods for clustering high-dimensional data.

Example 11.14 Clustering in a derived space. Consider the three clusters of points in Figure 11.9. It is not possible to cluster these points in any subspace of the original space, $X \times Y$, because

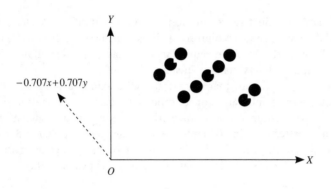

Figure 11.9 Clustering in a derived space may be more effective.

all three clusters would end up being projected onto overlapping areas in the x and y axes. What if, instead, we construct a new dimension, $-\frac{\sqrt{2}}{2}x + \frac{\sqrt{2}}{2}y$ (shown as a dashed line in the figure)? By projecting the points onto this new dimension, the three clusters become apparent. ∎

Although Example 11.14 involves only two dimensions, the idea of constructing a new space (so that any clustering structure that is hidden in the data becomes well manifested) can be extended to high-dimensional data. Preferably, the newly constructed space should have low dimensionality.

There are many dimensionality reduction methods. A straightforward approach is to apply feature selection and extraction methods to the data set such as those discussed in Chapter 3. However, such methods may not be able to detect the clustering structure. Therefore, methods that combine feature extraction and clustering are preferred. In this section, we introduce *spectral clustering*, a group of methods that are effective in high-dimensional data applications.

Figure 11.10 shows the general framework for spectral clustering approaches. The Ng-Jordan-Weiss algorithm is a spectral clustering method. Let's have a look at each step of the framework. In doing so, we also note special conditions that apply to the Ng-Jordan-Weiss algorithm as an example.

Given a set of objects, $o_1, \ldots, o_n$, the distance between each pair of objects, $dist(o_i, o_j)$ $(1 \leq i, j \leq n)$, and the desired number k of clusters, a spectral clustering approach works as follows.

1. Using the distance measure, calculate an *affinity matrix*, W, such that

$$W_{ij} = e^{-\frac{dist(o_i, o_j)}{\sigma^2}},$$

where σ is a scaling parameter that controls how fast the affinity W_{ij} decreases as $dist(o_i, o_j)$ increases. In the Ng-Jordan-Weiss algorithm, W_{ii} is set to 0.

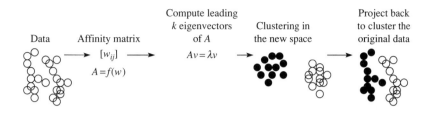

Figure 11.10 The framework of spectral clustering approaches. *Source:* Adapted from Slide 8 at *http://videolectures.net/micued08_azran_mcl/*.

2. Using the affinity matrix W, derive a matrix $A = f(W)$. The way in which this is done can vary. The Ng-Jordan-Weiss algorithm defines a matrix, D, as a diagonal matrix such that D_{ii} is the sum of the ith row of W, that is,

$$D_{ii} = \sum_{j=1}^{n} W_{ij}. \tag{11.24}$$

A is then set to

$$A = D^{-\frac{1}{2}} W D^{-\frac{1}{2}}. \tag{11.25}$$

3. Find the k leading eigenvectors of A. Recall that the *eigenvectors* of a square matrix are the nonzero vectors that remain proportional to the original vector after being multiplied by the matrix. Mathematically, a vector v is an eigenvector of matrix A if $Av = \lambda v$, where λ is called the corresponding *eigenvalue*. This step derives k new dimensions from A, which are based on the affinity matrix W. Typically, k should be much smaller than the dimensionality of the original data.

    The Ng-Jordan-Weiss algorithm computes the k eigenvectors with the largest eigenvalues $x_1, \ldots, x_k$ of A.

4. Using the k leading eigenvectors, project the original data into the new space defined by the k leading eigenvectors, and run a clustering algorithm such as k-means to find k clusters.

    The Ng-Jordan-Weiss algorithm stacks the k largest eigenvectors in columns to form a matrix $X = [x_1 x_2 \cdots x_k] \in \mathbb{R}^{n \times k}$. The algorithm forms a matrix Y by renormalizing each row in X to have unit length, that is,

$$Y_{ij} = \frac{X_{ij}}{\sqrt{\sum_{j=1}^{k} X_{ij}^2}}. \tag{11.26}$$

The algorithm then treats each row in Y as a point in the k-dimensional space $\mathbb{R}^k$, and runs k-means (or any other algorithm serving the partitioning purpose) to cluster the points into k clusters.

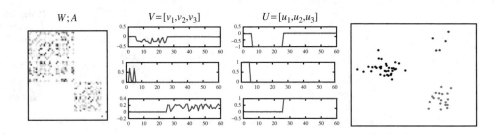

Figure 11.11 The new dimensions and the clustering results of the Ng-Jordan-Weiss algorithm. *Source:* Adapted from Slide 9 at *http://videolectures.net/micued08_azran_mcl/*.

5. Assign the original data points to clusters according to how the transformed points are assigned in the clusters obtained in step 4.

In the Ng-Jordan-Weiss algorithm, the original object o_i is assigned to the jth cluster if and only if matrix Y's row i is assigned to the jth cluster as a result of step 4.

In spectral clustering methods, the dimensionality of the new space is set to the desired number of clusters. This setting expects that each new dimension should be able to manifest a cluster.

Example 11.15 The Ng-Jordan-Weiss algorithm. Consider the set of points in Figure 11.11. The data set, the affinity matrix, the three largest eigenvectors, and the normalized vectors are shown. Note that with the three new dimensions (formed by the three largest eigenvectors), the clusters are easily detected. ∎

Spectral clustering is effective in high-dimensional applications such as image processing. Theoretically, it works well when certain conditions apply. Scalability, however, is a challenge. Computing eigenvectors on a large matrix is costly. Spectral clustering can be combined with other clustering methods, such as biclustering. Additional information on other dimensionality reduction clustering methods, such as kernel PCA, can be found in the bibliographic notes (Section 11.7).

11.3 Clustering Graph and Network Data

Cluster analysis on graph and network data extracts valuable knowledge and information. Such data are increasingly popular in many applications. We discuss applications and challenges of clustering graph and network data in Section 11.3.1. Similarity measures for this form of clustering are given in Section 11.3.2. You will learn about graph clustering methods in Section 11.3.3.

In general, the terms *graph* and *network* can be used interchangeably. In the rest of this section, we mainly use the term *graph*.

11.3.1 Applications and Challenges

As a customer relationship manager at *AllElectronics*, you notice that a lot of data relating to customers and their purchase behavior can be preferably modeled using graphs.

Example 11.16 **Bipartite graph.** The customer purchase behavior at *AllElectronics* can be represented in a *bipartite graph*. In a bipartite graph, vertices can be divided into two disjoint sets so that each edge connects a vertex in one set to a vertex in the other set. For the *AllElectronics* customer purchase data, one set of vertices represents customers, with one customer per vertex. The other set represents products, with one product per vertex. An edge connects a customer to a product, representing the purchase of the product by the customer. Figure 11.12 shows an illustration.

"*What kind of knowledge can we obtain by a cluster analysis of the customer-product bipartite graph?*" By clustering the customers such that those customers buying similar sets of products are placed into one group, a customer relationship manager can make product recommendations. For example, suppose Ada belongs to a customer cluster in which most of the customers purchased a digital camera in the last 12 months, but Ada has yet to purchase one. As manager, you decide to recommend a digital camera to her.

Alternatively, we can cluster products such that those products purchased by similar sets of customers are grouped together. This clustering information can also be used for product recommendations. For example, if a digital camera and a high-speed flash memory card belong to the same product cluster, then when a customer purchases a digital camera, we can recommend the high-speed flash memory card. ∎

Bipartite graphs are widely used in many applications. Consider another example.

Example 11.17 **Web search engines.** In web search engines, search logs are archived to record user queries and the corresponding *click-through information*. (The click-through information tells us on which pages, given as a result of a search, the user clicked.) The query and click-through information can be represented using a bipartite graph, where the two sets

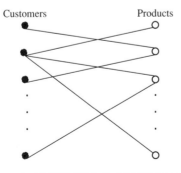

Customers   Products

Figure 11.12 Bipartite graph representing customer-purchase data.

of vertices correspond to queries and web pages, respectively. An edge links a query to a web page if a user clicks the web page when asking the query. Valuable information can be obtained by cluster analyses on the query–web page bipartite graph. For instance, we may identify queries posed in different languages, but that mean the same thing, if the click-through information for each query is similar.

As another example, all the web pages on the Web form a directed graph, also known as the *web graph*, where each web page is a vertex, and each hyperlink is an edge pointing from a source page to a destination page. Cluster analysis on the web graph can disclose communities, find hubs and authoritative web pages, and detect web spams. ■

In addition to bipartite graphs, cluster analysis can also be applied to other types of graphs, including general graphs, as elaborated Example 11.18.

Example 11.18 **Social network.** A *social network* is a social structure. It can be represented as a graph, where the vertices are individuals or organizations, and the links are interdependencies between the vertices, representing friendship, common interests, or collaborative activities. *AllElectronics'* customers form a social network, where each customer is a vertex, and an edge links two customers if they know each other.

As customer relationship manager, you are interested in finding useful information that can be derived from *AllElectronics'* social network through cluster analysis. You obtain clusters from the network, where customers in a cluster know each other or have friends in common. Customers within a cluster may influence one another regarding purchase decision making. Moreover, communication channels can be designed to inform the "heads" of clusters (i.e., the "best" connected people in the clusters), so that promotional information can be spread out quickly. Thus, you may use customer clustering to promote sales at *AllElectronics*.

As another example, the authors of scientific publications form a social network, where the authors are vertices and two authors are connected by an edge if they co-authored a publication. The network is, in general, a weighted graph because an edge between two authors can carry a weight representing the strength of the collaboration such as how many publications the two authors (as the end vertices) coauthored. Clustering the coauthor network provides insight as to communities of authors and patterns of collaboration. ■

"Are there any challenges specific to cluster analysis on graph and network data?" In most of the clustering methods discussed so far, objects are represented using a set of attributes. A unique feature of graph and network data is that only objects (as vertices) and relationships between them (as edges) are given. No dimensions or attributes are explicitly defined. To conduct cluster analysis on graph and network data, there are two major new challenges.

■ *"How can we measure the similarity between two objects on a graph accordingly?"* Typically, we cannot use conventional distance measures, such as Euclidean distance. Instead, we need to develop new measures to quantify the similarity. Such measures often are not metric, and thus raise new challenges regarding the development of efficient clustering methods. Similarity measures for graphs are discussed in Section 11.3.2.

■ *"How can we design clustering models and methods that are effective on graph and network data?"* Graph and network data are often complicated, carrying topological structures that are more sophisticated than traditional cluster analysis applications. Many graph data sets are large, such as the web graph containing at least tens of billions of web pages in the publicly indexable Web. Graphs can also be sparse where, on average, a vertex is connected to only a small number of other vertices in the graph. To discover accurate and useful knowledge hidden deep in the data, a good clustering method has to accommodate these factors. Clustering methods for graph and network data are introduced in Section 11.3.3.

11.3.2 Similarity Measures

"How can we measure the similarity or distance between two vertices in a graph?" In our discussion, we examine two types of measures: *geodesic distance* and *distance based on random walk.*

Geodesic Distance

A simple measure of the distance between two vertices in a graph is the shortest path between the vertices. Formally, the **geodesic distance** between two vertices is the length in terms of the number of edges of the shortest path between the vertices. For two vertices that are not connected in a graph, the geodesic distance is defined as infinite.

Using geodesic distance, we can define several other useful measurements for graph analysis and clustering. Given a graph $G = (V, E)$, where V is the set of vertices and E is the set of edges, we define the following:

■ For a vertext $v \in V$, the **eccentricity** of v, denoted $eccen(v)$, is the largest geodesic distance between v and any other vertex $u \in V - \{v\}$. The eccentricity of v captures how far away v is from its remotest vertex in the graph.

■ The **radius** of graph G is the minimum eccentricity of all vertices. That is,

$$r = \min_{v \in V} eccen(v). \tag{11.27}$$

The radius captures the distance between the "most central point" and the "farthest border" of the graph.

■ The **diameter** of graph G is the maximum eccentricity of all vertices. That is,

$$d = \max_{v \in V} eccen(v). \tag{11.28}$$

The diameter represents the largest distance between any pair of vertices.

■ A **peripheral vertex** is a vertex that achieves the diameter.

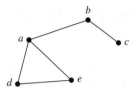

Figure 11.13 A graph, G, where vertices c, d, and e are peripheral.

Example 11.19 **Measurements based on geodesic distance.** Consider graph G in Figure 11.13. The eccentricity of a is 2, that is, $eccen(a) = 2$, $eccen(b) = 2$, and $eccen(c) = eccen(d) = eccen(e) = 3$. Thus, the radius of G is 2, and the diameter is 3. Note that it is not necessary that $d = 2 \times r$. Vertices c, d, and e are peripheral vertices. ∎

SimRank: Similarity Based on Random Walk and Structural Context

For some applications, geodesic distance may be inappropriate in measuring the similarity between vertices in a graph. Here we introduce SimRank, a similarity measure based on random walk and on the structural context of the graph. In mathematics, a *random walk* is a trajectory that consists of taking successive random steps.

Example 11.20 **Similarity between people in a social network.** Let's consider measuring the similarity between two vertices in the *AllElectronics* customer social network of Example 11.18. Here, similarity can be explained as the closeness between two participants in the network, that is, how close two people are in terms of the relationship represented by the social network.

"*How well can the geodesic distance measure similarity and closeness in such a network?*" Suppose Ada and Bob are two customers in the network, and the network is undirected. The geodesic distance (i.e., the length of the shortest path between Ada and Bob) is the shortest path that a message can be passed from Ada to Bob and vice versa. However, this information is not useful for *AllElectronics*' customer relationship management because the company typically does not want to send a specific message from one customer to another. Therefore, geodesic distance does not suit the application.

"*What does similarity mean in a social network?*" We consider two ways to define similarity:

■ Two customers are considered similar to one another if they have similar neighbors in the social network. This heuristic is intuitive because, in practice, two people receiving recommendations from a good number of common friends often make similar decisions. This kind of similarity is based on the local structure (i.e., the *neighborhoods*) of the vertices, and thus is called *structural context–based similarity*.

▪ Suppose *AllElectronics* sends promotional information to both Ada and Bob in the social network. Ada and Bob may randomly forward such information to their friends (or *neighbors*) in the network. The closeness between Ada and Bob can then be measured by the likelihood that other customers simultaneously receive the promotional information that was originally sent to Ada and Bob. This kind of similarity is based on the random walk reachability over the network, and thus is referred to as *similarity based on random walk*.   ■

Let's have a closer look at what is meant by similarity based on structural context, and similarity based on random walk.

The intuition behind similarity based on structural context is that two vertices in a graph are similar if they are connected to similar vertices. To measure such similarity, we need to define the notion of individual neighborhood. In a directed graph $G = (V, E)$, where V is the set of vertices and $E \subseteq V \times V$ is the set of edges, for a vertex $v \in V$, the *individual in-neighborhood* of v is defined as

$$I(v) = \{u | (u, v) \in E\}. \tag{11.29}$$

Symmetrically, we define the *individual out-neighborhood* of v as

$$O(v) = \{w | (v, w) \in E\}. \tag{11.30}$$

Following the intuition illustrated in Example 11.20, we define SimRank, a structural-context similarity, with a value that is between 0 and 1 for any pair of vertices. For any vertex, $v \in V$, the similarity between the vertex and itself is $s(v, v) = 1$ because the neighborhoods are identical. For vertices $u, v \in V$ such that $u \neq v$, we can define

$$s(u, v) = \frac{C}{|I(u)||I(v)|} \sum_{x \in I(u)} \sum_{y \in I(v)} s(x, y), \tag{11.31}$$

where C is a constant between 0 and 1. A vertex may not have any in-neighbors. Thus, we define Eq. (11.31) to be 0 when either $I(u)$ or $I(v)$ is $\emptyset$. Parameter C specifies the rate of decay as similarity is propagated across edges.

"*How can we compute SimRank?*" A straightforward method iteratively evaluates Eq. (11.31) until a fixed point is reached. Let $s_i(u, v)$ be the SimRank score calculated at the ith round. To begin, we set

$$s_0(u, v) = \begin{cases} 0 & \text{if } u \neq v \\ 1 & \text{if } u = v. \end{cases} \tag{11.32}$$

We use Eq. (11.31) to compute s_{i+1} from s_i as

$$s_{i+1}(u, v) = \frac{C}{|I(u)||I(v)|} \sum_{x \in I(u)} \sum_{y \in I(v)} s_i(x, y). \tag{11.33}$$

It can be shown that $\lim_{i \to \infty} s_i(u, v) = s(u, v)$. Additional methods for approximating SimRank are given in the bibliographic notes (Section 11.7).

Now, let's consider similarity based on random walk. A directed graph is *strongly connected* if, for any two nodes u and v, there is a path from u to v and another path from v to u. In a strongly connected graph, $G = (V, E)$, for any two vertices, $u, v \in V$, we can define the *expected distance* from u to v as

$$d(u, v) = \sum_{t: u \rightsquigarrow v} P[t] l(t), \tag{11.34}$$

where $u \rightsquigarrow v$ is a path starting from u and ending at v that may contain cycles but does not reach v until the end. For a *traveling tour*, $t = w_1 \to w_2 \to \cdots \to w_k$, its length is $l(t) = k - 1$. The probability of the tour is defined as

$$P[t] = \begin{cases} \prod_{i=1}^{k-1} \frac{1}{|O(w_i)|} & \text{if } l(t) > 0 \\ 0 & \text{if } l(t) = 0. \end{cases} \tag{11.35}$$

To measure the probability that a vertex w receives a message that originated simultaneously from u and v, we extend the expected distance to the notion of *expected meeting distance*, that is,

$$m(u, v) = \sum_{t: (u,v) \rightsquigarrow (x,x)} P[t] l(t), \tag{11.36}$$

where $(u, v) \rightsquigarrow (x, x)$ is a pair of tours $u \rightsquigarrow x$ and $v \rightsquigarrow x$ of the same length. Using a constant C between 0 and 1, we define the *expected meeting probability* as

$$p(u, v) = \sum_{t: (u,v) \rightsquigarrow (x,x)} P[t] C^{l(t)}, \tag{11.37}$$

which is a similarity measure based on random walk. Here, the parameter C specifies the probability of continuing the walk at each step of the trajectory.

It has been shown that $s(u, v) = p(u, v)$ for any two vertices, u and v. That is, SimRank is based on both structural context and random walk.

11.3.3 Graph Clustering Methods

Let's consider how to conduct clustering on a graph. We first describe the intuition behind graph clustering. We then discuss two general categories of graph clustering methods.

To find clusters in a graph, imagine cutting the graph into pieces, each piece being a cluster, such that the vertices within a cluster are well connected and the vertices in different clusters are connected in a much weaker way. Formally, for a graph, $G = (V, E)$, a **cut**, $C = (S, T)$, is a partitioning of the set of vertices V in G, that is, $V = S \cup T$ and $S \cap T = \emptyset$. The *cut set* of a cut is the set of edges, $\{(u, v) \in E | u \in S, v \in T\}$. The *size* of the cut is the number of edges in the cut set. For weighted graphs, the size of a cut is the sum of the weights of the edges in the cut set.

"*What kinds of cuts are good for deriving clusters in graphs?*" In graph theory and some network applications, a minimum cut is of importance. A cut is *minimum* if the cut's size is not greater than any other cut's size. There are polynomial time algorithms to compute minimum cuts of graphs. Can we use these algorithms in graph clustering?

Example 11.21 **Cuts and clusters.** Consider graph G in Figure 11.14. The graph has two clusters: $\{a, b, c, d, e, f\}$ and $\{g, h, i, j, k\}$, and one outlier vertex, l.

Consider cut $C_1 = (\{a, b, c, d, e, f, g, h, i, j, k\}, \{l\})$. Only one edge, namely, (e, l), crosses the two partitions created by C_1. Therefore, the cut set of C_1 is $\{(e, l)\}$ and the size of C_1 is 1. (Note that the size of any cut in a connected graph cannot be smaller than 1.) As a minimum cut, C_1 does not lead to a good clustering because it only separates the outlier vertex, l, from the rest of the graph.

Cut $C_2 = (\{a, b, c, d, e, f, l\}, \{g, h, i, j, k\})$ leads to a much better clustering than C_1. The edges in the cut set of C_2 are those connecting the two "natural clusters" in the graph. Specifically, for edges (d, h) and (e, k) that are in the cut set, most of the edges connecting d, h, e, and k belong to one cluster. ∎

Example 11.21 indicates that using a minimum cut is unlikely to lead to a good clustering. We are better off choosing a cut where, for each vertex u that is involved in an edge in the cut set, most of the edges connecting to u belong to one cluster. Formally, let $deg(u)$ be the degree of u, that is, the number of edges connecting to u. The *sparsity* of a cut $C = (S, T)$ is defined as

$$\Phi = \frac{\text{cut size}}{\min\{|S|, |T|\}}. \tag{11.38}$$

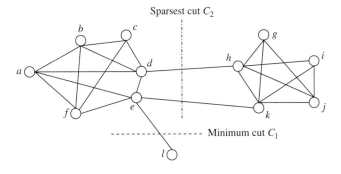

Figure 11.14 A graph G and two cuts.

A cut is *sparsest* if its sparsity is not greater than the sparsity of any other cut. There may be more than one sparsest cut.

In Example 11.21 and Figure 11.14, C_2 is a sparsest cut. Using sparsity as the objective function, a sparsest cut tries to minimize the number of edges crossing the partitions and balance the partitions in size.

Consider a clustering on a graph $G = (V, E)$ that partitions the graph into k clusters. The **modularity** of a clustering assesses the quality of the clustering and is defined as

$$Q = \sum_{i=1}^{k} \left(\frac{l_i}{|E|} - \left(\frac{d_i}{2|E|} \right)^2 \right), \tag{11.39}$$

where l_i is the number of edges between vertices in the ith cluster, and d_i is the sum of the degrees of the vertices in the ith cluster. The modularity of a clustering of a graph is the difference between the fraction of all edges that fall into individual clusters and the fraction that would do so if the graph vertices were randomly connected. The optimal clustering of graphs maximizes the modularity.

Theoretically, many graph clustering problems can be regarded as finding good cuts, such as the sparsest cuts, on the graph. In practice, however, a number of challenges exist:

- **High computational cost:** Many graph cut problems are computationally expensive. The sparsest cut problem, for example, is NP-hard. Therefore, finding the optimal solutions on large graphs is often impossible. A good trade-off between efficiency/scalability and quality has to be achieved.

- **Sophisticated graphs:** Graphs can be more sophisticated than the ones described here, involving weights and/or cycles.

- **High dimensionality:** A graph can have many vertices. In a similarity matrix, a vertex is represented as a vector (a row in the matrix) with a dimensionality that is the number of vertices in the graph. Therefore, graph clustering methods must handle high dimensionality.

- **Sparsity:** A large graph is often sparse, meaning each vertex on average connects to only a small number of other vertices. A similarity matrix from a large sparse graph can also be sparse.

There are two kinds of methods for clustering graph data, which address these challenges. One uses clustering methods for high-dimensional data, while the other is designed specifically for clustering graphs.

The first group of methods is based on generic clustering methods for high-dimensional data. They extract a similarity matrix from a graph using a similarity measure such as those discussed in Section 11.3.2. A generic clustering method can then be applied on the similarity matrix to discover clusters. Clustering methods for high-dimensional data are typically employed. For example, in many scenarios, once a similarity matrix is obtained, spectral clustering methods (Section 11.2.4) can be applied. Spectral clustering can approximate optimal graph cut solutions. For additional information, please refer to the bibliographic notes (Section 11.7).

The second group of methods is specific to graphs. They search the graph to find well-connected components as clusters. Let's look at a method called **SCAN** (Structural Clustering Algorithm for Networks) as an example.

Given an undirected graph, $G = (V, E)$, for a vertex, $u \in V$, the neighborhood of u is $\Gamma(u) = \{v | (u, v) \in E\} \cup \{u\}$. Using the idea of structural-context similarity, SCAN measures the similarity between two vertices, $u, v \in V$, by the normalized common neighborhood size, that is,

$$\sigma(u, v) = \frac{|\Gamma(u) \cap \Gamma(v)|}{\sqrt{|\Gamma(u)||\Gamma(v)|}}. \tag{11.40}$$

The larger the value computed, the more similar the two vertices. SCAN uses a similarity threshold ε to define the cluster membership. For a vertex, $u \in V$, the ε-*neighborhood* of u is defined as $N_\varepsilon(u) = \{v \in \Gamma(u) | \sigma(u, v) \geq \varepsilon\}$. The ε-neighborhood of u contains all neighbors of u with a structural-context similarity to u that is at least ε.

In SCAN, a *core vertex* is a vertex inside of a cluster. That is, $u \in V$ is a core vertex if $|N_\varepsilon(u)| \geq \mu$, where μ is a popularity threshold. SCAN grows clusters from core vertices. If a vertex v is in the ε-neighborhood of a core u, then v is assigned to the same cluster as u. This process of growing clusters continues until no cluster can be further grown. The process is similar to the density-based clustering method, DBSCAN (Chapter 10).

Formally, a vertex v can be *directly reached* from a core u if $v \in N_\varepsilon(u)$. Transitively, a vertex v can be *reached* from a core u if there exist vertices $w_1, \ldots, w_n$ such that w_1 can be reached from u, w_i can be reached from w_{i-1} for $1 < i \leq n$, and v can be reached from w_n. Moreover, two vertices, $u, v \in V$, which may or may not be cores, are said to be *connected* if there exists a core w such that both u and v can be reached from w. All vertices in a cluster are connected. A cluster is a maximum set of vertices such that every pair in the set is connected.

Some vertices may not belong to any cluster. Such a vertex u is a *hub* if the neighborhood $\Gamma(u)$ of u contains vertices from more than one cluster. If a vertex does not belong to any cluster, and is not a hub, it is an *outlier*.

The SCAN algorithm is shown in Figure 11.15. The search framework closely resembles the cluster-finding process in DBSCAN. SCAN finds a cut of the graph, where each cluster is a set of vertices that are connected based on the transitive similarity in a structural context.

An advantage of SCAN is that its time complexity is linear with respect to the number of edges. In very large and sparse graphs, the number of edges is in the same scale of the number of vertices. Therefore, SCAN is expected to have good scalability on clustering large graphs.

Algorithm: SCAN for clusters on graph data.
Input: a graph $G = (V, E)$, a similarity threshold ε, and a
    population threshold μ
Output: a set of clusters
Method: set all vertices in V unlabeled
    for all unlabeled vertex u **do**
        if u is a core **then**
            generate a new cluster-id c
            insert all $v \in N_\varepsilon (u)$ into a queue Q
            while $Q \neq$ **do**
                $w \leftarrow$ the first vertex in Q
                $R \leftarrow$ the set of vertices that can be directly reached from w
                for all $s \in R$ **do**
                    if s is not unlabeled or labeled as nonmember **then**
                        assign the current cluster-id c to s
                    endif
                    if s is unlabeled **then**
                        insert s into queue Q
                    endif
                endfor
                remove w from Q
            end while
        else
            label u as nonmember
        endif
    endfor
    for all vertex u labeled nonmember **do**
        if $\exists x, y \in \Gamma(u) : x$ and y have different cluster-ids **then**
            label u as hub
         else
             label u as outlier
        endif
    endfor

Figure 11.15 SCAN algorithm for cluster analysis on graph data.

11.4 Clustering with Constraints

Users often have background knowledge that they want to integrate into cluster analysis. There may also be application-specific requirements. Such information can be modeled as clustering constraints. We approach the topic of clustering with constraints in two steps. Section 11.4.1 categorizes the types of constraints for clustering graph data. Methods for clustering with constraints are introduced in Section 11.4.2.

11.4.1 Categorization of Constraints

This section studies how to categorize the constraints used in cluster analysis. Specifically, we can categorize constraints according to the subjects on which they are set, or on how strongly the constraints are to be enforced.

As discussed in Chapter 10, cluster analysis involves three essential aspects: objects as instances of clusters, clusters as groups of objects, and the similarity among objects. Therefore, the first method we discuss categorizes constraints according to what they are applied to. We thus have three types: *constraints on instances, constraints on clusters,* and *constraints on similarity measurement.*

Constraints on instances: A *constraint on instances* specifies how a pair or a set of instances should be grouped in the cluster analysis. Two common types of constraints from this category include:

- **Must-link constraints.** If a must-link constraint is specified on two objects x and y, then x and y should be grouped into one cluster in the output of the cluster analysis. These must-link constraints are transitive. That is, if must-link(x, y) and must-link(y, z), then must-link(x, z).

- **Cannot-link constraints.** Cannot-link constraints are the opposite of must-link constraints. If a cannot-link constraint is specified on two objects, x and y, then in the output of the cluster analysis, x and y should belong to different clusters. Cannot-link constraints can be entailed. That is, if cannot-link(x, y), must-link(x, x'), and must-link(y, y'), then cannot-link(x', y').

A constraint on instances can be defined using specific instances. Alternatively, it can also be defined using instance variables or attributes of instances. For example, a constraint,

$$Constraint(x, y) : \text{must-link}(x, y) \text{ if } dist(x, y) \leq \epsilon,$$

uses the distance between objects to specify a must-link constraint.

Constraints on clusters: A *constraint on clusters* specifies a requirement on the clusters, possibly using attributes of the clusters. For example, a constraint may specify the minimum number of objects in a cluster, the maximum diameter of a cluster, or the shape of a cluster (e.g., a convex). The number of clusters specified for partitioning clustering methods can be regarded as a constraint on clusters.

Constraints on similarity measurement: Often, a similarity measure, such as Euclidean distance, is used to measure the similarity between objects in a cluster analysis. In some applications, exceptions apply. A *constraint on similarity measurement* specifies a requirement that the similarity calculation must respect. For example, to cluster people as moving objects in a plaza, while Euclidean distance is used to give the walking distance between two points, a constraint on similarity measurement is that the trajectory implementing the shortest distance cannot cross a wall.

There can be more than one way to express a constraint, depending on the category. For example, we can specify a constraint on clusters as

$Constraint_1$: the diameter of a cluster cannot be larger than d.

The requirement can also be expressed using a constraint on instances as

$$Constraint'_1: \text{cannot-link}(x, y) \text{ if } dist(x, y) > d. \tag{11.41}$$

Example 11.22 Constraints on instances, clusters, and similarity measurement. *AllElectronics* clusters its customers so that each group of customers can be assigned to a customer relationship manager. Suppose we want to specify that all customers at the same address are to be placed in the same group, which would allow more comprehensive service to families. This can be expressed using a must-link constraint on instances:

$$Constraint_{family}(x, y) : \text{must-link}(x, y) \text{ if } x.address = y.address.$$

AllElectronics has eight customer relationship managers. To ensure that they each have a similar workload, we place a constraint on clusters such that there should be eight clusters, and each cluster should have at least 10% of the customers and no more than 15% of the customers. We can calculate the spatial distance between two customers using the driving distance between the two. However, if two customers live in different countries, we have to use the flight distance instead. This is a constraint on similarity measurement. ∎

Another way to categorize clustering constraints considers how firmly the constraints have to be respected. A constraint is **hard** if a clustering that violates the constraint is unacceptable. A constraint is **soft** if a clustering that violates the constraint is not preferable but acceptable when no better solution can be found. Soft constraints are also called *preferences*.

Example 11.23 Hard and soft constraints. For *AllElectronics*, $Constraint_{family}$ in Example 11.22 is a hard constraint because splitting a family into different clusters could prevent the company from providing comprehensive services to the family, leading to poor customer satisfaction. The constraint on the number of clusters (which corresponds to the number of customer relationship managers in the company) is also hard. Example 11.22 also has a constraint to balance the size of clusters. While satisfying this constraint is strongly preferred, the company is flexible in that it is willing to assign a senior and more capable customer relationship manager to oversee a larger cluster. Therefore, the constraint is soft. ∎

Ideally, for a specific data set and a set of constraints, all clusterings satisfy the constraints. However, it is possible that there may be no clustering of the data set that satisfies all the constraints. Trivially, if two constraints in the set conflict, then no clustering can satisfy them at the same time.

Example 11.24 Conflicting constraints. Consider these constraints:

$$\text{must-link}(x, y) \text{ if } dist(x, y) < 5$$

$$\text{cannot-link}(x, y) \text{ if } dist(x, y) > 3.$$

If a data set has two objects, x, y, such that $dist(x, y) = 4$, then no clustering can satisfy both constraints simultaneously.

Consider these two constraints:

$$\text{must-link}(x, y) \text{ if } dist(x, y) < 5$$

$$\text{must-link}(x, y) \text{ if } dist(x, y) < 3.$$

The second constraint is redundant given the first. Moreover, for a data set where the distance between any two objects is at least 5, every possible clustering of the objects satisfies the constraints. ■

"*How can we measure the quality and the usefulness of a set of constraints?*" In general, we consider either their informativeness, or their coherence. The **informativeness** is the amount of information carried by the constraints that is beyond the clustering model. Given a data set, D, a clustering method, $\mathcal{A}$, and a set of constraints, $\mathcal{C}$, the informativeness of $\mathcal{C}$ with respect to $\mathcal{A}$ on D can be measured by the fraction of constraints in $\mathcal{C}$ that are unsatisfied by the clustering computed by $\mathcal{A}$ on D. The higher the informativeness, the more specific the requirements and background knowledge that the constraints carry. The **coherence** of a set of constraints is the degree of agreement among the constraints themselves, which can be measured by the redundancy among the constraints.

11.4.2 Methods for Clustering with Constraints

Although we can categorize clustering constraints, applications may have very different constraints of specific forms. Consequently, various techniques are needed to handle specific constraints. In this section, we discuss the general principles of handling hard and soft constraints.

Handling Hard Constraints

A general strategy for handling hard constraints is to strictly respect the constraints in the cluster assignment process. To illustrate this idea, we will use partitioning clustering as an example.

Given a data set and a set of constraints on instances (i.e., must-link or cannot-link constraints), how can we extend the *k*-means method to satisfy such constraints? The **COP-*k*-means algorithm** works as follows:

1. **Generate superinstances for must-link constraints.** Compute the transitive closure of the must-link constraints. Here, all must-link constraints are treated as an equivalence relation. The closure gives one or multiple subsets of objects where all objects in a subset must be assigned to one cluster. To represent such a subset, we replace all those objects in the subset by the mean. The superinstance also carries a weight, which is the number of objects it represents.

   After this step, the must-link constraints are always satisfied.

2. **Conduct modified k-means clustering.** Recall that, in *k*-means, an object is assigned to the closest center. What if a nearest-center assignment violates a cannot-link constraint? To respect cannot-link constraints, we modify the center assignment process in *k*-means to a *nearest feasible center assignment*. That is, when the objects are assigned to centers in sequence, at each step we make sure the assignments so far do not violate any cannot-link constraints. An object is assigned to the nearest center so that the assignment respects all cannot-link constraints.

Because COP-*k*-means ensures that no constraints are violated at every step, it does not require any backtracking. It is a greedy algorithm for generating a clustering that satisfies all constraints, provided that no conflicts exist among the constraints.

Handling Soft Constraints

Clustering with soft constraints is an optimization problem. When a clustering violates a soft constraint, a penalty is imposed on the clustering. Therefore, the optimization goal of the clustering contains two parts: optimizing the clustering quality and minimizing the constraint violation penalty. The overall objective function is a combination of the clustering quality score and the penalty score.

To illustrate, we again use partitioning clustering as an example. Given a data set and a set of soft constraints on instances, the **CVQE (Constrained Vector Quantization Error) algorithm** conducts *k*-means clustering while enforcing constraint violation penalties. The objective function used in CVQE is the sum of the distance used in *k*-means, adjusted by the constraint violation penalties, which are calculated as follows.

- **Penalty of a must-link violation.** If there is a must-link constraint on objects x and y, but they are assigned to two different centers, c_1 and c_2, respectively, then the constraint is violated. As a result, $dist(c_1, c_2)$, the distance between c_1 and c_2, is added to the objective function as the penalty.

- **Penalty of a cannot-link violation.** If there is a cannot-link constraint on objects x and y, but they are assigned to a common center, c, then the constraint is violated.

The distance, $dist(c, c')$, between c and c' is added to the objective function as the penalty.

Speeding up Constrained Clustering

Constraints, such as on similarity measurements, can lead to heavy costs in clustering. Consider the following **clustering with obstacles** problem: To cluster people as moving objects in a plaza, Euclidean distance is used to measure the walking distance between two points. However, a constraint on similarity measurement is that the trajectory implementing the shortest distance cannot cross a wall (Section 11.4.1). Because obstacles may occur between objects, the distance between two objects may have to be derived by geometric computations (e.g., involving triangulation). The computational cost is high if a large number of objects and obstacles are involved.

The clustering with obstacles problem can be represented using a graphical notation. First, a point, p, is **visible** from another point, q, in the region R if the straight line joining p and q does not intersect any obstacles. A **visibility graph** is the graph, $VG = (V, E)$, such that each vertex of the obstacles has a corresponding node in V and two nodes, v_1 and v_2, in V are joined by an edge in E if and only if the corresponding vertices they represent are visible to each other. Let $VG' = (V', E')$ be a visibility graph created from VG by adding two additional points, p and q, in V'. E' contains an edge joining two points in V' if the two points are mutually visible. The shortest path between two points, p and q, will be a subpath of VG', as shown in Figure 11.16(a). We see that it begins with an edge from p to either v_1, v_2, or v_3, goes through a path in VG, and then ends with an edge from either v_4 or v_5 to q.

To reduce the cost of distance computation between any two pairs of objects or points, several preprocessing and optimization techniques can be used. One method groups points that are close together into microclusters. This can be done by first triangulating the region R into triangles, and then grouping nearby points in the same triangle into microclusters, using a method similar to BIRCH or DBSCAN, as shown in Figure 11.16(b). By processing microclusters rather than individual points, the overall computation is reduced. After that, precomputation can be performed to build two

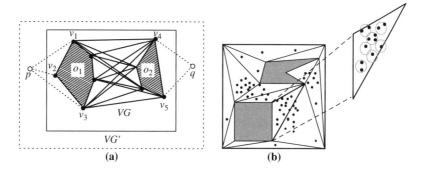

(a)   **(b)**

Figure 11.16 Clustering with obstacle objects (o_1 and o_2): (a) a visibility graph and (b) triangulation of regions with microclusters. *Source:* Adapted from Tung, Hou, and Han [THH01].

kinds of join indices based on the computation of the shortest paths: (1) *VV indices*, for any pair of obstacle vertices, and (2) *MV indices*, for any pair of microcluster and obstacle vertex. Use of the indices helps further optimize the overall performance.

Using such precomputation and optimization strategies, the distance between any two points (at the granularity level of a microcluster) can be computed efficiently. Thus, the clustering process can be performed in a manner similar to a typical efficient *k*-medoids algorithm, such as CLARANS, and achieve good clustering quality for large data sets.

11.5 Summary

- In conventional cluster analysis, an object is assigned to one cluster exclusively. However, in some applications, there is a need to assign an object to one or more clusters in a fuzzy or probabilistic way. **Fuzzy clustering** and **probabilistic model-based clustering** allow an object to belong to one or more clusters. A **partition matrix** records the membership degree of objects belonging to clusters.

- **Probabilistic model-based clustering** assumes that a cluster is a parameterized distribution. Using the data to be clustered as the observed samples, we can estimate the parameters of the clusters.

- A **mixture model** assumes that a set of observed objects is a mixture of instances from multiple probabilistic clusters. Conceptually, each observed object is generated independently by first choosing a probabilistic cluster according to the probabilities of the clusters, and then choosing a sample according to the probability density function of the chosen cluster.

- An **expectation-maximization algorithm** is a framework for approaching maximum likelihood or maximum a posteriori estimates of parameters in statistical models. Expectation-maximization algorithms can be used to compute fuzzy clustering and probabilistic model-based clustering.

- **High-dimensional data** pose several challenges for cluster analysis, including how to model high-dimensional clusters and how to search for such clusters.

- There are two major categories of clustering methods for high-dimensional data: subspace clustering methods and dimensionality reduction methods. **Subspace clustering methods** search for clusters in subspaces of the original space. Examples include **subspace search methods**, **correlation-based clustering methods**, and **biclustering methods**. **Dimensionality reduction methods** create a new space of lower dimensionality and search for clusters there.

- **Biclustering methods** cluster objects and attributes simultaneously. Types of biclusters include biclusters with **constant values**, **constant values on rows/columns**, **coherent values**, and **coherent evolutions on rows/columns**. Two major types of biclustering methods are **optimization-based methods** and **enumeration methods**.

- **Spectral clustering** is a **dimensionality reduction method**. The general idea is to construct new dimensions using an affinity matrix.

- **Clustering graph and network data** has many applications such as social network analysis. Challenges include how to measure the similarity between objects in a graph, and how to design clustering models and methods for graph and network data.

- **Geodesic distance** is the number of edges between two vertices on a graph. It can be used to measure similarity. Alternatively, similarity in graphs, such as social networks, can be measured using structural context and random walk. **SimRank** is a similarity measure that is based on both structural context and random walk.

- Graph clustering can be modeled as computing **graph cuts**. A **sparsest cut** may lead to a good clustering, while **modularity** can be used to measure the clustering quality.

- **SCAN** is a graph clustering algorithm that searches graphs to identify well-connected components as clusters.

- **Constraints** can be used to express application-specific requirements or background knowledge for cluster analysis. Constraints for clustering can be categorized as constraints on **instances**, on **clusters**, or on **similarity measurement**. Constraints on instances include **must-link** and **cannot-link** constraints. A constraint can be **hard** or **soft**.

- **Hard constraints for clustering** can be enforced by strictly respecting the constraints in the cluster assignment process. **Clustering with soft constraints** can be considered an optimization problem. Heuristics can be used to speed up constrained clustering.

11.6 Exercises

11.1 Traditional clustering methods are rigid in that they require each object to belong exclusively to only one cluster. Explain why this is a special case of fuzzy clustering. You may use k-means as an example.

11.2 *AllElectronics* carries 1000 products, $P_1, \ldots, P_{1000}$. Consider customers Ada, Bob, and Cathy such that Ada and Bob purchase three products in common, P_1, P_2, and P_3. For the other 997 products, Ada and Bob independently purchase seven of them randomly. Cathy purchases 10 products, randomly selected from the 1000 products. In Euclidean distance, what is the probability that $dist(\text{Ada}, \text{Bob}) > dist(\text{Ada}, \text{Cathy})$? What if Jaccard similarity (Chapter 2) is used? What can you learn from this example?

11.3 Show that $I \times J$ is a bicluster with coherent values if and only if, for any $i_1, i_2 \in I$ and $j_1, j_2 \in J$, $e_{i_1 j_1} - e_{i_2 j_1} = e_{i_1 j_2} - e_{i_2 j_2}$.

11.4 Compare the MaPle algorithm (Section 11.2.3) with the frequent closed itemset mining algorithm, CLOSET (Pei, Han, and Mao [PHM00]). What are the major similarities and differences?

11.5 SimRank is a similarity measure for clustering graph and network data.

(a) Prove $\lim_{i \to \infty} s_i(u, v) = s(u, v)$ for SimRank computation.

(b) Show $s(u, v) = p(u, v)$ for SimRank.

11.6 In a large sparse graph where on average each node has a low degree, is the similarity matrix using SimRank still sparse? If so, in what sense? If not, why? Deliberate on your answer.

11.7 Compare the SCAN algorithm (Section 11.3.3) with DBSCAN (Section 10.4.1). What are their similarities and differences?

11.8 Consider partitioning clustering and the following constraint on clusters: The number of objects in each cluster must be between $\frac{n}{k}(1 - \delta)$ and $\frac{n}{k}(1 + \delta)$, where n is the total number of objects in the data set, k is the number of clusters desired, and δ in $[0, 1)$ is a parameter. Can you extend the k-means method to handle this constraint? Discuss situations where the constraint is hard and soft.

11.7 Bibliographic Notes

Höppner Klawonn, Kruse, and Runkler [HKKR99] provide a thorough discussion of fuzzy clustering. The fuzzy c-means algorithm (on which Example 11.7 is based) was proposed by Bezdek [Bez81]. Fraley and Raftery [FR02] give a comprehensive overview of model-based cluster analysis and probabilistic models. McLachlan and Basford [MB88] present a systematic introduction to mixture models and applications in cluster analysis.

Dempster, Laird, and Rubin [DLR77] are recognized as the first to introduce the EM algorithm and give it its name. However, the idea of the EM algorithm had been "proposed many times in special circumstances" before, as admitted in Dempster, Laird, and Rubin [DLR77]. Wu [Wu83] gives the correct analysis of the EM algorithm.

Mixture models and EM algorithms are used extensively in many data mining applications. Introductions to model-based clustering, mixture models, and EM algorithms can be found in recent textbooks on machine learning and statistical learning—for example, Bishop [Bis06], Marsland [Mar09], and Alpaydin [Alp11].

The increase of dimensionality has severe effects on distance functions, as indicated by Beyer et al. [BGRS99]. It also has had a dramatic impact on various techniques for classification, clustering, and semisupervised learning (Radovanović, Nanopoulos, and Ivanović [RNI09]).

Kriegel, Kröger, and Zimek [KKZ09] present a comprehensive survey on methods for clustering high-dimensional data. The CLIQUE algorithm was developed by Agrawal, Gehrke, Gunopulos, and Raghavan [AGGR98]. The PROCLUS algorithm was proposed by Aggawal, Procopiuc, Wolf, et al. [APW$^+$99].

The technique of biclustering was initially proposed by Hartigan [Har72]. The term *biclustering* was coined by Mirkin [Mir98]. Cheng and Church [CC00] introduced biclustering into gene expression data analysis. There are many studies on biclustering models and methods. The notion of δ-pCluster was introduced by Wang, Wang, Yang, and Yu [WWYY02]. For informative surveys, see Madeira and Oliveira [MO04] and Tanay, Sharan, and Shamir [TSS04]. In this chapter, we introduced the δ-cluster algorithm by Cheng and Church [CC00] and MaPle by Pei, Zhang, Cho, et al. [PZC$^+$03] as examples of optimization-based methods and enumeration methods for biclustering, respectively.

Donath and Hoffman [DH73] and Fiedler [Fie73] pioneered spectral clustering. In this chapter, we use an algorithm proposed by Ng, Jordan, and Weiss [NJW01] as an example. For a thorough tutorial on spectral clustering, see Luxburg [Lux07].

Clustering graph and network data is an important and fast-growing topic. Schaeffer [Sch07] provides a survey. The SimRank measure of similarity was developed by Jeh and Widom [JW02a]. Xu et al. [XYFS07] proposed the SCAN algorithm. Arora, Rao, and Vazirani [ARV09] discuss the sparsest cuts and approximation algorithms.

Clustering with constraints has been extensively studied. Davidson, Wagstaff, and Basu [DWB06] proposed the measures of informativeness and coherence. The COP-k-means algorithm is given by Wagstaff et al. [WCRS01]. The CVQE algorithm was proposed by Davidson and Ravi [DR05]. Tung, Han, Lakshmanan, and Ng [THLN01] presented a framework for constraint-based clustering based on user-specified constraints. An efficient method for constraint-based spatial clustering in the existence of physical obstacle constraints was proposed by Tung, Hou, and Han [THH01].

Outlier Detection

Imagine that you are a transaction auditor in a credit card company. To protect your customers from credit card fraud, you pay special attention to card usages that are rather different from typical cases. For example, if a purchase amount is much bigger than usual for a card owner, and if the purchase occurs far from the owner's resident city, then the purchase is suspicious. You want to detect such transactions as soon as they occur and contact the card owner for verification. This is common practice in many credit card companies. *What data mining techniques can help detect suspicious transactions?*

Most credit card transactions are normal. However, if a credit card is stolen, its transaction pattern usually changes dramatically—the locations of purchases and the items purchased are often very different from those of the authentic card owner and other customers. An essential idea behind credit card fraud detection is to identify those transactions that are very different from the norm.

Outlier detection (also known as *anomaly detection*) is the process of finding data objects with behaviors that are very different from expectation. Such objects are called **outliers** or **anomalies**. Outlier detection is important in many applications in addition to fraud detection such as medical care, public safety and security, industry damage detection, image processing, sensor/video network surveillance, and intrusion detection.

Outlier detection and clustering analysis are two highly related tasks. Clustering finds the majority patterns in a data set and organizes the data accordingly, whereas outlier detection tries to capture those exceptional cases that deviate substantially from the majority patterns. Outlier detection and clustering analysis serve different purposes.

In this chapter, we study outlier detection techniques. Section 12.1 defines the different types of outliers. Section 12.2 presents an overview of outlier detection methods. In the rest of the chapter, you will learn about outlier detection methods in detail. These approaches, organized here by category, are statistical (Section 12.3), proximity-based (Section 12.4), clustering-based (Section 12.5), and classification-based (Section 12.6). In addition, you will learn about mining contextual and collective outliers (Section 12.7) and outlier detection in high-dimensional data (Section 12.8).

12.1 Outliers and Outlier Analysis

Let us first define what outliers are, categorize the different types of outliers, and then discuss the challenges in outlier detection at a general level.

12.1.1 What Are Outliers?

Assume that a given statistical process is used to generate a set of data objects. An **outlier** is a data object that deviates significantly from the rest of the objects, as if it were generated by a different mechanism. For ease of presentation within this chapter, we may refer to data objects that are not outliers as "normal" or expected data. Similarly, we may refer to outliers as "abnormal" data.

Example 12.1   Outliers. In Figure 12.1, most objects follow a roughly Gaussian distribution. However, the objects in region R are significantly different. It is unlikely that they follow the same distribution as the other objects in the data set. Thus, the objects in R are outliers in the data set. ∎

Outliers are different from noisy data. As mentioned in Chapter 3, noise is a random error or variance in a measured variable. In general, noise is not interesting in data analysis, including outlier detection. For example, in credit card fraud detection, a customer's purchase behavior can be modeled as a random variable. A customer may generate some "noise transactions" that may seem like "random errors" or "variance," such as by buying a bigger lunch one day, or having one more cup of coffee than usual. Such transactions should not be treated as outliers; otherwise, the credit card company would incur heavy costs from verifying that many transactions. The company may also lose customers by bothering them with multiple false alarms. As in many other data analysis and data mining tasks, noise should be removed before outlier detection.

Outliers are interesting because they are suspected of not being generated by the same mechanisms as the rest of the data. Therefore, in outlier detection, it is important to

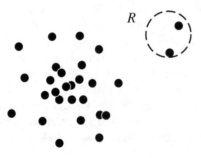

Figure 12.1   The objects in region R are outliers.

justify *why* the outliers detected are generated by some other mechanisms. This is often achieved by making various assumptions on the rest of the data and showing that the outliers detected violate those assumptions significantly.

Outlier detection is also related to *novelty detection* in evolving data sets. For example, by monitoring a social media web site where new content is incoming, novelty detection may identify new topics and trends in a timely manner. Novel topics may initially appear as outliers. To this extent, outlier detection and novelty detection share some similarity in modeling and detection methods. However, a critical difference between the two is that in novelty detection, once new topics are confirmed, they are usually incorporated into the model of normal behavior so that follow-up instances are not treated as outliers anymore.

12.1.2 Types of Outliers

In general, outliers can be classified into three categories, namely global outliers, contextual (or conditional) outliers, and collective outliers. Let's examine each of these categories.

Global Outliers

In a given data set, a data object is a **global outlier** if it deviates significantly from the rest of the data set. Global outliers are sometimes called *point anomalies*, and are the simplest type of outliers. Most outlier detection methods are aimed at finding global outliers.

Example 12.2 **Global outliers.** Consider the points in Figure 12.1 again. The points in region *R* significantly deviate from the rest of the data set, and hence are examples of global outliers. ■

To detect global outliers, a critical issue is to find an appropriate measurement of deviation with respect to the application in question. Various measurements are proposed, and, based on these, outlier detection methods are partitioned into different categories. We will come to this issue in detail later.

Global outlier detection is important in many applications. Consider intrusion detection in computer networks, for example. If the communication behavior of a computer is very different from the normal patterns (e.g., a large number of packages is broadcast in a short time), this behavior may be considered as a global outlier and the corresponding computer is a suspected victim of hacking. As another example, in trading transaction auditing systems, transactions that do not follow the regulations are considered as global outliers and should be held for further examination.

Contextual Outliers

"The temperature today is 28° C. Is it exceptional (i.e., an outlier)?" It depends, for example, on the time and location! If it is in winter in Toronto, yes, it is an outlier. If it is a summer day in Toronto, then it is normal. Unlike global outlier detection, in this case,

whether or not today's temperature value is an outlier depends on the context—the date, the location, and possibly some other factors.

In a given data set, a data object is a **contextual outlier** if it deviates significantly with respect to a specific context of the object. Contextual outliers are also known as *conditional outliers* because they are conditional on the selected context. Therefore, in contextual outlier detection, the context has to be specified as part of the problem definition. Generally, in contextual outlier detection, the attributes of the data objects in question are divided into two groups:

- **Contextual attributes**: The contextual attributes of a data object define the object's context. In the temperature example, the contextual attributes may be date and location.

- **Behavioral attributes**: These define the object's characteristics, and are used to evaluate whether the object is an outlier in the context to which it belongs. In the temperature example, the behavioral attributes may be the temperature, humidity, and pressure.

Unlike global outlier detection, in contextual outlier detection, whether a data object is an outlier depends on not only the behavioral attributes but also the contextual attributes. A configuration of behavioral attribute values may be considered an outlier in one context (e.g., 28°C is an outlier for a Toronto winter), but not an outlier in another context (e.g., 28°C is not an outlier for a Toronto summer).

Contextual outliers are a generalization of local outliers, a notion introduced in density-based outlier analysis approaches. An object in a data set is a **local outlier** if its density significantly deviates from the local area in which it occurs. We will discuss local outlier analysis in greater detail in Section 12.4.3.

Global outlier detection can be regarded as a special case of contextual outlier detection where the set of contextual attributes is empty. In other words, global outlier detection uses the whole data set as the context. Contextual outlier analysis provides flexibility to users in that one can examine outliers in different contexts, which can be highly desirable in many applications.

Example 12.3 **Contextual outliers.** In credit card fraud detection, in addition to global outliers, an analyst may consider outliers in different contexts. Consider customers who use more than 90% of their credit limit. If one such customer is viewed as belonging to a group of customers with low credit limits, then such behavior may not be considered an outlier. However, similar behavior of customers from a high-income group may be considered outliers if their balance often exceeds their credit limit. Such outliers may lead to business opportunities—raising credit limits for such customers can bring in new revenue.

∎

The quality of contextual outlier detection in an application depends on the meaningfulness of the contextual attributes, in addition to the measurement of the deviation of an object to the majority in the space of behavioral attributes. More often than not, the contextual attributes should be determined by domain experts, which can be regarded as part of the input background knowledge. In many applications, neither obtaining sufficient information to determine contextual attributes nor collecting high-quality contextual attribute data is easy.

"How can we formulate meaningful contexts in contextual outlier detection?" A straightforward method simply uses group-bys of the contextual attributes as contexts. This may not be effective, however, because many group-bys may have insufficient data and/or noise. A more general method uses the proximity of data objects in the space of contextual attributes. We discuss this approach in detail in Section 12.4.

Collective Outliers

Suppose you are a supply-chain manager of *AllElectronics*. You handle thousands of orders and shipments every day. If the shipment of an order is delayed, it may not be considered an outlier because, statistically, delays occur from time to time. However, you have to pay attention if 100 orders are delayed on a single day. Those 100 orders as a whole form an outlier, although each of them may not be regarded as an outlier if considered individually. You may have to take a close look at those orders collectively to understand the shipment problem.

Given a data set, a subset of data objects forms a **collective outlier** if the objects as a whole deviate significantly from the entire data set. Importantly, the individual data objects may not be outliers.

Example 12.4 Collective outliers. In Figure 12.2, the black objects as a whole form a collective outlier because the density of those objects is much higher than the rest in the data set. However, every black object individually is not an outlier with respect to the whole data set.

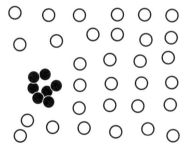

Figure 12.2 The black objects form a collective outlier.

Collective outlier detection has many important applications. For example, in intrusion detection, a denial-of-service package from one computer to another is considered normal, and not an outlier at all. However, if several computers keep sending denial-of-service packages to each other, they as a whole should be considered as a collective outlier. The computers involved may be suspected of being compromised by an attack. As another example, a stock transaction between two parties is considered normal. However, a large set of transactions of the same stock among a small party in a short period are collective outliers because they may be evidence of some people manipulating the market.

Unlike global or contextual outlier detection, in collective outlier detection we have to consider not only the behavior of individual objects, but also that of groups of objects. Therefore, to detect collective outliers, we need background knowledge of the relationship among data objects such as distance or similarity measurements between objects.

In summary, a data set can have multiple types of outliers. Moreover, an object may belong to more than one type of outlier. In business, different outliers may be used in various applications or for different purposes. Global outlier detection is the simplest. Context outlier detection requires background information to determine contextual attributes and contexts. Collective outlier detection requires background information to model the relationship among objects to find groups of outliers.

12.1.3 Challenges of Outlier Detection

Outlier detection is useful in many applications yet faces many challenges such as the following:

- **Modeling normal objects and outliers effectively.** Outlier detection quality highly depends on the modeling of normal (nonoutlier) objects and outliers. Often, building a comprehensive model for data normality is very challenging, if not impossible. This is partly because it is hard to enumerate all possible normal behaviors in an application.

    The border between data normality and abnormality (outliers) is often not clear cut. Instead, there can be a wide range of gray area. Consequently, while some outlier detection methods assign to each object in the input data set a label of either "normal" or "outlier," other methods assign to each object a score measuring the "outlier-ness" of the object.

- **Application-specific outlier detection.** Technically, choosing the similarity/distance measure and the relationship model to describe data objects is critical in outlier detection. Unfortunately, such choices are often application-dependent. Different applications may have very different requirements. For example, in clinic data analysis, a small deviation may be important enough to justify an outlier. In contrast, in marketing analysis, objects are often subject to larger fluctuations, and consequently a substantially larger deviation is needed to justify an outlier. Outlier detection's high dependency on the application type makes it impossible to develop a universally applicable outlier detection method. Instead, individual outlier detection methods that are dedicated to specific applications must be developed.

- **Handling noise in outlier detection.** As mentioned earlier, outliers are different from noise. It is also well known that the quality of real data sets tends to be poor. Noise often unavoidably exists in data collected in many applications. Noise may be present as deviations in attribute values or even as missing values. Low data quality and the presence of noise bring a huge challenge to outlier detection. They can distort the data, blurring the distinction between normal objects and outliers. Moreover, noise and missing data may "hide" outliers and reduce the effectiveness of outlier detection—an outlier may appear "disguised" as a noise point, and an outlier detection method may mistakenly identify a noise point as an outlier.

- **Understandability.** In some application scenarios, a user may want to not only detect outliers, but also understand why the detected objects are outliers. To meet the understandability requirement, an outlier detection method has to provide some justification of the detection. For example, a statistical method can be used to justify the degree to which an object may be an outlier based on the likelihood that the object was generated by the same mechanism that generated the majority of the data. The smaller the likelihood, the more unlikely the object was generated by the same mechanism, and the more likely the object is an outlier.

The rest of this chapter discusses approaches to outlier detection.

12.2 Outlier Detection Methods

There are many outlier detection methods in the literature and in practice. Here, we present two orthogonal ways to categorize outlier detection methods. First, we categorize outlier detection methods according to whether the sample of data for analysis is given with domain expert–provided labels that can be used to build an outlier detection model. Second, we divide methods into groups according to their assumptions regarding normal objects versus outliers.

12.2.1 Supervised, Semi-Supervised, and Unsupervised Methods

If expert-labeled examples of normal and/or outlier objects can be obtained, they can be used to build outlier detection models. The methods used can be divided into supervised methods, semi-supervised methods, and unsupervised methods.

Supervised Methods

Supervised methods model data normality and abnormality. Domain experts examine and label a sample of the underlying data. Outlier detection can then be modeled as a classification problem (Chapters 8 and 9). The task is to learn a classifier that can recognize outliers. The sample is used for training and testing. In some applications, the experts may label just the normal objects, and any other objects not matching the model of normal objects are reported as outliers. Other methods model the outliers and treat objects not matching the model of outliers as normal.

Although many classification methods can be applied, challenges to supervised outlier detection include the following:

- The two classes (i.e., normal objects versus outliers) are imbalanced. That is, the population of outliers is typically much smaller than that of normal objects. Therefore, methods for handling imbalanced classes (Section 8.6.5) may be used, such as over-sampling (i.e., replicating) outliers to increase their distribution in the training set used to construct the classifier. Due to the small population of outliers in data, the sample data examined by domain experts and used in training may not even sufficiently represent the outlier distribution. The lack of outlier samples can limit the capability of classifiers built as such. To tackle these problems, some methods "make up" artificial outliers.

- In many outlier detection applications, catching as many outliers as possible (i.e., the sensitivity or recall of outlier detection) is far more important than not mislabeling normal objects as outliers. Consequently, when a classification method is used for supervised outlier detection, it has to be interpreted appropriately so as to consider the application interest on recall.

In summary, supervised methods of outlier detection must be careful in how they train and how they interpret classification rates due to the fact that outliers are rare in comparison to the other data samples.

Unsupervised Methods

In some application scenarios, objects labeled as "normal" or "outlier" are not available. Thus, an unsupervised learning method has to be used.

Unsupervised outlier detection methods make an implicit assumption: The normal objects are somewhat "clustered." In other words, an unsupervised outlier detection method expects that normal objects follow a pattern far more frequently than outliers. Normal objects do not have to fall into one group sharing high similarity. Instead, they can form multiple groups, where each group has distinct features. However, an outlier is expected to occur far away in feature space from any of those groups of normal objects.

This assumption may not be true all the time. For example, in Figure 12.2, the normal objects do not share any strong patterns. Instead, they are uniformly distributed. The collective outliers, however, share high similarity in a small area. Unsupervised methods cannot detect such outliers effectively. In some applications, normal objects are diversely distributed, and many such objects do not follow strong patterns. For instance, in some intrusion detection and computer virus detection problems, normal activities are very diverse and many do not fall into high-quality clusters. In such scenarios, unsupervised methods may have a high false positive rate—they may mislabel many normal objects as outliers (intrusions or viruses in these applications), and let many actual outliers go undetected. Due to the high similarity between intrusions and viruses (i.e., they have to attack key resources in the target systems), modeling outliers using supervised methods may be far more effective.

Many clustering methods can be adapted to act as unsupervised outlier detection methods. The central idea is to find clusters first, and then the data objects not belonging to any cluster are detected as outliers. However, such methods suffer from two issues. First, a data object not belonging to any cluster may be noise instead of an outlier. Second, it is often costly to find clusters first and then find outliers. It is usually assumed that there are far fewer outliers than normal objects. Having to process a large population of nontarget data entries (i.e., the normal objects) before one can touch the real meat (i.e., the outliers) can be unappealing. The latest unsupervised outlier detection methods develop various smart ideas to tackle outliers directly without explicitly and completely finding clusters. You will learn more about these techniques in Sections 12.4 and 12.5 on proximity-based and clustering-based methods, respectively.

Semi-Supervised Methods

In many applications, although obtaining some labeled examples is feasible, the number of such labeled examples is often small. We may encounter cases where only a small set of the normal and/or outlier objects are labeled, but most of the data are unlabeled. Semi-supervised outlier detection methods were developed to tackle such scenarios.

Semi-supervised outlier detection methods can be regarded as applications of semi-supervised learning methods (Section 9.7.2). For example, when some labeled normal objects are available, we can use them, together with unlabeled objects that are close by, to train a model for normal objects. The model of normal objects then can be used to detect outliers—those objects not fitting the model of normal objects are classified as outliers.

If only some labeled outliers are available, semi-supervised outlier detection is trickier. A small number of labeled outliers are unlikely to represent all the possible outliers. Therefore, building a model for outliers based on only a few labeled outliers is unlikely to be effective. To improve the quality of outlier detection, we can get help from models for normal objects learned from unsupervised methods.

For additional information on semi-supervised methods, interested readers are referred to the bibliographic notes at the end of this chapter (Section 12.11).

12.2.2 Statistical Methods, Proximity-Based Methods, and Clustering-Based Methods

As discussed in Section 12.1, outlier detection methods make assumptions about outliers versus the rest of the data. According to the assumptions made, we can categorize outlier detection methods into three types: statistical methods, proximity-based methods, and clustering-based methods.

Statistical Methods

Statistical methods (also known as **model-based methods**) make assumptions of data normality. They assume that normal data objects are generated by a statistical (stochastic) model, and that data not following the model are outliers.

Example 12.5 **Detecting outliers using a statistical (Gaussian) model.** In Figure 12.1, the data points except for those in region R fit a Gaussian distribution g_D, where for a location $\boldsymbol{x}$ in the data space, $g_D(\boldsymbol{x})$ gives the probability density at $\boldsymbol{x}$. Thus, the Gaussian distribution g_D can be used to model the normal data, that is, most of the data points in the data set. For each object $\boldsymbol{y}$ in region, R, we can estimate $g_D(\boldsymbol{y})$, the probability that this point fits the Gaussian distribution. Because $g_D(\boldsymbol{y})$ is very low, $\boldsymbol{y}$ is unlikely generated by the Gaussian model, and thus is an outlier. ∎

The effectiveness of statistical methods highly depends on whether the assumptions made for the statistical model hold true for the given data. There are many kinds of statistical models. For example, the statistic models used in the methods may be parametric or nonparametric. Statistical methods for outlier detection are discussed in detail in Section 12.3.

Proximity-Based Methods

Proximity-based methods assume that an object is an outlier if the nearest neighbors of the object are far away in feature space, that is, the proximity of the object to its neighbors significantly deviates from the proximity of most of the other objects to their neighbors in the same data set.

Example 12.6 **Detecting outliers using proximity.** Consider the objects in Figure 12.1 again. If we model the proximity of an object using its three nearest neighbors, then the objects in region R are substantially different from other objects in the data set. For the two objects in R, their second and third nearest neighbors are dramatically more remote than those of any other objects. Therefore, we can label the objects in R as outliers based on proximity. ∎

The effectiveness of proximity-based methods relies heavily on the proximity (or distance) measure used. In some applications, such measures cannot be easily obtained. Moreover, proximity-based methods often have difficulty in detecting a group of outliers if the outliers are close to one another.

There are two major types of proximity-based outlier detection, namely *distance-based* and *density-based* outlier detection. Proximity-based outlier detection is discussed in Section 12.4.

Clustering-Based Methods

Clustering-based methods assume that the normal data objects belong to large and dense clusters, whereas outliers belong to small or sparse clusters, or do not belong to any clusters.

Example 12.7 **Detecting outliers using clustering.** In Figure 12.1, there are two clusters. Cluster C_1 contains all the points in the data set except for those in region R. Cluster C_2 is tiny, containing just two points in R. Cluster C_1 is large in comparison to C_2. Therefore, a clustering-based method asserts that the two objects in R are outliers. ∎

There are many clustering methods, as discussed in Chapters 10 and 11. Therefore, there are many clustering-based outlier detection methods as well. Clustering is an expensive data mining operation. A straightforward adaptation of a clustering method for outlier detection can be very costly, and thus does not scale up well for large data sets. Clustering-based outlier detection methods are discussed in detail in Section 12.5.

12.3 Statistical Approaches

As with statistical methods for clustering, statistical methods for outlier detection make assumptions about data normality. They assume that the normal objects in a data set are generated by a stochastic process (a generative model). Consequently, normal objects occur in regions of high probability for the stochastic model, and objects in the regions of low probability are outliers.

The general idea behind statistical methods for outlier detection is to learn a generative model fitting the given data set, and then identify those objects in low-probability regions of the model as outliers. However, there are many different ways to learn generative models. In general, statistical methods for outlier detection can be divided into two major categories: *parametric methods* and *nonparametric methods*, according to how the models are specified and learned.

A **parametric method** assumes that the normal data objects are generated by a parametric distribution with parameter Θ. The *probability density function* of the parametric distribution $f(x, \Theta)$ gives the probability that object x is generated by the distribution. The smaller this value, the more likely x is an outlier.

A **nonparametric method** does not assume an a priori statistical model. Instead, a nonparametric method tries to determine the model from the input data. Note that most nonparametric methods do not assume that the model is completely parameter-free. (Such an assumption would make learning the model from data almost mission impossible.) Instead, nonparametric methods often take the position that the number and nature of the parameters are flexible and not fixed in advance. Examples of nonparametric methods include histogram and kernel density estimation.

12.3.1 Parametric Methods

In this subsection, we introduce several simple yet practical parametric methods for outlier detection. We first discuss methods for univariate data based on normal distribution. We then discuss how to handle multivariate data using multiple parametric distributions.

Detection of Univariate Outliers Based on Normal Distribution

Data involving only one attribute or variable are called *univariate data*. For simplicity, we often choose to assume that data are generated from a normal distribution. We can then learn the parameters of the normal distribution from the input data, and identify the points with low probability as outliers.

Let's start with univariate data. We will try to detect outliers by assuming the data follow a normal distribution.

Example 12.8   Univariate outlier detection using maximum likelihood. Suppose a city's average temperature values in July in the last 10 years are, in value-ascending order, 24.0°C, 28.9°C, 28.9°C, 29.0°C, 29.1°C, 29.1°C, 29.2°C, 29.2°C, 29.3°C, and 29.4°C. Let's assume that the average temperature follows a normal distribution, which is determined by two parameters: the mean, μ, and the standard deviation, σ.

We can use the *maximum likelihood method* to estimate the parameters μ and σ. That is, we maximize the *log-likelihood function*

$$\ln \mathcal{L}(\mu, \sigma^2) = \sum_{i=1}^{n} \ln f(x_i|(\mu, \sigma^2)) = -\frac{n}{2}\ln(2\pi) - \frac{n}{2}\ln \sigma^2 - \frac{1}{2\sigma^2}\sum_{i=1}^{n}(x_i - \mu)^2, \quad (12.1)$$

where n is the total number of samples, which is 10 in this example.

Taking derivatives with respect to μ and σ^2 and solving the resulting system of first-order conditions leads to the following *maximum likelihood estimates*:

$$\hat{\mu} = \bar{x} = \frac{1}{n}\sum_{i=1}^{n}x_i \quad (12.2)$$

$$\hat{\sigma}^2 = \frac{1}{n}\sum_{i=1}^{n}(x_i - \bar{x})^2. \quad (12.3)$$

In this example, we have

$$\hat{\mu} = \frac{24.0 + 28.9 + 28.9 + 29.0 + 29.1 + 29.1 + 29.2 + 29.2 + 29.3 + 29.4}{10} = 28.61$$

$$\hat{\sigma}^2 = ((24.1 - 28.61)^2 + (28.9 - 28.61)^2 + (28.9 - 28.61)^2 + (29.0 - 28.61)^2$$
$$+ (29.1 - 28.61)^2 + (29.1 - 28.61)^2 + (29.2 - 28.61)^2 + (29.2 - 28.61)^2$$
$$+ (29.3 - 28.61)^2 + (29.4 - 28.61)^2)/10 \simeq 2.29.$$

Accordingly, we have $\hat{\sigma} = \sqrt{2.29} = 1.51$.

The most deviating value, 24.0°C, is 4.61°C away from the estimated mean. We know that the $\mu \pm 3\sigma$ region contains 99.7% data under the assumption of normal

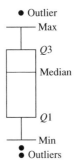

Figure 12.3 Using a boxplot to visualize outliers.

distribution. Because $\frac{4.61}{1.51} = 3.04 > 3$, the probability that the value 24.0°C is generated by the normal distribution is less than 0.15%, and thus can be identified as an outlier. ∎

Example 12.8 elaborates a simple yet practical outlier detection method. It simply labels any object as an outlier if it is more than 3σ away from the mean of the estimated distribution, where σ is the standard deviation.

Such straightforward methods for statistical outlier detection can also be used in visualization. For example, the *boxplot method* (described in Chapter 2) plots the univariate input data using a five-number summary (Figure 12.3): the smallest nonoutlier value (Min), the lower quartile (Q1), the median (Q2), the upper quartile (Q3), and the largest nonoutlier value (Max). The *interquantile range (IQR)* is defined as Q3 − Q1. Any object that is more than $1.5 \times IQR$ smaller than Q1 or $1.5 \times IQR$ larger than Q3 is treated as an outlier because the region between $Q1 - 1.5 \times IQR$ and $Q3 + 1.5 \times IQR$ contains 99.3% of the objects. The rationale is similar to using 3σ as the threshold for normal distribution.

Another simple statistical method for univariate outlier detection using normal distribution is the *Grubb's test* (also known as the *maximum normed residual test*). For each object x in a data set, we define a z-score as

$$z = \frac{|x - \bar{x}|}{s}, \tag{12.4}$$

where $\bar{x}$ is the mean, and s is the standard deviation of the input data. An object x is an outlier if

$$z \geq \frac{N-1}{\sqrt{N}} \sqrt{\frac{t^2_{\alpha/(2N),N-2}}{N - 2 + t^2_{\alpha/(2N),N-2}}}, \tag{12.5}$$

where $t^2_{\alpha/(2N),N-2}$ is the value taken by a t-distribution at a significance level of $\alpha/(2N)$, and N is the number of objects in the data set.

Detection of Multivariate Outliers

Data involving two or more attributes or variables are *multivariate data*. Many univariate outlier detection methods can be extended to handle multivariate data. The central idea is to transform the multivariate outlier detection task into a univariate outlier detection problem. Here, we use two examples to illustrate this idea.

Example 12.9 Multivariate outlier detection using the Mahalanobis distance. For a multivariate data set, let $\bar{o}$ be the mean vector. For an object, o, in the data set, the Mahalanobis distance from o to $\bar{o}$ is

$$MDist(o, \bar{o}) = (o - \bar{o})^T S^{-1} (o - \bar{o}), \tag{12.6}$$

where S is the covariance matrix.

$MDist(o, \bar{o})$ is a univariate variable, and thus Grubb's test can be applied to this measure. Therefore, we can transform the multivariate outlier detection tasks as follows:

1. Calculate the mean vector from the multivariate data set.

2. For each object o, calculate $MDist(o, \bar{o})$, the Mahalanobis distance from o to $\bar{o}$.

3. Detect outliers in the transformed univariate data set, $\{MDist(o, \bar{o}) | o \in D\}$.

4. If $MDist(o, \bar{o})$ is determined to be an outlier, then o is regarded as an outlier as well.

∎

Our second example uses the χ^2-statistic to measure the distance between an object to the mean of the input data set.

Example 12.10 Multivariate outlier detection using the χ^2-statistic. The χ^2-statistic can also be used to capture multivariate outliers under the assumption of normal distribution. For an object, o, the χ^2-statistic is

$$\chi^2 = \sum_{i=1}^{n} \frac{(o_i - E_i)^2}{E_i}, \tag{12.7}$$

where o_i is the value of o on the ith dimension, E_i is the mean of the i-dimension among all objects, and n is the dimensionality. If the χ^2-statistic is large, the object is an outlier. ∎

Using a Mixture of Parametric Distributions

If we assume that the data were generated by a normal distribution, this works well in many situations. However, this assumption may be overly simplified when the actual data distribution is complex. In such cases, we instead assume that the data were generated by a mixture of parametric distributions.

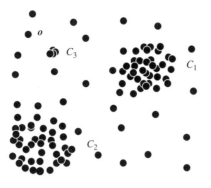

Figure 12.4 A complex data set.

Example 12.11 **Multivariate outlier detection using multiple parametric distributions.** Consider the data set in Figure 12.4. There are two big clusters, C_1 and C_2. To assume that the data are generated by a normal distribution would not work well here. The estimated mean is located between the two clusters and not inside any cluster. The objects between the two clusters cannot be detected as outliers since they are close to the mean. ∎

To overcome this problem, we can instead assume that the normal data objects are generated by multiple normal distributions, two in this case. That is, we assume two normal distributions, $\Theta_1(\mu_1, \sigma_1)$ and $\Theta_2(\mu_2, \sigma_2)$. For any object, o, in the data set, the probability that o is generated by the mixture of the two distributions is given by

$$Pr(o|\Theta_1, \Theta_2) = f_{\Theta_1}(o) + f_{\Theta_2}(o),$$

where f_{Θ_1} and f_{Θ_2} are the probability density functions of Θ_1 and Θ_2, respectively. We can use the *expectation-maximization* (EM) algorithm (Chapter 11) to learn the parameters $\mu_1, \sigma_1, \mu_2, \sigma_2$ from the data, as we do in mixture models for clustering. Each cluster is represented by a learned normal distribution. An object, o, is detected as an outlier if it does not belong to any cluster, that is, the probability is very low that it was generated by the combination of the two distributions.

Example 12.12 **Multivariate outlier detection using multiple clusters.** Most of the data objects shown in Figure 12.4 are in either C_1 or C_2. Other objects, representing noise, are uniformly distributed in the data space. A small cluster, C_3, is highly suspicious because it is not close to either of the two major clusters, C_1 and C_2. The objects in C_3 should therefore be detected as outliers.

Note that identifying the objects in C_3 as outliers is difficult, whether or not we assume that the given data follow a normal distribution or a mixture of multiple distributions. This is because the probability of the objects in C_3 will be higher than some of the noise objects, like o in Figure 12.4, due to a higher local density in C_3. ∎

To tackle the problem demonstrated in Example 12.12, we can assume that the normal data objects are generated by a normal distribution, or a mixture of normal distributions, whereas the outliers are generated by another distribution. Heuristically, we can add constraints on the distribution that is generating outliers. For example, it is reasonable to assume that this distribution has a larger variance if the outliers are distributed in a larger area. Technically, we can assign $\sigma_{outlier} = k\sigma$, where k is a user-specified parameter and σ is the standard deviation of the normal distribution generating the normal data. Again, the EM algorithm can be used to learn the parameters.

12.3.2 Nonparametric Methods

In nonparametric methods for outlier detection, the model of "normal data" is learned from the input data, rather than assuming one a priori. Nonparametric methods often make fewer assumptions about the data, and thus can be applicable in more scenarios.

Example 12.13 Outlier detection using a histogram. *AllElectronics* records the purchase amount for every customer transaction. Figure 12.5 uses a histogram (refer to Chapters 2 and 3) to graph these amounts as percentages, given all transactions. For example, 60% of the transaction amounts are between $0.00 and $1000.

We can use the histogram as a nonparametric statistical model to capture outliers. For example, a transaction in the amount of $7500 can be regarded as an outlier because only $1 - (60\% + 20\% + 10\% + 6.7\% + 3.1\%) = 0.2\%$ of transactions have an amount higher than $5000. On the other hand, a transaction amount of $385 can be treated as normal because it falls into the bin (or bucket) holding 60% of the transactions.

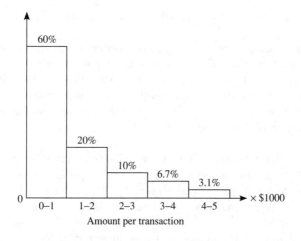

Figure 12.5 Histogram of purchase amounts in transactions.

■

As illustrated in the previous example, the histogram is a frequently used nonparametric statistical model that can be used to detect outliers. The procedure involves the following two steps.

Step 1: Histogram construction. In this step, we construct a histogram using the input data (training data). The histogram may be univariate as in Example 12.13, or multivariate if the input data are multidimensional.

Note that although nonparametric methods do not assume any a priori statistical model, they often do require user-specified parameters to learn models from data. For example, to construct a good histogram, a user has to specify the type of histogram (e.g., equal width or equal depth) and other parameters (e.g., the number of bins in the histogram or the size of each bin). Unlike parametric methods, these parameters do not specify types of data distribution (e.g., Gaussian).

Step 2: Outlier detection. To determine whether an object, o, is an outlier, we can check it against the histogram. In the simplest approach, if the object falls in one of the histogram's bins, the object is regarded as normal. Otherwise, it is considered an outlier.

For a more sophisticated approach, we can use the histogram to assign an outlier score to the object. In Example 12.13, we can let an object's outlier score be the inverse of the volume of the bin in which the object falls. For example, the outlier score for a transaction amount of $7500 is $\frac{1}{0.2\%} = 500$, and that for a transaction amount of $385 is $\frac{1}{60\%} = 1.67$. The scores indicate that the transaction amount of $7500 is much more likely to be an outlier than that of $385.

A drawback to using histograms as a nonparametric model for outlier detection is that it is hard to choose an appropriate bin size. On the one hand, if the bin size is set too small, many normal objects may end up in empty or rare bins, and thus be misidentified as outliers. This leads to a high false positive rate and low precision. On the other hand, if the bin size is set too high, outlier objects may infiltrate into some frequent bins and thus be "disguised" as normal. This leads to a high false negative rate and low recall.

To overcome this problem, we can adopt kernel density estimation to estimate the probability density distribution of the data. We treat an observed object as an indicator of high probability density in the surrounding region. The probability density at a point depends on the distances from this point to the observed objects. We use a *kernel function* to model the influence of a sample point within its neighborhood. A kernel $K()$ is a non-negative real-valued integrable function that satisfies the following two conditions:

- $\int_{-\infty}^{+\infty} K(u)\,du = 1$.

- $K(-u) = K(u)$ for all values of u.

A frequently used kernel is a standard Gaussian function with mean 0 and variance 1:

$$K\left(\frac{x - x_i}{h}\right) = \frac{1}{\sqrt{2\pi}} e^{-\frac{(x-x_i)^2}{2h^2}}. \tag{12.8}$$

Let $x_1, \ldots, x_n$ be an independent and identically distributed sample of a random variable f. The kernel density approximation of the probability density function is

$$\hat{f}_h(x) = \frac{1}{nh} \sum_{i=1}^{n} K\left(\frac{x - x_i}{h}\right), \tag{12.9}$$

where $K()$ is a kernel and h is the bandwidth serving as a smoothing parameter.

Once the probability density function of a data set is approximated through kernel density estimation, we can use the estimated density function $\hat{f}$ to detect outliers. For an object, $o, \hat{f}(o)$ gives the estimated probability that the object is generated by the stochastic process. If $\hat{f}(o)$ is high, then the object is likely normal. Otherwise, o is likely an outlier. This step is often similar to the corresponding step in parametric methods.

In summary, statistical methods for outlier detection learn models from data to distinguish normal data objects from outliers. An advantage of using statistical methods is that the outlier detection may be statistically justifiable. Of course, this is true only if the statistical assumption made about the underlying data meets the constraints in reality.

The data distribution of high-dimensional data is often complicated and hard to fully understand. Consequently, statistical methods for outlier detection on high-dimensional data remain a big challenge. Outlier detection for high-dimensional data is further addressed in Section 12.8.

The computational cost of statistical methods depends on the models. When simple parametric models are used (e.g., a Gaussian), fitting the parameters typically takes linear time. When more sophisticated models are used (e.g., mixture models, where the EM algorithm is used in learning), approximating the best parameter values often takes several iterations. Each iteration, however, is typically linear with respect to the data set's size. For kernel density estimation, the model learning cost can be up to quadratic. Once the model is learned, the outlier detection cost is often very small per object.

12.4 Proximity-Based Approaches

Given a set of objects in feature space, a distance measure can be used to quantify the similarity between objects. Intuitively, objects that are far from others can be regarded as outliers. Proximity-based approaches assume that the proximity of an outlier object to its nearest neighbors significantly deviates from the proximity of the object to most of the other objects in the data set.

There are two types of proximity-based outlier detection methods: distance-based and density-based methods. A *distance-based outlier detection method* consults the **neighborhood** of an object, which is defined by a given radius. An object is then considered an outlier if its neighborhood does not have enough other points. A *density-based outlier detection method* investigates the density of an object and that of its neighbors. Here, an object is identified as an outlier if its density is relatively much lower than that of its neighbors.

Let's start with distance-based outliers.

12.4.1 Distance-Based Outlier Detection and a Nested Loop Method

A representative method of proximity-based outlier detection uses the concept of **distance-based outliers**. For a set, D, of data objects to be analyzed, a user can specify a distance threshold, r, to define a reasonable neighborhood of an object. For each object, o, we can examine the number of other objects in the r-neighborhood of o. If most of the objects in D are far from o, that is, not in the r-neighborhood of o, then o can be regarded as an outlier.

Formally, let r ($r \geq 0$) be a *distance threshold* and π ($0 < \pi \leq 1$) be a fraction threshold. An object, o, is a $DB(r, \pi)$-**outlier** if

$$\frac{\|\{o' | dist(o, o') \leq r\}\|}{\|D\|} \leq \pi, \tag{12.10}$$

where $dist(\cdot, \cdot)$ is a distance measure.

Equivalently, we can determine whether an object, o, is a $DB(r, \pi)$-outlier by checking the distance between o and its k-nearest neighbor, o_k, where $k = \lceil \pi \|D\| \rceil$. Object o is an outlier if $dist(o, o_k) > r$, because in such a case, there are fewer than k objects except for o that are in the r-neighborhood of o.

"*How can we compute $DB(r, \pi)$-outliers?*" A straightforward approach is to use nested loops to check the r-neighborhood for every object, as shown in Figure 12.6. For any object, o_i ($1 \leq i \leq n$), we calculate the distance between o_i and the other object, and count the number of other objects in the r-neighborhood of o_i. Once we find $\pi \cdot n$ other

Algorithm: Distance-based outlier detection.

Input:

- a set of objects $D = \{o_1, \ldots, o_n\}$, threshold r ($r > 0$) and π ($0 < \pi \leq 1$);

Output: $DB(r, \pi)$ outliers in D.

Method:

    for $i = 1$ to n **do**
        $count \leftarrow 0$
        for $j = 1$ to n **do**
            if $i \neq j$ and $dist(o_i, o_j) \leq r$ **then**
                $count \leftarrow count + 1$
                if $count \geq \pi \cdot n$ **then**
                    exit {o_i cannot be a $DB(r, \pi)$ outlier}
                endif
            endif
        endfor
        print o_i {o_i is a $DB(r, \pi)$ outlier according to (Eq. 12.10)}
    endfor;

Figure 12.6 Nested loop algorithm for $DB(r, \pi)$-outlier detection.

objects within a distance r from o_i, the inner loop can be terminated because o_i already violates (Eq. 12.10), and thus is not a $DB(r,\pi)$-outlier. On the other hand, if the inner loop completes for o_i, this means that o_i has less than $\pi \cdot n$ neighbors in a radius of r, and thus is a $DB(r,\pi)$-outlier.

The straightforward nested loop approach takes $O(n^2)$ time. Surprisingly, the actual CPU runtime is often linear with respect to the data set size. For most nonoutlier objects, the inner loop terminates early when the number of outliers in the data set is small, which should be the case most of the time. Correspondingly, only a small fraction of the data set is examined.

When mining large data sets where the complete set of objects cannot be held in main memory, the nested loop approach is still costly. Suppose the main memory has m pages for the mining. Instead of conducting the inner loop object by object, in such a case, the outer loop uses $m-1$ pages to hold as many objects as possible and uses the remaining one page to run the inner loop. The inner loop cannot stop until all objects in the $m-1$ pages are identified as not being outliers, which is very unlikely to happen. Correspondingly, it is likely that the algorithm has to incur $O((\frac{n}{b})^2)$ input/output (I/O) cost, where b is the number of objects that can be held in one page.

The major cost in the nested loop method comes from two aspects. First, to check whether an object is an outlier, the nested loop method tests the object against the whole data set. To improve, we need to explore how to determine the outlierness of an object from the neighbors that are close to the object. Second, the nested loop method checks objects one by one. To improve, we should try to group objects according to their proximity, and check the outlierness of objects group by group most of the time. Section 12.4.2 introduces how to implement the preceding ideas.

12.4.2 A Grid-Based Method

CELL is a grid-based method for distance-based outlier detection. In this method, the data space is partitioned into a multidimensional grid, where each cell is a hypercube that has a diagonal of length $\frac{r}{2}$, where r is a distance threshold parameter. In other words, if there are l dimensions, the length of each edge of a cell is $\frac{r}{2\sqrt{l}}$.

Consider a 2-D data set, for example. Figure 12.7 shows part of the grid. The length of each edge of a cell is $\frac{r}{2\sqrt{2}}$.

Consider the cell C in Figure 12.7. The neighboring cells of C can be divided into two groups. The cells immediately next to C constitute the *level-1* cells (labeled "1" in the figure), and the cells one or two cells away from C in any direction constitute the *level-2* cells (labeled "2" in the figure). The two levels of cells have the following properties:

- **Level-1 cell property**: Given any possible point, x of C, and any possible point, y, in a level-1 cell, then $dist(x,y) \leq r$.

- **Level-2 cell property**: Given any possible point, x of C, and any point, y, such that $dist(x,y) \geq r$, then y is in a level-2 cell.

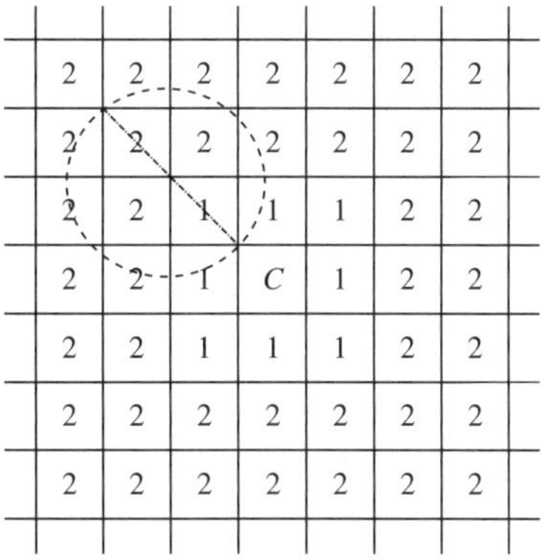

Figure 12.7 Grids in the CELL method.

Let a be the number of objects in cell C, b_1 be the total number of objects in the level-1 cells, and b_2 be the total number of objects in the level-2 cells. We can apply the following rules.

- **Level-1 cell pruning rule**: Based on the level-1 cell property, if $a + b_1 > \lceil \pi n \rceil$, then every object o in C is not a $DB(r,\pi)$-outlier because all those objects in C and the level-1 cells are in the r-neighborhood of o, and there are at least $\lceil \pi n \rceil$ such neighbors.

- **Level-2 cell pruning rule**: Based on the level-2 cell property, if $a + b_1 + b_2 < \lceil \pi n \rceil + 1$, then all objects in C are $DB(r,\pi)$-outliers because each of their r-neighborhoods has less than $\lceil \pi n \rceil$ other objects.

Using the preceding two rules, the CELL method organizes objects into groups using a grid—all objects in a cell form a group. For groups satisfying one of the two rules, we can determine that either all objects in a cell are outliers or nonoutliers, and thus do not need to check those objects one by one. Moreover, to apply the two rules, we need only check a limited number of cells close to a target cell instead of the whole data set.

Using the previous two rules, many objects can be determined as being either nonoutliers or outliers. We only need to check the objects that cannot be pruned using the two rules. Even for such an object, o, we need only compute the distance between o and the objects in the level-2 cells with respect to o. This is because all objects in the level-1 cells have a distance of at most r to o, and all objects not in a level-1 or level-2 cell must have a distance of more than r from o, and thus cannot be in the r-neighborhood of o.

When the data set is very large so that most of the data are stored on disk, the CELL method may incur many random accesses to disk, which is costly. An alternative method was proposed, which uses a very small amount of main memory (around 1% of the data set) to mine all outliers by scanning the data set three times. First, a sample, S, is created of the given data set, D, using sampling by replacement. Each object in S is considered the centroid of a partition. The objects in D are assigned to the partitions based on distance. The preceding steps are completed in one scan of D. Candidate outliers are identified in a second scan of D. After a third scan, all $DB(r, \pi)$-outliers have been found.

12.4.3 Density-Based Outlier Detection

Distance-based outliers, such as $DB(r, \pi)$-outliers, are just one type of outlier. Specifically, distance-based outlier detection takes a global view of the data set. Such outliers can be regarded as "global outliers" for two reasons:

- A $DB(r, \pi)$-outlier, for example, is far (as quantified by parameter r) from at least $(1 - \pi) \times 100\%$ of the objects in the data set. In other words, an outlier as such is remote from the majority of the data.

- To detect distance-based outliers, we need two global parameters, r and π, which are applied to every outlier object.

Many real-world data sets demonstrate a more complex structure, where objects may be considered outliers with respect to their local neighborhoods, rather than with respect to the global data distribution. Let's look at an example.

Example 12.14 **Local proximity-based outliers.** Consider the data points in Figure 12.8. There are two clusters: C_1 is dense, and C_2 is sparse. Object o_3 can be detected as a distance-based outlier because it is far from the majority of the data set.

Now, let's consider objects o_1 and o_2. Are they outliers? On the one hand, the distance from o_1 and o_2 to the objects in the dense cluster, C_1, is smaller than the average distance between an object in cluster C_2 and its nearest neighbor. Thus, o_1 and o_2 are not distance-based outliers. In fact, if we were to categorize o_1 and o_2 as $DB(r, \pi)$-outliers, we would have to classify all the objects in clusters C_2 as $DB(r, \pi)$-outliers.

On the other hand, o_1 and o_2 can be identified as outliers when they are considered locally with respect to cluster C_1 because o_1 and o_2 deviate significantly from the objects in C_1. Moreover, o_1 and o_2 are also far from the objects in C_2.

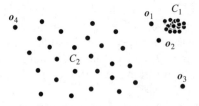

Figure 12.8 Global outliers and local outliers.

To summarize, distance-based outlier detection methods cannot capture local outliers like o_1 and o_2. Note that the distance between object o_4 and its nearest neighbors is much greater than the distance between o_1 and its nearest neighbors. However, because o_4 is local to cluster C_2 (which is sparse), o_4 is not considered a local outlier. ∎

"How can we formulate the local outliers as illustrated in Example 12.14?" The critical idea here is that we need to compare the density around an object with the density around its local neighbors. The basic assumption of density-based outlier detection methods is that the density around a nonoutlier object is similar to the density around its neighbors, while the density around an outlier object is significantly different from the density around its neighbors.

Based on the preceding, density-based outlier detection methods use the relative density of an object against its neighbors to indicate the degree to which an object is an outlier.

Now, let's consider how to measure the *relative density* of an object, o, given a set of objects, D. The *k-distance* of o, denoted by $dist_k(o)$, is the distance, $dist(o, p)$, between o and another object, $p \in D$, such that

- There are at least k objects $o' \in D-\{o\}$ such that $dist(o, o') \leq dist(o, p)$.
- There are at most $k-1$ objects $o'' \in D-\{o\}$ such that $dist(o, o'') < dist(o, p)$.

In other words, $dist_k(o)$ is the distance between o and its k-nearest neighbor. Consequently, the *k-distance neighborhood* of o contains all objects of which the distance to o is not greater than $dist_k(o)$, the k-distance of o, denoted by

$$N_k(o) = \{o'|o' \in D, dist(o,o') \leq dist_k(o)\}. \tag{12.11}$$

Note that $N_k(o)$ may contain more than k objects because multiple objects may each be the same distance away from o.

We can use the average distance from the objects in $N_k(o)$ to o as the measure of the local density of o. However, such a straightforward measure has a problem: If o has very close neighbors o' such that $dist(o, o')$ is very small, the statistical fluctuations of the distance measure can be undesirably high. To overcome this problem, we can switch to the following reachability distance measure by adding a smoothing effect.

For two objects, o and o', the *reachability distance* from o' to o is $dist(o \leftarrow o')$ if $dist(o, o') > dist_k(o)$, and $dist_k(o)$ otherwise. That is,

$$reachdist_k(o \leftarrow o') = \max\{dist_k(o), dist(o,o')\}. \tag{12.12}$$

Here, k is a user-specified parameter that controls the smoothing effect. Essentially, k specifies the minimum neighborhood to be examined to determine the local density of an object. Importantly, reachability distance is not symmetric, that is, in general, $reachdist_k(o \leftarrow o') \neq reachdist_k(o' \leftarrow o)$.

Now, we can define the *local reachability density* of an object, o, as

$$lrd_k(o) = \frac{\|N_k(o)\|}{\sum_{o' \in N_k(o)} reachdist_k(o' \leftarrow o)}. \tag{12.13}$$

There is a critical difference between the density measure here for outlier detection and that in density-based clustering (Section 12.5). In density-based clustering, to determine whether an object can be considered a core object in a density-based cluster, we use two parameters: a radius parameter, r, to specify the range of the neighborhood, and the minimum number of points in the r-neighborhood. Both parameters are global and are applied to every object. In contrast, as motivated by the observation that relative density is the key to finding local outliers, we use the parameter k to quantify the neighborhood and do not need to specify the minimum number of objects in the neighborhood as a requirement of density. We instead calculate the local reachability density for an object and compare it with that of its neighbors to quantify the degree to which the object is considered an outlier.

Specifically, we define the *local outlier factor* of an object o as

$$LOF_k(o) = \frac{\sum_{o' \in N_k(o)} \frac{lrd_k(o')}{lrd_k(o)}}{\|N_k(o)\|} = \sum_{o' \in N_k(o)} lrd_k(o') \cdot \sum_{o' \in N_k(o)} reachdist_k(o' \leftarrow o). \tag{12.14}$$

In other words, the local outlier factor is the average of the ratio of the local reachability density of o and those of o's k-nearest neighbors. The lower the local reachability density of o (i.e., the smaller the item $\sum_{o' \in N_k(o)} reachdist_k(o' \leftarrow o)$) and the higher the local reachability densities of the k-nearest neighbors of o, the higher the LOF value is. This exactly captures a local outlier of which the local density is relatively low compared to the local densities of its k-nearest neighbors.

The local outlier factor has some nice properties. First, for an object deep within a consistent cluster, such as the points in the center of cluster C_2 in Figure 12.8, the local outlier factor is close to 1. This property ensures that objects inside clusters, no matter whether the cluster is dense or sparse, will not be mislabeled as outliers.

Second, for an object o, the meaning of $LOF(o)$ is easy to understand. Consider the objects in Figure 12.9, for example. For object o, let

$$direct_{min}(o) = \min\{reachdist_k(o' \leftarrow o)|o' \in N_k(o)\} \tag{12.15}$$

be the minimum reachability distance from o to its k-nearest neighbors. Similarly, we can define

$$direct_{max}(o) = \max\{reachdist_k(o' \leftarrow o)|o' \in N_k(o)\}. \tag{12.16}$$

We also consider the neighbors of o's k-nearest neighbors. Let

$$indirect_{min}(o) = \min\{reachdist_k(o'' \leftarrow o')|o' \in N_k(o) \text{ and } o'' \in N_k(o')\} \tag{12.17}$$

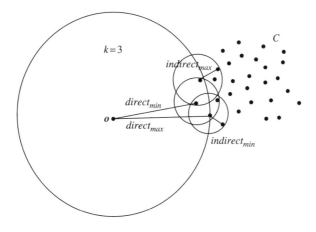

Figure 12.9 A property of $LOF(o)$.

and

$$indirect_{max}(o) = \max\{reachdist_k(o'' \leftarrow o')|o' \in N_k(o) \text{ and } o'' \in N_k(o')\}. \qquad (12.18)$$

Then, it can be shown that $LOF(o)$ is bounded as

$$\frac{direct_{min}(o)}{indirect_{max}(o)} \leq LOF(o) \leq \frac{direct_{max}(o)}{indirect_{min}(o)}. \qquad (12.19)$$

This result clearly shows that LOF captures the relative density of an object.

12.5 Clustering-Based Approaches

The notion of outliers is highly related to that of clusters. Clustering-based approaches detect outliers by examining the relationship between objects and clusters. Intuitively, an outlier is an object that belongs to a small and remote cluster, or does not belong to any cluster.

This leads to three general approaches to clustering-based outlier detection. Consider an object.

- Does the object belong to any cluster? If not, then it is identified as an outlier.

- Is there a large distance between the object and the cluster to which it is closest? If yes, it is an outlier.

- Is the object part of a small or sparse cluster? If yes, then all the objects in that cluster are outliers.

Let's look at examples of each of these approaches.

Example 12.15 **Detecting outliers as objects that do not belong to any cluster.** Gregarious animals (e.g., goats and deer) live and move in flocks. Using outlier detection, we can identify outliers as animals that are not part of a flock. Such animals may be either lost or wounded.

In Figure 12.10, each point represents an animal living in a group. Using a density-based clustering method, such as DBSCAN, we note that the black points belong to clusters. The white point, a, does not belong to any cluster, and thus is declared an outlier. ■

The second approach to clustering-based outlier detection considers the distance between an object and the cluster to which it is closest. If the distance is large, then the object is likely an outlier with respect to the cluster. Thus, this approach detects individual outliers with respect to clusters.

Example 12.16 **Clustering-based outlier detection using distance to the closest cluster.** Using the k-means clustering method, we can partition the data points shown in Figure 12.11 into three clusters, as shown using different symbols. The center of each cluster is marked with a $+$.

For each object, o, we can assign an outlier score to the object according to the distance between the object and the center that is closest to the object. Suppose the closest center to o is c_o; then the distance between o and c_o is $dist(o, c_o)$, and the average

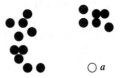

Figure 12.10 Object a is an outlier because it does not belong to any cluster.

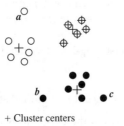

+ Cluster centers

Figure 12.11 Outliers (a, b, c) are far from the clusters to which they are closest (with respect to the cluster centers).

distance between c_o and the objects assigned to o is l_{c_o}. The ratio $\frac{dist(o,c_o)}{l_{c_o}}$ measures how $dist(o, c_o)$ stands out from the average. The larger the ratio, the farther away o is relative from the center, and the more likely o is an outlier. In Figure 12.11, points a, b, and c are relatively far away from their corresponding centers, and thus are suspected of being outliers.   ∎

This approach can also be used for intrusion detection, as described in Example 12.17.

Example 12.17 **Intrusion detection by clustering-based outlier detection.** A bootstrap method was developed to detect intrusions in TCP connection data by considering the similarity between data points and the clusters in a training data set. The method consists of three steps.

1. A training data set is used to find patterns of normal data. Specifically, the TCP connection data are segmented according to, say, dates. Frequent itemsets are found in each segment. The frequent itemsets that are in a majority of the segments are considered patterns of normal data and are referred to as "base connections."

2. Connections in the training data that contain base connections are treated as attack-free. Such connections are clustered into groups.

3. The data points in the original data set are compared with the clusters mined in step 2. Any point that is deemed an outlier with respect to the clusters is declared as a possible attack.   ∎

Note that each of the approaches we have seen so far detects only individual objects as outliers because they compare objects one at a time against clusters in the data set. However, in a large data set, some outliers may be similar and form a small cluster. In intrusion detection, for example, hackers who use similar tactics to attack a system may form a cluster. The approaches discussed so far may be deceived by such outliers.

To overcome this problem, a third approach to cluster-based outlier detection identifies small or sparse clusters and declares the objects in those clusters to be outliers as well. An example of this approach is the *FindCBLOF* algorithm, which works as follows.

1. Find clusters in a data set, and sort them according to decreasing size. The algorithm assumes that most of the data points are not outliers. It uses a parameter α ($0 \leq \alpha \leq 1$) to distinguish large from small clusters. Any cluster that contains at least a percentage α (e.g., $\alpha = 90\%$) of the data set is considered a "large cluster." The remaining clusters are referred to as "small clusters."

2. To each data point, assign a *cluster-based local outlier factor* (CBLOF). For a point belonging to a large cluster, its CBLOF is the product of the cluster's size and the similarity between the point and the cluster. For a point belonging to a small cluster, its CBLOF is calculated as the product of the size of the small cluster and the similarity between the point and the closest large cluster.

CBLOF defines the similarity between a point and a cluster in a statistical way that represents the probability that the point belongs to the cluster. The larger the value, the more similar the point and the cluster are. The CBLOF score can detect outlier points that are far from any clusters. In addition, small clusters that are far from any large cluster are considered to consist of outliers. The points with the lowest CBLOF scores are suspected outliers.

Example 12.18 **Detecting outliers in small clusters.** The data points in Figure 12.12 form three clusters: large clusters, C_1 and C_2, and a small cluster, C_3. Object o does not belong to any cluster.

Using CBLOF, *FindCBLOF* can identify o as well as the points in cluster C_3 as outliers. For o, the closest large cluster is C_1. The CBLOF is simply the similarity between o and C_1, which is small. For the points in C_3, the closest large cluster is C_2. Although there are three points in cluster C_3, the similarity between those points and cluster C_2 is low, and $|C_3| = 3$ is small; thus, the CBLOF scores of points in C_3 are small.   ∎

Clustering-based approaches may incur high computational costs if they have to find clusters before detecting outliers. Several techniques have been developed for improved efficiency. For example, **fixed-width clustering** is a linear-time technique that is used in some outlier detection methods. The idea is simple yet efficient. A point is assigned to a cluster if the center of the cluster is within a predefined distance threshold from the point. If a point cannot be assigned to any existing cluster, a new cluster is created. The distance threshold may be learned from the training data under certain conditions.

Clustering-based outlier detection methods have the following advantages. First, they can detect outliers without requiring any labeled data, that is, in an unsupervised way. They work for many data types. Clusters can be regarded as summaries of the data. Once the clusters are obtained, clustering-based methods need only compare any object against the clusters to determine whether the object is an outlier. This process is typically fast because the number of clusters is usually small compared to the total number of objects.

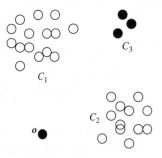

Figure 12.12 Outliers in small clusters.

A weakness of clustering-based outlier detection is its effectiveness, which depends highly on the clustering method used. Such methods may not be optimized for outlier detection. Clustering methods are often costly for large data sets, which can serve as a bottleneck.

12.6 Classification-Based Approaches

Outlier detection can be treated as a classification problem if a training data set with class labels is available. The general idea of classification-based outlier detection methods is to train a classification model that can distinguish normal data from outliers.

Consider a training set that contains samples labeled as "normal" and others labeled as "outlier." A classifier can then be constructed based on the training set. Any classification method can be used (Chapters 8 and 9). This kind of brute-force approach, however, does not work well for outlier detection because the training set is typically heavily biased. That is, the number of normal samples likely far exceeds the number of outlier samples. This imbalance, where the number of outlier samples may be insufficient, can prevent us from building an accurate classifier. Consider intrusion detection in a system, for example. Because most system accesses are normal, it is easy to obtain a good representation of the normal events. However, it is infeasible to enumerate all potential intrusions, as new and unexpected attempts occur from time to time. Hence, we are left with an insufficient representation of the outlier (or intrusion) samples.

To overcome this challenge, classification-based outlier detection methods often use a *one-class model*. That is, a classifier is built to describe only the normal class. Any samples that do not belong to the normal class are regarded as outliers.

Example 12.19 Outlier detection using a one-class model. Consider the training set shown in Figure 12.13, where white points are samples labeled as "normal" and black points are samples labeled as "outlier." To build a model for outlier detection, we can learn the decision boundary of the normal class using classification methods such as SVM (Chapter 9), as illustrated. Given a new object, if the object is within the decision boundary of the normal class, it is treated as a normal case. If the object is outside the decision boundary, it is declared an outlier.

An advantage of using only the model of the normal class to detect outliers is that the model can detect new outliers that may not appear close to any outlier objects in the training set. This occurs as long as such new outliers fall outside the decision boundary of the normal class. ∎

The idea of using the decision boundary of the normal class can be extended to handle situations where the normal objects may belong to multiple classes such as in fuzzy clustering (Chapter 11). For example, *AllElectronics* accepts returned items. Customers can return items for a number of reasons (corresponding to class categories) such as "product design defects" and "product damaged during shipment." Each such

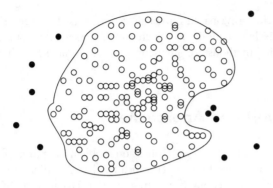

Figure 12.13 Learning a model for the normal class.

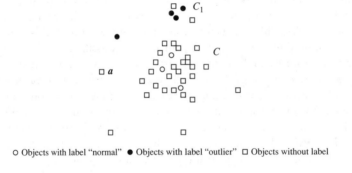

○ Objects with label "normal" ● Objects with label "outlier" □ Objects without label

Figure 12.14 Detecting outliers by semi-supervised learning.

class is regarded as normal. To detect outlier cases, *AllElectronics* can learn a model for each normal class. To determine whether a case is an outlier, we can run each model on the case. If the case does not fit any of the models, then it is declared an outlier.

Classification-based methods and clustering-based methods can be combined to detect outliers in a semi-supervised learning way.

Example 12.20 **Outlier detection by semi-supervised learning.** Consider Figure 12.14, where objects are labeled as either "normal" or "outlier," or have no label at all. Using a clustering-based approach, we find a large cluster, C, and a small cluster, C_1. Because some objects in C carry the label "normal," we can treat all objects in this cluster (including those without labels) as normal objects. We use the one-class model of this cluster to identify normal objects in outlier detection. Similarly, because some objects in cluster C_1 carry the label "outlier," we declare all objects in C_1 as outliers. Any object that does not fall into the model for C (e.g., a) is considered an outlier as well. ∎

Classification-based methods can incorporate human domain knowledge into the detection process by learning from the labeled samples. Once the classification model is constructed, the outlier detection process is fast. It only needs to compare the objects to be examined against the model learned from the training data. The quality of classification-based methods heavily depends on the availability and quality of the training set. In many applications, it is difficult to obtain representative and high-quality training data, which limits the applicability of classification-based methods.

12.7 Mining Contextual and Collective Outliers

An object in a given data set is a **contextual outlier** (or *conditional outlier*) if it deviates significantly with respect to a specific context of the object (Section 12.1). The context is defined using **contextual attributes**. These depend heavily on the application, and are often provided by users as part of the contextual outlier detection task. Contextual attributes can include spatial attributes, time, network locations, and sophisticated structured attributes. In addition, **behavioral attributes** define characteristics of the object, and are used to evaluate whether the object is an outlier in the context to which it belongs.

Example 12.21 **Contextual outliers.** To determine whether the temperature of a location is exceptional (i.e., an outlier), the attributes specifying information about the location can serve as contextual attributes. These attributes may be spatial attributes (e.g., longitude and latitude) or location attributes in a graph or network. The attribute *time* can also be used. In customer-relationship management, whether a customer is an outlier may depend on other customers with similar profiles. Here, the attributes defining customer profiles provide the context for outlier detection. ■

In comparison to outlier detection in general, identifying contextual outliers requires analyzing the corresponding contextual information. Contextual outlier detection methods can be divided into two categories according to whether the contexts can be clearly identified.

12.7.1 Transforming Contextual Outlier Detection to Conventional Outlier Detection

This category of methods is for situations where the contexts can be clearly identified. The idea is to transform the contextual outlier detection problem into a typical outlier detection problem. Specifically, for a given data object, we can evaluate whether the object is an outlier in two steps. In the first step, we identify the context of the object using the contextual attributes. In the second step, we calculate the outlier score for the object in the context using a conventional outlier detection method.

Example 12.22 **Contextual outlier detection when the context can be clearly identified.** In customer-relationship management, we can detect outlier customers in the context of customer groups. Suppose *AllElectronics* maintains customer information on four attributes, namely *age_group* (i.e., under 25, 25-45, 45-65, and over 65), *postal_code*, *number_of_transactions_per_year*, and *annual_total_transaction_amount*. The attributes *age_group* and *postal_code* serve as contextual attributes, and the attributes *number_of_transactions_per_year* and *annual_total_transaction_amount* are behavioral attributes. ∎

To detect contextual outliers in this setting, for a customer, *c*, we can first locate the context of *c* using the attributes *age_group* and *postal_code*. We can then compare *c* with the other customers in the same group, and use a conventional outlier detection method, such as some of the ones discussed earlier, to determine whether *c* is an outlier.

Contexts may be specified at different levels of granularity. Suppose *AllElectronics* maintains customer information at a more detailed level for the attributes *age*, *postal_code*, *number_of_transactions_per_year*, and *annual_total_transaction_amount*. We can still group customers on *age* and *postal_code*, and then mine outliers in each group. What if the number of customers falling into a group is very small or even zero? For a customer, *c*, if the corresponding context contains very few or even no other customers, the evaluation of whether *c* is an outlier using the exact context is unreliable or even impossible.

To overcome this challenge, we can assume that customers of similar age and who live within the same area should have similar normal behavior. This assumption can help to generalize contexts and makes for more effective outlier detection. For example, using a set of training data, we may learn a mixture model, *U*, of the data on the contextual attributes, and another mixture model, *V*, of the data on the behavior attributes. A mapping $p(V_i|U_j)$ is also learned to capture the probability that a data object *o* belonging to cluster U_j on the contextual attributes is generated by cluster V_i on the behavior attributes. The outlier score can then be calculated as

$$S(o) = \sum_{U_j} p(o \in U_j) \sum_{V_i} p(o \in V_i) p(V_i|U_j). \tag{12.20}$$

Thus, the contextual outlier problem is transformed into outlier detection using mixture models.

12.7.2 Modeling Normal Behavior with Respect to Contexts

In some applications, it is inconvenient or infeasible to clearly partition the data into contexts. For example, consider the situation where the online store of *AllElectronics* records customer browsing behavior in a search log. For each customer, the data log contains the sequence of products searched for and browsed by the customer. *AllElectronics* is interested in contextual outlier behavior, such as if a customer suddenly purchased a product that is unrelated to those she recently browsed. However, in this application, contexts cannot be easily specified because it is unclear how many products browsed earlier should be considered as the context, and this number will likely differ for each product.

This second category of contextual outlier detection methods models the normal behavior with respect to contexts. Using a training data set, such a method trains a model that predicts the expected behavior attribute values with respect to the contextual attribute values. To determine whether a data object is a contextual outlier, we can then apply the model to the contextual attributes of the object. If the behavior attribute values of the object significantly deviate from the values predicted by the model, then the object can be declared a contextual outlier.

By using a prediction model that links the contexts and behavior, these methods avoid the explicit identification of specific contexts. A number of classification and prediction techniques can be used to build such models such as regression, Markov models, and finite state automaton. Interested readers are referred to Chapters 8 and 9 on classification and the bibliographic notes for further details (Section 12.11).

In summary, contextual outlier detection enhances conventional outlier detection by considering contexts, which are important in many applications. We may be able to detect outliers that cannot be detected otherwise. Consider a credit card user whose income level is low but whose expenditure patterns are similar to those of millionaires. This user can be detected as a contextual outlier if the income level is used to define context. Such a user may not be detected as an outlier without contextual information because she does share expenditure patterns with many millionaires. Considering contexts in outlier detection can also help to avoid false alarms. Without considering the context, a millionaire's purchase transaction may be falsely detected as an outlier if the majority of customers in the training set are not millionaires. This can be corrected by incorporating contextual information in outlier detection.

12.7.3 Mining Collective Outliers

A group of data objects forms a **collective outlier** if the objects as a whole deviate significantly from the entire data set, even though each individual object in the group may not be an outlier (Section 12.1). To detect collective outliers, we have to examine the *structure* of the data set, that is, the relationships between multiple data objects. This makes the problem more difficult than conventional and contextual outlier detection.

"How can we explore the data set structure?" This typically depends on the nature of the data. For outlier detection in temporal data (e.g., time series and sequences), we explore the structures formed by time, which occur in segments of the time series or subsequences. To detect collective outliers in spatial data, we explore local areas. Similarly, in graph and network data, we explore subgraphs. Each of these structures is inherent to its respective data type.

Contextual outlier detection and collective outlier detection are similar in that they both explore structures. In contextual outlier detection, the structures are the contexts, as specified by the contextual attributes explicitly. The critical difference in collective outlier detection is that the structures are often not explicitly defined, and have to be discovered as part of the outlier detection process.

As with contextual outlier detection, collective outlier detection methods can also be divided into two categories. The first category consists of methods that reduce the problem to conventional outlier detection. Its strategy is to identify *structure units*, treat each structure unit (e.g., a subsequence, a time-series segment, a local area, or a subgraph) as a data object, and extract features. The problem of collective outlier detection is thus transformed into outlier detection on the set of "structured objects" constructed as such using the extracted features. A structure unit, which represents a group of objects in the original data set, is a collective outlier if the structure unit deviates significantly from the expected trend in the space of the extracted features.

Example 12.23 **Collective outlier detection on graph data.** Let's see how we can detect collective outliers in *AllElectronics'* online social network of customers. Suppose we treat the social network as an unlabeled graph. We then treat each possible subgraph of the network as a structure unit. For each subgraph, S, let $|S|$ be the number of vertices in S, and $freq(S)$ be the frequency of S in the network. That is, $freq(S)$ is the number of different subgraphs in the network that are isomorphic to S. We can use these two features to detect outlier subgraphs. An *outlier subgraph* is a collective outlier that contains multiple vertices.

In general, a small subgraph (e.g., a single vertex or a pair of vertices connected by an edge) is expected to be frequent, and a large subgraph is expected to be infrequent. Using the preceding simple method, we can detect small subgraphs that are of very low frequency or large subgraphs that are surprisingly frequent. These are outlier structures in the social network. ∎

Predefining the structure units for collective outlier detection can be difficult or impossible. Consequently, the second category of methods models the expected behavior of structure units directly. For example, to detect collective outliers in temporal sequences, one method is to learn a Markov model from the sequences. A subsequence can then be declared as a collective outlier if it significantly deviates from the model.

In summary, collective outlier detection is subtle due to the challenge of exploring the structures in data. The exploration typically uses heuristics, and thus may be application-dependent. The computational cost is often high due to the sophisticated mining process. While highly useful in practice, collective outlier detection remains a challenging direction that calls for further research and development.

12.8 Outlier Detection in High-Dimensional Data

In some applications, we may need to detect outliers in high-dimensional data. The dimensionality curse poses huge challenges for effective outlier detection. As the dimensionality increases, the distance between objects may be heavily dominated by noise. That is, the distance and similarity between two points in a high-dimensional space may not reflect the real relationship between the points. Consequently, conventional outlier detection methods, which mainly use proximity or density to identify outliers, deteriorate as dimensionality increases.

Ideally, outlier detection methods for high-dimensional data should meet the challenges that follow.

- **Interpretation of outliers:** They should be able to not only detect outliers, but also provide an interpretation of the outliers. Because many features (or dimensions) are involved in a high-dimensional data set, detecting outliers without providing any interpretation as to why they are outliers is not very useful. The interpretation of outliers may come from, for example, specific subspaces that manifest the outliers or an assessment regarding the "outlier-ness" of the objects. Such interpretation can help users to understand the possible meaning and significance of the outliers.

- **Data sparsity:** The methods should be capable of handling sparsity in high-dimensional spaces. The distance between objects becomes heavily dominated by noise as the dimensionality increases. Therefore, data in high-dimensional spaces are often sparse.

- **Data subspaces:** They should model outliers appropriately, for example, adaptive to the subspaces signifying the outliers and capturing the local behavior of data. Using a fixed-distance threshold against all subspaces to detect outliers is not a good idea because the distance between two objects monotonically increases as the dimensionality increases.

- **Scalability with respect to dimensionality:** As the dimensionality increases, the number of subspaces increases exponentially. An exhaustive combinatorial exploration of the search space, which contains all possible subspaces, is not a scalable choice.

Outlier detection methods for high-dimensional data can be divided into three main approaches. These include extending conventional outlier detection (Section 12.8.1), finding outliers in subspaces (Section 12.8.2), and modeling high-dimensional outliers (Section 12.8.3).

12.8.1 Extending Conventional Outlier Detection

One approach for outlier detection in high-dimensional data extends conventional outlier detection methods. It uses the conventional proximity-based models of outliers. However, to overcome the deterioration of proximity measures in high-dimensional spaces, it uses alternative measures or constructs subspaces and detects outliers there.

The **HilOut** algorithm is an example of this approach. HilOut finds distance-based outliers, but uses the ranks of distance instead of the absolute distance in outlier detection. Specifically, for each object, o, HilOut finds the k-nearest neighbors of o, denoted by $nn_1(o), \ldots, nn_k(o)$, where k is an application-dependent parameter. The weight of object o is defined as

$$w(o) = \sum_{i=1}^{k} dist(o, nn_i(o)).$$

(12.21)

All objects are ranked in weight-descending order. The top-*l* objects in weight are output as outliers, where *l* is another user-specified parameter.

Computing the *k*-nearest neighbors for every object is costly and does not scale up when the dimensionality is high and the database is large. To address the scalability issue, HilOut employs space-filling curves to achieve an approximation algorithm, which is scalable in both running time and space with respect to database size and dimensionality.

While some methods like HilOut detect outliers in the full space despite the high dimensionality, other methods reduce the high-dimensional outlier detection problem to a lower-dimensional one by dimensionality reduction (Chapter 3). The idea is to reduce the high-dimensional space to a lower-dimensional space where normal instances can still be distinguished from outliers. If such a lower-dimensional space can be found, then conventional outlier detection methods can be applied.

To reduce dimensionality, general feature selection and extraction methods may be used or extended for outlier detection. For example, principal components analysis (PCA) can be used to extract a lower-dimensional space. Heuristically, the principal components with low variance are preferred because, on such dimensions, normal objects are likely close to each other and outliers often deviate from the majority.

By extending conventional outlier detection methods, we can reuse much of the experience gained from research in the field. These new methods, however, are limited. First, they cannot detect outliers with respect to subspaces and thus have limited interpretability. Second, dimensionality reduction is feasible only if there exists a lower-dimensional space where normal objects and outliers are well separated. This assumption may not hold true.

12.8.2 Finding Outliers in Subspaces

Another approach for outlier detection in high-dimensional data is to search for outliers in various subspaces. A unique advantage is that, if an object is found to be an outlier in a subspace of much lower dimensionality, the subspace provides critical information for interpreting *why* and *to what extent* the object is an outlier. This insight is highly valuable in applications with high-dimensional data due to the overwhelming number of dimensions.

Example 12.24 Outliers in subspaces. As a customer-relationship manager at *AllElectronics*, you are interested in finding outlier customers. *AllElectronics* maintains an extensive customer information database, which contains many attributes and the transaction history of customers. The database is high dimensional.

Suppose you find that a customer, Alice, is an outlier in a lower-dimensional subspace that contains the dimensions *average_transaction_amount* and *purchase_frequency*, such that her average transaction amount is substantially larger than the majority of the customers, and her purchase frequency is dramatically lower. The subspace itself speaks for why and to what extent Alice is an outlier. Using this information, you strategically decide to approach Alice by suggesting options that could improve her purchase frequency at *AllElectronics*.   ∎

"How can we detect outliers in subspaces?" We use a *grid-based subspace outlier detection method* to illustrate. The major ideas are as follows. We consider projections of the data onto various subspaces. If, in a subspace, we find an area that has a density that is much lower than average, then the area may contain outliers. To find such projections, we first discretize the data into a grid in an equal-depth way. That is, each dimension is partitioned into ϕ equal-depth ranges, where each range contains a fraction, f, of the objects $\left(f = \frac{1}{\phi} \right)$. Equal-depth partitioning is used because data along different dimensions may have different localities. An equal-width partitioning of the space may not be able to reflect such differences in locality.

Next, we search for regions defined by ranges in subspaces that are significantly sparse. To quantify what we mean by "significantly sparse," let's consider a k-dimensional cube formed by k ranges on k dimensions. Suppose the data set contains n objects. If the objects are independently distributed, the expected number of objects falling into a k-dimensional region is $\left(\frac{1}{\phi} \right)^k n = f^k n$. The standard deviation of the number of points in a k-dimensional region is $\sqrt{f^k(1 - f^k)n}$. Suppose a specific k-dimensional cube C has $n(C)$ objects. We can define the **sparsity coefficient** of C as

$$S(C) = \frac{n(C) - f^k n}{\sqrt{f^k(1 - f^k)n}}. \tag{12.22}$$

If $S(C) < 0$, then C contains fewer objects than expected. The smaller the value of $S(C)$ (i.e., the more negative), the sparser C is and the more likely the objects in C are outliers in the subspace.

By assuming $S(C)$ follows a normal distribution, we can use normal distribution tables to determine the probabilistic significance level for an object that deviates dramatically from the average for an a priori assumption of the data following a uniform distribution. In general, the assumption of uniform distribution does not hold. However, the sparsity coefficient still provides an intuitive measure of the "outlier-ness" of a region.

To find cubes of significantly small sparsity coefficient values, a brute-force approach is to search every cube in every possible subspace. The cost of this, however, is immediately exponential. An *evolutionary search* can be conducted, which improves efficiency at the expense of accuracy. For details, please refer to the bibliographic notes (Section 12.11). The objects contained by cubes of very small sparsity coefficient values are output as outliers.

In summary, searching for outliers in subspaces is advantageous in that the outliers found tend to be better understood, owing to the context provided by the subspaces. Challenges include making the search efficient and scalable.

12.8.3 Modeling High-Dimensional Outliers

An alternative approach for outlier detection methods in high-dimensional data tries to develop new models for high-dimensional outliers directly. Such models typically avoid proximity measures and instead adopt new heuristics to detect outliers, which do not deteriorate in high-dimensional data.

Let's examine *angle-based outlier detection* (ABOD) as an example.

Example 12.25 **Angle-based outliers.** Figure 12.15 contains a set of points forming a cluster, with the exception of *c*, which is an outlier. For each point *o*, we examine the angle $\angle xoy$ for every pair of points *x*, *y* such that $x \neq o, y \neq o$. The figure shows angle $\angle dae$ as an example.

Note that for a point in the center of a cluster (e.g., *a*), the angles formed as such differ widely. For a point that is at the border of a cluster (e.g., *b*), the angle variation is smaller. For a point that is an outlier (e.g., *c*), the angle variable is substantially smaller. This observation suggests that we can use the variance of angles for a point to determine whether a point is an outlier. ∎

We can combine angles and distance to model outliers. Mathematically, for each point *o*, we use the distance-weighted angle variance as the outlier score. That is, given a set of points, *D*, for a point, $o \in D$, we define the **angle-based outlier factor** (ABOF) as

$$ABOF(o) = VAR_{x,y \in D, x \neq o, y \neq o} \frac{\langle \vec{ox}, \vec{oy} \rangle}{dist(o,x)^2 \, dist(o,y)^2}, \tag{12.23}$$

where $\langle , \rangle$ is the scalar product operator, and $dist(,)$ is a norm distance.

Clearly, the farther away a point is from clusters and the smaller the variance of the angles of a point, the smaller the ABOF. The ABOD computes the ABOF for each point, and outputs a list of the points in the data set in ABOF-ascending order.

Computing the exact ABOF for every point in a database is costly, requiring a time complexity of $O(n^3)$, where *n* is the number of points in the database. Obviously, this exact algorithm does not scale up for large data sets. Approximation methods have been developed to speed up the computation. The angle-based outlier detection idea has been generalized to handle arbitrary data types. For additional details, see the bibliographic notes (Section 12.11).

Developing native models for high-dimensional outliers can lead to effective methods. However, finding good heuristics for detecting high-dimensional outliers is difficult. Efficiency and scalability on large and high-dimensional data sets are major challenges.

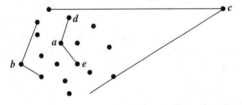

Figure 12.15 Angle-based outliers.

12.9 Summary

- Assume that a given statistical process is used to generate a set of data objects. An **outlier** is a data object that deviates significantly from the rest of the objects, as if it were generated by a different mechanism.

- **Types of outliers** include global outliers, contextual outliers, and collective outliers. An object may be more than one type of outlier.

- **Global outliers** are the simplest form of outlier and the easiest to detect. A **contextual outlier** deviates significantly with respect to a specific context of the object (e.g., a Toronto temperature value of 28°C is an outlier if it occurs in the context of winter). A subset of data objects forms a **collective outlier** if the objects as a whole deviate significantly from the entire data set, even though the individual data objects may not be outliers. Collective outlier detection requires background information to model the relationships among objects to find outlier groups.

- **Challenges** in outlier detection include finding appropriate data models, the dependence of outlier detection systems on the application involved, finding ways to distinguish outliers from noise, and providing justification for identifying outliers as such.

- Outlier detection methods can be **categorized** according to whether the sample of data for analysis is given with expert-provided labels that can be used to build an outlier detection model. In this case, the detection methods are *supervised, semi-supervised,* or *unsupervised.* Alternatively, outlier detection methods may be organized according to their assumptions regarding normal objects versus outliers. This categorization includes *statistical* methods, *proximity-based* methods, and *clustering-based* methods.

- **Statistical outlier detection methods** (or **model-based methods**) assume that the normal data objects follow a statistical model, where data not following the model are considered outliers. Such methods may be *parametric* (they assume that the data are generated by a parametric distribution) or *nonparametric* (they learn a model for the data, rather than assuming one a priori). Parametric methods for multivariate data may employ the Mahalanobis distance, the χ^2-statistic, or a mixture of multiple parametric models. Histograms and kernel density estimation are examples of nonparametric methods.

- **Proximity-based outlier detection methods** assume that an object is an outlier if the proximity of the object to its nearest neighbors significantly deviates from the proximity of most of the other objects to their neighbors in the same data set. *Distance-based outlier detection methods* consult the *neighborhood* of an object, defined by a given radius. An object is an outlier if its neighborhood does not have enough other points. In *density-based outlier detection methods*, an object is an outlier if its density is relatively much lower than that of its neighbors.

- **Clustering-based outlier detection methods** assume that the normal data objects belong to large and dense clusters, whereas outliers belong to small or sparse clusters, or do not belong to any clusters.

- **Classification-based outlier detection methods** often use a one-class model. That is, a classifier is built to describe only the normal class. Any samples that do not belong to the normal class are regarded as outliers.

- **Contextual outlier detection** and **collective outlier detection** explore structures in the data. In contextual outlier detection, the structures are defined as contexts using contextual attributes. In collective outlier detection, the structures are implicit and are explored as part of the mining process. To detect such outliers, one approach transforms the problem into one of conventional outlier detection. Another approach models the structures directly.

- **Outlier detection methods for high-dimensional data** can be divided into three main approaches. These include extending conventional outlier detection, finding outliers in subspaces, and modeling high-dimensional outliers.

12.10 Exercises

12.1 Give an application example where global outliers, contextual outliers, and collective outliers are all interesting. What are the attributes, and what are the contextual and behavioral attributes? How is the relationship among objects modeled in collective outlier detection?

12.2 Give an application example of where the border between normal objects and outliers is often unclear, so that the degree to which an object is an outlier has to be well estimated.

12.3 Adapt a simple semi-supervised method for outlier detection. Discuss the scenario where you have (a) only some labeled examples of normal objects, and (b) only some labeled examples of outliers.

12.4 Using an equal-depth histogram, design a way to assign an object an outlier score.

12.5 Consider the nested loop approach to mining distance-based outliers (Figure 12.6). Suppose the objects in a data set are arranged randomly, that is, each object has the same probability to appear in a position. Show that when the number of outlier objects is small with respect to the total number of objects in the whole data set, the expected number of distance calculations is linear to the number of objects.

12.6 In the density-based outlier detection method of Section 12.4.3, the definition of local reachability density has a potential problem: $lrd_k(o) = \infty$ may occur. Explain why this may occur and propose a fix to the issue.

12.7 Because clusters may form a hierarchy, outliers may belong to different granularity levels. Propose a clustering-based outlier detection method that can find outliers at different levels.

12.8 In outlier detection by semi-supervised learning, what is the advantage of using objects without labels in the training data set?

12.9 To understand why angle-based outlier detection is a heuristic method, give an example where it does not work well. Can you come up with a method to overcome this issue?

12.11 Bibliographic Notes

Hawkins [Haw80] defined outliers from a statistics angle. For surveys or tutorials on the subject of outlier and anomaly detection, see Chandola, Banerjee, and Kumar [CBK09]; Hodge and Austin [HA04]; Agyemang, Barker, and Alhajj [ABA06]; Markou and Singh [MS03a, MS03b]; Patcha and Park [PP07]; Beckman and Cook [BC83]; Ben-Gal [B-G05]; and Bakar, Mohemad, Ahmad, and Deris [BMAD06]. Song, Wu, Jermaine, et al. [SWJR-07] proposed the notion of conditional anomaly and contextual outlier detection.

Fujimaki, Yairi, and Machida [FYM05] presented an example of semi-supervised outlier detection using a set of labeled "normal" objects. For an example of semi-supervised outlier detection using labeled outliers, see Dasgupta and Majumdar [DM02].

Shewhart [She31] assumed that most objects follow a Gaussian distribution and used 3σ as the threshold for identifying outliers, where σ is the standard deviation. Boxplots are used to detect and visualize outliers in various applications such as medical data (Horn, Feng, Li, and Pesce [HFLP01]). Grubb's test was described by Grubbs [Gru69], Stefansky [Ste72], and Anscombe and Guttman [AG60]. Laurikkala, Juhola, and Kentala [LJK00] and Aggarwal and Yu [AY01] extended Grubb's test to detect multivariate outliers. Use of the χ^2-statistic to detect multivariate outliers was studied by Ye and Chen [YC01].

Agarwal [Aga06] used Gaussian mixture models to capture "normal data." Abraham and Box [AB79] assumed that outliers are generated by a normal distribution with a substantially larger variance. Eskin [Esk00] used the EM algorithm to learn mixture models for normal data and outliers.

Histogram-based outlier detection methods are popular in the application domain of intrusion detection (Eskin [Esk00] and Eskin, Arnold, Prerau, et al. [EAP$^+$02]) and fault detection (Fawcett and Provost [FP97]).

The notion of distance-based outliers was developed by Knorr and Ng [KN97]. The index-based, nested loop–based, and grid-based approaches were explored (Knorr and Ng [KN98] and Knorr, Ng, and Tucakov [KNT00]) to speed up distance-based outlier detection. Bay and Schwabacher [BS03] and Jin, Tung, and Han [JTH01] pointed out that the CPU runtime of the nested loop method is often scalable with respect to database size. Tao, Xiao, and Zhou [TXZ06] presented an algorithm that finds all distance-based outliers by scanning the database three times with fixed main memory. For larger memory size, they proposed a method that uses only one or two scans.

The notion of density-based outliers was first developed by Breunig, Kriegel, Ng, and Sander [BKNS00]. Various methods proposed with the theme of density-based outlier detection include Jin, Tung, and Han [JTH01]; Jin, Tung, Han, and Wang [JTHW06]; and Papadimitriou, Kitagawa, Gibbons, et al. [PKG-F03]. The variations differ in how they estimate density.

The bootstrap method discussed in Example 12.17 was developed by Barbara, Li, Couto, et al. [BLC+03]. The FindCBOLF algorithm was given by He, Xu, and Deng [HXD03]. For the use of fixed-width clustering in outlier detection methods, see Eskin, Arnold, and Prerau, et al. [EAP+02]; Mahoney and Chan [MC03]; and He, Xu, and Deng [HXD03]. Barbara, Wu, and Jajodia [BWJ01] used multiclass classification in network intrusion detection.

Song, Wu, Jermaine, et al. [SWJR07] and Fawcet and Provost [FP97] presented a method to reduce the problem of contextual outlier detection to one of conventional outlier detection. Yi, Sidiropoulos, Johnson, Jagadish, et al. [YSJJ+00] used regression techniques to detect contextual outliers in co-evolving sequences. The idea in Example 12.22 for collective outlier detection on graph data is based on Noble and Cook [NC03].

The HilOut algorithm was proposed by Angiulli and Pizzuti [AP05]. Aggarwal and Yu [AY01] developed the sparsity coefficient–based subspace outlier detection method. Kriegel, Schubert, and Zimek [KSZ08] proposed angle-based outlier detection.

Data Mining Trends and Research Frontiers

As a young research field, data mining has made significant progress and covered a broad spectrum of applications since the 1980s. Today, data mining is used in a vast array of areas. Numerous commercial data mining systems and services are available. Many challenges, however, still remain. In this final chapter, we introduce the mining of complex data types as a prelude to further in-depth study readers may choose to do. In addition, we focus on trends and research frontiers in data mining. Section 13.1 presents an overview of methodologies for mining complex data types, which extend the concepts and tasks introduced in this book. Such mining includes mining time-series, sequential patterns, and biological sequences; graphs and networks; spatiotemporal data, including geospatial data, moving-object data, and cyber-physical system data; multimedia data; text data; web data; and data streams. Section 13.2 briefly introduces other approaches to data mining, including statistical methods, theoretical foundations, and visual and audio data mining.

In Section 13.3, you will learn more about data mining applications in business and in science, including the financial retail, and telecommunication industries, science and engineering, and recommender systems. The social impacts of data mining are discussed in Section 13.4, including ubiquitous and invisible data mining, and privacy-preserving data mining. Finally, in Section 13.5 we speculate on current and expected data mining trends that arise in response to new challenges in the field.

13.1 Mining Complex Data Types

In this section, we outline the major developments and research efforts in mining complex data types. Complex data types are summarized in Figure 13.1. Section 13.1.1 covers mining sequence data such as time-series, symbolic sequences, and biological sequences. Section 13.1.2 discusses mining graphs and social and information networks. Section 13.1.3 addresses mining other kinds of data, including spatial data, spatiotemporal data, moving-object data, cyber-physical system data, multimedia data, text data,

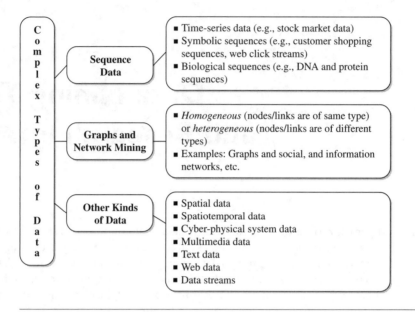

Figure 13.1 Complex data types for mining.

web data, and data streams. Due to the broad scope of these themes, this section presents only a high-level overview; these topics are not discussed in-depth in this book.

13.1.1 Mining Sequence Data: Time-Series, Symbolic Sequences, and Biological Sequences

A **sequence** is an ordered list of events. Sequences may be categorized into three groups, based on the characteristics of the events they describe: (1) *time-series data*, (2) *symbolic sequence data*, and (3) *biological sequences*. Let's consider each type.

In **time-series data**, sequence data consist of long sequences of numeric data, recorded at equal time intervals (e.g., per minute, per hour, or per day). Time-series data can be generated by many natural and economic processes such as stock markets, and scientific, medical, or natural observations.

Symbolic sequence data consist of long sequences of event or nominal data, which typically are not observed at equal time intervals. For many such sequences, *gaps* (i.e., lapses between recorded events) do not matter much. Examples include customer shopping sequences and web click streams, as well as sequences of events in science and engineering and in natural and social developments.

Biological sequences include DNA and protein sequences. Such sequences are typically very long, and carry important, complicated, but hidden semantic meaning. Here, gaps are usually important.

Let's look into data mining for each of these sequence data types.

Similarity Search in Time-Series Data

A **time-series data set** consists of sequences of numeric values obtained over repeated measurements of time. The values are typically measured at equal time intervals (e.g., every minute, hour, or day). Time-series databases are popular in many applications such as stock market analysis, economic and sales forecasting, budgetary analysis, utility studies, inventory studies, yield projections, workload projections, and process and quality control. They are also useful for studying natural phenomena (e.g., atmosphere, temperature, wind, earthquake), scientific and engineering experiments, and medical treatments.

Unlike normal database queries, which find data that match a given query *exactly*, a **similarity search** finds data sequences that *differ only slightly* from the given query sequence. Many time-series similarity queries require **subsequence matching**, that is, finding a set of sequences that contain subsequences that are similar to a given query sequence.

For similarity search, it is often necessary to first perform *data or dimensionality reduction and transformation* of time-series data. Typical *dimensionality reduction* techniques include (1) the *discrete Fourier transform (DFT)*, (2) *discrete wavelet transforms (DWT)*, and (3) *singular value decomposition (SVD)* based on *principle components analysis (PCA)*. Because we touched on these concepts in Chapter 3, and because a thorough explanation is beyond the scope of this book, we will not go into great detail here. With such techniques, the data or signal is mapped to a signal in a *transformed space*. A small subset of the "strongest" transformed coefficients are saved as features.

These features form a *feature space*, which is a projection of the transformed space. Indices can be constructed on the original or transformed time-series data to speed up a search. For a query-based similarity search, techniques include normalization transformation, atomic matching (i.e., finding pairs of gap-free windows of a small length that are similar), window stitching (i.e., stitching similar windows to form pairs of large similar subsequences, allowing gaps between atomic matches), and subsequence ordering (i.e., linearly ordering the subsequence matches to determine whether enough similar pieces exist). Numerous software packages exist for a similarity search in time-series data.

Recently, researchers have proposed transforming time-series data into piecewise aggregate approximations so that the data can be viewed as a sequence of symbolic representations. The problem of similarity search is then transformed into one of matching subsequences in symbolic sequence data. We can identify *motifs* (i.e., frequently occurring sequential patterns) and build index or hashing mechanisms for an efficient search based on such motifs. Experiments show this approach is fast and simple, and has comparable search quality to that of DFT, DWT, and other dimensionality reduction methods.

Regression and Trend Analysis in Time-Series Data

Regression analysis of time-series data has been studied substantially in the fields of statistics and signal analysis. However, one may often need to go beyond pure regression

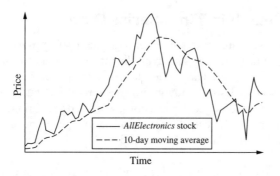

Figure 13.2 Time-series data for the stock price of *AllElectronics* over time. The *trend* is shown with a dashed curve, calculated by a moving average.

analysis and perform *trend analysis* for many practical applications. Trend analysis builds an integrated model using the following four major *components* or *movements* to characterize time-series data:

1. **Trend or long-term movements**: These indicate the general direction in which a time-series graph is moving over time, for example, using *weighted moving average* and the *least squares* methods to find *trend curves* such as the dashed curve indicated in Figure 13.2.

2. **Cyclic movements**: These are the long-term oscillations about a trend line or curve.

3. **Seasonal variations**: These are nearly identical patterns that a time series appears to follow during corresponding seasons of successive years such as holiday shopping seasons. For effective trend analysis, the data often need to be "deseasonalized" based on a **seasonal index** computed by autocorrelation.

4. **Random movements**: These characterize sporadic changes due to chance events such as labor disputes or announced personnel changes within companies.

Trend analysis can also be used for **time-series forecasting**, that is, finding a mathematical function that will approximately generate the historic patterns in a time series, and using it to make long-term or short-term predictions of future values. *ARIMA (auto-regressive integrated moving average)*, *long-memory time-series modeling*, and *autoregression* are popular methods for such analysis.

Sequential Pattern Mining in Symbolic Sequences

A **symbolic sequence** consists of an ordered set of elements or events, recorded with or without a concrete notion of time. There are many applications involving data of symbolic sequences such as customer shopping sequences, web click streams, program execution sequences, biological sequences, and sequences of events in science and engineering and in natural and social developments. Because biological sequences carry very complicated semantic meaning and pose many challenging research issues, most investigations are conducted in the field of bioinformatics.

Sequential pattern mining has focused extensively on mining symbolic sequences. A sequential pattern is a frequent subsequence existing in a single sequence or a set of sequences. A sequence $\alpha = \langle a_1 a_2 \cdots a_n \rangle$ is a **subsequence** of another sequence $\beta = \langle b_1 b_2 \cdots b_m \rangle$ if there exist integers $1 \leq j_1 < j_2 < \cdots < j_n \leq m$ such that $a_1 \subseteq b_{j_1}$, $a_2 \subseteq b_{j_2}, \ldots, a_n \subseteq b_{j_n}$. For example, if $\alpha = \langle \{ab\}, d \rangle$ and $\beta = \langle \{abc\}, \{be\}, \{de\}, a \rangle$, where a, b, c, d, and e are items, then α is a subsequence of β. Mining of sequential patterns consists of mining the set of subsequences that are frequent in one sequence or a set of sequences. Many scalable algorithms have been developed as a result of extensive studies in this area. Alternatively, we can mine only the *set of closed* sequential patterns, where a sequential pattern s is **closed** if there exists no sequential pattern s', where s is a *proper* subsequence of s', and s' has the same (frequency) support as s. Similar to its frequent pattern mining counterpart, there are also studies on efficient mining of **multidimensional, multilevel sequential patterns**.

As with constraint-based frequent pattern mining, user-specified constraints can be used to reduce the search space in sequential pattern mining and derive only the patterns that are of interest to the user. This is referred to as **constraint-based sequential pattern mining**. Moreover, we may relax constraints or enforce additional constraints on the problem of sequential pattern mining to derive different kinds of patterns from sequence data. For example, we can enforce gap constraints so that the patterns derived contain only consecutive subsequences or subsequences with very small gaps. Alternatively, we may derive periodic sequential patterns by folding events into proper-size windows and finding recurring subsequences in these windows. Another approach derives *partial order patterns* by relaxing the requirement of strict sequential ordering in the mining of subsequence patterns. Besides mining partial order patterns, sequential pattern mining methodology can also be extended to mining trees, lattices, episodes, and some other ordered patterns.

Sequence Classification

Most classification methods perform model construction based on feature vectors. However, sequences do not have explicit features. Even with sophisticated feature selection techniques, the dimensionality of potential features can still be very high and the sequential nature of features is difficult to capture. This makes sequence classification a challenging task.

Sequence classification methods can be organized into three categories: (1) feature-based classification, which transforms a sequence into a feature vector and then applies conventional classification methods; (2) sequence distance–based classification, where the distance function that measures the similarity between sequences determines the quality of the classification significantly; and (3) model-based classification such as using hidden Markov model (HMM) or other statistical models to classify sequences.

For time-series or other numeric-valued data, the feature selection techniques for symbolic sequences cannot be easily applied to time-series data without discretization. However, discretization can cause information loss. A recently proposed time-series *shapelets method* uses the time-series subsequences that can maximally represent a class as the features. It achieves quality classification results.

Alignment of Biological Sequences

Biological sequences generally refer to sequences of nucleotides or amino acids. **Biological sequence analysis** compares, aligns, indexes, and analyzes biological sequences and thus plays a crucial role in bioinformatics and modern biology.

Sequence alignment is based on the fact that all living organisms are related by evolution. This implies that the nucleotide (DNA, RNA) and protein sequences of species that are closer to each other in evolution should exhibit more similarities. An **alignment** is the process of lining up sequences to achieve a maximal identity level, which also expresses the degree of similarity between sequences. Two sequences are **homologous** if they share a common ancestor. The degree of similarity obtained by sequence alignment can be useful in determining the possibility of homology between two sequences. Such an alignment also helps determine the relative positions of multiple species in an evolution tree, which is called a **phylogenetic tree**.

The problem of alignment of biological sequences can be described as follows: *Given two or more input biological sequences, identify similar sequences with long conserved subsequences.* If the number of sequences to be aligned is exactly two, the problem is known as **pairwise sequence alignment**; otherwise, it is **multiple sequence alignment**. The sequences to be compared and aligned can be either nucleotides (DNA/RNA) or amino acids (proteins). For nucleotides, two symbols align if they are identical. However, for amino acids, two symbols align if they are identical, or if one can be derived from the other by substitutions that are likely to occur in nature. There are two kinds of alignments: *local alignments* and *global alignments*. The former means that only portions of the sequences are aligned, whereas the latter requires alignment over the entire length of the sequences.

For either nucleotides or amino acids, insertions, deletions, and substitutions occur in nature with different probabilities. **Substitution matrices** are used to represent the probabilities of substitutions of nucleotides or amino acids and probabilities of insertions and deletions. Usually, we use the gap character, −, to indicate positions where it is preferable not to align two symbols. To evaluate the quality of alignments, a *scoring* mechanism is typically defined, which usually counts identical or similar symbols as positive scores and gaps as negative ones. The algebraic sum of the scores is taken as the alignment measure. The goal of alignment is to achieve the maximal score among all the possible alignments. However, it is very expensive (more exactly, an NP-hard problem) to find optimal alignment. Therefore, various heuristic methods have been developed to find suboptimal alignments.

The dynamic programming approach is commonly used for sequence alignments. Among many available analysis packages, BLAST (Basic Local Alignment Search Tool) is one of the most popular tools in biosequence analysis.

Hidden Markov Model for Biological Sequence Analysis

Given a biological sequence, biologists would like to analyze what that sequence represents. To represent the structure or statistical regularities of sequence classes, biologists construct various probabilistic models such as *Markov chains* and *hidden Markov models*. In both models, the probability of a state depends only on that of the previous state; therefore, they are particularly useful for the analysis of biological sequence data. The most common methods for constructing hidden Markov models are the forward algorithm, the Viterbi algorithm, and the Baum-Welch algorithm. Given a sequence of symbols, x, the *forward algorithm* finds the probability of obtaining x in the model; the *Viterbi algorithm* finds the most probable path (corresponding to x) through the model, whereas the *Baum-Welch algorithm* learns or adjusts the model parameters so as to best explain a set of training sequences.

13.1.2 Mining Graphs and Networks

Graphs represents a more general class of structures than sets, sequences, lattices, and trees. There is a broad range of graph applications on the Web and in social networks, information networks, biological networks, bioinformatics, chemical informatics, computer vision, and multimedia and text retrieval. Hence, graph and network mining have become increasingly important and heavily researched. We overview the following major themes: (1) graph pattern mining; (2) statistical modeling of networks; (3) data cleaning, integration, and validation by network analysis; (4) clustering and classification of graphs and homogeneous networks; (5) clustering, ranking, and classification of heterogeneous networks; (6) role discovery and link prediction in information networks; (7) similarity search and OLAP in information networks; and (8) evolution of information networks.

Graph Pattern Mining

Graph pattern mining is the mining of *frequent subgraphs* (also called (**sub**)**graph patterns**) in one or a set of graphs. Methods for mining graph patterns can be categorized into Apriori-based and pattern growth–based approaches. Alternatively, we can mine the set of *closed graphs* where a graph g is *closed* if there exists no proper supergraph g' that carries the same support count as g. Moreover, there are many *variant graph patterns*, including approximate frequent graphs, coherent graphs, and dense graphs. User-specified constraints can be pushed deep into the graph pattern mining process to improve mining efficiency.

Graph pattern mining has many interesting applications. For example, it can be used to generate compact and effective *graph index structures* based on the concept of frequent and discriminative graph patterns. Approximate *structure similarity search* can be achieved by exploring graph index structures and multiple graph features. Moreover, classification of graphs can also be performed effectively using frequent and discriminative subgraphs as features.

Statistical Modeling of Networks

A **network** consists of a set of *nodes*, each corresponding to an *object* associated with a set of properties, and a set of *edges* (or *links*) connecting those nodes, representing relationships between objects. A network is **homogeneous** if all the nodes and links are of the same type, such as a friend network, a coauthor network, or a web page network. A network is **heterogeneous** if the nodes and links are of different types, such as publication networks (linking together authors, conferences, papers, and contents), and health-care networks (linking together doctors, nurses, patients, diseases, and treatments).

Researchers have proposed multiple statistical models for modeling homogeneous networks. The most well-known generative models are the random graph model (i.e., the Erdös-Rényi model), the Watts-Strogatz model, and the scale-free model. The scale-free model assumes that the network follows the *power law distribution* (also known as the *Pareto distribution* or the *heavy-tailed distribution*). In most large-scale social networks, a **small-world phenomenon** is observed, that is, the network can be characterized as having a high degree of local clustering for a small fraction of the nodes (i.e., these nodes are interconnected with one another), while being no more than a few degrees of separation from the remaining nodes.

Social networks exhibit certain evolutionary characteristics. They tend to follow the **densification power law**, which states that networks become increasingly *dense* over time. **Shrinking diameter** is another characteristic, where the effective diameter often *decreases* as the network grows. Node *out-degrees* and *in-degrees* typically follow a heavy-tailed distribution.

Data Cleaning, Integration, and Validation by Information Network Analysis

Real-world data are often incomplete, noisy, uncertain, and unreliable. Information redundancy may exist among the multiple pieces of data that are interconnected in a large network. Information redundancy can be explored in such networks to perform quality data cleaning, data integration, information validation, and trustability analysis by network analysis. For example, we can distinguish authors who share the same names by examining the networked connections with other heterogeneous objects such as coauthors, publication venues, and terms. In addition, we can identify inaccurate author information presented by booksellers by exploring a network built based on author information provided by multiple booksellers.

Sophisticated information network analysis methods have been developed in this direction, and in many cases, portions of the data serve as the "training set." That is, relatively clean and reliable data or a consensus of data from multiple information providers can be used to help consolidate the remaining, unreliable portions of the data. This reduces the costly efforts of labeling the data by hand and of training on massive, dynamic, real-world data sets.

Clustering and Classification of Graphs and Homogeneous Networks

Large graphs and networks have cohesive structures, which are often hidden among their massive, interconnected nodes and links. Cluster analysis methods have been developed on large networks to uncover network structures, discover hidden communities, hubs, and outliers based on network topological structures and their associated properties. Various kinds of network clustering methods have been developed and can be categorized as either partitioning, hierarchical, or density-based algorithms. Moreover, given human-labeled training data, the discovery of network structures can be guided by human-specified heuristic constraints. Supervised classification and semi-supervised classification of networks are recent hot topics in the data mining research community.

Clustering, Ranking, and Classification of Heterogeneous Networks

A heterogeneous network contains interconnected nodes and links of different types. Such interconnected structures contain rich information, which can be used to mutually enhance nodes and links, and propagate knowledge from one type to another. Clustering and ranking of such heterogeneous networks can be performed hand-in-hand in the context that highly ranked nodes/links in a cluster may contribute more than their lower-ranked counterparts in the evaluation of the cohesiveness of a cluster. Clustering may help consolidate the high ranking of objects/links dedicated to the cluster. Such mutual enhancement of ranking and clustering prompted the development of an algorithm called RankClus. Moreover, users may specify different ranking rules or present labeled nodes/links for certain data types. Knowledge of one type can be propagated to other types. Such propagation reaches the nodes/links of the same type via heterogeneous-type connections. Algorithms have been developed for supervised learning and semi-supervised learning in heterogeneous networks.

Role Discovery and Link Prediction in Information Networks

There exist many hidden roles or relationships among different nodes/links in a heterogeneous network. Examples include advisor–advisee and leader–follower relationships in a research publication network. To discover such hidden roles or relationships, experts can specify constraints based on their background knowledge. Enforcing such constraints may help cross-checking and validation in large interconnected networks. Information redundancy in a network can often be used to help weed out objects/links that do not follow such constraints.

Similarly, *link prediction* can be performed based on the assessment of the ranking of the expected relationships among the candidate nodes/links. For example, we may predict which papers an author may write, read, or cite, based on the author's recent publication history and the trend of research on similar topics. Such studies often require analyzing the proximity of network nodes/links and the trends and connections of their similar neighbors. Roughly speaking, people refer to link prediction as **link mining**; however, link mining covers additional tasks including *link-based object classification*, *object type prediction*, *link type prediction*, *link existence prediction*, *link cardinality estimation*, and *object reconciliation* (which predicts whether two objects are, in fact, the same). It also includes *group detection* (which clusters objects), as well as *subgraph identification* (which finds characteristic subgraphs within networks) and *metadata mining* (which uncovers schema-type information regarding unstructured data).

Similarity Search and OLAP in Information Networks

Similarity search is a primitive operation in database and web search engines. A heterogeneous information network consists of multityped, interconnected objects. Examples include bibliographic networks and social media networks, where two objects are considered similar if they are linked in a similar way with multityped objects. In general, object similarity within a network can be determined based on network structures and object properties, and with similarity measures. Moreover, network clusters and hierarchical network structures help organize objects in a network and identify subcommunities, as well as facilitate similarity search. Furthermore, similarity can be defined differently per user. By considering different linkage paths, we can derive various similarity semantics in a network, which is known as *path-based similarity*.

By organizing networks based on the notion of similarity and clusters, we can generate multiple hierarchies within a network. Online analytical processing (OLAP) can then be performed. For example, we can drill down or dice information networks based on different levels of abstraction and different angles of views. OLAP operations may generate multiple, interrelated networks. The relationships among such networks may disclose interesting hidden semantics.

Evolution of Social and Information Networks

Networks are dynamic and constantly evolving. Detecting evolving communities and evolving regularities or anomalies in homogeneous or heterogeneous networks can help people better understand the structural evolution of networks and predict trends and irregularities in evolving networks. For homogeneous networks, the evolving communities discovered are subnetworks consisting of objects of the same type such as a set of friends or coauthors. However, for heterogeneous networks, the communities discovered are subnetworks consisting of objects of different types, such as a connected set of papers, authors, venues, and terms, from which we can also derive a set of evolving objects for each type, like evolving authors and themes.

13.1.3 Mining Other Kinds of Data

In addition to sequences and graphs, there are many other kinds of semi-structured or unstructured data, such as spatiotemporal, multimedia, and hypertext data, which have interesting applications. Such data carry various kinds of semantics, are either stored in or dynamically streamed through a system, and call for specialized data mining methodologies. Thus, mining multiple kinds of data, including *spatial data, spatiotemporal data, cyber-physical system data, multimedia data, text data, web data,* and *data streams,* are increasingly important tasks in data mining. In this subsection, we overview the methodologies for mining these kinds of data.

Mining Spatial Data

Spatial data mining discovers patterns and knowledge from spatial data. Spatial data, in many cases, refer to geospace-related data stored in geospatial data repositories. The data can be in "vector" or "raster" formats, or in the form of imagery and geo-referenced multimedia. Recently, large *geographic data warehouses* have been constructed by integrating thematic and geographically referenced data from multiple sources. From these, we can construct *spatial data cubes* that contain spatial dimensions and measures, and support *spatial OLAP* for *multidimensional spatial data analysis*. Spatial data mining can be performed on spatial data warehouses, spatial databases, and other geospatial data repositories. Popular topics on geographic knowledge discovery and spatial data mining include *mining spatial associations and co-location patterns, spatial clustering, spatial classification, spatial modeling,* and *spatial trend and outlier analysis*.

Mining Spatiotemporal Data and Moving Objects

Spatiotemporal data are data that relate to both space and time. **Spatiotemporal data mining** refers to the process of discovering patterns and knowledge from spatiotemporal data. Typical examples of spatiotemporal data mining include discovering the evolutionary history of cities and lands, uncovering weather patterns, predicting earthquakes and hurricanes, and determining global warming trends. Spatiotemporal data mining has become increasingly important and has far-reaching implications, given the popularity of mobile phones, GPS devices, Internet-based map services, weather services, and digital Earth, as well as satellite, RFID, sensor, wireless, and video technologies.

Among many kinds of spatiotemporal data, *moving-object data* (i.e., data about moving objects) are especially important. For example, animal scientists attach telemetry equipment on wildlife to analyze ecological behavior, mobility managers embed GPS in cars to better monitor and guide vehicles, and meteorologists use weather satellites and radars to observe hurricanes. Massive-scale moving-object data are becoming rich, complex, and ubiquitous. Examples of **moving-object data mining** include mining *movement patterns of multiple moving objects* (i.e., the discovery of relationships among multiple moving objects such as moving clusters, leaders and followers, merge, convoy, swarm, and pincer, as well as other collective movement patterns). Other examples of moving-object data mining include mining *periodic patterns* for one or a set of moving objects, and mining *trajectory patterns, clusters, models,* and *outliers.*

Mining Cyber-Physical System Data

A **cyber-physical system** (CPS) typically consists of a large number of interacting physical and information components. CPS systems may be interconnected so as to form large heterogeneous *cyber-physical networks.* Examples of cyber-physical networks include a patient care system that links a patient monitoring system with a network of patient/medical information and an emergency handling system; a transportation system that links a transportation monitoring network, consisting of many sensors and video cameras, with a traffic information and control system; and a battlefield commander system that links a sensor/reconnaissance network with a battlefield information analysis system. Clearly, cyber-physical systems and networks will be ubiquitous and form a critical component of modern information infrastructure.

Data generated in cyber-physical systems are dynamic, volatile, noisy, inconsistent, and interdependent, containing rich spatiotemporal information, and they are critically important for real-time decision making. In comparison with typical spatiotemporal data mining, mining cyber-physical data requires linking the current situation with a large information base, performing real-time calculations, and returning prompt responses. Research in the area includes rare-event detection and anomaly analysis in cyber-physical data streams, reliability and trustworthiness in cyber-physical data analysis, effective spatiotemporal data analysis in cyber-physical networks, and the integration of stream data mining with real-time automated control processes.

Mining Multimedia Data

Multimedia data mining is the discovery of interesting patterns from multimedia databases that store and manage large collections of multimedia objects, including image data, video data, audio data, as well as sequence data and hypertext data containing text, text markups, and linkages. Multimedia data mining is an interdisciplinary field that integrates image processing and understanding, computer vision, data mining, and pattern recognition. Issues in multimedia data mining include *content-based retrieval and similarity search,* and *generalization and multidimensional analysis.* Multimedia data cubes contain additional dimensions and measures for multimedia information. Other topics in multimedia mining include *classification and prediction analysis, mining associations,* and *video and audio data mining* (Section 13.2.3).

Mining Text Data

Text mining is an interdisciplinary field that draws on information retrieval, data mining, machine learning, statistics, and computational linguistics. A substantial portion of information is stored as text such as news articles, technical papers, books, digital libraries, email messages, blogs, and web pages. Hence, research in text mining has been very active. An important goal is to derive high-quality information from text. This is typically done through the discovery of patterns and trends by means such as statistical pattern learning, topic modeling, and statistical language modeling. Text mining usually requires structuring the input text (e.g., parsing, along with the addition of some derived linguistic features and the removal of others, and subsequent insertion into a database). This is followed by deriving patterns within the structured data, and evaluation and interpretation of the output. "High quality" in text mining usually refers to a combination of relevance, novelty, and interestingness.

Typical text mining tasks include text categorization, text clustering, concept/entity extraction, production of granular taxonomies, sentiment analysis, document summarization, and entity-relation modeling (i.e., learning relations between named entities). Other examples include multilingual data mining, multidimensional text analysis, contextual text mining, and trust and evolution analysis in text data, as well as text mining applications in security, biomedical literature analysis, online media analysis, and analytical customer relationship management. Various kinds of text mining and analysis software and tools are available in academic institutions, open-source forums, and industry. Text mining often also uses WordNet, Sematic Web, Wikipedia, and other information sources to enhance the understanding and mining of text data.

Mining Web Data

The World Wide Web serves as a huge, widely distributed, global information center for news, advertisements, consumer information, financial management, education, government, and e-commerce. It contains a rich and dynamic collection of information about web page contents with hypertext structures and multimedia, hyperlink information, and access and usage information, providing fertile sources for data mining. **Web mining** is the application of data mining techniques to discover patterns, structures, and knowledge from the Web. According to analysis targets, web mining can be organized into three main areas: *web content mining*, *web structure mining*, and *web usage mining*.

Web content mining analyzes web content such as text, multimedia data, and structured data (within web pages or linked across web pages). This is done to understand the content of web pages, provide scalable and informative keyword-based page indexing, entity/concept resolution, web page relevance and ranking, web page content summaries, and other valuable information related to web search and analysis. Web pages can reside either on the *surface web* or on the *deep Web*. The *surface web* is that portion of the Web that is indexed by typical search engines. The *deep Web* (or *hidden Web*) refers to web content that is not part of the surface web. Its contents are provided by underlying database engines.

Web content mining has been studied extensively by researchers, search engines, and other web service companies. Web content mining can build links across multiple web pages for individuals; therefore, it has the potential to inappropriately disclose personal information. Studies on privacy-preserving data mining address this concern through the development of techniques to protect personal privacy on the Web.

Web structure mining is the process of using graph and network mining theory and methods to analyze the nodes and connection structures on the Web. It extracts patterns from hyperlinks, where a hyperlink is a structural component that connects a web page to another location. It can also mine the document structure within a page (e.g., analyze the treelike structure of page structures to describe HTML or XML tag usage). Both kinds of web structure mining help us understand web contents and may also help transform web contents into relatively structured data sets.

Web usage mining is the process of extracting useful information (e.g., user click streams) from server logs. It finds patterns related to general or particular groups of users; understands users' search patterns, trends, and associations; and predicts what users are looking for on the Internet. It helps improve search efficiency and effectiveness, as well as promotes products or related information to different groups of users at the right time. Web search companies routinely conduct web usage mining to improve their quality of service.

Mining Data Streams

Stream data refer to data that flow into a system in vast volumes, change dynamically, are possibly infinite, and contain multidimensional features. Such data cannot be stored in traditional database systems. Moreover, most systems may only be able to read the stream once in sequential order. This poses great challenges for the effective mining of stream data. Substantial research has led to progress in the development of efficient methods for mining data streams, in the areas of mining frequent and sequential patterns, multidimensional analysis (e.g., the construction of stream cubes), classification, clustering, outlier analysis, and the online detection of rare events in data streams. The general philosophy is to develop single-scan or a-few-scan algorithms using limited computing and storage capabilities.

This includes collecting information about stream data in sliding windows or *tilted time windows* (where the most recent data are registered at the finest granularity and the more distant data are registered at a coarser granularity), and exploring techniques like microclustering, limited aggregation, and approximation. Many applications of stream data mining can be explored—for example, real-time detection of anomalies in computer network traffic, botnets, text streams, video streams, power-grid flows, web searches, sensor networks, and cyber-physical systems.

13.2 Other Methodologies of Data Mining

Due to the broad scope of data mining and the large variety of data mining methodologies, not all methodologies of data mining can be thoroughly covered in this book. In this section, we briefly discuss several interesting methodologies that were not fully addressed in the previous chapters. These methodologies are listed in Figure 13.3.

13.2.1 Statistical Data Mining

The data mining techniques described in this book are primarily drawn from computer science disciplines, including data mining, machine learning, data warehousing, and algorithms. They are designed for the efficient handling of huge amounts of data that are

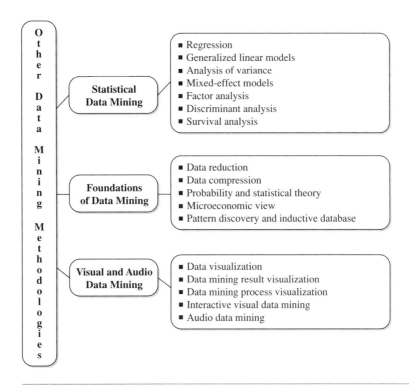

Figure 13.3 Other data mining methodologies.

typically multidimensional and possibly of various complex types. There are, however, many well-established statistical techniques for data analysis, particularly for numeric data. These techniques have been applied extensively to scientific data (e.g., data from experiments in physics, engineering, manufacturing, psychology, and medicine), as well as to data from economics and the social sciences. Some of these techniques, such as principal components analysis (Chapter 3) and clustering (Chapters 10 and 11), have already been addressed in this book. A thorough discussion of major statistical methods for data analysis is beyond the scope of this book; however, several methods are mentioned here for the sake of completeness. Pointers to these techniques are provided in the bibliographic notes (Section 13.8).

- **Regression**: In general, these methods are used to predict the value of a *response* (dependent) variable from one or more *predictor* (independent) variables, where the variables are numeric. There are various forms of regression, such as linear, multiple, weighted, polynomial, nonparametric, and robust (robust methods are useful when errors fail to satisfy normalcy conditions or when the data contain significant outliers).

- **Generalized linear models**: These models, and their generalization (*generalized additive models*), allow a *categorical* (nominal) response variable (or some transformation of it) to be related to a set of predictor variables in a manner similar to the modeling of a numeric response variable using linear regression. Generalized linear models include logistic regression and Poisson regression.

- **Analysis of variance**: These techniques analyze experimental data for two or more populations described by a numeric response variable and one or more categorical variables (*factors*). In general, an ANOVA (single-factor analysis of variance) problem involves a comparison of k population or treatment means to determine if at least two of the means are different. More complex ANOVA problems also exist.

- **Mixed-effect models**: These models are for analyzing grouped data—data that can be classified according to one or more grouping variables. They typically describe relationships between a response variable and some covariates in data grouped according to one or more factors. Common areas of application include multilevel data, repeated measures data, block designs, and longitudinal data.

- **Factor analysis**: This method is used to determine which variables are combined to generate a given factor. For example, for many psychiatric data, it is not possible to measure a certain factor of interest directly (e.g., intelligence); however, it is often possible to measure other quantities (e.g., student test scores) that reflect the factor of interest. Here, none of the variables is designated as dependent.

- **Discriminant analysis**: This technique is used to predict a categorical response variable. Unlike generalized linear models, it assumes that the independent variables follow a multivariate normal distribution. The procedure attempts to determine several discriminant functions (linear combinations of the independent variables) that discriminate among the groups defined by the response variable. Discriminant analysis is commonly used in social sciences.

- **Survival analysis**: Several well-established statistical techniques exist for survival analysis. These techniques originally were designed to predict the probability that a patient undergoing a medical treatment would survive at least to time t. Methods for survival analysis, however, are also commonly applied to manufacturing settings to estimate the life span of industrial equipment. Popular methods include Kaplan-Meier estimates of survival, Cox proportional hazards regression models, and their extensions.

- **Quality control**: Various statistics can be used to prepare charts for quality control, such as Shewhart charts and CUSUM charts (both of which display group summary statistics). These statistics include the mean, standard deviation, range, count, moving average, moving standard deviation, and moving range.

13.2.2 Views on Data Mining Foundations

Research on the theoretical foundations of data mining has yet to mature. A solid and systematic theoretical foundation is important because it can help provide a coherent framework for the development, evaluation, and practice of data mining technology. Several theories for the basis of data mining include the following:

- **Data reduction**: In this theory, the basis of data mining is to reduce the data representation. Data reduction trades accuracy for speed in response to the need to obtain quick approximate answers to queries on very large databases. Data reduction techniques include singular value decomposition (the driving element behind principal components analysis), wavelets, regression, log-linear models, histograms, clustering, sampling, and the construction of index trees.

- **Data compression**: According to this theory, the basis of data mining is to compress the given data by encoding in terms of bits, association rules, decision trees, clusters, and so on. Encoding based on the *minimum description length principle* states that the "best" theory to infer from a data set is the one that minimizes the length of the theory and of the data when encoded, using the theory as a predictor for the data. This encoding is typically in bits.

- **Probability and statistical theory**: According to this theory, the basis of data mining is to discover joint probability distributions of random variables, for example, Bayesian belief networks or hierarchical Bayesian models.

- **Microeconomic view**: The microeconomic view considers data mining as the task of finding patterns that are interesting only to the extent that they can be used in the decision-making process of some enterprise (e.g., regarding marketing strategies and production plans). This view is one of utility, in which patterns are considered interesting if they can be acted on. Enterprises are regarded as facing optimization problems, where the object is to maximize the utility or value of a decision. In this theory, data mining becomes a nonlinear optimization problem.

- **Pattern discovery and inductive databases**: In this theory, the basis of data mining is to discover patterns occurring in the data such as associations, classification models, sequential patterns, and so on. Areas such as machine learning, neural network, association mining, sequential pattern mining, clustering, and several other subfields contribute to this theory. A knowledge base can be viewed as a database consisting of data and patterns. A user interacts with the system by querying the data and the theory (i.e., patterns) in the knowledge base. Here, the knowledge base is actually an inductive database.

These theories are not mutually exclusive. For example, pattern discovery can also be seen as a form of data reduction or data compression. Ideally, a theoretical framework should be able to model typical data mining tasks (e.g., association, classification, and clustering), have a probabilistic nature, be able to handle different forms of data, and consider the iterative and interactive essence of data mining. Further efforts are required to establish a well-defined framework for data mining that satisfies these requirements.

13.2.3 **Visual and Audio Data Mining**

Visual data mining discovers implicit and useful knowledge from large data sets using data and/or knowledge visualization techniques. The human visual system is controlled by the eyes and brain, the latter of which can be thought of as a powerful, highly parallel processing and reasoning engine containing a large knowledge base. Visual data mining essentially combines the power of these components, making it a highly attractive and effective tool for the comprehension of data distributions, patterns, clusters, and outliers in data.

Visual data mining can be viewed as an integration of two disciplines: data visualization and data mining. It is also closely related to computer graphics, multimedia systems, human–computer interaction, pattern recognition, and high-performance computing. In general, data visualization and data mining can be integrated in the following ways:

- **Data visualization**: Data in a database or data warehouse can be viewed at different granularity or abstraction levels, or as different combinations of attributes or dimensions. Data can be presented in various visual forms, such as boxplots, 3-D cubes, data distribution charts, curves, surfaces, and link graphs, as shown in the data visualization section of Chapter 2. Figures 13.4 and 13.5 from StatSoft show

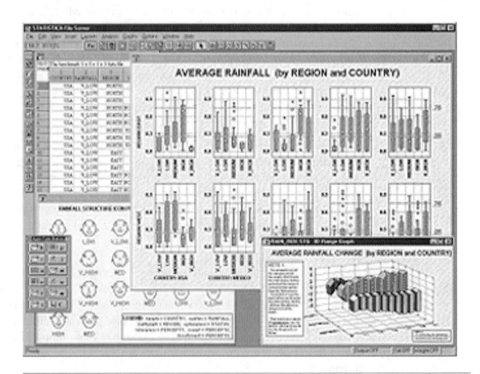

Figure 13.4 Boxplots showing multiple variable combinations in StatSoft. *Source: www.statsoft.com.*

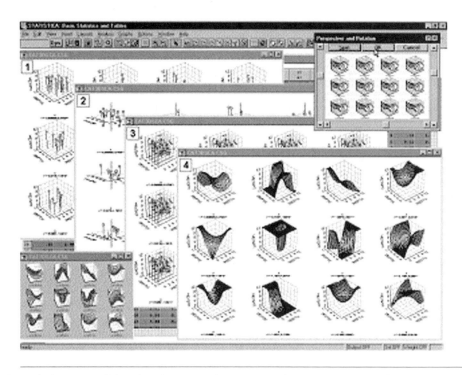

Figure 13.5 Multidimensional data distribution analysis in StatSoft. *Source: www.statsoft.com.*

data distributions in multidimensional space. Visual display can help give users a clear impression and overview of the data characteristics in a large data set.

- **Data mining result visualization**: Visualization of data mining results is the presentation of the results or knowledge obtained from data mining in visual forms. Such forms may include scatter plots and boxplots (Chapter 2), as well as decision trees, association rules, clusters, outliers, and generalized rules. For example, scatter plots are shown in Figure 13.6 from SAS Enterprise Miner. Figure 13.7, from MineSet, uses a plane associated with a set of pillars to describe a set of association rules mined from a database. Figure 13.8, also from MineSet, presents a decision tree. Figure 13.9, from IBM Intelligent Miner, presents a set of clusters and the properties associated with them.

- **Data mining process visualization**: This type of visualization presents the various processes of data mining in visual forms so that users can see how the data are extracted and from which database or data warehouse they are extracted, as well as how the selected data are cleaned, integrated, preprocessed, and mined. Moreover, it may also show which method is selected for data mining, where the results are stored, and how they may be viewed. Figure 13.10 shows a visual presentation of data mining processes by the Clementine data mining system.

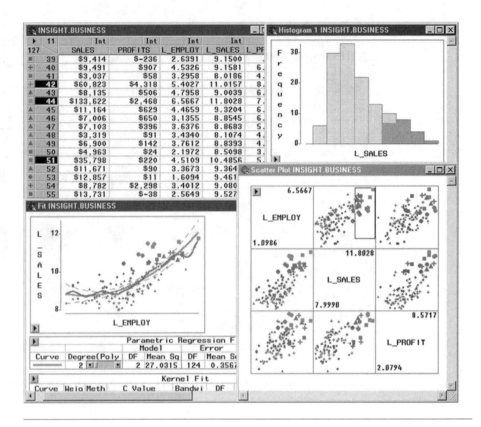

Figure 13.6 Visualization of data mining results in SAS Enterprise Miner.

- **Interactive visual data mining**: In (interactive) visual data mining, visualization tools can be used in the data mining process to help users make smart data mining decisions. For example, the data distribution in a set of attributes can be displayed using colored sectors (where the whole space is represented by a circle). This display helps users determine which sector should first be selected for classification and where a good split point for this sector may be. An example of this is shown in Figure 13.11, which is the output of a perception-based classification (PBC) system developed at the University of Munich.

Audio data mining uses audio signals to indicate the patterns of data or the features of data mining results. Although visual data mining may disclose interesting patterns using graphical displays, it requires users to concentrate on watching patterns and identifying interesting or novel features within them. This can sometimes be quite tiresome. If patterns can be transformed into sound and music, then instead of watching pictures, we can listen to pitchs, rhythm, tune, and melody to identify anything interesting or unusual. This may relieve some of the burden of visual concentration and be more

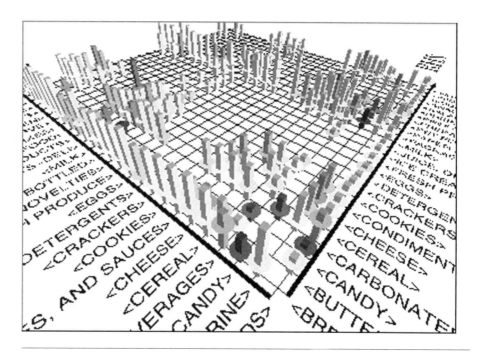

Figure 13.7 Visualization of association rules in MineSet.

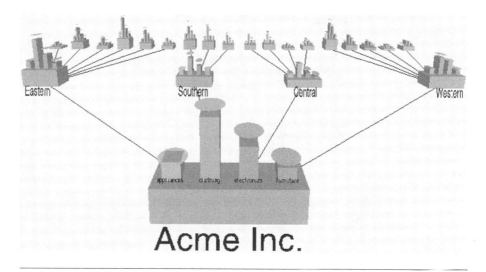

Figure 13.8 Visualization of a decision tree in MineSet.

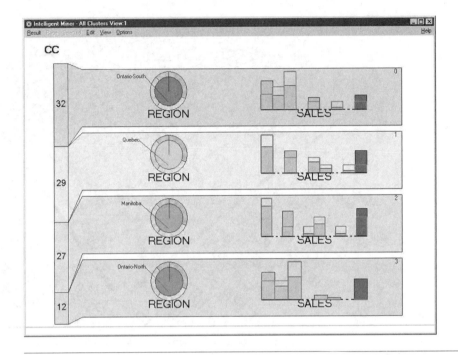

Figure 13.9 Visualization of cluster groupings in IBM Intelligent Miner.

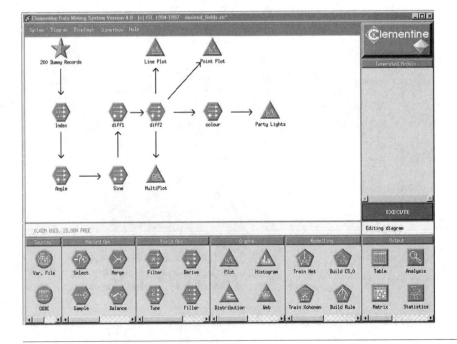

Figure 13.10 Visualization of data mining processes by Clementine.

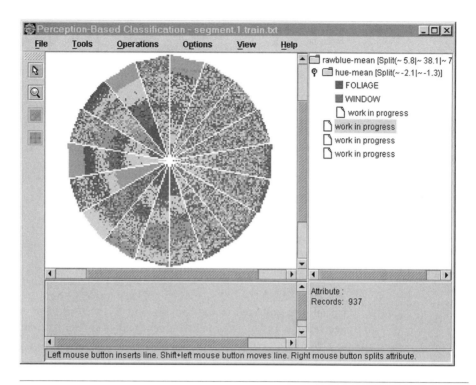

Figure 13.11 Perception-based classification, an interactive visual mining approach.

relaxing than visual mining. Therefore, audio data mining is an interesting complement to visual mining.

13.3 Data Mining Applications

In this book, we have studied principles and methods for mining relational data, data warehouses, and complex data types. Because data mining is a relatively young discipline with wide and diverse applications, there is still a nontrivial gap between general principles of data mining and application-specific, effective data mining tools. In this section, we examine several application domains, as listed in Figure 13.12. We discuss how customized data mining methods and tools should be developed for such applications.

13.3.1 Data Mining for Financial Data Analysis

Most banks and financial institutions offer a wide variety of banking, investment, and credit services (the latter include business, mortgage, and automobile loans and credit cards). Some also offer insurance and stock investment services.

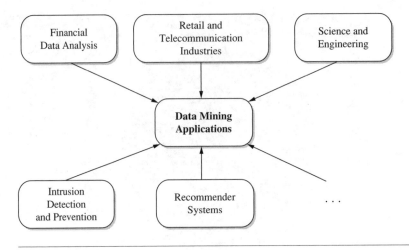

Figure 13.12 Common data mining application domains.

Financial data collected in the banking and financial industry are often relatively complete, reliable, and of high quality, which facilitates systematic data analysis and data mining. Here we present a few typical cases.

- **Design and construction of data warehouses for multidimensional data analysis and data mining:** Like many other applications, data warehouses need to be constructed for banking and financial data. Multidimensional data analysis methods should be used to analyze the general properties of such data. For example, a company's financial officer may want to view the debt and revenue changes by month, region, and sector, and other factors, along with maximum, minimum, total, average, trend, deviation, and other statistical information. Data warehouses, data cubes (including advanced data cube concepts such as multifeature, discovery-driven, regression, and prediction data cubes), characterization and class comparisons, clustering, and outlier analysis will all play important roles in financial data analysis and mining.

- **Loan payment prediction and customer credit policy analysis:** Loan payment prediction and customer credit analysis are critical to the business of a bank. Many factors can strongly or weakly influence loan payment performance and customer credit rating. Data mining methods, such as attribute selection and attribute relevance ranking, may help identify important factors and eliminate irrelevant ones. For example, factors related to the risk of loan payments include loan-to-value ratio, term of the loan, debt ratio (total amount of monthly debt versus total monthly income), payment-to-income ratio, customer income level, education level, residence region, and credit history. Analysis of the customer payment history may find that, say, payment-to-income ratio is a dominant factor, while education level and debt ratio are not. The bank may then decide to adjust its loan-granting policy so as to grant loans to those customers whose applications were previously denied but whose profiles show relatively low risks according to the critical factor analysis.

- **Classification and clustering of customers for targeted marketing:** Classification and clustering methods can be used for customer group identification and targeted marketing. For example, we can use classification to identify the most crucial factors that may influence a customer's decision regarding banking. Customers with similar behaviors regarding loan payments may be identified by multidimensional clustering techniques. These can help identify customer groups, associate a new customer with an appropriate customer group, and facilitate targeted marketing.

- **Detection of money laundering and other financial crimes:** To detect money laundering and other financial crimes, it is important to integrate information from multiple, heterogeneous databases (e.g., bank transaction databases and federal or state crime history databases), as long as they are potentially related to the study. Multiple data analysis tools can then be used to detect unusual patterns, such as large amounts of cash flow at certain periods, by certain groups of customers. Useful tools include data visualization tools (to display transaction activities using graphs by time and by groups of customers), linkage and information network analysis tools (to identify links among different customers and activities), classification tools (to filter unrelated attributes and rank the highly related ones), clustering tools (to group different cases), outlier analysis tools (to detect unusual amounts of fund transfers or other activities), and sequential pattern analysis tools (to characterize unusual access sequences). These tools may identify important relationships and patterns of activities and help investigators focus on suspicious cases for further detailed examination.

13.3.2 Data Mining for Retail and Telecommunication Industries

The retail industry is a well-fit application area for data mining, since it collects huge amounts of data on sales, customer shopping history, goods transportation, consumption, and service. The quantity of data collected continues to expand rapidly, especially due to the increasing availability, ease, and popularity of business conducted on the Web, or **e-commerce**. Today, most major chain stores also have web sites where customers can make purchases online. Some businesses, such as Amazon.com (*www.amazon.com*), exist solely online, without any brick-and-mortar (i.e., physical) store locations. Retail data provide a rich source for data mining.

Retail data mining can help identify customer buying behaviors, discover customer shopping patterns and trends, improve the quality of customer service, achieve better customer retention and satisfaction, enhance goods consumption ratios, design more effective goods transportation and distribution policies, and reduce the cost of business.

A few examples of data mining in the retail industry are outlined as follows:

- **Design and construction of data warehouses:** Because retail data cover a wide spectrum (including sales, customers, employees, goods transportation, consumption, and services), there can be many ways to design a data warehouse for this industry. The levels of detail to include can vary substantially. The outcome of preliminary data mining exercises can be used to help guide the design and development of data warehouse structures. This involves deciding which dimensions and levels to include and what preprocessing to perform to facilitate effective data mining.

■ **Multidimensional analysis of sales, customers, products, time, and region:** The retail industry requires timely information regarding customer needs, product sales, trends, and fashions, as well as the quality, cost, profit, and service of commodities. It is therefore important to provide powerful multidimensional analysis and visualization tools, including the construction of sophisticated data cubes according to the needs of data analysis. The *advanced data cube structures* introduced in Chapter 5 are useful in retail data analysis because they facilitate analysis on multidimensional aggregates with complex conditions.

■ **Analysis of the effectiveness of sales campaigns:** The retail industry conducts sales campaigns using advertisements, coupons, and various kinds of discounts and bonuses to promote products and attract customers. Careful analysis of the effectiveness of sales campaigns can help improve company profits. Multidimensional analysis can be used for this purpose by comparing the amount of sales and the number of transactions containing the sales items during the sales period versus those containing the same items before or after the sales campaign. Moreover, association analysis may disclose which items are likely to be purchased together with the items on sale, especially in comparison with the sales before or after the campaign.

■ **Customer retention—analysis of customer loyalty:** We can use customer loyalty card information to register sequences of purchases of particular customers. Customer loyalty and purchase trends can be analyzed systematically. Goods purchased at different periods by the same customers can be grouped into sequences. Sequential pattern mining can then be used to investigate changes in customer consumption or loyalty and suggest adjustments on the pricing and variety of goods to help retain customers and attract new ones.

■ **Product recommendation and cross-referencing of items:** By mining associations from sales records, we may discover that a customer who buys a digital camera is likely to buy another set of items. Such information can be used to form product recommendations. *Collaborative recommender systems* (Section 13.3.5) use data mining techniques to make personalized product recommendations during live customer transactions, based on the opinions of other customers. Product recommendations can also be advertised on sales receipts, in weekly flyers, or on the Web to help improve customer service, aid customers in selecting items, and increase sales. Similarly, information, such as "hot items this week" or attractive deals, can be displayed together with the associative information to promote sales.

■ **Fraudulent analysis and the identification of unusual patterns:** Fraudulent activity costs the retail industry millions of dollars per year. It is important to (1) identify potentially fraudulent users and their atypical usage patterns; (2) detect attempts to gain fraudulent entry or unauthorized access to individual and organizational accounts; and (3) discover unusual patterns that may need special attention. Many of these patterns can be discovered by multidimensional analysis, cluster analysis, and outlier analysis.

As another industry that handles huge amounts of data, the **telecommunication industry** has quickly evolved from offering local and long-distance telephone services to providing many other comprehensive communication services. These include cellular phone, smart phone, Internet access, email, text messages, images, computer and web data transmissions, and other data traffic. The integration of telecommunication, computer network, Internet, and numerous other means of communication and computing has been under way, changing the face of telecommunications and computing. This has created a great demand for data mining to help understand business dynamics, identify telecommunication patterns, catch fraudulent activities, make better use of resources, and improve service quality.

Data mining tasks in telecommunications share many similarities with those in the retail industry. Common tasks include constructing large-scale data warehouses, performing multidimensional visualization, OLAP, and in-depth analysis of trends, customer patterns, and sequential patterns. Such tasks contribute to business improvements, cost reduction, customer retention, fraud analysis, and sharpening the edges of competition. There are many data mining tasks for which customized data mining tools for telecommunication have been flourishing and are expected to play increasingly important roles in business.

Data mining has been popularly used in many other industries, such as *insurance, manufacturing, and health care*, as well as for the *analysis of governmental and institutional administration data*. Although each industry has its own characteristic data sets and application demands, they share many common principles and methodologies. Therefore, through effective mining in one industry, we may gain experience and methodologies that can be transferred to other industrial applications.

13.3.3 Data Mining in Science and Engineering

In the past, many scientific data analysis tasks tended to handle relatively small and homogeneous data sets. Such data were typically analyzed using a *"formulate hypothesis, build model, and evaluate results"* paradigm. In these cases, statistical techniques were typically employed for their analysis (see Section 13.2.1). Massive data collection and storage technologies have recently changed the landscape of scientific data analysis. Today, scientific data can be amassed at much higher speeds and lower costs. This has resulted in the accumulation of huge volumes of high-dimensional data, stream data, and heterogenous data, containing rich spatial and temporal information. Consequently, scientific applications are shifting from the *"hypothesize-and-test"* paradigm toward a *"collect and store data, mine for new hypotheses, confirm with data or experimentation"* process. This shift brings about new challenges for data mining.

Vast amounts of data have been collected from scientific domains (including geosciences, astronomy, meteorology, geology, and biological sciences) using sophisticated telescopes, multispectral high-resolution remote satellite sensors, global positioning systems, and new generations of biological data collection and analysis technologies. Large data sets are also being generated due to fast numeric simulations in various fields such as climate and ecosystem modeling, chemical engineering, fluid dynamics, and structural mechanics. Here we look at some of the challenges brought about by emerging scientific applications of data mining.

- **Data warehouses and data preprocessing**: Data preprocessing and data warehouses are critical for information exchange and data mining. Creating a warehouse often requires finding means for resolving inconsistent or incompatible data collected in multiple environments and at different time periods. This requires reconciling semantics, referencing systems, geometry, measurements, accuracy, and precision. Methods are needed for integrating data from heterogeneous sources and for identifying events.

  For instance, consider climate and ecosystem data, which are spatial and temporal and require cross-referencing geospatial data. A major problem in analyzing such data is that there are too many events in the spatial domain but too few in the temporal domain. For example, El Nino events occur only every four to seven years, and previous data on them might not have been collected as systematically as they are today. Methods are also needed for the efficient computation of sophisticated spatial aggregates and the handling of spatial-related data streams.

- **Mining complex data types**: Scientific data sets are heterogeneous in nature. They typically involve semi-structured and unstructured data, such as multimedia data and georeferenced stream data, as well as data with sophisticated, deeply hidden semantics (e.g., genomic and proteomic data). Robust and dedicated analysis methods are needed for handling spatiotemporal data, biological data, related concept hierarchies, and complex semantic relationships. For example, in bioinformatics, a research problem is to identify regulatory influences on genes. *Gene regulation* refers to how genes in a cell are switched on (or off) to determine the cell's functions. Different biological processes involve different sets of genes acting together in precisely regulated patterns. Thus, to understand a biological process we need to identify the participating genes and their regulators. This requires the development of sophisticated data mining methods to analyze large biological data sets for clues about regulatory influences on specific genes, by finding DNA segments ("regulatory sequences") mediating such influence.

- **Graph-based and network-based mining**: It is often difficult or impossible to model several physical phenomena and processes due to limitations of existing modeling approaches. Alternatively, labeled graphs and networks may be used to capture many of the spatial, topological, geometric, biological, and other relational characteristics present in scientific data sets. In graph or network modeling, each object to be mined is represented by a vertex in a graph, and edges between vertices represent relationships between objects. For example, graphs can be used to model chemical structures, biological pathways, and data generated by numeric simulations such as fluid-flow simulations. The success of graph or network modeling, however, depends on improvements in the scalability and efficiency of many graph-based data mining tasks such as classification, frequent pattern mining, and clustering.

- **Visualization tools and domain-specific knowledge**: High-level graphical user interfaces and visualization tools are required for scientific data mining systems. These should be integrated with existing domain-specific data and information systems to guide researchers and general users in searching for patterns, interpreting and visualizing discovered patterns, and using discovered knowledge in their decision making.

Data mining in engineering shares many similarities with data mining in science. Both practices often collect massive amounts of data, and require data preprocessing, data warehousing, and scalable mining of complex types of data. Both typically use visualization and make good use of graphs and networks. Moreover, many engineering processes need real-time responses, and so mining data streams in real time often becomes a critical component.

Massive amounts of human communication data pour into our daily life. Such communication exists in many forms, including news, blogs, articles, web pages, online discussions, product reviews, twitters, messages, advertisements, and communications, both on the Web and in various kinds of social networks. Hence, **data mining in social science and social studies** has become increasingly popular. Moreover, user or reader feedback regarding products, speeches, and articles can be analyzed to deduce general opinions and sentiments on the views of those in society. The analysis results can be used to predict trends, improve work, and help in decision making.

Computer science generates unique kinds of data. For example, computer programs can be long, and their execution often generates huge-size traces. Computer networks can have complex structures and the network flows can be dynamic and massive. Sensor networks may generate large amounts of data with varied reliability. Computer systems and databases can suffer from various kinds of attacks, and their system/data accessing may raise security and privacy concerns. These unique kinds of data provide fertile land for data mining.

Data mining in computer science can be used to help monitor system status, improve system performance, isolate software bugs, detect software plagiarism, analyze computer system faults, uncover network intrusions, and recognize system malfunctions. Data mining for software and system engineering can operate on static or dynamic (i.e., stream-based) data, depending on whether the system dumps traces beforehand for postanalysis or if it must react in real time to handle online data.

Various methods have been developed in this domain, which integrate and extend methods from machine learning, data mining, software/system engineering, pattern recognition, and statistics. Data mining in computer science is an active and rich domain for data miners because of its unique challenges. It requires the further development of sophisticated, scalable, and real-time data mining and software/system engineering methods.

13.3.4 **Data Mining for Intrusion Detection and Prevention**

The security of our computer systems and data is at continual risk. The extensive growth of the Internet and the increasing availability of tools and tricks for intruding and attacking networks have prompted **intrusion detection and prevention** to become a critical component of networked systems. An intrusion can be defined as any set of actions that threaten the integrity, confidentiality, or availability of a network resource (e.g., user accounts, file systems, system kernels, and so on). Intrusion detection systems and intrusion prevention systems both monitor network traffic and/or system executions for malicious activities. However, the former produces reports whereas the latter is placed in-line and is able to actively prevent/block intrusions that are detected. The main functions of an intrusion prevention system are to identify malicious activity, log information about said activity, attempt to block/stop activity, and report activity.

The majority of intrusion detection and prevention systems use either *signature-based detection* or *anomaly-based detection.*

- **Signature-based detection**: This method of detection utilizes *signatures*, which are attack patterns that are preconfigured and predetermined by domain experts. A signature-based intrusion prevention system monitors the network traffic for matches to these signatures. Once a match is found, the intrusion detection system will report the anomaly and an intrusion prevention system will take additional appropriate actions. Note that since the systems are usually quite dynamic, the signatures need to be updated laboriously whenever new software versions arrive or changes in network configuration or other situations occur. Another drawback is that such a detection mechanism can only identify cases that match the signatures. That is, it is unable to detect new or previously unknown intrusion tricks.

- **Anomaly-based detection**: This method builds models of normal network behavior (called *profiles*) that are then used to detect new patterns that significantly deviate from the profiles. Such deviations may represent actual intrusions or simply be new behaviors that need to be added to the profiles. The main advantage of anomaly detection is that it may detect novel intrusions that have not yet been observed. Typically, a human analyst must sort through the deviations to ascertain which represent real intrusions. A limiting factor of anomaly detection is the high percentage of false positives. New patterns of intrusion can be added to the set of signatures to enhance signature-based detection.

Data mining methods can help an intrusion detection and prevention system to enhance its performance in various ways as follows.

- **New data mining algorithms for intrusion detection**: Data mining algorithms can be used for both signature-based and anomaly-based detection. In signature-based detection, training data are labeled as either "normal" or "intrusion." A classifier can then be derived to detect known intrusions. Research in this area has included the application of classification algorithms, association rule mining, and cost-sensitive modeling. Anomaly-based detection builds models of normal behavior and automatically detects significant deviations from it. Methods include the application of clustering, outlier analysis, and classification algorithms and statistical approaches. The techniques used must be efficient and scalable, and capable of handling network data of high volume, dimensionality, and heterogeneity.

- **Association, correlation, and discriminative pattern analyses help select and build discriminative classifiers**: Association, correlation, and discriminative pattern mining can be applied to find relationships between system attributes describing the network data. Such information can provide insight regarding the selection of useful attributes for intrusion detection. New attributes derived from aggregated data may also be helpful such as summary counts of traffic matching a particular pattern.

- **Analysis of stream data**: Due to the transient and dynamic nature of intrusions and malicious attacks, it is crucial to perform intrusion detection in the data stream environment. Moreover, an event may be normal on its own, but considered malicious if viewed as part of a sequence of events. Thus, it is necessary to study what sequences of events are frequently encountered together, find sequential patterns, and identify outliers. Other data mining methods for finding evolving clusters and building dynamic classification models in data streams are also necessary for real-time intrusion detection.

- **Distributed data mining**: Intrusions can be launched from several different locations and targeted to many different destinations. Distributed data mining methods may be used to analyze network data from several network locations to detect these distributed attacks.

- **Visualization and querying tools**: Visualization tools should be available for viewing any anomalous patterns detected. Such tools may include features for viewing associations, discriminative patterns, clusters, and outliers. Intrusion detection systems should also have a graphical user interface that allows security analysts to pose queries regarding the network data or intrusion detection results.

In summary, computer systems are at continual risk of breaks in security. Data mining technology can be used to develop strong intrusion detection and prevention systems, which may employ signature-based or anomaly-based detection.

13.3.5 Data Mining and Recommender Systems

Today's consumers are faced with millions of goods and services when shopping online. **Recommender systems** help consumers by making product recommendations that are likely to be of interest to the user such as books, CDs, movies, restaurants, online news articles, and other services. Recommender systems may use either a *content-based* approach, a *collaborative* approach, or a *hybrid* approach that combines both content-based and collaborative methods.

The **content-based approach** recommends items that are similar to items the user preferred or queried in the past. It relies on product features and textual item descriptions. The **collaborative approach** (or *collaborative filtering approach*) may consider a user's social environment. It recommends items based on the opinions of other customers who have similar tastes or preferences as the user. Recommender systems use a broad range of techniques from information retrieval, statistics, machine learning, and data mining to search for similarities among items and customer preferences. Consider Example 13.1.

Example 13.1 **Scenarios of using a recommender system.** Suppose that you visit the web site of an online bookstore (e.g., Amazon) with the intention of purchasing a book that you have been wanting to read. You type in the name of the book. This is not the first time you have visited the web site. You have browsed through it before and even made purchases from it last Christmas. The web store remembers your previous visits, having stored click stream information and information regarding your past purchases. The system displays the description and price of the book you have just specified. It compares your interests with other customers having similar interests and recommends additional book titles, saying *"Customers who bought the book you have specified also bought these other titles as well."* From surveying the list, you see another title that sparks your interest and decide to purchase that one as well.

Now suppose you go to another online store with the intention of purchasing a digital camera. The system suggests additional items to consider based on previously mined sequential patterns, such as *"Customers who buy this kind of digital camera are likely to buy a particular brand of printer, memory card, or photo editing software within three months."* You decide to buy just the camera, without any additional items. A week later, you receive coupons from the store regarding the additional items. ∎

An advantage of recommender systems is that they provide *personalization* for customers of e-commerce, promoting one-to-one marketing. Amazon, a pioneer in the use of collaborative recommender systems, offers "a personalized store for every customer" as part of their marketing strategy. Personalization can benefit both consumers and the company involved. By having more accurate models of their customers, companies gain a better understanding of customer needs. Serving these needs can result in greater success regarding cross-selling of related products, upselling, product affinities, one-to-one promotions, larger baskets, and customer retention.

The recommendation problem considers a set, C, of users and a set, S, of items. Let u be a utility function that measures the usefulness of an item, s, to a user, c. The utility is commonly represented by a rating and is initially defined only for items previously rated by users. For example, when joining a movie recommendation system, users are typically asked to rate several movies. The space $C \times S$ of all possible users and items is huge. The recommendation system should be able to extrapolate from known to unknown ratings so as to predict item–user combinations. Items with the highest predicted rating/utility for a user are recommended to that user.

"How is the utility of an item estimated for a user?" In content-based methods, it is estimated based on the utilities assigned by the same user to other items that are similar. Many such systems focus on recommending items containing textual information, such as web sites, articles, and news messages. They look for commonalities among items. For movies, they may look for similar genres, directors, or actors. For articles, they may look for similar terms. Content-based methods are rooted in information theory. They make use of keywords (describing the items) and user profiles that contain information about users' tastes and needs. Such profiles may be obtained explicitly (e.g., through questionnaires) or learned from users' transactional behavior over time.

A collaborative recommender system tries to predict the utility of items for a user, u, based on items previously rated by other users who are similar to u. For example, when recommending books, a collaborative recommender system tries to find other users who have a history of agreeing with u (e.g., they tend to buy similar books, or give similar ratings for books). Collaborative recommender systems can be either memory (or heuristic) based or model based.

Memory-based methods essentially use heuristics to make rating predictions based on the entire collection of items previously rated by users. That is, the unknown rating of an item–user combination can be estimated as an aggregate of ratings of the most similar users for the same item. Typically, a k-nearest-neighbor approach is used, that is, we find the k other users (or neighbors) that are most similar to our target user, u. Various approaches can be used to compute the similarity between users. The most popular approaches use either Pearson's correlation coefficient (Section 3.3.2) or cosine similarity (Section 2.4.7). A weighted aggregate can be used, which adjusts for the fact that different users may use the rating scale differently. Model-based collaborative recommender systems use a collection of ratings to learn a model, which is then used to make rating predictions. For example, probabilistic models, clustering (which finds clusters of like-minded customers), Bayesian networks, and other machine learning techniques have been used.

Recommender systems face major challenges such as scalability and ensuring quality recommendations to the consumer. For example, regarding scalability, collaborative recommender systems must be able to search through millions of potential neighbors in real time. If the site is using browsing patterns as indications of product preference, it may have thousands of data points for some of its customers. Ensuring quality recommendations is essential to gain consumers' trust. If consumers follow a system recommendation but then do not end up liking the product, they are less likely to use the recommender system again.

As with classification systems, recommender systems can make two types of errors: false negatives and false positives. Here, *false negatives* are products that the system fails to recommend, although the consumer would like them. *False positives* are products that are recommended, but which the consumer does not like. False positives are less desirable because they can annoy or anger consumers. Content-based recommender systems are limited by the features used to describe the items they recommend.

Another challenge for both content-based and collaborative recommender systems is how to deal with new users for which a buying history is not yet available.

Hybrid approaches integrate both content-based and collaborative methods to achieve further improved recommendations. The Netflix Prize was an open competition held by an online DVD-rental service, with a payout of $1,000,000 for the best recommender algorithm to predict user ratings for films, based on previous ratings. The competition and other studies have shown that the predictive accuracy of a recommender system can be substantially improved when blending multiple predictors, especially by using an ensemble of many substantially different methods, rather than refining a single technique.

Collaborative recommender systems are a form of **intelligent query answering**, which consists of analyzing the intent of a query and providing generalized, neighborhood, or associated information relevant to the query. For example, rather than simply returning the book description and price in response to a customer's query, returning additional information that is related to the query but that was not explicitly asked for (e.g., book evaluation comments, recommendations of other books, or sales statistics) provides an intelligent answer to the same query.

13.4 Data Mining and Society

For most of us, data mining is part of our daily lives, although we may often be unaware of its presence. Section 13.4.1 looks at several examples of "ubiquitous and invisible" data mining, affecting everyday things from the products stocked at our local supermarket, to the ads we see while surfing the Internet, to crime prevention. Data mining can offer the individual many benefits by improving customer service and satisfaction as well as lifestyle, in general. However, it also has serious implications regarding one's right to privacy and data security. These issues are the topic of Section 13.4.2.

13.4.1 Ubiquitous and Invisible Data Mining

Data mining is present in many aspects of our daily lives, whether we realize it or not. It affects how we shop, work, and search for information, and can even influence our leisure time, health, and well-being. In this section, we look at examples of such **ubiquitous** (or ever-present) **data mining**. Several of these examples also represent **invisible data mining**, in which "smart" software, such as search engines, customer-adaptive web services (e.g., using recommender algorithms), "intelligent" database systems, email managers, ticket masters, and so on, incorporates data mining into its functional components, often unbeknownst to the user.

From grocery stores that print personalized coupons on customer receipts to online stores that recommend additional items based on customer interests, data mining has innovatively influenced what we buy, the way we shop, and our experience while shopping. One example is Wal-Mart, which has hundreds of millions of customers visiting its tens of thousands of stores every week. Wal-Mart allows suppliers to access data on their products and perform analyses using data mining software. This allows suppliers to identify customer buying patterns at different stores, control inventory and product placement, and identify new merchandising opportunities. All of these affect which items (and how many) end up on the stores' shelves—something to think about the next time you wander through the aisles at Wal-Mart.

Data mining has shaped the online shopping experience. Many shoppers routinely turn to online stores to purchase books, music, movies, and toys. Recommender systems, discussed in Section 13.3.5, offer personalized product recommendations based on the opinions of other customers. Amazon.com was at the forefront of using such a personalized, data mining–based approach as a marketing strategy. It has observed that in traditional brick-and-mortar stores, the hardest part is getting the customer into the store. Once the customer is there, he or she is likely to buy something, since the cost of going to another store is high. Therefore, the marketing for brick-and-mortar stores tends to emphasize drawing customers in, rather than the actual in-store customer experience. This is in contrast to online stores, where customers can "walk out" and enter another online store with just a click of the mouse. Amazon.com capitalized on this difference, offering a "personalized store for every customer." They use several data mining techniques to identify customer's likes and make reliable recommendations.

While we are on the topic of shopping, suppose you have been doing a lot of buying with your credit cards. Nowadays, it is not unusual to receive a phone call from one's credit card company regarding suspicious or unusual patterns of spending. Credit card companies use data mining to detect fraudulent usage, saving billions of dollars a year.

Many companies increasingly use data mining for **customer relationship management (CRM)**, which helps provide more customized, personal service addressing individual customer's needs, in lieu of mass marketing. By studying browsing and purchasing patterns on web stores, companies can tailor advertisements and promotions to customer profiles, so that customers are less likely to be annoyed with unwanted mass mailings or junk mail. These actions can result in substantial cost savings for companies. The customers further benefit in that they are more likely to be notified of offers that are actually of interest, resulting in less waste of personal time and greater satisfaction.

Data mining has greatly influenced the ways in which people use computers, search for information, and work. Once you get on the Internet, for example, you decide to check your email. Unbeknownst to you, several annoying emails have already been deleted, thanks to a spam filter that uses classification algorithms to recognize spam. After processing your email, you go to Google (*www.google.com*), which provides access to information from billions of web pages indexed on its server. Google is one of the most popular and widely used Internet search engines. Using Google to search for information has become a way of life for many people.

Google is so popular that it has even become a new verb in the English language, meaning "to search for (something) on the Internet using the Google search engine or, by extension, any comprehensive search engine."[1] You decide to type in some keywords

---

[1] *http://open-dictionary.com.*

for a topic of interest. Google returns a list of web sites on your topic, mined, indexed, and organized by a set of data mining algorithms including PageRank. Moreover, if you type "Boston New York," Google will show you bus and train schedules from Boston to New York; however, a minor change to "Boston Paris" will lead to flight schedules from Boston to Paris. Such smart offerings of information or services are likely based on the frequent patterns mined from the click streams of many previous queries.

While you are viewing the results of your Google query, various ads pop up relating to your query. Google's strategy of tailoring advertising to match the user's interests is one of the typical services being explored by every Internet search provider. This also makes you happier, because you are less likely to be pestered with irrelevant ads.

Data mining is omnipresent, as can be seen from these daily-encountered examples. We could go on and on with such scenarios. In many cases, data mining is invisible, as users may be unaware that they are examining results returned by data mining or that their clicks are actually fed as new data into some data mining functions. For data mining to become further improved and accepted as a technology, continuing research and development are needed in the many areas mentioned as challenges throughout this book. These include efficiency and scalability, increased user interaction, incorporation of background knowledge and visualization techniques, effective methods for finding interesting patterns, improved handling of complex data types and stream data, real-time data mining, web mining, and so on. In addition, the *integration* of data mining into existing business and scientific technologies, to provide domain-specific data mining tools, will further contribute to the advancement of the technology. The success of data mining solutions tailored for e-commerce applications, as opposed to generic data mining systems, is an example.

13.4.2 Privacy, Security, and Social Impacts of Data Mining

With more and more information accessible in electronic forms and available on the Web, and with increasingly powerful data mining tools being developed and put into use, there are increasing concerns that data mining may pose a threat to our privacy and data security. However, it is important to note that many data mining applications do not even touch personal data. Prominent examples include applications involving natural resources, the prediction of floods and droughts, meteorology, astronomy, geography, geology, biology, and other scientific and engineering data. Furthermore, most studies in data mining research focus on the development of scalable algorithms and do not involve personal data.

The focus of data mining technology is on the *discovery of general or statistically significant patterns*, not on specific information regarding individuals. In this sense, we believe that the real privacy concerns are with unconstrained access to individual records, especially access to privacy-sensitive information such as credit card transaction records, health-care records, personal financial records, biological traits, criminal/justice investigations, and ethnicity. For the data mining applications that do involve personal data, in many cases, simple methods such as removing sensitive IDs from data may protect the privacy of most individuals. Nevertheless, privacy concerns exist wherever *personally identifiable information* is collected and stored in digital form, and data mining programs are able to access such data, even during data preparation.

Improper or nonexistent disclosure control can be the root cause of privacy issues. To handle such concerns, numerous data security-enhancing techniques have been developed. In addition, there has been a great deal of recent effort on developing *privacy-preserving* data mining methods. In this section, we look at some of the advances in protecting privacy and data security in data mining.

"What can we do to secure the privacy of individuals while collecting and mining data?" Many **data security–enhancing techniques** have been developed to help protect data. Databases can employ a *multilevel security model* to classify and restrict data according to various security levels, with users permitted access to only their authorized level. It has been shown, however, that users executing specific queries at their authorized security level can still infer more sensitive information, and that a similar possibility can occur through data mining. *Encryption* is another technique in which individual data items may be encoded. This may involve *blind signatures* (which build on public key encryption), *biometric encryption* (e.g., where the image of a person's iris or fingerprint is used to encode his or her personal information), and *anonymous databases* (which permit the consolidation of various databases but limit access to personal information only to those who need to know; personal information is encrypted and stored at different locations). Intrusion detection is another active area of research that helps protect the privacy of personal data.

Privacy-preserving data mining is an area of data mining research in response to privacy protection in data mining. It is also known as *privacy-enhanced* or *privacy-sensitive* data mining. It deals with obtaining valid data mining results without disclosing the underlying sensitive data values. Most privacy-preserving data mining methods use some form of transformation on the data to perform privacy preservation. Typically, such methods reduce the granularity of representation to preserve privacy. For example, they may generalize the data from individual customers to customer groups. This reduction in granularity causes loss of information and possibly of the usefulness of the data mining results. This is the natural trade-off between information loss and privacy. Privacy-preserving data mining methods can be classified into the following categories.

- **Randomization methods**: These methods add noise to the data to mask some attribute values of records. The noise added should be sufficiently large so that individual record values, especially sensitive ones, cannot be recovered. However, it should be added skillfully so that the final results of data mining are basically preserved. Techniques are designed to derive aggregate distributions from the perturbed data. Subsequently, data mining techniques can be developed to work with these aggregate distributions.

- **The *k*-anonymity and *l*-diversity methods**: Both of these methods alter individual records so that they cannot be uniquely identified. In the *k-anonymity method*, the granularity of data representation is reduced sufficiently so that any given record maps onto at least *k* other records in the data. It uses techniques like generalization and suppression. The *k*-anonymity method is weak in that, if there is a homogeneity of sensitive values within a group, then those values may be inferred for the altered records. The *l-diversity model* was designed to handle this weakness by enforcing intragroup diversity of sensitive values to ensure anonymization. The goal is to make it sufficiently difficult for adversaries to use combinations of record attributes to exactly identify individual records.

- **Distributed privacy preservation**: Large data sets could be partitioned and distributed either *horizontally* (i.e., the data sets are partitioned into different subsets of records and distributed across multiple sites) or *vertically* (i.e., the data sets are partitioned and distributed by their attributes), or even in a combination of both. While the individual sites may not want to share their entire data sets, they may consent to limited information sharing with the use of a variety of protocols. The overall effect of such methods is to maintain privacy for each individual object, while deriving aggregate results over all of the data.

- **Downgrading the effectiveness of data mining results**: In many cases, even though the data may not be available, the output of data mining (e.g, association rules and classification models) may result in violations of privacy. The solution could be to downgrade the effectiveness of data mining by either modifying data or mining results, such as hiding some association rules or slightly distorting some classification models.

Recently, researchers proposed new ideas in privacy-preserving data mining such as the notion of **differential privacy**. The general idea is that, for any two data sets that are close to one another (i.e., that differ only on a tiny data set such as a single element), a given *differentially private algorithm* will behave approximately the same on both data sets. This definition gives a strong guarantee that the presence or absence of a tiny data set (e.g., representing an individual) will not affect the final output of the query significantly. Based on this notion, a set of differential privacy-preserving data mining algorithms have been developed. Research in this direction is ongoing. We expect more powerful privacy-preserving data publishing and data mining algorithms in the near future.

Like any other technology, data mining can be misused. However, we must not lose sight of all the benefits that data mining research can bring, ranging from insights gained from medical and scientific applications to increased customer satisfaction by helping companies better suit their clients' needs. We expect that computer scientists, policy experts, and counterterrorism experts will continue to work with social scientists, lawyers, companies, and consumers to take responsibility in building solutions to ensure data privacy protection and security. In this way, we may continue to reap the benefits of data mining in terms of time and money savings and the discovery of new knowledge.

13.5 Data Mining Trends

The diversity of data, data mining tasks, and data mining approaches poses many challenging research issues in data mining. The development of efficient and effective data mining methods, systems and services, and interactive and integrated data mining environments is a key area of study. The use of data mining techniques to solve large or sophisticated application problems is an important task for data mining researchers and data mining system and application developers. This section describes some of the trends in data mining that reflect the pursuit of these challenges.

- **Application exploration:** Early data mining applications put a lot of effort into helping businesses gain a competitive edge. The exploration of data mining for businesses continues to expand as e-commerce and e-marketing have become mainstream in the retail industry. Data mining is increasingly used for the exploration of applications in other areas such as web and text analysis, financial analysis, industry, government, biomedicine, and science. Emerging application areas include data mining for counterterrorism and mobile (wireless) data mining. Because generic data mining systems may have limitations in dealing with application-specific problems, we may see a trend toward the development of more application-specific data mining systems and tools, as well as invisible data mining functions embedded in various kinds of services.

- **Scalable and interactive data mining methods:** In contrast with traditional data analysis methods, data mining must be able to handle huge amounts of data efficiently and, if possible, interactively. Because the amount of data being collected continues to increase rapidly, scalable algorithms for individual and integrated data mining functions become essential. One important direction toward improving the overall efficiency of the mining process while increasing user interaction is **constraint-based mining**. This provides users with added control by allowing the specification and use of constraints to guide data mining systems in their search for interesting patterns and knowledge.

- **Integration of data mining with search engines, database systems, data warehouse systems, and cloud computing systems:** Search engines, database systems, data warehouse systems, and cloud computing systems are mainstream information processing and computing systems. It is important to ensure that data mining serves as an essential data analysis component that can be smoothly integrated into such an information processing environment. A data mining subsystem/service should be tightly coupled with such systems as a seamless, unified framework or as an invisible function. This will ensure data availability, data mining portability, scalability, high performance, and an integrated information processing environment for multi-dimensional data analysis and exploration.

- **Mining social and information networks:** Mining social and information networks and link analysis are critical tasks because such networks are ubiquitous and complex. The development of scalable and effective knowledge discovery methods and applications for large numbers of network data is essential, as outlined in Section 13.1.2.

- **Mining spatiotemporal, moving-objects, and cyber-physical systems:** Cyber-physical systems as well as spatiotemporal data are mounting rapidly due to the popular use of cellular phones, GPS, sensors, and other wireless equipment. As outlined in Section 13.1.3, there are many challenging research issues realizing real-time and effective knowledge discovery with such data.

- **Mining multimedia, text, and web data:** As outlined in Section 13.1.3, mining such kinds of data is a recent focus in data mining research. Great progress has been made, yet there are still many open issues to be solved.

- **Mining biological and biomedical data:** The unique combination of complexity, richness, size, and importance of biological and biomedical data warrants special attention in data mining. Mining DNA and protein sequences, mining high-dimensional microarray data, and biological pathway and network analysis are just a few topics in this field. Other areas of biological data mining research include mining biomedical literature, link analysis across heterogeneous biological data, and information integration of biological data by data mining.

- **Data mining with software engineering and system engineering:** Software programs and large computer systems have become increasingly bulky in size, sophisticated in complexity, and tend to originate from the integration of multiple components developed by different implementation teams. This trend has made it an increasingly challenging task to ensure software robustness and reliability. The analysis of the executions of a buggy software program is essentially a data mining process—tracing the data generated during program executions may disclose important patterns and outliers that could lead to the eventual automated discovery of software bugs. We expect that the further development of data mining methodologies for software/system debugging will enhance software robustness and bring new vigor to software/system engineering.

- **Visual and audio data mining:** Visual and audio data mining is an effective way to integrate with humans' visual and audio systems and discover knowledge from huge amounts of data. A systematic development of such techniques will facilitate the promotion of human participation for effective and efficient data analysis.

- **Distributed data mining and real-time data stream mining:** Traditional data mining methods, designed to work at a centralized location, do not work well in many of the distributed computing environments present today (e.g., the Internet, intranets, local area networks, high-speed wireless networks, sensor networks, and cloud computing). Advances in distributed data mining methods are expected. Moreover, many applications involving stream data (e.g., e-commerce, Web mining, stock analysis, intrusion detection, mobile data mining, and data mining for counterterrorism) require dynamic data mining models to be built in real time. Additional research is needed in this direction.

- **Privacy protection and information security in data mining:** An abundance of personal or confidential information available in electronic forms, coupled with increasingly powerful data mining tools, poses a threat to data privacy and security. Growing interest in data mining for counterterrorism also adds to the concern.

Further development of privacy-preserving data mining methods is foreseen. The collaboration of technologists, social scientists, law experts, governments, and companies is needed to produce a rigorous privacy and security protection mechanism for data publishing and data mining.

With confidence, we look forward to the next generation of data mining technology and the further benefits that it will bring.

13.6 Summary

- Mining complex data types poses challenging issues, for which there are many dedicated lines of research and development. This chapter presents a high-level overview of **mining complex data types**, which includes *mining sequence data* such as time series, symbolic sequences, and biological sequences; *mining graphs and networks*; and mining other kinds of data, including *spatiotemporal and cyber-physical system data*, *multimedia, text and Web data*, and *data streams*.

- Several well-established **statistical methods** have been proposed for data analysis such as regression, generalized linear models, analysis of variance, mixed-effect models, factor analysis, discriminant analysis, survival analysis, and quality control. Full coverage of statistical data analysis methods is beyond the scope of this book. Interested readers are referred to the statistical literature cited in the bibliographic notes (Section 13.8).

- Researchers have been striving to build **theoretical foundations** for data mining. Several interesting proposals have appeared, based on data reduction, data compression, probability and statistics theory, microeconomic theory, and pattern discovery–based inductive databases.

- **Visual data mining** integrates data mining and data visualization to discover implicit and useful knowledge from large data sets. Visual data mining includes *data visualization, data mining result visualization, data mining process visualization,* and *interactive visual data mining.* **Audio data mining** uses audio signals to indicate data patterns or features of data mining results.

- Many customized data mining tools have been developed for **domain-specific applications**, including finance, the retail and telecommunication industries, science and engineering, intrusion detection and prevention, and recommender systems. Such application domain-based studies integrate domain-specific knowledge with data analysis techniques and provide mission-specific data mining solutions.

- **Ubiquitous data mining** is the constant presence of data mining in many aspects of our daily lives. It can influence how we shop, work, search for information, and use a computer, as well as our leisure time, health, and well-being. In **invisible data mining**, "smart" software, such as search engines, customer-adaptive web services (e.g., using recommender algorithms), email managers, and so on, incorporates data mining into its functional components, often unbeknownst to the user.

■ A major social concern of data mining is the issue of *privacy and data security*. **Privacy-preserving data mining** deals with obtaining valid data mining results without disclosing underlying sensitive values. Its goal is to ensure privacy protection and security while preserving the overall quality of data mining results.

■ **Data mining trends** include further efforts toward the exploration of new application areas; improved scalable, interactive, and constraint-based mining methods; the integration of data mining with web service, database, warehousing, and cloud computing systems; and mining social and information networks. Other trends include the mining of spatiotemporal and cyber-physical system data, biological data, software/system engineering data, and multimedia and text data, in addition to web mining, distributed and real-time data stream mining, visual and audio mining, and privacy and security in data mining.

13.7 Exercises

13.1 Sequence data are ubiquitous and have diverse applications. This chapter presented a general overview of sequential pattern mining, sequence classification, sequence similarity search, trend analysis, biological sequence alignment, and modeling. However, we have not covered sequence clustering. Present an overview of methods for *sequence clustering*.

13.2 This chapter presented an overview of sequence pattern mining and graph pattern mining methods. Mining tree patterns and partial order patterns is also studied in research. *Summarize the methods for mining structured patterns*, including sequences, trees, graphs, and partial order relationships. Examine what kinds of structural pattern mining have not been covered in research. Propose applications that can be created for such new mining problems.

13.3 Many studies analyze homogeneous information networks (e.g., social networks consisting of friends linked with friends). However, many other applications involve *heterogeneous information networks* (i.e., networks linking multiple types of object such as research papers, conference, authors, and topics). What are the major differences between methodologies for mining heterogeneous information networks and methods for their homogeneous counterparts?

13.4 Research and describe a *data mining application* that was not presented in this chapter. Discuss how different forms of data mining can be used in the application.

13.5 Why is the establishment of *theoretical foundations* important for data mining? Name and describe the main theoretical foundations that have been proposed for data mining. Comment on how they each satisfy (or fail to satisfy) the requirements of an ideal theoretical framework for data mining.

13.6 (**Research project**) Building a theory of data mining requires setting up a *theoretical framework* so that the major data mining functions can be explained under this framework. Take one theory as an example (e.g., data compression theory) and examine how the major data mining functions fit into this framework. If some functions do not fit well into the current theoretical framework, can you propose a way to extend the framework to explain these functions?

13.7 There is a strong linkage between *statistical data analysis* and data mining. Some people think of data mining as automated and scalable methods for statistical data analysis. Do you agree or disagree with this perception? Present one statistical analysis method that can be automated and/or scaled up nicely by integration with current data mining methodology.

13.8 What are the differences between *visual data mining* and *data visualization*? Data visualization may suffer from the data abundance problem. For example, it is not easy to visually discover interesting properties of network connections if a social network is huge, with complex and dense connections. Propose a visualization method that may help people see through the network topology to the interesting features of a social network.

13.9 Propose a few implementation methods for *audio data mining*. Can we integrate audio and *visual data mining* to bring fun and power to data mining? Is it possible to develop some video data mining methods? State some scenarios and your solutions to make such integrated audiovisual mining effective.

13.10 General-purpose computers and domain-independent relational database systems have become a large market in the last several decades. However, many people feel that generic data mining systems will not prevail in the data mining market. What do you think? For data mining, should we focus our efforts on developing *domain-independent* data mining tools or on developing *domain-specific* data mining solutions? Present your reasoning.

13.11 What is a *recommender system*? In what ways does it differ from a customer or product-based clustering system? How does it differ from a typical classification or predictive modeling system? Outline one method of collaborative filtering. Discuss why it works and what its limitations are in practice.

13.12 Suppose that your local bank has a data mining system. The bank has been studying your debit card usage patterns. Noticing that you make many transactions at home renovation stores, the bank decides to contact you, offering information regarding their special loans for home improvements.

(a) Discuss how this may conflict with your right to *privacy*.

(b) Describe another situation in which you feel that data mining can infringe on your privacy.

(c) Describe a *privacy-preserving data mining* method that may allow the bank to perform customer pattern analysis without infringing on its customers' right to privacy.

(d) What are some examples where data mining could be used to help society? Can you think of ways it could be used that may be detrimental to society?

13.13 What are the major challenges faced in bringing data mining research to *market*? Illustrate one data mining research issue that, in your view, may have a strong impact on the market and on society. Discuss how to approach such a research issue.

13.14 Based on your view, what is the most *challenging research problem* in data mining? If you were given a number of years and a good number of researchers and implementors, what would your plan be to make good progress toward an effective solution to such a problem?

13.15 Based on your experience and knowledge, suggest a *new frontier* in data mining that was not mentioned in this chapter.

13.8 Bibliographic Notes

For mining complex data types, there are many research papers and books covering various themes. We list here some recent books and well-cited survey or research articles for references.

Time-series analysis has been studied in statistics and computer science communities for decades, with many textbooks such as Box, Jenkins, and Reinsel [BJR08]; Brockwell and Davis [BD02]; Chatfield [Cha03b]; Hamilton [Ham94]; and Shumway and Stoffer [SS05]. A fast subsequence matching method in time-series databases was presented by Faloutsos, Ranganathan, and Manolopoulos [FRM94]. Agrawal, Lin, Sawhney, and Shim [ALSS95] developed a method for fast **similarity search** in the presence of noise, scaling, and translation in time-series databases. Shasha and Zhu present an overview of the methods for high-performance discovery in time series [SZ04].

Sequential pattern mining methods have been studied by many researchers, including Agrawal and Srikant [AS95]; Zaki [Zak01]; Pei, Han, Mortazavi-Asl, et al. [PHM-A^{+}04]; and Yan, Han, and Afshar [YHA03]. The study on **sequence classification** includes Ji, Bailey, and Dong [JBD05] and Ye and Keogh [YK09], with a survey by Xing, Pei, and Keogh [XPK10]. Dong and Pei [DP07] provide an overview on **sequence data mining** methods.

Methods for **analysis of biological sequences** including **Markov chains** and **hidden Markov models** are introduced in many books or tutorials such as Waterman [Wat95]; Setubal and Meidanis [SM97]; Durbin, Eddy, Krogh, and Mitchison [DEKM98]; Baldi and Brunak [BB01]; Krane and Raymer [KR03]; Rabiner [Rab89]; Jones and Pevzner [JP04]; and Baxevanis and Ouellette [BO04]. Information about BLAST (see also Korf, Yandell, and Bedell [KYB03]) can be found at the NCBI web site *www.ncbi.nlm.nih.gov/BLAST/*.

Graph pattern mining has been studied extensively, including Holder, Cook, and Djoko [HCD94]; Inokuchi, Washio, and Motoda [IWM98]; Kuramochi and Karypis [KK01]; Yan and Han [YH02, YH03a]; Borgelt and Berthold [BB02]; Huan, Wang, Bandyopadhyay, et al. [HWB^{+}04]; and the Gaston tool by Nijssen and Kok [NK04].

There has been a great deal of research on **social and information network analysis**, including Newman [New10]; Easley and Kleinberg [EK10]; Yu, Han, and Faloutsos [YHF10]; Wasserman and Faust [WF94]; Watts [Wat03]; and Newman, Barabasi, and Watts [NBW06]. **Statistical modeling of networks** is studied popularly such as Albert and Barbasi [AB99]; Watts [Wat03]; Faloutsos, Faloutsos, and Faloutsos [FFF99]; Kumar, Raghavan, Rajagopalan, et al. [KRR$^+$00]; and Leskovec, Kleinberg, and Faloutsos [LKF05]. **Data cleaning, integration, and validation by information network analysis** was studied by many, including Bhattacharya and Getoor [BG04] and Yin, Han, and Yu [YHY07, YHY08].

Clustering, ranking, and classification in networks has been studied extensively, including in Brin and Page [BP98]; Chakrabarti, Dom, and Indyk [CDI98]; Kleinberg [Kle99]; Getoor, Friedman, Koller, and Taskar [GFKT01]; Newman and M. Girvan [NG04]; Yin, Han, Yang, and Yu [YHYY04]; Yin, Han, and Yu [YHY05]; Xu, Yuruk, Feng, and Schweiger [XYFS07]; Kulis, Basu, Dhillon, and Mooney [KBDM09]; Sun, Han, Zhao, et al. [SHZ$^+$09]; Neville, Gallaher, and Eliassi-Rad [NGE-R09]; and Ji, Sun, Danilevsky et al. [JSD$^+$10]. **Role discovery and link prediction in information networks** have been studied extensively as well, such as by Krebs [Kre02]; Kubica, Moore, and Schneider [KMS03]; Liben-Nowell and Kleinberg [L-NK03]; and Wang, Han, Jia, et al. [WHJ$^+$10].

Similarity search and OLAP in information networks has been studied by many, including Tian, Hankins, and Patel [THP08] and Chen, Yan, Zhu, et al. [CYZ$^+$08]. **Evolution of social and information networks** has been studied by many researchers, such as Chakrabarti, Kumar, and Tomkins [CKT06]; Chi, Song, Zhou, et al. [CSZ$^+$07]; Tang, Liu, Zhang, and Nazeri [TLZN08]; Xu, Zhang, Yu, and Long [XZYL08]; Kim and Han [KH09]; and Sun, Tang, and Han [STH$^+$10].

Spatial and spatiotemporal data mining has been studied extensively, with a collection of papers by Miller and Han [MH09], and was introduced in some textbooks, such as Shekhar and Chawla [SC03] and Hsu, Lee, and Wang [HLW07]. Spatial clustering algorithms have been studied extensively in Chapters 10 and 11 of this book. Research has been conducted on spatial warehouses and OLAP, such as by Stefanovic, Han, and Koperski [SHK00], and spatial and spatiotemporal data mining, such as by Koperski and Han [KH95]; Mamoulis, Cao, Kollios, Hadjieleftheriou, et al. [MCK$^+$04]; Tsoukatos and Gunopulos [TG01]; and Hadjieleftheriou, Kollios, Gunopulos, and Tsotras [HKGT03]. **Mining moving-object data** has been studied by many, such as Vlachos, Gunopulos, and Kollios [VGK02]; Tao, Faloutsos, Papadias, and Liu [TFPL04]; Li, Han, Kim, and Gonzalez [LHKG07]; Lee, Han, and Whang [LHW07]; and Li, Ding, Han, et al. [LDH$^+$10]. For the bibliography of temporal, spatial, and spatiotemporal data mining research, see a collection by Roddick, Hornsby, and Spiliopoulou [RHS01].

Multimedia data mining has deep roots in image processing and pattern recognition, which have been studied extensively in many textbooks, including Gonzalez and Woods [GW07]; Russ [Rus06]; Duda, Hart, and Stork [DHS01]; and Z. Zhang and R. Zhang [ZZ09]. Searching and mining of multimedia data has been studied by many (see, e.g., Fayyad and Smyth [FS93]; Faloutsos and Lin [FL95]; Natsev, Rastogi, and

Shim [NRS99]; and Zaïane, Han, and Zhu [ZHZ00]). An overview of image mining methods is given by Hsu, Lee, and Zhang [HLZ02].

Text data analysis has been studied extensively in information retrieval, with many textbooks and survey articles such as Croft, Metzler, and Strohman [CMS09]; S. Buttcher, C. Clarke, G. Cormack [BCC10]; Manning, Raghavan, and Schutze [MRS08]; Grossman and Frieder [GR04]; Baeza-Yates and Riberio-Neto [BYRN11]; Zhai [Zha08]; Feldman and Sanger [FS06]; Berry [Ber03]; and Weiss, Indurkhya, Zhang, and Damerau [WIZD04]. Text mining is a fast-developing field with numerous papers published in recent years, covering many topics such as topic models (e.g., Blei and Lafferty [BL09]); sentiment analysis (e.g., Pang and Lee [PL07]); and contextual text mining (e.g., Mei and Zhai [MZ06]).

Web mining is another focused theme, with books like Chakrabarti [Cha03a], Liu [Liu06], and Berry [Ber03]. Web mining has substantially improved search engines with a few influential milestone works, such as Brin and Page [BP98]; Kleinberg [Kle99]; Chakrabarti, Dom, Kumar, et al. [CDK+99]; and Kleinberg and Tomkins [KT99]. Numerous results have been generated since then, such as search log mining (e.g., Silvestri [Sil10]); blog mining (e.g., Mei, Liu, Su, and Zhai [MLSZ06]); and mining online forums (e.g., Cong, Wang, Lin, et al. [CWL+08]).

Books and surveys on stream data systems and stream data processing include Babu and Widom [BW01]; Babcock, Babu, Datar, et al. [BBD+02]; Muthukrishnan [Mut05]; and Aggarwal [Agg06].

Stream data mining research covers stream cube models (e.g., Chen, Dong, Han, et al. [CDH+02]), stream frequent pattern mining (e.g., Manku and Motwani [MM02] and Karp, Papadimitriou and Shenker [KPS03]), stream classification (e.g., Domingos and Hulten [DH00]; Wang, Fan, Yu, and Han [WFYH03]; Aggarwal, Han, Wang, and Yu [AHWY04b]), and stream clustering (e.g., Guha, Mishra, Motwani, and O'Callaghan [GMMO00] and Aggarwal, Han, Wang, and Yu [AHWY03]).

There are many books that discuss **data mining applications**. For financial data analysis and financial modeling, see, for example, Benninga [Ben08] and Higgins [Hig08]. For retail data mining and customer relationship management, see, for example, books by Berry and Linoff [BL04] and Berson, Smith, and Thearling [BST99]. For telecommunication-related data mining, see, for example, Horak [Hor08]. There are also books on scientific data analysis, such as Grossman, Kamath, Kegelmeyer, et al. [GKK+01] and Kamath [Kam09].

Issues in the **theoretical foundations of data mining** have been addressed by many researchers. For example, Mannila presents a summary of studies on the foundations of data mining in [Man00]. The data reduction view of data mining is summarized in *The New Jersey Data Reduction Report* by Barbará, DuMouchel, Faloutos, et al. [BDF+97]. The data compression view can be found in studies on the minimum description length principle, such as Grunwald and Rissanen [GR07].

The pattern discovery point of view of data mining is addressed in numerous machine learning and data mining studies, ranging from association mining, to decision tree induction, sequential pattern mining, clustering, and so on. The probability theory point of view is popular in the statistics and machine learning literature, such as Bayesian networks and hierarchical Bayesian models in Chapter 9, and probabilistic graph models (e.g., Koller and Friedman [KF09]). Kleinberg, Papadimitriou, and Raghavan [KPR98] present a microeconomic view, treating data mining as an optimization problem. Studies on the inductive database view include Imielinski and Mannila [IM96] and de Raedt, Guns, and Nijssen [RGN10].

Statistical methods for data analysis are described in many books, such as Hastie, Tibshirani, Friedman [HTF09]; Freedman, Pisani, and Purves [FPP07]; Devore [Dev03]; Kutner, Nachtsheim, Neter, and Li [KNNL04]; Dobson [Dob01]; Breiman, Friedman, Olshen, and Stone [BFOS84]; Pinheiro and Bates [PB00]; Johnson and Wichern [JW02b]; Huberty [Hub94]; Shumway and Stoffer [SS05]; and Miller [Mil98].

For **visual data mining**, popular books on the visual display of data and information include those by Tufte [Tuf90, Tuf97, Tuf01]. A summary of techniques for visualizing data is presented in Cleveland [Cle93]. A dedicated visual data mining book, *Visual Data Mining: Techniques and Tools for Data Visualization and Mining*, is by Soukup and Davidson [SD02]. The book *Information Visualization in Data Mining and Knowledge Discovery*, edited by Fayyad, Grinstein, and Wierse [FGW01], contains a collection of articles on visual data mining methods.

Ubiquitous and invisible data mining has been discussed in many texts including John [Joh99], and some articles in a book edited by Kargupta, Joshi, Sivakumar, and Yesha [KJSY04]. The book *Business @ the Speed of Thought: Succeeding in the Digital Economy* by Gates [Gat00] discusses e-commerce and customer relationship management, and provides an interesting perspective on data mining in the future. Mena [Men03] has an informative book on the use of data mining to detect and prevent crime. It covers many forms of criminal activities, ranging from fraud detection, money laundering, insurance crimes, identity crimes, and intrusion detection.

Data mining issues regarding **privacy and data security** are addressed popularly in literature. Books on privacy and security in data mining include Thuraisingham [Thu04]; Aggarwal and Yu [AY08]; Vaidya, Clifton, and Zhu [VCZ10]; and Fung, Wang, Fu, and Yu [FWFY10]. Research articles include Agrawal and Srikant [AS00]; Evfimievski, Srikant, Agrawal, and Gehrke [ESAG02]; and Vaidya and Clifton [VC03]. Differential privacy was introduced by Dwork [Dwo06] and studied by many such as Hay, Rastogi, Miklau, and Suciu [HRMS10].

There have been many discussions on **trends and research directions of data mining** in various forums. Several books are collections of articles on these issues such as Kargupta, Han, Yu, et al. [KHY+08].

Bibliography

[AAD+96]   S. Agarwal, R. Agrawal, P. M. Deshpande, A. Gupta, J. F. Naughton, R. Ramakrishnan, and S. Sarawagi. On the computation of multidimensional aggregates. In *Proc. 1996 Int. Conf. Very Large Data Bases (VLDB'96)*, pp. 506–521, Bombay, India, Sept. 1996.

[AAP01]   R. Agarwal, C. C. Aggarwal, and V. V. V. Prasad. A tree projection algorithm for generation of frequent itemsets. *J. Parallel and Distributed Computing*, 61:350–371, 2001.

[AB79]   B. Abraham and G. E. P. Box. Bayesian analysis of some outlier problems in time series. *Biometrika*, 66:229–248, 1979.

[AB99]   R. Albert and A.-L. Barabasi. Emergence of scaling in random networks. *Science*, 286:509–512, 1999.

[ABA06]   M. Agyemang, K. Barker, and R. Alhajj. A comprehensive survey of numeric and symbolic outlier mining techniques. *Intell. Data Anal.*, 10:521–538, 2006.

[ABKS99]   M. Ankerst, M. Breunig, H.-P. Kriegel, and J. Sander. OPTICS: Ordering points to identify the clustering structure. In *Proc. 1999 ACM-SIGMOD Int. Conf. Management of Data (SIGMOD'99)*, pp. 49–60, Philadelphia, PA, June 1999.

[AD91]   H. Almuallim and T. G. Dietterich. Learning with many irrelevant features. In *Proc. 1991 Nat. Conf. Artificial Intelligence (AAAI'91)*, pp. 547–552, Anaheim, CA, July 1991.

[AEEK99]   M. Ankerst, C. Elsen, M. Ester, and H.-P. Kriegel. Visual classification: An interactive approach to decision tree construction. In *Proc. 1999 Int. Conf. Knowledge Discovery and Data Mining (KDD'99)*, pp. 392–396, San Diego, CA, Aug. 1999.

[AEMT00]   K. M. Ahmed, N. M. El-Makky, and Y. Taha. A note on "beyond market basket: Generalizing association rules to correlations." *SIGKDD Explorations*, 1:46–48, 2000.

[AG60]   F. J. Anscombe, and I. Guttman. Rejection of outliers. *Technometrics*, 2:123–147, 1960.

[Aga06]   D. Agarwal. Detecting anomalies in cross-classified streams: A Bayesian approach. *Knowl. Inf. Syst.*, 11:29–44, 2006.

[AGAV09]   E. Amigó, J. Gonzalo, J. Artiles, and F. Verdejo. A comparison of extrinsic clustering evaluation metrics based on formal constraints. *Information Retrieval*, 12(4):461–486, 2009.

[Agg06]   C. C. Aggarwal. *Data Streams: Models and Algorithms*. Kluwer Academic, 2006.

[AGGR98]   R. Agrawal, J. Gehrke, D. Gunopulos, and P. Raghavan. Automatic subspace clustering of high dimensional data for data mining applications. In *Proc. 1998 ACM-SIGMOD Int. Conf. Management of Data (SIGMOD'98)*, pp. 94–105, Seattle, WA, June 1998.

[AGM04]   F. N. Afrati, A. Gionis, and H. Mannila. Approximating a collection of frequent sets. In *Proc. 2004 ACM SIGKDD Int. Conf. Knowledge Discovery in Databases (KDD'04)*, pp. 12–19, Seattle, WA, Aug. 2004.

[AGS97]   R. Agrawal, A. Gupta, and S. Sarawagi. Modeling multidimensional databases. In *Proc. 1997 Int. Conf. Data Engineering (ICDE'97)*, pp. 232–243, Birmingham, England, Apr. 1997.

[Aha92]   D. Aha. Tolerating noisy, irrelevant, and novel attributes in instance-based learning algorithms. *Int. J. Man-Machine Studies*, 36:267–287, 1992.

[AHS96]   P. Arabie, L. J. Hubert, and G. De Soete. *Clustering and Classification*. World Scientific, 1996.

[AHWY03]   C. C. Aggarwal, J. Han, J. Wang, and P. S. Yu. A framework for clustering evolving data streams. In *Proc. 2003 Int. Conf. Very Large Data Bases (VLDB'03)*, pp. 81–92, Berlin, Germany, Sept. 2003.

[AHWY04a]   C. C. Aggarwal, J. Han, J. Wang, and P. S. Yu. A framework for projected clustering of high dimensional data streams. In *Proc. 2004 Int. Conf. Very Large Data Bases (VLDB'04)*, pp. 852–863, Toronto, Ontario, Canada, Aug. 2004.

[AHWY04b]   C. C. Aggarwal, J. Han, J. Wang, and P. S. Yu. On demand classification of data streams. In *Proc. 2004 ACM SIGKDD Int. Conf. Knowledge Discovery in Databases (KDD'04)*, pp. 503–508, Seattle, WA, Aug. 2004.

[AIS93]   R. Agrawal, T. Imielinski, and A. Swami. Mining association rules between sets of items in large databases. In *Proc. 1993 ACM-SIGMOD Int. Conf. Management of Data (SIGMOD'93)*, pp. 207–216, Washington, DC, May 1993.

[AK93]   T. Anand and G. Kahn. Opportunity explorer: Navigating large databases using knowledge discovery templates. In *Proc. AAAI-93 Workshop Knowledge Discovery in Databases*, pp. 45–51, Washington, DC, July 1993.

[AL99]   Y. Aumann and Y. Lindell. A statistical theory for quantitative association rules. In *Proc. 1999 Int. Conf. Knowledge Discovery and Data Mining (KDD'99)*, pp. 261–270, San Diego, CA, Aug. 1999.

[All94]   B. P. Allen. Case-based reasoning: Business applications. *Communications of the ACM*, 37:40–42, 1994.

[Alp11]   E. Alpaydin. *Introduction to Machine Learning* (2nd ed.). Cambridge, MA: MIT Press, 2011.

[ALSS95]   R. Agrawal, K.-I. Lin, H. S. Sawhney, and K. Shim. Fast similarity search in the presence of noise, scaling, and translation in time-series databases. In *Proc. 1995 Int. Conf. Very Large Data Bases (VLDB'95)*, pp. 490–501, Zurich, Switzerland, Sept. 1995.

[AMS+96]   R. Agrawal, H. Mannila, R. Srikant, H. Toivonen, and A. I. Verkamo. Fast discovery of association rules. In U. M. Fayyad, G. Piatetsky-Shapiro, P. Smyth, and R. Uthurusamy (eds.), *Advances in Knowledge Discovery and Data Mining*, pp. 307–328. AAAI/MIT Press, 1996.

[Aok98]   P. M. Aoki. Generalizing "search" in generalized search trees. In *Proc. 1998 Int. Conf. Data Engineering (ICDE'98)*, pp. 380–389, Orlando, FL, Feb. 1998.

[AP94]   A. Aamodt and E. Plazas. Case-based reasoning: Foundational issues, methodological variations, and system approaches. *AI Communications*, 7:39–52, 1994.

[AP05]   F. Angiulli, and C. Pizzuti. Outlier mining in large high-dimensional data sets. *IEEE Trans. on Knowl. and Data Eng.*, 17:203–215, 2005.

[APW+99]   C. C. Aggarwal, C. Procopiuc, J. Wolf, P. S. Yu, and J.-S. Park. Fast algorithms for projected clustering. In *Proc. 1999 ACM-SIGMOD Int. Conf. Management of Data (SIGMOD'99)*, pp. 61–72, Philadelphia, PA, June 1999.

[ARV09]   S. Arora, S. Rao, and U. Vazirani. Expander flows, geometric embeddings and graph partitioning. *J. ACM*, 56(2):1–37, 2009.

[AS94a]   R. Agrawal and R. Srikant. Fast algorithm for mining association rules in large databases. In *Research Report RJ 9839*, IBM Almaden Research Center, San Jose, CA, June 1994.

[AS94b]   R. Agrawal and R. Srikant. Fast algorithms for mining association rules. In *Proc. 1994 Int. Conf. Very Large Data Bases (VLDB'94)*, pp. 487–499, Santiago, Chile, Sept. 1994.

[AS95]   R. Agrawal and R. Srikant. Mining sequential patterns. In *Proc. 1995 Int. Conf. Data Engineering (ICDE'95)*, pp. 3–14, Taipei, Taiwan, Mar. 1995.

[AS96]   R. Agrawal and J. C. Shafer. Parallel mining of association rules: Design, implementation, and experience. *IEEE Trans. Knowledge and Data Engineering*, 8:962–969, 1996.

[AS00]   R. Agrawal and R. Srikant. Privacy-preserving data mining. In *Proc. 2000 ACM-SIGMOD Int. Conf. Management of Data (SIGMOD'00)*, pp. 439–450, Dallas, TX, May 2000.

[ASS00]   E. Allwein, R. Shapire, and Y. Singer. Reducing multiclass to binary: A unifying approach for margin classifiers. *Journal of Machine Learning Research*, 1:113–141, 2000.

[AV07]   D. Arthur and S. Vassilvitskii. K-means++: The advantages of careful seeding. In *Proc. 2007 ACM-SIAM Symp. on Discrete Algorithms (SODA'07)*, pp. 1027–1035, Tokyo, 2007.

[Avn95]   S. Avner. Discovery of comprehensible symbolic rules in a neural network. In *Proc. 1995 Int. Symp. Intelligence in Neural and Biological Systems*, pp. 64–67, Washington, DC, 1995.

[AY99]   C. C. Aggarwal and P. S. Yu. A new framework for itemset generation. In *Proc. 1998 ACM Symp. Principles of Database Systems (PODS'98)*, pp. 18–24, Seattle, WA, June 1999.

[AY01]   C. C. Aggarwal and P. S. Yu. Outlier detection for high dimensional data. In *Proc. 2001 ACM-SIGMOD Int. Conf. Management of Data (SIGMOD'01)*, pp. 37–46, Santa Barbara, CA, May 2001.

[AY08]   C. C. Aggarwal and P. S. Yu. *Privacy-Preserving Data Mining: Models and Algorithms*. New York: Springer, 2008.

[BA97]   L. A. Breslow and D. W. Aha. Simplifying decision trees: A survey. *Knowledge Engineering Rev.*, 12:1–40, 1997.

[Bay98]   R. J. Bayardo. Efficiently mining long patterns from databases. In *Proc. 1998 ACM-SIGMOD Int. Conf. Management of Data (SIGMOD'98)*, pp. 85–93, Seattle, WA, June 1998.

[BB98]   A. Bagga and B. Baldwin. Entity-based cross-document coreferencing using the vector space model. In *Proc. 1998 Annual Meeting of the Association for Computational Linguistics and Int. Conf. Computational Linguistics (COLING-ACL'98)*, Montreal, Quebec, Canada, Aug. 1998.

[BB01]   P. Baldi and S. Brunak. *Bioinformatics: The Machine Learning Approach* (2nd ed.). Cambridge, MA: MIT Press, 2001.

[BB02]   C. Borgelt and M. R. Berthold. Mining molecular fragments: Finding relevant substructures of molecules. In *Proc. 2002 Int. Conf. Data Mining (ICDM'02)*, pp. 211–218, Maebashi, Japan, Dec. 2002.

[BBD$^+$02]   B. Babcock, S. Babu, M. Datar, R. Motwani, and J. Widom. Models and issues in data stream systems. In *Proc. 2002 ACM Symp. Principles of Database Systems (PODS'02)*, pp. 1–16, Madison, WI, June 2002.

[BC83]   R. J. Beckman and R. D. Cook. Outlier...s. *Technometrics*, 25:119–149, 1983.

[BCC10]   S. Buettcher, C. L. A. Clarke, and G. V. Cormack. *Information Retrieval: Implementing and Evaluating Search Engines.* Cambridge, MA: MIT Press, 2010.

[BCG01]   D. Burdick, M. Calimlim, and J. Gehrke. MAFIA: A maximal frequent itemset algorithm for transactional databases. In *Proc. 2001 Int. Conf. Data Engineering (ICDE'01),* pp. 443–452, Heidelberg, Germany, Apr. 2001.

[BCP93]   D. E. Brown, V. Corruble, and C. L. Pittard. A comparison of decision tree classifiers with backpropagation neural networks for multimodal classification problems. *Pattern Recognition,* 26:953–961, 1993.

[BD01]   P. J. Bickel and K. A. Doksum. *Mathematical Statistics: Basic Ideas and Selected Topics,* Vol. 1. Prentice-Hall, 2001.

[BD02]   P. J. Brockwell and R. A. Davis. *Introduction to Time Series and Forecasting* (2nd ed.). New York: Springer, 2002.

[BDF$^+$97] D. Barbará, W. DuMouchel, C. Faloutsos, P. J. Haas, J. H. Hellerstein, Y. Ioannidis, H. V. Jagadish, T. Johnson, R. Ng, V. Poosala, K. A. Ross, and K. C. Servcik. The New Jersey data reduction report. *Bull. Technical Committee on Data Engineering,* 20:3–45, Dec. 1997.

[BDG96]   A. Bruce, D. Donoho, and H.-Y. Gao. Wavelet analysis. *IEEE Spectrum,* 33:26–35, Oct. 1996.

[BDJ$^+$05] D. Burdick, P. Deshpande, T. S. Jayram, R. Ramakrishnan, and S. Vaithyanathan. OLAP over uncertain and imprecise data. In *Proc. 2005 Int. Conf. Very Large Data Bases (VLDB'05),* pp. 970–981, Trondheim, Norway, Aug. 2005.

[Ben08]   S. Benninga. *Financial Modeling* (3rd. ed.). Cambridge, MA: MIT Press, 2008.

[Ber81]   J. Bertin. *Graphics and Graphic Information Processing.* Walter de Gruyter, Berlin, 1981.

[Ber03]   M. W. Berry. *Survey of Text Mining: Clustering, Classification, and Retrieval.* New York: Springer, 2003.

[Bez81]   J. C. Bezdek. *Pattern Recognition with Fuzzy Objective Function Algorithms.* Plenum Press, 1981.

[BFOS84] L. Breiman, J. Friedman, R. Olshen, and C. Stone. *Classification and Regression Trees.* Wadsworth International Group, 1984.

[BFR98]   P. Bradley, U. Fayyad, and C. Reina. Scaling clustering algorithms to large databases. In *Proc. 1998 Int. Conf. Knowledge Discovery and Data Mining (KDD'98),* pp. 9–15, New York, Aug. 1998.

[BG04]   I. Bhattacharya and L. Getoor. Iterative record linkage for cleaning and integration. In *Proc. SIGMOD 2004 Workshop on Research Issues on Data Mining and Knowledge Discovery (DMKD'04),* pp. 11–18, Paris, France, June 2004.

[B-G05]   I. Ben-Gal. Outlier detection. In O. Maimon and L. Rockach (eds.), *Data Mining and Knowledge Discovery Handbook: A Complete Guide for Practitioners and Researchers.* Kluwer Academic, 2005.

[BGKW03] C. Bucila, J. Gehrke, D. Kifer, and W. White. DualMiner: A dual-pruning algorithm for itemsets with constraints. *Data Mining and Knowledge Discovery,* 7:241–272, 2003.

[BGMP03] F. Bonchi, F. Giannotti, A. Mazzanti, and D. Pedreschi. ExAnte: Anticipated data reduction in constrained pattern mining. In *Proc. 7th European Conf. Principles and Pratice of Knowledge Discovery in Databases (PKDD'03),* Vol. 2838/2003, pp. 59–70, Cavtat-Dubrovnik, Croatia, Sept. 2003.

[BGRS99] K. S. Beyer, J. Goldstein, R. Ramakrishnan, and U. Shaft. When is "nearest neighbor" meaningful? In *Proc. 1999 Int. Conf. Database Theory (ICDT'99)*, pp. 217–235, Jerusalem, Israel, Jan. 1999.

[BGV92] B. Boser, I. Guyon, and V. N. Vapnik. A training algorithm for optimal margin classifiers. In *Proc. Fifth Annual Workshop on Computational Learning Theory*, pp. 144–152, ACM Press, San Mateo, CA, 1992.

[Bis95] C. M. Bishop. *Neural Networks for Pattern Recognition.* Oxford University Press, 1995.

[Bis06] C. M. Bishop. *Pattern Recognition and Machine Learning.* New York: Springer, 2006.

[BJR08] G. E. P. Box, G. M. Jenkins, and G. C. Reinsel. *Time Series Analysis: Forecasting and Control* (4th ed.). Prentice-Hall, 2008.

[BKNS00] M. M. Breunig, H.-P. Kriegel, R. Ng, and J. Sander. LOF: Identifying density-based local outliers. In *Proc. 2000 ACM-SIGMOD Int. Conf. Management of Data (SIGMOD'00)*, pp. 93–104, Dallas, TX, May 2000.

[BL99] M. J. A. Berry and G. Linoff. *Mastering Data Mining: The Art and Science of Customer Relationship Management.* John Wiley & Sons, 1999.

[BL04] M. J. A. Berry and G. S. Linoff. *Data Mining Techniques: For Marketing, Sales, and Customer Relationship Management.* John Wiley & Sons, 2004.

[BL09] D. Blei and J. Lafferty. Topic models. In A. Srivastava and M. Sahami (eds.), *Text Mining: Theory and Applications*, Taylor and Francis, 2009.

[BLC⁺03] D. Barbará, Y. Li, J. Couto, J.-L. Lin, and S. Jajodia. Bootstrapping a data mining intrusion detection system. In *Proc. 2003 ACM Symp. on Applied Computing (SAC'03)*, Melbourne, FL, March 2003.

[BM98] A. Blum and T. Mitchell. Combining labeled and unlabeled data with co-training. In *Proc. 11th Conf. Computational Learning Theory (COLT'98)*, pp. 92–100, Madison, WI, 1998.

[BMAD06] Z. A. Bakar, R. Mohemad, A. Ahmad, and M. M. Deris. A comparative study for outlier detection techniques in data mining. In *Proc. 2006 IEEE Conf. Cybernetics and Intelligent Systems*, pp. 1–6, Bangkok, Thailand, 2006.

[BMS97] S. Brin, R. Motwani, and C. Silverstein. Beyond market basket: Generalizing association rules to correlations. In *Proc. 1997 ACM-SIGMOD Int. Conf. Management of Data (SIGMOD'97)*, pp. 265–276, Tucson, AZ, May 1997.

[BMUT97] S. Brin, R. Motwani, J. D. Ullman, and S. Tsur. Dynamic itemset counting and implication rules for market basket analysis. In *Proc. 1997 ACM-SIGMOD Int. Conf. Management of Data (SIGMOD'97)*, pp. 255–264, Tucson, AZ, May 1997.

[BN92] W. L. Buntine and T. Niblett. A further comparison of splitting rules for decision-tree induction. *Machine Learning*, 8:75–85, 1992.

[BO04] A. Baxevanis and B. F. F. Ouellette. *Bioinformatics: A Practical Guide to the Analysis of Genes and Proteins* (3rd ed.). John Wiley & Sons, 2004.

[BP92] J. C. Bezdek and S. K. Pal. *Fuzzy Models for Pattern Recognition: Methods That Search for Structures in Data.* IEEE Press, 1992.

[BP98] S. Brin and L. Page. The anatomy of a large-scale hypertextual web search engine. In *Proc. 7th Int. World Wide Web Conf. (WWW'98)*, pp. 107–117, Brisbane, Australia, Apr. 1998.

[BPT97]   E. Baralis, S. Paraboschi, and E. Teniente. Materialized view selection in a multidimensional database. In *Proc. 1997 Int. Conf. Very Large Data Bases (VLDB'97)*, pp. 98–12, Athens, Greece, Aug. 1997.

[BPW88]   E. R. Bareiss, B. W. Porter, and C. C. Weir. Protos: An exemplar-based learning apprentice. *Int. J. Man-Machine Studies*, 29:549–561, 1988.

[BR99]   K. Beyer and R. Ramakrishnan. Bottom-up computation of sparse and iceberg cubes. In *Proc. 1999 ACM-SIGMOD Int. Conf. Management of Data (SIGMOD'99)*, pp. 359–370, Philadelphia, PA, June 1999.

[Bre96]   L. Breiman. Bagging predictors. *Machine Learning*, 24:123–140, 1996.

[Bre01]   L. Breiman. Random forests. *Machine Learning*, 45:5–32, 2001.

[BS97]   D. Barbará and M. Sullivan. Quasi-cubes: Exploiting approximation in multidimensional databases. *SIGMOD Record*, 26:12–17, 1997.

[BS03]   S. D. Bay and M. Schwabacher. Mining distance-based outliers in near linear time with randomization and a simple pruning rule. In *Proc. 2003 ACM SIGKDD Int. Conf. Knowledge Discovery and Data Mining (KDD'03)*, pp. 29–38, Washington, DC, Aug. 2003.

[BST99]   A. Berson, S. J. Smith, and K. Thearling. *Building Data Mining Applications for CRM*. McGraw-Hill, 1999.

[BT99]   D. P. Ballou and G. K. Tayi. Enhancing data quality in data warehouse environments. *Communications of the ACM*, 42:73–78, 1999.

[BU95]   C. E. Brodley and P. E. Utgoff. Multivariate decision trees. *Machine Learning*, 19:45–77, 1995.

[Bun94]   W. L. Buntine. Operations for learning with graphical models. *J. Artificial Intelligence Research*, 2:159–225, 1994.

[Bur98]   C. J. C. Burges. A tutorial on support vector machines for pattern recognition. *Data Mining and Knowledge Discovery*, 2:121–168, 1998.

[BW00]   D. Barbará and X. Wu. Using loglinear models to compress datacubes. In *Proc. 1st Int. Conf. Web-Age Information Management (WAIM'00)*, pp. 311–322, Shanghai, China, 2000.

[BW01]   S. Babu and J. Widom. Continuous queries over data streams. *SIGMOD Record*, 30: 109–120, 2001.

[BYRN11]   R. A. Baeza-Yates and B. A. Ribeiro-Neto. *Modern Information Retrieval* (2nd ed.). Boston: Addison-Wesley, 2011.

[Cat91]   J. Catlett. *Megainduction: Machine Learning on Very large Databases*. Ph.D. Thesis, University of Sydney, 1991.

[CBK09]   V. Chandola, A. Banerjee, and V. Kumar. Anomaly detection: A survey. *ACM Computing Surveys*, 41:1–58, 2009.

[CC00]   Y. Cheng and G. Church. Biclustering of expression data. In *Proc. 2000 Int. Conf. Intelligent Systems for Molecular Biology (ISMB'00)*, pp. 93–103, La Jolla, CA, Aug. 2000.

[CCH91]   Y. Cai, N. Cercone, and J. Han. Attribute-oriented induction in relational databases. In G. Piatetsky-Shapiro and W. J. Frawley (eds.), *Knowledge Discovery in Databases*, pp. 213–228. AAAI/MIT Press, 1991.

[CCLR05]   B.-C. Chen, L. Chen, Y. Lin, and R. Ramakrishnan. Prediction cubes. In *Proc. 2005 Int. Conf. Very Large Data Bases (VLDB'05)*, pp. 982–993, Trondheim, Norway, Aug. 2005.

[CCS93]   E. F. Codd, S. B. Codd, and C. T. Salley. Beyond decision support. *Computer World*, 27(30):5–12, July 1993.

[CD97]   S. Chaudhuri and U. Dayal. An overview of data warehousing and OLAP technology. *SIGMOD Record*, 26:65–74, 1997.

[CDH+02]   Y. Chen, G. Dong, J. Han, B. W. Wah, and J. Wang. Multidimensional regression analysis of time-series data streams. In *Proc. 2002 Int. Conf. Very Large Data Bases (VLDB'02)*, pp. 323–334, Hong Kong, China, Aug. 2002.

[CDH+06]   Y. Chen, G. Dong, J. Han, J. Pei, B. W. Wah, and J. Wang. Regression cubes with lossless compression and aggregation. *IEEE Trans. Knowledge and Data Engineering*, 18:1585–1599, 2006.

[CDI98]   S. Chakrabarti, B. E. Dom, and P. Indyk. Enhanced hypertext classification using hyper-links. In *Proc. 1998 ACM-SIGMOD Int. Conf. Management of Data (SIGMOD'98)*, pp. 307–318, Seattle, WA, June 1998.

[CDK+99]   S. Chakrabarti, B. E. Dom, S. R. Kumar, P. Raghavan, S. Rajagopalan, A. Tomkins, D. Gibson, and J. M. Kleinberg. Mining the web's link structure. *COMPUTER*, 32:60–67, 1999.

[CGC94]   A. Chaturvedi, P. Green, and J. Carroll. *k*-means, *k*-medians and *k*-modes: Special cases of partitioning multiway data. In *The Classification Society of North America (CSNA) Meeting Presentation*, Houston, TX, 1994.

[CGC01]   A. Chaturvedi, P. Green, and J. Carroll. *k*-modes clustering. *J. Classification*, 18:35–55, 2001.

[CH67]   T. Cover and P. Hart. Nearest neighbor pattern classification. *IEEE Trans. Information Theory*, 13:21–27, 1967.

[CH92]   G. Cooper and E. Herskovits. A Bayesian method for the induction of probabilistic networks from data. *Machine Learning*, 9:309–347, 1992.

[CH07]   D. J. Cook and L. B. Holder. *Mining Graph Data*. John Wiley & Sons, 2007.

[Cha03a]   S. Chakrabarti. *Mining the Web: Discovering Knowledge from Hypertext Data*. Morgan Kaufmann, 2003.

[Cha03b]   C. Chatfield. *The Analysis of Time Series: An Introduction* (6th ed.). Chapman & Hall, 2003.

[CHN+96]   D. W. Cheung, J. Han, V. Ng, A. Fu, and Y. Fu. A fast distributed algorithm for mining association rules. In *Proc. 1996 Int. Conf. Parallel and Distributed Information Systems*, pp. 31–44, Miami Beach, FL, Dec. 1996.

[CHNW96]   D. W. Cheung, J. Han, V. Ng, and C. Y. Wong. Maintenance of discovered association rules in large databases: An incremental updating technique. In *Proc. 1996 Int. Conf. Data Engineering (ICDE'96)*, pp. 106–114, New Orleans, LA, Feb. 1996.

[CHY96]   M. S. Chen, J. Han, and P. S. Yu. Data mining: An overview from a database perspective. *IEEE Trans. Knowledge and Data Engineering*, 8:866–883, 1996.

[CK98]   M. Carey and D. Kossman. Reducing the braking distance of an SQL query engine. In *Proc. 1998 Int. Conf. Very Large Data Bases (VLDB'98)*, pp. 158–169, New York, Aug. 1998.

[CKT06]   D. Chakrabarti, R. Kumar, and A. Tomkins. Evolutionary clustering. In *Proc. 2006 ACM SIGKDD Int. Conf. Knowledge Discovery in Databases (KDD'06)*, pp. 554–560, Philadelphia, PA, Aug. 2006.

[Cle93]   W. Cleveland. *Visualizing Data*. Hobart Press, 1993.

[CSZ06]   O. Chapelle, B. Schölkopf, and A. Zien. *Semi-supervised Learning.* Cambridge, MA: MIT Press, 2006.

[CM94]   S. P. Curram and J. Mingers. Neural networks, decision tree induction and discriminant analysis: An empirical comparison. *J. Operational Research Society,* 45:440–450, 1994.

[CMC05]   H. Cao, N. Mamoulis, and D. W. Cheung. Mining frequent spatio-temporal sequential patterns. In *Proc. 2005 Int. Conf. Data Mining (ICDM'05),* pp. 82–89, Houston, TX, Nov. 2005.

[CMS09]   B. Croft, D. Metzler, and T. Strohman. *Search Engines: Information Retrieval in Practice.* Boston: Addison-Wesley, 2009.

[CN89]   P. Clark and T. Niblett. The CN2 induction algorithm. *Machine Learning,* 3:261–283, 1989.

[Coh95]   W. Cohen. Fast effective rule induction. In *Proc. 1995 Int. Conf. Machine Learning (ICML'95),* pp. 115–123, Tahoe City, CA, July 1995.

[Coo90]   G. F. Cooper. The computational complexity of probabilistic inference using Bayesian belief networks. *Artificial Intelligence,* 42:393–405, 1990.

[CPS98]   K. Cios, W. Pedrycz, and R. Swiniarski. *Data Mining Methods for Knowledge Discovery.* Kluwer Academic, 1998.

[CR95]   Y. Chauvin and D. Rumelhart. *Backpropagation: Theory, Architectures, and Applications.* Lawrence Erlbaum, 1995.

[Cra89]   S. L. Crawford. Extensions to the CART algorithm. *Int. J. Man-Machine Studies,* 31:197–217, Aug. 1989.

[CRST06] B.-C. Chen, R. Ramakrishnan, J. W. Shavlik, and P. Tamma. Bellwether analysis: Predicting global aggregates from local regions. In *Proc. 2006 Int. Conf. Very Large Data Bases (VLDB'06),* pp. 655–666, Seoul, Korea, Sept. 2006.

[CS93a]   P. K. Chan and S. J. Stolfo. Experiments on multistrategy learning by metalearning. In *Proc. 2nd. Int. Conf. Information and Knowledge Management (CIKM'93),* pp. 314–323, Washington, DC, Nov. 1993.

[CS93b]   P. K. Chan and S. J. Stolfo. Toward multi-strategy parallel & distributed learning in sequence analysis. In *Proc. 1st Int. Conf. Intelligent Systems for Molecular Biology (ISMB'93),* pp. 65–73, Bethesda, MD, July 1993.

[CS96]   M. W. Craven and J. W. Shavlik. Extracting tree-structured representations of trained networks. In D. Touretzky, M. Mozer, and M. Hasselmo (eds.), *Advances in Neural Information Processing Systems.* Cambridge, MA: MIT Press, 1996.

[CS97]   M. W. Craven and J. W. Shavlik. Using neural networks in data mining. *Future Generation Computer Systems,* 13:211–229, 1997.

[CS-T00] N. Cristianini and J. Shawe-Taylor. *An Introduction to Support Vector Machines and Other Kernel-Based Learning Methods.* Cambridge University Press, 2000.

[CSZ+07] Y. Chi, X. Song, D. Zhou, K. Hino, and B. L. Tseng. Evolutionary spectral clustering by incorporating temporal smoothness. In *Proc. 2007 ACM SIGKDD Intl. Conf. Knowledge Discovery and Data Mining (KDD'07),* pp. 153–162, San Jose, CA, Aug. 2007.

[CTTX05] G. Cong, K.-Lee Tan, A. K. H. Tung, and X. Xu. Mining top-k covering rule groups for gene expression data. In *Proc. 2005 ACM-SIGMOD Int. Conf. Management of Data (SIGMOD'05),* pp. 670–681, Baltimore, MD, June 2005.

[CWL+08]   G. Cong, L. Wang, C.-Y. Lin, Y.-I. Song, and Y. Sun. Finding question-answer pairs from online forums. In *Proc. 2008 Int. ACM SIGIR Conf. Research and Development in Information Retrieval (SIGIR'08)*, pp. 467–474, Singapore, July 2008.

[CYHH07]   H. Cheng, X. Yan, J. Han, and C.-W. Hsu. Discriminative frequent pattern analysis for effective classification. In *Proc. 2007 Int. Conf. Data Engineering (ICDE'07)*, pp. 716–725, Istanbul, Turkey, Apr. 2007.

[CYHY08]   H. Cheng, X. Yan, J. Han, and P. S. Yu. Direct discriminative pattern mining for effective classification. In *Proc. 2008 Int. Conf. Data Engineering (ICDE'08)*, pp. 169–178, Cancun, Mexico, Apr. 2008.

[CYZ+08]   C. Chen, X. Yan, F. Zhu, J. Han, and P. S. Yu. Graph OLAP: Towards online analytical processing on graphs. In *Proc. 2008 Int. Conf. Data Mining (ICDM'08)*, pp. 103–112, Pisa, Italy, Dec. 2008.

[Dar10]   A. Darwiche. Bayesian networks. *Communications of the ACM*, 53:80–90, 2010.

[Das91]   B. V. Dasarathy. *Nearest Neighbor (NN) Norms: NN Pattern Classification Techniques*. IEEE Computer Society Press, 1991.

[Dau92]   I. Daubechies. *Ten Lectures on Wavelets*. Capital City Press, 1992.

[DB95]   T. G. Dietterich and G. Bakiri. Solving multiclass learning problems via error-correcting output codes. *J. Artificial Intelligence Research*, 2:263–286, 1995.

[DBK+97]   H. Drucker, C. J. C. Burges, L. Kaufman, A. Smola, and V. N. Vapnik. Support vector regression machines. In M. Mozer, M. Jordan, and T. Petsche (eds.), *Advances in Neural Information Processing Systems 9*, pp. 155–161. Cambridge, MA: MIT Press, 1997.

[DE84]   W. H. E. Day and H. Edelsbrunner. Efficient algorithms for agglomerative hierarchical clustering methods. *J. Classification*, 1:7–24, 1984.

[De01]   S. Dzeroski and N. Lavrac (eds.). *Relational Data Mining*. New York: Springer, 2001.

[DEKM98]   R. Durbin, S. Eddy, A. Krogh, and G. Mitchison. *Biological Sequence Analysis: Probability Models of Proteins and Nucleic Acids*. Cambridge University Press, 1998.

[Dev95]   J. L. Devore. *Probability and Statistics for Engineering and the Sciences* (4th ed.). Duxbury Press, 1995.

[Dev03]   J. L. Devore. *Probability and Statistics for Engineering and the Sciences* (6th ed.). Duxbury Press, 2003.

[DH73]   W. E. Donath and A. J. Hoffman. Lower bounds for the partitioning of graphs. *IBM J. Research and Development*, 17:420–425, 1973.

[DH00]   P. Domingos and G. Hulten. Mining high-speed data streams. In *Proc. 2000 ACM SIGKDD Int. Conf. Knowledge Discovery in Databases (KDD'00)*, pp. 71–80, Boston, MA, Aug. 2000.

[DHL+01]   G. Dong, J. Han, J. Lam, J. Pei, and K. Wang. Mining multi-dimensional constrained gradients in data cubes. In *Proc. 2001 Int. Conf. Very Large Data Bases (VLDB'01)*, pp. 321–330, Rome, Italy, Sept. 2001.

[DHL+04]   G. Dong, J. Han, J. Lam, J. Pei, K. Wang, and W. Zou. Mining constrained gradients in multi-dimensional databases. *IEEE Trans. Knowledge and Data Engineering*, 16:922–938, 2004.

[DHS01]   R. O. Duda, P. E. Hart, and D. G. Stork. *Pattern Classification* (2nd ed.). John Wiley & Sons, 2001.

[DJ03]   T. Dasu and T. Johnson. *Exploratory Data Mining and Data Cleaning*. John Wiley & Sons, 2003.

[DJMS02]   T. Dasu, T. Johnson, S. Muthukrishnan, and V. Shkapenyuk. Mining database structure; or how to build a data quality browser. In *Proc. 2002 ACM-SIGMOD Int. Conf. Management of Data (SIGMOD'02)*, pp. 240–251, Madison, WI, June 2002.

[DL97]   M. Dash and H. Liu. Feature selection methods for classification. *Intelligent Data Analysis*, 1:131–156, 1997.

[DL99]   G. Dong and J. Li. Efficient mining of emerging patterns: Discovering trends and differences. In *Proc. 1999 Int. Conf. Knowledge Discovery and Data Mining (KDD'99)*, pp. 43–52, San Diego, CA, Aug. 1999.

[DLR77]   A. P. Dempster, N. M. Laird, and D. B. Rubin. Maximum likelihood from incomplete data via the EM algorithm. *J. Royal Statistical Society, Series B*, 39:1–38, 1977.

[DLY97]   M. Dash, H. Liu, and J. Yao. Dimensionality reduction of unsupervised data. In *Proc. 1997 IEEE Int. Conf. Tools with AI (ICTAI'97)*, pp. 532–539, Newport Beach, CA, IEEE Computer Society, 1997.

[DM02]   D. Dasgupta and N. S. Majumdar. Anomaly detection in multidimensional data using negative selection algorithm. In *Proc. 2002 Congress on Evolutionary Computation (CEC'02)*, Chapter 12, pp. 1039–1044, Washington, DC, 2002.

[DNR^{+}97] P. Deshpande, J. Naughton, K. Ramasamy, A. Shukla, K. Tufte, and Y. Zhao. Cubing algorithms, storage estimation, and storage and processing alternatives for OLAP. *Bull. Technical Committee on Data Engineering*, 20:3–11, 1997.

[Dob90]   A. J. Dobson. *An Introduction to Generalized Linear Models*. Chapman & Hall, 1990.

[Dob01]   A. J. Dobson. *An Introduction to Generalized Linear Models* (2nd ed.). Chapman & Hall, 2001.

[Dom94]   P. Domingos. The RISE system: Conquering without separating. In *Proc. 1994 IEEE Int. Conf. Tools with Artificial Intelligence (TAI'94)*, pp. 704–707, New Orleans, LA, 1994.

[Dom99]   P. Domingos. The role of Occam's razor in knowledge discovery. *Data Mining and Knowledge Discovery*, 3:409–425, 1999.

[DP96]   P. Domingos and M. Pazzani. Beyond independence: Conditions for the optimality of the simple Bayesian classifier. In *Proc. 1996 Int. Conf. Machine Learning (ML'96)*, pp. 105–112, Bari, Italy, July 1996.

[DP97]   J. Devore and R. Peck. *Statistics: The Exploration and Analysis of Data*. Duxbury Press, 1997.

[DP07]   G. Dong and J. Pei. *Sequence Data Mining*. New York: Springer, 2007.

[DR99]   D. Donjerkovic and R. Ramakrishnan. Probabilistic optimization of top N queries. In *Proc. 1999 Int. Conf. Very Large Data Bases (VLDB'99)*, pp. 411–422, Edinburgh, UK, Sept. 1999.

[DR05]   I. Davidson and S. S. Ravi. Clustering with constraints: Feasibility issues and the *k*-means algorithm. In *Proc. 2005 SIAM Int. Conf. Data Mining (SDM'05)*, Newport Beach, CA, Apr. 2005.

[DT93]   V. Dhar and A. Tuzhilin. Abstract-driven pattern discovery in databases. *IEEE Trans. Knowledge and Data Engineering*, 5:926–938, 1993.

[Dun03]   M. Dunham. *Data Mining: Introductory and Advanced Topics.* Prentice-Hall, 2003.

[DWB06]   I. Davidson, K. L. Wagstaff, and S. Basu. Measuring constraint-set utility for partitional clustering algorithms. In *Proc. 10th European Conf. Principles and Practice of Knowledge Discovery in Databases (PKDD'06)*, pp. 115–126, Berlin, Germany, Sept. 2006.

[Dwo06]   C. Dwork. Differential privacy. In *Proc. 2006 Int. Col. Automata, Languages and Programming (ICALP)*, pp. 1–12, Venice, Italy, July 2006.

[DYXY07] W. Dai, Q. Yang, G. Xue, and Y. Yu. Boosting for transfer learning. In *Proc. 24th Intl. Conf. Machine Learning*, pp. 193–200, Corvallis, OR, June 2007.

[Ega75]   J. P. Egan. *Signal Detection Theory and ROC Analysis.* Academic Press, 1975.

[EK10]   D. Easley and J. Kleinberg. *Networks, Crowds, and Markets: Reasoning about a Highly Connected World.* Cambridge University Press, 2010.

[Esk00]   E. Eskin. Anomaly detection over noisy data using learned probability distributions. In *Proc. 17th Int. Conf. Machine Learning (ICML'00)*, Stanford, CA, 2000.

[EKSX96] M. Ester, H.-P. Kriegel, J. Sander, and X. Xu. A density-based algorithm for discovering clusters in large spatial databases. In *Proc. 1996 Int. Conf. Knowledge Discovery and Data Mining (KDD'96)*, pp. 226–231, Portland, OR, Aug. 1996.

[EKX95]   M. Ester, H.-P. Kriegel, and X. Xu. Knowledge discovery in large spatial databases: Focusing techniques for efficient class identification. In *Proc. 1995 Int. Symp. Large Spatial Databases (SSD'95)*, pp. 67–82, Portland, ME, Aug. 1995.

[Elk97]   C. Elkan. Boosting and naïve Bayesian learning. In *Technical Report CS97-557*, Dept. Computer Science and Engineering, University of California at San Diego, Sept. 1997.

[Elk01]   C. Elkan. The foundations of cost-sensitive learning. In *Proc. 17th Intl. Joint Conf. Artificial Intelligence (IJCAI'01)*, pp. 973–978, Seattle, WA, 2001.

[EN10]   R. Elmasri and S. B. Navathe. *Fundamentals of Database Systems* (6th ed.). Boston: Addison-Wesley, 2010.

[Eng99]   L. English. *Improving Data Warehouse and Business Information Quality: Methods for Reducing Costs and Increasing Profits.* John Wiley & Sons, 1999.

[ESAG02] A. Evfimievski, R. Srikant, R. Agrawal, and J. Gehrke. Privacy preserving mining of association rules. In *Proc. 2002 ACM SIGKDD Int. Conf. Knowledge Discovery and Data Mining (KDD'02)*, pp. 217–228, Edmonton, Alberta, Canada, July 2002.

[ET93]   B. Efron and R. Tibshirani. *An Introduction to the Bootstrap.* Chapman & Hall, 1993.

[FB74]   R. A. Finkel and J. L. Bentley. Quad-trees: A data structure for retrieval on composite keys. *ACTA Informatica*, 4:1–9, 1974.

[FB08]   J. Friedman and E. P. Bogdan. Predictive learning via rule ensembles. *Ann. Applied Statistics*, 2:916–954, 2008.

[FBF77]   J. H. Friedman, J. L. Bentley, and R. A. Finkel. An algorithm for finding best matches in logarithmic expected time. *ACM Transactions on Math Software*, 3:209–226, 1977.

[FFF99]   M. Faloutsos, P. Faloutsos, and C. Faloutsos. On power-law relationships of the internet topology. In *Proc. ACM SIGCOMM'99 Conf. Applications, Technologies, Architectures, and Protocols for Computer Communication*, pp. 251–262, Cambridge, MA, Aug. 1999.

[FG02]   M. Fishelson and D. Geiger. Exact genetic linkage computations for general pedigrees. *Disinformation*, 18:189–198, 2002.

[FGK⁺05]   R. Fagin, R. V. Guha, R. Kumar, J. Novak, D. Sivakumar, and A. Tomkins. Multi-structural databases. In *Proc. 2005 ACM SIGMOD-SIGACT-SIGART Symp. Principles of Database Systems (PODS'05)*, pp. 184–195, Baltimore, MD, June 2005.

[FGW01]   U. Fayyad, G. Grinstein, and A. Wierse. *Information Visualization in Data Mining and Knowledge Discovery*. Morgan Kaufmann, 2001.

[FH51]   E. Fix and J. L. Hodges Jr. Discriminatory analysis, non-parametric discrimination: Consistency properties. In *Technical Report 21-49-004(4)*, USAF School of Aviation Medicine, Randolph Field, Texas, 1951.

[FH87]   K. Fukunaga and D. Hummels. Bayes error estimation using Parzen and *k-nn* procedure. *IEEE Trans. Pattern Analysis and Machine Learning*, 9:634–643, 1987.

[FH95]   Y. Fu and J. Han. Meta-rule-guided mining of association rules in relational databases. In *Proc. 1995 Int. Workshop Integration of Knowledge Discovery with Deductive and Object-Oriented Databases (KDOOD'95)*, pp. 39–46, Singapore, Dec. 1995.

[FI90]   U. M. Fayyad and K. B. Irani. What should be minimized in a decision tree? In *Proc. 1990 Nat. Conf. Artificial Intelligence (AAAI'90)*, pp. 749–754, Boston, MA, 1990.

[FI92]   U. M. Fayyad and K. B. Irani. The attribute selection problem in decision tree generation. In *Proc. 1992 Nat. Conf. Artificial Intelligence (AAAI'92)*, pp. 104–110, San Jose, CA, 1992.

[FI93]   U. Fayyad and K. Irani. Multi-interval discretization of continuous-valued attributes for classification learning. In *Proc. 1993 Int. Joint Conf. Artificial Intelligence (IJCAI'93)*, pp. 1022–1029, Chambery, France, 1993.

[Fie73]   M. Fiedler. Algebraic connectivity of graphs. *Czechoslovak Mathematical J.*, 23:298–305, 1973.

[FL90]   S. Fahlman and C. Lebiere. The cascade-correlation learning algorithm. In *Technical Report CMU-CS-90-100*, Computer Sciences Department, Carnegie Mellon University, 1990.

[FL95]   C. Faloutsos and K.-I. Lin. FastMap: A fast algorithm for indexing, data-mining and visualization of traditional and multimedia datasets. In *Proc. 1995 ACM-SIGMOD Int. Conf. Management of Data (SIGMOD'95)*, pp. 163–174, San Jose, CA, May 1995.

[Fle87]   R. Fletcher. *Practical Methods of Optimization*. John Wiley & Sons, 1987.

[FMMT96]   T. Fukuda, Y. Morimoto, S. Morishita, and T. Tokuyama. Data mining using two-dimensional optimized association rules: Scheme, algorithms, and visualization. In *Proc. 1996 ACM-SIGMOD Int. Conf. Management of Data (SIGMOD'96)*, pp. 13–23, Montreal, Quebec, Canada, June 1996.

[FP05]   J. Friedman and B. E. Popescu. Predictive learning via rule ensembles. In *Technical Report*, Department of Statistics, Stanford University, 2005.

[FPP07]   D. Freedman, R. Pisani, and R. Purves. *Statistics* (4th ed.). W. W. Norton & Co., 2007.

[FPSS+96]   U. M. Fayyad, G. Piatetsky-Shapiro, P. Smyth, and R. Uthurusamy (eds.). *Advances in Knowledge Discovery and Data Mining*. AAAI/MIT Press, 1996.

[FP97]   T. Fawcett and F. Provost. Adaptive fraud detection. *Data Mining and Knowledge Discovery*, 1:291–316, 1997.

[FR02]   C. Fraley and A. E. Raftery. Model-based clustering, discriminant analysis, and density estimation. *J. American Statistical Association*, 97:611–631, 2002.

[Fri77]   J. H. Friedman. A recursive partitioning decision rule for nonparametric classifiers. *IEEE Trans. Computer*, 26:404–408, 1977.

[Fri01]   J. H. Friedman. Greedy function approximation: A gradient boosting machine. *Ann. Statistics*, 29:1189–1232, 2001.

[Fri03]   N. Friedman. Pcluster: Probabilistic agglomerative clustering of gene expression profiles. In *Technical Report 2003-80*, Hebrew University, 2003.

[FRM94]   C. Faloutsos, M. Ranganathan, and Y. Manolopoulos. Fast subsequence matching in time-series databases. In *Proc. 1994 ACM-SIGMOD Int. Conf. Management of Data (SIGMOD'94)*, pp. 419–429, Minneapolis, MN, May 1994.

[FS93]   U. Fayyad and P. Smyth. Image database exploration: Progress and challenges. In *Proc. AAAI'93 Workshop Knowledge Discovery in Databases (KDD'93)*, pp. 14–27, Washington, DC, July 1993.

[FS97]   Y. Freund and R. E. Schapire. A decision-theoretic generalization of on-line learning and an application to boosting. *J. Computer and System Sciences*, 55:119–139, 1997.

[FS06]   R. Feldman and J. Sanger. *The Text Mining Handbook: Advanced Approaches in Analyzing Unstructured Data*. Cambridge University Press, 2006.

[FSGM+98] M. Fang, N. Shivakumar, H. Garcia-Molina, R. Motwani, and J. D. Ullman. Computing iceberg queries efficiently. In *Proc. 1998 Int. Conf. Very Large Data Bases (VLDB'98)*, pp. 299–310, New York, NY, Aug. 1998.

[FW94]   J. Furnkranz and G. Widmer. Incremental reduced error pruning. In *Proc. 1994 Int. Conf. Machine Learning (ICML'94)*, pp. 70–77, New Brunswick, NJ, 1994.

[FWFY10]   B. C. M. Fung, K. Wang, A. W.-C. Fu, and P. S. Yu. *Introduction to Privacy-Preserving Data Publishing: Concepts and Techniques*. Chapman & Hall/CRC, 2010.

[FYM05]   R. Fujimaki, T. Yairi, and K. Machida. An approach to spacecraft anomaly detection problem using kernel feature space. In *Proc. 2005 Int. Workshop Link Discovery (LinkKDD'05)*, pp. 401–410, Chicago, IL, 2005.

[Gal93]   S. I. Gallant. *Neural Network Learning and Expert Systems*. Cambridge, MA: MIT Press, 1993.

[Gat00]   B. Gates. *Business @ the Speed of Thought: Succeeding in the Digital Economy*. Warner Books, 2000.

[GCB+97] J. Gray, S. Chaudhuri, A. Bosworth, A. Layman, D. Reichart, M. Venkatrao, F. Pellow, and H. Pirahesh. Data cube: A relational aggregation operator generalizing group-by, cross-tab and sub-totals. *Data Mining and Knowledge Discovery*, 1:29–54, 1997.

[GFKT01]   L. Getoor, N. Friedman, D. Koller, and B. Taskar. Learning probabilistic models of relational structure. In *Proc. 2001 Int. Conf. Machine Learning (ICML'01)*, pp. 170–177, Williamstown, MA, 2001.

[GFS+01]   H. Galhardas, D. Florescu, D. Shasha, E. Simon, and C.-A. Saita. Declarative data cleaning: Language, model, and algorithms. In *Proc. 2001 Int. Conf. Very Large Data Bases (VLDB'01)*, pp. 371–380, Rome, Italy, Sept. 2001.

[GG92]   A. Gersho and R. M. Gray. *Vector Quantization and Signal Compression*. Kluwer Academic, 1992.

[GG98]   V. Gaede and O. Günther. Multidimensional access methods. *ACM Computing Surveys*, 30:170–231, 1998.

[GGR99]   V. Ganti, J. E. Gehrke, and R. Ramakrishnan. CACTUS—clustering categorical data using summaries. In *Proc. 1999 Int. Conf. Knowledge Discovery and Data Mining (KDD'99)*, pp. 73–83, San Diego, CA, 1999.

[GGRL99]   J. Gehrke, V. Ganti, R. Ramakrishnan, and W.-Y. Loh. BOAT—optimistic decision tree construction. In *Proc. 1999 ACM-SIGMOD Int. Conf. Management of Data (SIGMOD'99)*, pp. 169–180, Philadelphia, PA, June 1999.

[GHL06]   H. Gonzalez, J. Han, and X. Li. Flowcube: Constructuing RFID flowcubes for multi-dimensional analysis of commodity flows. In *Proc. 2006 Int. Conf. Very Large Data Bases (VLDB'06)*, pp. 834–845, Seoul, Korea, Sept. 2006.

[GHLK06]   H. Gonzalez, J. Han, X. Li, and D. Klabjan. Warehousing and analysis of massive RFID data sets. In *Proc. 2006 Int. Conf. Data Engineering (ICDE'06)*, p. 83, Atlanta, GA, Apr. 2006.

[GKK$^+$01] R. L. Grossman, C. Kamath, P. Kegelmeyer, V. Kumar, and R. R. Namburu. *Data Mining for Scientific and Engineering Applications*. Kluwer Academic, 2001.

[GKR98]   D. Gibson, J. M. Kleinberg, and P. Raghavan. Clustering categorical data: An approach based on dynamical systems. In *Proc. 1998 Int. Conf. Very Large Data Bases (VLDB'98)*, pp. 311–323, New York, NY, Aug. 1998.

[GM99]   A. Gupta and I. S. Mumick. *Materialized Views: Techniques, Implementations, and Applications*. Cambridge, MA: MIT Press, 1999.

[GMMO00]   S. Guha, N. Mishra, R. Motwani, and L. O'Callaghan. Clustering data streams. In *Proc. 2000 Symp. Foundations of Computer Science (FOCS'00)*, pp. 359–366, Redondo Beach, CA, 2000.

[GMP$^+$09] J. Ginsberg, M. H. Mohebbi, R. S. Patel, L. Brammer, M. S. Smolinski, and L. Brilliant. Detecting influenza epidemics using search engine query data. *Nature*, 457:1012–1014, Feb. 2009.

[GMUW08]   H. Garcia-Molina, J. D. Ullman, and J. Widom. *Database Systems: The Complete Book* (2nd ed.). Prentice Hall, 2008.

[GMV96]   I. Guyon, N. Matic, and V. Vapnik. Discoverying informative patterns and data cleaning. In U. M. Fayyad, G. Piatetsky-Shapiro, P. Smyth, and R. Uthurusamy (eds.), *Advances in Knowledge Discovery and Data Mining*, pp. 181–203. AAAI/MIT Press, 1996.

[Gol89]   D. Goldberg. *Genetic Algorithms in Search, Optimization, and Machine Learning*. Reading, MA: Addison-Wesley, 1989.

[GR04]   D. A. Grossman and O. Frieder. *Information Retrieval: Algorithms and Heuristics*. New York: Springer, 2004.

[GR07]   P. D. Grunwald and J. Rissanen. *The Minimum Description Length Principle*. Cambridge, MA: MIT Press, 2007.

[GRG98]   J. Gehrke, R. Ramakrishnan, and V. Ganti. RainForest: A framework for fast decision tree construction of large datasets. In *Proc. 1998 Int. Conf. Very Large Data Bases (VLDB'98)*, pp. 416–427, New York, NY, Aug. 1998.

[GRS98]   S. Guha, R. Rastogi, and K. Shim. CURE: An efficient clustering algorithm for large databases. In *Proc. 1998 ACM-SIGMOD Int. Conf. Management of Data (SIGMOD'98)*, pp. 73–84, Seattle, WA, June 1998.

[GRS99]   S. Guha, R. Rastogi, and K. Shim. ROCK: A robust clustering algorithm for categorical attributes. In *Proc. 1999 Int. Conf. Data Engineering (ICDE'99)*, pp. 512–521, Sydney, Australia, Mar. 1999.

[Gru69]   F. E. Grubbs. Procedures for detecting outlying observations in samples. *Technometrics*, 11:1–21, 1969.

[Gup97]   H. Gupta. Selection of views to materialize in a data warehouse. In *Proc. 7th Int. Conf. Database Theory (ICDT'97)*, pp. 98–112, Delphi, Greece, Jan. 1997.

[Gut84]   A. Guttman. R-Tree: A dynamic index structure for spatial searching. In *Proc. 1984 ACM-SIGMOD Int. Conf. Management of Data (SIGMOD'84)*, pp. 47–57, Boston, MA, June 1984.

[GW07]   R. C. Gonzalez and R. E. Woods. *Digital Image Processing* (3rd ed.). Prentice Hall, 2007.

[GZ03a]   B. Goethals and M. Zaki. An introduction to workshop frequent itemset mining implementations. In *Proc. ICDM'03 Int. Workshop Frequent Itemset Mining Implementations (FIMI'03)*, pp. 1–13, Melbourne, FL, Nov. 2003.

[GZ03b]   G. Grahne and J. Zhu. Efficiently using prefix-trees in mining frequent itemsets. In *Proc. ICDM'03 Int. Workshop on Frequent Itemset Mining Implementations (FIMI'03)*, Melbourne, FL, Nov. 2003.

[HA04]   V. J. Hodge, and J. Austin. A survey of outlier detection methodologies. *Artificial Intelligence Review*, 22:85–126, 2004.

[HAC+99]   J. M. Hellerstein, R. Avnur, A. Chou, C. Hidber, C. Olston, V. Raman, T. Roth, and P. J. Haas. Interactive data analysis: The control project. *IEEE Computer*, 32:51–59, 1999.

[Ham94]   J. Hamilton. *Time Series Analysis*. Princeton University Press, 1994.

[Han98]   J. Han. Towards on-line analytical mining in large databases. *SIGMOD Record*, 27:97–107, 1998.

[Har68]   P. E. Hart. The condensed nearest neighbor rule. *IEEE Trans. Information Theory*, 14:515–516, 1968.

[Har72]   J. Hartigan. Direct clustering of a data matrix. *J. American Stat. Assoc.*, 67:123–129, 1972.

[Har75]   J. A. Hartigan. *Clustering Algorithms*. John Wiley & Sons, 1975.

[Haw80]   D. M. Hawkins. *Identification of Outliers*. Chapman & Hall, 1980.

[Hay99]   S. S. Haykin. *Neural Networks: A Comprehensive Foundation*. Prentice-Hall, 1999.

[Hay08]   S. Haykin. *Neural Networks and Learning Machines*. Prentice-Hall, 2008.

[HB87]   S. J. Hanson and D. J. Burr. Minkowski-r back-propagation: Learning in connectionist models with non-euclidian error signals. In *Neural Information Proc. Systems Conf.*, pp. 348–357, Denver, CO, 1987.

[HBV01]   M. Halkidi, Y. Batistakis, and M. Vazirgiannis. On clustering validation techniques. *J. Intelligent Information Systems*, 17:107–145, 2001.

[HCC93]   J. Han, Y. Cai, and N. Cercone. Data-driven discovery of quantitative rules in relational databases. *IEEE Trans. Knowledge and Data Engineering*, 5:29–40, 1993.

[HCD94]   L. B. Holder, D. J. Cook, and S. Djoko. Substructure discovery in the subdue system. In *Proc. AAAI'94 Workshop on Knowledge Discovery in Databases (KDD'94)*, pp. 169–180, Seattle, WA, July 1994.

[Hec96]   D. Heckerman. Bayesian networks for knowledge discovery. In U. M. Fayyad, G. Piatetsky-Shapiro, P. Smyth, and R. Uthurusamy (eds.), *Advances in Knowledge Discovery and Data Mining*, pp. 273–305. Cambridge, MA: MIT Press, 1996.

[HF94]   J. Han and Y. Fu. Dynamic generation and refinement of concept hierarchies for knowledge discovery in databases. In *Proc. AAAI'94 Workshop Knowledge Discovery in Databases (KDD'94)*, pp. 157–168, Seattle, WA, July 1994.

[HF95]   J. Han and Y. Fu. Discovery of multiple-level association rules from large databases. In *Proc. 1995 Int. Conf. Very Large Data Bases (VLDB'95)*, pp. 420–431, Zurich, Switzerland, Sept. 1995.

[HF96]   J. Han and Y. Fu. Exploration of the power of attribute-oriented induction in data mining. In U. M. Fayyad, G. Piatetsky-Shapiro, P. Smyth, and R. Uthurusamy (eds.), *Advances in Knowledge Discovery and Data Mining*, pp. 399–421. AAAI/MIT Press, 1996.

[HFLP01]   P. S. Horn, L. Feng, Y. Li, and A. J. Pesce. Effect of outliers and nonhealthy individuals on reference interval estimation. *Clinical Chemistry*, 47:2137–2145, 2001.

[HG05]   K. A. Heller and Z. Ghahramani. Bayesian hierarchical clustering. In *Proc. 22nd Int. Conf. Machine Learning (ICML'05)*, pp. 297–304, Bonn, Germany, 2005.

[HG07]   A. Hinneburg and H.-H. Gabriel. DENCLUE 2.0: Fast clustering based on kernel density estimation. In *Proc. 2007 Int. Conf. Intelligent Data Analysis (IDA'07)*, pp. 70–80, Ljubljana, Slovenia, 2007.

[HGC95]   D. Heckerman, D. Geiger, and D. M. Chickering. Learning Bayesian networks: The combination of knowledge and statistical data. *Machine Learning*, 20:197–243, 1995.

[HH01]   R. J. Hilderman and H. J. Hamilton. *Knowledge Discovery and Measures of Interest*. Kluwer Academic, 2001.

[HHW97]   J. Hellerstein, P. Haas, and H. Wang. Online aggregation. In *Proc. 1997 ACM-SIGMOD Int. Conf. Management of Data (SIGMOD'97)*, pp. 171–182, Tucson, AZ, May 1997.

[Hig08]   R. C. Higgins. *Analysis for Financial Management with S&P Bind-In Card*. Irwin/McGraw-Hill, 2008.

[HK91]   P. Hoschka and W. Klösgen. A support system for interpreting statistical data. In G. Piatetsky-Shapiro and W. J. Frawley (eds.), *Knowledge Discovery in Databases*, pp. 325–346. AAAI/MIT Press, 1991.

[HK98]   A. Hinneburg and D. A. Keim. An efficient approach to clustering in large multimedia databases with noise. In *Proc. 1998 Int. Conf. Knowledge Discovery and Data Mining (KDD'98)*, pp. 58–65, New York, NY, Aug. 1998.

[HKGT03]   M. Hadjieleftheriou, G. Kollios, D. Gunopulos, and V. J. Tsotras. Online discovery of dense areas in spatio-temporal databases. In *Proc. 2003 Int. Symp. Spatial and Temporal Databases (SSTD'03)*, pp. 306–324, Santorini Island, Greece, July 2003.

[HKKR99]   F. Höppner, F. Klawonn, R. Kruse, and T. Runkler. *Fuzzy Cluster Analysis: Methods for Classification, Data Analysis and Image Recognition*. Wiley, 1999.

[HKP91]   J. Hertz, A. Krogh, and R. G. Palmer. *Introduction to the Theory of Neural Computation*. Reading, MA: Addison-Wesley, 1991.

[HLW07]   W. Hsu, M. L. Lee, and J. Wang. *Temporal and Spatio-Temporal Data Mining*. IGI Publishing, 2007.

[HLZ02]   W. Hsu, M. L. Lee, and J. Zhang. Image mining: Trends and developments. *J. Intelligent Information Systems*, 19:7–23, 2002.

[HMM86]   J. Hong, I. Mozetic, and R. S. Michalski. Incremental learning of attribute-based descriptions from examples, the method and user's guide. In *Report ISG 85-5, UIUCDCS-F-86-949*, Department of Computer Science, University of Illinois at Urbana-Champaign, 1986.

[HMS66]   E. B. Hunt, J. Marin, and P. T. Stone. *Experiments in Induction*. Academic Press, 1966.

[HMS01]   D. J. Hand, H. Mannila, and P. Smyth. *Principles of Data Mining (Adaptive Computation and Machine Learning)*. Cambridge, MA: MIT Press, 2001.

[HN90]   R. Hecht-Nielsen. *Neurocomputing*. Reading, MA: Addison-Wesley, 1990.

[Hor08]   R. Horak. *Telecommunications and Data Communications Handbook* (2nd ed.). Wiley-Interscience, 2008.

[HP07]   M. Hua and J. Pei. Cleaning disguised missing data: A heuristic approach. In *Proc. 2007 ACM SIGKDD Intl. Conf. Knowledge Discovery and Data Mining (KDD'07)*, pp. 950–958, San Jose, CA, Aug. 2007.

[HPDW01]   J. Han, J. Pei, G. Dong, and K. Wang. Efficient computation of iceberg cubes with complex measures. In *Proc. 2001 ACM-SIGMOD Int. Conf. Management of Data (SIGMOD'01)*, pp. 1–12, Santa Barbara, CA, May 2001.

[HPS97]   J. Hosking, E. Pednault, and M. Sudan. A statistical perspective on data mining. *Future Generation Computer Systems*, 13:117–134, 1997.

[HPY00]   J. Han, J. Pei, and Y. Yin. Mining frequent patterns without candidate generation. In *Proc. 2000 ACM-SIGMOD Int. Conf. Management of Data (SIGMOD'00)*, pp. 1–12, Dallas, TX, May 2000.

[HRMS10]   M. Hay, V. Rastogi, G. Miklau, and D. Suciu. Boosting the accuracy of differentially-private queries through consistency. In *Proc. 2010 Int. Conf. Very Large Data Bases (VLDB'10)*, pp. 1021–1032, Singapore, Sept. 2010.

[HRU96]   V. Harinarayan, A. Rajaraman, and J. D. Ullman. Implementing data cubes efficiently. In *Proc. 1996 ACM-SIGMOD Int. Conf. Management of Data (SIGMOD'96)*, pp. 205–216, Montreal, Quebec, Canada, June 1996.

[HS05]   J. M. Hellerstein and M. Stonebraker. *Readings in Database Systems* (4th ed.). Cambridge, MA: MIT Press, 2005.

[HSG90]   S. A. Harp, T. Samad, and A. Guha. Designing application-specific neural networks using the genetic algorithm. In D. S. Touretzky (ed.), *Advances in Neural Information Processing Systems II*, pp. 447–454. Morgan Kaufmann, 1990.

[HT98]   T. Hastie and R. Tibshirani. Classification by pairwise coupling. *Ann. Statistics*, 26:451–471, 1998.

[HTF09]   T. Hastie, R. Tibshirani, and J. Friedman. *The Elements of Statistical Learning: Data Mining, Inference, and Prediction* (2nd ed.). Springer Verlag, 2009.

[Hua98]   Z. Huang. Extensions to the k-means algorithm for clustering large data sets with categorical values. *Data Mining and Knowledge Discovery*, 2:283–304, 1998.

[Hub94]   C. H. Huberty. *Applied Discriminant Analysis*. Wiley-Interscience, 1994.

[Hub96]   B. B. Hubbard. *The World According to Wavelets*. A. K. Peters, 1996.

[HWB$^+$04]   J. Huan, W. Wang, D. Bandyopadhyay, J. Snoeyink, J. Prins, and A. Tropsha. Mining spatial motifs from protein structure graphs. In *Proc. 8th Int. Conf. Research in Computational Molecular Biology (RECOMB)*, pp. 308–315, San Diego, CA, Mar. 2004.

[HXD03]   Z. He, X. Xu, and S. Deng. Discovering cluster-based local outliers. *Pattern Recognition Lett.*, 24:1641–1650, June, 2003.

[IGG03]   C. Imhoff, N. Galemmo, and J. G. Geiger. *Mastering Data Warehouse Design: Relational and Dimensional Techniques.* John Wiley & Sons, 2003.

[IKA02]   T. Imielinski, L. Khachiyan, and A. Abdulghani. Cubegrades: Generalizing association rules. *Data Mining and Knowledge Discovery*, 6:219–258, 2002.

[IM96]   T. Imielinski and H. Mannila. A database perspective on knowledge discovery. *Communications of the ACM*, 39:58–64, 1996.

[Inm96]   W. H. Inmon. *Building the Data Warehouse.* John Wiley & Sons, 1996.

[IWM98]   A. Inokuchi, T. Washio, and H. Motoda. An apriori-based algorithm for mining frequent substructures from graph data. In *Proc. 2000 European Symp. Principles of Data Mining and Knowledge Discovery (PKDD'00)*, pp. 13–23, Lyon, France, Sept. 1998.

[Jac88]   R. Jacobs. Increased rates of convergence through learning rate adaptation. *Neural Networks*, 1:295–307, 1988.

[Jai10]   A. K. Jain. Data clustering: 50 years beyond k-means. *Pattern Recognition Lett.*, 31(8):651–666, 2010.

[Jam85]   M. James. *Classification Algorithms.* John Wiley & Sons, 1985.

[JBD05]   X. Ji, J. Bailey, and G. Dong. Mining minimal distinguishing subsequence patterns with gap constraints. In *Proc. 2005 Int. Conf. Data Mining (ICDM'05)*, pp. 194–201, Houston, TX, Nov. 2005.

[JD88]   A. K. Jain and R. C. Dubes. *Algorithms for Clustering Data.* Prentice-Hall, 1988.

[Jen96]   F. V. Jensen. *An Introduction to Bayesian Networks.* Springer Verlag, 1996.

[JL96]   G. H. John and P. Langley. Static versus dynamic sampling for data mining. In *Proc. 1996 Int. Conf. Knowledge Discovery and Data Mining (KDD'96)*, pp. 367–370, Portland, OR, Aug. 1996.

[JMF99]   A. K. Jain, M. N. Murty, and P. J. Flynn. Data clustering: A survey. *ACM Computing Surveys*, 31:264–323, 1999.

[Joh97]   G. H. John. *Enhancements to the Data Mining Process.* Ph.D. Thesis, Computer Science Department, Stanford University, 1997.

[Joh99]   G. H. John. Behind-the-scenes data mining: A report on the KDD-98 panel. *SIGKDD Explorations*, 1:6–8, 1999.

[JP04]   N. C. Jones and P. A. Pevzner. *An Introduction to Bioinformatics Algorithms.* Cambridge, MA: MIT Press, 2004.

[JSD+10]   M. Ji, Y. Sun, M. Danilevsky, J. Han, and J. Gao. Graph regularized transductive classification on heterogeneous information networks. In *Proc. 2010 European Conf. Machine Learning and Principles and Practice of Knowledge Discovery in Databases (ECMLPKDD'10)*, pp. 570–586, Barcelona, Spain, Sept. 2010.

[JTH01]   W. Jin, K. H. Tung, and J. Han. Mining top-n local outliers in large databases. In *Proc. 2001 ACM SIGKDD Int. Conf. Knowledge Discovery in Databases (KDD'01)*, pp. 293–298, San Fransisco, CA, Aug. 2001.

[JTHW06]   W. Jin, A. K. H. Tung, J. Han, and W. Wang. Ranking outliers using symmetric neighborhood relationship. In *Proc. 2006 Pacific-Asia Conf. Knowledge Discovery and Data Mining (PAKDD'06)*, Singapore, Apr. 2006.

[JW92]   R. A. Johnson and D. A. Wichern. *Applied Multivariate Statistical Analysis* (3rd ed.). Prentice-Hall, 1992.

[JW02a]   G. Jeh and J. Widom. SimRank: A measure of structural-context similarity. In *Proc. 2002 ACM SIGKDD Int. Conf. Knowledge Discovery and Data Mining (KDD'02)*, pp. 538–543, Edmonton, Alberta, Canada, July 2002.

[JW02b]   R. A. Johnson and D. A. Wichern. *Applied Multivariate Statistical Analysis* (5th ed.). Prentice Hall, 2002.

[Kam09]   C. Kamath. *Scientific Data Mining: A Practical Perspective.* Society for Industrial and Applied Mathematic (SIAM), 2009.

[Kas80]   G. V. Kass. An exploratory technique for investigating large quantities of categorical data. *Applied Statistics*, 29:119–127, 1980.

[KBDM09]   B. Kulis, S. Basu, I. Dhillon, and R. Mooney. Semi-supervised graph clustering: A kernel approach. *Machine Learning*, 74:1–22, 2009.

[Kec01]   V. Kecman. *Learning and Soft Computing.* Cambridge, MA: MIT Press, 2001.

[Kei97]   D. A. Keim. Visual techniques for exploring databases. In *Tutorial Notes, 3rd Int. Conf. Knowledge Discovery and Data Mining (KDD'97)*, Newport Beach, CA, Aug. 1997.

[Ker92]   R. Kerber. ChiMerge: Discretization of numeric attributes. In *Proc. 1992 Nat. Conf. Artificial Intelligence (AAAI'92)*, pp. 123–128, San Jose, CA, 1992.

[KF09]   D. Koller and N. Friedman. *Probabilistic Graphical Models: Principles and Techniques.* Cambridge, MA: MIT Press, 2009.

[KH95]   K. Koperski and J. Han. Discovery of spatial association rules in geographic information databases. In *Proc. 1995 Int. Symp. Large Spatial Databases (SSD'95)*, pp. 47–66, Portland, ME, Aug. 1995.

[KH97]   I. Kononenko and S. J. Hong. Attribute selection for modeling. *Future Generation Computer Systems*, 13:181–195, 1997.

[KH09]   M.-S. Kim and J. Han. A particle-and-density based evolutionary clustering method for dynamic networks. In *Proc. 2009 Int. Conf. Very Large Data Bases (VLDB'09)*, Lyon, France, Aug. 2009.

[KHC97]   M. Kamber, J. Han, and J. Y. Chiang. Metarule-guided mining of multi-dimensional association rules using data cubes. In *Proc. 1997 Int. Conf. Knowledge Discovery and Data Mining (KDD'97)*, pp. 207–210, Newport Beach, CA, Aug. 1997.

[KHK99]   G. Karypis, E.-H. Han, and V. Kumar. CHAMELEON: A hierarchical clustering algorithm using dynamic modeling. *COMPUTER*, 32:68–75, 1999.

[KHY+08]   H. Kargupta, J. Han, P. S. Yu, R. Motwani, and V. Kumar. *Next Generation of Data Mining.* Chapman & Hall/CRC, 2008.

[KJ97]   R. Kohavi and G. H. John. Wrappers for feature subset selection. *Artificial Intelligence*, 97:273–324, 1997.

[KJSY04]   H. Kargupta, A. Joshi, K. Sivakumar, and Y. Yesha. *Data Mining: Next Generation Challenges and Future Directions.* Cambridge, MA: AAAI/MIT Press, 2004.

[KK01]   M. Kuramochi and G. Karypis. Frequent subgraph discovery. In *Proc. 2001 Int. Conf. Data Mining (ICDM'01)*, pp. 313–320, San Jose, CA, Nov. 2001.

[KKW+10]   H. S. Kim, S. Kim, T. Weninger, J. Han, and T. Abdelzaher. NDPMine: Efficiently mining discriminative numerical features for pattern-based classification. In *Proc. 2010 European Conf. Machine Learning and Principles and Practice of Knowledge Discovery in Databases (ECMLPKDD'10)*, Barcelona, Spain, Sept. 2010.

[KKZ09]   H.-P. Kriegel, P. Kroeger, and A. Zimek. Clustering high-dimensional data: A survey on subspace clustering, pattern-based clustering, and correlation clustering. *ACM Trans. Knowledge Discovery from Data (TKDD)*, 3(1):1–58, 2009.

[KLA+08]   M. Khan, H. Le, H. Ahmadi, T. Abdelzaher, and J. Han. DustMiner: Troubleshooting interactive complexity bugs in sensor networks. In *Proc. 2008 ACM Int. Conf. Embedded Networked Sensor Systems (SenSys'08)*, pp. 99–112, Raleigh, NC, Nov. 2008.

[Kle99]   J. M. Kleinberg. Authoritative sources in a hyperlinked environment. *J. ACM*, 46: 604–632, 1999.

[KLV+98]   R. L. Kennedy, Y. Lee, B. Van Roy, C. D. Reed, and R. P. Lippman. *Solving Data Mining Problems Through Pattern Recognition*. Prentice-Hall, 1998.

[KM90]   Y. Kodratoff and R. S. Michalski. *Machine Learning, An Artificial Intelligence Approach*, Vol. 3. Morgan Kaufmann, 1990.

[KM94]   J. Kivinen and H. Mannila. The power of sampling in knowledge discovery. In *Proc. 13th ACM Symp. Principles of Database Systems*, pp. 77–85, Minneapolis, MN, May 1994.

[KMN+02]   T. Kanungo, D. M. Mount, N. S. Netanyahu, C. D. Piatko, R. Silverman, and A. Y. Wu. An efficient k-means clustering algorithm: Analysis and implementation. *IEEE Trans. Pattern Analysis and Machine Intelligence (PAMI)*, 24:881–892, 2002.

[KMR+94]   M. Klemettinen, H. Mannila, P. Ronkainen, H. Toivonen, and A. I. Verkamo. Finding interesting rules from large sets of discovered association rules. In *Proc. 3rd Int. Conf. Information and Knowledge Management*, pp. 401–408, Gaithersburg, MD, Nov. 1994.

[KMS03]   J. Kubica, A. Moore, and J. Schneider. Tractable group detection on large link data sets. In *Proc. 2003 Int. Conf. Data Mining (ICDM'03)*, pp. 573–576, Melbourne, FL, Nov. 2003.

[KN97]   E. Knorr and R. Ng. A unified notion of outliers: Properties and computation. In *Proc. 1997 Int. Conf. Knowledge Discovery and Data Mining (KDD'97)*, pp. 219–222, Newport Beach, CA, Aug. 1997.

[KNNL04]   M. H. Kutner, C. J. Nachtsheim, J. Neter, and W. Li. *Applied Linear Statistical Models with Student CD*. Irwin, 2004.

[KNT00]   E. M. Knorr, R. T. Ng, and V. Tucakov. Distance-based outliers: Algorithms and applications. *The VLDB J.*, 8:237–253, 2000.

[Koh95]   R. Kohavi. A study of cross-validation and bootstrap for accuracy estimation and model selection. In *Proc. 14th Joint Int. Conf. Artificial Intelligence (IJCAI'95)*, Vol. 2, pp. 1137–1143, Montreal, Quebec, Canada, Aug. 1995.

[Kol93]   J. L. Kolodner. *Case-Based Reasoning*. Morgan Kaufmann, 1993.

[Kon95]   I. Kononenko. On biases in estimating multi-valued attributes. In *Proc. 14th Joint Int. Conf. Artificial Intelligence (IJCAI'95)*, Vol. 2, pp. 1034–1040, Montreal, Quebec, Canada, Aug. 1995.

[Kot88]   P. Koton. Reasoning about evidence in causal explanation. In *Proc. 7th Nat. Conf. Artificial Intelligence (AAAI'88)*, pp. 256–263, St. Paul, MN, Aug. 1988.

[KPR98]   J. M. Kleinberg, C. Papadimitriou, and P. Raghavan. A microeconomic view of data mining. *Data Mining and Knowledge Discovery*, 2:311–324, 1998.

[KPS03]   R. M. Karp, C. H. Papadimitriou, and S. Shenker. A simple algorithm for finding frequent elements in streams and bags. *ACM Trans. Database Systems*, 28:51–55, 2003.

[KR90]   L. Kaufman and P. J. Rousseeuw. *Finding Groups in Data: An Introduction to Cluster Analysis*. John Wiley & Sons, 1990.

[KR02]   R. Kimball and M. Ross. *The Data Warehouse Toolkit: The Complete Guide to Dimensional Modeling* (2nd ed.). John Wiley & Sons, 2002.

[KR03]   D. Krane and R. Raymer. *Fundamental Concepts of Bioinformatics*. Benjamin Cummings, 2003.

[Kre02]   V. Krebs. Mapping networks of terrorist cells. *Connections*, 24:43–52 (Winter), 2002.

[KRR+00]   R. Kumar, P. Raghavan, S. Rajagopalan, D. Sivakumar, A. Tomkins, and E. Upfal. Stochastic models for the web graph. In *Proc. 2000 IEEE Symp. Foundations of Computer Science (FOCS'00)*, pp. 57–65, Redondo Beach, CA, Nov. 2000.

[KRTM08]   R. Kimball, M. Ross, W. Thornthwaite, and J. Mundy. *The Data Warehouse Lifecycle Toolkit*. Hoboken, NJ: John Wiley & Sons, 2008.

[KSZ08]   H.-P. Kriegel, M. Schubert, and A. Zimek. Angle-based outlier detection in high-dimensional data. In *Proc. 2008 ACM SIGKDD Int. Conf. Knowledge Discovery and Data Mining (KDD'08)*, pp. 444–452, Las Vegas, NV, Aug. 2008.

[KT99]   J. M. Kleinberg and A. Tomkins. Application of linear algebra in information retrieval and hypertext analysis. In *Proc. 18th ACM Symp. Principles of Database Systems (PODS'99)*, pp. 185–193, Philadelphia, PA, May 1999.

[KYB03]   I. Korf, M. Yandell, and J. Bedell. *BLAST*. Sebastopol, CA: O'Reilly Media, 2003.

[Lam98]   W. Lam. Bayesian network refinement via machine learning approach. *IEEE Trans. Pattern Analysis and Machine Intelligence*, 20:240–252, 1998.

[Lau95]   S. L. Lauritzen. The EM algorithm for graphical association models with missing data. *Computational Statistics and Data Analysis*, 19:191–201, 1995.

[LCH+09]   D. Lo, H. Cheng, J. Han, S. Khoo, and C. Sun. Classification of software behaviors for failure detection: A discriminative pattern mining approach. In *Proc. 2009 ACM SIGKDD Int. Conf. Knowledge Discovery and Data Mining (KDD'09)*, pp. 557–566, Paris, France, June 2009.

[LDH+08]   C. X. Lin, B. Ding, J. Han, F. Zhu, and B. Zhao. Text cube: Computing IR measures for multidimensional text database analysis. In *Proc. 2008 Int. Conf. Data Mining (ICDM'08)*, pp. 905–910, Pisa, Italy, Dec. 2008.

[LDH+10]   Z. Li, B. Ding, J. Han, R. Kays, and P. Nye. Mining periodic behaviors for moving objects. In *Proc. 2010 ACM SIGKDD Conf. Knowledge Discovery and Data Mining (KDD'10)*, pp. 1099–1108, Washington, DC, July 2010.

[LDR00]   J. Li, G. Dong, and K. Ramamohanrarao. Making use of the most expressive jumping emerging patterns for classification. In *Proc. 2000 Pacific-Asia Conf. Knowledge Discovery and Data Mining (PAKDD'00)*, pp. 220–232, Kyoto, Japan, Apr. 2000.

[LDS90]   Y. Le Cun, J. S. Denker, and S. A. Solla. Optimal brain damage. In D. Touretzky (ed.), *Advances in Neural Information Processing Systems*. Morgan Kaufmann, 1990.

[Lea96]   D. B. Leake. CBR in context: The present and future. In D. B. Leake (ed.), *Cased-Based Reasoning: Experiences, Lessons, and Future Directions*, pp. 3–30. AAAI Press, 1996.

[LGT97]   S. Lawrence, C. L. Giles, and A. C. Tsoi. Symbolic conversion, grammatical inference and rule extraction for foreign exchange rate prediction. In Y. Abu-Mostafa, A. S. Weigend, and P. N. Refenes (eds.), *Neural Networks in the Capital Markets*. London: World Scientific, 1997.

[LHC97]   B. Liu, W. Hsu, and S. Chen. Using general impressions to analyze discovered classification rules. In *Proc. 1997 Int. Conf. Knowledge Discovery and Data Mining (KDD'97)*, pp. 31–36, Newport Beach, CA, Aug. 1997.

[LHF98]   H. Lu, J. Han, and L. Feng. Stock movement and *n*-dimensional inter-transaction association rules. In *Proc. 1998 SIGMOD Workshop Research Issues on Data Mining and Knowledge Discovery (DMKD'98)*, pp. 12:1–12:7, Seattle, WA, June 1998.

[LHG04]   X. Li, J. Han, and H. Gonzalez. High-dimensional OLAP: A minimal cubing approach. In *Proc. 2004 Int. Conf. Very Large Data Bases (VLDB'04)*, pp. 528–539, Toronto, Ontario, Canada, Aug. 2004.

[LHKG07]   X. Li, J. Han, S. Kim, and H. Gonzalez. Roam: Rule- and motif-based anomaly detection in massive moving object data sets. In *Proc. 2007 SIAM Int. Conf. Data Mining (SDM'07)*, Minneapolis, MN, Apr. 2007.

[LHM98]   B. Liu, W. Hsu, and Y. Ma. Integrating classification and association rule mining. In *Proc. 1998 Int. Conf. Knowledge Discovery and Data Mining (KDD'98)*, pp. 80–86, New York, Aug. 1998.

[LHP01]   W. Li, J. Han, and J. Pei. CMAR: Accurate and efficient classification based on multiple class-association rules. In *Proc. 2001 Int. Conf. Data Mining (ICDM'01)*, pp. 369–376, San Jose, CA, Nov. 2001.

[LHTD02]   H. Liu, F. Hussain, C. L. Tan, and M. Dash. Discretization: An enabling technique. *Data Mining and Knowledge Discovery*, 6:393–423, 2002.

[LHW07]   J.-G. Lee, J. Han, and K. Whang. Clustering trajectory data. In *Proc. 2007 ACM-SIGMOD Int. Conf. Management of Data (SIGMOD'07)*, Beijing, China, June 2007.

[LHXS06]   H. Liu, J. Han, D. Xin, and Z. Shao. Mining frequent patterns on very high dimensional data: A top-down row enumeration approach. In *Proc. 2006 SIAM Int. Conf. Data Mining (SDM'06)*, Bethesda, MD, Apr. 2006.

[LHY$^+$08]   X. Li, J. Han, Z. Yin, J.-G. Lee, and Y. Sun. Sampling Cube: A framework for statistical OLAP over sampling data. In *Proc. 2008 ACM SIGMOD Int. Conf. Management of Data (SIGMOD'08)*, pp. 779–790, Vancouver, British Columbia, Canada, June 2008.

[Liu06]   B. Liu. *Web Data Mining: Exploring Hyperlinks, Contents, and Usage Data*. New York: Springer, 2006.

[LJK00]   J. Laurikkala, M. Juhola, and E. Kentala. Informal identification of outliers in medical data. In *Proc. 5th Int. Workshop on Intelligent Data Analysis in Medicine and Pharmacology*, Berlin, Germany, Aug. 2000.

[LKCH03]   Y.-K. Lee, W.-Y. Kim, Y. D. Cai, and J. Han. CoMine: Efficient mining of correlated patterns. In *Proc. 2003 Int. Conf. Data Mining (ICDM'03)*, pp. 581–584, Melbourne, FL, Nov. 2003.

[LKF05]   J. Leskovec, J. Kleinberg, and C. Faloutsos. Graphs over time: Densification laws, shrinking diameters and possible explanations. In *Proc. 2005 ACM SIGKDD Int. Conf. Knowledge Discovery and Data Mining (KDD'05)*, pp. 177–187, Chicago, IL, Aug. 2005.

[LLLY03]   G. Liu, H. Lu, W. Lou, and J. X. Yu. On computing, storing and querying frequent patterns. In *Proc. 2003 ACM SIGKDD Int. Conf. Knowledge Discovery and Data Mining (KDD'03)*, pp. 607–612, Washington, DC, Aug. 2003.

[LLMZ04]   Z. Li, S. Lu, S. Myagmar, and Y. Zhou. CP-Miner: A tool for finding copy-paste and related bugs in operating system code. In *Proc. 2004 Symp. Operating Systems Design and Implementation (OSDI'04)*, pp. 20–22, San Francisco, CA, Dec. 2004.

[Llo57]   S. P. Lloyd. Least squares quantization in PCM. *IEEE Trans. Information Theory*, 28:128–137, 1982 (original version: Technical Report, Bell Labs, 1957).

[LLS00]   T.-S. Lim, W.-Y. Loh, and Y.-S. Shih. A comparison of prediction accuracy, complexity, and training time of thirty-three old and new classification algorithms. *Machine Learning*, 40:203–228, 2000.

[LM97]   K. Laskey and S. Mahoney. Network fragments: Representing knowledge for constructing probabilistic models. In *Proc. 13th Annual Conf. Uncertainty in Artificial Intelligence*, pp. 334–341, San Francisco, CA, Aug. 1997.

[LM98a]   H. Liu and H. Motoda. *Feature Selection for Knowledge Discovery and Data Mining*. Kluwer Academic, 1998.

[LM98b]   H. Liu and H. Motoda (eds.). *Feature Extraction, Construction, and Selection: A Data Mining Perspective*. Kluwer Academic, 1998.

[LNHP99]   L. V. S. Lakshmanan, R. Ng, J. Han, and A. Pang. Optimization of constrained frequent set queries with 2-variable constraints. In *Proc. 1999 ACM-SIGMOD Int. Conf. Management of Data (SIGMOD'99)*, pp. 157–168, Philadelphia, PA, June 1999.

[L-NK03]   D. Liben-Nowell and J. Kleinberg. The link prediction problem for social networks. In *Proc. 2003 Int. Conf. Information and Knowledge Management (CIKM'03)*, pp. 556–559, New Orleans, LA, Nov. 2003.

[Los01]   D. Loshin. *Enterprise Knowledge Management: The Data Quality Approach*. Morgan Kaufmann, 2001.

[LP97]   A. Lenarcik and Z. Piasta. Probabilistic rough classifiers with mixture of discrete and continuous variables. In T. Y. Lin and N. Cercone (eds.), *Rough Sets and Data Mining: Analysis for Imprecise Data*, pp. 373–383, Kluwer Academic, 1997.

[LPH02]   L. V. S. Lakshmanan, J. Pei, and J. Han. Quotient cube: How to summarize the semantics of a data cube. In *Proc. 2002 Int. Conf. Very Large Data Bases (VLDB'02)*, pp. 778–789, Hong Kong, China, Aug. 2002.

[LPWH02]   J. Liu, Y. Pan, K. Wang, and J. Han. Mining frequent itemsets by opportunistic projection. In *Proc. 2002 ACM SIGKDD Int. Conf. Knowledge Discovery in Databases (KDD'02)*, pp. 239–248, Edmonton, Alberta, Canada, July 2002.

[LPZ03]   L. V. S. Lakshmanan, J. Pei, and Y. Zhao. QC-Trees: An efficient summary structure for semantic OLAP. In *Proc. 2003 ACM-SIGMOD Int. Conf. Management of Data (SIGMOD'03)*, pp. 64–75, San Diego, CA, June 2003.

[LS95]   H. Liu and R. Setiono. Chi2: Feature selection and discretization of numeric attributes. In *Proc. 1995 IEEE Int. Conf. Tools with AI (ICTAI'95)*, pp. 388–391, Washington, DC, Nov. 1995.

[LS97]   W. Y. Loh and Y. S. Shih. Split selection methods for classification trees. *Statistica Sinica*, 7:815–840, 1997.

[LSBZ87]   P. Langley, H. A. Simon, G. L. Bradshaw, and J. M. Zytkow. *Scientific Discovery: Computational Explorations of the Creative Processes*. Cambridge, MA: MIT Press, 1987.

[LSL95]   H. Lu, R. Setiono, and H. Liu. Neurorule: A connectionist approach to data mining. In *Proc. 1995 Int. Conf. Very Large Data Bases (VLDB'95)*, pp. 478–489, Zurich, Switzerland, Sept. 1995.

[LSW97]   B. Lent, A. Swami, and J. Widom. Clustering association rules. In *Proc. 1997 Int. Conf. Data Engineering (ICDE'97)*, pp. 220–231, Birmingham, England, Apr. 1997.

[Lux07]   U. Luxburg. A tutorial on spectral clustering. *Statistics and Computing*, 17:395–416, 2007.

[LV88]   W. Y. Loh and N. Vanichsetakul. Tree-structured classificaiton via generalized discriminant analysis. *J. American Statistical Association*, 83:715–728, 1988.

[LZ05]   Z. Li and Y. Zhou. PR-Miner: Automatically extracting implicit programming rules and detecting violations in large software code. In *Proc. 2005 ACM SIGSOFT Symp. Foundations of Software Engineering (FSE'05)*, Lisbon, Portugal, Sept. 2005.

[MA03]   S. Mitra and T. Acharya. *Data Mining: Multimedia, Soft Computing, and Bioinformatics.* John Wiley & Sons, 2003.

[MAE05]   A. Metwally, D. Agrawal, and A. El Abbadi. Efficient computation of frequent and top-k elements in data streams. In *Proc. 2005 Int. Conf. Database Theory (ICDT'05)*, pp. 398–412, Edinburgh, Scotland, Jan. 2005.

[Mac67]   J. MacQueen. Some methods for classification and analysis of multivariate observations. In *Proc. 5th Berkeley Symp. Math. Stat. Prob.*, 1:281–297, Berkeley, CA, 1967.

[Mag94]   J. Magidson. The CHAID approach to segmentation modeling: CHI-squared automatic interaction detection. In R. P. Bagozzi (ed.), *Advanced Methods of Marketing Research*, pp. 118–159. Blackwell Business, 1994.

[Man00]   H. Mannila. Theoretical frameworks of data mining. *SIGKDD Explorations*, 1:30–32, 2000.

[MAR96]   M. Mehta, R. Agrawal, and J. Rissanen. SLIQ: A fast scalable classifier for data mining. In *Proc. 1996 Int. Conf. Extending Database Technology (EDBT'96)*, pp. 18–32, Avignon, France, Mar. 1996.

[Mar09]   S. Marsland. *Machine Learning: An Algorithmic Perspective.* Chapman & Hall/CRC, 2009.

[MB88]   G. J. McLachlan and K. E. Basford. *Mixture Models: Inference and Applications to Clustering.* John Wiley & Sons, 1988.

[MC03]   M. V. Mahoney and P. K. Chan. Learning rules for anomaly detection of hostile network traffic. In *Proc. 2003 Int. Conf. Data Mining (ICDM'03)*, Melbourne, FL, Nov. 2003.

[MCK+04]   N. Mamoulis, H. Cao, G. Kollios, M. Hadjieleftheriou, Y. Tao, and D. Cheung. Mining, indexing, and querying historical spatiotemporal data. In *Proc. 2004 ACM SIGKDD Int. Conf. Knowledge Discovery in Databases (KDD'04)*, pp. 236–245, Seattle, WA, Aug. 2004.

[MCM83]   R. S. Michalski, J. G. Carbonell, and T. M. Mitchell. *Machine Learning, An Artificial Intelligence Approach*, Vol. 1. Morgan Kaufmann, 1983.

[MCM86]   R. S. Michalski, J. G. Carbonell, and T. M. Mitchell. *Machine Learning, An Artificial Intelligence Approach*, Vol. 2. Morgan Kaufmann, 1986.

[MD88]   M. Muralikrishna and D. J. DeWitt. Equi-depth histograms for extimating selectivity factors for multi-dimensional queries. In *Proc. 1988 ACM-SIGMOD Int. Conf. Management of Data (SIGMOD'88)*, pp. 28–36, Chicago, IL, June 1988.

[Mei03]   M. Meilă. Comparing clusterings by the variation of information. In *Proc. 16th Annual Conf. Computational Learning Theory (COLT'03)*, pp. 173–187, Washington, DC, Aug. 2003.

[Mei05]   M. Meilă. Comparing clusterings: An axiomatic view. In *Proc. 22nd Int. Conf. Machine Learning (ICML'05)*, pp. 577–584, Bonn, Germany, 2005.

[Men03]   J. Mena. *Investigative Data Mining with Security and Criminal Detection.* Butterworth-Heinemann, 2003.

[MFS95]   D. Malerba, E. Floriana, and G. Semeraro. A further comparison of simplification methods for decision tree induction. In D. Fisher and H. Lenz (eds.), *Learning from Data: AI and Statistics*. Springer Verlag, 1995.

[MH95]   J. K. Martin and D. S. Hirschberg. The time complexity of decision tree induction. In *Technical Report ICS-TR 95-27*, pp. 1–27, Department of Information and Computer Science, University of California, Irvine, CA, Aug. 1995.

[MH09]   H. Miller and J. Han. *Geographic Data Mining and Knowledge Discovery* (2nd ed.). Chapman & Hall/CRC, 2009.

[Mic83]   R. S. Michalski. A theory and methodology of inductive learning. In R. S. Michalski, J. G. Carbonell, and T. M. Mitchell (eds.), *Machine Learning: An Artificial Intelligence Approach*, Vol. 1, pp. 83–134. Morgan Kaufmann, 1983.

[Mic92]   Z. Michalewicz. *Genetic Algorithms + Data Structures = Evolution Programs*. Springer Verlag, 1992.

[Mil98]   R. G. Miller. *Survival Analysis*. Wiley-Interscience, 1998.

[Min89]   J. Mingers. An empirical comparison of pruning methods for decision-tree induction. *Machine Learning*, 4:227–243, 1989.

[Mir98]   B. Mirkin. Mathematical classification and clustering. *J. Global Optimization*, 12:105–108, 1998.

[Mit96]   M. Mitchell. *An Introduction to Genetic Algorithms*. Cambridge, MA: MIT Press, 1996.

[Mit97]   T. M. Mitchell. *Machine Learning*. McGraw-Hill, 1997.

[MK91]   M. Manago and Y. Kodratoff. Induction of decision trees from complex structured data. In G. Piatetsky-Shapiro and W. J. Frawley (eds.), *Knowledge Discovery in Databases*, pp. 289–306. AAAI/MIT Press, 1991.

[MLSZ06]   Q. Mei, C. Liu, H. Su, and C. Zhai. A probabilistic approach to spatiotemporal theme pattern mining on weblogs. In *Proc. 15th Int. Conf. World Wide Web (WWW'06)*, pp. 533–542, Edinburgh, Scotland, May 2006.

[MM95]   J. Major and J. Mangano. Selecting among rules induced from a hurricane database. *J. Intelligent Information Systems*, 4:39–52, 1995.

[MM02]   G. Manku and R. Motwani. Approximate frequency counts over data streams. In *Proc. 2002 Int. Conf. Very Large Data Bases (VLDB'02)*, pp. 346–357, Hong Kong, China, Aug. 2002.

[MN89]   M. Mézard and J.-P. Nadal. Learning in feedforward layered networks: The tiling algorithm. *J. Physics*, 22:2191–2204, 1989.

[MO04]   S. C. Madeira and A. L. Oliveira. Biclustering algorithms for biological data analysis: A survey. *IEEE/ACM Trans. Computational Biology and Bioinformatics*, 1(1):24–25, 2004.

[MP69]   M. L. Minsky and S. Papert. *Perceptrons: An Introduction to Computational Geometry*. Cambridge, MA: MIT Press, 1969.

[MRA95]   M. Metha, J. Rissanen, and R. Agrawal. MDL-based decision tree pruning. In *Proc. 1995 Int. Conf. Knowledge Discovery and Data Mining (KDD'95)*, pp. 216–221, Montreal, Quebec, Canada, Aug. 1995.

[MRS08]   C. D. Manning, P. Raghavan, and H. Schutze. *Introduction to Information Retrieval*. Cambridge University Press, 2008.

[MS03a]   M. Markou and S. Singh. Novelty detection: A review—part 1: Statistical approaches. *Signal Processing*, 83:2481–2497, 2003.

[MS03b]   M. Markou and S. Singh. Novelty detection: A review—part 2: Neural network based approaches. *Signal Processing*, 83:2499–2521, 2003.

[MST94]   D. Michie, D. J. Spiegelhalter, and C. C. Taylor. *Machine Learning, Neural and Statistical Classification.* Chichester, England: Ellis Horwood, 1994.

[MT94]   R. S. Michalski and G. Tecuci. *Machine Learning, A Multistrategy Approach*, Vol. 4. Morgan Kaufmann, 1994.

[MTV94]   H. Mannila, H. Toivonen, and A. I. Verkamo. Efficient algorithms for discovering association rules. In *Proc. AAAI'94 Workshop Knowledge Discovery in Databases (KDD'94)*, pp. 181–192, Seattle, WA, July 1994.

[MTV97]   H. Mannila, H. Toivonen, and A. I. Verkamo. Discovery of frequent episodes in event sequences. *Data Mining and Knowledge Discovery*, 1:259–289, 1997.

[Mur98]   S. K. Murthy. Automatic construction of decision trees from data: A multi-disciplinary survey. *Data Mining and Knowledge Discovery*, 2:345–389, 1998.

[Mut05]   S. Muthukrishnan. *Data Streams: Algorithms and Applications.* Now Publishers, 2005.

[MXC+07]   Q. Mei, D. Xin, H. Cheng, J. Han, and C. Zhai. Semantic annotation of frequent patterns. *ACM Trans. Knowledge Discovery from Data (TKDD)*, 15:321–348, 2007.

[MY97]   R. J. Miller and Y. Yang. Association rules over interval data. In *Proc. 1997 ACM-SIGMOD Int. Conf. Management of Data (SIGMOD'97)*, pp. 452–461, Tucson, AZ, May 1997.

[MZ06]   Q. Mei and C. Zhai. A mixture model for contextual text mining. In *Proc. 2006 ACM SIGKDD Int. Conf. Knowledge Discovery in Databases (KDD'06)*, pp. 649–655, Philadelphia, PA, Aug. 2006.

[NB86]   T. Niblett and I. Bratko. Learning decision rules in noisy domains. In M. A. Brammer (ed.), *Expert Systems '86: Research and Development in Expert Systems III*, pp. 25–34. British Computer Society Specialist Group on Expert Systems, Dec. 1986.

[NBW06]   M. Newman, A.-L. Barabasi, and D. J. Watts. *The Structure and Dynamics of Networks.* Princeton University Press, 2006.

[NC03]   C. C. Noble and D. J. Cook. Graph-based anomaly detection. In *Proc. 2003 ACM SIGKDD Int. Conf. Knowledge Discovery and Data Mining (KDD'03)*, pp. 631–636, Washington, DC, Aug. 2003.

[New10]   M. Newman. *Networks: An Introduction.* Oxford University Press, 2010.

[NG04]   M. E. J. Newman and M. Girvan. Finding and evaluating community structure in networks. *Physical Rev. E*, 69:113–128, 2004.

[NGE-R09]   J. Neville, B. Gallaher, and T. Eliassi-Rad. Evaluating statistical tests for within-network classifiers of relational data. In *Proc. 2009 Int. Conf. Data Mining (ICDM'09)*, pp. 397–406, Miami, FL, Dec. 2009.

[NH94]   R. Ng and J. Han. Efficient and effective clustering method for spatial data mining. In *Proc. 1994 Int. Conf. Very Large Data Bases (VLDB'94)*, pp. 144–155, Santiago, Chile, Sept. 1994.

[NJW01]   A. Y. Ng, M. I. Jordan, and Y. Weiss. On spectral clustering: Analysis and an algorithm. In T. G. Dietterich, S. Becker, and Z. Ghahramani (eds.), *Advances in Neural Information Processing Systems 14.* pp. 849–856, Cambridge, MA: MIT Press, 2001.

[NK04]   S. Nijssen and J. Kok. A quick start in frequent structure mining can make a difference. In *Proc. 2004 ACM SIGKDD Int. Conf. Knowledge Discovery in Databases (KDD'04)*, pp. 647–652, Seattle, WA, Aug. 2004.

[NKNW96] J. Neter, M. H. Kutner, C. J. Nachtsheim, and L. Wasserman. *Applied Linear Statistical Models* (4th ed.). Irwin, 1996.

[NLHP98] R. Ng, L. V. S. Lakshmanan, J. Han, and A. Pang. Exploratory mining and pruning optimizations of constrained associations rules. In *Proc. 1998 ACM-SIGMOD Int. Conf. Management of Data (SIGMOD'98)*, pp. 13–24, Seattle, WA, June 1998.

[NRS99] A. Natsev, R. Rastogi, and K. Shim. Walrus: A similarity retrieval algorithm for image databases. In *Proc. 1999 ACM-SIGMOD Int. Conf. Management of Data (SIGMOD'99)*, pp. 395–406, Philadelphia, PA, June 1999.

[NW99] J. Nocedal and S. J. Wright. *Numerical Optimization.* Springer Verlag, 1999.

[OFG97] E. Osuna, R. Freund, and F. Girosi. An improved training algorithm for support vector machines. In *Proc. 1997 IEEE Workshop Neural Networks for Signal Processing (NNSP'97)*, pp. 276–285, Amelia Island, FL, Sept. 1997.

[OG95] P. O'Neil and G. Graefe. Multi-table joins through bitmapped join indices. *SIGMOD Record*, 24:8–11, Sept. 1995.

[Ols03] J. E. Olson. *Data Quality: The Accuracy Dimension.* Morgan Kaufmann, 2003.

[Omi03] E. Omiecinski. Alternative interest measures for mining associations. *IEEE Trans. Knowledge and Data Engineering*, 15:57–69, 2003.

[OMM+02] L. O'Callaghan, A. Meyerson, R. Motwani, N. Mishra, and S. Guha. Streaming-data algorithms for high-quality clustering. In *Proc. 2002 Int. Conf. Data Engineering (ICDE'02)*, pp. 685–696, San Fransisco, CA, Apr. 2002.

[OQ97] P. O'Neil and D. Quass. Improved query performance with variant indexes. In *Proc. 1997 ACM-SIGMOD Int. Conf. Management of Data (SIGMOD'97)*, pp. 38–49, Tucson, AZ, May 1997.

[ORS98] B. Özden, S. Ramaswamy, and A. Silberschatz. Cyclic association rules. In *Proc. 1998 Int. Conf. Data Engineering (ICDE'98)*, pp. 412–421, Orlando, FL, Feb. 1998.

[Pag89] G. Pagallo. Learning DNF by decision trees. In *Proc. 1989 Int. Joint Conf. Artificial Intelligence (IJCAI'89)*, pp. 639–644, San Francisco, CA, 1989.

[Paw91] Z. Pawlak. *Rough Sets, Theoretical Aspects of Reasoning about Data.* Kluwer Academic, 1991.

[PB00] J. C. Pinheiro and D. M. Bates. *Mixed Effects Models in S and S-PLUS.* Springer Verlag, 2000.

[PBTL99] N. Pasquier, Y. Bastide, R. Taouil, and L. Lakhal. Discovering frequent closed itemsets for association rules. In *Proc. 7th Int. Conf. Database Theory (ICDT'99)*, pp. 398–416, Jerusalem, Israel, Jan. 1999.

[PCT+03] F. Pan, G. Cong, A. K. H. Tung, J. Yang, and M. Zaki. CARPENTER: Finding closed patterns in long biological datasets. In *Proc. 2003 ACM SIGKDD Int. Conf. Knowledge Discovery and Data Mining (KDD'03)*, pp. 637–642, Washington, DC, Aug. 2003.

[PCY95a] J. S. Park, M. S. Chen, and P. S. Yu. An effective hash-based algorithm for mining association rules. In *Proc. 1995 ACM-SIGMOD Int. Conf. Management of Data (SIGMOD'95)*, pp. 175–186, San Jose, CA, May 1995.

[PCY95b] J. S. Park, M. S. Chen, and P. S. Yu. Efficient parallel mining for association rules. In *Proc. 4th Int. Conf. Information and Knowledge Management*, pp. 31–36, Baltimore, MD, Nov. 1995.

[Pea88] J. Pearl. *Probabilistic Reasoning in Intelligent Systems.* Morgan Kaufmann, 1988.

[PHL01]   J. Pei, J. Han, and L. V. S. Lakshmanan. Mining frequent itemsets with convertible constraints. In *Proc. 2001 Int. Conf. Data Engineering (ICDE'01)*, pp. 433–442, Heidelberg, Germany, Apr. 2001.

[PHL⁺01]   J. Pei, J. Han, H. Lu, S. Nishio, S. Tang, and D. Yang, H-Mine: Hyper-Structure Mining of Frequent Patterns in Large Databases. In *Proc. 2001 Int. Conf. Data Mining (ICDM'01)*, pp. 441–448, San Jose, CA, Nov. 2001.

[PHL04]   L. Parsons, E. Haque, and H. Liu. Subspace clustering for high dimensional data: A review. *SIGKDD Explorations*, 6:90–105, 2004.

[PHM00]   J. Pei, J. Han, and R. Mao. CLOSET: An efficient algorithm for mining frequent closed itemsets. In *Proc. 2000 ACM-SIGMOD Int. Workshop Data Mining and Knowledge Discovery (DMKD'00)*, pp. 11–20, Dallas, TX, May 2000.

[PHM-A⁺01]   J. Pei, J. Han, B. Mortazavi-Asl, H. Pinto, Q. Chen, U. Dayal, and M.-C. Hsu. PrefixSpan: Mining sequential patterns efficiently by prefix-projected pattern growth. In *Proc. 2001 Int. Conf. Data Engineering (ICDE'01)*, pp. 215–224, Heidelberg, Germany, Apr. 2001.

[PHM-A⁺04]   J. Pei, J. Han, B. Mortazavi-Asl, J. Wang, H. Pinto, Q. Chen, U. Dayal, and M.-C. Hsu. Mining sequential patterns by pattern-growth: The prefixSpan approach. *IEEE Trans. Knowledge and Data Engineering*, 16:1424–1440, 2004.

[PI97]   V. Poosala and Y. Ioannidis. Selectivity estimation without the attribute value independence assumption. In *Proc. 1997 Int. Conf. Very Large Data Bases (VLDB'97)*, pp. 486–495, Athens, Greece, Aug. 1997.

[PKGF03]   S. Papadimitriou, H. Kitagawa, P. B. Gibbons, and C. Faloutsos. Loci: Fast outlier detection using the local correlation integral. In *Proc. 2003 Int. Conf. Data Engineering (ICDE'03)*, pp. 315–326, Bangalore, India, Mar. 2003.

[PKMT99]   A. Pfeffer, D. Koller, B. Milch, and K. Takusagawa. SPOOK: A system for probabilistic object-oriented knowledge representation. In *Proc. 15th Annual Conf. Uncertainty in Artificial Intelligence (UAI'99)*, pp. 541–550, Stockholm, Sweden, 1999.

[PKZT01]   D. Papadias, P. Kalnis, J. Zhang, and Y. Tao. Efficient OLAP operations in spatial data warehouses. In *Proc. 2001 Int. Symp. Spatial and Temporal Databases (SSTD'01)*, pp. 443–459, Redondo Beach, CA, July 2001.

[PL07]   B. Pang and L. Lee. Opinion mining and sentiment analysis. *Foundations and Trends in Information Retrieval*, 2:1–135, 2007.

[Pla98]   J. C. Platt. Fast training of support vector machines using sequential minimal optimization. In B. Schölkopf, C. J. C. Burges, and A. Smola (eds.), *Advances in Kernel Methods—Support Vector Learning*, pp. 185–208. Cambridge, MA: MIT Press, 1998.

[PP07]   A. Patcha, and J.-M. Park. An overview of anomaly detection techniques: Existing solutions and latest technological trends. *Computer Networks*, 51(12):3448–3470, 2007.

[PS85]   F. P. Preparata and M. I. Shamos. *Computational Geometry: An Introduction*. Springer Verlag, 1985.

[P-S91]   G. Piatetsky-Shapiro. *Notes AAAI'91 Workshop Knowledge Discovery in Databases (KDD'91)*. Anaheim, CA, July 1991.

[P-SF91]   G. Piatetsky-Shapiro and W. J. Frawley. *Knowledge Discovery in Databases*. AAAI/MIT Press, 1991.

[PTCX04]   F. Pan, A. K. H. Tung, G. Cong, and X. Xu. COBBLER: Combining column and row enumeration for closed pattern discovery. In *Proc. 2004 Int. Conf. Scientific and Statistical Database Management (SSDBM'04)*, pp. 21–30, Santorini Island, Greece, June 2004.

[PTVF07]   W. H. Press, S. A. Teukolosky, W. T. Vetterling, and B. P. Flannery. *Numerical Recipes: The Art of Scientific Computing*. Cambridge: Cambridge University Press, 2007.

[PY10]   S. J. Pan and Q. Yang. A survey on transfer learning. *IEEE Trans. Knowledge and Data Engineering*, 22:1345–1359, 2010.

[Pyl99]   D. Pyle. *Data Preparation for Data Mining*. Morgan Kaufmann, 1999.

[PZC$^+$03] J. Pei, X. Zhang, M. Cho, H. Wang, and P. S. Yu. Maple: A fast algorithm for maximal pattern-based clustering. In *Proc. 2003 Int. Conf. Data Mining (ICDM'03)*, pp. 259–266, Melbourne, FL, Dec. 2003.

[QC-J93]   J. R. Quinlan and R. M. Cameron-Jones. FOIL: A midterm report. In *Proc. 1993 European Conf. Machine Learning (ECML'93)*, pp. 3–20, Vienna, Austria, 1993.

[QR89]   J. R. Quinlan and R. L. Rivest. Inferring decision trees using the minimum description length principle. *Information and Computation*, 80:227–248, Mar. 1989.

[Qui86]   J. R. Quinlan. Induction of decision trees. *Machine Learning*, 1:81–106, 1986.

[Qui87]   J. R. Quinlan. Simplifying decision trees. *Int. J. Man-Machine Studies*, 27:221–234, 1987.

[Qui88]   J. R. Quinlan. An empirical comparison of genetic and decision-tree classifiers. In *Proc. 1988 Int. Conf. Machine Learning (ICML'88)*, pp. 135–141, Ann Arbor, MI, June 1988.

[Qui89]   J. R. Quinlan. Unknown attribute values in induction. In *Proc. 1989 Int. Conf. Machine Learning (ICML'89)*, pp. 164–168, Ithaca, NY, June 1989.

[Qui90]   J. R. Quinlan. Learning logic definitions from relations. *Machine Learning*, 5:139–166, 1990.

[Qui93]   J. R. Quinlan. *C4.5: Programs for Machine Learning*. Morgan Kaufmann, 1993.

[Qui96]   J. R. Quinlan. Bagging, boosting, and C4.5. In *Proc. 1996 Nat. Conf. Artificial Intelligence (AAAI'96)*, Vol. 1, pp. 725–730, Portland, OR, Aug. 1996.

[RA87]   E. L. Rissland and K. Ashley. HYPO: A case-based system for trade secret law. In *Proc. 1st Int. Conf. Artificial Intelligence and Law*, pp. 60–66, Boston, MA, May 1987.

[Rab89]   L. R. Rabiner. A tutorial on hidden Markov models and selected applications in speech recognition. *Proc. IEEE*, 77:257–286, 1989.

[RBKK95]   S. Russell, J. Binder, D. Koller, and K. Kanazawa. Local learning in probabilistic networks with hidden variables. In *Proc. 1995 Joint Int. Conf. Artificial Intelligence (IJCAI'95)*, pp. 1146–1152, Montreal, Quebec, Canada, Aug. 1995.

[RC07]   R. Ramakrishnan and B.-C. Chen. Exploratory mining in cube space. *Data Mining and Knowledge Discovery*, 15:29–54, 2007.

[Red92]   T. Redman. *Data Quality: Management and Technology*. Bantam Books, 1992.

[Red01]   T. Redman. *Data Quality: The Field Guide*. Digital Press (Elsevier), 2001.

[RG03]   R. Ramakrishnan and J. Gehrke. *Database Management Systems* (3rd ed.). McGraw-Hill, 2003.

[RGN10]   L. De Raedt, T. Guns, and S. Nijssen. Constraint programming for data mining and machine learning. In *Proc. 2010 AAAI Conf. Artificial Intelligence (AAAI'10)*, pp. 1671–1675, Atlanta, GA, July 2010.

[RH01]   V. Raman and J. M. Hellerstein. Potter's wheel: An interactive data cleaning system. In *Proc. 2001 Int. Conf. Very Large Data Bases (VLDB'01)*, pp. 381–390, Rome, Italy, Sept. 2001.

[RH07]   A. Rosenberg and J. Hirschberg. V-measure: A conditional entropy-based external cluster evaluation measure. In *Proc. 2007 Joint Conf. Empirical Methods in Natural Language Processing and Computational Natural Language Learning (EMNLP-CoNLL'07)*, pp. 410–420, Prague, Czech Republic, June 2007.

[RHS01]   J. F. Roddick, K. Hornsby, and M. Spiliopoulou. An updated bibliography of temporal, spatial, and spatio-temporal data mining research. In J. F. Roddick and K. Hornsby (eds.), TSDM 2000, *Lecture Notes in Computer Science 2007*, pp. 147–163. New York: Springer, 2001.

[RHW86]   D. E. Rumelhart, G. E. Hinton, and R. J. Williams. Learning internal representations by error propagation. In D. E. Rumelhart and J. L. McClelland (eds.), *Parallel Distributed Processing*. Cambridge, MA: MIT Press, 1986.

[Rip96]   B. D. Ripley. *Pattern Recognition and Neural Networks*. Cambridge University Press, 1996.

[RM86]   D. E. Rumelhart and J. L. McClelland. *Parallel Distributed Processing*. Cambridge, MA: MIT Press, 1986.

[RMS98]   S. Ramaswamy, S. Mahajan, and A. Silberschatz. On the discovery of interesting patterns in association rules. In *Proc. 1998 Int. Conf. Very Large Data Bases (VLDB'98)*, pp. 368–379, New York, Aug. 1998.

[RN95]   S. Russell and P. Norvig. *Artificial Intelligence: A Modern Approach*. Prentice-Hall, 1995.

[RNI09]   M. Radovanović, A. Nanopoulos, and M. Ivanović. Nearest neighbors in high-dimensional data: The emergence and influence of hubs. In *Proc. 2009 Int. Conf. Machine Learning (ICML'09)*, pp. 865–872, Montreal, Quebec, Canada, June 2009.

[Ros58]   F. Rosenblatt. The perceptron: A probabilistic model for information storage and organization in the brain. *Psychological Rev.*, 65:386–498, 1958.

[RS89]   C. Riesbeck and R. Schank. *Inside Case-Based Reasoning*. Lawrence Erlbaum, 1989.

[RS97]   K. Ross and D. Srivastava. Fast computation of sparse datacubes. In *Proc. 1997 Int. Conf. Very Large Data Bases (VLDB'97)*, pp. 116–125, Athens, Greece, Aug. 1997.

[RS98]   R. Rastogi and K. Shim. Public: A decision tree classifer that integrates building and pruning. In *Proc. 1998 Int. Conf. Very Large Data Bases (VLDB'98)*, pp. 404–415, New York, Aug. 1998.

[RS01]   F. Ramsey and D. Schafer. *The Statistical Sleuth: A Course in Methods of Data Analysis*. Duxbury Press, 2001.

[RSC98]   K. A. Ross, D. Srivastava, and D. Chatziantoniou. Complex aggregation at multiple granularities. In *Proc. Int. Conf. Extending Database Technology (EDBT'98)*, pp. 263–277, Valencia, Spain, Mar. 1998.

[Rus06]   J. C. Russ. *The Image Processing Handbook* (5th ed.). CRC Press, 2006.

[SA95]   R. Srikant and R. Agrawal. Mining generalized association rules. In *Proc. 1995 Int. Conf. Very Large Data Bases (VLDB'95)*, pp. 407–419, Zurich, Switzerland, Sept. 1995.

[SA96]   R. Srikant and R. Agrawal. Mining sequential patterns: Generalizations and performance improvements. In *Proc. 5th Int. Conf. Extending Database Technology (EDBT'96)*, pp. 3–17, Avignon, France, Mar. 1996.

[SAM96]   J. Shafer, R. Agrawal, and M. Mehta. SPRINT: A scalable parallel classifier for data mining. In *Proc. 1996 Int. Conf. Very Large Data Bases (VLDB'96)*, pp. 544–555, Bombay, India, Sept. 1996.

[SAM98]   S. Sarawagi, R. Agrawal, and N. Megiddo. Discovery-driven exploration of OLAP data cubes. In *Proc. Int. Conf. Extending Database Technology (EDBT'98)*, pp. 168–182, Valencia, Spain, Mar. 1998.

[SBSW99]   B. Schölkopf, P. L. Bartlett, A. Smola, and R. Williamson. Shrinking the tube: A new support vector regression algorithm. In M. S. Kearns, S. A. Solla, and D. A. Cohn (eds.), *Advances in Neural Information Processing Systems 11*, pp. 330–336. Cambridge, MA: MIT Press, 1999.

[SC03]   S. Shekhar and S. Chawla. *Spatial Databases: A Tour.* Prentice-Hall, 2003.

[Sch86]   J. C. Schlimmer. Learning and representation change. In *Proc. 1986 Nat. Conf. Artificial Intelligence (AAAI'86)*, pp. 511–515, Philadelphia, PA, 1986.

[Sch07]   S. E. Schaeffer. Graph clustering. *Computer Science Rev.*, 1:27–64, 2007.

[SCZ98]   G. Sheikholeslami, S. Chatterjee, and A. Zhang. WaveCluster: A multi-resolution clustering approach for very large spatial databases. In *Proc. 1998 Int. Conf. Very Large Data Bases (VLDB'98)*, pp. 428–439, New York, Aug. 1998.

[SD90]   J. W. Shavlik and T. G. Dietterich. *Readings in Machine Learning.* Morgan Kaufmann, 1990.

[SD02]   T. Soukup and I. Davidson. *Visual Data Mining: Techniques and Tools for Data Visualization and Mining.* Wiley, 2002.

[SDJL96]   D. Srivastava, S. Dar, H. V. Jagadish, and A. V. Levy. Answering queries with aggregation using views. In *Proc. 1996 Int. Conf. Very Large Data Bases (VLDB'96)*, pp. 318–329, Bombay, India, Sept. 1996.

[SDN98]   A. Shukla, P. M. Deshpande, and J. F. Naughton. Materialized view selection for multidimensional datasets. In *Proc. 1998 Int. Conf. Very Large Data Bases (VLDB'98)*, pp. 488–499, New York, Aug. 1998.

[SE10]   G. Seni and J. F. Elder. *Ensemble Methods in Data Mining: Improving Accuracy Through Combining Predictions.* Morgan and Claypool, 2010.

[Set10]   B. Settles. Active learning literature survey. In *Computer Sciences Technical Report 1648*, University of Wisconsin–Madison, 2010.

[SF86]   J. C. Schlimmer and D. Fisher. A case study of incremental concept induction. In *Proc. 1986 Nat. Conf. Artificial Intelligence (AAAI'86)*, pp. 496–501, Philadelphia, PA, 1986.

[SFB99]   J. Shanmugasundaram, U. M. Fayyad, and P. S. Bradley. Compressed data cubes for OLAP aggregate query approximation on continuous dimensions. In *Proc. 1999 Int. Conf. Knowledge Discovery and Data Mining (KDD'99)*, pp. 223–232, San Diego, CA, Aug. 1999.

[SG92]   P. Smyth and R. M. Goodman. An information theoretic approach to rule induction. *IEEE Trans. Knowledge and Data Engineering*, 4:301–316, 1992.

[She31]   W. A. Shewhart. *Economic Control of Quality of Manufactured Product.* D. Van Nostrand, 1931.

[Shi99]   Y.-S. Shih. Families of splitting criteria for classification trees. *Statistics and Computing*, 9:309–315, 1999.

[SHK00]   N. Stefanovic, J. Han, and K. Koperski. Object-based selective materialization for efficient implementation of spatial data cubes. *IEEE Trans. Knowledge and Data Engineering*, 12:938–958, 2000.

[Sho97]   A. Shoshani. OLAP and statistical databases: Similarities and differences. In *Proc. 16th ACM Symp. Principles of Database Systems*, pp. 185–196, Tucson, AZ, May 1997.

[Shu88]   R. H. Shumway. *Applied Statistical Time Series Analysis.* Prentice-Hall, 1988.

[SHX04]   Z. Shao, J. Han, and D. Xin. MM-Cubing: Computing iceberg cubes by factorizing the lattice space. In *Proc. 2004 Int. Conf. Scientific and Statistical Database Management (SSDBM'04)*, pp. 213–222, Santorini Island, Greece, June 2004.

[SHZ⁺09]   Y. Sun, J. Han, P. Zhao, Z. Yin, H. Cheng, and T. Wu. RankClus: Integrating clustering with ranking for heterogeneous information network analysis. In *Proc. 2009 Int. Conf. Extending Data Base Technology (EDBT'09)*, pp. 565–576, Saint Petersburg, Russia, Mar. 2009.

[Sil10]   F. Silvestri. Mining query logs: Turning search usage data into knowledge. *Foundations and Trends in Information Retrieval*, 4:1–174, 2010.

[SK08]   J. Shieh and E. Keogh. iSAX: Indexing and mining terabyte sized time series. In *Proc. 2008 ACM SIGKDD Int. Conf. Knowledge Discovery and Data Mining (KDD'08)*, pp. 623–631, Las Vegas, NV, Aug. 2008.

[SKS10]   A. Silberschatz, H. F. Korth, and S. Sudarshan. *Database System Concepts* (6th ed.). McGraw-Hill, 2010.

[SLT⁺01]   S. Shekhar, C.-T. Lu, X. Tan, S. Chawla, and R. R. Vatsavai. Map cube: A visualization tool for spatial data warehouses. In H. J. Miller and J. Han (eds.), *Geographic Data Mining and Knowledge Discovery*, pp. 73–108. Taylor and Francis, 2001.

[SM97]   J. C. Setubal and J. Meidanis. *Introduction to Computational Molecular Biology*. PWS Publishing Co., 1997.

[SMT91]   J. W. Shavlik, R. J. Mooney, and G. G. Towell. Symbolic and neural learning algorithms: An experimental comparison. *Machine Learning*, 6:111–144, 1991.

[SN88]   K. Saito and R. Nakano. Medical diagnostic expert system based on PDP model. In *Proc. 1988 IEEE Int. Conf. Neural Networks*, pp. 225–262, San Mateo, CA, 1988.

[SOMZ96]   W. Shen, K. Ong, B. Mitbander, and C. Zaniolo. Metaqueries for data mining. In U. M. Fayyad, G. Piatetsky-Shapiro, P. Smyth, and R. Uthurusamy (eds.), *Advances in Knowledge Discovery and Data Mining*, pp. 375–398. AAAI/MIT Press, 1996.

[SON95]   A. Savasere, E. Omiecinski, and S. Navathe. An efficient algorithm for mining association rules in large databases. In *Proc. 1995 Int. Conf. Very Large Data Bases (VLDB'95)*, pp. 432–443, Zurich, Switzerland, Sept. 1995.

[SON98]   A. Savasere, E. Omiecinski, and S. Navathe. Mining for strong negative associations in a large database of customer transactions. In *Proc. 1998 Int. Conf. Data Engineering (ICDE'98)*, pp. 494–502, Orlando, FL, Feb. 1998.

[SR81]   R. Sokal and F. Rohlf. *Biometry*. Freeman, 1981.

[SR92]   A. Skowron and C. Rauszer. The discernibility matrices and functions in information systems. In R. Slowinski (ed.), *Intelligent Decision Support, Handbook of Applications and Advances of the Rough Set Theory*, pp. 331–362. Kluwer Academic, 1992.

[SS88]   W. Siedlecki and J. Sklansky. On automatic feature selection. *Int. J. Pattern Recognition and Artificial Intelligence*, 2:197–220, 1988.

[SS94]   S. Sarawagi and M. Stonebraker. Efficient organization of large multidimensional arrays. In *Proc. 1994 Int. Conf. Data Engineering (ICDE'94)*, pp. 328–336, Houston, TX, Feb. 1994.

[SS01]   G. Sathe and S. Sarawagi. Intelligent rollups in multidimensional OLAP data. In *Proc. 2001 Int. Conf. Very Large Data Bases (VLDB'01)*, pp. 531–540, Rome, Italy, Sept. 2001.

[SS05] R. H. Shumway and D. S. Stoffer. *Time Series Analysis and Its Applications*. New York: Springer, 2005.

[ST96] A. Silberschatz and A. Tuzhilin. What makes patterns interesting in knowledge discovery systems. *IEEE Trans. Knowledge and Data Engineering*, 8:970–974, Dec. 1996.

[STA98] S. Sarawagi, S. Thomas, and R. Agrawal. Integrating association rule mining with relational database systems: Alternatives and implications. In *Proc. 1998 ACM-SIGMOD Int. Conf. Management of Data (SIGMOD'98)*, pp. 343–354, Seattle, WA, June 1998.

[STH⁺10] Y. Sun, J. Tang, J. Han, M. Gupta, and B. Zhao. Community evolution detection in dynamic heterogeneous information networks. In *Proc. 2010 KDD Workshop Mining and Learning with Graphs (MLG'10)*, Washington, DC, July 2010.

[Ste72] W. Stefansky. Rejecting outliers in factorial designs. *Technometrics*, 14:469–479, 1972.

[Sto74] M. Stone. Cross-validatory choice and assessment of statistical predictions. *J. Royal Statistical Society*, 36:111–147, 1974.

[SVA97] R. Srikant, Q. Vu, and R. Agrawal. Mining association rules with item constraints. In *Proc. 1997 Int. Conf. Knowledge Discovery and Data Mining (KDD'97)*, pp. 67–73, Newport Beach, CA, Aug. 1997.

[SW49] C. E. Shannon and W. Weaver. *The Mathematical Theory of Communication*. University of Illinois Press, 1949.

[Swe88] J. Swets. Measuring the accuracy of diagnostic systems. *Science*, 240:1285–1293, 1988.

[Swi98] R. Swiniarski. Rough sets and principal component analysis and their applications in feature extraction and selection, data model building and classification. In S. K. Pal and A. Skowron (eds.), *Rough Fuzzy Hybridization: A New Trend in Decision-Making*, Springer Verlag, Singapore, 1999.

[SWJR07] X. Song, M. Wu, C. Jermaine, and S. Ranka. Conditional anomaly detection. *IEEE Trans. on Knowledge and Data Engineering*, 19(5):631–645, 2007.

[SZ04] D. Shasha and Y. Zhu. *High Performance Discovery in Time Series: Techniques and Case Studies*. New York: Springer, 2004.

[TD02] D. M. J. Tax and R. P. W. Duin. Using two-class classifiers for multiclass classification. In *Proc. 16th Intl. Conf. Pattern Recognition (ICPR'2002)*, pp. 124–127, Montreal, Quebec, Canada, 2002.

[TFPL04] Y. Tao, C. Faloutsos, D. Papadias, and B. Liu. Prediction and indexing of moving objects with unknown motion patterns. In *Proc. 2004 ACM-SIGMOD Int. Conf. Management of Data (SIGMOD'04)*, pp. 611–622, Paris, France, June 2004.

[TG01] I. Tsoukatos and D. Gunopulos. Efficient mining of spatiotemporal patterns. In *Proc. 2001 Int. Symp. Spatial and Temporal Databases (SSTD'01)*, pp. 425–442, Redondo Beach, CA, July 2001.

[THH01] A. K. H. Tung, J. Hou, and J. Han. Spatial clustering in the presence of obstacles. In *Proc. 2001 Int. Conf. Data Engineering (ICDE'01)*, pp. 359–367, Heidelberg, Germany, Apr. 2001.

[THLN01] A. K. H. Tung, J. Han, L. V. S. Lakshmanan, and R. T. Ng. Constraint-based clustering in large databases. In *Proc. 2001 Int. Conf. Database Theory (ICDT'01)*, pp. 405–419, London, Jan. 2001.

[THP08] Y. Tian, R. A. Hankins, and J. M. Patel. Efficient aggregation for graph summarization. In *Proc. 2008 ACM SIGMOD Int. Conf. Management of Data (SIGMOD'08)*, pp. 567–580, Vancouver, British Columbia, Canada, June 2008.

[Thu04]   B. Thuraisingham. Data mining for counterterrorism. In H. Kargupta, A. Joshi, K. Sivakumar, and Y. Yesha (eds.), *Data Mining: Next Generation Challenges and Future Directions*, pp. 157–183. AAAI/MIT Press, 2004.

[TK08]   S. Theodoridis and K. Koutroumbas. *Pattern Recognition* (4th ed.) Academic Press, 2008.

[TKS02]   P.-N. Tan, V. Kumar, and J. Srivastava. Selecting the right interestingness measure for association patterns. In *Proc. 2002 ACM SIGKDD Int. Conf. Knowledge Discovery in Databases (KDD'02)*, pp. 32–41, Edmonton, Alberta, Canada, July 2002.

[TLZN08]   L. Tang, H. Liu, J. Zhang, and Z. Nazeri. Community evolution in dynamic multi-mode networks. In *Proc. 2008 ACM SIGKDD Int. Conf. Knowledge Discovery and Data Mining (KDD'08)*, pp. 677–685, Las Vegas, NV, Aug. 2008.

[Toi96]   H. Toivonen. Sampling large databases for association rules. In *Proc. 1996 Int. Conf. Very Large Data Bases (VLDB'96)*, pp. 134–145, Bombay, India, Sept. 1996.

[TS93]   G. G. Towell and J. W. Shavlik. Extracting refined rules from knowledge-based neural networks. *Machine Learning*, 13:71–101, Oct. 1993.

[TSK05]   P. N. Tan, M. Steinbach, and V. Kumar. *Introduction to Data Mining*. Boston: Addison-Wesley, 2005.

[TSS04]   A. Tanay, R. Sharan, and R. Shamir. Biclustering algorithms: A survey. In S. Aluru (ed.), *Handbook of Computational Molecular Biology*, pp. 26:1–26:17. London: Chapman & Hall, 2004.

[Tuf83]   E. R. Tufte. *The Visual Display of Quantitative Information*. Graphics Press, 1983.

[Tuf90]   E. R. Tufte. *Envisioning Information*. Graphics Press, 1990.

[Tuf97]   E. R. Tufte. *Visual Explanations: Images and Quantities, Evidence and Narrative*. Graphics Press, 1997.

[Tuf01]   E. R. Tufte. *The Visual Display of Quantitative Information* (2nd ed.). Graphics Press, 2001.

[TXZ06]   Y. Tao, X. Xiao, and S. Zhou. Mining distance-based outliers from large databases in any metric space. In *Proc. 2006 ACM SIGKDD Int. Conf. Knowledge Discovery in Databases (KDD'06)*, pp. 394–403, Philadelphia, PA, Aug. 2006.

[UBC97]   P. E. Utgoff, N. C. Berkman, and J. A. Clouse. Decision tree induction based on efficient tree restructuring. *Machine Learning*, 29:5–44, 1997.

[UFS91]   R. Uthurusamy, U. M. Fayyad, and S. Spangler. Learning useful rules from inconclusive data. In G. Piatetsky-Shapiro and W. J. Frawley (eds.), *Knowledge Discovery in Databases*, pp. 141–157. AAAI/MIT Press, 1991.

[Utg88]   P. E. Utgoff. An incremental ID3. In *Proc. Fifth Int. Conf. Machine Learning (ICML'88)*, pp. 107–120, San Mateo, CA, 1988.

[Val87]   P. Valduriez. Join indices. *ACM Trans. Database Systems*, 12:218–246, 1987.

[Vap95]   V. N. Vapnik. *The Nature of Statistical Learning Theory*. Springer Verlag, 1995.

[Vap98]   V. N. Vapnik. *Statistical Learning Theory*. John Wiley & Sons, 1998.

[VC71]   V. N. Vapnik and A. Y. Chervonenkis. On the uniform convergence of relative frequencies of events to their probabilities. *Theory of Probability and Its Applications*, 16:264–280, 1971.

[VC03]   J. Vaidya and C. Clifton. Privacy-preserving k-means clustering over vertically partitioned data. In *Proc. 2003 ACM SIGKDD Int. Conf. Knowledge Discovery and Data Mining (KDD'03)*, Washington, DC, Aug 2003.

[VC06]   M. Vuk and T. Curk. ROC curve, lift chart and calibration plot. *Metodološki zvezki*, 3:89–108, 2006.

[VCZ10]   J. Vaidya, C. W. Clifton, and Y. M. Zhu. *Privacy Preserving Data Mining*. New York: Springer, 2010.

[VGK02]   M. Vlachos, D. Gunopulos, and G. Kollios. Discovering similar multidimensional trajectories. In *Proc. 2002 Int. Conf. Data Engineering (ICDE'02)*, pp. 673–684, San Fransisco, CA, Apr. 2002.

[VMZ06]   A. Veloso, W. Meira, and M. Zaki. Lazy associative classificaiton. In *Proc. 2006 Int. Conf. Data Mining (ICDM'06)*, pp. 645–654, Hong Kong, China, 2006.

[vR90]   C. J. van Rijsbergen. *Information Retrieval*. Butterworth, 1990.

[VWI98]   J. S. Vitter, M. Wang, and B. R. Iyer. Data cube approximation and histograms via wavelets. In *Proc. 1998 Int. Conf. Information and Knowledge Management (CIKM'98)*, pp. 96–104, Washington, DC, Nov. 1998.

[Wat95]   M. S. Waterman. *Introduction to Computational Biology: Maps, Sequences, and Genomes (Interdisciplinary Statistics)*. CRC Press, 1995.

[Wat03]   D. J. Watts. *Six Degrees: The Science of a Connected Age*. W. W. Norton & Company, 2003.

[WB98]   C. Westphal and T. Blaxton. *Data Mining Solutions: Methods and Tools for Solving Real-World Problems*. John Wiley & Sons, 1998.

[WCH10]   T. Wu, Y. Chen, and J. Han. Re-examination of interestingness measures in pattern mining: A unified framework. *Data Mining and Knowledge Discovery*, 21(3):371–397, 2010.

[WCRS01]   K. Wagstaff, C. Cardie, S. Rogers, and S. Schrödl. Constrained k-means clustering with background knowledge. In *Proc. 2001 Int. Conf. Machine Learning (ICML'01)*, pp. 577–584, Williamstown, MA, June 2001.

[Wei04]   G. M. Weiss. Mining with rarity: A unifying framework. *SIGKDD Explorations*, 6:7–19, 2004.

[WF94]   S. Wasserman and K. Faust. *Social Network Analysis: Methods and Applications*. Cambridge University Press, 1994.

[WF05]   I. H. Witten and E. Frank. *Data Mining: Practical Machine Learning Tools and Techniques* (2nd ed.). Morgan Kaufmann, 2005.

[WFH11]   I. H. Witten, E. Frank, and M. A. Hall. *Data Mining: Practical Machine Learning Tools and Techniques with Java Implementations* (3rd ed.). Boston: Morgan Kaufmann, 2011.

[WFYH03]   H. Wang, W. Fan, P. S. Yu, and J. Han. Mining concept-drifting data streams using ensemble classifiers. In *Proc. 2003 ACM SIGKDD Int. Conf. Knowledge Discovery and Data Mining (KDD'03)*, pp. 226–235, Washington, DC, Aug. 2003.

[WHH00]   K. Wang, Y. He, and J. Han. Mining frequent itemsets using support constraints. In *Proc. 2000 Int. Conf. Very Large Data Bases (VLDB'00)*, pp. 43–52, Cairo, Egypt, Sept. 2000.

[WHJ+10]   C. Wang, J. Han, Y. Jia, J. Tang, D. Zhang, Y. Yu, and J. Guo. Mining advisor-advisee relationships from research publication networks. In *Proc. 2010 ACM SIGKDD Conf. Knowledge Discovery and Data Mining (KDD'10)*, Washington, DC, July 2010.

[WHLT05]   J. Wang, J. Han, Y. Lu, and P. Tzvetkov. TFP: An efficient algorithm for mining top-k frequent closed itemsets. *IEEE Trans. Knowledge and Data Engineering*, 17:652–664, 2005.

[WHP03]   J. Wang, J. Han, and J. Pei. CLOSET+: Searching for the best strategies for mining frequent closed itemsets. In *Proc. 2003 ACM SIGKDD Int. Conf. Knowledge Discovery and Data Mining (KDD'03)*, pp. 236–245, Washington, DC, Aug. 2003.

[WI98]   S. M. Weiss and N. Indurkhya. *Predictive Data Mining*. Morgan Kaufmann, 1998.

[Wid95]   J. Widom. Research problems in data warehousing. In *Proc. 4th Int. Conf. Information and Knowledge Management*, pp. 25–30, Baltimore, MD, Nov. 1995.

[WIZD04]   S. Weiss, N. Indurkhya, T. Zhang, and F. Damerau. *Text Mining: Predictive Methods for Analyzing Unstructured Information*. New York: Springer, 2004.

[WK91]   S. M. Weiss and C. A. Kulikowski. *Computer Systems That Learn: Classification and Prediction Methods from Statistics, Neural Nets, Machine Learning, and Expert Systems*. Morgan Kaufmann, 1991.

[WK05]   J. Wang and G. Karypis. HARMONY: Efficiently mining the best rules for classification. In *Proc. 2005 SIAM Conf. Data Mining (SDM'05)*, pp. 205–216, Newport Beach, CA, Apr. 2005.

[WLFY02]   W. Wang, H. Lu, J. Feng, and J. X. Yu. Condensed cube: An effective approach to reducing data cube size. In *Proc. 2002 Int. Conf. Data Engineering (ICDE'02)*, pp. 155–165, San Fransisco, CA, Apr. 2002.

[WRL94]   B. Widrow, D. E. Rumelhart, and M. A. Lehr. Neural networks: Applications in industry, business and science. *Communications of the ACM*, 37:93–105, 1994.

[WSF95]   R. Wang, V. Storey, and C. Firth. A framework for analysis of data quality research. *IEEE Trans. Knowledge and Data Engineering*, 7:623–640, 1995.

[Wu83]   C. F. J. Wu. On the convergence properties of the EM algorithm. *Ann. Statistics*, 11:95–103, 1983.

[WW96]   Y. Wand and R. Wang. Anchoring data quality dimensions in ontological foundations. *Communications of the ACM*, 39:86–95, 1996.

[WWYY02]   H. Wang, W. Wang, J. Yang, and P. S. Yu. Clustering by pattern similarity in large data sets. In *Proc. 2002 ACM-SIGMOD Int. Conf. Management of Data (SIGMOD'02)*, pp. 418–427, Madison, WI, June 2002.

[WXH08]   T. Wu, D. Xin, and J. Han. ARCube: Supporting ranking aggregate queries in partially materialized data cubes. In *Proc. 2008 ACM SIGMOD Int. Conf. Management of Data (SIGMOD'08)*, pp. 79–92, Vancouver, British Columbia, Canada, June 2008.

[WXMH09]   T. Wu, D. Xin, Q. Mei, and J. Han. Promotion analysis in multi-dimensional space. In *Proc. 2009 Int. Conf. Very Large Data Bases (VLDB'09)*, 2(1):109–120, Lyon, France, Aug. 2009.

[WYM97]   W. Wang, J. Yang, and R. Muntz. STING: A statistical information grid approach to spatial data mining. In *Proc. 1997 Int. Conf. Very Large Data Bases (VLDB'97)*, pp. 186–195, Athens, Greece, Aug. 1997.

[XCYH06]   D. Xin, H. Cheng, X. Yan, and J. Han. Extracting redundancy-aware top-k patterns. In *Proc. 2006 ACM SIGKDD Int. Conf. Knowledge Discovery in Databases (KDD'06)*, pp. 444–453, Philadelphia, PA, Aug. 2006.

[XHCL06]   D. Xin, J. Han, H. Cheng, and X. Li. Answering top-k queries with multi-dimensional selections: The ranking cube approach. In *Proc. 2006 Int. Conf. Very Large Data Bases (VLDB'06)*, pp. 463–475, Seoul, Korea, Sept. 2006.

[XHLW03]   D. Xin, J. Han, X. Li, and B. W. Wah. Star-cubing: Computing iceberg cubes by top-down and bottom-up integration. In *Proc. 2003 Int. Conf. Very Large Data Bases (VLDB'03)*, pp. 476–487, Berlin, Germany, Sept. 2003.

[XHSL06]   D. Xin, J. Han, Z. Shao, and H. Liu. C-cubing: Efficient computation of closed cubes by aggregation-based checking. In *Proc. 2006 Int. Conf. Data Engineering (ICDE'06)*, p. 4, Atlanta, GA, Apr. 2006.

[XHYC05]   D. Xin, J. Han, X. Yan, and H. Cheng. Mining compressed frequent-pattern sets. In *Proc. 2005 Int. Conf. Very Large Data Bases (VLDB'05)*, pp. 709–720, Trondheim, Norway, Aug. 2005.

[XOJ00]   Y. Xiang, K. G. Olesen, and F. V. Jensen. Practical issues in modeling large diagnostic systems with multiply sectioned Bayesian networks. *Intl. J. Pattern Recognition and Artificial Intelligence (IJPRAI)*, 14:59–71, 2000.

[XPK10]   Z. Xing, J. Pei, and E. Keogh. A brief survey on sequence classification. *SIGKDD Explorations*, 12:40–48, 2010.

[XSH+04]   H. Xiong, S. Shekhar, Y. Huang, V. Kumar, X. Ma, and J. S. Yoo. A framework for discovering co-location patterns in data sets with extended spatial objects. In *Proc. 2004 SIAM Int. Conf. Data Mining (SDM'04)*, Lake Buena Vista, FL, Apr. 2004.

[XYFS07]   X. Xu, N. Yuruk, Z. Feng, and T. A. J. Schweiger. SCAN: A structural clustering algorithm for networks. In *Proc. 2007 ACM SIGKDD Int. Conf. Knowledge Discovery in Databases (KDD'07)*, pp. 824–833, San Jose, CA, Aug. 2007.

[XZYL08]   T. Xu, Z. M. Zhang, P. S. Yu, and B. Long. Evolutionary clustering by hierarchical Dirichlet process with hidden Markov state. In *Proc. 2008 Int. Conf. Data Mining (ICDM'08)*, pp. 658–667, Pisa, Italy, Dec. 2008.

[YC01]   N. Ye and Q. Chen. An anomaly detection technique based on a chi-square statistic for detecting intrusions into information systems. *Quality and Reliability Engineering International*, 17:105–112, 2001.

[YCHX05]   X. Yan, H. Cheng, J. Han, and D. Xin. Summarizing itemset patterns: A profile-based approach. In *Proc. 2005 ACM SIGKDD Int. Conf. Knowledge Discovery in Databases (KDD'05)*, pp. 314–323, Chicago, IL, Aug. 2005.

[YFB01]   C. Yang, U. Fayyad, and P. S. Bradley. Efficient discovery of error-tolerant frequent itemsets in high dimensions. In *Proc. 2001 ACM SIGKDD Int. Conf. Knowledge Discovery in Databases (KDD'01)*, pp. 194–203, San Fransisco, CA, Aug. 2001.

[YFM+97]   K. Yoda, T. Fukuda, Y. Morimoto, S. Morishita, and T. Tokuyama. Computing optimized rectilinear regions for association rules. In *Proc. 1997 Int. Conf. Knowledge Discovery and Data Mining (KDD'97)*, pp. 96–103, Newport Beach, CA, Aug. 1997.

[YH02]   X. Yan and J. Han. gSpan: Graph-based substructure pattern mining. In *Proc. 2002 Int. Conf. Data Mining (ICDM'02)*, pp. 721–724, Maebashi, Japan, Dec. 2002.

[YH03a]   X. Yan and J. Han. CloseGraph: Mining closed frequent graph patterns. In *Proc. 2003 ACM SIGKDD Int. Conf. Knowledge Discovery and Data Mining (KDD'03)*, pp. 286–295, Washington, DC, Aug. 2003.

[YH03b]   X. Yin and J. Han. CPAR: Classification based on predictive association rules. In *Proc. 2003 SIAM Int. Conf. Data Mining (SDM'03)*, pp. 331–335, San Fransisco, CA, May 2003.

[YHA03]   X. Yan, J. Han, and R. Afshar. CloSpan: Mining closed sequential patterns in large datasets. In *Proc. 2003 SIAM Int. Conf. Data Mining (SDM'03)*, pp. 166–177, San Fransisco, CA, May 2003.

[YHF10]   P. S. Yu, J. Han, and C. Faloutsos. *Link Mining: Models, Algorithms and Applications*. New York: Springer, 2010.

[YHY05]   X. Yin, J. Han, and P. S. Yu. Cross-relational clustering with user's guidance. In *Proc. 2005 ACM SIGKDD Int. Conf. Knowledge Discovery in Databases (KDD'05)*, pp. 344–353, Chicago, IL, Aug. 2005.

[YHY07]   X. Yin, J. Han, and P. S. Yu. Object distinction: Distinguishing objects with identical names by link analysis. In *Proc. 2007 Int. Conf. Data Engineering (ICDE'07)*, Istanbul, Turkey, Apr. 2007.

[YHY08]   X. Yin, J. Han, and P. S. Yu. Truth discovery with multiple conflicting information providers on the Web. *IEEE Trans. Knowledge and Data Engineering*, 20:796–808, 2008.

[YHYY04]   X. Yin, J. Han, J. Yang, and P. S. Yu. CrossMine: Efficient classification across multiple database relations. In *Proc. 2004 Int. Conf. Data Engineering (ICDE'04)*, pp. 399–410, Boston, MA, Mar. 2004.

[YK09]   L. Ye and E. Keogh. Time series shapelets: A new primitive for data mining. In *Proc. 2009 ACM SIGKDD Int. Conf. Knowledge Discovery and Data Mining (KDD'09)*, pp. 947–956, Paris, France, June 2009.

[YWY07]   J. Yuan, Y. Wu, and M. Yang. Discovery of collocation patterns: From visual words to visual phrases. In *Proc. IEEE Conf. Computer Vision and Pattern Recognition (CVPR'07)*, pp. 1–8, Minneapolis, MN, June 2007.

[YYH03]   H. Yu, J. Yang, and J. Han. Classifying large data sets using SVM with hierarchical clusters. In *Proc. 2003 ACM SIGKDD Int. Conf. Knowledge Discovery and Data Mining (KDD'03)*, pp. 306–315, Washington, DC, Aug. 2003.

[YYH05]   X. Yan, P. S. Yu, and J. Han. Graph indexing based on discriminative frequent structure analysis. *ACM Trans. Database Systems*, 30:960–993, 2005.

[YZ94]   R. R. Yager and L. A. Zadeh. *Fuzzy Sets, Neural Networks and Soft Computing*. Van Nostrand Reinhold, 1994.

[YZYH06]   X. Yan, F. Zhu, P. S. Yu, and J. Han. Feature-based substructure similarity search. *ACM Trans. Database Systems*, 31:1418–1453, 2006.

[Zad65]   L. A. Zadeh. Fuzzy sets. *Information and Control*, 8:338–353, 1965.

[Zad83]   L. Zadeh. Commonsense knowledge representation based on fuzzy logic. *Computer*, 16:61–65, 1983.

[Zak00]   M. J. Zaki. Scalable algorithms for association mining. *IEEE Trans. Knowledge and Data Engineering*, 12:372–390, 2000.

[Zak01]   M. Zaki. SPADE: An efficient algorithm for mining frequent sequences. *Machine Learning*, 40:31–60, 2001.

[ZDN97]   Y. Zhao, P. M. Deshpande, and J. F. Naughton. An array-based algorithm for simultaneous multidimensional aggregates. In *Proc. 1997 ACM-SIGMOD Int. Conf. Management of Data (SIGMOD'97)*, pp. 159–170, Tucson, AZ, May 1997.

[ZH02]   M. J. Zaki and C. J. Hsiao. CHARM: An efficient algorithm for closed itemset mining. In *Proc. 2002 SIAM Int. Conf. Data Mining (SDM'02)*, pp. 457–473, Arlington, VA, Apr. 2002.

[Zha08]   C. Zhai. *Statistical Language Models for Information Retrieval.* Morgan and Claypool, 2008.

[ZHL⁺98]   O. R. Zaïane, J. Han, Z. N. Li, J. Y. Chiang, and S. Chee. MultiMedia-Miner: A system prototype for multimedia data mining. In *Proc. 1998 ACM-SIGMOD Int. Conf. Management of Data (SIGMOD'98)*, pp. 581–583, Seattle, WA, June 1998.

[Zhu05]   X. Zhu. Semi-supervised learning literature survey. In *Computer Sciences Technical Report 1530*, University of Wisconsin–Madison, 2005.

[ZHZ00]   O. R. Zaïane, J. Han, and H. Zhu. Mining recurrent items in multimedia with progressive resolution refinement. In *Proc. 2000 Int. Conf. Data Engineering (ICDE'00)*, pp. 461–470, San Diego, CA, Feb. 2000.

[Zia91]   W. Ziarko. The discovery, analysis, and representation of data dependencies in databases. In G. Piatetsky-Shapiro and W. J. Frawley (eds.), *Knowledge Discovery in Databases*, pp. 195–209. AAAI Press, 1991.

[ZL06]   Z.-H. Zhou and X.-Y. Liu. Training cost-sensitive neural networks with methods addressing the class imbalance problem. *IEEE Trans. Knowledge and Data Engineering*, 18:63–77, 2006.

[ZPOL97]   M. J. Zaki, S. Parthasarathy, M. Ogihara, and W. Li. Parallel algorithm for discovery of association rules. *Data Mining and Knowledge Discovery*, 1:343–374, 1997.

[ZRL96]   T. Zhang, R. Ramakrishnan, and M. Livny. BIRCH: An efficient data clustering method for very large databases. In *Proc. 1996 ACM-SIGMOD Int. Conf. Management of Data (SIGMOD'96)*, pp. 103–114, Montreal, Quebec, Canada, June 1996.

[ZS02]   N. Zapkowicz and S. Stephen. The class imbalance program: A systematic study. *Intelligence Data Analysis*, 6:429–450, 2002.

[ZYH⁺07]   F. Zhu, X. Yan, J. Han, P. S. Yu, and H. Cheng. Mining colossal frequent patterns by core pattern fusion. In *Proc. 2007 Int. Conf. Data Engineering (ICDE'07)*, pp. 706–715, Istanbul, Turkey, Apr. 2007.

[ZYHY07]   F. Zhu, X. Yan, J. Han, and P. S. Yu. gPrune: A constraint pushing framework for graph pattern mining. In *Proc. 2007 Pacific-Asia Conf. Knowledge Discovery and Data Mining (PAKDD'07)*, pp. 388–400, Nanjing, China, May 2007.

[ZZ09]   Z. Zhang and R. Zhang. *Multimedia Data Mining: A Systematic Introduction to Concepts and Theory.* Chapman & Hall, 2009.

[ZZH09]   D. Zhang, C. Zhai, and J. Han. Topic cube: Topic modeling for OLAP on multidimensional text databases. In *Proc. 2009 SIAM Int. Conf. Data Mining (SDM'09)*, pp. 1123–1134, Sparks, NV, Apr. 2009.

Index